Praise for *Namath: A Biography*

"Excellent . . . plenty of blood and guts."   —*The New York Times Book Review*

"Irreverent and highly entertaining."   —*Los Angeles Times Book Review*

"Superb . . . subtly shaded, beautifully nuanced, and, ultimately, heartbreakingly sad."   —*Chicago Tribune*

"Fascinating, meticulously researched."   —*USA Today*

"Punchy, refreshingly gutter-mouthed. . . . Kriegel does a magnificent job of getting across Namath's greatness as a player and his natural capacity as a celebrity."   —*San Francisco Chronicle*

"Meticulous and lively. . . . Kriegel's a master: In the end, his subject emerges as being flawed and lovable, egocentric and unassuming, giddy and downright compelling."   —*People*

"You can taste the scotch and smell the perfume in this rich portrayal of the ultimate playboy, but Kriegel's burrowing reveals the physical and emotional anguish Namath endured. Life after football isn't always pretty for Broadway Joe; Kriegel shows Namath is all the more fascinating for being flawed."   —*Sports Illustrated*

"Excellent . . . Kriegel excels in getting beyond Namath the star quarterback to explore Namath the cultural phenomenon. . . . Mark Kriegel wins [us over], too, with this outstanding portrait."   —*Boston Herald*

"Fantastically vivid . . . *Namath* goes down as one of the top sports biographies of the decade."   —*Newsday*

"Penetrating . . . through dogged reporting and insightful writing, reveals a Namath we didn't know. . . . As sports biographies go, this is on a level with David Maraniss' book on Vince Lombardi and Richard Ben Cramer's on Joe DiMaggio. And that's the big leagues."   —Dan McGrath, *Chicago Tribune*

"Kriegel has meticulously reconstructed Namath's life and accomplishments with a thoroughness that historian David McCullough would admire."   —Allen Barra, *The Atlanta Journal-Constitution*

"Always solid, often brilliant. . . . This is a life-and-times book, and Kriegel is as good on the times as he is the life . . . a superb reporter. . . . All these things Kriegel tells in the gripping prose of a novelist."   —Henry Kisor, *Chicago Sun-Times*

"Definitive and hugely entertaining." —Ron Rapoport, *Chicago Sun-Times*

"An almost Shakespearean drama of triumph and tragedy, told with a flair as dazzling as Joe Willie Namath in his prime." —*The Dallas Morning News*

"A sympathetic but not fawning portrait of a man far more complex, intelligent and reflective than his boozy, skirt-chasing public personality ever suggested. Kriegel turns phrases with the precision of a craftsman and paces Namath's story so adroitly that the book moves quickly." —*The Philadelphia Inquirer*

"A terrific read, an all encompassing look at an American icon."
—Ron Cook, *Pittsburgh Post-Gazette*

"Kriegel's biography . . . doesn't blink, whether his subject is in the locker room or at the bar." —*The Boston Globe*

"Exquisitely written and deeply researched . . . It delivers a hundred scoops—some tabloid, some Freudian. . . . The book displays taste in probing Mr. Namath's interior life; it is never cheap, but always true."
—Jack Newfield, *The New York Sun*

"An illuminating book . . . Ostensibly about a sports figure, it is truly a comment on America and how it views, and forgets, its heroes." —Associated Press

"Avoiding the pitfalls of mythology while telling a larger-than-life story is never easy, but Kriegel does it grandly in this landmark portrait of the 1960s icon. . . . Elegantly told . . . Kriegel has written a remarkable book: a feel-good sports story still abundant with insight and social commentary."
—*Publishers Weekly* (starred)

"Entertaining . . . the only [biography of Namath] that can be called comprehensive." —*St. Louis Post-Dispatch*

"A terrific read." —*The San Diego Union-Tribune*

"Meticulously researched . . . Kriegel shows a command of both the narrative form and the world of professional sports. . . . [He] deftly places the man in the context of the times, showing the impact of one on the other."
—*The Oregonian*

"Marvelous . . . This is not just another sports book . . . this is literature."
—*Pro Football Weekly*

"Kriegel paints a moving portrait of a man who redefined the world of professional athletes." —*Rocky Mountain News*

"Excellent" —*Arkansas Democrat-Gazette*

PENGUIN BOOKS

NAMATH

Mark Kriegel is a former sports columnist for the *New York Daily News* and author of the novel *Bless Me, Father*. He lives in Brooklyn, New York, with his wife and daughter.

A Biography

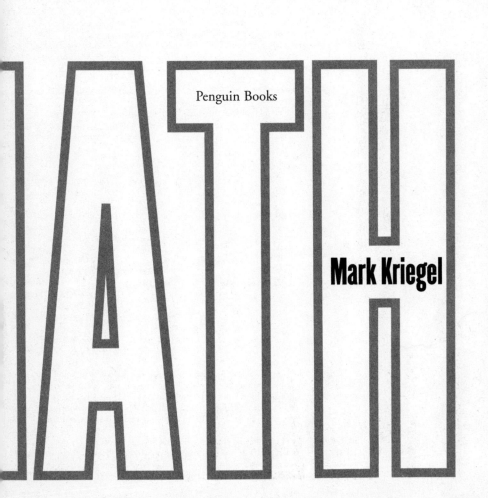

Penguin Books

Mark Kriegel

For Emily

PENGUIN BOOKS

Published by the Penguin Group

Penguin Group (USA) Inc., 375 Hudson Street, New York, New York 10014, U.S.A.
Penguin Group (Canada), 90 Eglinton Avenue East, Suite 700, Toronto, Ontario,
Canada M4P 2Y3 (a division of Pearson Penguin Canada Inc.)
Penguin Books Ltd, 80 Strand, London WC2R 0RL, England
Penguin Ireland, 25 St Stephen's Green, Dublin 2, Ireland (a division of Penguin Books Ltd)
Penguin Group (Australia), 250 Camberwell Road, Camberwell, Victoria 3124,
Australia (a division of Pearson Australia Group Pty Ltd)
Penguin Books India Pvt Ltd, 11 Community Centre, Panchsheel Park, New Delhi – 110 017, India
Penguin Group (NZ), 67 Apollo Drive, Rosedale, North Shore 0632, New Zealand
(a division of Pearson New Zealand Ltd)
Penguin Books (South Africa) (Pty) Ltd, 24 Sturdee Avenue, Rosebank, Johannesburg 2196, South Africa

Penguin Books Ltd, Registered Offices: 80 Strand, London WC2R 0RL, England

First published in the United States of America by Viking Penguin,
a member of Penguin Group (USA) Inc., 2004
Published in Penguin Books 2005

2 3 4 5 6 7 8 9 10

THE LIBRARY OF CONGRESS HAS CATALOGED THE HARDCOVER EDITION AS FOLLOWS:
Kriegel, Mark.
Namath : a biography / Mark Kriegel.
p. cm.
ISBN 0-670-03329-4 (hc.)
ISBN 978-0-14-303535-0 (pbk.)
1. Namath, Joe Willie, 1943– . 2. Football players—United States—Biography. I. Title.
GV939.N28K75 2004
796.322'092—dc22
[B]   2004049619

Printed in the United States of America
Set in Adobe Garamond   Designed by Jaye Zimet

Contents

January 27, 1999 "What about Joe Namath?"

He repeats the words, announcing himself again and again, reciting the line as both declaration and question, as if he were hearing his name for the first time. He varies the cadence, the accent, the timbre. He says it slow and sly and with an extra dollop of that southern syrup. He tries different styles: first, an anchorman; next, a color commentator; then, with the enthusiastic baritone of a game show host. *What about Jo-o-o-e Namath?*

In accordance with his ancestors' instructions, he had learned to speak American. He was fluent in those dialects heard
on television. After all, he had studied
voice. "The voice," he had been taught,
"reveals us completely."

PROLOGUE

But what of a man with many voices?

What about Joe Namath?

Now he eyes the sportswriter suspiciously. This rehearsal, preparation for a voice-over, will not be part of the story. The sportswriter will gladly agree to these terms. They always do. The sportswriter belongs to the generation that adores him most. Even as a president once listed him as an enemy of the re-public, kids rushed to buy popcorn makers and chocolate milk on his say-so. This sportswriter had been one of those kids. With each passing year, they love him more, but know him less.

The interview is to take place here, in a vacant locker room at the Orange Bowl. He had always been great in January in the Orange Bowl. In 1963, as a sophomore, with John F. Kennedy in attendance, he began by throwing a touchdown in a shutout of Oklahoma. After the game, all the writers wanted to know: How do you spell that boy's name? *N-A-M-A-T-H,* said Coach Bryant. *Y'all be learning it soon enough.* In '65, he made his debut in living color, becoming MVP of the first prime-time bowl game. The night served as a pilot for a new kind of action series. He was cast as its leading man—"Broad-way Joe"—a role that culminated in its greatest glory thirty years ago this month, in the Super Bowl. They called him an antihero. But really, there's no such thing. Antiheroes morph into heroes. It's the American way.

Still, little in Namath's current appearance suggests such heroism. As standing can be painful, even on artificial knees of metal and plastic, he sits on a folding chair. The famous stoop in his shoulders seems more pronounced. He slouches, shirtless, a tuft of gray protruding from his chest. He is tan and thin. There is less of him than the sportswriter imagined. He doesn't look like Broadway Joe. Rather, he looks not unlike the sportswriter. He looks like somebody's father.

So what about Joe Namath?

At the height of his fame, he made—or rather, had made for him—a cult of his bachelorhood. Broadway Joe was a high priest of lush life, his affections sought by a sugar-frosted society of starlets and stews, all of whom sought to worship at an altar adorned with llama-skin rugs.

But now, the star seems a bit unsure at the sound of his own name. He's still practicing his voice-over. For what, the sportswriter does not know, doesn't care. Namath is selling something. Of course, he is. This is the Super Bowl, the game he made, that highest sabbath in the American religion, the an-nual consecration of corporate culture, an event that celebrates thirty-second spots as sagas and bookmakers as theologians. The Super Bowl evokes a star-spangled yin and yang, all those equal but opposing forces that create a prime-time culture: Coke and Pepsi, Miller and Bud, McDonald's and Burger King, Disney and Fox, Bloods and Crips, AFC and NFC. Only two things you can do here at the Super Bowl; you're buying, or you're selling.

The sportswriter understands his end of the transaction. He's purchasing another piece of the Guarantee.

Thirty years have passed since the Jets were 18-point underdogs to the Bal-timore Colts. Namath was high on scotch when he promised a Jets victory.

I guarantee it.

For a generation raised on canned laughter, the Guarantee qualifies as a kind of performance art. He was live. He was alive. He was bigger news than the astronauts returning from the moon. At least that's how they make it sound today.

In fact, the Guarantee didn't even make the New York papers. Not until after the game. But, hey, what do you want from sportswriters? Now they come around like pilgrims. Each year they become more devout.

They all want to know about the Good Old Days. They must have been good, a time before clogged arteries and enlarged prostates, before secondhand smoke, before pills to keep you happy and hard.

Broadway Joe was the coolest kid in America, an object of affection for girls and gangsters, a source of bafflement for bookmakers everywhere. What bookies saw as a 7-to-1 long shot—Jets over the Colts—Joe saw as a sure thing. Fuck the points, he told the bartender, take the odds. Such a gifted hustler. He made debonair comedy of most likelihoods.

He walked off with Jagger's girls. He spilled drinks on Sinatra. He grinned his way through it all. The Raiders broke his face, and he caught a flight to Vegas, came back the next week, and set a single-season passing record.

Namath had a concussion when he hit Maynard in the AFL championship game. He was still drunk the day he threw three touchdowns against the Patriots in '66. He had a joint in his hand when the squad car showed up on Third Avenue. The cops could be heard over the loudspeaker. "That him?" "Nah, can't be." They drove off.

Another sure thing.

But that's not the stuff for a family newspaper. It's better to just play along with these writers and their need for nostalgia. "I'm getting goose bumps just thinking about it." That's what he usually says. Not today, though. No goose bumps today. "I get a special feeling when I'm here," he says, quite unconvincingly. His tone is glum, but it's the best he can do.

Not even the sportswriter believes him. The sportswriter leaves feeling deceived. But this regret won't last long. He'll give his editor what he wants, what the readers want, what everybody wants: the Guarantee and the Good Old Days. It's Super Bowl Week. It's all good, and it's all on the house, everything from the quotes to the beer to the lap dances.

But what about Joe Namath?

He survived fame and drink and orthopedic ruin. He became a husband and a father. The standard-bearer for booze and broads had become an apostle of family values, even as the first baby boomer president was hustling blow jobs down the hall from the Oval Office.

Salvation through fatherhood, that's what Joe Namath had come to believe in. That's all he believed in. The rest was bullshit.

Try explaining that to a sportswriter.

But now Broadway Joe needs a drink.

His wife has left him, ran off with a plastic surgeon from Beverly Hills.

So what's he supposed to say? Should he tell the guy there are no guarantees? Why ruin everything?

Oh, he wants a drink. A vodka, a beer.

So what's the spread on this one? What are the odds? Does he make a comeback?

What about Joe Namath?

NAM

On February 11, 1911, after nineteen days at sea, the RMS *Pannonia* dropped anchor in New York Harbor. The steamer had accommodations for 40 passengers in first class, 800 in steerage. Immigration officers directed their transfer to ferries, on which they were literally packed and delivered to Ellis Island. Among those bound for the Great Hall was Joe Namath's paternal grandfather. The ship's master entered his name in the manifest: Andras Nemet. He was Hungarian, of the Magyar race and the peasant class. He had been born a subject of Franz Josef, emperor of Austria and apostolic king of Hungary, and lived in a place called Raho, a village of several hundred on the Rima River in the foothills of the Carpathian Mountains. Andras Nemet was darkly complected with gray eyes and stood five-five, which, compared with others in the *Pannonia*'s manifest, was a healthy height for men whose diet

1. A DISTANT FABLED LAND

did not include much meat. He was thirty-nine, with the equivalent of $34 in his pocket. He swore he was neither a polygamist nor an anarchist. He was not crippled. He was in fine mental and physical condition, save for a common ailment known as *Amerika-laz,* American fever.

Magyar society—emanating from two classes, nobles and serfs—hadn't changed much through its first millennium, which had been celebrated in 1896. Hungary's national anthem proclaimed: "Here you must live and here you must die." Emigrants were denounced in Parliament and the press. American *fectris* were said to be so dangerous that real Americans wouldn't even work there—"not even Negroes," according to the *Budapest Notifier*. America's mills and mines represented nothing more than a new kind of servitude. A Magyar folk song warned of perils "in a distant fabled land." "We have lived and died here for a thousand years, Oh! Why, at your own danger, do you want to leave here now?"

America was not to be confused with El Dorado. Mines collapsed. Mill furnaces exploded. Men drowned in a lava of molten steel. Still, one didn't need theories of probability to understand the lure of the distant fabled land.

Why America?

More meat, more money. Better odds.

Andras Nemet took the bet. Years later, Janos, the third of his four sons, would remember: "My dad came to this country when I was a year or a year and a half old, and I stayed behind. The reason I stayed behind was because my older brother was learning the blacksmith trade and had two years to go, so my father wanted to leave him behind for those years. He asked my grandparents to remain with him and be his guardians. They said that they would do it only if one of the younger children also remained with them. So I was the one that was elected to stay there. That way they figured that my mother would come back and they would get to see their daughter again. My grandparents were wonderful."

Wonderful as they might have been, this couldn't have been an easy period for Janos, who grew up without a father. Two years went by, then two more, and so on, until almost a decade had passed. Finally, on December 4, 1920, Janos arrived at Ellis Island. He was eleven. The ship's master entered his name as "Nemeth."

Janos was accompanied by his kid brother Lazlo, nine, and their mother, Julia, who had traveled back to Hungary to reclaim him. Janos answered the same questions his father had. He was not a polygamist, an anarchist, or a cripple. But there was still one more question: How long would he be staying in the United States? Most immigrants left Hungary with ambitions to return, already dreaming of a glorious homecoming. Not Janos, though. The officer inquiring as to the length of his stay checked the box marked "Always." World War I had redrawn national boundaries; Janos's hometown was now part of Czechoslovakia. But his fate had nothing to do with politics. Or money. Or even the American fever.

For Janos Nemeth, repatriation wasn't a matter of country, but of kin. It was about making the family whole again. Janos wasn't ever going home. He was home.

By now his father had signed a "Declaration of Intention," a petition for citizenship, renouncing forever his allegiance to Charles, emperor of Austria and apostolic king of Hungary. Andras had settled in a place called Beaver Falls, about thirty miles northwest of Pittsburgh, where he worked as a laborer for the Armstrong Cork Works. It was in Beaver Falls that Andras Nemet became Andy Namath.

The oldest of his four sons, Andy Junior, had given up blacksmithing to work in the mill, pouring molten metal for a living. The three other boys still lived at home. There was Steve, a machinist at the Keystone Driller Company; Lazlo, better known as Lester, and Janos, who quickly became John.

"When I first came here my father told my brother to take me amongst the boys," John Namath would recall. "He didn't want to hear me talking Hungarian. Learn to talk American, he says, and learn it right."

John Namath mastered more than the language; he learned, quite quickly, to live American as well. Something about him was exquisitely adapted to life in the hardscrabble precincts of Beaver Falls. "He was tough," said Jeff Alford, whose family, descended from slaves, had come from Alabama. "Guys like that just didn't take no shit. You had to be tough to survive around there. Shee-it, lot of white guys could fight they ass off back then."

What young Namath evidenced was a kind of rugged egalitarianism. Race and religion were like athletic talent: granted by God. But you didn't judge a man by how God treated him; you judged him on how he treated you. This was a practical philosophy in a town like Beaver Falls, whose many tribes were known by pejorative proper nouns: Hunkies, Coloreds, Wops, Polacks, Micks, Krauts, Yids, even Chinamen. For each tribe, there were several churches and as many bars.

Prohibition never stopped anyone from getting a drink in Beaver Falls. Drink was a man's reward for breathing the exhaust fumes of progress. Just about everyone's father worked in a factory. Beaver Falls made glass, china, enamel, cork, steam drillers, and doors. But mostly, like all those towns along the Beaver River, it made steel. Moltrup made cold finished steel. Union Drawn made bars and rods. Standard Gauge produced crankshafts and taper pins. Babcock & Wilcox, the town's biggest employer, was known for seamless tubing.

After a shift in the mills, most men were too tired to do anything but drink. Their sons, however, could avail themselves of other amusements. Basketball was in its infancy, but still popular enough that the standings of club teams were dutifully printed in the local paper. Football, another very young game, had been popularized by college kids. But as it skirted the line between athleticism and violence, the sport seemed less suited for a bunch of swells than the rough-hewn sons of mill towns like Beaver Falls.

Still, basketball and football were mere curiosities compared to baseball. The Beaver Falls Athletics, the town's first entry in organized ball, had been around since 1896. In 1921 and '22, the Beaver Falls Elks were the reigning champions of semipro ball. There was a city league and a county league and any number of industrial leagues. The town had at least six ball fields, showcases for local legends with names like Heinie and Bennie and Lefty and Babyface.

Kids were crazy for baseball. In 1920, the year Janos became John, Babe Ruth hit fifty-four home runs, more than any single team had hit the season before. Baseball embodied an almost absurd sense of possibility, decidedly unEuropean, but no matter how Andy Namath tried to assimilate, the game and its value would remain beyond his comprehension.

That didn't stop John from playing. He just learned to sneak around, keeping his glove and his uniform at a friend's house. "My parents never allowed none of us to compete in any sport at all," John would remember. "They said, 'We didn't raise you boys up to go out there and cripple yourselves up.'"

America didn't want cripples. They were turned back at Ellis Island. Cripples couldn't work.

Zoltan Kovac, a Hungarian immigrant who came to know the Namath family, explains: "To an old-fashioned Magyar family, sport was wasting time. You have to work, to earn a living. They don't want you playing ball or painting pictures. You worked. That's how they were brought up. That's what they brought with them from Hungary."

All the Namath brothers left school early to get jobs. "I had a doctor change my birth certificate so that I could quit school when I was 15," John said.

He got a mill job, a standard fifty-five-hour week at 23 cents an hour. He worked in a glass factory for a quarter an hour. Then he worked as a "heater boy," heating rivets at the Penn Bridge Company. He worked at the Union Clothing Company. He worked at Armstrong Cork. He was still a kid.

What, then, made you a man?

Was it loss? Or the ability to endure it?

On November 10, 1926, Andy Junior died of septicemia—blood poisoning—not uncommon among America's industrial class. He was twenty-six, survived by his wife and young daughter. The cost of the funeral, including limousine, floral arrangements, and a deluxe "Belmont" casket, came to $643.50, a considerable sum at a time when steelworkers made about 50 cents an hour. Still, all the expense afforded the Namaths little peace. The poison would linger in the family's blood.

From the lead story in the *Beaver Falls Tribune,* May 17, 1927:

> Answering an alarm of fire which came over the telephone this morning shortly after 9:30 o'clock, the Beaver Falls fire department discovered upon arriving at 1315 Twenty-Third street, Mt. Washington, Beaver Falls, that instead of there being a fire, the man living in the house, Andy Namath, aged 56 years, had taken his life by hanging himself to supporting beams in the cellar of his own home. . . .
>
> It is said that the man had been in ill health for several weeks past and had brooded considerably over the death of his son about one year ago as well as his wife's present illness. Procuring a clothesline, he threw one end of it over the supporting rafter in the cellar while standing on the lower cellar steps, after which he stepped off. He then evidently bent his knees, causing slow strangulation.

There would be no $385 Belmont casket this time; the entire burial cost less than that. As a gambling man would say, why chase after bad money?

Andy Namath lost the bet he made as Andras Nemet. So much for those great odds in this distant fabled land.

■   ■   ■

In a little more than eight months, on January 30, 1928, Julia Namath would remarry. Her new husband, William Bartus, was a mill worker who had been widowed ten years before. They lived at 316 Ninth Avenue, on the lower end of Beaver Falls, a block populated by Americans of African, Polish, and Magyar descent. Suddenly, there was a family of ten: six children from his first marriage and two from hers. The 1930 census counts Lester and John Namath as Bartus's stepsons. By then, John was twenty-two, ready to go out and start a family of his own.

He didn't have to look far for a bride. Rose Juhasz lived on the very next block, at 408 Ninth Avenue, the second of four children from a good Hungarian family. The Juhaszes owned their own home, valued at $3,500. Both mother and father, a mill worker, were naturalized citizens. Their children had been born in this country. On April 11, 1930, when the census worker knocked on their door, Rose was still ten days shy of her eighteenth birthday.

She had attended St. Mary's, run by the Sisters of Divine Providence. But to her everlasting dismay, her schooling was cut short by her household duties, which included washing, cleaning, sewing, and tending to the furnace. She was also employed as a domestic for a well-to-do family up in the Patterson Heights section. "Women in mill towns were expected to work just as soon as they could, then find a husband," she would recall.

Rose, later described as a "handsome" woman, would not disappoint. Not only could she keep house, she was a talented cook and a devout Catholic. Rose was a very qualified spouse. And as she saw it, so was John Namath.

He had given up his great passion, baseball, but still played industrial league basketball and semipro football for the Beaver Falls Cardinals. Still, Rose wasn't marrying John for his athletic prowess. "He had a good job at the Moltrup Steel Company as a helper on a hot furnace, and he was a big, good-looking, hardworking man," she recalled. "But from my point of view, I was honestly less concerned about getting married than I was with the fact that at last I was finished with all the hard work around the Juhasz household."

John and Rose were married on April 14, 1931, at St. Ladislaus, the Hungarian Catholic church. Later that year, on December 1, John Alexander Namath was born. They'd call the baby Sonny. Sonny had great timing; the Great Depression was now in full swing.

Their newlywed years were a season of hardship. A good week was one that saw John get two days' work at the mill. He tried to make up for it by working as a salesman at Sedicoff's shoe store. Rose worked as a maid on Saturdays, nine hours for a buck. She stretched the family budget by making everything from scratch: soup, bread, apple butter, even soap from scraps of animal fat. She cooked a lot of rabbit, which they raised for food. Sometimes John would fish the Beaver River for their dinner.

He had finally retired from the Beaver Falls Cardinals with a bad ankle. For entertainment, the young couple would play cards, pop popcorn, and listen to the radio. Rose loved *Amos 'n Andy*.

On October 6, 1934, Robert Namath was born. Another mouth to feed. Another baby wailing to suckle at two in the morning. Another set of diapers. After Bobby, the young couple decided not to have any more kids, at least not for a while. This moratorium came to an end on January 5, 1938, with the birth of a third son, Franklin.

Fortunately, the worst of the Depression was over. The family had survived. Soon enough the mills would thrive as never before. Beaver Falls would be a boomtown.

There was just one thing bothering Rose Namath. She wanted a girl.

■   ■   ■

On May 31, 1943, Rose went to see her doctor. She was near the end of yet another pregnancy, though this one would conclude differently. Unlike the three boys, all of whom were born at home, the Namaths had arranged for this baby to be born in Providence Hospital.

"I thought little girls deserved something special," Rose would say. She had no doubt. In anticipation of the infant princess, Rose had already painted the baby's room pink. There was a pink crib, pink blankets, pink sweaters.

Dr. James Smith assured her that everything was fine, right on schedule. In another two weeks or so, she would be reporting for a shift of hard labor in the delivery room. And yes, Rose Namath would indeed be having a girl. Maybe it was the way she was carrying. Perhaps it was Dr. Smith's many years of experience. Whatever the case, the physician was absolutely certain as to one thing: The baby would be a girl.

"I guarantee you," he said.

■   ■   ■

Later that day, after hanging the laundry out to dry, John and Rose walked the three blocks to Providence Hospital.

The baby was dimpled, but dark. Very dark. Almost Spanish-looking.

"Oh, no," Rose told the nurse. "This couldn't be mine."

Congratulations. It's a boy.

He was baptized Joseph William Namath—the middle name commemorating the birthday he shared with William Bartus—and he howled while cutting his teeth. That agony prompted what Rose would recall as "his first taste of the hard stuff," an introduction to liquor's analgesic properties:

"He just cried and cried and cried from the pain. I took out a special bottle of clear liquid we always kept around the house and rubbed some on his gums. From that day on there was never any problem. He turned into a marvelous baby, always so happy and playful. I think that maybe even today when Joey gets a toothache, a stiff shoulder, or a sore leg, he might occasionally take a sip of our old magic potion."

2. THE LOWER END

Rose cared for Joey as she had for her other sons. But he was not like her others, or anyone else's. He was different. That much was apparent by the time he arrived at St. Mary's elementary school.

Unfortunately, the Sisters of Divine Providence regarded difference as a kind of deviltry. There might be sixty or more kids in a single classroom, but they were expected to act in unison, to speak with one voice, though only when spoken to. Children would stand when a nun entered the room, and wait for permission to sit. The day began with hands folded. Everyone recited the Our Father. Then they were drilled in the *Baltimore Catechism*, a nun's questions followed by the students' answers:

Who made us?
God made us.
Who is God?
God is the Supreme Being who made all things.

"They'd slap you one if you didn't give the right answer," recalls Frances Morelli-Pickard, a classmate of Namath's.

"All the stories you hear about the nuns are true," says Frances Pinchotti. "They were so strict. March in line. No talking."

Children who insisted on being different were sent to stand in a corner. If humiliation didn't work, a steel ruler probably would. The nuns would bring it right down on your hands. No one would challenge them. Their authority was divine.

"Even the parents, they looked at the nuns as being next to God," says Morelli-Pickard, who became a teacher herself. "I can remember thinking that a poor student was bad, meaning: a bad child." But little Joey Namath was already testing and twisting her notions of good and bad. "He wasn't afraid of the nuns," she says.

A St. Mary's education was based on fear; but Joey had none. Instead, he had a smile so sweet it bordered on blasphemy. "He got a lot of mileage out of that grin," says the former Joyce Hupp. "I think even the nuns were charmed."

Some of the girls would carry their crushes all the way through high school and beyond. "He was always so cute," says Pinchotti. "He wore real colorful shirts. His mom must have done a real nice job with the laundry."

"Even in high school," recalls Hupp, "the creases in his slacks were perfect. *Perfect.* His mother bent over backwards: The way she took care of his clothes, the way she ironed, the way she'd make him whatever he wanted to eat. She always babied him."

■ ■ ■

World War II wasn't bad for steelworkers. The federal government mandated all sorts of new rules, like wage freezes and forty-eight-hour weeks. But everybody was working, and you couldn't beat the overtime. By one estimate, steelworkers' average annual earnings rose 26 percent between 1940 and 1945. Still, the concept of prosperity was a relative one in Beaver Falls. People read the stock pages, but only for the last three digits of total shares traded on the New York Stock Exchange. That figure was the daily number, which Rose played with great regularity.

She would divine her three digits, write them on a slip of paper, and give it to Joey with a quarter. A few other ladies from the neighborhood did the same. As Rose recalled, Joey ran the slips "down to the nice man at the corner drugstore."

Beaver Falls, a scaled-down version of a big city, was full of numbers bankers. Prohibitions against gambling were just as effective as the prohibition against alcohol. To gamble went against Pennsylvania law; not to gamble went against human nature.

Rose, who'd never do anything to offend her plaster saints, knew she wouldn't burn in hell for making a bet. What's more, numbers were the most democratic system of wagering. Back in the old country, there were *kascinos,* betting salons for men of the moneyed classes. Here, anybody could bet. You didn't need much money. You didn't need to be a wizard. You didn't have to worry about the fighter, the pitcher, or the horse (whose dignity was less easily compromised than that of men). The numbers required nothing—except faith. And faith was something women like Rose possessed in abundance.

As it happened, the Namaths even bought their home from a local numbers man, Louis Sacco, who took bets at his record shop. Sacco's deed to the property at 802 Sixth Street was transferred to the Namaths at 11:01 A.M., March 3, 1944. The two-story white frame house, its only bathroom in the basement, cost $4,400. The Lower End, as the neighborhood was called, was bordered to the east by the Beaver River and to the west by the Pennsylvania Railroad, which ran through the Allegheny foothills below well-to-do Patterson Heights. Andras Nemet's grandsons, among the few white kids on the block, now belonged to the landed class.

By 1949, Rose finally got her wish. As she remembered: "There was the cutest twelve-year-old girl—just a month older than Franklin—who came from a broken home, and it seemed as though God intended for her to be mine. She lived with us for six months before the courts saw how much she needed us and how much John and I needed her, and it wasn't long before her name was officially changed to Rita Namath. Finally I had a daughter. . . . Now, at last our family was complete."

They were seven now. Seven wasn't a bad number. Still, for Joey, the family didn't end with Rita. Directly across the street, at 606 Eighth Avenue, lived a kid named Linwood Alford, just seven months his junior. The Alfords, like the Namaths, had come from a faraway place where men toiled over tiny patches of earth—Eufaula, Alabama. Linwood, like Joey, had three older brothers and an older sister.

They were inseparable. Linwood attended services at St. Ladislaus, where Joey served mass. Joey accompanied the Alfords to Tabernacle Baptist, even going to the church picnic. Joey ate Mrs. Alford's fried chicken and greens. Linny feasted on Mrs. Namath's goulash and "Hunky soup," one of Joey's favorite dishes, a broth loaded with square noodles, beef, and chunks of cabbage. Under threat of physical harm, the boys were forced into servitude, popping corn and fetching soft drinks for Bobby Namath and his girlfriends. They fished the Beaver River, baiting their hooks with doughballs to snare catfish and carp, hearty species of bottom feeders immune to the industrial-strength pollutants being dumped by the mills. They saw *The Thing from Another World* at the Granada, an old-fashioned movie palace up on Seventh Avenue. They ran home holding hands.

Even more frightening than "The Thing" was their adventure in Powell's Funeral Home on Seventh Street. They used to pretend the empty caskets were motorboats. Then, one day, the boys commandeered a vessel already inhabited by a corpse. "Cat's laying up in there in his Sunday best with his arms crossed, looked like 'Blacula,'" Alford remembers. "We cut out so fast. I hid under the bed. I'm sure Joe ran up into his mama's arms."

Joey and Linwood were not known for their sense of caution. Linwood re-members them setting a barn on fire. "Burned to the ground," he says. Then they had the brilliant idea of hanging from the railroad trestle. "We were laughing," says Linwood. "We held on till the train went by, then we climbed back up. Joe's father gave us some whupping that day, boy."

It was the least John could do. In 1947, when Linwood was three, his fa-ther died of lung cancer. He had worked at Richmond Radiator in nearby Monaca. "He worked without a mask or anything," says Linwood. "It killed him. It killed a lot of people."

The Alfords got by on disability payments. John Namath, who knew what it was like to grow up without a father, tried to help out with Linwood. Some-times, that meant Linwood got a whupping. But that wasn't all he got. Lin-wood would always remember Mr. Namath going off to work: "If he kissed Joe good-bye, he kissed me good-bye, too."

On Saturday afternoons in the summer the boys went to the Morado Pool up on College Hill, a tonier neighborhood up by Geneva College. Blacks didn't go to the Morado Pool. "Never saw anybody black in there but me," says Linwood. "I think Joe's dad had something to do with that."

But John Namath couldn't always be there to run interference. When the boys were nine, a woman in a pizzeria refused to serve Linwood. "Called me a nigger," he remembers. "First time I ever got hit with that."

The kids left together, more puzzled than hurt. The pizza lady was herself a distinct minority. Down in the Lower End, poisoned blood and sick lungs were common maladies. But the boys remained uninfected by another sick-ness, the American preoccupation with race. Alford still laughs at the recollec-tion of Joey, maybe six years old, with his face covered in brown shoe polish. Joey told his mother he wanted to look like Linwood. "For a long time," says Alford, "I really don't think Joe thought of himself as black or white."

He was of the Lower End. That was his tribe, and his advantage, too. Boys from the Lower End tended to be tougher and slicker than those from other parts of town. Joey and Linny were already in touch with their inner hustler.

At the age of ten or eleven, they went into business, setting up shop right there on Fifth Street. For the right price, a man could get anything on Fifth Street: a drink, a woman, or a bettor's chance. Fifth Street had the bars, the whorehouses, the bookmakers. And now, it had two little kids with a shine box. Joey and Linwood never considered another location. "That's where the hus-tlers were," says Alford. "A town like this, town full of workingmen, the only ones need shined shoes is the hustlers."

Also, the hustlers knew how to tip.

■   ■   ■

Joey and Linwood found plenty of other hustles. Benny Rose had a junkyard on Eighth Street. After dark, the boys would hop the fence and help themselves to some of Benny's best inventory. The next morning, they'd sell it back to him. Already, they knew rudimentary sleight of hand, how to fill their pockets with assorted candies, the most prized being Clark Bars pinched from Snowden's drugstore.

Then there was the bottle scam. Joey would knock on somebody's front door and ask if there were any bottles he could return for the deposit. Soda bottles were worth two cents; milk jugs a nickel. As Joey filibustered the mark, Linwood was already out back, taking inventory of the empties.

Eventually, Rita alerted Mrs. Namath to the con. But Joey had an explanation for his mother: "If they said we couldn't take any, we didn't. But if they said they didn't have any and Linny found some out back, then we took 'em, 'cause they were lyin' ."

In other words: Hustlers were okay. But liars were no damn good.

The nicety of this distinction was lost on some, including Beaver Falls police officer John Jackson Jr., whose beat was the Lower End. Big John, as he was called, didn't look like the average cop; he was black, six-three, almost 300 pounds of muscle. He specialized in keeping apprentice hustlers in line. There was the time when one of Linwood's brothers got drunk, and Big John hung him way up on a telephone pole, let him get sober at the proper altitude. Big John might give you a smack, but that required an extraordinary circumstance, feloniousness of a type that was beyond Joey and Linwood.

For all the boys' hustles, Big John can't remember ever laying a hand on them. "I didn't have to give many whuppings," he says. "If I brung a kid home, he'd be getting a whupping from his parents."

Being a cop was easier back then. Parents were one reason. But there was another. "Television," says Big John. "There was no damn television."

After more than half a century, the memory remains undiminished. "There was this basketball game," recalls Frances Morelli-Pickard, Namath's classmate at St. Mary's. "The gym looks precisely as it does today. There wasn't any place to sit. But I can remember that people were crowding in anyway because there was this little boy playing. There was something about him people were drawn to."

Part mother, part father. From their ferment came his nature; from their nurture came his character. A mother's touch was evident in everything from the crease in Joey's clothes. But there were other gifts his father had cultivated. The dimpled smile and slight frame camouflaged uncommon physical prowess.

3. PLAY BALL

All the Namaths could play ball. John proved that as a teenager just off the boat. Even after he became a father, he continued playing for the St. Ladislaus team in the city basketball league, his name still appearing in the *News-Tribune*'s box scores. Sonny, who left to join the army when Joey was just six, was the first Namath to play high school football. In two of his three years as a varsity lineman, Sonny played with Jim Mutscheller, a star end who went on to a career with Notre Dame and the Baltimore Colts. Bobby Namath, the second son, acquired a reputation as a formidably talented quarterback while still in junior high. Frank was thicker, a plugger, but also a formidable ballplayer: a catcher in baseball, a lineman in football. Joey's athleticism, however, was different, more abundant.

"It was God's gift," said John Namath.

The father never credited himself as the source of Joey's ability, but he felt a duty to indulge and foster it. "I knew I would always do anything that I could for my kids," he said. At Joey's age, Janos had been left back in Hungary. As a teenager, he endured his own father's prohibition against sport. "Nothing hurts a kid more," he would say.

Having had to sneak his games, John Namath made a vow: "I said this: If I get married and I have boys I am going to let them play anything and everything that they want. I am not going to tell them they have to or that they are not allowed. If they want to play, I'll sign for it. Let them play." John would go into hock if he had to, just to keep his kids in pads and helmets and balls and bats. *Let them play.* In the old country, fields were for tilling and toiling. But here, they represented nothing less than a new way of life. To men like Andras Nemet, football fields and baseball diamonds must have seemed profligate, a waste of good soil. But wasn't that why families left their fallow fields back in Europe, so that their children might actually have the opportunity to enjoy themselves? *Let them play.* The creed elevated sport to a kind of patriotic act. In John Namath's America, the games of boys were an inalienable right, and not to be squandered.

By the time he was six or seven, Joey was already being schooled in the rudiments of America's pastime. As he was scrawny, his talent was easier to spot in baseball than in football. His modest dimensions did not detract from his naturally graceful swing. He had a live arm, too. John Namath had pegged a plate into the dirt street in front of the house. He would get down on his haunches and tell Joey to pitch, urging him, "Hit me right in the chin."

They worked on situations: where to throw the ball or how to run, based on the count or the number of outs. As a pitcher, Joey learned to hit the corners. His father only permitted him to throw fastballs, no curves. John had taken boys to tryouts with the Pittsburgh Pirates; he knew that the scouts were interested in control, not curveballs. Later, in Legion ball, he'd tell the managers not to let Joey throw any curves. Once, when Joey was around ten and pitching for the Elks in Little League, John noticed him dipping his shoulder after releasing the pitch. It was some sort of championship game. But John had his son taken out. The Elks would lose. So what? John Namath could tell his son was hurting. He knew. He always knew.

"I used to rub Joe's arm when it was sore," he once said.

John Namath knew his kid's arm. He knew his kid's head, too. Joey was eight when he first came home with his Elks uniform. "That's real nice, son. Fits you good."

Joey was the smallest kid on that team. He was the youngest, too, probably by a year. "You know, Daddy, those other kids are so good," he said. "They're bigger than I am. . . . I don't have a chance."

"Well, you take that uniform off right now," his father said. "Take it back to the manager and tell him that you can't make the team because the other boys are better than you are."

Joey looked at his father with those sad, dreamy eyes. "Oh, no, Daddy. I can't do that."

"If you can't make the team, what's the use of keeping the uniform?"

"But Daddy," he said, "they're so good."

"You're good, too. You can field grounders. You can hit the ball. You know where to make the plays."

John gave the boy a choice: return the uniform or practice with the team.

If, after the practice, he didn't feel that he was better than every other kid, he should quit.

Joey said he'd try.

As it happened, he turned out to be the best player on that Elks team and the ones to follow. John Namath liked to recall his youngest boy's Little League career with a game at Moltrup. The mill had a field all the way on the east side of town, bordered by the train tracks that ran along the Beaver River.

"I arrived late and I asked this colored fellow, who was at all of the games, what the score was, and he said well there are no outs, the score is tied at 3 all and the bases are loaded, but don't worry. They just put the little Namath kid in to pitch."

John was a stranger to the colored guy, and didn't bother to introduce himself. It was enough to be there, to see the gift that had traveled through his blood.

Joey, who'd been playing left field, began by striking out the first batter.

The next batter grounded back to the pitcher.

Then Frank Walton came to the plate. Walton, two years older than Joey, was also from a family of athletes. The Waltons were football royalty in Beaver Falls. Frank's father, Tiger Walton, and his brother, Joe, were both All-Americans at Pitt. Frank would play there, too. "He was an enormous size," John Namath would remember.

Joey's first pitch was a ball, the second a strike. Then another ball, something Walton wouldn't bite on. He bit on the next pitch, though, swing and a miss. Then Joey reared back for his good fastball. The ball cut the plate—just like his daddy had taught him. Walton stepped off for the ump to call a ball.

"The kid stood back, and the umpire said, 'You're out!'" John recalled. "It was beautiful. When Walton struck out he threw his bat over the railroad tracks down into the river.

"So the score was now tied. Joe was the last man up, and no one was on. He hit the ball over the boxcars for a home run."

See what a little confidence could do? Father knew best. Talent *was* God's gift. And like God, it didn't do much for you if you didn't believe in it. For Joey, belief began the day his father told him to give back the uniform. "From that time when I talked to him he started to develop confidence," said John Namath.

If you came from Beaver Falls, confidence was just a nice way of saying cocky. What it came down to, John Namath's premier postulate, was this: "What you should feel is that you are better than anyone out there."

■   ■   ■

There were other games that lacked the organized trappings of Little League. Joey's first experience with team sports might have been in the foothills above

the Lower End. There, kids threw rocks to gain strategic control of tiny terri-
tories that appeared on no map, places they called Bunny Hill and Jungle Hill.
Their teams were like little gangs. There were all-black teams from Bridge
Street and Harmony Dwellings, a housing project that went up in 1941.
White kids from Patterson Township called themselves the Hilltop Boys, not
to be confused with the white boys from Downtown or College Hill, a relatively affluent neighborhood near Geneva College.

Then there was the Lower End crew. As they had to throw uphill, kids
from the Lower End were said to be more cunning, with better arms. Later,
Namath would recall those rock fights with amusement: "Maybe that's how I
developed my arm."

Metal ash can covers served as shields to protect from incoming fire.
Those rocks hurt. "You'd get a big knot on your head," says Alford. "But so
what?" They were honor-bound to protect their claim to Jungle Hill. It was
nothing more than a mound strewn with scrap metal. "But it was our territory," says Alford.

Basketball, unlike rock fighting, was merely a metaphor for combat. But
the difference was lost on Joey. His was an abnormal disdain for defeat. He'd
go to war over electric football, stickball, even sockball—in which four or five
old socks were bunched together, forming a lumpy object that could be hit,
thrown, or shot.

"The most competitive kid I ever met," says Alford. "One time we were
playing fastpitch, and something happened. I don't remember how or why. But
I remember how it ended. He just smacked me upside the head—didn't even
close his fist. Boy, did that hurt. Joe just had natural power."

Such ferocity belied his appearance. The dimpled sprite who delighted
girls at St. Mary's drew a smirk when he arrived with Linwood at Third Street.
The challenge was made earlier in the day at the public elementary school: if
Linwood had a partner, he could get a game, two-on-two basketball. "Third
Street was the Lower-*lower* end," says Alford. "This was the first time those
guys had met Joe because he went to St. Mary's. They were all laughing like:
who's this little scrawny kid? How you gonna win with this white guy?"

A bucket had been affixed to a light pole, some coins tossed in a hat,
maybe two bucks total. That was the pot.

The game was played a little differently here. The kids had already acquired an insolent body language, a bop, the beginnings of a swagger. Guys
like Benny Singleton could dribble behind their backs and between their legs.
But this sport was more than slick tricks. You played through split lips and
bloody noses.

Joe fit right in. He had quickness, a good enough shot, and no fear going
to the basket. "You knocked him down, he got right back up," says Alford. "Joe
wasn't no pretty boy."

But he looked like one. And that altar boy look proved a fantastic hustle in itself.

"Kid had a lot of confidence," says Benny Singleton.

Joey won more than the pot that day. He won new respect, new friends. Soon, he'd be sneaking his pals into the gym at St. Mary's. Was it a crack in the door? An open window? Or did he have a key? Who remembers? Once, in seventh or eighth grade, the janitor walked in, interrupting the game in progress. Even an aspiring hustler like Joe couldn't talk his way out of that one.

"Somebody had to pay the price, and it wasn't going to be any of us," recalls Singleton. "No black kids went to Saint Mary's. So Joe got suspended for a while."

It wouldn't be the last time. Joe kept on sneaking into gyms. It was lot better than having to shovel snow off the court at projects or shooting at a bucket on a light pole. The guys from Third Street would always remember the day he took their money. Who could have known the little kid had that kind of game?

Actually, there was a clue, if anybody thought to look. "Joe always had big hands," says Alford. "Even as a little kid, he almost looked deformed, they were so big."

"I had pretty good-size hands," says Butch Ryan, who came out of the Harmony Dwellings projects. "And Joe's were a full knuckle bigger than mine. But all we knew is, he could throw the ball. Any kind of ball."

■   ■   ■

Those hands alone qualified him for service as a quarterback. Sandlot football teams were roughly organized along the same lines as the rock-fighting crews, with makeshift fields at Harmony Dwellings and the Moltrup Steel mill. Joey was easy to recognize. The kid who could barely see over the center's ass was one of the few with equipment: helmet, shoulder pads, even football pants.

"Joe had things the rest of us didn't have," says Ryan. "If he didn't get it from his Mama and Daddy, he got it from his big brothers."

The brothers gave him more than their hand-me-downs. Each of John Namath's sons was responsible for the next. Sonny, now a GI fighting in Korea, had been Bobby's tutor. Bobby, who dropped out of high school to get work at a mill, was still known throughout the Beaver Valley as a wizard of the sandlots. A quarterback, he had been working with Joey since he was six. Bobby, Namath would recall, "showed me how to grip the ball and, right from the beginning, he taught me how not to wind up, but to throw from my ear. He taught me how to get rid of the ball fast; he taught me quick release, even though I'm sure neither of us had ever heard the expression then."

Bobby's lessons would burn memory-deep in his muscles. Throwing a football requires more than mere arm strength. Power comes from the rotation of the torso, a coil wound from the hip. Soon, Frank joined Bobby and started drilling the kid, too. Joey was ordered to throw the ball over telephone wires and trees. The brothers Namath were grim taskmasters. "They put a lot of pressure on Joe," says Alford. "They made sure he got it right. If Joe didn't do it right, they'd slap him upside the head. Sometimes, they'd hit Joe so hard with the football they'd knock him down."

Rita would stick her head out the window and yell: "Don't throw so hard at that little kid."

No one messed with Rita. "Not only could Rita throw the ball herself," says Butch Ryan, "Rita could kick your ass, too. If we got out of line, Rita would kick our asses. It was a long time before I found out she was adopted. She was like one of the boys. Probably, coming into that family, she had no choice."

Joey didn't have much choice, either, certainly not with Frank around. It was Frank, more than anybody, who served as Joey's keeper. He was tough, strong, and a little square, like a drill sergeant. "Frank was the hard-ass," says Alford.

"All the brothers were tough on him, but Frank was *really* tough," recalled Jake Lotz, who became a close friend of Joe's in junior high.

Frank, a catcher in high school, was good enough for the Baltimore Orioles to offer a $20,000 bonus for his services. That kind of money usually meant the catcher had a gun for an arm. Frank had aimed that gun right between Joey's eyes. Joey was about nine then. Frank put him up against the side of the house, gave him a mitt, and started burning them in as hard as he could. The boy caught everything Frank threw.

"If I didn't," Namath said, "he'd have killed me."

Frank's ass had been kicked by Bobby, whose ass had been kicked by Sonny. Now it was Frank's turn to kick some ass. But unlike Bobby, who was known as a rebel, Frank always did the right thing. He was on the homemaking club, the trampoline club, and the pep club. He played three years of varsity baseball and was captain of the football team. Frank was a catcher and a lineman, positions that called for strength and steadfastness. "He was a strong kid," Dom Casey, the local American Legion coach, once recalled. "But he couldn't move like Joe." Frank was plodding and powerful; Joey was a wisp, full of cool magic. Perhaps Frank's love for Joey was tinged with envy. But his overriding instinct was a sense of responsibility. Frank was always the responsible one. Frank would make sure Joey's gifts were not wasted. He just wanted to help his kid brother. And sometimes, the best way to help Joey was to kick his ass.

The notion of Janos Nemeth, the Hungarian boy separated from those of his own blood, haunted Joey. It would remain with him always. "He was the last one from his family to come to America," Namath would say. "I often have thought about that, what it's like to be left behind."

Joey did not fear much from physical harm. He would hang off a train trestle. He could take all his brothers would give, all those beatings served up as disciplinary medicine. But these mere thoughts—of separation, of fractures in the family, of being left behind—disturbed him deeply.

Consider a day that the Namaths went to visit Rose's brother in Masillon, Ohio. The trip was unremarkable but for the absence of Linwood, who usually came along on these family outings. Without Linwood, Joey fell into a mood of unrelenting despair. He was still sobbing on the way back to Beaver Falls. Perhaps this reaction was extreme—but not for Joey. Joey thought of Linwood as family.

As a man, Joe Namath would enjoy a reputation for candor. He would

4. BOY AT THE TOP OF THE STAIRS

be advertised as a man who told it like it was. In fact, Namath didn't tell much at all. He was much closer to the strong and silent archetype. Joe Namath did not reveal himself. He didn't surrender intimacies. Sure, he'd be happy to rehash the Guarantee, especially for a fee. But his emotional life—*family life*—that was never part of the deal. He'd show the famous scars on his knees. He'd even let you touch that grapefruit-sized ball of mangled tissue on his hamstring. But he'd give not a glimpse of, or even a hint at, the internal scar tissue. He'd talk about concussions and broken bones. But never the broken heart, his original wound. Years later, at the beginning of a new millennium, this is as much as he would allow: "I can remember as a three- or four-year-old, to this day, hearing them downstairs talking or arguing about something. I was upstairs and I came to the top of the steps and I was crying because it got me scared."

He had reason to be scared. Perhaps the fear was in his bones, something from his own father's boyhood lodged in the marrow, the knowledge that separation is inevitable. Families fracture. You *can* get left behind.

■ ■ ■

A photograph of John Namath hints of his longing for another life: more gentle, more genteel, the good life. At his side are two sons, the oldest and the youngest. Sonny looks to be in high school. Joey's still a kid, his hair wet, perfectly parted. He comes up to the stickpin on his father's tie. The occasion is unknown, but it might as well be a celebration of John Namath himself.

Andras Nemet would have been proud. His son had learned American. And to study the photograph is to see just how American John Namath had become. His full head of hair is swept back, jet black but for a bolt of silver. His nose is prominent, his hands meaty. But unlike so many of his fellow mill workers, John Namath didn't have a beer gut. He didn't like beer much, anyway. He'd rather have a gin and Squirt.

The guys at the mill didn't wear stickpins, either. His looks to be a pearl. Clothes might not make the man, but the good stuff doesn't hurt. His tie is striped and knotted, set off by a crisp white shirt. The shoes are two-toned, white and saddle brown. He's wearing a suit: slacks comfortably pleated and cuffed, a single button fastened on the jacket. The suit is white.

The man in the white suit looks as if he could own a racehorse. He could be a Wall Streeter on vacation in Havana. He could even be a movie star. But not a Hunky steelworker.

John Namath was not one to call attention to himself. But here he seems unusually dapper for a workingman. Just the *idea* of a white suit was slightly absurd in Beaver Falls. The mill furnaces were always belching out foul clouds, leaving people of the Beaver Valley in a sooty miasma. Tiny flakes of ash fluttered to the ground. They got in your hair, your clothes, your car, even in the back of your throat. The air was bitter, acrid. In the winter, when the fumes were most moist, you could taste the mills, the flavor of the slag heaps. You could taste the coal people burned for heat. There were no white Christmases, only gray. Mothers warned their children to stick their tongues back in their mouths. "Honey, don't eat the black snow."

And there's John Namath in his white suit, an act of splendid defiance for a man who toiled in a mill.

Namath worked for Babcock & Wilcox, the largest mill in town. B & W made steel tubing. The process started with scrap metal. The scrap was melted in the furnace, where it became a molten soup. The soup was poured into a mold, making ingots. Then the ingots were cut into square blooms. Blooms were divided into bars. Bars became billets. Billets were rolled and plugged into tubes.

John Namath would spend fifty-one years at B & W, most of them as a roller on Hot Mill #2. It was a job that required both seniority and skill. The roller, he once said, "is the top man. It's real hot work. You're on your feet all the time. You get a piece of hollow steel pipe dropped down in the trough by the operator. You got to plug her. You got a bar in the middle with a hole in the end of it. You put a pin in it and on that pin you run a plug. Maybe this piece of hollow would only be 8 or 9 or 10 feet long. . . . You stretch it out maybe 15, 18, 20 feet."

In a town known for black snow, John Namath worked at the source of the soot. The billets were 2,100 degrees Fahrenheit when they were pierced in the hot mills. "Even in the summer when it was 100 degrees outside," said John Namath, "we had to wear long underwear to keep from getting burned."

Workers didn't wear protective masks. John Namath would develop emphysema, which, considering the incidence of lung cancer, wasn't such a bad break. He wondered if he had gotten it from smoking. No, the doctor told him: "It's all that damn dirt and steel dust you guys have been breathing all them years. . . . Your lungs are just full of it."

Kids like Joey could spot a veteran steelworker in a second. Mill work turned white men shades of gray. Men of fifty who looked seventy shuffled through the town. They could be seen coughing into handkerchiefs, spitting up their lungs.

Most boys expected to become what their fathers were. Fathers expected it, too. But not John Namath. This wasn't the old country. Mill workers were just modern serfs. John Namath wanted better for his boys. Maybe Joey most of all. The father could handle himself in a bar or a ball field or at the mill. In his own home, his word was law. But for all that toughness, there was also tenderness. When Joey was in first grade, he made a card for his father. It read: "Daddy Will You Be My Valentine?" John Namath kept it folded in his wallet.

Joey's father responded in kind, with many tokens of his affection. There were the electric football games and a baseball glove. There were countless days and nights spent in the stands watching Joey play ball. They had their father-and-son outings, too. John even took Joey to a lake, where he fished off a boat and caught a trout. It was a puny trout, but his first. That alone was enough for a memorable day. Still, their day on the lake was not nearly the success that their day at the mill was.

Joey was eleven when his father took him to B & W. "It was terrifying," he would recall. "The noise. The heat. The molten metal. I vowed I would never work in such a place, and to this day I'm convinced that's why he took me there."

■   ■   ■

By the summer of 1955, not long after his twelfth birthday, Joey was the only kid left in the house. Sonny was in the army. Bobby was working in the mill. Rita and Frank had just graduated from high school. Frank, who won an athletic scholarship to the University of Kentucky, would be the first Namath to go to college.

But the marriage of John and Rose remained troubled, not much changed since the day that Joey stood crying at the top of the stairs. The love John Namath felt for his children did not extend to his wife. Though a fine father, he left something to be desired as a husband. The man in the white suit had found a lover.

Esther Mae Armour, eleven years younger than John, was an attractive divorcée from New Brighton, the town just across the river. On December 14, 1938, she married one Lawrence Armour. By July of 1942, Armour had left her and their two young sons. He told her there was another woman. Esther waited for him to come to his senses. She waited four years. By then, her husband had found another mistress in Detroit. Finally, on October 1, 1947, Judge Robert E. McCreary granted Esther's petition for divorce. She had, in the language of the law, suffered "such indignities as to render her condition intolerable and life burdensome."

But as sometimes happens, one woman's indignities become another's. For Rose, the first among them was her discovery that John had purchased a diamond ring and cameo set. Later, the court papers would refer to these as "articles for feminine use." But Rose had a clearer understanding. They were trinkets of the good life, not intended for a housewife making Hunky soup in Beaver Falls.

John told her to mind her own business.

Then she found the rubbers.

They must be Bobby's, he said.

Maybe she believed him. Lord knows she wanted to. But John didn't make it easy. He went out most evenings, leaving the house shortly after six P.M. Rose would ask where he was going. Bowling, he said, then to the club.

Funny, John didn't look like that when he took *her* bowling. All of a sudden, John Namath had become the world's best-dressed bowler. He didn't keep bowlers' hours, either, returning home at one A.M. on work nights.

By now, word of John Namath and Esther Armour was all over town. Rose waited for this misbehavior to pass. And when mere patience proved fruitless, she hired a private detective. Finally, she started following him herself. She watched as John took Esther to the Blackhawk golf course. She watched as they ducked into the bar. Some hours later, she watched as her husband denied it all.

The next morning, John drove Rose to her job at W. T. Grant's, a five-and-dime store where she worked as a clerk. He hadn't even bothered to remove the evidence. The back seat was still littered with love-nut shells and tissues smeared with lipstick. Esther had left her sunglasses, too. "Look what I found," said Rose. "Whose are these?"

John grabbed the glasses and put them in his pocket. His capacity for denial was spectacular, but this tragically dishonest ritual of accusation and refutation was coming to an end. Finally, the preponderance of evidence forced him to admit his adulterous conduct. Yes, he acknowledged, he had had an affair with Esther Armour, and yes, the ring and cameo set had been for her. But that was all in the past. It was over, he promised.

In fact, it had just begun. For Joey, who wasn't a little boy anymore, the pain was no longer a matter of imagination or anticipation. His brothers and Rita were gone. This was all he had feared at the top of the stairs. He'd been left behind.

"His daddy left him when he was in the seventh grade," says Jack Hicks, for many years a devoted friend of Namath's. "He told me that was the saddest day of his life."

The house at 802 Sixth Street was sold for $7,000 on September 17, 1956. "Joey and I were suddenly out on our own," Rose would recall. "The next several years were the most trying ones of his life—and mine. It was hard for me to find steady employment. I was only forty-three, but I had spent all of my life raising a family, and good jobs just weren't that easy to come by. We moved around from apartment to apartment, and just when we got settled into one place it seemed as though we would have to move out and look for another. For the most part, people sincerely tried to be helpful, and they were. But we often ran into cruel individuals who cared only about themselves, like one landlord I'll never forget who rented us a house knowing very well it was going to be torn down three weeks later.

"It was a struggle, but Joey was a great help to my spirits and somehow we managed. He couldn't possibly have known all of my frustrations, but I think he sensed them. And when he did, he'd always calm me by saying, 'Don't worry, Mom. Things will be okay.'"

Don't worry, Mom. That was the very best of him, of both the boy and the man he would become, a magnificent demonstration of virtues associated with masculinity: gallantry, strength, stoicism, confidence. *Things will be okay.* Suddenly, the boy quaking and crying at the top of the stairs had become the man of the house. The bond between mother and son intensified.

"He got more affection, more love, more pain," said Zoltan Kovac, a Hungarian immigrant who became friendly with Rose after her separation. "When she cried, Joe was there. There was nobody else, just him. She had nobody else but Joe."

Suddenly Joey had to be responsible—for his own mother. He felt obligated, bound by honor, duty, and love. But the truth was, he didn't like this feeling, the idea that he could disappoint her. It made him literally sick to his stomach. Love was responsibility. Love was a stomachache. But he never let on. He never told her.

It was during these years that the umbilical circuits were rerouted. The child she once nursed now nursed her faith. "Looking into those sleepy, mischievous eyes," said Rose, "I just had to believe him."

Such a belief required more faith than playing the numbers. Rose and Joey were not exactly betting favorites here. Years later, Joe Namath became famous for winning the Super Bowl, beating the point spread, issuing the Guarantee. But he would never be more contemptuous of the odds than he was then, as a kid. *Don't worry, Mom. Things will be okay.*

Rose's account *Namath: My Son Joe* devotes less than a page to the family's domestic difficulties. In striking contrast is her explanation to the court-appointed master, who identified Rose as plaintiff and her husband as defendant: "When plaintiff tried to talk with the defendant about their difficulties, the defendant stated that the plaintiff and Mrs. Armour could not be compared; that Esther Armour was a lady, intimating that his wife was not, and that Esther Armour was built nice and his wife was old. Thereafter, the defendant frequently made similar remarks, which, of course, made the plaintiff feel very bad.

"When the plaintiff would reproach the defendant, the defendant would clench his fist as though to strike her and tell her to shut up, and on one occasion said that he would kill her."

As her situation grew more desperate, loan companies threatened to take her furniture. Tough luck, said John, who told her that he was now making less than $300 a month. She had him arrested for nonsupport. At the hearing, it was determined that his annual salary was about $8,500.

John would come to W. T. Grant's when she was at the cashier's and loudly demand a divorce. She had him arrested after he came to her house and threatened her. She dropped the charge.

From the master's report: "The plaintiff's health has been adversely affected. She had become nervous and sick and underwent an operation because of her nerves. Psychiatry has been recommended for her. She lost twenty pounds after her separation from her husband because of his bothering her."

Such were the offenses that rendered her condition intolerable and her life burdensome. These were the indignities of Rose Namath.

But they were also Joey's. He had no court to petition, no way to air grievances or to redress wrongs. All Joey could do was take it. His indignities were just that, *his.* They were not to be shared, discussed, or mentioned, not even with his friends.

"Before they moved, Joe's mom would come over to our house and go over her troubles with my mother," says Linwood Alford. "But Joe never talked about it with me, and I considered myself one of his best friends."

"He held it inside, and I'm glad he did," says Butch Ryan. "What happens in your household should stay there. There were things that happened in most of our households. It wasn't something you just go out and talk about."

What are families but blood and secrets? Giving them up would make a boy less of a man.

As the ninth grade began, Joey was living with his mother above a gin mill on Twenty-third Street at the north end of town. Having left St. Mary's when he left the neighborhood, he was now attending the local middle school, where his football ability remained largely unknown. "We always knew he was a quarterback," says Alford. "We knew before anybody." What passed for common knowledge on the Lower End was more difficult to fathom at the middle school. At five feet tall, 115 pounds, Joe was barely visible as he slouched behind the center, big Jimmy Seaburn. "You couldn't hardly see him over Seaburn," said Jake Lotz, the first-stringer.

5. PINT-SIZED QUARTER-BACK

Lotz, heir apparent as Beaver Falls' next high school quarterback, was eight or nine inches taller than Joey. "I was bigger than most kids," he says. "And I was fast."

But the day before the first game of the junior high season, Jake and Joey and some other kids snuck into the field house at Geneva College, turned on the lights, and started playing ball. They did this all the time. But for some reason that day, Jake was possessed by the inexplicable urge to start punching a pillar—"just goofing around, acting like a thirteen-year-old"—and broke a finger. Jake missed the season, his finger in a cast. "We only played five games," he recalls. "By the time it was healed, the season was over."

In his absence Joey got the starting job and his first mention in the sporting press. The *Beaver Falls News-Tribune* described him as the "pint-sized Quarterback." In his second game, he threw a pair of touchdowns in the first quarter, as the Beaver Falls Tiger Cubs beat Midland 31–0. The following week, they beat Ambridge, 7–0, on a touchdown pass from the pint-sized quarterback to Tommy Krzemienski late in the fourth quarter. The newspaper called Joey's crew "one of the most devastating offenses for a junior high team witnessed in several seasons."

Though impressive as Lotz's understudy, Joe drew even more notice on the court than the football field. Homeroom basketball became an adventure, with only three guys in the class: Joe, Benny Singleton, and a kid named Tommy. "Tommy, keep your hands up all the time," Joe instructed him. That was enough. With Joe and Benny, they could beat the other homerooms, three on five.

"By ninth grade, you could just tell with Joe," recalls Chuck Knox, then coaching junior high basketball in the neighboring town of Ellwood City. "The long arms, the big hands, the way he moved—very gracefully."

Knox couldn't have been more impressed. A good coach saw a kid not as he was, but as he could be. In Joe's case, the grace was augmented by a natural confidence, something in the way he carried himself.

Lotz recalls a game against Midland, Beaver Falls down by three in the last minute, when the coach called time-out: "Coach says, 'Nobody shoot but Namath. He's the one. He's going to take the shot.'" And that's just what happened. Joe hit the shot. Then, as the final seconds ticked off the clock, he stole the ball and sank the winning layup.

"Boy, could he handle the ball," says Lotz. "Even then, he knew where everybody should be." They became good friends, perhaps because Jake didn't consider Joey much of a threat as a quarterback. Joey was good for a couple of quick steps, but then he slowed down. Physically, he was still very much a boy. Jake, on the other hand, was already on the far side of puberty.

"I felt like I'd beat him out the next year," said Lotz. "And I did."

On the last week of August 1958—in accordance with a tradition established by the Beaver Falls booster club—Jake Lotz was among thirty-five or so of the best varsity players selected to report to Camp Lillian Taylor, a home for wayward girls in Mars, Pennsylvania. With two, sometimes three, daily workouts, those hot days at camp could be brutal. But they were even worse for the boys who had to spend them at home.

Joe was so hurt over not being invited that he told the coach, Bill Ross, that he was quitting football. Ross had seen the same talent that Chuck Knox had seen. He'd been watching Joey going all the way back to Little League. He'd known all the Namath boys. They were plenty big enough. This slouchy runt would grow, too. Quitting, he told Joe, would be a big mistake.

Beaver Falls had never been much of a football power. Ross, in the words of his successor, was just "too nice of a guy." After three losing seasons as coach at Beaver Falls, this would be his last. The Tigers went 3–6–1 in 1958 and were outscored 179 to 72. But that was also the year Bill Ross made his everlasting contribution to Beaver Falls, seeing to it that Joe Namath stuck around.

Joe didn't dress for all the games, but he practiced with the varsity. Later he would say, "Mr. Ross gave me the idea that he thought someday I might develop into a pretty good football player. I don't know whether he really believed that or not. He didn't believe it enough to use me at quarterback in a single game. The one chance I got to play all year, I played defensive halfback."

Practices were another story. An old assistant named Leland Schackern took an interest in Namath. "I'm going to make a passer out of you," he said. Schackern took over where Bobby and Frank had left off. "Mr. Schackern showed me how to throw the ball at different speeds and at different angles, how to loop one kind of pass and how to bullet another," Namath recalled. "While most kids my age were just hoping they could throw the ball the same way every time, I was varying my speed and my trajectory."

He was beginning to understand the position, the peculiar calculus of quarterbacking, the science of angles. There were two kinds of angles: those determined by distance, and those born of deception.

"He just had a way with the ball," says Lotz. "I remember being in the gym on a rainy day, and we were running a belly series. You ride the fullback through and pull it back at the last second. The way Joe did it, you couldn't tell if the fullback or the halfback had the ball. He could fake, and you never knew who had it."

Lotz was still a head taller than Joey. But Joey's arm had outpaced the rest of his body. "I couldn't throw the ball as well as he could," says Lotz. "I could see it coming. I knew he was better than me."

Lotz told the coaches he wanted to come back next season as the left halfback.

■   ■   ■

On November 15, 1958, Jake, Joe, and another friend of theirs snuck into the gym at Geneva College. There, they found that the equipment room just happened to be unlocked and helped themselves to an assortment of football shoes and jerseys belonging to Geneva's Golden Tornadoes. Then they hauled ass to their respective homes, where, some hours later, uniformed cops showed up to arrest them.

The case was adjudicated in downtown Beaver. Jake recalls waiting for the judge, scared to death that he would send them to the juvenile home, "juvie," as it was called. Joe sat with his parents. Jake knew Mrs. Namath and recognized her estranged husband as the one who attended his son's games so faithfully. "He was at all the games—from pony league to basketball," says Lotz.

Jake's mother gave him a nudge. She didn't want him talking to Joey. She didn't want him to have anything to do with that Namath boy. "You can't run around with him anymore," she said. "That kid is a bad influence."

Still, the judge figured he hadn't crossed the line into delinquency. Joe and his cohorts were released to the custody of their parents, who, it was safe to assume, would be far less merciful than His Honor. Nine years later, a report prepared for J. Edgar Hoover would list the disposition of this incident as "turned over to parents."

For Joe, it could have been a lot worse. Worse even than juvie. He could have been turned over to Frank.

■   ■   ■

Frank had left for Kentucky without any idea that the Orioles had offered him a $20,000 bonus. "His father and I never let him find out about it," Rose would write. "We just sat down at the kitchen table one day and decided college was more important." Though Rose described this as a joint decision, it's difficult to imagine John being very upset at the prospect of his son playing professional baseball. After all, John Namath believed in a boy's right to play whatever he wanted. John didn't express regret about being a high school dropout. He put work before school. And twenty grand represented a whole lot of work, nearly two and a half years in the mill.

Rose, on the other hand, always mourned her lack of education. College conferred a higher social standing, as enjoyed by those families up in Patterson Heights where she worked as a maid. She never regretted not telling Frank: "I think we made the right decision for him."

Frank was livid when he finally learned of the Orioles offer. But by then it was too late. University of Kentucky media guides reveal an unfulfilled collegiate career. In his first year, Frank led the freshman baseball team in home runs. But the following autumn, as a center for Blanton Collier's football team, he appeared in only five games, a total of nine minutes and fifty-three seconds, not enough to earn a letter. The 1957 media guide predicts bigger things for Frank: "You've got to find a place for fellows like Namath to play . . . tough and talented . . . should see more action than last year."

As it happened, though, '57 was his last year in Lexington. Dude Hennessey, then Kentucky's defensive line coach, recalls Frank as "a pretty good player," but also a torn one. "He said he was going to go home a couple times," recalls Hennessey. "Finally, the third time, he went."

Frank had a lot on his mind. His father was shacking up with Esther. Now Bobby, like Sonny, had gone off and joined the army. Rose and Joe were alone, and suddenly Frank had his own wife, with a baby on the way. With the birth of his son Michael on April 27, 1958, Frank became a kind of young patriarch, the one to reestablish the natural family order. He had never been easy on Joe, but now, in the absence of their father and older brothers, Frank became the prime authority figure.

"Frank was almost like a father," says Lotz. "Joe was always saying, 'I don't want Frank to know.' He was scared to death of Frank.

"I remember one time me and Joe went over to Frank's house. He was in the other room, and we were talking to his wife. She had a glass of wine, and me and Joe were taking sips from it. It made us goofy, and we were giggling like hell. Frank says, 'Yins sound like a bunch of girls in there.' It's a good thing he didn't walk in. If he'd have seen us drinking, he'd have kicked our asses."

Frank would kick Joey's ass if he caught him drinking. Frank would kick Joey's ass if he caught him smoking. Frank was stricter than their own father. By ninth and tenth grades, the cool guys were wearing their hair in pompadours lubed with pomade. Not Joe, though. Joe wasn't crazy enough to be that cool. "Everything was crew cut for Joe," says Lotz. "Frank wouldn't have had it any other way."

■   ■   ■

The Lotz family left Beaver Falls for California on June 3, 1959. By then, Jake had a pretty good idea that his pal would make a decent high school quarterback. After that? Well, at fifteen, he wasn't thinking much beyond that. But in the years to come, Jake Lotz would take great delight in the idea of Joe Namath as a squire to leading ladies. Whatever the harbingers of Joey's eventual success as a cocksman, Jake missed them. Rather, he recalls a dance they attended as sophomores, not long before he moved away. The pint-sized quarterback's powerful belief in himself had suddenly evaporated. He just looked down, without saying a word. Jake had never seen this before: Joe was scared. "I could tell by just looking at him," he says.

Then again, looking at Joe proved nothing. There were things about him that would always remain unknowable, off-limits. Perhaps the most inscrutable part of him involved women. He had his secrets. He didn't share them. You didn't ask. Asking him about girls was like asking about his mother. "Some stuff," says Linwood Alford, "Joe just kept to himself."

Even as he spent the dance staring at his shoes, Joe was about to get his first taste, a morsel to inaugurate a decades-long feast. He was barely sixteen when he lost his virginity. He had gone with a friend to the girl's house. She was a senior. She told the friend to wait downstairs. She wanted the pint-sized quarterback. As Namath would recall: "We went into her bedroom and we didn't even get undressed. It was just like lifting up her skirt and—surprise! It was kind of funny, and kind of nice."

That was always the best way, Broadway Joe's favorite brand: Kind of funny, kind of nice. Nothing too serious. Make sex, not love. You should feel it in your cock, not your gut. And that's just what happened when you got too serious, too attached, too tied down. You got an upset stomach.

Consider his experience with Frances Pinchotti, who lived above the grocery store across the street. Joe used to play ball with her older brother. Frances, a lithe brunette cheerleader, was a year behind him at the high school. In Beaver Falls, men of a certain age remember her cheerleading routines as full-fledged events, cartwheels and flips imparting a sexually charged tingle.

But for Joe, that tingle was less than the sensation she stirred in his gut, that invisible vise around his chest. He loved Frances. "The first girl I ever loved," he once said. "She was part of an Italian family and was a beautiful person inside. But God, I got this pain in my chest and my stomach and I hated it."

In the world of the pint-sized quarterback, where divorce informed all things, commitment meant angst. Love led to loss. Love was pain, physical and emotional. Sooner or later, it would hurt you. Look what it had done to his mother.

He would always recall that day she sent him to the store. He must have been fifteen or sixteen. He bought whatever she had sent him for and started walking home with her change. Then he ducked into the pool hall, the Blue Room. Joe went on to do a good bit of hustling at the Blue Room. But on this day, he was the one who got hustled.

A little change was a lot of money to Rose. Now he'd let his mother down, betrayed her trust. Then it hit him: the bad stomach, the pain. Even as a man in his thirties, he'd think of that ache as a driving force in his life: "She was waiting on the money and I lost it. I was so sick leaving that pool room I wanted to die. And all the way home I had that awful feeling inside, suffering. That stuck with me, remembering the damn thing." For Joe, love was a terrible responsibility, in a mother or a lover. "It might be one of the reasons I never got married or seriously involved with a girl."

Little wonder, then, that Namath became so famously unattached. As America's perennial bachelor, he liked to have a good time, to feel as if he were lifting that senior girl's skirt again and again. Bachelorhood was also good business: married men who bought shaving cream and cologne wanted to feel as if they, too, had a hand in lifting that skirt. But it wasn't a love of money or good times that would keep Namath single so long. It was fear of that old grief in his guts. Part of him remained the pint-sized quarterback, knowing that kind-of-funny, kind-of-nice was preferable to love, and a whole lot easier on the system.

■   ■   ■

There were, however, mother's medicines for the dread in his belly. These included chicken paprika, stuffed peppers, goulash, and dumpling-laden soup. His pals counted themselves lucky to be around as Rose set one of her dishes on the table. "Man, she slaved over that stove cooking for him," recalls Wibby Glover, a friend of Joe's.

 Zoltan Kovac, now good friends with Rose, implored her to teach his own wife to cook. Rose cooked as if she came from the old country, her culinary skill infused with a spirit much older than she, as if ancient Magyar instincts had been preserved in her American blood. Her work in the kitchen was a little like prayer, devotional and therapeutic. Watching Joey eat gave her some rare moments of happiness.

For the first time since the Depression, Rose was poor. Pennsylvania's divorce statutes included no provision for alimony. John, who had been a generous father, now became stingy with the support money. "He was pissed off he had to pay support," says Kovac. "He had a young sweetheart, and so Rose was a burden to him. Let me tell you, it was no love lost between those two."

"There was a lot of hate," says Wibby Glover. "The older boys, Frank and Bobby and Johnny, felt like the father left their mother high and dry."

Mr. Namath would take Joe to buy clothes at Taylor's department store. But nothing for Rose. Wibby remembers giving her his sweater. It was black and red and new; he'd just bought it at Berkman's. But Rose was obviously cold. "Take it," he insisted.

Occasionally, Rose would go bowling, or to the Hungarian Club in Ellwood City. That's where she met Stephen Szolnoki, a quiet man recovering from his own misfortune. Szolnoki had been among the mass of "displaced persons" left in Hungary after the war. He came to America in 1949 and became a widower in January 1957. Kovac knew him from the Westinghouse plant, where he was a welder and Szolnoki a drill press operator. As Szolnoki didn't have much interest in speaking or learning English, Kovac acted as his translator.

Kovac was there the night his friends met at the Hungarian Club. Szolnoki was eleven years older than Rose. It wasn't love at first sight. "I don't think so," says Kovac. "She more likely married him because he had a house. She was renting on a pretty poor block at Twenty-third and Eighth Avenue. But Steve had a nice house on Twelfth Street and Fourth Avenue."

Rose and Joe were already living there, at 1207 Fourth Avenue, by August 24, 1959, the day she finally filed for divorce. Her petition was granted before the year was over, Judge Morgan H. Sohn ruling that Rose had demonstrated sufficient indignities "as to render her condition intolerable and life burdensome." She and John—who never showed up or testified for the proceedings—were now free to go on with their lives "as if they had never been married." *As if they had never been married.* Try explaining that to Joe. Some months later, on March 4, 1960, Rose and Stephen Szolnoki would be joined in holy matrimony.

"The way Joe figures, Steve is interfering with the *family*," says Kovac. "The old man tried to give him good advice. But he don't want to listen." Out of respect to his mother, Joe didn't talk back to Szolnoki. But *listen*? He sure as shit wasn't going to listen. This Szolnoki was a stranger to Joe. He wasn't blood. He wasn't cool. He didn't even speak American. Who was he to be eating his mother's dumplings?

Following the 1958 season, the fourth straight losing campaign for the Beaver Falls Tigers, Bill Ross was promoted to athletic director, and was thereby relieved of his responsibilities as football coach. As his replacement, he chose Larry Bruno, who had done well coaching football, basketball, and track in the nearby town of Monaca. Ross had known Bruno since their days at Geneva College.

Bruno played halfback, well enough to be selected for the 1946 East-West Shrine Game. That December, the Pittsburgh Steelers selected him with the 129th pick in the National Football League's annual draft. Bruno had a good showing in training camp, but left after Monaca offered him a full-time position teaching and coaching. He wanted to be a coach. Besides, back then pro football was not to be confused with a real job.

6. MAGIC

The son of a tailor from Naples, Bruno had grown up in East Liverpool, Ohio. The family lost its home during the Depression, and Larry and his sister were consigned to the back of their father's shop. A row of clothes separated the children's quarters from the customers' domain. They had no hot water, no bathtub, just a commode.

For Bruno, two endeavors offered respite from poverty. The first was football, which earned him a scholarship to Geneva and kept him out of the mills. The other was magic. He had been fascinated by magic since his father had made an exhibition of the knife trick, whereby spots would disappear and reappear on either side of a blade. Later, while playing basketball for Geneva, he stayed at the Plymouth Hotel in New York City. Next door was a novelty shop, a "magic store," as Bruno calls it, with an assortment of tricks in the window. He spent his last dollar on spongeballs and a deck of cards.

Bruno never thought of magic in spooky or supernatural terms. Rather, he delighted in deception. Give him a little room in the auditorium or the Kiwanis Club, and he could pull rabbits from hats and doves from saucepans. He could make his wife, Ginny, vanish in a box that had been run through with swords. There was no magic, of course. There was only a fake, a move that got the audience looking the other way. "I believed in faking," he says.

This belief informed his theory of the game. "Magic is the same as football," he says. "Now you see it, now you don't. It's all misdirection." Football, as taught by Larry Bruno, required more than size (which was fortunate, considering that Beaver Falls didn't have a starter bigger than 195 pounds). It required craft, some of which Bruno learned from Babe Parilli, the great faking quarterback from nearby Rochester who had played for Bear Bryant at Kentucky. Bruno took extra time with his skilled players, his backs and ends. He offered a special tutorial in the game's magic arts. Under Bruno, quarterbacks were expected to fake flawlessly. The hand went into the back's belly, wrist deep—*always* wrist deep. You had to sell a fake. You had to get them looking the other way. It all came down to sleight of hand. Small, subtle movements caused a defense to suspend its disbelief. Fakes froze the linebackers. Now you see it, now you don't. You can't tackle the guy with the ball if you don't know who has it. The offense began with the fake. The fake began with the quarterback.

Fake was just another word for a hustle. And Joe, now a pool hall regular, had been honing his hustling skills most of his life, ever since his larcenous instincts and unnaturally big hands led him to palm Clark Bars from Snowden's drugstore.

"Everybody said he was going to be a great quarterback—if you could handle him," recalls Bruno. "He had a bad reputation. But that was other people's version of Joe."

Where others saw a delinquent, Bruno saw a prince. In regard to Joe, Bruno engaged in a different kind of misdirection—getting himself to look the other way. Take, for example, his prohibition against smoking. Players caught smoking were suspended. Joe smoked. But the trick was not catching him. "I never tried to," he says.

Same with curfew. When Bruno became coach, he started calling players' homes at night to make sure they were tucked in safe and sound. Bruno would phone third-stringers, scrubs. But somehow, he never got around to ringing his starting quarterback, though the kid was already known for keeping very late hours.

Then there was the gym. Bruno knew all about Joe's history of breaking and entering gymnasiums, from St. Mary's to Geneva College. But he couldn't be accused of breaking into the high school gym. Not after Bruno gave him a set of keys.

Bruno tried not to show favoritism. But like most coaches, he did. Joe's talent made it inevitable. "You only had to tell him once," says Bruno. "He just had the right moves." In Joe, the coach saw an embodiment of the attributes he held dear: deception, speed, craft, the makings of an ideal magician.

Joe still wasn't ready—not yet. Programs for the 1959 season list him, a bit generously perhaps, at five-nine, 156 pounds. Rich Niedbala, the returning starter, was six-one, 195. Niedbala was also a senior, good enough to win a scholarship to the University of Miami. Bruno could wait. You didn't rush a kid like Joe. This was the kid who could make your career.

Still, Bruno's feelings for Joe were based on more than just talent. Joe didn't lie. He wouldn't allow himself to be insulted. You couldn't ride him too hard, couldn't call him names. But if you gave Joe respect, he'd give it back in spades. He wanted a little fathering. Bruno understood all too well.

"My mother and dad got divorced, and I know what that was like," says Bruno. "Of course, when something like that happens, everybody goes against the father. Joe's brothers, they weren't speaking to the dad. They thought he was the worst guy in the world. They would tell Joe how bad his father was, how he was this and that. And he sort of listened. You could tell, he would've wanted to speak with his dad. But his brothers said not to. Something like that.

"But I would tell him, 'Joe, you know my mother and dad were divorced. I loved my mother and I loved my dad. And nobody's gonna tell me any different.' I'd tell him 'Joe, no matter what happens, he's still your father.'

"We were very close, me and Joe. Little stuff like that I could throw at him and he'd listen. But you had to do it delicately."

■   ■   ■

Joe might have been forty pounds lighter than Rich Niedbala, but his presence was immense. "You could feel it," says Niedbala. "I remember when we were in Little League, the Optimists and the Elks, and the manager gave him the ball to pitch. You wondered where all his velocity came from. He was all bones and skin. But he always had that swagger, that confidence."

Niedbala had size, strength, and experience. But now he'd be sharing the quarterback duties. He might even lose his starting spot. "I knew there was a chance," he says. "I knew Joe's ability."

Neither Niedbala nor Joe complained. Joe played some halfback, and a little defensive back, but mostly quarterback. In the second game, a 33–19 loss to Sharon, he was impressive enough to be named "Back of the Week," courtesy of Kane's Men's Store on Seventh Avenue. He even got his picture in the paper.

Niedbala asked Larry Bruno if he could play safety. But the coach still didn't want to move too fast. He was thinking of next year, not this one.

As the season came to a close, the town was not in good spirits. A 116-day steelworkers strike had come to a halt when President Eisenhower invoked the Taft-Hartley Act. One local sage compared it to "taking the ball to the goal line and then being penalized 15 yards." The metaphor seemed particularly apropos in Beaver Falls, where people had become accustomed to losing football. Going into their final game, the Tigers were 3–5–1. Nineteen-fifty-nine would be another losing season. But as it ended, it didn't feel that way.

On November 13, the Tigers faced New Brighton, the town on the other side of the Beaver River. According to tradition, they played for a mud jug, a symbol of bragging rights. But this game would signal a break from a dismal tradition for Beaver Falls. Namath came on in the second quarter with the Tigers already up 14–0. His first pass was a touchdown, a twenty-four-yarder to the gifted end Tom Krzemienski. It was the first of three touchdown passes for Joe. He ran for one, too.

"We were winning pretty good," recalls Bruno, "so I put in next year's team with Joe at quarterback. They were terrific. They were better than the team I had."

Bruno had suspected that his underclassmen might be this impressive. But here was proof. Krzemienski and Tony Golmont, the ends, were brilliant. The backfield of Butch Ryan and Bo Hayden was as good as anyone's—and they were only sophomores. Hayden ran ninety-one yards for a touchdown on the last play of the game. Another touchdown came on Namath's "jump pass," a specialty of his, which, as the name implied, had him throwing from a leap in midair. Joe didn't need to plant his feet. The jump pass demonstrated an astonishing contempt for gravity. What's more, his play selection demonstrated a precocious knowledge of football's finer points. Joe called his own game, the plays in the huddle and the audibles at the line of scrimmage. Teachers might complain about Joe and his C-minus average, but as far as Bruno was concerned, they didn't understand the boy. Joe knew something you didn't get from textbooks. He knew the angles. Some he knew intuitively, others through study. He watched game films. He made careful observation of his opponent's nature. He listened. "Never had a kid with a higher football IQ," said Bruno. "He might've been able to call the plays better than me."

In his account of the game, the *News-Tribune*'s Joe Tronzo also noticed Namath's "amazing" knack for making "excellent calls on the line, changing the signals when he saw an opening." Beaver Falls easily won the mud jug. The final score was 52–7. But by then, who was counting? Bruno understood what he had waiting for him next year.

■   ■   ■

Many adults thought of the Blue Room as a finishing school for ne'er-do-wells. Coach Bruno was not among them. The pool hall, where hustlers were held in highest esteem, was actually good for a kid like Joe. He could sharpen his knack for the fake, not to mention his hand-eye coordination.

The Blue Room, 1422 Seventh Avenue, had been converted from a bowling alley to a pool hall in 1948. You entered through a luncheonette off the street. Behind the dining area were the tables: a dozen Gold Crown Brunswicks with ashtrays atop each corner pocket. They cost Pete Greco, the owner, about $900 apiece. But only nine dimes bought you an hour on one of the prime tables in the front. The back tables were even cheaper, six dimes an hour, a penny a minute. Suspended above each table was a four-foot fluorescent bulb and a shade fashioned from metal and porcelain. The harsh light had an enchanting effect. Its glow transformed cigarette smoke into a kind of incense, a holy haze for boys who wanted to think of themselves as men.

You went to the Blue Room when you cut class. You went to the Blue Room when you didn't want to go home. You went to the Blue Room because you were too old to play pinball at Earl's Dairy, but not yet old enough to drink at the bar. You went to loaf, to lie about girls, to smoke (Joe puffed Salems when Frank wasn't around). You went to be cool. Cool was the religion of adolescent males, and the Blue Room one of its temples.

Cool made American boys different from their immigrant fathers. Cool was the bop in your step, the pearl in your cap, the cigarette dangling from your lip. Cool was the way you kept a secret and the way you played ball.

At the cusp of a new decade, the coolest kids in Beaver Falls were the football players. Coming off that win against New Brighton, Joe wasn't yet recognized as the best, but he was the coolest. He was cool in a way that belied his flat-top haircut or still-undersized physique. To see Joe operate at those Brunswick tables was to understand. Pool was about angles, real and metaphorical. Again, there were better players in town—those more practiced or technically able—but none who could wink so well at the odds, or the stakes.

"I probably should have gotten my high school diploma from the Blue Room," he once said.

The etiquette of pool was itself an advanced seminar in cool. Guys came dressed for success: peak-billed berets, straight-legged pants, and "Italians," calfskin shoes you could only buy in Pittsburgh. "Italians were a big deal," recalls Linwood Alford. "So soft you could fold them up in your pocket." Socks were important, too. You had to display a design of suitable cool on your ankle. An embroidered red diamond was always good. You had to look the part. The hustler learns young that style and substance are indivisible.

They played eight-ball, nine-ball, and a game called Charlie. Charlie began with two numbered pills being tossed from a shaker. The number on the first pill determined the order in which you shot. The second pill was your ball, the one you had to put down. If another player knocked in your ball, you won. Seven or eight guys might be playing at one table. Charlie was a quick game, and an expensive one, too. With enough players doubling their bets, you could win or lose forty, fifty bucks on a single shot. Charlie required skill. But even more, it called for luck. Then again, luck was a kind of skill. Making people believe in your luck was, perhaps, the greatest skill. *That* was magic.

Once a guy believes you're lucky, you got him. His money is yours.

Playing for money changed the nature of the game. Joe learned that much as a child, going back to the day that he and Linwood won the money in the hat. Even if you were just playing for quarters, money meant pressure. Playing for money made guys play not to lose. There was shame in losing your money. The possibility of failure raised a tremor in your blood. But not Joe's. At least that's what you were thinking, looking at him across the table. Joe might have been desperate for your quarter. But he never let on. He made it look easy, as easy as that senior sweetie lifting her skirt. That's what he wanted you to think. In a way, that was his genius.

"Didn't matter if Joe had twenty dollars in his pocket or five cents," says Fred Klages, a three-sport star from nearby Ambridge. "He'd play you for a hundred. He should have played the Hustler instead of Jackie Gleason."

"He had more guts than you could imagine," recalls Butch Ryan. "The money was not a factor for him. Money was not going to put the pressure on him to blow a shot that he shouldn't blow."

"If it was a shot that had, say, a ten percent probability, Joe approached it like it was ninety-nine percent, a gimme," says Rich Niedbala.

"He would snicker a lot," Alford remembers. "He would look at you and smile, like: 'you know you can't beat me.' He'd be messing with your mind. I seen him beat guys who were better than him. They'd be cussing Joe out, and Joe would just laugh."

In retrospect, one wonders if Namath incited any discussion among the local bookies operating out of Dom & John's Sports Bar, next door to the Blue Room. As bookmakers belong to a fraternal society—a network of wise men who traffic in information—there might have been an early line on the Namath kid. Instead, he would go on to surprise them, again and again.

All they had to do was watch him shoot pool. Joe believed he was better than anyone out there. Not only that, but he made the other kids believe it, too. They wanted what he had, and they'd back him up to get a little touch of it.

Rich Niedbala still remembers that day the Blue Room waitress brought him his sandwich. It wasn't what Joe had ordered. The waitress, Pete Greco's niece, gave Joe some lip. Joe, then a junior, gave her some lip right back. She went and got her uncle, who threw Joe out.

"Next day," says Niedbala, "there was like a boycott. Nobody went in. All of a sudden the dimes weren't popping on those tables."

Joe didn't have anything to do with it. That would have meant he was hurt, that he cared. It wouldn't have been cool. The boycott wasn't a day old before Pete Greco folded. He missed those dimes. This was a money game, and Joe, that little hustler, had him beat.

■　　■　　■

Joe's nascent brilliance—his daring aptitude for the angles—did not extend to academic pursuits. He could usually convince his mother or one of his nonsteady girlfriends to do his homework. Who needed school anyway? He wanted to be a baseball player. And if baseball didn't work out, he kind of liked the idea of going into the air force and flying planes.

Still, in anticipation of the many colleges that would soon be courting him as a football star, Coach Bruno suggested that Joe attend summer school. The extra courses, explained the coach, would placate the tweedy types in the admissions offices. John Namath was impressed with Bruno's argument, and offered his son an incentive: "I'd make sure he had enough money and I'd even let him use my car a couple nights a week."

But shortly before junior year ended Joe called his dad, telling him that his mother was *buying* him a car.

Oh, that burned John's ass. A judge had recently ordered him to pay Rose's court costs for the divorce. Now Rose had found another way to stick it to him. So much for summer school, he told his son.

No, said Joe, he'd still go to summer school.

He never did, though, preferring to tool around in a 1951 Ford.

"An old piece of junk it was," said John Namath.

"*Famous* junk," Zoltan Kovac qualifies. "That car was famous junk around here."

It was Kovac who found the car, which was grayish black—primer, not paint—and seems to have been pushed as often as driven. Friends who recall the old Ford estimate its value as scrap metal. But Kovac puts the price at about $200. He should know. He lent Rose the money.

"I was on the father's shit list for a long time because I helped Joe get that car," says Kovac. "John said, 'Why don't you give him the money to buy gas, too?' "

Actually, Joe had a job that should've kept him in gas money—caddying at the Blackhawk Country Club. Then again, most of the time, it was easier to siphon gas from other cars.

Famous junk indeed. When he could get it to run, that car announced him, his peculiar presence: part prankster, part punk, part prince. He siphoned gas. He went double the speed limit. He'd even drive that big old Ford up on the sidewalk, right on Seventh Avenue, an evasive maneuver in a game of bumper tag. The Ford might have been a wreck, but guys loved to ride with Joe, to share in the feeling of his luck.

Step on the pedal. Roll down the window. Feel the wind. Wheels gave you wings. You weren't tasting black snow anymore. Your mother wasn't shacked up with some guy from the old country. You were flying. You could head down Blackhawk Road to Negley, Ohio, where the drinking age was eighteen and they gladly accepted fake ID. The beer was only 3.2 percent alcohol, piss water. But you didn't need much back then. What a wonderful world it was, buzzed on beer. You'd fly high back from Negley.

"Negley was a fifteen-minute drive, ten the way Joe drove," says Rich Niedbala. "I don't know how many times we got pulled over with Joe driving, and for whatever reason, the cops never seemed to give him a ticket."

One night Joe was driving to an American Legion baseball game with Butch Ryan, Rich, and his cousin Billy, who wasn't playing due to the fact that he had broken his jaw sliding into home some weeks before. They were late for the game, so Joe tried a shortcut: the wrong way down a one-way street in New Brighton. The cops pulled him over, siren lights whirring. "Didn't you see the sign?" said the cop. "One-way."

"We ain't going but one way," said Joe.

Another kid might have gotten a beating with his ticket. Another kid might have spent the night in jail. But Joe wasn't another kid. The cops started laughing. If the boy had enough balls to say that, he wasn't getting a ticket.

That same night, after the game, Joe put pedal to metal on the way home. "He was flying," says Butch Ryan. "And I mean *flying*." Again, the cops pulled him over. Joe watched them in the rearview mirror as they got out of the marked car. Then he told Billy Niedbala, whose jaw was wired shut, "Start acting hurt. Really hurt."

As the cop asked for Joe's license, Billy started moaning.

"Look at this guy," said Joe. "We gotta get him to Providence Hospital."

The cop didn't quite know what to do. The moaning kid sure didn't look too good.

"Officer," said Joe, nodding back at Billy. "We gotta get going."

The cop tried to look suspicious. He knew he might be getting played. But he didn't have the nerve to write the ticket.

The boys were laughing their asses off as Joe floored it again, peeling out on Route 65, flying home in his famous junker.

■   ■   ■

Spring and summer were for baseball. American Legion Post 261 had a renowned team, "the Tommies," so named for Colonel Joseph H. Thompson, a son of Beaver Falls whose valor during the Battle of the Marne earned him a Congressional Medal of Honor. In 1960, as managed by Dom Casey, the Tommies won county, district, and area-level championships. Casey's roster was blessed with the same kids as Bruno's: Niedbala, Ryan, Krzemienski, and of course Namath. Joe loved the game. Casey would recall Joe showing up for a game immediately after the dentist pulled his tooth. He pitched five innings of one-hit ball that day. That's how Joe was. If it was his turn to pitch, he took the ball. The days he didn't pitch, he played the outfield. "Joe could charge a ball and make the play at the plate better than anybody, that's the reason I played him in left field," Casey once said. "He acted like an infielder playing the outfield."

At the plate, he was a hitter of fierce line drives. He was growing, too. Before the summer was over Joe would be six-one, 175 pounds. No longer did coaches have to imagine him as a man. He was all but there. Joe could be a player in the mold of his baseball idol, Roberto Clemente, or another of his favorites, Mickey Mantle. Major league scouts were already telling Casey how much money the kid could make in baseball.

Coach Bruno had other ideas, though. Casey had been winning championships since 1948, but to Bruno he remained "an asshole first class . . . who thought he knew more than he did." Even in the sunny season, Bruno wanted Joe focused on football. He scheduled practices at a field by his house in East Liverpool, about twenty miles from Beaver Falls. Attendance for backs and receivers was considered mandatory.

"We worked on steps: three-step drops, five-step drops, rollouts, all that," Bruno recalls. Namath credited Bruno with eliminating a "false step"—a left-footed hitch—as he took the snap from center. But Namath wasn't exactly a project. There wasn't much you had to tell him. "Joe's brothers had already worked on him," says Bruno. "They like to get credit. But they didn't make Joe Namath."

Nor did Bruno. He always knew that. A coach didn't make that kind of talent. But that talent could make the coach.

Linwood Alford often accompanied Joe to Bruno's house. "We would go down there two, three times a week, all on the sly," says Alford. "He would teach Joe the routes, how to throw, how to handle the ball, how to step into the throw. And I would be the wide receiver. You could *hear* it when Joe threw the ball. If you didn't catch it right, it would knock the wind out of you. Joe would just laugh. We didn't do nothing but laugh."

"Bruno's the one who taught Joe to be a magician," says Tony Golmont. "The bootleg was a big play for us. But it's really all deception, sleight of hand. You look at Joe's hand, that's a big hand. He could hide a ball in that hand. He could give it to you and take it back and you'd never know."

In Bruno's scheme, backs had to block, too. Once again Beaver Falls' biggest starter would weigh less than 200 pounds. Bruno was determined to make up with craft what he lacked in size. "Tackles at schools like Butler went as big as two-thirty, two-forty," says Butch Ryan. "Larry's blocking schemes were all geared to give small people advantages: angle blocking, trap blocking. You didn't have to knock a man down. All you had to do was shield him like a basketball screen."

There was a lot to teach these kids: steps, throws, fakes, and blocks. Even the practices themselves required some stealth. Under the rules of the Western Pennsylvania Interscholastic Athletic League these sessions were illegal. But what the WPIAL didn't know wouldn't hurt anybody. Bruno couldn't be bothered with mere rules. He knew what he had seen against New Brighton. This was his chance. He had his quarterback, a natural hustler through whom he could choreograph his theories of misdirection. Larry Bruno wasn't teaching balls and strikes. This wasn't some cheap trick Dom Casey could signal with a stream of tobacco juice from the dugout. This was magic.

As Namath began his senior year, the game's greatest quarterback was Johnny Unitas of the Baltimore Colts. Though football ranked below baseball, boxing, and horse racing in the pantheon of professional sport, the Colts had an avid following in Beaver Falls. Their tight end, Jim "Bucky" Mutscheller, was from Beaver Falls, class of '48. Back in ninth grade, when Joe was a pint-sized quarterback and Mutscheller led the NFL with eight touchdown receptions, Beaver Falls players had been studying Colts game films. Kids like Namath knew all about Johnny Unitas, who wore number 19.

Unitas had a decent enough arm, but more than that, he had brains and balls. Unitas grew up in Pittsburgh and played his college ball at Louisville. He was drafted in the ninth round by his hometown Steelers, who cut him in the summer of '55. After a

7. JOEY U

season playing semipro ball—six bucks a game for the Bloomfield Rams of the Greater Pittsburgh League—he caught on with Baltimore. The Colts, coached by Weeb Ewbank, had long been a losing operation. But Unitas changed all that. From 1957 through 1960, the years coinciding with Namath's high school football career, Unitas led the National Football League in touchdown passes.

A famous photograph of Unitas, taken during the 1958 championship game, captures him as he stands to deliver in a trench of fighting, falling men. The ball is cocked way back in anticipation of a mighty heave, his left arm extended, pointing, onward and upward. His form, suggesting a javelin thrower more than a quarterback, evokes a classical heroism. The photograph was taken December 28, 1958, at Yankee Stadium in New York City. There, as dusk gave way to dark, in the overtime period of a championship game, Unitas went against the urgings of his coach and called a pass play with the Colts at the Giants' 8-yard line. Unitas had noticed that the Giants' strong-side linebacker was playing to the inside of Mutscheller. So instead of going with a safe running play to set up the game-winning field goal, Unitas called for Mutscheller to run a "diagonal" to the sideline. He caught the ball a yard from the end zone. If Mutscheller had fallen backward instead of sideways, he would have scored the winning touchdown. As it happened, that honor went to Al Ameche, who barreled into the end zone on the next play. Not only had the Colts won the championship, 23–17, they had beaten the 3½-point spread.

In the winning locker room reporters kept asking Unitas if his decision to go for the touchdown instead of the field goal had anything to do with the betting line.

Then a man from *Sport* magazine came in and told him he'd won a red Corvette. The next day Unitas appeared on *The Pat Boone Chevy Show.* That night Johnny and his wife were welcomed at the Harwyn Club, where Liz Taylor had embarked on her amorous adventure with Eddie Fisher.

Unitas had played great, thrilling games before. But this was different. Everyone talked of "sudden death," but in fact the game portended new life for the NFL. The '58 championship may not have been as billed, the greatest game ever played. But to that point it was the greatest game ever played on national television. Fathers and sons, 50 million kids of all ages, would remember the game airing on NBC affiliates around the country. It was television that conferred a special status on the game and its players. As Johnny Unitas could tell you from his table in the Harwyn Club, television made you famous.

Fame, in turn, made you money. But fame was also a form of insanity. People who didn't know you started having feelings for you. They loved you, hated you, admired you—without ever having met you. In Unitas's case, these admirers included Joe Namath. Around Beaver Falls, they were already calling Namath "Joey U." He chose to wear 19 as his number on the white home uniform, and 29 (the closest number in the Beaver Falls inventory) on the road. They were nice new jerseys with V-neck collars, designed by Coach Bruno in anticipation of the 1960 season.

Sam Allen recalls Namath's uniform as well as anyone. As a high school sophomore, secretly impressed with Robert Frost, Allen harbored some vague ambition to become a poet. But as his father, a radio repairman, had different ideas, he went out for football. He was the fourth-string end, a designation that earned him the right to put away Joe Namath's equipment.

Allen's stint as a valet left him with certain indelible memories. First, there was the matter of Namath's improbable physique, a young man's washboard stomach with an old man's stooped shoulders. Then the cleats: most guys wore black high-tops for extra ankle support. Not Joe. He wore a sporty low-cut model, so much lighter than the clodhoppers issued to scrubs like Sam Allen. Most striking of all was the way Namath looked right through him as he took his equipment to drape on an iron hanger. Allen doesn't like to think of this as arrogance, but rather, as evidence of the naturally occurring caste system that pervades all locker rooms.

On Fridays, game days, Bruno's boys wore ties and orange blazers. They attended a prayer service at a church of their choice. Then there were the pep rallies, also full of religiosity. Held in the gymnasium, they provided both ornamented hierarchy and fervent testimonial. Allen recalls only one player who never spoke. Joe just sat there looking cool, the sainted hustler.

Nineteen-sixty was a memorable autumn in Beaver Falls. The Pirates won the World Series on Bill Mazeroski's famous homer in the ninth inning of the seventh game. John F. Kennedy spoke in front of City Hall. Sam Allen was pressured into attending by his father—perhaps the only registered Republican in town—who kept yelling at the Democratic presidential nominee. It was not a wise move, calling him a mick; Beaver Falls loved Kennedy almost as much as it loved Mazeroski.

Still, as those months are recalled in Beaver Falls, the Pirates second baseman and the first Catholic president seem like cameo roles. The season belonged to a high school quarterback. Sam Allen carries his remembrances everywhere, like a wallet fat with snapshots, one image connecting to another, and all of them, in some way, connecting to Namath.

Before the season began, Joe contracted pleurisy, a painful inflammation of the membrane between the lungs and the ribs. It was unclear if he would even suit up for the first game, scheduled for Friday, September 9, against Midland. But sometime that week, he made an appearance at practice, wearing street clothes and sunglasses. His torso was trussed in bandages.

Allen remembers: "We were on the practice field right behind the high school, and Tommy Krzemienski was about fifty yards downfield when he started taunting Namath, calling him a pussy, saying that Namath couldn't reach him. Finally, Namath heard enough, and picked up a ball. It looked like one of those souvenir mini footballs in his hands. He couldn't even take a step, wrapped up like he was. So he just threw, nothing but arm.

"It was a beautiful, clear day, and the ball looked like a missile. I remember just watching it recede in the distance."

Namath hit Krzemienski, without breaking his stride, fifty, maybe sixty yards downfield. It was an absurdly long throw, challenging Allen's sense of distance. Wow, he thought, this guy is going places. Maybe even college.

"I was fifteen," he says. "What did I know?"

■　　■　　■

The home opener, like all home games, would be played in Reeves Stadium at Geneva College. In those years the Tigers, like many mill-town high school teams, were a lock to sell out. These fans loved their football; the spectators and the sport had achieved a state of congruence, something even baseball couldn't touch. "Tough people liked a tough game," says Butch Ryan. "Friday night was their holiday."

Workingmen liked to celebrate their holidays with a beer and a bet. High school football was no exception. If you couldn't speculate on the chances of your own children, then who? One of those pro teams? Not with all those rumors about players throwing games and giving points, messing with the point spread. Better to bet on boys from your own town; you could trust them. So what was the harm in a little wager? A man was going to make a bet somehow. Besides, the nearest race track, Waterford Park, was thirty miles away in Chester, West Virginia.

"High school betting was big around here," says Ryan. "There was a lot of it."

"I'm sure there was some," says Bruno. "But I never got into that. I never even wanted to know."

Some things you just couldn't avoid, though. Sam Allen, who played three years under Bruno, recalls the coach once declaring in exasperation, "Anybody who bets on high school games is crazy."

As it pertains to sports played by teenage boys, bookmaking is a very inexact science. Kids might not cheat, but even the wise men remain ignorant of their real capabilities and probabilities.

Beaver Falls began its first series of the season with the ball on its own 38. Namath called a sweep to the halfback, Bo Hayden, who got two yards. Next, Namath called a 38 Ride, sending the fullback, Bert Kerstetter, to the outside hole.

Forty-two years later, Bruno loves nothing better than to watch the tape and narrate the action from his own TV room. You want magic? How about the VCR as a time machine? "Joe shows the ball," says Bruno, holding the remote control like a wand. "He rides it one step, just one step. . . . Now you see it, now you don't. . . . Puts it in there wrist deep. . . . Look at that: two guys just crush the fullback, maul him."

But then, to Bruno's everlasting glee, the Midland defenders, crushers and maulers of fullback Bert Kerstetter, discover that he doesn't have the ball.

The ball is, in fact, with Namath. During the scrum, he broke to the outside. Now he's long gone. The Midland defenders can see his number, the back of his uniform. Johnny Unitas never ran like that. A sixty-yard touchdown run: Not a bad way to start a season. What were the wise men saying now? Their science paled before this magic.

In the fourth quarter, Namath made sixty yards and a touchdown in another way—with four passes, one to Whitey Harris and three to his favorite receiver, Krzemienski. From the press box the *News-Tribune*'s Joe Tronzo wrote: "If this boy wants to be he can rank with the greatest quarterbacks ever developed in Beaver Falls as he has few weaknesses."

The final score was 43–13. But Bruno saw some things he wanted to work on while they were still fresh in the kids' minds. The team was in good spirits for the bus ride back to the high school. Joe was sitting in his usual seat next to Bruno when the coach got up to announce a new Tiger tradition: Saturday-morning practices. That was Joe's cue. Suddenly, Namath—who never said a word at the pep rallies—burst into cheers. Judging from Joe's reaction, Saturday practice (now but hours away) might as well have meant free beer and girls. A silent beat passed. Then another. Now the rest of the bus started whooping and hollering.

"Joe did his lines perfectly," said Bruno.

The coach knew: as Joe goes, so do the rest of the kids. If Joe said Saturday-morning practice was cool, it was cool.

The following Friday, Beaver Falls beat Sharon 39–7. Butch Ryan had an eighty-one-yard touchdown run. Namath was 8 for 9 passing. He also ran the ball four times. Through the first two games he was averaging better than twelve yards a carry. But those were just numbers, their sum less than the boy. Actually, he wasn't even a boy. "A magician," wrote Tronzo.

■   ■   ■

Joe Tronzo covered his first sporting event for the *Beaver Falls News-Tribune* in 1936. He was twelve, and the occasion was a Polish Falcons track meet. In 1942, he enlisted as an infantryman. "I was small, only five feet, five inches tall and 128 pounds, but I felt I could do as much as any big man, and this was a good way to prove it," he would say. Proof of his mettle was provided by a mortar shell, the shrapnel from which lodged in his ass. In the spring of 1947, following his discharge, he started full-time at the *News-Tribune* covering local sports, everything from high school to Little League to midget football. He held that assignment until his retirement in 1991.

The sportswriter's maxim forbids cheering in the press box. Whether Tronzo, whose Marsh Wheeling stogie did much to offend his colleagues' olfactory senses, observed this prohibition is unknown. But he did cheer in his copy, which reduced the world around Beaver Falls to a simple scheme, easily understood by a generation that had served in World War II. There were two teams: us and them. Under Tronzo's byline, a synonym for them—the kids who weren't in orange and black—was "the enemy." Tronzo was a homer, and wore the designation with pride. Beneath his game story leads was the exhortation: "Take 'Em Tigers!"

Tronzo considered his mission more civic than journalistic. He did not interview players. He believed in coaches, that they were all but infallible. Tronzo knew the batting average of Little Leaguers. In many ways, they were his heroes; a good game story mentioned even the benchwarmers in a favorable light. "Some I liked better than others, but they were all pretty good kids," he would say, explaining his theory of sportswriting. "I had nothing to do with their athletic abilities. But I hope I had something to do with their confidence. I never wrote anything negative about a kid."

Tronzo knew there were grown men who kept his yellowing columns with their most prized possessions. A mention in the paper bestowed a kind of

celebrity. For most of the kids, Tronzo's column was their first and final taste
of fame. For Joe Namath, it was just the beginning. Fame, as he would learn, is
to be loved and loathed. Fame is a kind of poison. Take just enough, and it allows you to see things you might have missed. Take a lot, it leaves you retching
and sick. Fame is a fine, ferocious bitch. But you'd never know it from the way
she dressed for Joe Tronzo, so gently did he introduce her to Joe.

Despite the fact that he persisted in spelling the quarterback's name
Nameth, Tronzo informed Namath's enduring feelings on his sportswriter heralds and his mistress, Fame. Joe liked her best when she was agreeable, compliant, an easy, grateful lay. As for the sportswriters, he didn't like too many
questions. He didn't like the ones who stirred up shit. He liked them like
Tronzo.

■   ■   ■

Beaver Falls hadn't played New Castle since 1943, when the rivalry was suspended. As the Tigers hadn't scored against the Castlemen since 1927, it had
become difficult to consider this game much of a sporting proposition. But in
1960, as their competition began anew, Beaver Falls looked to the New Castle
game with great anticipation. "The team is a confident club led by brash Joe
Nameth, a sleight of hand artist who has more nerve than a pickpocket at an
FBI convention," Tronzo wrote in his game advance. However, unknown to
Tronzo was the fact that Joe had a sore ankle. As Joe also did the Tigers'
punting, Bruno had reason to be worried. But Joe just put his arm around
Bruno and swore a grinning oath: "Don't worry, coach, we won't have to
punt."

About 8,500 were on hand at New Castle's Taggart Stadium to watch Joey
U throw his first interception of the season. It didn't seem to bother him,
though. Interceptions never taxed his composure. "If he threw a pass that was
intercepted, he wouldn't give up on it," says Bruno. "He'd call it again."

Namath finished the day completing 8 of 12 passes for 174 yards. Most of
those went to Krzemienski—"The Hungarian-Polish Alliance," as Tronzo
called it. Namath also ran 8 times for 66 yards and two touchdowns. The
paper featured a big photo on the front page, above the news from Cape
Canaveral: Bad weather had delayed the launch of a spacecraft "designed to
orbit the moon and make the most extensive study ever attempted of the lunar
environment." But really, who gave a shit? Beaver Falls had shut out New Castle, 39–0.

Next up was Ambridge. "We felt they were the one team that could stay
with us," says Butch Ryan. Ambridge had good players on either side of the
ball, including Fred Klages, a three-sport star who'd go on to pitch in the major leagues.

Ambridge scored first. Then Namath was hurt on an option play; one tackler had him by the ankles as another hit him high. "The Ambridge stands," wrote Tronzo, "went wild and sent up a burst of cheers. The band beat the drums and went into ecstasy.

"On the field, the Ambridge players were all happy and showed it with a burst of enthusiasm. . . . Here were members of the race sent into realms of the greatest happiness because a 17-year-old boy was down on the field with an injury."

"They thought they had us when they knocked Joe out of the game," says Ryan, who subbed at quarterback while Namath was examined on the sideline. The shoulder was hurt, though not enough for the tastes of the Ambridge fans. With 2:50 left in the half, Namath hit Krzemienski for ten, the Tigers' first first down of the game. Now they were at their own 46-yard line. Namath missed open receivers on the next two plays. He was in obvious pain, recalls Ryan, "with his left arm hanging down at the side." On third and ten, with 2:16 left in the half, Namath went back to pass again.

"That's the play I remember most the whole year," Krzemienski would recall. "Joe rolled to the right, and I ran a flag pattern to the left. I guess the defensive back didn't feel Joe would be able to throw the ball that far."

Fred Klages, the back covering Krzemienski, admits giving up on the ball. Klages played pool. He understood the angles, too. To hit Krzemienski, the injured Namath would have to throw upfield, across the field, and most difficult, across his own body. "I just turned around," says Klages. "But Krzemienski kept on running. I'm thinking: This is insane. Nobody can throw the ball this far. And as I'm telling myself this, the ball is spiraling over my head, hits Krzemienski on a dead run."

Touchdown. Klages had seen enough of Namath in the Blue Room to know what had happened. He had just gotten hustled. The score was tied, but the game had changed irrevocably. Beaver Falls would win 25–13. "Speaking frankly," wrote Tronzo, "I must admit that I sweated enough to ruin two armpits from a good rummage sale shirt."

Namath completed 3 of 15 passes. Statistically, it was his worst game. Of course, no statistic reflected his separated shoulder. From here on, Namath regarded both statistics and shoulders the same way: You didn't need either if you had balls.

■   ■   ■

John Namath kept close tabs on his youngest son's progress as a football player. He even attended Joe's practices. "Faithfully," recalls Ernie Neale, the team's trainer. "His dad would keep a watchful eye. He would sit outside the chain-link fence, where the cars are parked, and talk to coach Bruno. You *knew* his dad was there. Joe knew he was there."

After the Ambridge game, John insisted on taking his son to the doctor. He wanted to know what was wrong with his boy.

Joe returned with his arm in a sling and tears in his eyes. "Joe crying—that was unusual," says Bruno. The doctor had told him his football days were over. Bruno then brought him to an orthopedist who quickly provided a less catastrophic diagnosis. He showed Bruno how to tape the shoulder. It would hurt like hell. But if the kid could take it, he could play.

John Namath, who would gladly have given his own shoulder for Joe's, must have been overjoyed. Still, Joe's injury would heal more rapidly than their relationship. During that 1960 season, the team held a Dad's Night, in which players were introduced at Geneva College with their proud fathers. But Joe balked. "Joe said he wasn't going to walk with his dad," recalls Bruno. "I said, Joe, you're walking with your dad. He's your father. If you don't, one day you're going to realize you made a big mistake."

Get your ass out there or else. It was an empty threat; fortunately, Joe didn't call Bruno's bluff. It would have broken his father's heart. Perhaps at seventeen, Joe already knew that one broken heart didn't deserve another.

■   ■   ■

The shoulder was no longer much of a problem as Beaver Falls handed Butler its first loss of the season, 26–6. "Nameth turned in a brilliant game. His play selections were perfect. . . . When he needed the yardage he called on his magical arm and the fine receiving of Krzemienski," wrote Tronzo, who had begun to refer to the duo as "the Hungarian Howitzer and the Polish Picker."

The following Friday was a bye-week for Beaver Falls—just as well, considering that most people were still recovering from events of the day before. At 3:36 P.M. on October 13, 1960, the Pittsburgh Pirates' Bill Mazeroski hit a home run in the bottom of the ninth that beat the Yankees in the seventh game of the World Series at Forbes Field. Namath would recall watching it from the Blue Room. By the time he got to practice, his pals were already a little nuts. Sam Allen recalls Whitey Harris yelling that there would be free pussy in Pittsburgh that night. (Indeed, the Associated Press correspondent in downtown Pittsburgh reported, "Girls grabbed strangers and kissed them.") In the midst of this locker-room revelry, Namath showed up in sunglasses. He said nothing, just grinned.

The good mood lasted through the following night when the crew traveled to watch New Castle play Farrell, Beaver Falls' next opponent. This was only partially a scouting mission. "Joe had a girl up there," says Ernie Pelaia, a Beaver Falls guard who made the trip that night. Butch Ryan had a honey in New Castle, too.

Girls loved them. How could they not, the way they bopped into the stands with their varsity jackets, black leather sleeves, names embroidered on their chests? "We were the untouchables of football," Ryan says wistfully.

Sitting close by were the untouchables of New Castle, local bookmakers who made the high school line. The kids from Beaver Falls spotted them easy. Mill workers looked like your dad. But the bookies wore fedoras and slacks. And their shoes—Italians, of course.

"We knew who they were," says Ryan. "We knew they were part of the, if you want to say, mafia up there. But they treated us good. It wasn't hostile."

The Farrell Steelers were a perennial powerhouse. They beat New Castle 35–0 that night. Beaver Falls wouldn't be that much of a problem. Beaver Falls might have been off to a good start, but the Tigers hadn't beaten mighty Farrell since 1954.

Now the bookies looked over at the kids in the varsity jackets and started breaking balls. How many points? they asked. How many points should we give you?

Scoring against Farrell was not a likely scenario. In six games that season, the Steelers had allowed a total of 19 points.

The kids from Beaver Falls didn't know what to say. Except for Joe. He was insulted. Fuck the points.

The bookies looked at the other kids. Who is this guy, this Joe fucking Namath? This kid a little *stunad*? He been drinking too much of that homemade wine?

The kids in the varsity jackets shook their heads. Nah. Joe was serious.

Joe says, Take your points. Give the points to Farrell. Farrell's gonna need them.

The week that followed was another big one in Beaver Falls. John F. Kennedy, the Democratic nominee for president, came to town. The guy who had made Nixon look bad on television spoke in front of City Hall. The next day's *Beaver County Times* noted: "A large number of those who came out to hear and see Sen. Kennedy were young people, particularly young women."

Seven thousand people showed up for Kennedy—still fewer than turned out Friday night for Beaver Falls–Farrell. From Tronzo's lead: "The sleight of hand magician, Joe Nameth, sparked the Tigers to a 33–18 verdict over the Farrell team at Reeves Stadium."

The bookies should've listened. Farrell could have used the points.

On October 28, Beaver Falls beat Aliquippa 34–7. Namath—"a brash youngster with more nerve than a sore tooth," wrote Tronzo—was 13 for 17, 232 yards. A week later, the Tigers traveled to Ellwood City. There, Joe kept calling Bo Hayden's number. Hayden, a fast, shifty junior halfback, had the county scoring title in his grasp. The Hungarian Howitzer was just taking care of his guy, who scored four touchdowns that day. "Several times he could have selfishly scored from a yard or so out but each time attempted to give it to the boy who put the Tigers in scoring position," wrote Tronzo.

Frank Walton, the big kid Namath struck out in Little League, was in the stands that night. Walton was now a lineman at Pitt. From there, he'd go on to a career as a coach. But even after a lifetime of football, that evening at Ellwood stands apart in his recollection. Three times he saw the officials whistle a play dead, run in to clear the pile and spot the ball, only to discover that the ball was already upfield, resting comfortably in Namath's outsize hands. In forty years of football, says Walton, "he was the best high school quarterback I've ever seen."

"He acts like he is the best quarterback in the state," wrote Tronzo. "And who is to deny it as his record shows."

The final score was 26–0. The victory over Ellwood City, combined with an upset loss by Monessen, gave Beaver Falls the championship of the Western Pennsylvania Interscholastic Athletic League. The Tigers still had a nonleague game against New Brighton. But that was a mere formality; they won 40–6.

On the front page of the *News-Tribune,* above Tronzo's byline, the championship announcement was made in banner type of immense dimension:

BEAVER FALLS WINS "AA" TITLE!
WHIPS ELLWOOD CITY, 26 TO 0
Namath-Krz Spark Passing Game; Hayden Scores Four

In Beaver Falls, such an immodest proclamation seemed to cause more debate than the election. (Seven of the town's eight voting precincts went overwhelmingly for Kennedy.) Meanwhile, the *News-Tribune* was besieged with complaints. The coverage was unseemly, lacking any sense of proportion. After all, it was noted, the paper didn't even mark the end of the war with headlines that large.

But Joe Tronzo knew better. He knew what he had seen, the great glories swirling around the brash Hungarian Howitzer: Namath. He even promised to spell the name correctly now, attributing his inconsistencies to "an incident between the Hungarians and the Italians back in 1822." Still, how could these people compare wars with high school championships? They could stick their complaints with the shrapnel those army medics pulled out of his ass.

"Wars," wrote Tronzo, "are common occurrences."

Through his season as Namath's valet, Sam Allen became a keen observer of the quarterback and his mannerisms. But to his everlasting dismay, he was unable to master what he now calls the "we-bad strut," the bopping gait that announced the Namath crew. No matter how hard he tried, cool was beyond him. He was doomed to spend high school as a straight-A student. Still, one Friday night, his quest for cool brought him to the Blue Room, where Namath made short work of him, running the table and taking his money.

It was only a buck or two. But money was pride, and the loss of it, shame. Sam's father, whom he was always trying to please, felt this chagrin even more acutely than his son. Losing money in a pool hall was bad enough. But losing the money to Joe Namath moved Keith Allen to give his son a smack.

8. SMALL-TOWN HERO

"That Namath is no good," said the father. "He's nothing but trouble."

Mr. Allen might have been a Republican in a Democratic town. But in regard to young Joe Namath, his views echoed the mainstream. In the minds of most adults, Namath dwelled at the epicenter of bad infuences. He bet. He smoked. He drank. (By now, Joe had been introduced to the joys of homemade *vino*.) And of course, he was out to screw everyone's daughter.

Beaver Falls combined big-city vices with a small-town mentality. Everybody knew your business. And Joe's business, such as it was, drew little compassion. Divorce was looked upon as a kind of disease. Everyone knew that a "broken home" incubated a boy's delinquent tendencies. In Joe's case, people remembered all offenses, real and imagined, petty and otherwise. Clark Bars, pilfered jerseys, siphoned gas, stolen hubcaps, cut classes, and broken hearts—they all collected in a vat where facts fermented with rumor. There it brewed, a kid's reputation.

Not even Frank knew what to make of his kid brother. Just before football season, Joe had been seen in a bar. "The word spread through town pretty fast," he recalled. In fact, he had only gone in the bar to get Rich Pinchotti,

Frances's older brother. But news of the sighting didn't travel with that disclaimer. Frank showed up at the Szolnoki house and started swinging. It took a while for him to calm down and hear Joe out. By then, Joe was holding a butcher knife.

Joe wasn't the only kid with a reputation. But within the realm of Beaver Falls, he had become famous. Winning a championship made Joe a hero. As people inevitably confused victory with virtue, they wanted their ballplayers to be heroes. But something about fame also brought out a darker rooting interest. People wanted to tear their heroes down, too.

On November 15, 1960, three days after football season ended, Joe Tronzo did something he was loath to do, addressing the issue of Namath's reputation in print. He never wrote pieces like this, not about a kid. Then again, he had never covered a kid who generated such heat:

> Probably more rumors have cropped up about Joe Namath than any other high school kid since I have been covering sports. . . .
>
> Among the stories are that he sawed a cow in half in the auditorium of the high school, punched a pregnant woman, punched a school administrator, bombed school board members' houses, poured gasoline on a fifth grader and set him afire, threw eggs at Richard Nixon. . . .
>
> There are some who have said that I have made a hero out of the worst juvenile since Cain took a sling to Abel.
>
> Actually, even if Joe did all the above plus a few others, I would write him up in the same way. I am not interested in what a kid does off the field.
>
> I mean that my primary job is to report what goes on in the sport scene. If he is a hero on the field he is a hero on the sport page.
>
> If a kid has bad habits that is up to his parents, teachers and preachers to correct. Certainly it is not our job. It must be remembered that in Beaver Falls there are more parents, teachers and preachers than there are sports writers.
>
> However, I do want to defend this Namath lad . . . he is not the ogre that he has been made out.

Tronzo goes on to argue that Namath's much-noted brashness was in fact an asset: "The key to his grid success is his extreme confidence." After talking with Joe's teachers, he refutes the charge that "the only thing that Namath has passed so far in high school is a football." He allows that Namath is a bright kid who hasn't applied himself despite his chance for a college football scholarship.

"I am not saying that Namath hasn't been in trouble," he continues. "He has pulled some pranks but never anything serious."

Tronzo specifies neither the trouble nor the pranks. Rather, in closing he cites the enthusiastic endorsement of a football coach: "Coach Larry Bruno is high on the boy, both on and off the field."

Unmentioned in the column was the fact that Bruno had had to get Namath out of jail just days earlier.

The night before the New Brighton game, Joe and some friends—Wibby Glover, Whitey Harris and Red Christley, all easily identified by their "we-bad strut"—had an inspired idea. They would climb the roof of Sahli Chevrolet, a Seventh Avenue dealership just blocks from the pool hall. There, they would abscond with a great helium-filled balloon, painting over the ad for used Chevys and replacing it with school colors and the legend: TAKE 'EM TIGERS WPIAL CHAMPS! Unfortunately, such spirit didn't enthrall the cops who showed up, guns drawn, and took the boys to the police station, where they remained behind bars until Coach Bruno arrived.

The boys were released as a favor to Bruno. It wasn't the first time, or the last, that a coach would intercede on behalf of Joe. Where others saw a kid trading on the privilege due a star athlete, Bruno saw envy. "A lot of people were jealous of Joe," he says. "This one teacher, he'd say—not to my face— that I was Al Capone, the head of the mafia, and that Joe belonged to the mafia. One time, some kid knocks the books out of Joe's hand, you know, kidding around. But it was right in front of this teacher's door. So this guy—he taught social studies—tells Joe to pick up the books. Joe says, 'I didn't knock 'em down, I'm not gonna pick 'em up.' The teacher tells Joe to go to the principal's office. But Joe comes to me instead. He wasn't gonna do what *this guy* told him. So when the period ends I went down there and closed the door and I told this social studies teacher, I said you been picking on Joe. Now it better stop or you and I are going outside.' "

The social studies instructor was not alone in his disparagement of Joe. Joyce Hupp, then a senior cheerleader, recalls teachers warning her not to go with Joe to the prom. "He had the wrong reputation," she says.

The prom was quite a production. A lot of girls had their dates booked a year in advance. Joyce had been hoping Joe would ask her, but she wasn't counting on it. A girl didn't count on Joe like that.

Then one night at a postgame dance, Joe announced, "I'd like to ask you something, but I don't think you'll say yes."

"Just ask me," said Joyce.

"You'll probably say no."

Maybe Joe couldn't get the nerve to ask. Maybe he couldn't commit to the idea of being committed—if only for a night. Eventually, though—after he had skirted the question for more than an hour—the soft, seductive voice Joe used began to lose its charm. It now dawned on Joyce that this conversation was not a prelude to the prom. Joe was just being Joe; he probably just wanted her to do his homework again. "This is getting kind of ridiculous," she said.

So, finally, he asked. Joyce said yes. "Some of my teachers tried to talk me out of it," she says. "They didn't think that I should go with him. They said, 'You're going to be sitting alone all night.'"

Joyce disregarded the warning. She had liked Joey since St. Mary's. She didn't care about his reputation. Then again, maybe she did. That reputation had a funny effect on girls. The worse it got, the more they liked him.

■   ■   ■

Joyce's future husband was a big guy named Ron who had graduated the year before. He wasn't too happy when Namath called Joyce late one winter night, asking what she was doing. Ron grabbed the receiver. They had words.

"You know how black guys talk to each other?" Ron asks. That's how he heard Namath playing him, woofing on him. So Ron offered to settle their differences like men. He told Joe to meet him at the end of town, by the culvert. Joyce hollered after him as Ron jumped in his car, tires screeching. Joe wasn't there when he got to the culvert. But he waited. It was cold as hell. There, under the moonlight, steam must've been rising off him. Ron was so mad, thinking about all the things he was going to do to this Joe Namath. Ron waited. What was it? Fifteen minutes. An hour? Two hours?

Joe never showed. He must've been laughing his ass off.

He probably would have liked to ask Frances Pinchotti to the prom. She was the girl who lived above the grocery store when he lived above the bar. But she was a junior, and the senior prom was restricted to seniors. In a 1976 interview with the *Los Angeles Times,* Namath speaks of Frances, without identifying her, as his first love, the girl who made his insides gurgle. "I'm not aware of that quote," she says now. "He's never made a reference to me."

If it was love that Joe felt, Frances never knew. "I knew he cared about me," she says, choosing her words very carefully.

And what of the others? Bunny Kreshon was just a sophomore, also a cheerleader. One fall Friday in 1960, she got up enough courage to tap him on the shoulder and wish him good luck in that night's game. "After that," she says, "he began to wait for me after class and walk down the hall with me."

Frances. Bunny. Then there was a girl in Homewood. And another in New Castle. A girl here. A girl there. You wonder if they knew of one another. When it came to affairs of the heart—relationships, as they came to be known—Joe Namath was not to be taken seriously. Even his best friends didn't know what Joe was really up to.

"Lot of stories about Joe and the girls," says Butch Ryan. "Some can be verified. Some can't. But did he have a steady girl? No. Not as far as I knew. He might have a girlfriend who would last a week. But Joe was not one to be tied down."

"Joe kind of floated, if you know what I'm saying," said Rich Niedbala.

"Joe wasn't hung up on girls," says Linwood Alford. "But a lot of girls liked Joe. Not just white girls, black girls, too."

Linwood and Joe used to shoot pool and talk shit, playing the dozens as they sized up the table. Linwood would tease him about Ruby Jean Finley. He would have sworn Joe was seeing Ruby Jean on the sly.

"Everybody in Beaver Falls believes that," says Ruby Jean, now an attorney in Detroit. For the record, she dismisses the rumor: "Joe was a glamour guy, and I was just a homely black girl."

In fact, Ruby Jean Finley was a slender, good-looking girl from Bridge Street. She liked Joe, thought he was "cute," and enjoyed the way he "defied authority." But there was nothing romantic between them. "Just good friends," she says.

Still, Joe's inscrutable heart was as much of a mystery to her as it was to everyone else. "I don't remember Joe having any steady girlfriends," she says. "He was very secretive."

Secrets and rumors, the twined fibers of reputation. *Everybody in Beaver Falls believes that.* Even Ruby Jean's own father. "He was very disturbed by that," she says. "Really, really upset. Like I had done something terrible. Like, if I were to be with him I would degrade myself. I wouldn't be a lady."

Part of his disapproval was just being a father. Part of it was race. "The fact that he was white had something to do with it," she acknowledges. But the overriding objection was Joe himself. "He had that reputation," she says.

Her father, like most people, was a devout believer in reputation. He believed the friendship between his daughter and Joe Namath was less innocent than carnal. "My father went to his grave believing that," she says. "I know he did."

■   ■   ■

The various elements of Namath's reputation came together that winter on the basketball court. His attitude defied authority. But his talent defied reason.

At least that's how it seemed to Ray Brokos, who recalls the evening of December 27, 1960, with a sense of everlasting awe. "I was all over him," he says.

Beaver Falls and Ambridge were playing in a Christmas basketball tournament sponsored by the Hopewell Township Lions Club. Brokos, who'd attend Duquesne on a basketball scholarship, was a fine player, easily the section's leading scorer at more than 19 points a game. That night, he already had 12 at the half. By the third quarter, Ambridge was up 17.

"I thought I was hot shit," says Brokos.

But then Namath got hot. He had a long-distance set shot and some great moves to the basket. He used the entire repertoire that night. Namath, says

Brokos, "was an inch or two bigger than me, but he had that hunched look. He wasn't thin. But he wasn't a man yet, either."

Ambridge called time. "Let me take him," said Brokos.

Brokos was a good defensive player. But the next thing he knew, Namath had drilled one right over him. It went on like that, shot for shot, Namath and Brokos, the rest of the game. As the next day's *News-Tribune* reported: "Joe Namath of the Tigers waged a fourth period battle with the Bridger ace, Ray Brokos, and the result of this fray was to determine the outcome of the game."

"That's what it came down to," says Brokos. "Me and him."

As the final seconds ticked off, Beaver Falls was down, 63–62. Brokos had 26 points. By comparison, Namath only had 14. But he also had the ball. Freddy Klages, the Ambridge defensive back who had watched Namath's touchdown for Tom Krzemienski sail over his head, now watched Namath dribble as the fans counted down: *ten, nine, eight* . . . Joe keeps on dribbling . . . *seven, six, five* . . . still dribbling . . . *four, three, two* . . .

Benny Singleton, Beaver Falls' leading scorer, remembers: "I'm yelling, 'Give me the ball! Give me the ball, Joe!' But he's just looking at the clock. Just held it till there was one second, then he let it go."

"I was all over him," says Brokos.

They left their feet together. It felt as though they were up there for a while. "Namath could dunk," says Brokos. "There weren't a lot of guys who could do that." Joe's magic counteracted gravity, his leap obeying only the laws of metaphysics. When asked how high Namath jumped on that play, Brokos says: "As high as he had to get."

The shot was good from twenty-five feet. Beaver Falls won by a point as the final buzzer sounded. "If he'da missed," says Benny Singleton, "I'd have been yelling, 'Why didn't you give me the ball?'" But Benny had been playing with Joe since they were nine, since the day Linwood brought him around to hustle the money from the hat. That's long enough for Benny Singleton to understand the absurdity in his own hypothesis. "If he missed, it wouldn't have been Joe."

■   ■   ■

By now, colleges around the country were pursuing Joe as a quarterbacking prodigy. But it was basketball, not football, that always provided the most compelling proof of Namath's athleticism. The basketball player works closer to his audience. Nothing hides him—no visor, no helmet, no pads. After seeing him play basketball, a good coach would have recruited him to play any sport.

Roland Arrigoni, a University of Maryland football coach who sat in the stands for many of Joe's basketball games, was immediately struck by the hands: "Huge. Tremendously oversized. He could stop his dribble by palming the ball. I was there. I saw it happen."

The hands allowed him to put on Globetrotter-style exhibitions of his ball-handling skills. The legs made for another show. Namath didn't just dunk. He could dunk backward. Fans weren't accustomed to seeing that. The game was changing, its potential not yet understood. In 1958, Namath's freshman year, the ten top scorers in the National Basketball Association had one thing in common: they were white. By 1961, the league's top three scorers (Wilt Chamberlain, Elgin Baylor, and Oscar Robertson), its two top rebounders (Chamberlain and Bill Russell) and the leading assist man (Robertson) were black. There was a new style—players were now defined by their moves—and it was largely a function of race. The game Namath had learned on the Lower End was coming of age, and he with it. As a senior, Joe was the only white starter on the Beaver Falls varsity, a team that included Benny, Butch, Linwood, and Anthony Pugh, all from the Lower End.

Unfortunately, the coach was less than enamored with their style. Nate Lippe had coached Aliquippa from 1927 through 1947, during which time his basketball teams were 288–103, winning thirteen sectional championships. He didn't return to the game until 1960, when the Beaver Falls school board hired him. Lippe was supposed to provide the old-fashioned know-how the talented Tigers needed to win a championship. He disdained the newfangled game almost as much as the rhyming descriptions for it: shake and bake, run and gun, razzle-dazzle. Dunking was not something he approved of, nor was driving to the basket. Lippe insisted on a half-dozen passes before any of his players dared to shoot. He wanted them shooting fouls underhanded. What's more, though he was pushing sixty and could remember when the ball had laces, Lippe wanted to play for the future. He kept Linwood on the bench while playing a couple of six-three sophomores at center. "They were young, they were scared, and they couldn't catch a cold," says Singleton.

Coach Lippe, says Butch Ryan, "was in the dark ages. The game had passed him by. He didn't want us driving. He didn't want us shooting jump shots. It was like telling a greyhound to stay on the leash and walk."

As a junior Namath had led the team in scoring. As a senior he led the team in benchings. "I fooled around a lot," he later recalled. "I remember once some guy was guarding me awful tight, sticking his hand in my face all the time, so, finally, I took the ball and wound up and followed through just like I was going to throw the ball right in his face. Except, I held on to the ball. The coach took me out for that."

"Lippe really screwed him," says Arrigoni. To Lippe, Namath's game reflected a subversive sensibility. The dunks and behind-the-back passes challenged the natural order of things. Lippe wanted a symphony; but Namath and his boys from the Lower End played rock and roll. The promise evidenced in that Christmas tournament was lost to the conflict between the coach and players.

On Wednesday, January 31, 1961, in the second quarter against Farrell, Lippe benched Namath for the last time. In his account some years later, Joe could not recall his exact offense. Arrigoni says Namath had just faked a kid out of his jock, dribbled around him, and dunked. Then Lippe took him out of the game. "Joe threw the ball straight up in the air," says Linwood Alford. "He didn't *throw* it," corrects Ryan. "He just didn't give it to the officials in such a gracious way."

There is, however, near unanimity on what happened next. Instead of taking his seat on the bench, Joe kept walking to the locker room. No one had seen anything like that before—not in the mills or the churches or the schools, and certainly not on the fields or in the gyms. A coach's authority was almost absolute, less frequently challenged than a boss's or a priest's or a cop's. But Namath's stroll to the locker room made the challenge explicit. Lippe represented all the uncool, boneheaded adults. Namath's body language translated thusly: *Fuck you.* Sometime later in the game—it could have been the next play or the next quarter—Lippe benched Benny Singleton, who also went straight to the locker room. If Joe was quitting, Benny was, too.

Beaver Falls lost that day, 73–43. But the score was forgotten after Namath's subversive pageant. "It was a shock to everybody," recalls Sam Allen, who was sitting in the stands. "Everybody's jaw dropped to their chest."

But Joe Tronzo's game story contained no reference to the walkout. He didn't even mention the incident until Saturday's paper, four days after the fact. "I did not see it due to my position away from the Tiger bench," he wrote. By then, Lippe had announced that, contrary to popular belief, his leading scorers had not quit—they had been dropped from the team.

Tronzo, who surely wanted the story to go away, would have to devote his next three columns to the incident. The town's sentiments went squarely against Joe and Benny. They were selfish, slothful, quitters. But one letter to the editor, written by Wilson Young of 3407 Sixth Avenue, did defend the kids against Lippe's archaic notions: "We are now watching a basketball team of 1961 vintage performing with all the ghosts of the mid-1940's impeding their every move. . . . Shades of the old peach baskets."

Mr. Young went on, accusing Tronzo of nothing less than a cover-up: "The hope for this year's team rested with 'Joe' Namath. The fans idolized the Hungarian 'Howitzer' for the bombastic football heroics he provided them and were eagerly anticipating the same from a basketball standpoint. This hope was rudely disrupted on the eve of the section opening by a regrettable incident, the full details of which were withheld from the local fans. But with Namath now on probation as a result of this incident the stage had been set for an alibi."

Witholding information. Alibis. The coach and the sportswriter were now cited as conspirators. Was there ever a kid with such a natural talent for generating controversy? Not in Tronzo's lifetime.

His columns of that week are, in fact, works of masterful equivocation, defending the player, the coach, and the sportswriter. "Joe Namath being on school probation is rather a surprise," wrote Tronzo. "The incident he tells of is so small and of so little concern, it was passed off by this reporter.

"What it amounted to was Joe and a group of boys were playing basketball on the high school floor during an unauthorized time."

As for the coach, he wrote: "Nate Lippe proves one thing. He is the one boss, the only boss and no boy or boys are going to take over."

If only that were so. The Tigers didn't win another game that season. Lippe lasted just two more years at Beaver Falls. He was sixty-six when he died in 1967.

In retrospect, Tronzo's reluctance to address the attempted mutiny seems understandable. It was his worst nightmare, an affront to all he represented. For Tronzo, the 1960s might as well have begun with the Beaver Falls–Farrell game. First Namath walked off the court; then it seemed that many old accepted ways began to fall apart, disintegrating amid talk of assassination and copulation, liberation and hallucination.

What do you expect to happen when boys don't obey their coaches?

Namath's reputation scared off a few colleges. Joe Paterno, the young backfield coach from Penn State, didn't even bother with Joe, determining that the kid wasn't Penn State material. "He wasn't a good student," said Paterno. Then there was the assistant from Michigan who traveled all the way to Beaver Falls only to find Joe in front of the Blue Room, lying on the hood of a car. "He didn't bother to talk to me," Namath would recall. "I guess he decided I wasn't the University of Michigan type."

But for every college that took a pass, there were dozens who'd literally pay for a chance to play in the Joe Namath sweepstakes. And they all had to go through Larry Bruno. Sometimes there would be five coaches in his office at once, all making their case. Some did it better than others.

9. HIGHER EDUCATION

Bruno would always remember the guy who approached him on behalf of Indiana. He was a teacher at the high school, too. During football season, they were on lunch duty in the gymnasium when he winked and began to flip through an imaginary billfold. "I got six hundred bucks here if you get Joe to sign this letter of intent," he says.

Now that was a guy who could go fuck himself. Joe made for a championship season, and the season made Bruno. And now this guy—this same prick who used to call him "dago" behind his back—wanted him to sell the kid out for $600. Six hundred was a lot of money back then. But Joe was like a son to Bruno. He'd never sell Joe. And he'd never forget the insult, either. After they won the championship, Bruno ambled over to the Indiana recruiter and started counting his own imaginary billfold: "Dago didn't do so bad, did he?"

As for Joe's own billfold, it most likely remained closed to the blandishments of recruiters. "I knew there were some things thrown his way if he wanted them, but I don't know if he ever really accepted anything. I really don't," says Bruno.

"It was strange coming out of high school and having colleges offer me as much money as my father made in a year," Namath once said.

Perhaps, with Frank looking over his shoulder, Joe was just too damn scared to be on the take. If you play for cheaters, reasoned Frank, then you're one, too. And chances are, it's only a matter of time before they try to cheat you. "No doubt we could have used the money, my mother and everybody in the family was working," Namath would recall. "But Frank set me straight."

If Joe took anything, it couldn't have been much. After all, he was still driving that junker of a Ford. Frank was right: Joe didn't want to be bought. Money, by itself, wasn't enough. If it was just about money, he would've already signed with one of those baseball scouts. Before his senior year had even started, the St. Louis Cardinals had offered a $15,000 bonus.

The early favorite to win Joe's services was Notre Dame. For a Catholic kid, being recruited by Notre Dame was like being recruited by God. It was the kind of place that would make a mother proud—especially a mother like Joe's. At the university's request, Bruno delivered his three senior stars—Joe, Tom Krzemienski, and the other end, Tony Golmont—to the Golden Dome in his station wagon. But when the boys arrived, there was nobody there to meet them. They didn't have a place to stay. They didn't even have tickets for the game. And worst of all, Notre Dame didn't have girls. "They told me they had a women's college right across the lake," Joe would say. "What was I supposed to do—swim over to make a date?"

Joe liked to say that he eliminated Notre Dame as soon as he found out it was an all-male institution. But the truth—given Notre Dame's cachet and its hold on Mrs. Namath—was a bit more complicated. "Deep down in Joe's heart, he might have liked Notre Dame," says Bruno. "But they never showed that much interest."

"Everybody was pissed off we didn't go to Notre Dame," remembers Tony Golmont. "But they didn't treat us real good."

They had a better time at Arizona State. At least there they got to see frat boys lighting farts. "First time I ever seen that," says Golmont.

Namath, who stopped counting his scholarship offers at fifty-two, didn't let the recruiting process go to his head. He already had a justifiably high opinion of his abilities. Of all the high school quarterbacks, he once said, "I rated myself best in the country, and that's the truth." He visited seven colleges: Notre Dame, Arizona State, Minnesota, Iowa, Indiana, Maryland, and Miami, where he showed up with a goatee just before Christmas. It is doubtful that Miami's head coach, Andy Gustafson, ever saw a live goatee, certainly not on a football player. But Joe explained that he had grown it for a Christmas play back at school. "I'm playing Christ," he said.

Gustafson, an aging disciplinarian, seemed a bit perplexed by Namath. Rich Niedbala, then a freshman at Miami, remembers thinking: "I got to get Joe out of here before my ass is in a major wringer."

But Joe wasn't finished. He was having too good a time. "Yeah," he told Gustafson, "I'm a hell of an actor."

■ ■ ■

Roland Arrigoni must have gotten a kick out of that story. Arrigoni was the assistant coach at Maryland, whose recruiting territory included western Pennsylvania. He had already established a pipeline, signing some fine players from Aliquippa and Ambridge. But Namath of Beaver Falls was the prize, perfect for Maryland's wide-open passing offense. "The best quarterback in the country," says Lee Corso, then the Terps' quarterbacks coach. "It would have made our program if we could get him. Shit, there was nobody like Joe."

Signing Namath was more than a job for Arrigoni. It became a kind of calling. Something about Joe, apart from his talent and the pressure to acquire it, Roland just liked. "In my opinion, Joe overcame a lot," says Arrigoni. "His home life was not the greatest." The wreckage from his parents' divorce was obvious to the coach. The father would talk bad about the mother. The mother would talk bad about the father. "And there were people in town who would tell you, 'They're both right,'" he says.

Unsure how to handle this complicated family dynamic, Arrigoni went to Bruno. "Best thing you can do is not to touch it," said Bruno. "You'll be better off with Joe."

Almost every Sunday night, when Namath returned from his recruiting visits, Arrigoni was there to pick him up at the airport and take him out for a huge steak at the Palace in New Brighton. Later in the week, he'd return to watch one of Joe's basketball games or take him out after practice. "In those days," Arrigoni remembers, "you could spend as much time as you wanted with the recruits." Joe might've been a hustler, but Arrigoni knew he wouldn't get him by hustling. You signed a kid like Joe by *not* hustling. He had to believe you were straight up, that you cared.

One night Arrigoni showed up after basketball practice to take Joe to dinner. They stopped at home for Joe to change. It was cold as hell, so he turned up the thermostat. Next thing the coach knew, a guy was hollering in broken English. "The stepfather chewed Joe's ass out royally, talking about how nobody turns on the heat but him," Arrigoni recalls.

Joe was embarrassed. You could see it on his face as they left the house. "I'm sorry," he said.

"Never apologize for where you're from," said Arrigoni. "It's where you're going that counts."

■ ■ ■

Namath's visit to College Park, Maryland, went well, though different people recall it differently. Arrigoni remembers Joe waiting for him in a bar at Washington National Airport. As the coach approached, Joe quickly slid his glass across the bar. "That's okay, Joe," said the coach. "Why don't you finish your beer first."

Corso, the quarterback coach, remembers looking out from a second-story window in the football office, waiting for Joe. The kid showed up shortly after noon. "He was a little different," says Corso, who had never seen a prospect arrive for his official visit wearing a peaked-bill beret.

Tim Secor, an end from Aiken, South Carolina, remembers touring the campus with a group of recruits, most of them southerners. For many, it was the first time they had seen black students. Somebody made a remark. Joe didn't like it. "That's bullshit," he said. "That's nowhere." It was the last such comment Secor heard that entire weekend.

Joe's host was Al Hassan, the team's student manager. "There were a lot of recruits," says Hassan. "It was a big weekend for us. And the biggest thing was Joe." Hassan, known as "Hatchet," was from New Castle. He'd been hearing about Namath ever since his last visit home. Guys were sitting around the coffee shop talking about him: *Kid's a fucking magician.*

Hassan recalls the day they finally met: Friday, January 20, 1961, exactly a week after his father had died. Hassan's father, who came from Syria, had also worked in a mill. Joe and Hassan had a lot in common. They liked girls. They liked to shoot pool. They'd be friends for life.

Al was six years older, though, and had already done a hitch in the navy. So on their way in to meet Tom Nugent, Maryland's head coach, Hassan thought to share the wisdom of his years with his new pal. "Joe," he said, "put out the cigarette."

■   ■   ■

Back in Beaver Falls, Namath appeared to relish his role as bad boy of the senior class, as if he wanted everyone to remember him as James Dean in a jockstrap. After quitting varsity basketball, he played on a local all-star team with Ambridge's Freddy Klages.

"He shows up half gassed, with a jug of wine in his hands," Klages would recall. "He gets dressed for the game, then says to me 'let's go out there and give them a show right now.' I saw the other club is on the floor and we're not due for fifteen minutes. He says what's the difference so we go out there and he grabs the ball and put on the darndest dribbling exhibition you ever did see; behind him, through his legs, on his knees everything. He had the people standing up and cheering."

Later that season, Namath showed up for their team picture with sunglasses and facial hair. "You," says the photographer. "The one with the goatee. Take off the glasses while I shoot."

"Look, mister," said Namath, "if you want my picture, you take it with these glasses on."

Joe looked much the same in the baseball team photo in the high school yearbook. Most kids have their hands behind their backs, in an at-ease pose.

But Namath appears with a practiced slouch: legs crossed, arms folded, the only kid in the frame wearing sunglasses.

Dick Allen, the six-time major league all-star from Wampum, Pennsylvania, would always remember the sight of Namath, circa 1961: "He just sat on the bench. He was wearing a beret and smoking a cigarette in a long cigarette holder and his glove was hanging from his belt. The scouts asked him to play and he refused. He stuck his head up and shook his head: No. And he could play ball."

Beneath the pose, though, was another confused, conflicted teenager. On April 15, John Namath finally wed Esther Armour. What was Joe supposed to make of that? And what was he supposed to do with his life?

"He would sit in my kitchen and talk to my mother," says Frances Pinchotti, whose mother, like Rose, loved cooking for Joe. "He was torn, very confused."

The smart money had him headed to College Park. Joe trusted Arrigoni. Al Hassan, who wrote him every week, had become a close friend. With its passing schemes, Maryland was great for quarterbacks. And though his mother was still pushing for Notre Dame, she'd be happy that her son was going to college.

On the other hand, college wasn't a lock. The baseball scouts kept coming around, offering ever-bigger bonuses. By now, the Orioles, the Kansas City A's, and the Chicago Cubs were also courting Namath. How could they not?

On June 8, 1961, in the WPIAL semifinals, Joe made a stunning display of his power and speed, hitting a ball over 400 feet—a shot that seemed oblivious to the stiff incoming wind—for an inside-the-park homer. There wasn't even a play at the plate. Namath finished the afternoon with a homer, a single, and a pair of walks. Four days later—eight months after Mazeroski's famous homer—the Tigers won the championship at Forbes Field. Joe was 2 for 3 that day, and finished the season with his batting average hovering around the .450 mark. Soon, word was out: the Cubs would pay $50,000 for his rights.

Fifty grand entitled the bearer to a lot of rights. Joe even picked out a car—an Oldsmobile Starfire, a convertible with 330 horses under the hood. It had leather bucket seats, a tachometer on the dash, a Hydra-Matic shift on the floor, and broad bands of brushed aluminum on the sides. Joe would drive past the Olds dealership, trolling along in his busted-out Ford with its bogus inspection sticker he had purchased for five bucks. And there it was: the Starfire. "He would drool," says Hassan. With that baseball bonus, Joe could leave his junker where it belonged, rusting with the rest of Beaver Falls, and fly out of town in his V8 chariot.

"I knew he was never coming back," says Frances Pinchotti.

"We *all* knew he wasn't coming back," says the former Joyce Hupp. "But we were hoping that he would."

The girls might've wanted him to stay. But others wanted him gone already. What's more, there was a feeling that Joe's decision would reflect well on Beaver Falls if he chose college over baseball. Frances's father, a bus driver, implored him to pursue his education. Joe Tronzo argued the point in print, quoting a teacher who said, "He has a rich opportunity that comes to only a few."

But nobody wanted Joe in college more than Rose. She wanted her baby to have a degree—and all the status it conferred. "It was *very* important to her," recalls Hassan. "Rose wanted her son to go to college." More than likely, she was counting on Joe's matriculation to lessen her own sense of regret. In her autobiographical account *My Son Joe,* she writes: "I went to St. Mary's High School, but my education stopped when I graduated from the twelfth grade, which was not uncommon then." In fact, St. Mary's never went beyond eighth grade. There is no record of her graduation from the local public school, either. In the 1930 census, taken when she was still seventeen, Rose gives her occupation as "domestic." Asked if she had "attended school or college any time since Sept. 1, 1929," she answered "no." Still, her claim to have been a high school graduate seems less of a lie than an attempt to ease her own embarrassment. Circumstances of age, gender, and culture conspired against Rose Juhasz. Joey was her last opportunity to send a child through college. After all she had gone through, this was a chance to hold her head high.

By graduation, Joe was leaning toward Maryland. He had been hanging out with Hassan every day since May, when the college semester ended. They played cards. They bowled. They shot pool. They played golf, which was kind of like pool—a game of angles and confidence—in the great outdoors. Underneath all that cool, Hassan discovered, "the most competitive guy I've ever seen. Joe didn't want to beat you. He wanted to thrash you."

Eventually, Hassan prevailed, convincing Joe that College Park was the place to be. On August 2 Arrigoni arrived to get Namath's signature on a letter of intent, a document that guaranteed room, board, tuition, books, and $15 a month for laundry as long as the student-athlete maintained a C average and displayed adequate citizenship.

But Arrigoni added a condition. He knew how much Rose and others still wanted Joe to go to Notre Dame. He'd even heard that Joe had already signed another letter committing to Notre Dame. Though Namath's nature wasn't to double-cross, Arrigoni wanted to protect himself. He asked Joe to write Notre Dame, stating that he would not be attending in the fall. They sat at the dining room table as Joe wrote it, addressing coach Joe Kuharich. Then they got a stamp and walked to the corner mailbox. Next, Rose had to sign the scholarship papers to Maryland, which she did reluctantly. "She was upset about it," says Arrigoni. Rose had recently undergone a gallbladder operation, recalls the coach, and she'd been told that the procedure was free only as long as Joe went to Notre Dame.

About two weeks later, says Arrigoni, she received the bill. On the bright side, her son was finally headed off to college. All he needed was a few more points on his SAT score. After taking the exam in the spring, Joe had scored in the low 730s. Maryland required 750. That shouldn't have been much of a problem. After all, Joe had been studying all summer.

As Rose liked to say, Hatchet had become her son's "unofficial tutor." They hit the books almost every night. They'd shower, put on their pool hall best, and slap on some Old Spice. "I can't wait till tomorrow," said Al, checking himself out in the mirror.

"Why's that?" asked Joe.

" 'Cause I get better-looking every day."

Rose would ask where they were going. "To study," said Joe. Hatchet had a good studying place in New Castle. They served thirty-five-cent Seven and Sevens.

With that type of preparatory work, it's no wonder Joe still fell a few points short of the 750 score he needed. The real wonder is why he didn't get somebody to take the test for him. That kind of thing happened all the time. Hassan, then a sophomore drama major, didn't want to take the test for his friend. But he was waiting for Joe to ask. Joe never did, though. "He didn't cheat," says Hassan. "And he could have."

"Roland was devastated," says Lee Corso. "He started looking for a place for Joe to go."

Arrigoni asked Joe if he wanted to go to prep school. "If I don't go to college this year," he replied, "I'll never go."

It was already August. Arrigoni felt responsible for Joe. He had been a stand-up kid. Now the coach had to find him a school, preferably one that didn't have Maryland on its football schedule. Arrigoni's first call was to Kuharich, the Notre Dame coach. Kuharich told him that Notre Dame didn't want anyone's rejects. "Then I'd like to congratulate you on your national championship," said Arrigoni. "If you got enough talent that you can turn down a kid this good, then you're definitely going to win one."

Next, Arrigoni talked to Bernie Reid, his colleague on the Maryland staff. Bernie called Charley Bradshaw, an assistant at Alabama. Alabama was interested. Alabama would send a man up right away. Arrigoni apprised Joe of the school's interest.

"Alabama?" said Joe. "That's Bear Bryant, isn't it?"

As it happened, Coach Paul W. Bryant had already sent a delegation from Tuscaloosa. That was back in the winter when Clem Gryska, Bryant's chief recruiter, and Dude Hennessey, Frank's former line coach at Kentucky, paid

Coach Bruno a visit. Bruno sat them down in his kitchen, drew the shades, and started the projector. Bryant's men were mesmerized by Joe's magic flickering across the kitchen wall. "Boy, they went nuts," Bruno remembers. "They wanted Joe bad."

Joe, of course, had other ideas. None of them included Tuscaloosa, wherever that was, or Bear Bryant. Joe knew the man's reputation—the kind of taskmaster who made you play with broken bones.

Now, all these months later, Joe told Arrigoni thanks but no thanks. The Olds Starfire was still sitting there at the dealership. "I'm gonna sign with the Cubs," said Joe.

"I don't think that's the thing for you," said Arrigoni. "You're better off going to college than playing minor league baseball. What if something happens to your knee?"

Joe had already noticed a cyst on his knee. But what was a mere cyst to a kid like Joe? "Sure as hell didn't bother him, the way he could run and jump," says Arrigoni.

Before long a young Alabama assistant named Howard Schnellenberger showed up in Beaver Falls. "My job was to get Joe to Alabama for an official visit," says Schnellenberger. "The big thing was getting him out of Beaver Falls before the eastern schools got wind that he was free."

Schnellenberger, who brought enough money and clothes for a few days' visit, ended up staying almost a week. He didn't want to return and face Bryant without the kid. So he spent his days working on Rose, John, and Frank. Schnellenberger, from Louisville, had played for Bryant and Blanton Collier at Kentucky. He was a senior when Frank was on the freshman team. "Frank was very, very helpful," he says of his stay in Beaver Falls. "If it weren't for Frank, I doubt seriously that we would have been able to convince Joe to come."

Joe would finish what Frank had only started. College was the right thing. Besides, Frank had to love the idea of his kid brother playing for the Bear. It would be good for Joe, the ass-kicking of his life.

Still, as obliging as Frank was, Schnellenberger quickly learned whose opinion mattered most: As Rose went, so went Joe. "Finally, his mother invited me for dinner," recalls Schnellenberger. "She made chicken and dumplings. That's when I figured I had a chance."

As Joe recalled: "My mother took a liking to Coach Schnellenberger. My mother went upstairs, packed my bags and said, 'Take him.'"

Joe stepped off the plane in Birmingham wearing a loudly checked sport coat, from which dangled a chain and pocket watch. As he recalled: "I had longish hair and I was wearing a silvered blue-straw hat with a dark blue band around it and a little pearl on the side and I had a toothpick in my mouth." He looked like the hustlers whose shoes he once shined. But the real hustle had already been pulled off by Schnellenberger, whose unexpectedly long stay in Beaver Falls had left him temporarily impoverished. "Back in those days we traveled in cash," says the coach. "I ended up spending more days than I had money."

Most football people still assumed Joe was headed for Maryland, and Schnellenberger wanted him out of Pennsylvania before any of them learned otherwise. They left for Alabama just as soon as Namath agreed to visit the campus. Not wanting to wait for money to be wired, the coach wrote a check for Namath's ticket. Then, after a problem with their connecting flight in Atlanta—either lateness or fog, Schnellenberger can't remember—he

10. THE TOWER

wrote another check for the hotel room. In fact, the coach didn't have sufficient funds to cover either. Early the next morning, as they set out for Tuscaloosa, he bought Joe a cup of coffee. "I was just hoping he wouldn't ask for breakfast," says Schnellenberger, who had but a few dimes left in his pocket.

Back on campus, Schnellenberger's state of high dishevelment caused some hilarity among his fellow assistants. He was still wearing the same shirt he had on when he left. "It was a white shirt," recalls Dude Hennessey. "Now it was yellow."

He had no money. He stank. Still, he was feeling pretty good about himself. Howard Schnellenberger would much rather have faced a judge for writing bad checks than face Coach Bryant without Namath.

■   ■   ■

Paul Bryant was born in Arkansas, September 11, 1913, the eleventh of twelve children. Three of the twelve died in infancy. The rest lived without running water or electricity in a place called Moro Bottom, which was about as bottom as a white person could get. "Moro what?" a writer once asked.

"Bottom," replied Coach Bryant. "Like your ass."

The Bryants were subsistence farmers. By age ten, Paul was pushing a plow. He didn't have much choice, as his father was not a well man. Wilson Monroe Bryant, in the words of one biographer, "mostly sat around the house," though occasionally he would be found wandering through the woods at night. He died in 1931. The cause of his death was said to be pneumonia; the cause of his suffering was unknown. Ida Bryant, his wife, believed in the Almighty and hard work, but not in doctors. She was the force in the family, at home and on the farm.

On Saturdays Ida and her youngest son would head to nearby Fordyce in a mule-drawn wagon to sell what they had grown, churned, or milked on their patch of Moro Bottom. Fordyce, with a population of fewer than 4,000, felt like a metropolis to Bryant. The "city" boys would make fun of his sorry country ass. Half a century later Bryant would say, "I still remember the ones who did it."

The combination of poverties—familial and economic—produced a tough, angry mama's boy. By the age of thirteen Bryant was a little over six feet, 180 pounds, and mean as hell. That was the year a man with a black bear came to the Lyric Theater in downtown Fordyce, offering a dollar a minute for anybody who'd wrestle his muzzled sidekick. For that kind of money, Bryant was in. He and the bear reached an early stalemate. "Sensing the need for a little more drama, the bear's owner walked over to the beast and yanked off its muzzle," wrote Keith Dunnavant in *Coach*. "They tussled around some more, and then Bryant felt a burning sensation on his right ear. The bear had bitten him and he was dripping blood all over the stage. Having earned his dollar, he didn't feel the need to become permanently maimed, so he jumped from the stage and crash-landed in the front row of seats. The whole bout lasted no more than two or three minutes."

The man and the bear skipped town, leaving Bryant with nothing but a nickname. And though his players and coaches never used it, "Bear" suited him well. Though Bryant wasn't the most talented or graceful of football players, he was a ferocious son of a bitch, which was enough to earn a scholarship to the University of Alabama. In Tuscaloosa, he was known as "the other end," in distinction to his teammate who played on the left side, Don Hutson, an All-American and future Hall of Famer. As a junior Bryant played on the team that beat Stanford in the 1935 Rose Bowl. But the game that epitomized his virtues came his senior year, in Knoxville, against Tennessee. Bryant made his usual assortment of nice hits on both sides of the ball. More unusual was the touchdown pass he caught. But unusual to the point of freakishness was the fact that he did it all on a right leg he had broken the week before.

Broken bones were never much of an excuse to Bryant. Dude Hennessey, an undersized end who later played for him at Kentucky, recalled this conversation: "What's wrong with you, little partner?" asked Bryant.

"Coach, I broke my hand."

"You don't run on your hands, do you?"

Bryant walked off rather than wait for an answer.

In 1954, the year he left Kentucky for Texas A & M, Bryant led 115 young men to a grueling training camp in Junction, Texas. By day, they were denied water. By night, they were confined to oven-hot Quonset huts. Of the 115, 35 returned to play for the Aggies. In the mythology of Bryant, Junction is as famous as the black bear. Boys could vomit all they wanted, but they weren't getting any water. Bryant did not acknowledge heat stroke as a medical possibility. Junction wasn't much different than the training camps Bryant had run in Kentucky. Schnellenberger recalls those nights in Millersburg: after the day's three practices you could hear guys throw their suitcases out of a second-story dormitory window, then slide down the drainpipe. These escapes were only made under the cover of darkness. You didn't want to face Coach Bryant. You didn't want to live with that shame.

"It was like the Marine Corps," says Schnellenberger. "Those who survived developed a special bond. Coach Bryant was able to get more effort than kids thought they could give." While Schnellenberger describes the process as "separating the chaff from the wheat," Bryant himself used a phrase with more color, less metaphor: "separating the champions from the turds." He knew where it was, that Moro Bottom in a boy's soul. For many, his indoctrination seemed less military than religious. Upon meeting him for the first time in 1945, then–Kentucky quarterback George Blanda said, "This must be what God looks like."

In 1958 Bryant returned to Alabama. "Mama called," he said, and there wasn't a preacher or a politician who could have stated it better. "Alabama football has always been the love of the people," says Jack "Hoot Owl" Hicks, a manager on Bryant's early teams in Tuscaloosa. Bryant combined two cults—his own and that of Alabama football—to form a religion. In the deepest South, Coach Bryant was a living God of the white man. Wally Butts, the former Georgia coach, used to say: "In Alabama, an atheist is someone who doesn't believe in Bear Bryant." He was an Old Testament deity; his rule was based on fear. Under Bryant, fear of pain was nothing compared to the fear of humiliation. Typically, his assistants were drawn from the ranks of his champions. Men like Schnellenberger and Hennessey became his apostles, turds who became champions, their fear now leavened with devotion.

Mere preachers spoke from pulpits; Bryant ruled from a tower. You had to squint in the sun to behold what had risen from Moro Bottom. Thirty-three spiral steps led up to the platform from which he lorded over practice, an Olympus for one with a chain as its gate. From above, Bryant would oversee his coaches, his players, his trainers, his water boys, all of them, all of it, his. You lived in fear of having him call down at you. This wasn't some Cecil B.

DeMille picture. This was for real. "The voice of God," said Bart Starr, the Green Bay Packers Hall of Fame quarterback from Montgomery, Alabama.

But the last thing you wanted to hear, the harbinger of absolute doom, was the chain. "If something wasn't going good in the drills, he'd unhook it and drop it," recalls Clem Gryska, a longtime assistant. "You could hear that chain rattle. Everybody came to attention: players, coaches, managers, spectators, everyone. If he was coming down off that tower, that meant he was gonna *do* something."

"You did not want to be in his line of sight," agrees Dude Hennessey, wincing in remembrance.

No one—least of all the sporting press—thought to challenge Bryant's divine right to rip people new assholes. His predecessor, J. B. Whitworth, had won four games in three years. By 1961, Bryant's fourth season in Tuscaloosa, he had won a national championship. "Everybody saw him as a savior, and he was," says Clyde Bolton, who started at the *Birmingham News* during that memorable year.

Bryant did more than win championships. Alabama had always been the Moro Bottom of America. The coach—who famously proclaimed "I ain't never been nothin' but a winner"—enabled Caucasians of the Yellowhammer State, from poor white trash to postbellum aristocracy, to feel like winners, too. "Alabama is at or near the bottom of all the meaningful statistics like education, income—but in football we can kick your ass. That's the mentality," says Bolton.

"Those were pretty lean years," says Charles Land, the former sports editor of the *Tuscaloosa News,* who doubled as Alabama's sports information director in 1961. "A whole lot of people in the state of Alabama desperately needed something to feel good about."

People felt a little better watching *The Bear Bryant Show,* sponsored by Coca-Cola and Golden Flake Potato Chips, on Sunday afternoons. Something about television made Coach Bryant even more godlike. People would never forget that voice, cured with whiskey and unfiltered Chesterfields, three packs a day. Mitchum sounded like a sissy boy compared to Coach Bryant.

"The persona was great," says Land. "He'd get on there and say the same thing week after week. He'd talk about how somebody made a good tackle. And he'd talk about the boy's parents. He loved to talk about the mamas and the papas. But the main thing was, he won."

■   ■   ■

Judging from Namath's first appearance, Bryant's divine quality and the hallowed place of Alabama football were both lost on the hustler prince.

"Looked like he was from another country," said Schnellenberger.

Gryska had seen golfers with hats like that. But he'd never seen a golfer wear it that way. "Tilted," recalls Gryska. "Just the right way."

Some of the players started to snort and snicker. Is that a toothpick?

"Must be a sportswriter," said one.

"A nigger sportswriter."

"Y'all better not say anything about him," said Dude Hennessey. "Coach wants him. He'll get rid of five of y'all to keep him."

Right about then, it happened. Everyone heard it but Namath.

The chain dropped.

■ ■ ■

Several men are alleged to have visited Bryant atop his tower: Governor Wallace; Dr. Frank Rose, the university president; Happy Campbell, the baseball coach; and a comedian from Mississippi in whom Bryant took great delight. But these sightings are difficult to confirm. More certain are the facts concerning Namath's arrival at the practice field. There is no shortage of witnesses, all of whom recount with awe the moment when Joe Namath became the first and only player to so ascend.

"Everybody was just shocked," says Hicks, the manager. "Joe was up there thirty, forty minutes, and Coach Bryant talked the whole time. Joe said he could only understand one word: 'stud.' The whole time, 'stud' is the only word he could understand."

Bryant's accent was thick, even by Alabama standards. Still, across generations and cultures, the coach and the kid reached an accord up there. In time, it would become a bond. They were, each in his way, two wild-ass mama's boys, each having suffered the sins of fathers. Joe would by turns hate Bryant, fear him, and love him. He would bend for Bryant. Joe could feel what the southerners felt: the love of the people, the paternal will. In Bryant, Joe had found an outrageously outsized father figure, a man he wanted to please.

"It made you feel good to do things right," he would say. "It made you feel good to make him happy."

It was Hoot Owl Hicks, the team's student manager, who relayed Joe's request to Carney Laslie, the assistant athletic director. Hoot Owl, so nicknamed for a likeness to a funny-paper character named Henry Owl, had grown up in West Blocton, about thirty miles from the Tuscaloosa campus. He played tackle on a high school team that won thirty-eight of forty games. Four West Blocton players received scholarships to Alabama, including Hicks. "They wouldn't give me one as a player so they gave me one as a manager," he says. The son of a coal miner, Hicks never considered another school. To his mind, handing out jerseys in Tuscaloosa was a calling. He would gladly serve in any way he could, even if it meant tending to this strange, homesick Yankee.

11. COLORED WATER

Laslie, however, didn't care what number Joe wanted or Johnny Unitas or any of that. The university didn't have a number 19 jersey, and Laslie was too damn stingy to buy one. The boy would get number 12.

"I think Coach Bryant had something to do with that," says Clem Gryska. Unitas might have been a great quarterback, but he wasn't Pat Trammell. Trammell, who wore number 12, was Bryant's favorite player. A doctor's son from Scottsboro, Alabama, Trammell was voted the Southeastern Conference's outstanding defensive back in 1959. More important, he was a three-year starter at quarterback. "As a quarterback, Pat had no ability," said Bryant. "All he could do was beat you." In 1961 the Crimson Tide would record eleven straight victories, including a finale against Arkansas in the Sugar Bowl. Having won a national championship, Trammell enrolled in medical school. A shining exemplar of southern virtue, he seemed to have little in common with the young Yankee wearing 12 for the freshman team. But they shared a talent for victory, and in Bryant's scheme of the world, victory was virtue.

As Bryant's feelings toward Trammell were well known, Namath's new number evoked the greatest of expectations. "Word spread," remembers Clyde Bolton of the *Birmingham News*. "It was kind of like a beautiful girl had moved to town."

The anticipation did little to ease Joe's adjustment to the South, which was fraught with all sorts of peculiarities and partitions. Southerners spoke a different language. They dressed funny, what with their khakis and their cardigans. But the real difference, an almost insurmountable chasm, was the system of apartheid. The drinking fountains left Joe particularly mystified. "Colored water," says Hoot Owl Hicks, "Joe just couldn't understand that."

Tuscaloosa might have been a college town, but it was also home to Robert M. Shelton, imperial wizard of the United Klans of America, Knights of the Ku Klux Klan. To Namath, coming as he did from the Lower End, segregation was an especially repugnant ideology. But he never asked Hoot Owl to explain the South. He never sought reasons for life as it had evolved below the Mason-Dixon line. "He just wanted a friend, is all," says Hoot Owl.

Joe was something of a loner. He didn't need many friends, just good ones. Hoot Owl was a good one. Ray Abruzzese, a senior halfback, was another. "We never *said* anything to him," recalls Hicks. "We just tried to be his friend. He didn't know anybody. See, I lived close, but I didn't go home during the holidays, and Ray was always here. So if Joe needed anything he knew he could ask Ray and me. He knew we'd do it."

Ray was from the South, too—South Philly, which in Joe's estimation was kind of like being from the heavily Italian districts of New Castle or Youngstown. Through a series of accidents, Abruzzese had traveled from South Philadelphia High School to Hinds Junior College in Mississippi to the University of Alabama. Ray showed Joe around the town, such as it was. Ray took the former altar boy to mass, where, for the first time in Joe's life, dark-skinned Catholics were very much the minority. They played pool, keeping an eye out for a hustler called the Tuscaloosa Squirrel. They went to the movies. They did a lot of hanging out. Abruzzese, recalls Schnellenberger, "was a guy who had more problems staying off the street than Joe did."

"Ray Abruzzese is as fine a guy that ever walked," says Hicks. "Joe had a lot of respect for him because Ray had already proven hisself as a player."

In Joe's case, proof would have to wait. As freshmen were not varsity-eligible, there were only omens of his talent. Gryska remembers that first week of practice, a period devoted to fundamentals and, as he put it, "indoctrination." In one of the morning sessions a skeleton team of freshman backs and ends went against the starting defensive secondary, coached by Gene Stallings. The drill was intended to help the starters get their timing and confidence at the younger players' expense. "But Joe ate 'em up," says Gryska.

Stallings returned for the afternoon session a little steamed, complaining that Joe was taking too long to throw. So Gryska told him to hurry up, and Joe started getting rid of the ball very quickly. "He *still* ate 'em up," says Gryska.

In those days, Bryant's players played both offense and defense. That first week, Gryska had Joe playing a little safety. He had a knack for the position, what the coach remembers as "an uncanny ability to lay back, see what was happening on the field, and get a good break on the ball." Joe was just playing the same angles he played as a quarterback—in reverse.

But the beauty of this exercise was lost on Bryant, who sent a student manager to request his assistant's presence. "I was scared to death," Gryska recalls.

"Don't let that kid work at safety," said Bryant. "Just let him throw the ball."

That wasn't like Bryant. He didn't believe in babying players, and he didn't believe in throwing the ball, either. Though the coach loved long weekends in Vegas, he abhorred risk on the football field. In his mind, the passing game posed little but risk. A team that passed too much risked losing its toughness. Bryant favored a defense that knocked people down and a running game that knocked people over. But Joe's talent was such that it posed another kind of risk entirely. You didn't want to squander what that boy could do with his arm.

At the beginning of each new season that arm seemed to produce a moment of wonder and revelation. Butch Henry, then a sophomore end, recalls a kickoff drill during which the kicker was unable to get enough distance on the ball. So Coach Bryant called over Joe, still the silliest-looking Yankee anyone had ever seen. He'd come to practice with a kind of slicked-back crew cut, that damn toothpick, and tape he wound around his shoes to make them look white. He walked hunched over, too. But, damn, could that boy throw. "With just a flick of the wrist," says Henry, "he could put it in the end zone from about the 35-yard line. Everybody just looked at each other. I mean, other guys could take a running start and throw it that far. But they'd have to strain. Joe just did it with such ease. Like he was throwing a baseball. It looked so easy to him."

The 1961 freshman team played a short three-game season, ending in a 7–7 tie with Auburn. Before that came victories against Mississippi State and Tulane, afternoons during which Namath scored more touchdowns running than passing. Such was Alabama football. "We were so option-oriented," says Gryska. "Coach Bryant was very demanding about the option. He wanted the quarterback going into the line."

One Monday night, during a scrimmage between the freshman team and the varsity scrubs, Namath ran the option left. He was tackled just as he pitched the ball, which fell loose. Bryant stormed out on the field, oblivious to the tackler who still had Joe in his grasp. "It's not your job just to pitch the ball out and lay down there on the ground and not do anything," Bryant hollered. "You don't just lay there."

Bryant was still hollering when Namath rose and turned to walk back to the huddle. Then, as Namath recalled: "Suddenly he grabbed hold of my face mask and nearly lifted me off the ground. 'Namath,' he said, 'when I'm talking to you, boy, you say, "Yes, sir," and look me in the eye.' I said, 'Yes, sir, yes, sir.' He scared me half to death. From then on, if Coach Bryant just said, 'Joe,' even if I was sixty yards downfield, I'd sprint up to him, stop a yard away, come to attention and say 'Yes, sir.' "

■   ■   ■

As a freshman, Namath generated even more buzz on the basketball court than on the football field. The coaches had an office in the gymnasium building, where the football players had a regular pickup game. "Joe could dunk," says Gryska. "I can't remember anyone who could dunk, not on our team."

"He could dunk it backward, he could dunk it forward, he could dunk it any old way," recalls Hicks, his frequent partner in those two-on-two contests. Hoot Owl, by his own account, couldn't even play a little. "That should tell you how good Joe was. We would play the other athletes, the football players, and we never got beat. Butch Henry, he made all-state basketball in high school, and his team went to the playoffs, but Joe used to get up there and block Butch's shot, and it made him so mad. Butch never saw a guy who could jump like Joe."

"He used to brag that he quit playing varsity basketball his senior year because the coach wanted him and four black guys to play slow-down basketball," says Henry, a right end who had two inches and sixteen pounds on Joe, according to the 1962 football media guide. Henry, from Selma, became Joe's roommate second semester freshman year. "The coaches wanted him to become acclimated to the South," he recalls. It wasn't the easiest acclimation. Joe remained stubbornly different. Butch had never seen anyone spend so much time shining his shoes. But what set Namath apart weren't just matters of style. Joe's tales of the Lower End challenged the imaginations of those who'd never had even a sip of colored water. The only white guy on the starting five? What could the good old boys have thought of that, comedy or blasphemy?

"In my freshman year," Joe would say, "I was sitting in my room doing something and one of the fellas picked up a picture of the Beaver Falls High school football queen and her court. My girl at the time was the football queen and the crown bearer was a black girl. The guy asked, 'Hey Joe, is this your girl?' and I answered yes, thinking he was pointing at the queen. But he was pointing at the black girl. He said, 'Oh yeah?' and ran out and told everybody he could find that I was dating a black girl."

(In fact, the photograph from the 1961 yearbook shows Namath escorting a cheerleader named Mary Wogan, the homecoming's scepter bearer. Tom Krzemienski escorts the queen, Joyce Thompson. Bill Heistand, a guard, escorts Linda Harrison, a majorette and crown bearer. They're all white.)

"All I know is he had three pictures on his dresser: two white girls and a black girl," says Hoot Owl. "One of the white girls was his girlfriend, named

Pinchotti." The black girl, as Hicks understood it, was Ruby Jean Finley. "He had her picture up 'cause they was friends," says Hicks.

Friends, girlfriends—the distinction was lost on people in Tuscaloosa in 1961. "That's why they called him 'nigger,'" explains Hicks.

Later, Joe would laugh about it, his nickname. But back then, he didn't see the humor "I wanted to quit about 15 times during my freshman year," he said.

He called home, told his mother he was leaving. Frank took the receiver. "You see how they treat the blacks down there?" he said. "Well, that's nothing compared to the whipping you're getting if you come home."

Colored water was only part of Joe's problem with the South. Bryant had six other quarterbacks on the roster, including a transfer from Texas named Jack Hurlbut. When spring practice started, Joe was on the second team. "He couldn't stand that," recalls Hoot Owl. "He was thinking he wasn't gonna make it. But I kept telling him, me and Abruzzese: 'When all is said and done, you will be the quarterback.'"

Still, the only guarantee Joe had was the baseball money. That deal was still there, waiting for his signature. So was the Starfire. He was homesick, and more than that, he was worried about his mother. "He was concerned about how she was getting along," says Bebe Schreiber, his steadiest girlfriend at Alabama. "Family was very important to him. . . . He was in a twilight zone kind of place."

Joe had met Bebe after a football game in Birmingham. She was a sophomore: a cute, vivacious, short-haired brunette, and crazy about Joe from the start. With his hat and sunglasses, his toothpick and tapered slacks, he definitely wouldn't be mistaken for a southerner. But then, Bebe wasn't a southerner, either. She had lived in Atlanta before coming to Tuscaloosa. As her family had moved around a lot, she actually considered herself more of a Yankee. She had something else in common with Joe; Bebe's parents had split, too. "Kids of divorce," she says, "they always have this picture that the family can be whole again."

Soon, Bebe had another picture, this one of her and Joe. "I encouraged him to stay put," she says.

She wasn't alone. Bryant sent an old friend of his to have a talk with Joe. Bubba Church, a pitcher from Birmingham, had been 15–11 his second year with the Phillies. Then he hurt his arm. The Phillies traded him to Cincinnati, who then traded him to the Cubs. He was never much good after that, 13–20 over the last four seasons in the big leagues. Church explained all this to Joe: that it was better to stay in college, that baseball would leave him, too, with nothing but a sore arm.

But Church's sore arm wasn't Joe's concern. He just wanted to go home. "Right then and there," Joe recalled, "Bubba just pulled some money out of his wallet and said, 'You fly home. You can stay there if you like, but I think it would be better for you to come back.' Well, after I got home, I decided maybe Bubba was right and I decided to stick it out."

It turned out that Beaver Falls was just a mill town. Alabama had the good weather and the pretty girls like Bebe. He had started making friends in guys like Hoot Owl and Ray and a short, freckled kid from Jersey named Jimmy Walsh. That spring, they all jumped in Ray's car and drove down to Panama City, Florida. Joe had never been to Florida. You couldn't beat it—the sun, the sand, the girls. "When he saw that beach" says Hoot Owl, "that was it."

The way Hoot Owl remembers, their spring break excursion to Panama City closed the deal, kept Joe in school. Then, on May 19, he had a great game in the annual Red-White scrimmage. In front of 10,500 fans at Denny Stadium—not a bad crowd for a scrimmage—Namath marched the White team to two long touchdowns. He was 12 of 17 for 156 yards, big numbers for a quarterback in Bryant's offense. He even intercepted one of Hurlbut's passes. He'd be staying at Alabama.

But, really, Alabama's hold on him was only as strong as Bryant's. Some months later, Joe met up with Rich Niedbala back in Beaver Falls. He told him about turning his back on the coach during that Monday-night scrimmage. "I will never, ever mess with that fucker again," said Namath. Niedbala was more than a little surprised. After all, this was the same kid who walked off the bas-ketball court with most of the town looking on. Joe never let a challenge— much less a physical one—go unanswered. It was difficult to imagine him letting another man put his hands on him.

"He put the fear of God into me," said Joe.

A profane football coach had accomplished what an army of nuns had failed to do. By laying hands on Joe Willie, he put the fear of the Almighty in him, and may even have saved him. Something about Bryant—his manner, his magnitude—enabled the rebel to find a cause. For the first time in his life, Na-math acquiesced willingly. While the notion of Bryant's infallibility might not have extended much beyond Alabama, that was enough for Joe. He had what he wanted: a father without fault. It felt good to make him happy. What Bryant provided outweighed his misgivings about the South. Joe's choice to stay was personal, not political. He got a Great White Father, more than he asked for, but just enough for him to navigate those colored waters.

As Namath's freshman year ended, the Crimson Tide lost fourteen letter-men from the 1961 national championship team. Gone was Darwin Holt, a small but vicious hitter who, earlier that season, had earned a measure of un-wanted fame for a shot that busted up the face of Georgia Tech's Chick Graning. Also gone were Ray Abruzzese and Billy Neighbors, Bryant's best tackle, who had headed off to the cold northern cities of Buffalo and Boston to play for the newfangled American Football League. Pat Trammell, the coach's alter ego at quarterback, would be attending medical school.

Things got worse over the summer. Tom Bible, who was supposed to assume starting duties at right tackle, drowned in June. Full-back Mike Fracchia, voted the Sugar Bowl's outstanding player and the Southeastern Con-ference's leading rusher in 1961, would miss

12. STUD

the upcoming season with an injured knee. The second-string fullback, Dink Wall, had a bad knee, too. As for quarterbacks, Bryant still had six—but not one had really been tested. Jack Hurlbut, the twenty-one-year-old transfer from Rice, was big and strong, but he was coming back from a broken arm. The spring scrimmage was still fresh in the coach's mind. Namath looked good, despite that silly bandanna he had taken to wearing in practice. But he was just nineteen. You couldn't count on sophomore quarterbacks.

On top of that, the Tide was just plain small. It was, of course, a well-known fact that Bryant did his best work coaching runts—lean, mean, hungry boys like Darwin Holt who could hit bigger than they were. But the cheap shot (even Bryant had to acknowledge as much) that cost Graning three teeth and four weeks in a hospital turned Holt and his coach into symbols for the game's violent excesses. Nearly a year after the Georgia Tech game, the *Saturday Evening Post* would charge Bryant with teaching "brutal" football.

Certainly Holt epitomized one of Bryant's Moro Bottom maxims: "You have to out-mean people." But there was an ethic amid the brutality, and it was lost on those northern press people who put out the *Saturday Evening Post*. Holt began his college career at 152 pounds. Under Coach Bryant, though, a boy like Holt could compensate for deficits in size or talent. All he had to do was pay the price, a debt Bryant settled with sweat and blood.

"It was commando training," says Christ Vagotis, a lineman from Ohio. "In the off-season we went to 'football class.' They put on the heat until this little room was about 120 degrees. Then you had to rassle each other to get out. If you lost, you stayed. The only way out of that room was to win."

Namath would recall the first time he saw linemen engaged in the Kill or Be Killed drill: "Three guys got in a circle and they just started fighting when the whistle blew. Literally fighting: kicking, slugging, anything." Namath was told the drill would "toughen the boys up a bit." When the whistle blew again, trainers came for the kid on the ground, who'd been kicked in the mouth; the other two were excused. Then, another whistle, and three more boys went at it. While Namath thanked God he was not a lineman, he never questioned Bryant's drill, or the effect it would have on the guys who'd be blocking for him. "I knew it sure as hell made 'em tougher, the guys who survived," he said.

They'd have to be extra tough for the 1962 season. As it began, Alabama's starting offensive linemen averaged 198 pounds; the average at, say, Georgia Tech was 222.

Lean and mean was well and good, but this was too damn lean for Bryant's tastes. The lack of size, the injuries, and the players lost to graduation caused the coach to offer a dismal forecast: the Crimson Tide would finish with a record of 5–5, maybe 6–4. Coming off a championship season, Bryant's prediction probably raised more consternation than the Klan's imperial wizard, who was busy preparing the state's biggest-ever cross burning for Tuscaloosa.

Then Namath went back to pass in the opener against Georgia. And everything seemed to change.

"I can still see that first one," says Clem Gryska. "We were on national TV. Joe just rides that fullback in there. Georgia jumps all over it, and Joe drops back and just kinda lays it out there for Richard Williamson." Williamson recalls the first pass of the season as "an out-and-up off a play action." The ball came down over his left shoulder, and Williamson caught it without breaking stride, a fifty-two-yard touchdown, the first of three Namath would throw that day, his varsity debut, September 22, 1962, before 54,000 fans at Legion Field in Birmingham. "Pat Trammell couldn't throw it like that," says Williamson, then a senior out of Fort Deposit, Alabama. "We hadn't seen *anybody* who could throw it like that."

The year before, Trammell had established a new school passing record: 1,035 yards on 133 attempts. By comparison, Namath—the "cocky 185-pound Yankee sophomore" as one paper was already calling him—threw for 179 yards in his first game. His three touchdowns (not including the one he ran for) tied a school record. He would break Trammell's season record with a couple of games to spare. But before that, he'd break the template for Alabama football players. As Williamson put it: "Joe was a whole different deal."

Joe was a stud in a litter of runts. There was a brutal beauty in Bryant's game; a boy could earn what he lacked in talent. But what of the kid who already had enormous talent? What about Joe Namath? Pat Trammell and Darwin Holt were players in the mold of their coach, but Namath was the player that coach wanted to be. "Joe was the best athlete I have ever seen," Bryant would say. "Nothing came easier for him than football."

And football wasn't something that was supposed to come easily, especially as it was practiced in Tuscaloosa. Years later, recalling that first day when he invited the young hustler up on the tower, Bryant would say: "I would have *carried* him up if I'd known then how good he was."

■　　■　　■

Yet Bryant still planned to alternate quarterbacks. In his spectacular debut, that 35–0 win over Georgia, Namath played about three quarters. "He did beautifully," cautioned Bryant, "for a sophomore." The following week, in New Orleans against Tulane, he threw a couple of touchdowns in little more than a half. The Tide was already up 44–6 when he left the game. It wasn't until October 6, against Vanderbilt, that Namath threw his first interception, a ball that was tipped at the goal line. Bama was a 35-point favorite that day. But Joe, who treated the point spread as a kind of subversive math, never much liked being a favorite. "I was having a miserable day," Namath would recall. "Coach Bryant pulled me out of the game, and I was really angry. I threw my helmet down as I came off the field. Then I went over to the bench and sat down, and Coach Bryant came over and sat down next to me and put his arm around me. To the crowd, it must've looked like he was cheering me up. Cheering me up, hell; he was damn near squeezing my head off. 'Boy,' he said, 'don't let me ever see you come out of a ball game acting like that. Don't you ever do that again.'"

He never did, at least not in the presence of Bryant, who told another story of that game. A Vanderbilt tackler had just put a good hit on Joe, figured he knocked the Yankee quarterback a little silly. "Hey, number 12," he said, taunting, "what's your name?"

"You'll see it in the headlines tomorrow," said Joe, who threw a touchdown on the very next play.

As it happened, Vanderbilt beat the spread, but lost the game 17–7. Namath's "miserable day" was anything but for Richard Williamson, who caught three of his passes for 86 yards. As a junior, Williamson had led the team in receiving with 206 yards. Now, after just three games with Namath, he had 241 yards. "I'd have loved to play another year or two with Joe," he says wistfully.

Williamson, who'd make a career coaching NFL offenses, could feel the game changing. Namath seemed to stretch the field, redefining the sense of distance. Al Davis, then an assistant for the San Diego Chargers in the upstart American Football League, scouted Namath that season and returned with a breathless report for his boss, Sid Gillman.

"I saw a guy who tips the field," said Davis.

"What do you mean?" asked Gillman, an architect of the modern passing game.

"This sonofabitch is so good he plays like he's going downhill."

■ ■ ■

Bryant loved hearing stuff like that. But publicly, he tried to temper the hype swirling about Namath: "Joe is a real fine sophomore quarterback. Some people expect him to play like a senior all the time. I don't." Even Joe's interceptions got people talking. Gene Ritch, a Houston defensive back, ran one back sixty-nine yards to the Alabama 11-yard line. There, according to Charles Land of the *Tuscaloosa News,* "he fell down trying to elude Namath, who played off a blocker beautifully to save the touchdown." Only a stud could have done that, and fortunately for Bryant, Bama had two that year. The other was Lee Roy Jordan, who was something like Darwin Holt, just a whole lot bigger. Lee Roy led a defense that would allow just 39 points in eleven games that season.

Alabama was 7–0 as it prepared to play Miami, a contest advertised as a duel between Namath and the Hurricanes' George Mira. A junior All-American who could run as well as he threw, Mira was widely regarded by the sporting press as the nation's most talented quarterback. "That little boy might be *your* favorite," Bryant confided to one of the writers. "But I've got one who is going to make more money than any quarterback who ever lived."

The first half of the game did little for Bryant's reputation as a prophet. Mira moved his team despite a fearsome defense. Meanwhile, Namath—whose bandanna earned him the nickname "Injun Joe" in the *Anniston Star*—had fumbled and thrown a couple of interceptions before finishing the half with four straight incompletions.

The halftime score was 3–0, Miami. The final was 36–3, Alabama. From sports editor George Smith's game story in the *Anniston Star,* November 11, 1962:

> Ole Indian Joe Namath just doesn't take kindly to anyone stealing his thunder. George (The Matador) Mira of the University of Miami will testify to that little gem of knowledge this morning.
>
> It was Namath, a cocksure Yankee sophomore quarterback from Beaver Falls, Pa., who picked Alabama's Crimson Tide up by the seat of its pants and led it to one of the greatest comebacks in SEC history. . . .
>
> . . . Ole Joe must have taken stock of the situation during the half-time break. He decided nobody should make Ole Joe look like a bum.

As usual, great quarterbacking made for great sports journalism. The All-American Mira—"the fiery Spaniard," as Smith called him—attempted thirteen more passes than Namath, but accounted for 100 fewer yards. Namath completed twelve passes for 205 yards and ran the ball six times for another 65. Those were outrageous numbers for a quarterback of that era. Andy Gustafson, the Miami coach, was not quoted in Smith's account, but his must have been an awe to behold. After all, he'd just been beat by that strange goateed boy who had played Jesus in the Christmas play.

Bama went to Georgia Tech ranked number one in the country, with Namath needing just seven yards to beat Trammell's record. He got the record. He also got three balls intercepted as the Tide lost 7–6. "Joe didn't have a bad day," said Bryant, who blamed the defeat in part on his own play-calling. A year after Darwin Holt's cheap hit, Tech fans hit Bryant twice with whiskey bottles. Alabama's first loss in twenty-six games probably cost the Tide a national championship. It would cost Auburn, too. The following week, Bryant's boys took it out on their traditional rivals, outmeaning them 38–0.

Bryant removed Namath with almost a quarter to go, with Joe only 36 yards from the school record for total offense in a season. But he didn't complain. If the record meant that much to him, he'd have thrown the ball more than ten times. But who needed records? A record was just a number. He was a stud.

■　　■　　■

The Orange Bowl was built in 1937 with a $340,000 grant from the Works Progress Administration to aid the city of Miami. By January 1, 1963, the day of the Alabama-Oklahoma game, any trace of the Depression had long since vanished. Having just undergone a million-dollar renovation, the stadium, like the annual New Year's game, had become part of a grand televised fantasy, now delivered in living color on NBC. The *Miami Herald* described the Orange Bowl pageant as "an army of 5,000 bandsmen and 500 beautiful women and a corps of half a hundred splendiferous floats."

What could be better than a procession of bathing beauties—scented with Coppertone and Noxzema, straddling these caissons of corporate sponsorship—followed by a kick-ass game of football? Here was the true American spirit, a pagan festival remade for the media. Nothing could undermine the sun-kissed optimism, not even the likes of Tommy Devine of the *Miami News*. "I'm not impressed by Bryant's corn pone and chitlins routine nor his great white father act as the benevolent protector of the Alabama players against the forces of evil," Devine wrote. Angered that Alabama players weren't made available to the press, Devine called Bryant "a whip-cracking tyrant" who, under the guise of amateur athletics, was making a small fortune from television fees and the endorsement of potato chips and soft drinks.

Chips, pop, and TV? Someone should have reminded Mr. Devine that this was free enterprise. It was chips, pop, and TV that would win the war against communism. Even the president knew it; he showed up in Miami, the front page of the *Herald* proclaiming, "Everything's AOK"—an acronym for Alabama, Oklahoma, Kennedy. Kennedy was the first TV president; he understood, even if he did sit in the Oklahoma section. At halftime, he summoned Martha Campbell, a nineteen-year-old cheerleader from Scottsboro, Alabama, to his box. The meeting caused Miss Campbell to weep with joy for six whole minutes.

By then, the game was all but over. Namath hit Williamson for twenty-five yards and a touchdown back in the first quarter. That was all the Tide needed, what with the way Lee Roy was hitting and the Sooners were fumbling. Jordan had twenty-four tackles. The final was 17–0.

In the steamy postgame locker room, a *Herald* sportswriter named Luther Evans watched as Bryant was asked to pose for a photograph with his star quarterback. The coach was only too glad to bear-hug Joe in front of the cameras. "I've hugged Joe quite a few times that you fellows don't know about," he said.

A late-arriving photographer inquired as to the spelling of the kid's name. "That's Namath, son," said Bryant. "N-A-M-A-T-H. But don't worry about it. You'll learn how to spell his name in the next couple of years."

■ ■ ■

The following afternoon, Namath attended a luncheon at Tropical Park racetrack, where he presented a silver cup to the winning jockey in a race honoring Alabama's victory. The nineteen-year-old quarterback then demonstrated his proficiency as a handicapper, cashing a long-shot win ticket that paid $50.50. Robert M. Morgan, chairman of the Florida Racing Commission, ordered an investigation. "I am very upset over it," said the commissioner. "I hold the Orange Bowl responsible because they gave me a written guarantee that no one under 21 would go near any pari-mutuel window."

Orange Bowl committee president G. Jackson Baldwin seemed to agree, calling the situation "unfortunate." You couldn't be too careful, not when it came to gambling and football players, particularly young, impressionable ones. The very day that Chairman Morgan announced his investigation, NFL commissioner Pete Rozelle revealed an investigation of his own: players from the Chicago Bears and "three or four other" pro teams had been discovered consorting with "undesirable types."

That meant gamblers. "The wrong kind of people," said Rozelle.

Says who? They were Joe's kind of people.

On Christmas Eve, 1962, just after returning from midnight mass at St. Philomena's, Bunny Kreshon received a call. A friend of Joe's was on the line, relaying a message for him, telling her that he was back in Beaver Falls for the holidays, saying how much he would like to see her. Bunny was a high school senior now, and prettier than ever. She didn't think it was odd for Joe to have a friend phone on his behalf. When it came to Joe, she didn't question much. Bunny was more in love with him now than she had been as a starstruck sophomore cheerleader. In the year or so since he left, she had collected a passel of letters and valentines postmarked Tuscaloosa. Still, she told this friend that it wouldn't be a good idea just now. It was very late. Plus, the guy she was seeing had just walked her home. The guy knew what was going on. Bunny was trembling as she put down the receiver.

Maybe half an hour later, there was a knock at the door. It was Joe and some of his boys, including Wibby Glover and Hoot Owl, who was making his first trip north. With her family watching, Bunny turned him away. "I'll regret that to my dying day," she says.

As for Joe, he managed to get over it. In matters involving the opposite sex, he took the advice of his father. Before Joe left for Alabama, the old man had pulled him aside. "Son, be like Jesus," he said. "Love them all. Love them. And leave them."

13. OF SOUTHERN COMFORTS AND THE SCHOOL- HOUSE DOOR

John Namath wanted to apprise his youngest boy of a special species— "beautiful southern babes"—awaiting him below the Mason-Dixon line. He wanted Joe to get to know them all. These girls were a long banquet. Take a taste, then take another seat at the table. "You don't have to pick one right away," he said. "Stay out of trouble, son."

This wasn't some winking, leering father-son chat. John Namath was as serious as the day he brought Joe to the mill. There was no reason for a son to repeat his father's mistakes—not in this country, anyway. He wanted Joe to enjoy these women, just as he wanted him to enjoy playing ball. It was just another of John Namath's star-spangled desires. "I'd be doing the same thing," he said. "Any red-blooded American boy would." Joe would live the life his father could not. *Stay out of trouble, son.* He didn't want his boy to be trapped in marriage any more than he wanted him trapped in the mills.

It wasn't difficult advice for Joe to heed. The southern tradition held female beauty and breeding in the highest esteem. Indeed, the selection of a homecoming queen for the Alabama-Miami game qualified as front-page news in Tuscaloosa, right beneath an Associated Press dispatch concerning a failed gubernatorial candidate now leaving public life with the words: "You won't have Nixon to kick around anymore." Finalists for Top *Corolla* Beauty also merited the front page. *Corolla* was the university yearbook, and as this was a public university, reflecting the mores and values of Alabamians, it's worth noting the edition of 1965, Namath's graduating class. The pages reveal Governor George Wallace to be an enthusiastic presence at pep rallies. Also, there was a mock election in which students voted two-to-one for Barry Goldwater over Lyndon Johnson. None other than Johnny Mathis played a show at the Cotillion Club. But this volume's main event was the beautiful southern babes. Twenty-six pages are devoted to them—in teased bouffants and gowns, in Jackie O getups, beauty in every shade of Caucasian.

Namath developed a lifetime addiction. They were great, these magnolia missies, expert practitioners of kind-of-funny, kind-of-nice. "I like Southern girls," he once said. "For some reason, they seem sweeter, gentler."

Given beauty in such abundance, he could not quarrel with his old man's advice. As his professors lectured in class, Joe would make mental lists of his conquests. "Just to see how well I was doing," he said. Toward the end of his senior year, the list reached about 300. "But that's a conservative estimate," he acknowledged.

Still, there was that inscrutable heart. His father would have been mighty proud of 300 notches. But what of his mother? He knew what she wanted. She was the one he wanted to please. When Rose visited Tuscaloosa, Joe introduced her to Bebe Schreiber. "This is the girl I'm going to marry," he said.

That made Rose very happy, as it did Bebe. Still, it was difficult for Bebe to imagine them living happily ever after. Joe had some vague idea about eventually settling down and coaching. But she knew that was just talk. "When you're a child of divorce, you approach relationships in a much more circumspect way," she says. "You know the pavement is cracked, and there are potholes everywhere."

"Bebe was a very beautiful girl," says Hoot Owl. "She was a top-of-the-line person. She knew what to say and when to say it. And Joe loved her, too. But he wasn't ready back then.

"He was never ready."

■   ■   ■

The South, it turned out, could be a wonderful place where football was king and females were queens, a land shrouded in a languid magnolia mist. Joe had begun adjusting quite well. In Tuscaloosa there lived three middle-aged widows—Miss Bessie, Miss Ruth, and Miss Mary—in whom Joe stirred the most motherly instincts. "All of them did love him," says Hoot Owl. "Those three little ladies were always there for him," says Bebe. "Like a support group." A boy so far from home needed some looking after. He could go to them for a coffeepot or a good hot meal. Rose's Hungarian dishes were replaced by pork chops and corn bread. Then there was Butch Henry's mother in Selma. She loved cooking for Joe, too. "My family just adored him," said Henry. "He was always just the perfect gentleman." He was a great guest at Hoot Owl's, too. He even played on Hoot Owl's baseball team, a semipro outfit in West Blocton.

Soon Joe developed the characteristic southern drawl. In the style of all those Lee Roys and Billy Bobs, Namath became Joe Willie. He started signing autographs "Joe Willie Namath." He liked his new name, and he liked Alabama. He was entitled to all the rights and privileges due a football hero serving under General Bryant.

In 1963, the ballplayers moved into a special athletic dormitory. Paul W. Bryant Hall, as it was soon named by a unanimous vote of the state legislature, looked more like an antebellum mansion than a dorm. With its massive Greek columns and a large fireplace, the athletes' residence reminded Rose of something from *Gone With the Wind*. Bryant wanted his poor white trash to feel like they were to the manner born. "He gave us a dorm with wall-to-wall carpeting, maid service, color TV's and phones in our rooms," said Namath. "You went down to the dining room, ordered a steak and told them how you wanted it fixed, and they fixed it. We had powder rooms for our dates and guest rooms for our parents, we had silk jackets for traveling."

There were other benefits, too. Joe liked to say that Alabama and Maryland were the only schools that offered him "a straight scholarship," which at the time meant room, board, books, and $15 a month for laundry. But Bryant's players could turn a handsome profit with their ticket allotment. Varsity players received four tickets for each home game, with a half dozen more available for purchase at face value. Butch Henry remembers $5 tickets going for as much as

$50. But with the right buyer, you could do even better. There were no shortage of well-to-do boosters and alumni who were looking to buy from a kid like Joe. Guys liked buying from the star. "You could get a hundred apiece for a seven-dollar ticket," says Frank Cicatiello, who became Namath's good friend sophomore year. "But Joe could get more."

If they'd been better students, Frank and Joe would have played together at Maryland. Cicatiello was from Youngstown, Ohio, about thirty miles from Beaver Falls. As with Joe, Maryland had been his first choice of colleges. As with Joe, his SAT scores didn't make the cut. But unlike Joe, Frank enlisted the help of a brainiac to take the test for him. Cicatiello was admitted to Maryland, but his scholarship was soon rescinded. "Someone at my high school ratted me out," he says.

Cicatiello then transferred to Youngstown State, only to leave when he discovered that Alabama was interested in his services. Bryant would always have a place for a kid like Frank Cicatiello, a big, mean lineman who could hit. But Youngstown State called the NCAA and charged Alabama with poaching one of its players. "Youngstown State caused me problems," Cicatiello recalls. "Those assholes."

Still, Frank figured that he was better off down South than slogging through the black snow up North. Joe understood, for they had a lot in common. "Two guys from dead-end mill towns," says Cicatiello.

■   ■   ■

Among the few southern customs Joe did not appreciate was A Club, the fraternity for varsity lettermen. After earning his letter sophomore year, Joe refused induction. Ray Abruzzese hadn't gone for that fraternity stuff, and neither would Joe, as it went against his religion. A Club wasn't cool. Actually, it was about the uncoolest thing he could imagine: getting your head shaved, chugging Tabasco, and letting some redneck Bama boy hit you with a paddle.

"You know it's a tradition here at the school," said Coach Bryant.

"I don't go for that tradition," said Joe.

"You can't ever be a captain of the team if you don't go through A Club."

Captain? "I don't care about that."

"Well, Joe, I'd like for you to go through it."

Anyone else, Joe would've told to go fuck himself. But this was Coach Bryant. This was the man who took him up on the tower, who came up with the money when his mother needed $800 to fix the well back in Beaver Falls. This was the man who shot him full of fear and glory. You didn't turn this man down.

Namath was always a little sorry he agreed to join A Club. "It went against my principles," he insisted. But a principle, like youth or love, is a perishable commodity, diminishing with time. Joe got over it. And just as he did, he showed up to present Frank Cicatiello with his fuzzy head and a grand idea.

Let's go to New Orleans, he said. They didn't have the bread, but that was okay, because Joe knew a couple of girls. One of them had an Oldsmobile Starfire. The other, the more attractive one, had a husband. Cicatiello still needed some convincing. "The one I was supposed to be with, she didn't look that good," he remembers.

"We're just gonna ride down with them," says Joe.

And what a ride it was. They hit New Orleans. They hit the racetrack. Then they hit Bourbon Street, and a joint called Pat O'Brien's. Everybody was in a good mood now. The married girl and her friend started singing college fight songs. "Then Joe started having a few of them drinks, those Hurricanes," says Cicatiello. "Joe was very shy, but when he got a couple of drinks in him he'd say anything. Now Joe starts with the Alabama fight songs, and how Auburn and LSU were horseshit."

Up North, if you wanted a fight, you said something about a guy's mother. Down South, you said something about his football team. Joe was still carrying on after they hurried him out of the bar. A couple good old boys getting in their car didn't appreciate these sentiments. But Joe just walked on by them with the married girl, who had been kind enough to pick up the tab. Then Cicatiello spotted one of the good old boys coming from behind to sucker-punch Joe. Frank caught him with a forearm, knocked him back into the car.

Then his friend charged. As Frank recalls the sound effects: *Bap, boom.* The first good old boy was trying to get out of the car when Frank grabbed the second and cracked their heads together, knocking them cold.

The steel-town kids ran for their getaway car. The night had been great for kicks, and best of all, Joe never had to throw a punch. "Joe could fight, believe me he could fight," says Cicatiello. "But this was right before spring football. What if he hurt his hands? Coach Bryant would've blamed me."

It all worked out fine. They got in the Starfire and flew off—Frank, the pretty married girl, her not so pretty friend, and Joe, still singing hillbilly opera.

■   ■   ■

They returned to a town very much on edge. Even as Joe acquired an appreciation for the many comforts of southern life, the anticipation of trouble had been building ever since he arrived on campus.

On September 29, 1962—two days before the admission of a black student set off deadly riots at Ole Miss—the largest cross ever burned in the state of Alabama was set afire on the outskirts of Tuscaloosa. It was fashioned from large utility poles and wrapped in 700 pounds of diesel-soaked burlap. The pyrotechnics took place under the direction of Imperial Wizard Bobby Shelton, boss of all Klan bosses. The evening was occasioned by the induction of 150 new Klansmen, all determined to prevent in Tuscaloosa what was imminent in Oxford, Mississippi. Shelton, himself a Tuscaloosan, took some pride in noting that university students were well represented among his new recruits.

That November, as Injun Joe staked his claim as Dixie's best quarterback, George C. Wallace was elected governor. He won with an assist from Bobby Shelton's boys, a campaign slogan of "Segregation Forever," and a famous vow to "stand in the schoolhouse door." Later that month the public became aware of Vivian Malone, a twenty-year-old "Negro coed" from Mobile. Vivian was one of eight children from a working-class family that celebrated Emancipation Day. Though her older brothers had gone to Tuskegee Institute, she enrolled at Alabama A & M to study business education. But neither A & M nor Alabama State, the state's black colleges, was accredited. As Vivian intended a career in personnel management, she required classes offered at the great university in Tuscaloosa. "I think I will get in," she said. "I am not worried that any harm will come to me."

Forty years later, the former Vivian Malone says plainly: "Those are chances you just have to take." But her youthful confidence was not informed by a realistic sense of the odds. In fact, there was a strong likelihood that harm would come to her. The university's first black student, Autherine Lucy, had been admitted in 1956. After three days of abuse from a mob, she left the campus and was later expelled for accusing university officials of conspiring with the gang of thugs. Malone knew Lucy's story. She had also talked with James Meredith, whose enrollment at Ole Miss had touched off the rioting that left two dead. She had been warned of possible reprisals against her family.

In Tuscaloosa, a sniff of menace mingled with the scent of magnolia. After editorials advocating Negroes' rights appeared in the *Crimson White,* Mel Meyer—the school paper's former sports editor—received the protection of two private detectives. Such a precaution was certainly warranted. After all, the imperial wizard had long been bragging that the Klan had infiltrated all aspects of campus life.

It was a terrible season of firebombs and fire hoses, and it seemed destined for resolution at the schoolhouse door, where Joe Namath found himself on June 10, 1963. He was no more than twenty feet from where Governor Wallace stood, theatrically, at the entrance to Foster Auditorium, an imposing brick edifice with six Grecian columns where students registered for summer session classes. Namath, who had already registered, watched as Brigadier General Henry V. Graham, of the newly federalized Alabama National Guard, approached and saluted the governor.

"It is my sad duty to ask you to step aside, on order of the president of the United States."

Here, as ever, the politician held politics above his avowed principles. To the great relief of many eyeing those sharpshooters atop Foster Auditorium,

Wallace turned his great stand into a great publicity stunt. The governor, already wearing a microphone, informed the general that he would be making a statement. He left upon its conclusion, and at 3:37 P.M. James A. Hood, a "negro" student from Gadsden, Alabama, walked into Foster Auditorium accompanied by agents of the Justice Department. Five minutes later Vivian Malone went in to register. She wore a faint smile and a pink suit, her hair in a neatly banged bouffant. She was a very pretty girl.

"It was a thrill to see Vivian walk through that door," Namath would recall. "We talked sometimes, and you couldn't understand how much pressure she was under at the time."

Namath would see her at Mary Burke Hall, where she lived in the same dorm as Bebe. "There were a group of us who supported Vivian and tried to eat with her," says Bebe. "She withstood the assault against her, and she did so magnificently. She held her head high. She did not betray emotion. Absolutely beautiful." And very southern. "Always a lady."

Though the university held up its football players as white knights, Bryant's boys couldn't compete with Vivian Malone. She withstood tests Bryant could not have imagined. "There were threats that first summer," she says. But even as James Hood left campus, in the words of one dispatch, "on the verge of a nervous breakdown," Vivian stayed. A girl in a pink suit had shown more courage, more *class*, as Bryant liked to say, than an army of his old boys. But on the day of her enrollment Bryant was not to be found. He had left early for a clinic in Montana.

The coach's many loyalists defend him vigorously, trying to wash any segregationist stain from his legacy. They are quick to portray him as a man of enlightenment. Back in the 1940s, when he was coaching Kentucky, Bryant went to the university president to argue for the Wildcats' becoming the first Southeastern Conference team with black players. "I told him he could be the Branch Rickey of the league," Bryant wrote in his autobiography. "But I didn't get anywhere." He didn't get anywhere at Alabama, either. Then again, he didn't really try too hard. On the subject of race, Bryant's most courageous and forward-thinking act seems to have occurred in 1959, when he accepted a bid to the Liberty Bowl, where the Tide played Penn State, a team with five blacks on its roster. By playing an integrated team, Bryant risked the wrath of segregationists across Alabama. A member of the university's Board of Trustees even boycotted the game, which Bama lost 7–0, thanks, in large measure, to Penn State's black halfback, Charley Jenrett.

But even the staunchest segregationists forgave and forgot. Bryant won championships, and in doing so, won everlasting respect and admiration. But he never applied this goodwill to its greatest use. When it came to race, the Great White Father was just another football coach.

"We're a public institution, publicly funded," says Clem Gryska, now an administrator at the Paul W. Bryant Museum. "He couldn't go against the governor."

The writer Diane McWhorter, who grew up in Birmingham, describes Bryant and Governor Wallace as being inextricably linked from 1958. That was the year Bryant took the Bama job, declaring, "I ain't nothing but a winner." It was also the year that Wallace, coming off a failed gubernatorial bid, promised never "to be outniggered again." Wallace was a great patron of Alabama football. But even as he promised to stand in the schoolhouse door, Bryant was the most popular man in the state. He was, as McWhorter writes, the Good Father to Wallace's Prodigal Son, a spiritual leader as compared to the mad king.

"You don't change people's thinking overnight," Bryant explained in his autobiography. "When folks are ignorant, you don't condemn them, you teach 'em."

But Bryant didn't teach Wallace, or any other politician, much on the subject of race. When Alabama football finally desegregated (two years after the basketball team), it followed Florida, Kentucky, Tennessee, Georgia, Vanderbilt, and Auburn.

It wasn't until 1971 that a black player debuted for the Crimson Tide varsity. A turbulent decade had passed since Namath had been summoned to the tower. But through those years, and in all the time since, there is nothing to suggest that Namath ever questioned Bryant on the issue of race. Of course, the quarterback had no obligation to question his coach. He belonged to no movement. He was a kid playing football. But unlike his teammates, he grew up knowing better. As a citizen of the Lower End, he was raised to be color-blind.

But he had other blindnesses, too. In Bryant, he had found an authority he would not question.

"We absolutely . . . trusted his vision," said Namath.

And more than that was Namath's distaste for any kind of conflict—personal, social, and especially political. Politics were as uncool as A Club. He judged people by their treatment of him, not their affiliations. Namath had a way to deal with people's racial "hang-ups." "I get the hell out of the way," he once said. As it pertained to politics, he was agnostic. Still, as he became famous during the 1960s, Namath would be freely, if wrongly, associated with any number of causes. He would arouse the great paranoids of the age. Both J. Edgar Hoover and Richard Nixon kept tabs on him, finding something subversive in his lifestyle. As a generation was being radicalized on campus, they forgot that Namath was a boy who bowed to the Bear. And who was more Establishment than the Bear? Vivian Malone passed through the schoolhouse door in 1963, but Bryant still needed eight more years. By then, the girl in the pink dress had just started a new job with the Justice Department.

"Wow, eight years later?" asks Vivian Malone. "It did seem to take forever. I thought he was a good coach, no question about that, but if you're asking if he could have had black players before he did, yes, I'm sure he could have. He should have, anyway."

Despite the death threats, Vivian Malone considered herself a fan of the Crimson Tide. "We played against all-white teams, too," she says. "If one of them had to win, I wanted it to be Alabama."

Besides, she liked the quarterback. Compared to her classmates, she saw Namath much as the girls back at St. Mary's had. "He was so *different*," she recalls. Vivian Malone didn't expect Namath to make any sort of stand. She did what she did. He did what he did. Still, sport is the strangest theater, allowing real heroes to find righteousness in mere ballplayers. "I really did admire him," says Vivian Malone.

Jimmy Walsh wanted to attend Rutgers, in his hometown of New Brunswick, New Jersey. Instead, upon his graduation from St. Peter the Apostle High School, he had to settle for a job at a bank. He'd count other people's money while figuring out what to do with the rest of his life. The following March, on a bitter cold day, he ran into a friend of his sister. The guy said he had been attending the University of Alabama on the GI bill, and he couldn't wait to get back. The worst of March in Alabama was like the best of May in Jersey. Jimmy didn't need to know much more about Alabama; he already knew enough about Jersey. He sent off an application. The registrar sent back a telegram telling him he'd been accepted, Class of '63. "I don't think the standards were exceedingly high," Jimmy later reflected.

14. JIMMY

In Tuscaloosa Jimmy became good friends with Ray Abruzzese, who introduced him to Joe at the pool hall. Jimmy liked pool, and had become a great fan of a local hustler called the Tuscaloosa Squirrel. As for this Namath kid, Jimmy wasn't a fan at all. Who did this guy think he was, standing off to the side and popping off when it was Jimmy's turn to shoot? "Let me play this guy," said Joe.

"I resented him," said Jimmy. "I thought he was a cocky wise guy." Still, they'd bump into each other around campus—at the pool hall or the university chapel, where they were among the few students going to mass. "It was very much like being an outcast," remembered Jimmy. "Catholics were a small minority." Then one day, Jimmy and Joe happened to have breakfast together. They got to talking, and Joe mentioned that he was Hungarian. What do you know? Jimmy was Hungarian, too, on his mother's side. Her maiden name was Nagy. It was a pleasant conversation, and it changed their relationship, such as it was.

"Now I could say hello," said Jimmy. "I didn't feel uncomfortable." He didn't think of Joe as a wise guy anymore. Then again, Joe wasn't exactly a friend, either. "In my frame of reference," said Jimmy, "he was like a celebrity."

Aside from their Hungarian blood, Joe was everything Jimmy was not. He was tall, dark, and handsome while Jimmy was short, pale, and freckled. Joe was cool; Jimmy was a plugger. Joe walked around campus in a peaked-bill beret and sharkskin slacks; Jimmy wore a blazer. Jimmy, recalls Hoot Owl, "was always studying."

After graduation, Jimmy decided to remain in Tuscaloosa at the university's law school. But in September 1963, as he was about to begin his first year, Jimmy was having a hard time getting back to Tuscaloosa. He'd planned to drive from Jersey in a '49 Buick, but the car overheated before he hit Pennsylvania. Then some genius gas station attendant put cold water in the radiator, which caused the engine block to crack. Jimmy spent a day and a half in Jersey trying to get the damn thing fixed. Finally, his sister gave him money to fly down before it was too late to register. His plane got into Birmingham at two in the morning. Tuscaloosa was another sixty miles away, and he didn't have a ride. He'd already called everybody, all his so-called friends, who had better things to do than pick him up at the airport. He got off the plane thinking he was screwed, but then he heard someone hollering. "There's this guy who I barely knew," he said. "Joe Namath."

The football players were still in preseason camp, and Coach Bryant had strict rules about curfew. Then again, for Joe, a rule was only a rule if you got caught. Someone had told him Jimmy needed a ride; Joe drove to Birmingham to give it to him.

"I didn't realize he thought that much of me," said Jimmy.

■   ■   ■

Later that fall, when Joe told him that he needed money for one of his brothers, Jimmy went to the bank and withdrew funds he had saved for his tuition. By January, Joe had sold enough tickets to pay his debt in full, about $1,000. "Joe never forgot what I had done for him," said Jimmy. "After that we were the best of friends."

Their relationship would evolve from friendship to partnership, toward a peculiar maturity, a yin and yang that paired the plugger and the star, high-strung and laid-back, Percival and the playboy. Theirs was an unlikely symbiosis, but an enduring one. Ultimately, it would be impossible to consider one without the other. Jimmy would become Joe's buffer, his protector, the custodian of his affairs and his image. That image was a vehicle for both of them, and after a time, Joe was happy to let Jimmy drive it. You wonder, though—what was driving Jimmy?

His father was born on July 2, 1899, in Charlestown, County Mayo, the Moro Bottom of Ireland. By 1936, the year he applied for a social security card, James Patrick Walsh had found a new life, working as a gravedigger at St. Peter's Cemetery in New Brunswick. He had married the former Elsie Nagy.

They lived at 28 Main Street, across the street from the cemetery. Their daughter Elizabeth was born that same year. Jimmy was born on August 12, 1940.

It is said that Jimmy took after his father, and to understand Jimmy's father you'd need an idea of what it was like in the winter, taking pick and shovel to the frozen ground. "It was the kind of work you couldn't even get guys to do today," says Bill Carroll, the caretaker at St. Peter's. "To go through the frost you had to put extra hours on the grave. All the digging was done by hand in those days. We didn't even have a backhoe until the fifties."

By then James Patrick Walsh had added another job, as a maintenance man at St. Peter the Apostle High School, an institution run by the Sisters of Charity. "He broke his back," says Ed Susan, recalling the elder Walsh. "Work never scared him." Susan was a student when they met, a 121-pound end on the football team. In the off-season he'd help Mr. Walsh after school. When the work was done, says Susan, "He loved to drink a little bit." Sometimes, when Mr. Walsh drank, his brogue would turn bitter, speaking of the Black and Tans, a thug army sent forth from the British prisons, and how they threw him out of Ireland.

After graduation Susan enlisted and was sent to Korea, where on April 23, 1952, he suffered wounds to the arms, legs, and back from mortar shrapnel in the Kumhwa Valley. He was lucky to live through the night, and blessed to return home, where he got a job coaching football at St. Peter's. In 1957, Ed Susan's team went undefeated. The St. Peter's Cardinals had plenty of good players that year, but none Susan liked better than the 140-pound halfback who played sparingly, the gravedigger's son. "Jimmy was the sixth back," said Susan. "I liked him because he reminded me of me. Scrappy is the word. He got no favors. He hustled his way through everything."

One of the stars of that undefeated '57 team, and a captain on the '58 squad, was Steve Baffic. He lived a block from Jimmy, and they grew up good friends. One summer, when they were in high school, they found a rusty weight set someone had left for the garbageman. They built a bench with two-by-sixes in Jimmy's backyard and, long before it became the fashion, started pumping iron. There was Jimmy, Baffic, and the starting quarterback, Gene Murphy. "Pound for pound, Jimmy could lift more than any of us," says Baffic. "He would lift when we weren't there. He was determined. . . . I personally think that because he was small he had to prove he could run with the rest of the boys. He made up for being small by being very aggressive."

It was an instinct that Coach Susan, in constant pain from his war wounds, admired and encouraged. "Sometimes he had a hard time walking," says Baffic. "But he gave you the feeling that you could knock the other guy on his ass even if he was five hundred pounds."

Baffic himself was six-three, 205 pounds, which was about as big as they came in high school back then. Nevertheless, he had his problems tackling Jimmy in practice. "I knocked him down a couple of times," he remembers. "But he just got back up. You couldn't stop Jimmy unless you had a two-by-four."

Still, the memory that best epitomizes Jimmy dates to the sixth or seventh grade. "There were three bullies," recalls Baffic. "They were already in high school, maybe ninth grade." It wasn't much of a fight, what with Steve outnumbered. But then, from the corner of his eye, he saw Jimmy vaulting into the fray. Jimmy didn't care if these kids were ninth graders. He knew they were weak where everyone is weak. "He put a hurting on one of those kids," says Baffic.

Jimmy went right for the biggest one and kicked him square in the balls. The ninth graders backed off after that.

And this is what Joe Namath had in Jimmy Walsh: someone who would kick a guy in the balls for you. What more could you want in a friend?

In football, as in politics, Paul Bryant wasn't one to embrace change. But a great coach is also a keen opportunist. And Bryant recognized that Namath's talent was, in some respects, superior to his own schemes. In the spring of '63 Bryant hired Ken Meyer, a highly regarded assistant from Florida State, to work with the backs and loosen the offense—but just a little. "It took us until Joe's junior year before Bryant put in a drop-back passing game with two wide receivers," remembers Howard Schnellenberger, the offensive coordinator. "I had to give him my personal word that I wouldn't let us get soft on the line, that we'd maintain the same toughness."

As a sophomore, Namath had broken school records for passing yardage
(1,192) and completions (176), while
tying the marks for touchdown passes

15. SIPPIN'

in a season (13) and in a single game (3). Those numbers, combined with the reconfigured offense, raised exponentially the expectations for Joe's junior season. Even Bryant had stopped trying to temper them. Hell, he was bragging on Joe himself—right out there for everyone to see in the sports pages. The coach went so far as to predict that Joe Namath would go down as the finest college quarterback ever to come out of the South.

"He's great," Bryant declared.

No surprise, then, that the first points of the season were recorded on a forty-seven-yard touchdown pass from Namath to Charlie Stephens, as Bama began its ritual beating of Georgia, 32–7, in Athens. Next, the Tide shut out Tulane, 28–0, before running over Vanderbilt, 21–6. And though these margins were huge, the quarterback was not what people were expecting. He was running the option as well as anyone. But Bama fans had seen quarterbacks run the option before. They wanted this boy to throw the damn ball, and he wasn't. Against Vanderbilt, for example, Namath was only 4 of 6 for 45 yards. Bryant dismissed it as a "bad night."

"Doesn't mean anything if you've got class," he said. "And Namath has class." No one disagreed. There might have been a half-dozen beat writers covering every practice, but there were no dissenting opinions. On occasion, assistant coaches would enthusiastically endorse the party line. Players, however, were not made available. "You just didn't get to speak to them," says Charles Land, sports editor of the *Tuscaloosa News*.

"Bryant didn't want you interviewing his players," adds *Birmingham News*'s Clyde Bolton. "He had a total protective ass-kissing press. I went along with it. I was a young guy. I was following the policy of the paper." Then again, as Bolton makes clear, there wasn't much for a sportswriter to disagree with: "Hard to criticize him when they won all the time."

Well, not *all* the time. The very next game, against Florida, Namath threw twenty-six passes, more attempts than he recorded in any game except Georgia Tech the year before. Alabama lost that one, and they lost this as well. Florida, whose average lineman was twenty-one pounds heavier than Bama's, stopped the Tide twice at the goal line. But they also stopped Namath, intercepting him twice in the 91-degree heat. Joe engineered a late touchdown drive that made the final score 10–6. For Bryant, whose team had been favored by four-teen points, it was his first home loss at Denny Stadium. "We gave plumb out," said Bryant.

The coach was asked if his team would give plumb out again. "Depends how much class you've got," he replied.

The loss provoked Namath into making a full demonstration of his class. He threw three touchdowns and ran for another as the Tide beat Tennessee 35–0, the Volunteers' worst defeat since entering the Southeastern Conference in 1933. The following week, in beating Houston, Namath accounted for 151 yards—despite sitting out a good part of the second half. "Namath hurt his leg a little," explained Bryant. "But we wrapped it up and he went back in." In this coach's world, all but the most catastrophic hurts were "little." They were to be wrapped and taped, healed with aspirin, then played on, which is what Na-math did the following week when the Tide came from behind to beat Missis-sippi State by a point. Anyone could see Joe's leg was plenty strong. After all, he scored the winning touchdown on a quarterback sneak. Despite a crucial inter-ception, he had turned in another fine game: 10 for 16, with a forty-yard touch-down pass. Of his six incompletions, one was returned for a touchdown, two were dropped by his receivers, another two thrown out of bounds to stop the clock, and one thrown out of the end zone to avoid a sack.

"He could easily have had a perfect day," wrote Charles Land.

But perfection, as Namath already knew, couldn't be quantified. In fact, his best game of the season, the one that came closest to perfection, was the most statistically modest of his career. Georgia Tech was always a big game. In '61, the year Darwin Holt busted Chick Graning's jaw, it became a grudge match. In '62, it cost Bama an undefeated season, and perhaps the national championship. That 7–6 loss to Tech saw Namath throw an astounding thirty-one times. "Too many," Bryant had said. But now, as a junior, Namath got his revenge while offering an elegant proof of his quarterbacking intelligence. He threw only four times the entire game: an eleven-yard jump pass to Butch Henry, two incompletions, and another ball that resulted in a pass interference call, setting up the Tide's last touchdown. With a single completion, Namath orchestrated an attack that beat Tech 27–11.

By now, he understood that a quarterback's highest talent was in his head. Namath, known as a great passer, decided for himself not to pass. For a twenty-year-old blessed with such an arm, it was a remarkable show of maturity—not to mention a great hustle. After the game, Bryant revealed that Namath had called every play but one. What's more, as if to demonstrate Joe's complete mastery of the game, Bryant used him on defense—playing safety to protect against a long pass. Bryant believed in Namath's athleticism, of course. But his ability to anticipate—to read the developing angles on either side of the ball—was a kind of intuitive genius, part calculus, part magic. Tech's quarterback, Billy Lothridge, was honorable mention All-American that year. But he couldn't get one by Joe.

"I would have to say that Mr. Namath had his finest hour," said Bryant.

■　■　■

And just then, just as the world seemed so bright for Bryant's boys, tragedy struck. First, the president was assassinated in Dallas. Then, despite their coach's rare prediction of victory, they lost to Auburn. Finally, Joe Namath was thrown off the team.

The season-ending suspension was announced late on Monday, December 9, 1963, after a bye-week in the schedule. Many recall the open date as part of the mourning that followed Kennedy's death. In fact, it had more to do with television. Before the season began, CBS Sports, which owned the national broadcast rights to the Bama-Miami contest, had moved the game from November 9 to December 7. In light of the assassination, the annual Army-Navy game, also CBS property, was rescheduled for December 7, leaving Namath and Hoot Owl to their own devices for yet another Saturday.

They hadn't been out in a few days. And now, after a morning practice, they found themselves tooling around Tuscaloosa in a 1926 Ford with a rumble seat, occupied by an acquaintance of the quarterback's, a girl from Miami. "She loaned us some money," says Hoot Owl, "and we went downtown to get Joe a pair of pants. When Joe went into the store to get a pair of pants, I went around the corner to get a bottle of whiskey."

Hoot started sipping, but "Joe didn't drink any," he insists.

They drove back to campus, hung out at the quadrangle for a while, and then the dorm. After dark, they went to a fraternity party. From there, they set out—with Joe and some other ballplayers riding in the old Ford—for Sorority Row. After the girls' curfew, some of the football players decided to drive all the way to Birmingham. But Hoot and Joe just went to one of their regular places, Captain Cooke's.

Of that night, Hoot Owl Hicks recalls: "Every football player on the team was about drunk." Not Joe, though. Hoot Owl will go to his maker swearing that. "But he did drink a beer," says Hoot Owl. "He drank a can of beer that night."

And someone saw him. Maybe it was someone at Captain Cooke's, or maybe Sorority Row. "We don't know who told on us," says Hicks.

By then, it no longer mattered. Namath had broken every coach's first commandment: He got caught. What, exactly, he was caught doing remains a murky matter. Bryant heard that Joe had a party at a "woman's store." He'd heard that Joe was directing traffic while drunk in downtown Tuscaloosa. The coach heard a lot of things, all involving alcohol, and all therefore in violation of his vaunted precepts for in-season behavior. Bryant's Training Rules, as they were known, were to be obeyed more strictly than God's own Commandments. Word of Joe's fall left the coach physically nauseated.

On Monday, he found Joe at the dorm. Bryant asked him if he'd been directing traffic drunk.

Joe said he was watching the Army-Navy game.

Bryant asked if he had anything to drink on Saturday.

"A few sips," replied Joe. "Not even a full glass." He said nothing of the guys who'd been drinking with him.

Early that afternoon, just three weeks before Bama was to play Ole Miss in the Sugar Bowl, Bryant called a meeting of his apostles, informing his assistants that Joe had taken a drink. And though he had no intention of accepting anyone's advice on the matter, Bryant asked them to consider a just punishment. He began with Dude Hennessey, who didn't want to see Joe suspended.

"Aw, Dude, you're worried about your bowl bonus," said Bryant.

He wasn't the only one. Men like Hennessey and Gryska were making between five and six grand a year. The bonus for winning a bowl game was a month's salary. But even apart from that, a suspension seemed excessive. Most of Bryant's assistants could recall sneaking a drink during their own college days. The sole dissenter was Gene Stallings, the defensive coordinator, who had played for Bryant at Texas A & M and survived his infamous camp in Junction.

"If it'd been me," drawled Stallings, "you'd have kicked me off."

Bryant asked to be alone. Perhaps he didn't want to be seen weeping during his deliberation. Stallings was right, but Stallings didn't have Joe's talent. Bryant might have been willing to change the offense in deference to Joe's talent—but not the Training Rules. It was a matter of principle. Joe's transgression might have meant less had he not been *seen*. Joe was unlike any of his other players. People loved talking about him. The gossip could undermine a coach's authority, and for a man like Bryant, authority was a principle superior to all others.

Bryant called for his quarterback and his coaches and reconvened the meeting. He told Joe that all but one of them wanted him to play. Bryant said he could let him play, but then he'd have to resign, as it violated his principles.

"Sir," said Joe, "I don't want you to do that."

The suspension would last through the Sugar Bowl. Joe had to leave the athletes' dormitory. He would be given the chance to prove himself worthy and rejoin the team in the spring. If he couldn't accept those terms, Bryant would make arrangements for him to transfer or get a paying job in the Canadian Football League. Joe asked one favor. He wanted the coach to call his mother before the news hit the papers. He wanted him to tell her everything would be all right.

■　■　■

"Joe come out of there, he had tears," remembers Hoot Owl. "That's the one time I ever saw him with real tears in his eyes. It killed him."

Butch Henry, Joe's roommate, recalls differently: "The only time he threatened to leave was when he was suspended. He was very upset about that . . . just mad . . . real bitter."

Joe recovered, though. In fact, he spent that night, and the next several, in the basement of Bryant's house as a secret guest of the coach's wife, Mary Harmon. "She hid me out," said Namath. "I was hurt. . . . She knew that and responded by protecting me, helping in a motherly way."

Always, this was a rogue any mother could love. "I sent for him," Mary Harmon said years later. "When he got here, I hugged him and we both just cried like babies. I said, 'Joe, what happened? You couldn't do anything bad. You're just too good a boy to do anything bad.'"

■　■　■

The next day Joe was all over the front pages. Charles Land, Bryant's former sports information director, went so far as to run a statement from the fallen twenty-year-old quarterback: "I have thought about it, and I don't know of a thing to say that would help. . . . I'm sorry as can be that it happened. It certainly would never happen again."

The precise nature of Joe's offense was left to the imagination. The papers specified no more than a violation of team "training rules"—as if the truth might be too terrible to contemplate. "We know none of the background of Bryant's sudden action against his quarterback, and we aren't really interested," wrote Bob Phillips, columnist for the *Birmingham Post-Herald*. "We are confident it was justified."

As morality tales go, this was a fine one, reaffirming the Good Father and his sacrosanct principles. Bryant was willing to sacrifice his best player, before the season's biggest game, just because he took a few sips. It was the tidiest fable since George Washington copped to chopping down the cherry tree. In fact, Bryant did right by both his principles and his player.

But the suspension was about more than a beer. It was about Namath and a reputation that seems both earned and exaggerated. "There were all these rumors about him being out and about when he was sleeping in the bed next to mine," says Butch Henry. "Joe was one of those people with more rumor than fact swirling about him."

One such story had Namath and fullback Mike Fracchia brawling the night before the loss to Florida. "Never happened, we never had a cross word," says Fracchia. "People make up a lot of things."

Or did they? When asked of the suspension, Richard Williamson, the receiver who joined Bryant's staff after graduating in '63, answers somewhat cryptically: "Joe had some other situations that came up." (As Williamson went on to a coaching career, it's worth noting that "situation" is a coach's standard euphemism for nocturnal unpleasantness.) Even the sportswriters suspected something was amiss with the team, and that Joe was at the center of it. "There have been ugly and unconfirmed rumors for weeks concerning the Alabama football team," Bob Phillips wrote in the *Post-Herald*.

"The team was barely holding together," says Fracchia. "It just didn't have the same discipline."

"I just felt like Coach Bryant needed to get his attention," Stallings said of the suspension. "I felt it was in the best interests of Joe Namath."

Bebe Schreiber speaks elliptically of "a brief episode" in which Joe blew a curfew earlier that season. "He was pushing his limits with Coach Bryant," she says.

■   ■   ■

One wonders, given the conflicting accounts, how much Joe really drank the night of December 7, 1963.

And what about other nights?

Hoot Owl Hicks, ever Joe's defender, says: "One thing about Joe people didn't realize, he couldn't drink a whole lot. He was always quick to get drunk. I used to always say he was like an Indian. He drank, but how much he drank is another thing."

Whatever his tolerance for liquor, that abstemious, repentant character— *just a few sips, sir*—was an image of Namath's own creation. His FBI report refers to an arrest of that same year when he was charged with being drunk in Tuscaloosa. Though Hoot Owl doesn't recall the date, the warm weather and the arresting officer's jurisdiction suggest a night they had been drinking at a dive called the Jungle Club. They left the bar in a green 1953 Ford from which Hoot Owl had removed the doors. And though they claimed not to be drunk, neither Hoot Owl nor Joe was alert enough to spot the marked car that began following them and pulled them over some blocks later. Joe grabbed their beers and tossed them under the car. Unfortunately, as the Ford was parked at the top of a hill, the evidence wasn't hard to spot as it came rolling back down.

"Well, hello, Pain-suhl-vain-i-a kid," said one of the cops. He told Hoot and Joe to step out. "What the hell you doin'?" said Joe, as the cop started to frisk them.

"Y'awl are drunk," said the cop.

"Bullshit," said Joe. "We only had two beers."

Despite his outrage, Joe managed to be very much amused with Hoot Owl as he attempted to walk a straight line at the officer's command. "Just be quiet," said Hoot Owl as he proceeded to pass the test. Hoot Owl was charged only with reckless driving, but that didn't sit well with Joe. "Now I know what a guy does when he can't find a job," he said. "He becomes a cop."

In due time Don McDaniel—the team's publicity director and academic counselor—arrived at the police station, where Joe and Hoot Owl had been taken to while away the hours in the drunk tank. Hoot Owl was pacing nervously, but Joe had his hands behind his head and his feet up on the cot. These cops weren't going to see him sweat. Joe wouldn't give them the satisfaction. They told Coach Bryant's man that he could take Hoot Owl, but Pennsylvania Kid had to remain in the cell. Drunks had to stay the requisite number of hours.

The incident never made the papers. But the date specified in the FBI report was August 20, 1963, when Bryant's players were getting ready for camp, the start of a new season. For Joe, it would seem then that the '63 season ended as it began, sipping.

■   ■   ■

With Namath cast off from the team, justice was served. But what about the spread?

Alabama had been an 11-point favorite for its regular season finale against Miami. But the 11 became a 7 "the moment Namath's suspension was announced," wrote Bob Phillips in the *Birmingham Post-Herald*. As for the Sugar Bowl, it had been "taken off the line" while the bookies tried to calculate the effect of Namath's absence. As vices go, gambling and drinking (two of Bryant's favorites) were fraternal twins. But men like Phillips—so sanctimonious when it came to Joe's suspension—were able to ponder his effect on the betting odds without any moralizing. It wasn't a sportswriter's job to ask why; he was obliged only to serve his readers. And there are a few things fans always like: a nice story with a moral, and a point spread they can count on.

■   ■   ■

Joe went home to Pennsylvania that Christmas, and ran into Rich Niedbala drinking at D & J's, the bar next door to the Blue Room. D & J's, identified as a "sports bar" in the local telephone directory, was a big bookie hangout. Rich and Joe were shooting the shit over dime drafts when the TV announcers started talking about the upcoming Sugar Bowl, featuring Ole Miss and Bama, the latter minus its star quarterback.

Joe seemed bitter. Still, it must have been some comfort to know how his fall had fucked with the odds. "Shit," he said, looking up from his beer. "What do you think their chances are without me?"

The kid had a point. The bookies and the bettors knew it. Just then, Rich Niedbala watched all the wise men start scrambling for the pay phones.

The seasons progressed as if they were chapters written by Bryant himself. First, Alabama won the Sugar Bowl with a gutsy sophomore quarterback named Steve Sloan. Then Namath returned, the knight errant now eager to prove and to please. By the conclusion of spring practice, he had reclaimed his place as a prince in the coach's kingdom. Despite a sore arm and a bruised foot, Namath passed the red team to a 17–6 victory in a scrimmage before 14,500 fans at Denny Stadium. "Namath was terrific," said Bryant, "particularly when you consider that he's all banged up and shouldn't even have been playing." In point of fact, Bryant expected his boys to play hurt. The real virtue was in the victory. Hence, this scrimmage—then the most well attended in school history—provided incontrovertible evidence as to the reformation of Namath's character.

16. DOYLES-TOWN REDUX

The 1964 Crimson Tide football media guide lists him by his southern appellation, "Joe Willie." At twenty-one years old, six-two, and 194 pounds, he is described as the best athlete ever to play for Bryant: ". . . gets rid of the ball quicker . . . a punishing runner . . . shoots golf in the 70s . . . A true all-America candidate."

This was the year that everything would come together for Namath. He had his customarily spectacular opener—16 for 21 attempts—in another rout of Georgia. There was just one twist; this time he *ran* for three touchdowns (not including the eleven-yard run that was called back on a penalty). "Namath was the big difference," said Vince Dooley, the new Georgia coach. "We would do one thing, and he'd do another."

The Associated Press selected him as the Back of the Week. "I know that I speak for all of our backs when I thank our linemen for doing such a fine job," said Joe. The hustler sure sounded like an All-American.

By the third game of the season—a 24–0 win over Vanderbilt—Namath established himself as Alabama's career leader in touchdown passes. He threw for two that day in Birmingham, and ran for another. Joe's fifteen-yard dash into the end zone was a thing of beauty. He was running better than he ever had. "Physically, I was at my peak," Namath would remember. "I was fast and I could throw."

A week later, North Carolina State came to town. It was bright sunshine, 67 degrees with a whispering breeze that made "the men's wool suits a little less scratchy and the women's fur pieces a little more practical." Tony Golmont, of NC State by way of Beaver Falls, remembers it as the kind of crisp day that aroused the highest expectations for a football game. Golmont was no longer a receiver; now a right-side cornerback, he'd be across the field from his old buddy, Joe. All week people had been talking about the high school teammates going against each other. Maybe, with a little luck, Tony could pick one off, or maybe he'd just have to pop Joe one. He'd learned that much in college; he'd rather be the guy doing the hitting. It just felt better that way. "I became pretty aggressive," he says.

The game was scoreless into the second quarter, when Namath called an option, rolling out to his right. He was 7 for 8 at that point, and looking for a receiver. "But everyone was covered," says Golmont. "So he cut back to go upfield. Then he just . . . went down."

As Golmont knew well, the game is predicated on the Hit. Anticipation of the hit adrenalizes the contest. From the hit flows football's agony and ecstasy. Damn right, it felt good to lay a guy out. The hit provided the measure of a player; how he gave it and how he took it. Then there was Joe, shifting to cut upfield, then . . . crumpling. It was the craziest thing. In a hitting game, this was the lowest comedy. "Nobody touched him," says Golmont.

A groan could be heard through Denny Stadium. Everything slowed down. Golmont walked over to where Joe was laid out. "You okay?"

"It's my knee." Joe felt like he'd been shot.

"You'll be okay," Golmont told him, never doubting it. As a young player, you never think you'll get hurt. You're a stud. You're invincible—and no one more so than Joe. Tony Golmont knew that from when they were kids. Joe was the magician.

Jim Goostree, the trainer, went out to work on him. Then Bryant came out on the field. He stayed for a while and walked off, looking like a pallbearer. Finally, Namath made it to his feet and, through a gauntlet of cheers, hobbled to the locker room. With his knee wrapped in ice, he returned to the sideline in the third quarter, watching Steve Sloan lead Bama to a 21–0 win. "We were in the game until Joe got hurt," says Golmont, who would leave the game himself with busted ribs. "Then we kind of relaxed."

Namath's injury was described as a "twisted right knee." A team orthopedist who examined him after the game figured it was probably a sprain. He didn't see any reason why Joe wouldn't be back the following week against Tennessee.

But even after a weekend in the infirmary, the swelling didn't dissipate as hoped. The knee needed to be aspirated, a large syringe inserted to drain the blood and fluid. For Joe, aspiration would become a familiar rite, like contrition, an habitual act of temporary benefit. The swelling would always return, the bucket of blood on his right knee like a curse, something that had come back to haunt him.

Both Joe and his mother associated the injury with an incident that happened when he was about seven. Joe and his father had traveled with Frank's baseball team to Doylestown, Pennsylvania, for a tournament. Once there, Joe fell ill. He started to run a high fever; his legs began to ache. Afraid that his boy was coming down with polio, John Namath took him to a doctor who provided medicine, administered throughout a troubled night by Frank and his teammates. The fever and that wicked ache left as suddenly as they came. Then, the following spring, it returned. "I was put in the hospital for three weeks," Joe would recall. "I got a shot every day, and then I felt all right again. The next spring, the legs acted up again, and my father took me to an orthopedic man, who looked me over and said all I needed was exercise."

Perhaps it was exercise that kept him healthy until October 10, 1964. Eventually, Joe's injury would be properly diagnosed: torn cartilage and ligaments. But in his mother's mind, the problem still went back to Doylestown. "I always wondered whether his legs might have been somehow weakened then," she would say.

Joe himself could never be sure. Maybe the same God who let him dunk backward and jump pass now found something blasphemous in his contempt for gravity. Or maybe the knee was the price Joe paid for violating his own superstition. Joe had always wrapped his cleats with white tape. He liked the support, but even more, he liked the look. This binding was his ritual before every game of his college career—except North Carolina State.

Although Bryant didn't want to play him the following week against Tennessee, he called on Namath to relieve Sloan in the fourth quarter of a 19–8 victory. Next up was Florida, the ninth-ranked team in the nation, a worthy opponent for Bama's homecoming weekend. *Tuscaloosa News* columnist Charles Land expected that Namath, honored when Bryant named him a co-captain for the game, would be in "fine fettle" for the Gators. But the coach wasn't so sure: "He moves like a human now. He did move like a cat."

The betting line—printed in a paper that treated pool hall "gambling raids" as front page news and football parlay sheets as contraband—had the Tide favored at Denny Stadium by 6½ points. Land saw the game 20–10, for the home team. As it happened, Bama won by a field goal—despite losing

Namath in the first quarter. He had called his own number, running off-tackle for a first down before fumbling. The knee was reinjured as he scrambled for the ball.

"He was really suffering with that knee," says Bebe Schreiber, recalling that weekend. Bebe had by now graduated and moved to Florida, where she began a career as a speech therapist, but returned for homecoming to see Joe. She was still in love with him, though she could sense the beginning of their end. Bebe wanted to start settling down. But Joe, she says, "definitely had his reservations with what had happened in his family." And more than that, "the world was opening up for him."

There was already much talk of Joe Namath, pro quarterback. She could hear the whispers emanating from men who speculate in talent, whispers concerning his worth, which was not to be confused with his worthiness. This new American Football League might have lacked credibility, but not cash. AFL teams were driving up the prices for players like Joe. "He was going where the money train was taking him," she says.

Joe would gladly have taken that train, but boarding might prove to be a problem. "I remember the knee buckling," Bebe says of that weekend. "He didn't talk about it."

What was to talk about? Joe knew he might need a "cartilage operation" after the season, but then he'd be good as new—at least, that's what it said in the papers. Bryant told the writers what he had been told: the boy should be just fine. In the meantime, Joe wanted to win a championship—as did the coaching staff. "They just didn't know better," he would say.

So Joe kept trying to play. It became a cycle: playing, buckling, swelling, hurting. "Pain," says Dude Hennessey. "That boy was in lots of pain." And he hadn't even taken a real hit yet.

Three weeks would pass before Joe played another meaningful down. By then, the Tide would be in Atlanta against Georgia Tech. Though the schools had been playing each other since 1902, the increasingly acrimonious atmosphere around the game had resulted in a decision to end the rivalry. This was to be the finale. Anticipating the shower of whiskey bottles from a record-breaking crowd of 53,505 at Grant Field, Bryant took the field wearing a helmet. Namath wouldn't come on until late in the second quarter. The game was scoreless when, with 1:45 left in the half, Bama recovered a fumble at the Tech 49-yard line. Namath threw two incompletions followed by a forty-eight-yard bomb to end David Ray. Fullback Steve Bowman scored the touchdown on the next play. After Bama recovered an onsides kick, Namath hit halfback Ray Ogden for forty-five yards, all the way to the Tech 3. A couple plays later Namath found David Ray in the end zone for the touchdown. The extra point made it 14–0. Namath was done for the day. He'd given the team more than it would need, more than anyone could have bargained for: two touchdowns in

78 seconds. "This boy is great," declared Bryant. "If he doesn't sign one of the biggest professional contracts ever I'll be awfully surprised."

Namath walked out of Grant Stadium happily chewing on a big-ass cigar. Then, as if remembering something, he stopped abruptly to toss it. He didn't want any kids seeing him with the stogie. Joe was funny that way.

■ ■ ■

After Tech, only Auburn stood between Alabama and a national championship, which was then decided by a poll published in early December. Auburn was led by its senior star, Tucker Frederickson. As a fullback and defensive back, he was the team's best player on either side of the ball. The son of a veterinarian from Florida, Frederickson was everything football players were supposed to be. He was big (six-two, 215 pounds), blond, and handsome, all the southern football gods wanted in a young man, tacit proof of the superiority of Anglo-Saxon genes. Tucker was not seen chewing stogies or hanging out at the pool hall.

"Joe was the colorful rogue," said the *Birmingham News*'s Clyde Bolton. "But Tucker was the all-American boy you wanted your daughter to marry."

The game was held on Thanksgiving Day in Birmingham, with 68,000 on hand. Once again, Joe came on late in the second quarter to try another bomb. This time it was intercepted. A gambler takes that risk, then he moves on. Namath returned in the second half—after Steve Sloan hurt *his* knee—and faked the entire Auburn defense out of its collective jock before throwing a twenty-two-yard touchdown. Still, of the game's two big stars, it was Tucker who enjoyed the better day, wreaking havoc as a safetyman and running for 117 yards on 22 carries.

But that couldn't have bothered Joe, whose touchdown pass turned out to be the winning score in a 21–14 victory. The Tide was now 10–0. Beauty queens were handing him oranges. Come the New Year, they'd be in sunny Miami for the Orange Bowl. By then, Joe would be counting his money.

■ ■ ■

Four days earlier the New York Giants had lost 44–17 in front of 62,961 fans at Yankee Stadium. It was the second time that season the Giants had lost to the Pittsburgh Steelers. It was also the second time the Steelers had knocked Y. A. Tittle out of the game with a concussion.

Tittle, the Giants' quarterback, had been playing pro ball since 1948. He held NFL passing records for touchdowns, yardage, and attempts. Only the year before, at age thirty-seven, Tittle had been the league's most valuable player, throwing thirty-six touchdowns and leading the Giants to the championship game. But now, he was finished.

The first concussion produced a famous photograph taken by Morris

Berman of the *Pittsburgh Post-Gazette*. Tittle's image seems antithetical to that other iconic photo of the time—the heroic Unitas as he reared back to throw in the '58 championship game. Unitas launches the ball as if it were a burning spear. But in Berman's shot Tittle is forever kneeling in his black high-top cleats, a quarterback without his helmet, blood trickling down his bald pate. The slump across his neck and shoulders speaks of an inward gasp. His hands rest on his thighs, as if the pain had propelled him to a meditative state. There he is, the hero at the end, the quarterback's inevitable finale, bloodied and bowed, a supplicant before the Hit.

Now, two months later, the Steelers had done it again. "A mild concussion" was the diagnosis. After the game, Tittle was asked where the Giants were in the league standings.

The quarterback was unable to answer. However, it was common knowledge that the Giants, having their worst season in seventeen years, were in last place.

All this was considered great news for Joe Namath. For in just six days, the National Football League would conduct its annual draft of college players at the Summit Hotel in Manhattan. The order of selection was determined by a club's record, with the worst team picking first. Though a team could trade the "rights" to a player it had drafted, players remained bound to that franchise. A kid's best hope for bargaining leverage was to be selected by teams from both the NFL and the upstart American Football League, which held its draft the same day just blocks away, at the Waldorf-Astoria. Furiously escalating competition between the leagues had resulted in bidding wars for select players. Still, it was difficult to imagine how anything could come between the Giants and their plans. With the loss to Pittsburgh, the Giants had solidified their claim to the first pick in the draft. What's more, with Tittle going down, they had a job opening at quarterback.

Suddenly, the smart money had Joe going to the Giants. As Coach Bryant said, "If a pro team needed a quarterback and didn't take Namath, they ought to go out of business." Talk like that was just fine with Joe, who loved the idea of playing in New York. No more of this penny-loafer crap. In New York, guys wore slacks without cuffs. "That's class," said Namath. And so were the Giants. The Giants weren't one of these cockamamie AFL teams, but one of the National Football League's grand old franchises. Despite their current difficulties, they had gone to six of the last seven championship games. The Giants had been selling out Yankee Stadium—where Mickey Mantle himself played— since the dawn of time. The players were paid to appear on the *Ed Sullivan Show*. No doubt about it: New York was the place to be.

Just before the draft, Joe got a call from Sammy Baugh, the legendary quarterback who was coaching for the Houston Oilers. Their scout had filed a pretty straightforward report on Joe, just two words: "The Best." But Joe told Baugh not to bother drafting him. It was New York or bust.

Finally, two days after Bama beat Auburn, the NFL draft was held at the Summit Hotel in Manhattan. With the first pick, the Giants selected Tucker Frederickson. By then he had already signed a $100,000 contract in a Birmingham hotel. "We chose the No. 1 player in the nation," announced Wellington Mara, the Giants' vice president and part-owner.

The Giants had been in the Mara family since 1925, when Wellington's father, a well-connected bookmaker, paid $500 for the franchise. To Wellington, who also held the title of personnel coordinator, these drafts were very serious business. He only wanted young men of the finest character. Frederickson fit the bill perfectly, with an air much like the Giants' fair-haired stars Frank Gifford and Kyle Rote. The oddsmaker's son was partial to golden boys.

Tucker couldn't have been happier. The money was great, and he'd be playing *real* pro football. He never wanted to go to that AFL. "It was the National League all the way," he said.

As for Namath, ten more names were called out before the St. Louis Cardinals selected him with the twelfth pick. But as it happened, another New York team drafted him as well. This outfit, an AFL team, hadn't been around very long, and not many people had even heard of them. They'd just changed their name. They were calling themselves the Jets.

The Jets?

Who the hell were the Jets?

The Jets had only been the Jets since 1963. Before that, they were the Titans, one of the American Football League's original franchises. The league had been founded in 1959 by Lamar Hunt, then twenty-six, a former backup end at Southern Methodist University. His qualifications were a function of his father's fortune. The filthy richest of all the Texas oilmen, H. L. Hunt was a degenerate gambler who fancied himself a right-wing philosopher. His novel *Alpaca* outlines his version of utopian democracy as one in which the rich have more votes than the poor. Lamar, his youngest son, displayed none of H. L.'s eccentricities. He just wanted a football team. And since those old boys at the National Football League wouldn't let him buy one, he figured he'd start his own league. He got to talking with a bunch of folks, folks with oil money, like him, and hotel money and insurance money and trucking money. Then he found himself a commissioner, Joe Foss, a decorated fighter pilot who'd tend to league business from his native South Dakota. In its inaugural season, 1960, the American Football League had eight teams, the owners of which were dubbed "The Foolish Club."

17. HARRY WISMER'S TITANS OF NEW YORK

The head fool, the one who personified all that was amphigoric about the AFL, was Harry Wismer, owner of the New York Titans. Wismer had always been destined for greatness. In 1946 the Junior Chamber of Commerce named him one of American's Outstanding Young Men, an honor he shared with John F. Kennedy. But unlike the young congressman from Massachusetts, a mere politician, Wismer was already a nationally known football announcer. He called games for Notre Dame, the Detroit Lions, and the Washington Redskins (a franchise of which Wismer—oblivious to any conflicts of interest—had a piece). Listeners became accustomed to hearing Harry welcome his many dear old friends—from President Truman to Humphrey Bogart, Albert Schweitzer to Charles de Gaulle—into the radio booth. But these guests, like much of Harry's genius, were apparent only to Harry.

Wismer's most intense fits of fantasy concerned Wismer. News organizations requesting team pictures of the Titans or photos of individual players were sent publicity stills of Wismer. Subway placards alerted prospective fans to an exciting new team: "Harry Wismer's Titans of New York."

The team's corporate headquarters was located at 277 Park Avenue, Wismer's apartment in the Park Lane Hotel. The great man himself kept a desk and a secretary in the living room. The ticket office, such as it was, could be found in a bedroom. Coaches met in the dining room. And the public relations staff—typically consisting of one very harried man in need of temporary employment—occupied what was formerly the butler's pantry. Despite these formidable offices, the franchise's most crucial decisions were made over drinks at a nearby pub, the Bull and Bear, where Wismer drank his lunch (he was partial to "bullshots") over the course of several hours each afternoon. "He had a weasely intelligence," recalls Larry Fox, then a beat writer with the *World-Telegram and Sun*. "But you had to deal with him in the morning, before he got to the bullshots."

Harry was known to greet people with shouts of "Congratulations!"— figuring that most everyone, no matter his station in life, had accomplished something worthy of his good wishes. However, as he drank through the day, a darker instinct took over, and Wismer would threaten lawsuits and offer bogus "scoops." Sometimes, he would identify himself as a state trooper just returned from a horrific car wreck in which a body—usually an enemy of his—had been found. He had many enemies, only some of them imagined, but none so hated as the New York football Giants.

The owner wasn't alone in this sentiment. His players came to develop their own loathing for the Giants. Don Maynard, a thin, long-strided flanker from West Texas, had been cut by the Giants. He blamed assistant coach Allie Sherman for miscasting him as a halfback, a slight Maynard would never forget. In his cowboy hats and western boots, Maynard knew he didn't conform to the Giants' vaunted image. But that shouldn't have mattered. "I ran faster backwards than those guys could run forwards," he says.

Larry Grantham, another original Titan, recalls a time when players from both teams would get together for games of penny ante poker. The fellows got along, but there was an unspoken divide. The Giants had a lot more pennies to ante. "It was embarrassing," recalls Grantham, an undersized linebacker from Ole Miss. "We might all be invited to the same function. But they'd be sitting up on the podium. If the Giants got, say, five hundred bucks for an appearance, we'd be getting fifty."

In time, he says, the poker games ended as Giants management put out the word that their players were no longer allowed to fraternize with the Titans.

Grantham, from Mississippi, should have understood. There were two kinds of football players in New York; the Titans were the colored.

"It was a Giant town," says fullback Billy Mathis, another original Titan. "Everybody was always talking about the Giants."

While the Giants were winning championships and selling out majestic Yankee Stadium, Harry Wismer's Titans of New York were consigned to the Polo Grounds, an immense stadium on Coogan's Bluff overlooking the Harlem River. Formerly the home of the New York Giants baseball club, the Polo Grounds had been a great temple of New York's sporting set. In 1923, more than 90,000 saw Dempsey knock out Firpo there. In 1925, 70,000 gathered to watch Red Grange, "the Galloping Ghost," when the Chicago Bears came to town. In the 1954 World Series, 52,751 witnessed Willie Mays snag a 425-foot fly ball over his shoulder, the most famous catch in baseball history. And on September 11, 1960, an estimated crowd of 10,200 turned out to see the Titans make their debut, a 27–3 win over the Buffalo Bills. By then, the baseball Giants were playing in California. The stadium, already dilapidated when its previous tenants had left in '57, had fallen into an even deeper state of decrepitude. There was talk of replacing the Polo Grounds with a more cheerful edifice, a municipal housing project, and of building a new stadium in Queens, a borough that the baby boom had stocked with middle class families.

In the meantime, those Titan attendance figures—known as "Wismer Counts"—came to symbolize deep-seated doubts about the viability of the team and its owner. Dick Young, of the *Daily News,* said Wismer counted fingers instead of noses. Warren Pack, of the *Journal-American,* wrote: "Wismer announced the crowd as 20,898 today. Of this total, 19,000 came disguised as empty seats."

Congratulations, Harry!

"You'd look up in the stands, and there'd be nobody there," recalls Grantham. "It got so bad my wife had her own hot dog vendor."

"Wismer would've made it if the stinking news media hadn't stabbed him in the back like they did," insists Maynard. "Instead of writing the good things, they were always writing how we weren't as good as the Giants."

Unfortunately, the good things were not so readily apparent. By 1961, Wismer had fired his coach, Hall of Fame quarterback Sammy Baugh, and was immersed in a blood feud with commissioner Foss. "It would be better for New York," declared Foss, "if the Titans got a new owner." It might have been better for the players, too. By '62, their paychecks started bouncing.

"It got to the point where they would just laugh at you when you walked into the bank," says Grantham, who recalls in particular the game of October 28, 1962, a day the Titans were hosting the San Diego Chargers. Attendance figures put the crowd at 7,175 on that dark afternoon, easily the biggest of the season (the Titans averaged just over 5,000 fans a game that year). With the onset of twilight, the referee notified Titans coach Clyde "Bulldog" Turner that the stadium lights would have to be turned on. Turner forwarded the order to Wismer. The owner, in severe arrears for the electric bill, refused to switch on the lights and instead gave Bulldog a message for the ref: "You tell him we play pretty good in the dark."

"Everybody was just trying to hold on until they got that stadium built in Queens," says Grantham.

The Queens project had long been a sore subject for Wismer. He accused the Giants of conspiring to block legislative approval for the plan. As his source for this charge, he identified none other than Mayor Robert Wagner, leaving one to assume that the mayor was a close personal friend, much like Albert Schweitzer. A key agent in his vision of a Giants conspiracy was Harold Weissman, columnist for the *Mirror*. Weissman's son, charged Wismer, was a "mascot of the New York Giants."

In fact, Weissman had no children, but facts never dissuaded Harry. He did what he had to do, which was hustle. Lacking the financial resources of the AFL's other owners, he was forced to seek solvency through more creative measures. For lack of a rich daddy, he went after a rich wife. The scheme had worked before. The first Mrs. Harry Wismer was an heir to a niece's share of the Ford family fortune. On July 24, 1962, it became known to the newspapers that Harry had "secretly" taken another bride, the widow of deceased racketeer Longy Zwillman. What was truly secret was the fact that Harry had asked his nemesis, AFL commissioner Joe Foss, to serve as best man. Foss, the former fighter pilot, performed admirably at the reception, carrying a very drunk groom back to his room and helping to get him to bed without further incident. It had been another swell evening for Harry, who had cheerfully referred to the Wismer-Zwillman union as "a merger." Some months later came the announcement that Longy's widow had been named the team's "chief executive officer."

That announcement, like the marriage, generated some optimism among the players, who figured that their paychecks might now be subsidized by a vast bootlegging fortune. But much to their dismay, the Zwillman children had other, legally binding ideas concerning the disposition of Longy's patrimony.

By early 1963 the situation had become so dire as to overwhelm Wismer's extraordinary capacity for self-deception. On February 6, the Titans of New York filed for bankruptcy protection. The list of creditors in the bankruptcy court's docket stretches twenty-six pages, and speaks of debts large and small, 227 claims involving everybody from the taxman to the barman. Those dismal digits in the ledger were Wismer's undoing. A hustler unable to sustain the illusion of money inevitably loses his standing. When people can no longer believe in his luck, he's no longer a hustler, just a deadbeat.

Wismer never reached his promised land, the stadium in Queens. But he retains, curiously enough, the affection of the original Titans, players who sought to cash his rubber checks, men like Maynard and Mathis and Grantham. "He wasn't a bad guy," says Mathis, the Titans' all-league fullback. "Just undercapitalized."

Despite his bingeing and blather, Wismer deserves some kind consideration. Wondrous is the man who marries both a Ford and a Zwillman. And in fact, Harry Wismer deserves great credit for helping to keep the league alive. Before the AFL's inaugural game, he devised a scheme he would modestly call the Wismer Plan. In his mind, it would do for the league what George C. Marshall had done for Europe. Yet the characterization reflects more than Wismer's regard for Wismer. Even Joe Foss, the commissioner who had little use for him, acknowledged in his memoirs that "Harry Wismer came up with an idea that, in my opinion, despite his eccentricities, saved the life of pro football."

The AFL wasn't the first league to go up against the NFL. But unlike its doomed predecessors, the AFL came of age with the nascent industry of television. At the time, NFL teams cut their broadcast deals individually with local affiliates. But Wismer, Foss remembered, "proposed that our teams unite to sign one contract together for television rights and share broadcast revenues equally."

This kind of deal worked better for undercapitalized owners like Harry than it would for, say, Lamar Hunt. Old H. L. might have found such a money-sharing proposition a little red for his tastes. But it made a lot of green.

The American Broadcasting Company, itself a fledgling network, cut a five-year deal with the AFL. The first year was worth $1,785,000, escalating to $2,125,000 in year five. The payments were to be split equally among the teams. While that wasn't enough to save Harry, it did save the league.

Of course, Wismer's account of the Wismer Plan neglects the men who made it a reality. They included Tom Moore, the president of ABC; Jay Michaels, a very capable agent for the Music Corporation of America; and Michaels's boss, also from the Flatbush section of Brooklyn, Sonny Werblin, head of MCA's television division. Early in the negotiations, Moore was Werblin's guest at "21." By Sonny's standards, the deal wasn't very big, but the evening had incited his intense interest. Sonny had been going to the track since Al Jolson, his inside coat pocket stocked with twenty thousand-dollar bills, started taking him back in the 1930s. Sonny liked to make a bet, and this AFL was the best kind, a favorite disguised in the tattered silks of a long shot. The combination of football and TV made a great parlay, a winner if he ever saw one.

■   ■   ▩

Later, Wismer would attend a birthday party for Foss. This, too, was held at "21" and hosted by Werblin and his wife, Leah Ray, a former big-band singer.

Wismer got drunk and started in on Sonny. Foss recalled "a series of invectives . . . that ended with the word 'kike.'"

For a moment, it looked as if Sonny might deck Harry. But then he thought better of it. Sonny wanted to hurt his guy for real. "I'm going to own your club," he vowed.

And not long thereafter, just weeks after the bankruptcy filing, he did. On March 28, 1963, Sonny and his team of four investors—a consortium known to the court as the Gotham Football Club—purchased the Titans for $1 million.

In his memoir, *The Public Calls It Sport,* Wismer recounts a final fruitless effort to secure financial aid from his fellow owners. "They turned their backs," he said, "and in the wings, ready to administer the *coup de grace,* stood one of my own ilk, a hustler like myself."

Sonny was indeed a hustler, but a solvent one, still blessed by Jolson's thousand-dollar bills.

In the years that followed, Wismer did less congratulating and more drinking. He died on December 4, 1967, at the age of fifty-six, from injuries sustained falling down a flight of stairs. By then, the team he once owned was leading the league in attendance, drawing 62,000 every Sunday at the stadium in Queens.

Sonny's partners were horsemen. Three were fellow officers at New Jersey's Monmouth Park racetrack and members of its jockey club. Another, stockbrocker Donald Lillis, was president of the Bowie racecourse in Maryland. They had something else in common, too: their end of the partnership was to be silent, not by contract, but by agreement. It was decided that Sonny, who assumed the title of president, would act as the front man. The partners were wary of publicity, the burdens and indignities it can bring to wealthy men. Besides, Sonny had a gift for dealing with the press.

Any doubts as to his qualifications were erased on April 15, 1963, at Toots Shor's. It was only a press luncheon, but for Sonny, it might as well have been opening night.

The Titans, he announced, had ceased to exist. They were now the Jets. The name owed something to the mythical stadium being built in Queens, the borough of airports. The "ultra modern" facility was situated in Flushing Meadows, adjacent to the site of the 1964 World's Fair, itself a celebration of

18. SONNY, AS IN MONEY

the jet age. Also, Jets rhymed with Mets, the new National League baseball team. But mostly, they were the Jets because Sonny decided they were. The same was true of the uniforms, which were now white and kelly green. As Sonny was born on St. Patrick's Day, green was his favorite color.

To assume the duties of coach and general manager, Sonny hired one man: Wilbur Ewbank, fifty-five, a self-described "little Hoosier boy from the Midwest." Weeb, as he was known, was short and pudgy with a flat-top haircut. He conveyed, as one columnist put it, "the appearance of roundness." But roundness gave way to shrewdness when it came to evaluating talent, of which Weeb all but admitted that the Jets had little. But not to worry. "I've seen sicker cows than this get well," he said. In 1954 he had been appointed coach of the Baltimore Colts, then a 3–9 team. In 1956 he signed Johnny Unitas. And in 1958, in that famous overtime victory, the Colts won a championship. What took five years in Baltimore shouldn't take any longer in New York. Ewbank's Colts went on to win another championship in '59. Like the first, it came at the expense of the New York Giants, a fact that wasn't lost on Werblin.

Ewbank was hired at the recommendation of Jimmy Cannon, then writing for the *Journal-American*. Cannon, still the best known of the New York sports columnists, was famous as the city's hard-boiled tabloid poet. Sonny had phoned him in Fort Lauderdale, where he was covering the Yankees during spring training, asking his advice. But advice wasn't all he wanted. A call like the one he placed to Cannon laid the groundwork for a deal of the subtlest sort.

Sonny got raves for his opening-week performances as the new Jets owner. As *Daily News* columnist Gene Ward wrote of Werblin and his partners: "Success will take time, but, frankly, we don't see how they can miss." Cannon, however, went the extra step in his own column, offering a new paradigm whereby the Jets would actually flourish at the Giants' expense. He described Sonny as "a theatrical power," who had already "repaired some of the damage" inflicted by Wismer with just "his personality." His team was off to "a wise beginning" in hiring a coach who had twice beaten the "metropolitan pets."

As for the Giants: "Their popularity is spectacular despite the ability of their publicist, Don Smith, an obscure journalist before going on the Giants' payroll, to alienate the likes of me. I consider Smith among the Jets' assets."

All of a sudden, the newspaper guys were choosing sides. They couldn't help themselves. Sonny understood columnists' egos, their desire to exercise influence, their prejudices, the spectacular predilection to enlist in even the smallest intramural beef. The ensuing war between the Jets and the Giants would be fought with press agents before players. The Jets hadn't played a game, but they had already scored big points in the press box.

Werblin was regarded as a master agent, but such mastery began with his skill for dealing with the press. He had been a stringer extraordinaire while in college at Rutgers, covering football games for no fewer than seven New York papers. Upon graduation, he worked briefly as a sportswriter for the *Brooklyn Eagle* and a copy boy for the *New York Times*. But a sportswriter's salaried life was not what he wanted; the money was too meager. Still, Sonny took this knowledge of journalism to the bank. His experience had left him with an understanding that newspapermen were cheap dates.

In contrast to Wismer's animated antagonism, Werblin's tenure was marked by accessibility (you could get him on the phone day and night) and rare hospitality. "It was writers in first class, players in coach," says the *Amsterdam News*'s Howie Evans, recalling the Jets' charter flights. On Air Sonny, the stewardesses were quick to take your drink order. "Everybody would be bombed before the plane took off."

Then there was Sonny's day for the press at Monmouth Park. It ended with a sunset over the yacht club in Sea Bright, where the bar was open and the garbage cans piled high with fresh oysters. But it began at the track. Sonny would make the rounds, bullshitting with the guys, talking about a horse he liked in the third or the fourth or the fifth.

That was the horse you bet. "That horse would have to die to lose," recalls Jerry Izenberg, who had just left the *Herald-Tribune* to write a column at the *Newark Star-Ledger*.

The sportswriters were starting to believe in Sonny's green luck—even if the facts belied it. The 1963 Jets wound up 5–8–1, only marginally better than the 5–9 record they posted in their last season as the Titans. Even worse, the new Queens stadium Werblin was counting on wouldn't be ready for another year. Meanwhile, the Giants, who sold out every date at Yankee Stadium, went 11–3, all the way to the championship game.

Given these figures, it was easy to understand the Giants' arrogance, something Matt Snell first encountered that year. Snell, who had grown up in Carle Place, Long Island, had played linebacker and fullback at Ohio State. The Giants drafted him in the third round. Weeb Ewbank, who knew more about prospecting talent than anyone in the Giants front office, selected him with his very first pick.

Tim Mara, Wellington's nephew, was first to arrive in Columbus on behalf of the Giants. He offered Snell a $15,000 salary and a $5,000 signing bonus. Mara seemed to think those numbers were pretty sweet. "Besides," he told Snell, "you get to play for the Giants."

He kept playing up "that Giant thing," as Snell puts it. Mara had a point. Snell did grow up a Giants fan, and for a guy whose father made less than $300 a week as the head groundskeeper at the Nassau Country Club, the money seemed very big. Still, Snell had just enough presence of mind to wait. He wanted to see what this other team had to say.

Weeb's offer was $20,000 in salary and a $10,000 bonus.

Tim Mara got word of the Jets' bid and called Snell back. "Don't do anything," he said. "I'm coming back out. I want you to meet someone." Shortly thereafter, he arrived in a cab with Emlen Tunnell, a Hall of Fame defensive back who had retired in 1961. Tunnell, a Giants coach, had been the team's first black star and was now highly regarded as a mentor to players from all-black schools down South. But Tunnell's allegiance to the Giants cut across any racial line. Later, when one of his players became embroiled in a salary dispute with the Maras, Tunnell would tell him: "You should be paying them. It's an honor to play here."

Snell didn't know quite what to make of Tunnell. Snell was black, but not southern. Honor and tradition were cool; money was cooler. Now the Giants upped the ante, made their *final* offer: twenty grand in salary, and another twenty in an upfront bonus.

Snell could sense what Mara feared but refused to acknowledge: he didn't want to lose him to the Jets. In fact, the word "Jets" never crossed his lips, not once in any of their conversations. "They could never bring themselves to admit they were actually in competition with the Jets," he says.

Forty grand, guaranteed. Tim Mara had only one condition, that Snell sign immediately.

But Snell said he needed time. And in that time, Sonny Werblin pulled up in front of the Ohio State athletic department in a chauffered Cadillac limousine. Snell's first impression: tan, silver hair, glasses, looked you right in the eye, and that *suit*. Maybe it was the cut, maybe the fabric, or the shade of greenish gray. "You just knew," says Snell. "It was money."

Sonny offered a $30,000 bonus and $20,000 in salary. "We want you with the Jets," he said. He assured Snell's coach, Woody Hayes, that the AFL was here to stay and mentioned something about television. Snell took the deal. "Congratulations," said Werblin. "You're part of the family now." He gave Snell his home number and told him, "My wife's name is Leah." Then Werblin went back to New York.

Snell never heard from the Giants again. To the Maras, giving a third-round draft choice $50,000 was an act of reckless extravagance, insanity in which they declined to take part. The team's founder may have been a bookmaker, but his progeny had a fierce sense of rectitude. Wellington always seemed to have a priest in tow, a Father Dudley. The Giants were a good, God-fearing team. They had standards to uphold.

Sonny must've had himself a good laugh. Fifty grand didn't buy a pot to piss in. The Jets were prepared to lose money. "Maybe a million dollars," he said. "Money is no object." Talk like that horrified people like the Maras. They didn't get it, these NFL guys. *Schmucks*. They didn't understand. They *couldn't* understand. They still thought they were in the *football* business.

■   ■   ■

On May 9, 1961, Newton N. Minow, chairman of the Federal Communications Commission, addressed the National Association of Broadcasters, decrying network television as "a procession of game shows, violence, audience participation shows, formula comedies about totally unbelievable families, blood and thunder, mayhem, violence, sadism, murder, Western badmen, Western goodmen, private eyes, gangsters, more violence, and cartoons. And endlessly, commercials—many screaming, cajoling and offending. And most of all, boredom."

TV, he declared, was a "vast wasteland."

A month later NBC chairman Robert Sarnoff fired back in the *Saturday Evening Post*, defending his network, his industry, and popular tastes against the pretense of pointy-headed Adlai Stevenson Democrats like Minow. "I like

Westerns," declared Sarnoff. Among the programs he cited was *Wagon Train,* then the top-rated show in the country.

Wagon Train was an NBC show. And like so many NBC shows, it had been "packaged" by MCA, the most powerful force in American entertainment. By then, the Music Corporation of America had less to do with music than television. And the president of MCA-TV was Sonny Werblin. If the medium was indeed "a vast wasteland," then Sonny was a lord of the realm.

"He was the best salesman in the television industry, without question," said Al Rush, one of the agents who helped Sonny package *Wagon Train* for NBC.

Sonny sold from his table at "21." He sold while bonefishing with Sarnoff in the Florida Keys. He sold while his horse was being led around the paddock. If Sonny was breathing, he was selling.

But what made Sonny run?

Born on St. Patrick's Day, 1910, David Abraham Werblin grew up in Flatbush, Brooklyn. His father, part-owner of a company that manufactured paper bags, died of a heart attack when Sonny, as his mother called him, was fourteen. Sonny graduated from James Madison High School, Class of '27. Though he had been an undersized center on Madison's football team, his athletic career ended the following autumn when he injured his shoulder playing freshman ball at Rutgers. He majored in liberal arts and journalism. And despite his prolific apprenticeship as a sportswriter, Sonny's real education didn't begin until after his graduation, when he swore off newspapering and got a job with MCA in 1934.

Starting as a $21-a-week office boy, he worked for Billy Goodheart, a former piano player whose spinal deformity left him with a mangled five-foot-three-inch frame. Goodheart was an early partner of Jules Stein, an ophthalmologist who had founded the talent agency in 1924. He would sit on a raised office chair, a platform from which he could look down on his office boys while berating them. Goodheart, whose heart was anything but, was given to fits of rage and liked nothing better than to humiliate little pishers like Sonny. He would empty his inkwell and break the points off his pencils just to scream at the kid for not having his desk ready. But no amount of abuse could break Werblin's composure. In time, as one MCA historian put it, Goodheart became "a kind of dysfunctional father figure" to Sonny. But first, he gave Sonny a promotion. His new title was band boy for Guy Lombardo and his Royal Canadians.

A band boy looked after the instruments, ran errands, kept the books, and counted the house. Sonny learned how to judge the size of a theater and how to tell which locked doors were *really* locked. The gate—from which MCA took its cut—was sacrosanct. Sonny kept the receipts and the cash in a money belt. Once, after discovering that a dance hall promoter was swindling

Lombardo, Sonny asked the promoter to make change for a thousand-dollar bill he had in his belt. Sure, said the swindler, who started to empty his pockets. They were full of cash. "I just grabbed whatever I could and ran for the bus," Sonny would recall.

That sort of quick thinking came by way of instinct and ability. Sonny didn't need to be taught much. An MCA agent was to work without fatigue. An MCA agent should conduct himself with the manners of an English lord and the sensitivities of an assassin. An MCA agent kept the talent happy. That was the business, talent: finding it, developing it, and most of all, selling it.

Soon, Sonny was going to the track with Al Jolson, walking to the window with Jolie's thousand-dollar bills.

Then he discovered this crazy goddamn piano player, Liberace.

He signed Dean Martin. "My father was the one who insisted that Dean Martin get a nose job," says Sonny's youngest son, Tom Werblin. Taking care of that big Italian schnozzola made all the difference. Sonny's professional education had alerted him to the existence of a superior life form: the star. With the proper proboscis, Dean Martin became a huge one. And Sinatra. Who do you think was there, minding the gate as bobby-soxers wept for him?

Sonny was ever on the prowl for "star quality"—the indefinable gift that men of his ilk could convert into currency. You never knew where you could find it, but you had to hustle once you did. As one NBC executive likes to say, "Sonny could walk a cockroach through a screen test."

In terms of mass entertainment, Sonny was there at the Creation, that long period of gestation that resulted from the mating of stage acts with television. At MCA, this pregnancy produced what one federal judge called an "Octopus"—a beast with "tentacles reaching out to all phases and grasping at everything in show business." MCA had a firm grasp on show business because it had a firm grasp on its stars. At one time or another, Sonny's clients included Sinatra, Martin, Jackie Gleason, Elizabeth Taylor, Andy Williams, Eddie Fisher, Ed Sullivan, Jack Benny, Rosalind Russell, Gene Kelly, Betty Grable, Joan Crawford, Phil Silvers, Ronald Reagan, Abbott, Costello, and all the Nelsons, from Ozzie to Ricky.

Within MCA Sonny's power trumped everyone's except that of the founder, Jules Stein, and Lew Wasserman, Hollywood's Richelieu. In 1951 he became the president of MCA-TV, a title that led him to another, when *Variety* proclaimed him "the father of the package deal." The "package" was a scheme by which MCA stars, MCA directors, and MCA writers would get together at MCA's Revue studios to produce an MCA show for NBC, CBS, or ABC. "Werblin could play both sides of the fence with effortless dexterity," wrote *Variety*'s George Rosen. "On many days, he would appear in the offices of each of the three network presidents—often selling programs that he had plotted to be scheduled opposite each other. . . . He was a masterful practitioner of the time-honored show biz dodge of starting a war and selling ammunition to all sides."

Sonny kept the Octopus well fed. In 1953 he stopped by to see Pat Weaver, NBC's head of programming, concerning a little-known West Coast comic named George Gobel. The meeting wound up lasting five hours and formed the basis for a five-year deal worth between $6 and $7 million. At Sonny's suggestion Gobel and his manager, David O'Malley, created Gomalco, a company with interests as varied as motels and other television shows. Gomalco even went in with some other MCA clients to produce *Leave It to Beaver,* a show that was later sold to MCA's Revue Productions.

If you had the star, you had the power. In 1959, when Jack Benny's CBS deal expired, Werblin threatened to take his star elsewhere unless the network agreed to invest in a group of shows to be produced by Benny's company. These included such masterpieces as *Checkmate, The Marge and Gower Champion Show, Ichabod and Me,* and *The Gisele MacKenzie Show,* all of which were sold back to MCA's Revue studios after they became established on the network's schedule.

Sonny stocked the vast wasteland with a multitude of programs: *Markham, Mike Hammer, M Squad, Treasury Men in Action, Overland Trail, Twenty-One, Shotgun Slade, Johnny Staccato, Whispering Smith, The Deputy, My Three Sons, Laramie, Riverboat,* and *Bachelor Father.* But perhaps the greatest of all Sonny's packages was *Wagon Train.*

In 1962, the year after Minow's speech, Werblin asked NBC to renew the *Wagon Train* contract by purchasing 39 new episodes and all 189 reruns. But just as the deal lapsed, Sonny hustled over to ABC for what *Variety* described as a hasty "handshake deal" worth a reported $20 million. Then, almost as quickly, he sold NBC *The Virginian,* another MCA package, to compete in the same time slot as *Wagon Train.*

Sonny always had a soft spot for NBC. He counted David Sarnoff—the visionary behind RCA and its subsidiary NBC—and his son Robert, the network's chairman, among his close friends. It was also said, with some authority, that NBC president Robert Kintner owed his job to Sonny.

According to *Forbes,* a famous exchange between Sonny and Kintner occurred in the spring of 1957. "Sonny," said the NBC executive, "look at the schedule for next season; here are the empty spots, you fill them."

And of course he did, penciling in fourteen MCA shows.

Though the story was denied (more vehemently by Kintner than Werblin), it illuminated an uncontestable truth. Around the holidays, Tom Werblin would receive NBC promotional towels featuring the network's programming grid. "Pretty cool," he thought, noting that prime time was Werblin time: *The Virginian, Dragnet, Ozzie and Harriet, Peter Gunn, My Three Sons.*

"My dad would deliver to the network its night of programming," says

Tom Werblin, known as TD. "The network didn't have to go anywhere else. He would give them the variety show, the sitcom, and the movie. Sarnoff didn't have to go to six different guys. MCA would say, here's your week of prime time."

"People like to say that Sonny had the Sarnoffs and Kintner in his pocket," said Al Rush, an NBC lawyer before he went to work for Sonny. "But they didn't get hurt. Sonny delivered hit shows."

Sonny's kingdom might have been vast, but who was this Minow to call it a wasteland? It was a thing of beauty, the union of mass culture with commerce.

■   ■   ■

Given MCA's success, and its myriad conflicts of interest, a Justice Department investigation was inevitable. As a result, MCA ceased representing individuals as a talent agency in 1962. It was bad news for Sonny, who at his core remained an agent, a hustler of stars. Now, after more than three decades, the business left him cold. If you weren't selling talent, you might as well be selling tires. The hustle wasn't as much fun. He was getting tired of packaging. He was getting tired of MCA. It was Lew Wasserman's company, anyway, and had been for a while. Sonny needed a new hustle, and the Jets were everything he had been looking for.

The Justice Department might not have approved of Sonny's relationship with NBC, but the AFL certainly did. The wisdom of the revenue-sharing Wismer Plan had been quickly recognized by the NFL's slick young commissioner, a former West Coast PR man named Pete Rozelle. In 1962, using the AFL's deal with ABC as its template, the NFL finalized a $4.65 million contract for CBS to televise all regular-season games. But the established league's attractiveness as a television property was so great that it soon rendered that pact obsolete. On Friday, January 24, 1964, Rozelle and CBS Sports president Bill MacPhail would toast the largest television sports contract ever signed. CBS now tripled the previous rate, with a two-year deal paying the NFL $28.2 million. Under the new contract, each team would get about a million a year, approximately $800,000 more than those bush-league AFL teams were getting from NBC. The disparity between the leagues had never been more clearly demonstrated. From now on, a football league was only as big, or as small, as its TV deal.

But on the very day that Rozelle was lifting his glass at Toots Shor's, NBC Sports president Carl Lindemann—dejected by yet another defeat at the hands of the NFL and CBS—received an urgent, though cryptic note. Within a couple of hours he was meeting with AFL commissioner Joe Foss and Sonny, who insisted on taking him back to NBC in a limo. There, in the back seat, Werblin took out an envelope and pen. "You say the NFL got twenty-eight-two?"

Lindemann nodded mournfully.

Sonny scratched some numbers on the back of the envelope and handed it to Lindemann. "We have the following in mind, Carl."

His figure was $36 million for a five-year deal. Sonny was asking for almost five times what ABC had been paying. By Monday, he got it. The AFL still didn't have respect. But in an instant, before anybody really understood what had happened, it had parity, as measured by the most important number—television dollars. Under the new deal, AFL teams would receive about $900,000 a year from NBC. NFL teams got a million, but since they also carried more players, the difference was small change.

"That was a very easy deal because of Sonny's relationship with the Sarnoffs and Kintner," says Chet Simmons, then second in command at NBC Sports. "It was his deal, no question. Nobody else in that league knew anything about television or show business. They were in oil or insurance or trucking. Everybody deferred to Sonny."

Eight days before the draft that yielded Joe Namath, the neediest AFL teams (of which the Jets were still one) met at league headquarters to receive an advance. NBC cut five checks, a total of $1,250,000. The accelerated payment had an express purpose: to procure stars at the expense of the NFL.

"Go get 'em," said Lindemann.

The leagues were preparing for what had become an annual festival of dirty tricks. With talent at a premium, scouts and team executives from both leagues—"babysitters," as they were called—were dispatched to charm, bribe, and otherwise divert the attentions of college kids with professional potential. The prospects were plied with booze and broads, kept incommunicado in hotel rooms until they could be drafted and signed. The prices were spiraling out of control. According to no less a source than the *New York Times,* it was believed that Don Trull, a Baylor quarterback who had signed with Houston the year before, had received "a three-year no-cut contract which, with bonuses and benefits, exceeded $100,000."

A hundred grand? Where would it end?

With NBC's deep pockets, it didn't have to end. A hundred grand? A hundred grand was nothing. A hundred grand was the set on the *Dean Martin Show.* This was the TV business. Didn't they understand? The AFL was just another package Sonny hustled to NBC, doing for Sunday afternoon what he had done for prime time.

■   ■   ■

Shea Stadium finally opened in 1964. In just their first game at their new "ultra modern" home in Flushing, the Jets attracted a crowd of 44,497, more fans than they had drawn in the entire 1962 season. For each game at Shea, they would average about 30,000 more than the year before, their last at the Polo Grounds.

Ewbank and personnel director George Sauer, the only holdover from the Wismer era, were proving just how astute their judgment of talent really was. Winston Hill, a 270-pound offensive tackle cut by the Colts, was just beginning to show his potential. Rookie guard Dave Herman, a twenty-seventh-round draft pick, displayed a rare combination of craft and ferocity, as did Gerry Philbin, a rookie defensive end from, of all places, the University of Buffalo. Best of all was Matt Snell. Not only did he run for 948 yards and make 56 catches—he could block his ass off. Snell was ultimately named Rookie of the Year. Oh, the Giants had to be eating their hearts out. Nineteen sixty-four was also the year of the great Giant collapse, when they lost Tittle and finished last. Then again, the Jets didn't perform that much better. It was another 5–8–1 season for Werblin's team.

The Jets' greatest attraction, as far as many fans were concerned, was Wahoo McDaniel. A full-blooded Choctaw Indian, he played linebacker when he wasn't wrestling under the name "Big Chief Wahoo." McDaniel played well that opening day against the Denver Broncos. Sonny noticed how the fans seemed to like this wrestling Indian, how they cheered whenever the PA announcer said, "Tackle made by Wahoo McDaniel."

Sonny wasted no time in having a conversation with the guy on the PA system. After that, the announcer became more like an emcee. After McDaniel made a hit, he would ask, "Tackle by who?" "Wa-hoo!" the delighted crowd would respond.

Soon, as per Sonny's order, the name on his jersey was "WAHOO." The professional wrestler understood: "Wahoo, that spells money."

After all those Westerns, Sonny knew you couldn't lose with a crazy Indian. Wahoo was cute, a vaudeville gimmick. "He had nothing else to sell," says the *Newark Star-Ledger*'s Jerry Izenberg. "So he created this Wahoo thing." It's what he had, but not what he needed. Everything Sonny had learned from his days as a band boy told him the same thing. He could hear Billy Goodheart's ghost berating him: *You little shit, the best you could do is a wrestling Indian? Where is he, kid? Where the fuck is the star?*

No doubt about it. This show needed a leading man.

On November 8, 1964, Tulsa quarterback Jerry Rhome was in New York City to pick up yet another award for his gridiron prowess, and to be the guest of Mr. and Mrs. Sonny Werblin. Rhome, a Texan, the son of a football coach, was rewriting the NCAA passing records. The Jets had drafted him as a junior the year before and still held his rights.

With no great desire to play in New York, Rhome hadn't felt like making the trip. Memphis State had beaten him up pretty bad the day before. His ribs hurt, his ankle hurt, and he needed a crutch to walk after the game. The Jets drew an incredible 61,929 the following day at Shea, but for Rhome, the best thing about that whole weekend was the sauna and hot tub at the stadium. "They let me soak in there for three hours," he says.

19. HAPPY NEW YEAR

After the game, a 20–7 loss to the Bills, Rhome and his coach, Glenn Dobbs, were taken by limousine to Lüchow's, a venerable German dining hall in downtown Manhattan where the waiters wore lederhosen. Rhome, still in pain throughout the meal, didn't do much talking.

Tom Werblin's recollection of the evening is much sharper. By the age of nine, TD, as he was called, was already accustomed to hanging out with his parents, Sonny and the lovely Leah Ray. He liked the action, the celebrities. He enjoyed seeing people from television as they existed in real life. And he loved his dad's joints. How many nine-year-olds knew what the "21" burger tasted like? How many had been to Toots Shor's? Where else could you see Mickey Mantle, Frank Gifford, and Jimmy Hoffa? TD would never forget that. And for entirely different reasons, he'd never forget that night at Lüchow's. It was pouring rain when they came out of the restaurant. A chauffeur handed Rhome an umbrella, which the Tulsa quarterback took and headed straight for the limo, leaving Leah Ray to make a mad dash through the pouring rain.

As she did, TD could see his father's face darken. Sonny had a saying: Present the lady. *Always* present the lady. "Jerry Rhome committed the cardinal sin," says Tom Werblin.

This screen test was over. The kid could set all the passing records in the world. It wasn't going to work. Not here.

"This is not the guy I need," Sonny muttered.

Rhome's rights were traded to Houston for the second pick in the draft.

◼   ◼   ◼

After Rhome, the nation's leader in total yards was Craig Morton, a big quarterback from Cal. Clive Rush, one of two assistants assigned to the Jets offense, was particularly high on him. As for Namath, Rush was less concerned with his knees than his reputation. If Bear Bryant had suspended him for the Sugar Bowl, the kid had to be trouble.

The other assistant, Chuck Knox, came out big for Namath. Knox was from the Beaver Valley, where he used to coach junior high school basketball. He had never forgotten seeing Namath as a ninth-grader against his Ellwood City team. Neither quarterback's numbers meant much to Knox. Morton, like Rhome, played in a passing offense. What Namath had, now as then, defied easy quantification. The kid had become exactly what Knox had forecast back in Ellwood.

Knox's assessment was echoed in the Jets' own scouting report, filed in October 1964: "An outstanding passer with big, good hands and exceptionally fast delivery. Has good agility and sets-up very well—a fine 'scrambler.' Throws the short pass very well and can also throw the 'bomb' with great accuracy. Is smart and follows the 'game plan' perfectly. Is a fine Leader and the Team has great confidence in him. *Will be everyone's number one draft choice.*"

"We needed a quarterback, and he was the best one out there," says Knox. "I pushed Weeb very hard to take Joe."

"Chuck pressed for Joe like crazy," recalls Walt Michaels, one of Ewbank's defensive assistants. "It was a great debate. And I'm glad Clive lost. In the end, the difference came down to Sonny Werblin."

As Knox had argued, there was another side to Namath's reputation. The idea of Namath as a winner was greatly enhanced by the news of November 30, 1964, when just three days after the draft, an Associated Press poll declared Alabama national champions of college football. That afternoon, as Namath appeared in his letter sweater at a pep rally in Foster Auditorium, the AP was moving additional testimony regarding his qualifications. Weeb Ewbank was quoted saying that Namath had "the potential of being another Johnny Unitas." Werblin, for his part, said: "We want this boy real bad. And we plan to get him."

Shortly thereafter, two men from the St. Louis Cardinals paid Namath a visit at the dormitory. They wanted to know how much it would take. As per Coach Bryant's instructions, Joe asked for the outrageous sum of $200,000. You may only get half that, said Bryant, but it wouldn't hurt none to ask.

The men from the Cardinals reacted with shock and dismay. One of them fell right down on the bed. It was as if Joe had hit them in the gut. Two hundred thousand? Two hundred thousand. "Screaming like they were in agony," recalled Namath.

They seemed to recover soon enough, though. And as soon as they had, Joe said there was something else. He needed a car.

"What kind?"

"Lincoln Continental."

For all their protestations, the Cardinals didn't have much trouble meeting his price. But as Joe couldn't jeopardize the appearance of his amateur status, he wouldn't sign any agreement until after the Orange Bowl on New Year's Day. The intervening month guaranteed a nice little bidding war. Namath would not proceed further without the benefit of his counsel—Mike Bite, of the Birmingham law firm of Bite, Bite & Bite. An Alabamian of Lebanese extraction, Bite was a good-natured man who liked to have a drink and shoot a round of golf. Joe had met him on the golf course a couple years prior. As an undergraduate, Bite had also been student manager of the Alabama football team. Most important, he came with Bryant's blessing.

On the weekend of December 4, Chuck Knox flew to Birmingham, attended an A Club dinner there, and hustled Joe and Mike Bite onto a plane bound for Atlanta with a connecting flight to Los Angeles, not far from San Diego, where the Jets would be playing the Chargers. Namath met up with Sonny and Weeb in L.A. Sonny would recall the meeting as compelling evidence of Joe's star quality, his ability to charge a room. But this wasn't an audition. It was a negotiation.

While Mike Bite inquired as to his cut—was it part of the contract, or would it come off the top?—Joe had different concerns. He wanted to set some money aside, and he wanted to know about the tax implications of doing so. He was already thinking long-term.

"The basic framework of the deal," says Knox, "was done down there."

The basic framework was worth about $300,000. But the deal was far from done. Though Namath would have commanded top dollar in any market, this one seemed unnaturally energized. An invisible hand—several, in fact—was hard at work: bidding, dealing, and double-dealing, as the price kept ratcheting upward. None of this came as a surprise to Dallas Cowboys personnel chief Gil Brandt, who selected Craig Morton instead of Namath. "We didn't draft him because we couldn't afford him," said Brandt.

If the Cowboys couldn't afford Joe, then how could the Cardinals? From the outset, St. Louis's interest in Namath aroused more than mild suspicion. The Cardinals already had a fine young quarterback in Charley Johnson, who had thrown for twenty-eight touchdowns and 3,280 yards in '63 and would lead the league in yardage in '64. It didn't require a conspiracy theorist to figure that the Cardinals were actually working on behalf of a team that did need a quarterback—namely, the Giants. Perhaps the Giants wanted Namath more than they ever let on.

"St. Louis was the patsy for the Giants," says Walt Michaels. "They just couldn't stand the publicity if they lost him. Of course, you'll never get Wellington Mara to admit that."

Michaels's wasn't the minority point of view. Even as the numbers escalated, one peculiar aspect of the negotiation remained constant: Mike Bite could never get an immediate response from the Cardinals' owners, the Bidwells. They always said they'd have to get back to him—as if they needed permission to match and raise the stakes. Sonny became convinced the Bidwells were running everything past the Maras. Fearing that he might lose Namath, he cut a secret deal with the Jets' second-round pick, John Huarte of Notre Dame. Despite winning the Heisman Trophy, Huarte wasn't nearly the prospect that Namath was. But Sonny needed some insurance. Larry Fox, who broke the Huarte story for the *New York World-Telegram and Sun,* attributed the Werblin regime's uncustomary silence to a fear of losing Namath to the hated Maras. "The latest rumor has St. Louis trading his rights to the Giants in hopes of keeping him in the NFL," wrote Fox.

The story ran on December 19, the same day Cardinals co-owner Bill Bidwell said St. Louis had an "even chance" of signing Namath. As for the Giants rumor, he denied it all categorically. Still, he never bothered to explain why St. Louis, which already had a very good quarterback, would bid almost $400,000—the biggest offer any ballplayer in any sport had ever seen—for a kid with a bad knee who wanted to play in New York. It was time for St. Louis to turn over its cards.

"There came a time," recalls Namath, "when . . . the Cardinals wanted to know if I'd play for the Giants."

And there came a time for Joe to leave the country.

■　　■　　■

Because Sonny had always considered hospitality a form of persuasion, he called his friend Joe Hirsch, the urbane racing writer for the *Daily Telegraph,* who was in Miami covering the Thoroughbreds. "There's this kid I'm trying to sign," Sonny explained. "He's going to be at Tropical Park. If you see him, buy him a drink."

Hirsch knew horses, not college football players. The bartender had to point out Joe. They had a drink, then Hirsch lent him a sports jacket and took him to a first-class dinner. "I suppose you're majoring in basket-weaving," he said.

"Nah, that class was all filled up," the kid replied. "But I found an even easier one—journalism."

The kid had a natural wink. Less natural was his accent, southern. But it would go over big in New York. Hirsch liked him right away. Though he can't recall the date, it seems their meeting might have been a stopover for Joe on his way to the Bahamas.

The Werblins usually spent the holidays in Elberon, New Jersey, where they had an estate and horse farm. But that year, 1964, they vacationed in Lyford Cay, where TD and his mother found themselves decorating a Bahamian pine, trying their best to make it look like a Christmas tree. It didn't feel like Christmas, though. TD missed home. He missed the snow, and missed New Jersey. He was almost crying as he asked his mother, "Why are we here?"

Instead of giving him an answer, his father and older brothers went to the airport to meet and greet the guest of honor. *Joe* was coming. *Joe* was here. And he wasn't alone: he brought Jimmy Walsh, only a second-year law student but already apprenticing for a specialized practice as Namath's counsel.

Even by the Werblins' standards, the club at Lyford Cay was very exclusive. But Joe, still a boy from a mill town, seemed as if he belonged, taking in everything with an easy grace: snorkeling, lounging by the pool, having dinner with the family. Leah Ray took a quick liking to him. He had naturally exquisite manners; no one had to tell *him* to present the lady.

Though still a child, TD understood what he was seeing at Lyford Cay. As Sonny's progeny, he was attuned to the many varieties of star quality. He had felt the absurd weight in the sleeves of Liberace's stage coat, twenty pounds of sequins and rhinestones. He had listened as Alfred Hitchcock held a large table spellbound while delivering a kind of dissertation on the merits of a good meal. TD had already learned to gauge celebrities by reading the reactions they caused in other adults. But Joe elicited a buzz different from that of any of the stars who stayed at Elberon. "With Joe, the *wives* would melt," he says. "You could see them nudge their husbands and whisper, 'Introduce me.'"

After dinner, Sonny and Joe had a talk. Werblin was still very worried, mostly about the Giants, but Joe said he'd known for three weeks that the Giants had been dealing for him. Like Joe used to say: you can't con a con man. Besides, why would he want to play for a team that had to be sneaky about it? "I just want to tell you not to worry about anything you hear," Joe assured him.

For Sonny, it was beginning to feel a lot like Christmas.

■   ■   ■

TD always assumed that his father had been acting on the advice of a smart lawyer who told him to close the deal offshore. Later, Werblin would recall Lyford Cay as the place where Joe committed to the Jets. But Werblin called Bryant anyway. A handshake was nice, but he wanted a signature. "You don't need it," said Bryant. "He gave you his word, you don't need the paper."

Still, Sonny felt he couldn't be too careful. So as the action moved to

Miami for the Alabama-Texas game, Chuck Knox received his new assignment: "Don't come home without Joe."

Knox checked in with his pregnant wife, Shirley, at the Bal Harbour Inn, which happened to be where Joe's mother was staying. The way to Joe's heart had never changed. "You had to take care of Rose," says Knox. Shirley took Rose shopping. (Joe told her she could buy anything she wanted.) Chuck took Joe and Jimmy to dinner. And all the while, the couple was on the lookout for any sign of the Giants or the Cardinals. "We were more like cops than babysitters," Knox would recall. "We had them covered."

■　■　■

Namath was expected to start in the Orange Bowl. He seemed fresh in practice, as if all the rest had done him good. Besides, Steve Sloan's knee—injured in the Auburn game—was thought to be in even worse shape than Joe's. Bryant accordingly drew up a whole game plan based around Namath, and so did the bookies. Texas had lost only one game, and by a single point, but with Namath looking sharp the line favored Alabama by six. Then, at practice four days before the game, Namath rolled right for a handoff and collapsed. As he lay there writhing in pain, a sportswriter put the matter in perspective: "It's an even game now."

Later, Bryant would visit Joe in the training room, where his right knee was encased on ice. "Never heard of one of those things that killed anybody yet," said the coach.

"I'm okay, coach. I'll be ready."

Bryant, however, wasn't counting on it. He went out and told the press that Steve Sloan would start at quarterback. The coach had a big smile on his face. Why? asked the sportswriters.

"Because I'm an idiot," he said.

■　■　■

The next morning the *St. Louis Post-Dispatch* reported that the Cardinals had dropped out of the bidding for Namath. Later that day Cardinals owner Bill Bidwell said, "Namath let it be known that he preferred to play in New York. So we have just about abandoned hopes of getting him for St. Louis."

And suddenly the Giants were out, too. In the end, the Maras had no stomach for this kind of business. On Wednesday, December 30, Leo Levine of the *New York Herald Tribune* reported that Namath would sign a three-year deal with the Jets for approximately $389,000—"more money than any other professional athlete has ever received for signing a contract."

The Cardinals, wrote Levine, "turned the rights to negotiate with him over to the Giants, who it is believed would have drafted him in the first place but didn't want to get into an open bidding battle with their crosstown rivals.

"When the Giants went looking for him, Namath was unavailable. Yesterday the Giants said they weren't interested in any rookies for nearly $400,000, much less one with a history of a knee injury."

Judging from all the hand-wringing over the Namath deal, the Giants struck a blow for sanity. Where would it end? sportswriters asked. Perhaps this *was* the end. Then again, a few of them actually seemed to appreciate Werblin's coup and what it portended. Dick Young of the *Daily News,* with almost 4 million readers on Sundays, couldn't wait for this kid to get to town: "Namath should go great in New York. He hates to go to bed." Young was only encouraged by his suspension from the Sugar Bowl. "If you can get into that kind of trouble in Tuscaloosa, Ala., imagine what wonders await you on the Great White Way."

Sonny couldn't have written it better himself.

■   ■   ■

In anticipation of the Orange Bowl telecast, NBC chairman Bob Kintner called his sports department to express his displeasure with the way college football had been covered. He was sick and tired of watching CBS and ABC broadcast ball games in color while his own network—identified, after all, by a multihued peacock and the slogan "In Living Color"—still aired most of them in black and white. An even greater source of Kintner's wrath was the fact that RCA, the network's parent company, was the leading manufacturer of color television sets. Kintner's message, as recalled by one well-placed executive at NBC Sports, was: "We *make* the goddamn TVs. Now you guys better come up with something good for this game."

"There was a lot of pressure on us all," explains the executive, David Kennedy. They were therefore determined to do better than mere color. They would use powerful new lighting and place an increased emphasis on isolated videotape replay, which NBC now christened "instant replay." More important, the production would forever be distinguished by the decision to play the game in prime time. It would be the first major team sporting event to be broadcast at night, a privilege for which NBC paid the Orange Bowl Committee $600,000. The pregame would start at 7:30 P.M. EST, on New Year's Day, preempting Jack Benny, Jack Paar, and Bob Hope.

Like an MCA package, the New Year's Eve Orange Bowl Parade seemed particularly suited for television, viewed through a lens unable to distinguish between fantasy and reality, the banal from the bizarre. It was guaranteed to piss off Newt Minow. The 1965 procession was heavy with girls, girls, girls, rolling down Biscayne Boulevard atop or astride floats brought to lurid life through corporate sponsorship. Queen Linda Egland and her blond princesses went forth on an eighty-foot castle of shocking pink, courtesy of Minute Maid. A biblically themed float featuring Jesus and Mary was followed by

Cinderella, Snow White, Catherine the Great, Marie Antoinette in a thirty-two-pound jeweled gown, and Neptune's bathing beauties waving from giant ridged clamshells. And don't forget the stewardesses. They came dressed as stewardesses, as they had no need of anything else to evoke their charms.

The dignitaries on hand included Jackie Gleason, the parade's grand marshal; Richard Nixon, who picked Texas by a field goal; and Governor George Wallace, who got a good bit of airtime. "I'm an incurable parade goer," confessed the governor, who spent his days in Miami handing out autographed pictures of himself and posing for photos that would make the wires, including one with a dashing, injured quarterback.

Wallace, like Werblin and Kintner, understood that television made this event more than a mere football game. The broadcast from Miami would be seen by 25 million people. Prime-time sports were the future, an endless annoyance to sportswriters, who preferred to spend evenings at the bar. But advertisers envisioned games as great spectacles in celebration of the ideal consumer: a clean-shaven, well-groomed white man who earned his satisfaction driving and smoking and drinking the right products.

On New Year's Day the parade forces reassembled inside the Orange Bowl. The crowd of 72,647 was a sellout. Bathing beauties were stationed on "coral reefs" in the eastern end zone. Fresh oranges were Scotch-taped to trees in honor of the occasion. On the Alabama sideline, Bryant spoke to his trainer for the first time in a couple of days. Could Namath play any?

"Yes, sir," said Jim Goostree. Joe could play. After all, he'd had the finest sports medicine could offer: ice, rest, and Ace bandages. Plus, he was wearing soccer shoes with small cleats that didn't dig deep into the turf. Still, Joe remained a just-in-case option. Bryant would be dipped in shit before he played that boy.

Then Jackie Gleason, wearing a red carnation, with two blondies in tow, presided over the coin toss. Next thing you knew, Ernie Koy, Texas's 220-pound tailback, started running through the Bama defense, making Bryant's boys look as little as they were. Late in the first quarter, Koy went around end on a sweep, seventy-nine yards for a touchdown. On the Longhorns' next possession, quarterback Jim Hudson—better known as a big-hitting safety on defense—found flanker George Sauer Jr., son of the Jets' personnel man, on a fly pattern down the right side for a sixty-nine-yard score.

With 9:51 left in the first half and Bama already down 14–0, Bryant found himself dipped in shit. The Tide looked badly rattled, having just fumbled a kickoff and taken possession back at its own 13-yard line. But here comes Ole Joe shuffling onto the field, offering a first glimpse of that odd, heavy-legged gait that would identify him for a generation of football fans. The young man was already old in the legs. But wrapped in that cast of tape and bandage was a gift to the network, on this Friday night and for many

Sundays to come: the knee. "It didn't hurt the storyline," says NBC's Chet Simmons.

The Longhorns had not expected Namath to play. But his entrance didn't require a genius to modify the game plan. You got a passing quarterback who can't move, you send everybody after his sorry ass. You blitz the hell out him. And that's just what Texas did.

George Sauer, who also played some defense, recalls rushing at Namath. "Nobody's blocking me," he says. "I've got a clean shot at him. He doesn't even look like he's going to throw the ball. I'm thinking: 'I've got a sack.' Then all of a sudden the ball was gone." Magic. "I never saw anybody release the ball that quick."

Namath hit end Tom Tolleson for fifteen yards. He hit Wayne Cook for fourteen. He hit Ray Perkins twice, for thirty-four yards. Halfback Wayne Trimble also caught two balls, one for eleven and a seven-yarder for a touchdown. The drive lasted 4 minutes and 36 seconds and covered 87 yards, 81 on Namath's passing.

A freaky series of mishaps—blocked kick, fumble, penalty—put Texas in position for another touchdown, making the halftime score 21–7. But then Namath came back to lead a sixty-three-yard drive. He finished with a twenty-yard touchdown pass, threading the ball between two defenders into the hands of Ray Perkins. "Fabulous, fabulous, fabulous," said Weeb Ewbank, from the press box where he was watching this game of beat-the-blitz. "Reminds me of Unitas."

Another Namath drive stalled at the 8, where Bryant elected to kick a field goal that made the score 21–17 with 14:54 left. The Longhorns weren't blitzing anymore. "By this time," wrote Charles Land, "Texas was dropping six and seven men back to cover Namath's receivers."

"How do you stop him?" Texas coach Darrell Royal would ask later. "He makes any pass defense look ordinary."

An Alabama interception gave Namath one more chance at the lead. With two passes, he got the Tide down to the 3-yard line. Then he handed off to fullback Steve Bowman. Once. Twice. Three times. No touchdown. Finally, Namath took it himself. Later, Bryant would claim that he himself had called the play. But it was Namath. Everything about it was Namath. "I thought I saw an opening," he explained after the game. "The time before, we ran 34-over and I could see the linebacker moving. I thought I could make it."

He thought he did make it. Pete Lammons, the Texas linebacker tight end, estimates that Namath was about three fingers—about what a generous bartender might pour—shy of the goal. The officials saw it like Lammons. And everybody else saw it, again and again, on NBC's instant replay.

The rest of the game seems to have been forgotten. Forgotten are some of the balls dropped by Alabama's receivers. Forgotten was Lammons's great evening: two interceptions, a blocked field goal, and a catch that set up Texas's last touchdown. Forgotten were Namath's eighteen completions, then an Orange Bowl record.

The reviews were all raves. From the *New York Times*: "The 72,647 who filled the Orange Bowl Stadium were privileged to witness an exhibition that has hardly been surpassed in artistry, unruffled poise and deadly targetry."

The *Miami Herald*: "The only hero Texas wanted to talk about Friday night was Joe Namath."

The *St. Louis Post-Dispatch*: "Maybe he really is worth $400,000."

Dick Young in the *Daily News*: "The most exciting thing on television since Arthur Godfrey was a boy."

Namath—the first player to be named as an Orange Bowl MVP—didn't pick up his trophy. Instead, he limped to the losers' locker room with Bryant, where the assembled press momentarily suspended deadline work to applaud him. The gesture was lost on Joe; the defeat hurt more than his ravaged knee. But Sonny Werblin couldn't share his pain. In fact, Sonny couldn't have been happier. Victory might be a virtue, but Namath endowed defeat with nobility. His performance was a thing of undeniable beauty, an act of defiance to thrill the millions numbed by all those package deals from *Wagon Train* to *The Munsters*. This was for a generation suckled on canned laughter, for people who confused theme songs with anthems, for whom the ending was already known.

Neither Newton Minow nor Marshall McLuhan could challenge what Joe had accomplished. Any reasonable man would gladly endure the commercials, the bizarre and banal, the American processional that married Snow White and George Wallace, to have seen this show.

Fuck your Vast Wasteland. What Joe had done was *real*.

No, that knee sure didn't hurt the storyline. An Achilles now lived and breathed in your RCA Victor.

Not long after Namath failed at the goal line, someone told Werblin that he now stood to benefit from the greatest ever television pilot. But Sonny, of all people, didn't need to be told that. It was a new year, and here was his new star. As the game ended, Sonny Werblin stood on his seat in the Orange Bowl, screaming: "I'm not paying this kid enough!"

Werblin's resignation from MCA was reported in the January 13, 1965, editions of *Variety* under the headline, "Sonny . . . Just Like in Money":

> . . . the end of an era. . . . Werblin wielded more influence, made more money, made and broke more careers than perhaps any other show biz impresario in New York.
>
> If he was not broadcasting's greatest showman, he certainly qualified as its greatest promoter and salesman.
>
> No one had better contacts, knew more secrets, swapped more information, flew so many airline miles, ate more meals at "21," made more deals or sold so many hundreds of millions of dollars worth of programming.

20. FOUR HUNDRED GRAND

And no one but a select few on either coast knew who Sonny Werblin was. MCA agents—a breed of "discreetly ferocious hustlers," Jimmy Cannon called them—were taught to work in the shadows. Their interest in celebrity was limited to their clients, inasmuch as fame could be redeemed for cash. But now, the world would see Werblin unbound. All the hustles he had learned in thirty-five years at MCA would go into the selling of Joe Namath. Like the agency's biggest clients, Joe would be hyped in accordance with a sublime formula, a cocktail first mixed on old Broadway, equal parts brilliance and bullshit. But Joe was more than just a client. Joe would make Sonny a star.

It began with the $400,000. That couldn't be right, could it? "We don't care to divulge the figures," Sonny had said the morning after the Orange Bowl, "but to my knowledge it is the largest amount ever given to an athlete for his professional services." The dollar amount became a kind of Homeric epithet, obligatory on first reference: *Joe Namath, the $400,000 quarterback . . .* It inspired much debate about the quarterback's worth and the profligacy of his patron. "I'd have gone as high as $800,000," Sonny volunteered. And why not? It would've cost more to buy this kind of attention.

"The $400,000 did a great harm to the sport," proclaimed Art Modell, owner of the NFL champion Cleveland Browns.

"Utterly ridiculous," complained the *Times*'s Arthur Daley. "No untested collegian is worth half that much."

"I guess I'll have to ask for a raise of about $980,000," said the Browns' Frank Ryan, who threw a league-leading twenty-five touchdowns on his way to the NFL championship. "If a fellow who hasn't even pulled on his cleats in pro ball is worth $400,000, then I must be worth a million dollars."

Even the Jets' own quarterbacks were inclined to agree. "It sounds impossible," said Mike Taliaferro, who had just finished his rookie season. "I don't see how anybody coming out of college is worth that much," said the incumbent starter, Dick Wood, who had not one, but two very bad knees.

"If I prove myself, maybe they'll accept me for what I am," Namath responded from Mobile, Alabama, where he had limped off to play in the Senior Bowl. There, in the annual game's first sellout, Namath threw for 246 yards, including a fifty-three-yard bomb to Bob Hayes, a gold-medal Olympic sprinter. "Best passer I have ever seen," said Hayes. "He's worth every penny."

Hayes, Joe's first black receiver since high school, was also of the minority opinion. But he wasn't alone. Dick Young, a columnist who stocked his column with hot info, came out big for Namath. "The guy Sonny targeted and wrapped up completely was Dick Young," says Paul Zimmerman, a young football writer who'd make a name for himself at the *Post*. Indeed, Young's column of January 3, two days after the Orange Bowl, reads as if he had just gotten off the phone with the Jets' impresario: "After a look at Joe Namath in pulsating color, I'm convinced of one thing. The Jets aren't paying him enough. He's a steal at the alleged $400,000, and if Sonny Werblin were decent about it, he'd toss in a membership card in the Playboy Club because Joe is said to have a wholesome interest in bunnies."

Not surprisingly, Sonny was an early, avid promoter of Namath as the embodiment of Hugh Hefner's fantasy lifestyle. When asked about Joe's interests, Sonny would say: "girls and golf, girls and golf." Straitlaced Wellington Mara must have been thrilled. The quarterback he wound up drafting to groom as Tittle's replacement, Michigan's Bob Timberlake, was considering enrolling at Princeton Theological Seminary to study for the ministry.

Timberlake was the fourth player chosen by the Giants that year. The Jets' fourth pick was Bob Schweickert, a back from Virginia Tech. The Jets gave Schweickert $150,000—$50,000 more than Mickey Mantle's 1964 salary, but still $50,000 less than they gave John Huarte. Unlike Namath, Huarte wasn't expected to have much success in the pro ranks. But as a Notre Dame man and winner of the Heisman Trophy, he had cachet. How could Sonny resist? At these prices, how could he pass up another bargain?

■   ■   ■

While Timberlake considered the seminary, and Huarte spoke of attending business school at NYU or Columbia, Namath was a long shot even to graduate from Alabama. It was commonly supposed that the kid would now squander his fortune on Bunnies. Or would he?

The $400,000 was intended to convey the impression that Sonny's money was without end. But Joe's sole extravagance, the only part of the deal to be conspicuously consumed by Namath himself, was the "Jet green" Lincoln convertible. Otherwise, the contract stood in marked contrast to Namath's budding image, the terms laden with a young man's sense of familial responsibility and fiscal foresight, a suitable model for seminarians and business students everywhere. It was a three-year, no-cut, no-trade agreement with a salary of $25,000, and the bulk of the money to be paid in bonuses after the life of the contract ($25,000 was due on May 2, 1968, and $200,000 a year later). Coaches and sportswriters—all of whom spoke with the authority of orthopedists—believed the condition of Namath's knee to be temporary, easily alleviated by surgery. But Namath knew better. He'd be lucky to get four years out of this game. He wanted to be taken care of. But more than that, much more, he wanted to take care of his family.

At the age of twenty-one, Namath had already heard many thousands cheer his name. Fame had shot him up with its first full dose. It would help him grow—big, bigger, huge. But in other ways, Joe remained that little boy perched anxiously at the top of the stairs. The family was his first concern. If he couldn't make it right, he could make it better.

"In college, he started wanting to see his father," says Hoot Owl Hicks, who often accompanied Joe back to Beaver Falls. "He'd get Frank and John and Bobby to go and have a barbecue with the father. I'm telling you, Joe was the one who brought them back together."

And now, the contract that was supposed to finance his apprenticeship as America's playboy prince was, in fact, a windfall for his loved ones. His mother would get a house up in Patterson Heights, where she used to work as a maid. Frank, Bobby, and Rita's husband, Tommy Sims, each received three-year deals worth $30,000 to "scout" for the New York Jets.

All totaled, Namath's deal came to $427,000, a figure that included Mike Bite's $30,000 fee and the green Lincoln, which, for publicity purposes, was valued at $7,000.

Joe's father would always remember that car when it was still new. He had just come home from the mill, dirty and tired. It was a hot day. And there was Joe: washing the Lincoln in his driveway.

"Dad, you look awful," he said. "Your eyes are all sunken in." It had been ten years since his father had taken him to the mill. "Is it hard," he asked, "doing what you're doing?"

John Namath was sipping a gin and Squirt. "Not if you're used to it," he said.

"Why don't you retire right now?" said Joe. "I can take care of you."

■   ■   ■

Y. A. Tittle announced his retirement on January 22, 1965, at a well-attended press conference at Mama Leone's restaurant. Tittle, now thirty-eight, wore a black suit, which seemed appropriate, considering the funereal atmosphere. It was announced that his number would be retired. That, too, was fitting.

In his black high-top cleats and his old shoulder pads—he had worn the same pair since breaking into the pros in 1948—Tittle epitomized the quarterback's virtues. "The greatest passer of our time," said Giants coach Allie Sherman.

But that time was now up. Tittle was no damn good anymore, and worst of all, he knew it. The hits had damaged that which an athlete, particularly a quarterback, needs most: they had finally impaired his capacity for self-deception. He could no longer fool himself; he had nothing left. Still, someone thought to ask Yat, as he was called, if he'd come back for some of that silly money they were paying kids now. "For $400,000" he said, "I'd sweep the floor."

In the end, he'd settle for a monthly pension of $821. He could begin collecting in 1991, when he would be sixty-five. In the meantime, he sat in Leone's and listened to himself being eulogized. He had won championships. He had set records. And he had always played with courage. Yes, Y. A. Tittle was everything a quarterback was supposed to be. Except he was no longer a quarterback.

"This is a moment I have dreaded," he said.

■   ■   ■

Later that same afternoon the sporting press congregated again in the upstairs room at Toots Shor's, 33 West Fifty-second Street. The occasion was intended to introduce Namath to the same people to whom Tittle had just bade farewell.

This wasn't going to be like the first Namath press conference, the morning after the Orange Bowl. Sportswriters saw something almost unseemly about that one, as if it had been produced expressly for television. Joe, who had been critical of his own MVP performance ("Terrible . . . I was just throwing with my arm . . . lucky on a lot of passes"), wore a pink sports jacket and a tie with the Longhorns logo. "If you can't beat 'em . . . ," he quipped. But these were subtleties inevitably lost in televised images. Leo Levine's account in the *Herald Tribune* suggests how ignorant newsmen were of the newfangled apparatus of fame, how it would amplify Namath as it marginalized them: "Five sets of klieg lights, three cameras, various microphones and what have you." Namath was more easily seen from a distance of eighty yards at the Orange Bowl than from twenty feet at the press conference: "The television equipment and cameramen obscured almost everything."

But the afternoon at Shor's would be free of such unpleasantries. This one was for the newspaper guys. "Just a friendly get-together for you to meet Joe," explained Sonny. His choice of Shor's, gin mill for the drinking establishment, was an obvious one, though it suggested that not even Sonny fully understood what he had in Joe.

Shor's eponymous owner hailed from Philadelphia, where, as a Jewish kid in an Irish neighborhood, he acquired a certain pugilistic competence. When he was fourteen, his mother was decapitated in a car accident. Five years later his father committed suicide. Despite his grief and a burgeoning thirst that would eventually consume two bottles of brandy a day (none of Tootsie's good-time pallies ever seemed to link his loss to the liquor), he went to New York and became a great success—first as a speakeasy bouncer, and later as a saloonkeeper.

You never knew who'd walk into Shor's, which is why the press agents liked to sit at the far wall facing the revolving door. The best booths went to the most favored regulars, among them Cardinal Spellman, Joe DiMaggio, Jackie Gleason, and Jimmy Cannon. Shor's was held in the highest esteem by Gotham's most elite fraternities: the Yankees, the football Giants, and writers of the Hearst chain. Sportswriters loved the joint for dinner and drinks after a ball game. Plus, you couldn't beat the laughs. Frank Gifford, another of the owner's favorites, would warmly recall Gleason and Toots as they watched a mound of chopped meat turn gray. There was no limit to the wit, what with those bantering lines offered by Gleason: "Get a load of the fag tie on Toots."

Maybe you had to be there. Maybe you had to be sloshed. "Before the drug culture took over, New York was a booze town," remembered Gifford. "In those days, in that society, Tootsie was a god."

Of course, those days and that society—that *city*—were dying. Werblin still did business in Shor's, as did most of the TV guys. But by 1965 the place had become a parliament of purple-nosed has-beens. The sun was setting on Hearst's New York empire. The *Mirror* had folded, and the *Journal-American* had but another year to live. The Yankee dynasty was over, too. Except for Mantle, the pin-striped heroes had all retired; the Bombers would finish in sixth place that year. The Giants, coming off their last-place finish, were gone, too. That was the final season for Tittle, Alex Webster, and Gifford, who became a broadcaster.

Pete Hamill, then a twenty-nine-year-old columnist at the *Post*, recalls a place filled with "ballplayers who don't play ball and newspapermen who don't have newspapers."

There was something else the guys at Shor's didn't have. The rest of the city, like much of the country, was about to embark on a carnal riot. But Shor's remained outside the action. At Shor's, Mickey Mantle had the same shot as Cardinal Spellman, which is to say, none. You couldn't get laid at Shor's. There were no broads.

And into this lair of squares comes the $400,000 Kid. What to make of him? He says he's from a mill town in Pennsylvania, but he speaks with a rebel drawl. He's supposed to be a football player, but, as one of Sonny's guests noted, there's "a cleft in his chin as handsome as Cary Grant's." He's still a college boy, but in that rocks glass he's holding is a grown man's drink. And that slouch? What's *that*?

The friendly get-together Sonny had promised soon became something else entirely, a mass grilling of a twenty-one-year-old kid. Although it went on for almost two hours, the line of questioning scarcely changed. Was it really $400,000? More? Or less? How much?

Namath was hungry. Before him lay an array of Toots's finest hors d'oeuvres—everything from pigs in blankets to liver wrapped in bacon, the kind of fare that moved Jackie Gleason to order out for pizza. Joe asked the waiter for a ham sandwich.

How much? They were still asking.

The smart move would have been to tell them how much was going to his family. He should have told them about his desire to repay debts, those born of blood and others of money. It felt good to make his family feel good. Besides, he wouldn't see most of the money for a good long time, maybe even until after his career was over. But Joe simply refused to address the subject. There was a principle involved. *His* money was none of *their* damn business.

Finally, toward the end of the affair, the *Times*'s Lou Effrat asked: "Suppose you don't make it? What happens to the money?"

"I'll make it," answered Joe.

"We all just kind of smiled," recalls Dave Anderson, then a young writer covering the Jets for Hearst's *Journal-American*. Anderson was taken not only with what Namath said, but with the way he said it. The etiquette of sports was changing; there was a new beat of braggadocio. Anderson had recently interviewed the new heavyweight champ, Cassius Clay, who was already calling himself the Greatest. But Namath's remark had a different quality altogether. It lacked inflection, any hint of taunting patter. "He wasn't boasting," recalls Anderson. "He just said it."

Joe was only following his father's instructions: Believe you're the best. Then again, such self-confidence wasn't easy to come by, considering the circumstances. Namath had just undergone his first orthopedic examination for the New York Jets. It was conducted by Dr. James Nicholas, an orthopedist who had diagnosed John F. Kennedy with Addison's disease. Nicholas, one of the many owed money by the Titans, stayed on with the Jets, which was fortunate in that he was a pioneer in the field of sports medicine. He got his first look at Namath that day. As the press was arriving, Namath was sitting on the toilet in the Shor's men's room, his pants leg rolled up as Nicholas performed the requisite rotations and tugs. The session didn't take long; a knee this bad wasn't a mystery. "If I had known this before," Nicholas told him, "I would have told Sonny to forget you."

Then the doctor went back upstairs and found Weeb Ewbank. "Hope we've got another quarterback," he said.

Namath was soon booked into a $65-a-night room at Lenox Hill Hospital, the only orthopedic patient in a ward devoted to ear, nose, and throat problems. The Jets didn't want to keep his visit a secret so much as they wanted the illusion of secrecy, something Sonny could auction off to the press as exclusivity. Even if Namath couldn't play a down, Sonny would make sure he got $400,000 worth of ink for that knee. Pro football was full of bad knees, but this was the first that people would care about. The *Daily News* gave the knee front-page treatment. And Time-Life, despite the hospital's misgivings, even managed to get a photographer into the operating room. The knee merited two-thirds of a page in Henry Luce's flagship publication and another four full pages—including photos and diagrams—in *Sports Illustrated*, with a circulation of 1.1 million.

At 6:30 A.M. on a Monday morning, January 25, 1965, a nurse woke Namath with a flashlight. He combed his hair and brushed his teeth, then she shot him up with thiopental sodium.

Sonny and Mike Bite were already pacing and smoking in the waiting room when Dr. Nicholas made the first incision:

21. NOW APPEARING ON BROADWAY: MISTRESS MENISCUS

three inches long, just below and left of the kneecap. There she was: the medial meniscus. Normally, the piece of cartilage looks like a smooth half moon, and serves as a shock absorber between the femur and shinbone. But Namath's had been ripped from its moorings and shredded, a chunk of it lodging in the joint, like a doorjamb, preventing him from straightening his leg. After removing the medial meniscus, or what remained of it, Nicholas then located a damaged ligament, a cord connecting muscle tissue. Joe's had been stretched, spaghetti-like. The surgeon pleated and stitched the ligament to tighten it. Then he made an incision on the knee's outer half to check on the lateral meniscus, which appeared to be fine. Finally, he removed the cyst that had been there, at the back of the knee, for years.

The operation took an hour and thirteen minutes, after which Nicholas appeared in the waiting room and declared the procedure a success. Then again, success is a relative term when it comes to surgery. The twenty-one-year-old quarterback, noted the physician, "has the knees of a seventy-year-old man."

In the recovery room two nurses stood over him, still unconscious. "He's not as good-looking as they say," remarked the first.

The other pulled up his eyelid. "But look at those beautiful eyes," she said.

Finally Namath awoke, with Dr. Nicholas at the foot of his bed. The doctor immediately ordered him to lift the leg and straighten it. Initially, Joe would perform this excruciating raising and straightening ritual 50 times a day, along with 400 contractions of the quadriceps muscle. Later, the doctor would add a weight that dangled from the leg. The regimen was to be completed without exception or regard for the postoperative pain, which was much more intense than the original injury.

"I thought I'd die just from the pain," Namath recalled.

He'd already met the fickle mistress called Fame. Now he was meeting her wicked stepmother, Pain. She, too, would be here for the duration.

"He was all drugged up," recalls Al Hassan, who arrived at the hospital the next day. "I don't even think he knew who was visiting." Hassan would never forget that purplish crescent as it was before drying down into scar tissue: "Ugliest thing I've ever seen." But he never considered the possibility that Joe wouldn't be able to play. Not for a moment. After all, this was Joe.

And fortunately, being Joe, his hospital stay was made bearable by good-looking nurses and many enthusiastic correspondents. Some wrote from Beaver Falls; others, from Alabama, where they were now proud to claim him as their own. He got many requests for autographs and chin straps. The get-well cards covered three walls in Namath's room. These weren't from your average football fans either. The majority were female.

"Most girls are Beatle crazy," wrote one. "But I have gone Joe Namath crazy."

"I have a crush on you."

"I'm writing you in civics class and the teacher just caught me."

"I'm 19 years old, considered quite beautiful, have a marvelous figure and a nice personality. I am hereby inviting you to escort me to the Junior Prom of the University of Texas, all expenses paid. Daddy will fly you down and home in the company plane."

Joe wrote back, declining regretfully. "I already have a date that day."

Upon his release, after twelve days at Lenox Hill, the wires ran a shot of him being sent off by two young nurses. Joe is looking very natty—pocket square, cufflinks, tie—stretched out in the back seat of a limo. There was Sonny's four hundred grand, right there. This was better than Sinatra with the bobby-soxers.

For chrissakes, this was only knee surgery. The kid hadn't even played a game yet.

■   ■   ■

Joe completed his convalescence in Tuscaloosa. He left Paul W. Bryant Hall to live in a house whose boarders included Jimmy Walsh and Ray Abruzzese. Typical was the weekend that Joe and Ray went down to Pensacola while Jimmy the law student stayed behind to study. They returned late on a Sunday afternoon bearing a gift. "A beautiful girl," said Jimmy. "She was wonderful. She stayed for about two weeks."

Christ Vagotis, a guard from Ohio who also lived at the house, recalls other guests. "Some blondes, some brunettes, some redheads, anything you wanted. It was an unusually great time," says Vagotis, who counted himself lucky to be among Joe's running mates. "We didn't want his money. We were his friends."

There were friends. And then there was Jimmy. Vagotis could see the difference: "I know Joe trusted him more than anything else."

While Jimmy studied, Joe partied. By Namath's own account he'd finish fifteen hours short of a degree at the College of Education. Amid the revelry no one seemed too concerned—with the exception of his mother. Rose, always sensitive in matters of education, made Joe promise he'd get his diploma. For the moment, though, he had other priorities. "I don't think he was real serious about getting a degree," says Vagotis. "He was living large."

That spring Freddy Klages, formerly of Ambridge, Pennsylvania, came to town. He was pitching double A ball for Lynchburg in the White Sox organization. "We boogied hard for three days, me and Joe," he says. "I'll never forget riding in that Lincoln with the top down." They were speeding down a four-lane highway in Birmingham, and Klages can still feel the wind and the sun. The cop cars swooped in, converging on the Lincoln. The cops were wearing their mirrored glasses, but Klages could see their expressions change, the glint of recognition. The cops scattered as quickly as they had come. "The Alabama police saw it was Joe behind the wheel," says Klages. "And they just pulled away."

This young man was going places.

■   ■   ■

Sometime that winter, Joe paid a visit to the NBC offices at 30 Rock. Sonny was showing him around and showing him off when they ran into David Kennedy, son of NBA commissioner Walter Kennedy. Werblin took him aside. "I need a favor," he said.

Kennedy, whose career was rising fast under Chet Simmons and Carl Lindemann, was only twenty-four. But he was the kind of kid who'd always done the right thing. He went to Notre Dame. He went to mass. He went to Brooks Brothers. He wore the uniform: blue button-down shirt, gray flannel suit. "Standard issue for the young executive," says Kennedy, who acknowledged his individuality by daring to substitute tasseled loafers for wing tips. Clothes don't make the man, but in his case they reflected certain sensibilities and aspirations, not just Kennedy's, but also those of the middle-class generation into which he was born. "I was the ultimate organization man," he recalls.

"What do you need?" he asked Sonny.

"You're a nice kid, David. I need you to look after him. Show him around town." *Him?* Kennedy would not forget: Joe was wearing a polyester suit of robin's-egg blue with white patent leather shoes.

It was about the craziest thing Kennedy had ever heard. He's thinking: You want *me* to look after *him*?

Kennedy could barely imagine the extra hours this assignment would cost him in the confessional booth.

"Sure thing, Sonny."

Of course, Sonny, being Sonny, covered his bets and put other guys on the case, too. Joe Hirsch had already been looking after Joe. They would go to the track and occasionally double-date. With Hirsch leading the way, Namath saw Tito Puente play the Fontainebleau and Lucky Debonair win the Kentucky Derby. (Joe attended the races in a more subdued houndstooth check.) The two Joes got along so well, Namath figured they might as well room together when he moved to New York that summer. At Namath's suggestion Hirsch found a sublet on Manhattan's Upper East Side: two bedrooms, two bathrooms, and a terrace, for about $300. Rose Namath made drapes—"Jet green, of course," says Hirsch—and matching bathrobes with their initials. They were a good pair, Joe and Joe, though Namath was the immediate beneficiary of their arrangement. Hirsch, then thirty-six, was a polished sophisticate, welcome at the best joints. Joe, meanwhile, was still something of a rube.

He would spit tobacco juice into cups at "21." He would leer at the Bunnies as they got off their shifts at the Playboy Club. He was still a kid, not far removed from the Lower End and Tuscaloosa. He didn't know better. Hirsch had to give him a little class and a guided tour of the town.

Before the Jets' training camp, Hirsch brought Joe to a new rock-and-roll joint called the Rolling Stone and introduced him to a guy named Tad Dowd. Hirsch knew Tad from the track, although he could have known him from a lot of places. Tad got around.

Tad Dowd had grown up in Jersey, where his family owned a cemetery, Graceland Memorial Park. At nineteen, on the cusp of manhood, he came to understand what his father had been telling him for years: "A single drink is one too many and a hundred isn't enough." It was a realization that had escaped so many other Dowds. Tad had a drinking problem, and his ingenuous solution was in substituting addictions: action for booze. Tad had to be near the action. A well-known denizen of clubs and discotheques, he was reputed to be the best dancing white man in New York. He managed the singer Mary Wells and the fighter Oscar Bonavena. That summer he took particular pride in being the one to convince Bonavena to get a Beatles-style haircut. Still, despite his many and varied interests, Tad Dowd did not have a pot to piss in. Most nights he spent on the couch of his mentor, Eddie Jaffe, known as "the Press Agent of Lost Causes." Jaffe got his start feeding lines to Walter Winchell. He got his fame (or something like it) by representing a stable of burlesque talent that included Ann "the Sultan's Daughter" Corio; Lois De Fee, who, at six-foot-six, was the world's tallest stripper; Rosita Royce, whose thirty-nine trained doves undressed her nightly; and Margie Hart, whom Jaffe billed as "the poor man's Garbo." Newspapermen were willing marks for Jaffe's hustle. Who else could have convinced reporters that Zorita the Snake Charmer had fallen hopelessly in love with one of her snakes, or that Rosita's doves had suffered a collective nervous breakdown? As far back as 1955, the *Daily News* had referred to Jaffe as "the last of the old line Broadway press agents." But he evidenced a great talent for survival. A decade later, he was still there, his apartment at 156 West Forty-eighth Street still a haven for undiscovered stars and itinerant hustlers. Among the guests who had availed themselves of Jaffe's couch were Marlon Brando, Julie Newmar, Dorothy Dandridge, and now, Tad Dowd.

"I thought the kid had talent," said Jaffe.

He put it to great use promoting the Rolling Stone, which featured acts like Tom Jones, the Animals, and a kid named Jimi Hendrix. The guy at the door was the light-heavyweight contender Frankie DiPaula, another friend of Tad's. "The lines were around the door," says Dowd. "Everything was just starting then."

And here comes Joe Willie pulling up to the starting line, his engine idling loudly.

"I'd like you to meet my friend," said Hirsch. "He's new in town."

It was clear to Tad that Hirsch wanted to save the guy from the fossils at Shor's. Joe stood out. He was wearing a tie in a rock-and-roll joint, and he was laying that southern accent on heavy.

Tad was happy to help, quickly introducing Namath to the two finest girls in the place. They, too, were just starting out. Before the decade had passed, they would be legends for their beauty, each of them blessed with height, prominent cheekbones, and a kind of glow that men would remember across generations. Winona was the color of caramel; Emeretta was cinnamon. Emeretta was the feistier one. Tad remembers her wearing a fringed western outfit that night.

"Honey," she told Joe, "you better lose that accent."

It may have worked in Alabama, but this was New York. The girls seemed to disappear even before Joe could chuckle. Winona and Emeretta had something to do, someone to see, somewhere. Like the girl said, this was New York.

Joe shook his head sheepishly. "Man," he said, "how do you meet girls here?"

"Throw touchdowns," said Tad. "They'll be lined up out the door."

■   ■   ■

The idea had been to capture Namath at what photographers call "the magic hour," neither day nor dark, but a backlit dusk through which sky and skyline remain distinct. James Drake, a *Sports Illustrated* photographer, had been waiting for a while at the intersection of Broadway and Seventh Avenue. The shoot, conceived by Drake's bosses, owed to both the quarterback's reputation and Sonny's skill at exploiting it. Joe might have been the cover boy, but Sonny was the story. Indeed, "Show-Biz Sonny and His Quest for Stars," written by Robert Boyle for the magazine's July 19, 1965, issue, only deals with Namath (and Huarte, for that matter) as an extension of Sonny's ambition. The piece detailed his history with MCA and his religious devotion to Star Quality. It was Sonny's professional opinion that Joe could make a picture for Universal as easily as play quarterback. Hence the cover, with Namath on Broadway under the headline "Football Goes Show Biz." By then, the Broadway known to veterans like Eddie Jaffe was all but extinct. Palaces once glorified by Runyon and Winchell were becoming decrepit houses of the lowest cinematic genres: splatter, blaxploitation, and porno. Even as the photographer waited for Namath's arrival, the local theaters were showing such classics as *Olga's House of Terror, Nature Camp Diary,* and *Sinners à la Carte.*

But then, the reality of a place didn't matter so much as what that place evoked. Broadway society would die, but the idea of Broadway would endure, alive and well, in perpetuity. Stage, television, movies—it was all the same. Broadway was a state of mind, the mythical capital of American entertainment, a fable conceived by newspapermen, sustained by hustlers, and now tethered to Sonny's prince.

It was a new world, and Sonny was fluent in all its facets: media, myth, and money. The Jets, he claimed, had lost $1.348 million the previous two seasons.

But who was counting? "The NFL couldn't buy shoe polish from most of the owners in the AFL," he said. "Over there you have a bunch of jaded old guys who have been making a million a year on a gross of less than $3 million with no capital investment."

He knew he was scaring the shit out of the NFL. The Jets had sold 35,000 season tickets since signing Namath. That was more than enough for *SI* to want him as a cover boy.

The Broadway shoot itself proved a delicate operation. John Huarte, who had been photographed earlier that day with Werblin and Joe at Shea Stadium, had not been invited. Second, the paparazzi had gotten wind of it, and had to be shooed away every so often. Finally, of most concern, was Namath himself. He was more than an hour late.

He'd get there when he got there, by limo, accompanied by friends from Beaver Falls, Wibby Glover and Larry Patterson. They had come from a big Italian dinner with Joe Hirsch. "The spread," recalls Wibby, "was unbelievable." The good friends, good food, and good spirits conspired to put Joe in a very agreeable mood. The shoot would be easy. Unfortunately, the magic hour had long since passed, and with it, the skyline. The hoped-for effect was blown. So much for the Great White Way. "By the time Joe got there," recalls Drake, "it was totally dark."

The resulting cover featured a grinning quarterback in full uniform, helmet tucked under his arm. Broadway is his background, enveloping Namath in a neon mist, the image almost wet with nocturnal possibility.

"It wasn't supposed to look like that," says Drake. "But it worked."

They were waiting for him in the courtyard at the Peekskill Military Academy, a dilapidated boarding school in upstate New York where the Jets held preseason camp. Some players had gathered under the big oak from which a British spy had been hanged during the Revolutionary War; the linemen were perched on the stone wall. Everyone, it seemed, wanted to clock his arrival, which came at 5:55 P.M., July 14, five minutes before the deadline for players to report. "Don't see why he's so early," groused one of the veterans.

Namath appeared in a small black car driven by a photographer for *Life* magazine. The photographer was working on a profile of the Jets' famous rookie with W. C. Heinz, a renowned magazine writer whose specialty was finding courage in men who played the games of boys. At Heinz's advice, Namath left the Lincoln at home. The writer knew they'd be watching, the linemen most keenly. The biggest guys took home the smallest checks, a fact of which they didn't need a rich kid quarterback to remind them. "Drive up in something more modest," Heinz had told him. "These are the guys who are going to be protecting you."

22. WAMPUM

Joe unpacked, sat through a meeting, and headed for the dining room, where he regarded the meal set before him—a soggy attempt at fried chicken—with a muted combination of amusement and disgust. While nothing could compare with the antebellum splendor of Paul W. Bryant Hall, Peekskill Military Academy (whose students included Sonny's son Hubbard, named after the chairman of Pepsi) was, by any standard, a dump. As Joe would soon discover, the window screens all seemed to be broken or torn, and flies were everywhere. There was no air-conditioning. The springs on the cots were so old that those thin mattresses hung like hammocks. Laundry services were erratic. And of course, the food was slop.

Joe asked Heinz if their interview could resume over a bite somewhere off campus, and they were joined by the *Journal-American*'s Dave Anderson. Joe decided to stop first at a pool hall in a black neighborhood, but it didn't serve food. Finally, they found a place that served pizza. "Shit, man," drawled Namath. "I got news for you, there's going be some changes made."

He was referring to the conditions at Peekskill. A quote like that, coming from the $400,000 kid, would have made a nice nugget of news, and Joe would have found himself at the center of his first media shitstorm. But neither Heinz nor Anderson used it. They decided, with an impulse toward decency and discretion, that Joe just didn't know any better yet, so they cut him a break. Besides, for all his bluster, there was something they really liked about him. You had to get a kick out of this kid. " 'Shit, man,' " recalls Heinz. "That was his expression. Everything was 'Shit, man.' "

Namath insisted on paying for dinner, and they went back to the dorm in time to make curfew. Heinz was sleeping in a second-floor room when he woke up in the middle of the night. He heard a voice—not just any voice, but those rarest of notes in a football camp, the voice of a female. Was she giggling? Was she happy or sad? Heinz does not recall, just that it was female, at a place and time where females were forbidden. But her date sounded like quite the merry lad.

"Shit, man," he drawled, "we gone win *aawwwll* the games."

The kid was off to a great start.

■   ■   ■

Among the humiliations inflicted on Jet rookies was the fight song. First-year players, the most formidable of them still treated as boys, were expected to get up in front of the team and sing to the glory of their alma mater, to their everlasting chagrin. But before Joe could get out the first bar of "Yea, Alabama," his teammates drowned him out with a chorus of "There's No Business Like Show Business."

It was a goof. Sort of. Joe understood the subtext. "I could see where it would be upsetting to them . . . ," he said, "that Broadway Joe thing."

Broadway Joe. The moniker owed as much to a 300-pound tackle named Sherman Plunkett as to the *Sports Illustrated* cover, a copy of which was placed in each player's locker. Plunkett, who liked to spend his nights playing pinochle and feasting, studied Joe as he entered the locker room. "Look at him," said Plunkett, quite amused. "Cat's been out on Broadway all night. You Broadway, Joe. You Broadway. Broadway Joe."

Plunkett's was among Namath's warmest receptions at Peekskill, where most players, like most owners, continued to believe that they were in the football business. While the Jets were still negotiating with Namath, Ewbank had moved to re-sign some of his key veterans. Larry Grantham recalls Ewbank telling him, "We have the rights to this kid from Alabama, and I want you to sign a contract right away to prove that we're going to take care of the veterans." Grantham, whose playing weight hovered around 190, was pound-for-pound the best outside linebacker in the game. Though he lacked size, strength, and speed, he knew how to tackle, and understood the game even better than the coaches. "I had eyes in the back of my head," says Grantham. "I could close my eyes and tell you where all twenty-two players were." An original Titan, Grantham was also a key presence in the locker room, as a leader of three factions: the veterans, the defense, and the southern whites. It was important to keep Grantham happy.

So Weeb, cheap as they come, asked him to name his raise.

"Fifteen hundred," said Grantham, then concluding his fifth consecutive pro-bowl season.

Much to Grantham's surprise, Weeb didn't even bother throwing out a lowball number of his own. Instead, he extended his hand to shake on the deal. "I knew right away I should have asked for more," says Grantham. "If we all waited after Joe had signed we all would have asked for a lot more. But none of us knew he was going to be Broadway Joe."

Later, Ewbank would try to rationalize the $400,000 deal by saying that Namath's *salary* was in line with the rest of the team. But even at $25,000, Joe's paycheck was still a heavy number. With the average AFL player making between $10,000 and $15,000, the coach's argument became as transparent as his players' envy.

The first guy to make a move on Joe was Big Chief Wahoo. Namath's acquisition had left the wrestling Indian feeling unappreciated. In March, he told the *Times* that he had conducted his own informal poll, which revealed that "eight or ten" of his teammates would be asking for raises in the neighborhood of 30 percent. The story appeared under the headline "Wahoo on Warpath for Wampum," with a photo featuring the Jets middle linebacker in feathered headdress and beaded armbands. "The Jets left themselves wide open," he said, "they're going to have to give everybody a big raise." By July, under another "Wampum" headline in the *Journal-American,* Wahoo declared that he would settle for a $5,000 raise, bringing his salary to $20,000. That seemed reasonable. After all, he had been the team's big drawing card. Had been? More like has-been. Big Chief Wahoo would hear Sonny's response in the wind. It was the voice of Billy Goodheart himself, telling Wahoo to go fuck himself. *If you got a leading man, no one's gonna give a shit about a wrestling Indian.*

Quarterbacks often practiced in red jerseys, a sign warning the other employees not to damage the merchandise. But when it came to Joe, Wahoo was color-blind. "He hit him anyway," says Grantham. "He used to give Joe a hard time in practice." Once, when the team was running laps, Wahoo jumped him from behind. The players didn't rush in to get Wahoo off Joe's back.

"The veterans," says Billy Mathis, another original Titan, "they really didn't like him."

But they couldn't ignore the talent, either. "You could see it," says Matt Snell. "Just from the way he threw the ball." Dave Anderson recalls a session early in camp. Namath hadn't been sharp, and Weeb would nitpick. He'd look at a stopwatch and complain that Joe was getting rid of the ball too fast. Or he'd tell him he wasn't following through properly. On this particular day, Namath was long, overthrowing Don Maynard on a fly pattern by at least ten yards. "You don't have to show me your arm," said Weeb. "If you couldn't throw, you wouldn't be here."

Rookie quarterbacks are all arm. Then again, Anderson—who was standing on the field when Namath let fly—had never seen an arm quite like this. "*Nobody* overthrew Maynard," he says.

About a week later, the Jets rookies went to Lowell, Massachusetts, for an exhibition game against the Boston Patriots' rookies. Of Namath's nine completions, five went to George Sauer Jr., son of the Jets general manager. Sauer, whose patterns were already notable for their precision, had played on the Texas team that beat Alabama in the Orange Bowl. Another member of that team was also with the Jets now—Jim Hudson, who threw the sixty-nine-yard touchdown to Sauer in the Orange Bowl. Though none of the twenty-two pro teams had bothered to draft him, the Jets signed him as a free agent. Hudson was six-three, 205 pounds, and hit like a sumbitch. There wasn't a position he couldn't play. Already, people were talking about Hud as the sleeper of training camp.

The Jets rookies beat the Boston rookies, 23–6. It was a good night. As they filed out of the stadium, Namath suggested they stop for beer. He'd buy. He felt like celebrating. After all, the knee, sheathed in a brace of aluminum and elastic, hadn't given him any trouble.

A day or two later, though, it would be hurting enough to keep him from running with the team. The leading man hung his head as the rest of the guys did their laps.

"What's the matter, rookie? You too good to run? Your money weighing you down?"

On July 30, at an intrasquad scrimmage against real men, not rookies, Joe was 13 of 33 with two interceptions. Mike Taliaferro (pronounced "Toliver"), the second-year man, threw for 267 yards and three touchdowns.

The scrimmage didn't do much for Joe's cause, which wouldn't get easier anytime soon. John Huarte had been in Chicago, practicing for the annual game featuring the college all-stars versus the NFL champs, and his return would open up another front in the battle for starting quarterback. In many respects, and to many people, Huarte represented the antidote for Namath. An earnest, aspiring Organization Man, Huarte was given to statements like: "My main interest is to refrain from limiting my future." He even kept his Notre

Dame letter blanket (a subject of some mirth among the players) prominently displayed by his bed. With Joe cast as the leering, swarthy playboy, Huarte became the Great White Hope.

Namath, of course, did nothing to dissuade his doubters among the fans, some of whom were on hand for the practice of August 5. "Wait'll Huarte gets here!" one of them yelled from the stands.

Namath yelled right back at the guy. "Go fuck yourself!"

Larry Fox, the *World-Telegram* beat writer, was walking across the field with Billy Mathis when they heard the exchange. Not only had Namath cursed out a fan, but he did so on some kind of family picnic day. A crowd of kids were gathered alongside a restraining rope, watching the quarterbacks warm up.

"Yeah, you can go ahead and print that, too," said Namath, turning to Fox. "I don't give a fuck."

Fox was well within his rights. The $400,000 contract and the movie star press agentry made Namath fair game. Besides, Fox wasn't exactly eavesdropping. "It was public domain," he says. "There were little kids and mothers there."

Fox went back to the press room and started typing:

Is success spoiling Joe Namath?
     The answer has to be a qualified yes. . . .
     The pressure has been building, building, building, and no matter how rich, glib and famous Namath is, he still has just become old enough to vote.

With his story not yet finished, Fox left for dinner, his copy paper still in the typewriter. Someone on the Jets must have had a look at his piece, because when he returned, the phone wouldn't stop ringing. Bill Hampton, the equipment manager, called. Fox had known Hampton for years, since Hampton had been the stick boy for the New York Rangers hockey team. Now Hampton started telling him that Namath was really a good kid and asked him to kill the story. "Larry didn't go for it," recalls Hampton. "He said, 'I'm a reporter and I have to report it.'" Then Fox got a call from Joe Hirsch, with whom he'd gone to high school. Same request, same answer. He'd get four more calls: the assistant PR man, Frank Ramos; Weeb, Sonny, and finally Joe himself. Fox tried to explain that Namath was now a public figure. This wasn't Beaver Falls, where Joe Tronzo could turn a blind eye. This wasn't Tuscaloosa, where Coach Bryant determined what was fit to print. In New York, where all the papers were fighting for their lives, Namath was news. Joe figured he could live with that. Unlike the guys who had already argued on his behalf, Joe wouldn't beg and plead for Fox to kill the story. Nor would he deny it. He said what he said.

■ ■ ■

The following week, fresh from a promising performance in the college all-star game, Huarte and his Notre Dame letter blanket rejoined the team. And with three quarterbacks bunking together—Joe (who brought his golf clubs), Huarte (who came with a big black attaché case), and Mike Taliaferro (whose portable black-and-white TV represented the proceeds of his signing bonus)— Dave Anderson thought to do a feature on room 31 of the Peekskill Military Academy. In the course of the interviews either Huarte or Taliaferro mentioned, quite casually, that Namath had been classified 1-A for the draft.

Now *that* was news. President Johnson had just announced that the American military presence in Vietnam would rise to 125,000 men, while draft calls would double. "This is war," the president proclaimed. The *Journal-American* ran a banner front-page editorial by William Randolph Hearst Jr.—Anderson's boss many times removed—praising the speech as a Churchillian masterpiece, Johnson's "finest hour." Suddenly, the papers were full of stories about the draft, who was going and who wasn't.

"Why don't you get married?" Anderson asked Namath. "They're not taking married guys."

"I don't even have a steady girlfriend," replied Joe, grinning widely. "I'd rather fight those reds in Vietnam than get married. Too many pretty girls in this world."

The next day's *Journal-American* featured news of Namath's draft status on the front page, just where Hearst's ringing endorsement of the president had been: "400G Jet Rookie Facing Draft."

According to Anderson's story, Namath's draft status had been reclassified to 1-A—the first to be called up—when he left Alabama. Namath said his papers were being transferred from Beaver Falls to a draft board in New York, where his physical would be conducted. Joe wasn't getting married, and he wasn't going to graduate from school, either—another surefire way to score a deferment. Suddenly, the only thing between him and southeast Asia was a bum knee. "If he passes the physical," said a Selective Service official, "his induction would be very imminent."

The day the story ran, Joe posed grim-faced for a photographer, holding a copy of the *Journal-American* to display Anderson's banner exclusive. It was an old trick, getting the celebrity to endorse the story. As for Anderson—a promising newspaperman who'd soon move to the *Times*—he was still trying to get a handle on Namath. The kid who had said so matter-of-factly "I'll make it" at Shor's was also the kid who insisted on paying for dinner. Joe read the story in the press room. Anderson was already working on his follow-up piece, this one concerning Huarte's draft status. ("That's classified information," said the Heisman Trophy winner.) Anderson watched Namath, half expecting him to complain that the whole thing had been blown out of proportion. Instead, after reading the story, he turned to Anderson and said, "I was a phys. ed major at Alabama, not a business major."

As for the Vietnam-before-marriage line, Joe sure wished Anderson hadn't printed that. But again, this was one public figure who knew the deal. Not only had he said these words, they were true. Every word. Joe put down the newspaper. "See you tomorrow," he said.

The draft piece ran on August 11, a lousy day in a trying summer. The way things looked, Namath wouldn't even be the starter for the season opener. Politically, it would be easier for Weeb to go with the veteran, Taliaferro. Besides, to that point, Namath hadn't been overly impressive.

Their next exhibition took the Jets to the Allentown School District Stadium in Allentown, Pennsylvania. The driving rain and muddy field were not ideal conditions for a young quarterback trying to show what he could do. But after calling eight consecutive running plays, Namath threw the bomb. This time, he didn't overthrow Maynard. Instead, he hit him on the dead run, sixty yards for a touchdown. Most remarkable, though, was the ball's perfect trajectory, a path that defied the fierce elements. Anderson would follow Namath's entire career without ever seeing him play on two good legs. Then again, the arm was enough to make you forget about the legs. That arm could stretch the game, rendering conventional probabilities obsolete.

Almost forty years later Anderson says, "I can still see that ball, like an arrow, cutting through the rain like it didn't exist. That was the moment when you knew: this guy was different."

Earlier that same day, Beatles fans rioted outside the Warwick Hotel in New York City, as teenage girls busted through police barricades. Out on the West Coast, Watts was burning. America had entered an absurd season, lacking any sense of boundary. Football was not immune. All that had infected the country seeped into the Peekskill Military Academy: the excesses associated with fame, this war in Vietnam, and race. The Jets were divided along the same lines that separated the rest of the country: young and old, haves and have-nots, black and white.

Tackle Winston Hill, a black Texan, says the team "reflected the racial tone of the country. You had players from different parts expressing different views."

"We had this whole crew from the South," says Snell, "and there was a lot of hatred those guys still held on to."

Black and white didn't come together but to hit one another. You played cards with your own kind; you drank with your own kind. One night, a couple of black rookies made the mistake of walking into a place where Larry Grantham was getting hammered, something he did quite often. "Go find your own bar," he snapped.

"You have to look at my history," explains Grantham. "When you're raised like I was in Mississippi, you don't come to New York and all of a sudden make a one-hundred-and-eighty-degree turn. It wasn't until I was in the pros that I even played against blacks. It took a while."

Grantham had a reputation for great knowledge of the game, and great ignorance on the subject of race: "I tell Larry this to his face," says Snell. "Being from Mississippi and that environment, he was one of the worst offenders."

Among the offenses Snell recalls: "We had a little wide receiver named Alphonzo Lawson. He stuttered. Whenever he started trying to talk, he stuttered. So a bunch of the white guys went to their local pub. They used to put the beer away at night, and this night they talked Al into going with them. . . . The drunker they got, the more they made fun of him, the crueler it became. . . . When they got back to the dormitory, they decided they were going to pull this great big joke on Al. So they all went and got sheets, cut holes in them, and threw them over themselves. . . . I was sleeping and I hear this screaming, and they hung him from one of the light fixtures. They didn't hang him by his neck. Actually, what they did was tie him from underneath his arms and pull him up so it looked like he was hanging.

"He was half shitfaced, but it scared him to death. I hear this tremendous screaming, and get up and go down the hall. They're all running away. They got their sheets and they're laughing like hell."

Snell remembers taking Lawson down and waking up the coaches. "I want to see Sonny," he said.

Lawson, for his part, denies this mock lynching ever took place, and comments, "I don't see why Matt would say that." Lawson agrees that Grantham and Wahoo McDaniel were among the team's worst bigots, but recalls an entirely different incident, one that still causes Grantham to laugh out loud.

"I stuttered," acknowledges Lawson, now a psychologist who specializes in personality disorders and developmental issues. "I didn't talk much. Anyway, I was in the whirlpool and Wahoo came over and said, 'Hey, nigger, I want to have this whirlpool by the time I get back.' That meant I had to get the fuck out. He had his towel around him. He was just strolling around. When he made this announcement, everybody knew what was going on. They were watching what was going down: Larry, Bake Turner, Don Maynard, Sam DeLuca. Then Wahoo came back and he called me a nigger again and I reached under his towel and grabbed a whole handful of his testicles and squeezed on them and I said to him, 'As long as you got a hole in your ass, don't you ever call me nigger.' "

Lawson didn't make the team, but he won a measure of respect, anyway. Werblin came out to Peekskill to address the entire team. "I was very impressed with Sonny," says Lawson.

As Snell remembers: "Sonny said, 'The only two people who are essential to this team are Joe and Matt, and the rest of you can pack up and leave.' "

■   ■   ■

One final team meeting remained, just before the start of the season. No Sonny. No coaches. Just players. As it came to an end, Mike Hudock, an original Titan who started at center, asked if anybody had anything else on his mind.

Now it was Joe's turn to speak. He told the guys that he knew some of them didn't like him. He didn't like them right back. He told them to judge him on how he played, not what he made. If anyone had any problems with that, he should step up right now. If you want to take care of it outside, then let's go.

"A lot of guys were shocked that the so-called pretty boy would say that," says Snell. "Like: maybe he was tougher than they thought."

"I thought he could handle himself," says Grantham.

The offer hung there. *Anyone want to take it outside? You want to make a move, now's the time. How about you, Injun Wahoo, you want to go?* Nope. *Anyone else?* This wasn't show business. Shit, man, this was for real.

Unlike the counterfeit machismo used to produce so many showbiz myths, Broadway Joe wasn't a lie. The image was merely an amplification of the young man: his virtues, his faults, his peacock vanity—though none of those tricky feelings that made his stomach ache. The press barely let a day pass without mention of his hair, which was shaggy only by the standards of the game he played. "I can't see why, just because I'm a football player, that I have to wear my hair a certain way or be a different type of person than I really am," he said.

The expectations for football players, in both grooming and conduct, were almost military. And why not? Football was America's military sport, a theatrical union of violence and regimentation. But Namath—or at least the Broadway Joe version—refused to be regimented. He was still the boy who attended St. Mary's, the boy who was different, and those qualities first discerned by girls in grade school now delighted young women in the big city. "I love them all," Namath declared from Peekskill. "A filly with brown hair is all right. So is one with black hair. But blondes, they come first."

23. SALTED APPLES

This announced preference for blondes was something new, and it couldn't have pleased Bebe Schreiber. Blond was the hue for a distinctly American genus of female, full of sugars and artificial color, starlets and bombshells, star-spangled floozies descended from Harlow. Blond was Fame's easiest color. Bebe had hung in this long, but now she would lose him, finally and forever. "I was still dating Joe when he was with the Jets," she recalls. "He was getting on with a new life and enjoying it to the hilt. New York City rolled out the red carpet for him. It was strange for me to be with him. Tuscaloosa was one thing, but New York. . . . That kind of public attention was not something that was agreeable to me. That's where the road forked."

It was there that Joe Namath, the guy she loved, became Broadway Joe, the guy everybody loved. As Bebe says, "It was not a great ending."

■ ■ ■

That September, when Namath reported for duty at Shea Stadium, a gift was waiting in his locker: white football shoes, courtesy of Bill Hampton, the Jets' equipment manager. Before arriving at camp, Namath had explained that his shoes were to be laced right over left, and wound with tape until they looked white. "He was superstitious," says Hampton. And as Hampton had forty-seven other uniforms to maintain, he envisioned this taping business becoming a big pain in the ass. "I was looking to save me a problem," he says. So he called a guy at Magnus, a company that made football cleats. "I'd like you to make a pair of shoes in white."

"Are you crazy?" asks the guy.

"No, it's for Namath."

"We'll make 'em."

Magnus made them; Joe wore them, a flagrant violation of the game's military aesthetic. White shoes? After Y. A. Tittle had all but sanctified black high-tops, Joe Willie Whiteshoes seemed a harbinger of the apocalypse. Barry Skolnick, a bar owner who became friendly with Namath and sat near Joe's father at home games, recalls the first couple of years at Shea: "I used to feel bad for the guy. Everybody was yelling that Joe was a fag because he wore white shoes. The fans were pretty rough on him."

It didn't make sense to Joe, people getting themselves all worked up, as if his shoes represented a larger issue. Then again, perhaps they did. "For me to change at that point would be punking out, man," said Namath. "I don't punk out."

"I didn't know I was going to make history," says Hampton, the equipment man.

What was denounced as a pretty boy's vanity instead became a sign of his toughness. Namath had made himself a target, but he refused to tremble. "So what?" he said. "You wear black. I'll wear white." He was the only one who did. From the beginning, Joe was separate and more equal than his teammates. The cluster of cameramen and reporters in the locker room was a telltale sign of his presence. Even if he had wanted to, Joe could never be one of the guys. Hell, he came with his own guys. As the season began, the Jets acquired Ray Abruzzese, who had just been released by the Bills. The Jets might not have needed another defensive back, but their star could always use an additional "babysitter," a term Abruzzese himself would use from time to time. Abruzzese quickly moved in with Namath and Hirsch.

"I think everybody understood why Ray was on the team," says Matt Snell. "Put it this way: if Joe wasn't his best friend, Ray would have had a hard time sticking on the team. He was borderline. But he was Joe's confidant, his *goombah,* his whatever you want to call it."

Call it what it was; they were friends. Friends do for friends, and as roster spots were precious, Joe did for Ray. But the veterans, who saw their own friends cut and traded every year, considered Ray Abruzzese in the same terms as the Lincoln Continental and the white shoes. To them, he was another token of the special treatment afforded this Broadway Joe character.

■   ■   ■

Shortly after 6 A.M., September 15, 1965, the streets of the Upper East Side were still dark. But Joe, a notorious late sleeper, was already awake, looking wearily into the bathroom mirror. "Just think," he said, "if I was in the army, I'd be getting up this early all the time." Namath had spent the previous night studying the playbook with Ray and Al Atkinson, a rookie linebacker out of Villanova. Now, where was his draft notice? He looked through the stacks of paper detailing pass coverages and blocking schemes. He searched through a pile of fan mail. The notice was not to be found. Shit, man. He grabbed his sunglasses, two apples, a salt shaker, and finally a cab.

"A salt shaker?" he was asked.

"I always eat apples that way."

At 7:20 A.M. the cab pulled up in front of the Armed Services Induction Center at 39 Whitehall Street in Lower Manhattan. A gaggle of photographers and newsmen were waiting as Joe emerged with the apple in his mouth. Cameras started to click and pop. "Sacrificial boar," wrote the *Herald Tribune*'s Leo Levine, who had observed Namath so well throughout that morning. "The only thing that was missing was a plate."

That's not to say Namath was a willing sacrifice, as he refused, somewhat adamantly, the photographers' request to remove his dark sunglasses. As a result, the shot that moved on the wires became a stunning visual distillation of the Broadway Joe essence. Even as his audition for Vietnam begins, the apple is planted in his mouth. He looks like a French movie star with American muscles. It's not at all difficult to divine his thoughts, as if they were a bubble of comic book dialogue: "Fuck y'all. I'm getting my bite of the apple. Tastes good, too."

In the midst of the crush, someone handed him a protest leaflet: "What the War Is All About."

When he got to the door, a sergeant instructed him to throw it away.

"The apple?" asked Joe.

"The piece of paper," said the sergeant.

Namath walked into the waiting room, the media men still in tow. Other prospective inductees started buzzing. *Whozat? Namath? Who? The kid. The quarterback. You know, the one what got 400 G's.*

Joe put the salt shaker back in his pocket. Then a colonel came out and told the photographers to get lost. The ensuing examinations took more than four hours. He was seen by two orthopedists. Still, no decision was made.

On October 8 the knee was examined again. In contrast to their usual policy regarding anything Namath, the Jets didn't notify the press. Unlike most second exams for draft-eligible men, it was not conducted at the Naval Hospital in St. Alban's, but at Harkness Pavilion, part of the Columbia-Presbyterian Medical Center, by Dr. Frank E. Stinchfield, director of orthopedic surgery for the College of Physicians and Surgeons of Columbia University. Neither the army nor the doctor made any announcement regarding their conclusions. Nor did the Jets.

It would be another month before the army—no doubt concerned about a general public whose impressions were formed in that moment when the flashbulbs popped the sunglassed star biting down on the apple—circulated a statement among congressmen:

> It may seem illogical that an individual who is physically active in civilian athletics should be found unfit for military service. . . .
>
> When playing professional football, it must be presumed that Mr. Namath does so with the counsel and preparation of doctors and trainers. He is closely watched and professional assistance is close at hand at every game and practice session.
>
> In the military service, these conditions would not necessarily be present. In Vietnam, for example, the life and safety of his comrades could depend on Namath performing his duties under extremely adverse conditions.

According to the Pentagon, the doctors were unanimous: "There was no question that the knee condition made Mr. Namath unfit for military service."

Namath's case caused *Times* columnist Arthur Daley to invoke the case of Johnny Podres, who pitched for the Brooklyn Dodgers. He was classified 4-F for the Korean War. Then he won the seventh game of the 1955 World Series and was suddenly reclassified 1-A. "I blame it on gutless draft boards, gutless politicians, and gutless baseball writers," said Ted Williams, the great hitter who flew combat missions in both World War II and the Korean War. "The draft board leaves him alone until he gets famous and then gives him the works. It's a disgrace."

Before it was over, the entire Vietnam draft would abound in disgrace. Rich kids went to college. Poor kids—those from America's various Lower Ends—went to war. Joe's oldest brother, Sonny—a career soldier who had fought in Korea—would also serve in Vietnam. Namath had no *political* objections to being drafted. Joe would've done his hitch, too, though not gladly. "How can I win, man?" he said of the army's decision. "If I say I'm glad, I'm a traitor, and if I say I'm sorry, I'm a fool."

Turned out that things hadn't changed much since Johnny Podres's time.

Fame gives, and she takes away. There were more than a thousand professional football players, but one didn't hear much about their draft status, as they didn't drive Lincolns or wear white shoes or do backstage photo ops with Barbra Streisand (Sonny was pissed that Joe hadn't worn a tie).

At least his bad knee was finally good for something. Joe would never complain about the knee. Shit, man, if it wasn't for that knee he would've probably gotten his ass shot off in Vietnam.

On January 20, 1966, about six weeks after the army alerted congressmen as to Namath's draft status, Representative Paul Rogers (D–Fort Lauderdale) entered a constituent's letter into the record. It was written by a junior high school principal whose son was in Vietnam despite cartilage and ligament injuries suffered while playing high school football. The principal's son, a five-foot-seven-inch soldier who walked with a limp, had already engaged in hand-to-hand combat with the Vietcong.

"I would like to know why there is no menial duty that can be given to physical weaklings such as Joe Namath . . . so the physical giants such as my son can be freed to fight our country's battles," wrote the principal, who called the quarterback's rejection "the most asinine action of the year."

The House Armed Services Committee promptly elected to investigate procedures that resulted in the rejection of famous athletes.

Soon, the heavyweight champ would have his draft status suddenly reclassified to 1-A. "Why me?" bellowed Cassius Clay, aka Muhammad Ali.

By then, Joe Namath had been voted the AFL's reigning Rookie of the Year and the most valuable player in its All-Star game.

■　　■　　■

Despite the 98-degree temperature, the 1965 season had begun with 52,680 fans passing through the turnstiles at Houston's Rice Stadium. No doubt the AFL's new opening-day attendance record owed much to fans eager to see Namath's debut. But Namath never got off the bench. Mike Taliaferro, the second-year man from Illinois, presided over a sloppy, sweat-drenched 27–11 loss. Namath didn't beef about it. Before the season had even started, he said, "If I had to pick a quarterback for this team, I'd pick Mike." This wasn't false modesty, for he had come to see that the game moved much faster than it had in college. Namath wasn't the only gifted player anymore; it seemed as if everyone had been an All-American. The pros were also more intelligent about the game. You could see it in the Jets' own locker room: Larry Grantham would be huddled with a bunch of guys at halftime, smoking cigarettes and making defensive adjustments. Suddenly, Joe wasn't the only guy with an aptitude for the angles. He found himself questioning that which had been second nature, basics like timing and footwork. He had to relearn the game, and it wasn't much fun.

After the game, as the team bus idled outside Rice Stadium, Namath's teammates were somewhat amused to see a woman scream at him for not signing autographs. Joe was usually pretty good about these requests, but now he just tried to smile, red-faced, and looked away. Why the hell would anyone want the benchwarmer's autograph?

The following week saw another record-breaking crowd at Shea, 53,658 for the home opener. All those fans chanting "We want Joe!" didn't do much to boost the confidence of Taliaferro, who was woefully inexperienced himself. About six minutes into the second quarter, with Taliaferro 4 of 12 for 24 yards, Ewbank finally called on Namath, who entered the game amid great applause. He was 11 for 23 that day for 121 yards. He threw his first touchdown, a dart to Maynard. But the Jets still lost to the Kansas City Chiefs, 14–10. A week later, in his first start, Namath gave some notice as to his real abilities against the Buffalo Bills, the defending AFL champs. In a duel with Bills quarterback Jack Kemp, the rookie threw forty times in a desperate game of catch-up against the league's best defense. He'd finish with two touchdowns, 287 yards, and heaps of praise. But Joe, who always measured his performance against some imaginary "perfect game," saw nothing worthy of tribute. He'd thrown two interceptions in a 33–21 loss. "I made a lot of mistakes," was his judgment.

Mistakes were the stock-in-trade of young quarterbacks, of which the Jets still had three. Unfortunately for John Huarte, that Notre Dame letter blanket bestowed no particular qualification as a professional quarterback. Huarte didn't play a down that season, his last with the Jets. "I can't complain," he says now. "I was paid."

By contrast, Taliaferro had a powerful pro arm, which some thought as strong, if not stronger, than Joe's. "Mike could throw the ball," says Snell. "But Mike didn't have any touch. He threw a ten-yard pass the same speed as he threw a twenty-five-yard pass."

Through the first two months of the season neither Namath nor Taliaferro had established himself as the clear-cut starter. Then on November 7, with winds gusting through Kansas City's Municipal Stadium, Ewbank devised a game plan that called for short passes. But Taliaferro, with that great arm, kept throwing, as Larry Fox recalled, "one bomb after another . . . as if compelled by some private desperation."

The Jets were only down 10–6 at the half. Taliaferro was 9 of 17 with two interceptions. He was also finished as the Jets starter. At that moment, the Jets were 1–5–1. In eight weeks Namath had been on the losing end of more football games than he had in all the seasons since his junior year at Beaver Falls. Now, as the second half began, he put together a touchdown drive that won the game. The defense didn't allow another point. The second half effectively inaugurated a second season. Namath was now the starter. Taliaferro's strong arm would be of no use to the Jets, unless, as he later remarked, Namath hurt himself "falling off a barstool."

Instead he followed the Kansas City win with another over the Patriots in Boston. Ewbank could see the poise with which the kid handled the blitz. Namath called for the backs to stay back and block, leaving Maynard time to run long routes against a single outmatched defender. Twice Namath hit Maynard for touchdowns. "He recognized the defenses," said Ewbank, who was particularly impressed by Namath's use of Snell, whom the Patriots keyed on, as a blocking back for Billy Mathis, whom they did not.

The Jets won 30–20, and Namath got a hip pointer for his efforts. Back at the apartment, he asked Joe Hirsch for something to relieve the pain. "Whatever tastes the worst," he said. Hirsch poured him a glass of scotch, Johnnie Walker Red, as Namath remembers: "It did taste terrible, but it made the pain go away." In fact, it worked as well as the high-proof medicinal beverage his mother once rubbed on his gums.

The Boston win was a minor feat compared to that of the following week when, in a fuller display of Namath's talents, the Jets beat Houston 41–14. The rookie understood that his ability to pass depended on the team's ability to run. Snell ran for 135 yards, and Mathis 126, while Joe threw four touchdowns, including another two to Maynard. Again, the secret to quarterbacking wasn't in the arm, but in the head.

"He called a tremendous game," said Ewbank. "He made the right decisions. In that game he became a man."

"I'm checking off more plays now at the line of scrimmage," said Namath. "Maybe a third of the time I'll change the play there because the defense isn't what was expected. I think I'm calling the plays better. Each play has to have a purpose."

Improvisational skill at the line of scrimmage is a quality that would distinguish his entire career. He had a natural feel for calling audibles, refined through careful study. Namath was spending between two and three hours a day—after practice—brainstorming with coaches and watching game films. Most nights, he'd take the films home with him. Of course, this dedication to his craft was a subtlety lost on the television audience. Most people were just getting used to Namath, their impressions still being refracted through an NBC lens. The camera didn't stop following him, as it would other ballplayers, just because the play was dead. Rather, it stayed with him, even on the sideline. There was Joe warming up. There was Joe blowing a bubble. There was Joe, with blackout makeup under his eyes, talking on the phone line to the assistant coaches in the press box. There was Joe, with trainers kneeling before him, checking out that knee. Wherever the cameras placed your eyes, there was Joe. He was the first football player to be seen without his helmet, the first guy to be given a face, an identity apart from his regiment.

"We isolated the cameras on him all the time," says NBC's Chet Simmons. "Everything we could do, however we could do it, instant replay, whatever. He was the guy we were going to highlight. The lead story was going to be Joe."

■   ■   ■

That December, as the Jets caught a flight to Oakland, Namath ran into Mickey Mantle, and the two went off to have a drink in the airport lounge. Other players regarded this meeting of the two stars with some envy.

"Lot of green stamps in there," said one, referring to their healthy salaries.

But Mickey and Joe were linked by more than money. Mantle, the son of an Oklahoma lead miner, had been a stud, too, an extraordinary physical specimen. But he'd been hobbling around on ruined knees for a while now. He didn't belong to the TV generation. He was thirty-four. He was married with kids, and bound by all the conventions of appearance that applied to men who played for the New York Yankees.

What a lucky kid he must have seen in Joe. Unlike the Mick, who had his own considerable passions for booze and broads, Joe could indulge himself without having to sneak around. He was young, still at the beginning. He could be seen drinking at the bar. He could be seen with the ladies. He didn't have to look over his shoulder. He didn't have to pretend he was something he wasn't. He didn't have to lie. Joe could let his hair touch his damn ears if he wanted. Goddamn, that must've felt great.

■   ■   ■

Then again, Mantle never had to play the Oakland Raiders. Coach Al Davis, who first scouted Namath as an assistant for Sid Gillman's Chargers, fashioned his team after its buccaneer logo. They were marauders and outcasts—none more so than defensive end Ben Davidson. At six-eight, 275 pounds, Davidson had been among the biggest NFL rejects. But under Davis, he re-created himself as an abuser of quarterbacks. He wasn't the best, but with his red handlebar mustache, Big Ben was easily the most noticeable.

The Raiders had a simple game plan for Namath and the Jets. "We figured if we could intimidate him, we could intimidate the team," says Davidson, who was enthusiastically joined by fellow linemen Dan Birdwell and Ike Lassiter as they endeavored to beat the shit out of the $400,000 rookie. "They have no class at all," Namath would say after the game, a 24–14 loss for the Jets. "I take it every week and I don't cry. As long as it's straight I don't mind."

But this wasn't straight. They hit him late, and they hit him low. Davidson was the worst offender. Namath spoke obliquely about the big man trying to hurt him in a pile of bodies. From the press box it looked as if Davidson had given Joe's head a good twist in the thick mud at Frank Youell Stadium.

"Just trying to do my job," Davidson said cheerfully after the game. "I don't know what he's complaining about. He's getting paid enough."

Namath—who threw for 280 yards, two TDs, and three interceptions that day—wasn't specific as to the manner of Raider abuse. But years later, Dr. Nicholas spoke about it with football writer Paul Zimmerman. "Did you know that he nearly died in Oakland once?" asked Nicholas. "It was the last game in Frank Youell Field, and they had no grass there, and the mud used to get a foot thick. They tackled Joe and pushed his face in the mud, and he gasped and swallowed some of it.

"He was choking and he lost consciousness. I had to reach down his throat and pull the mud out. If the mud cakes down there, he could die."

But Namath was not to be deterred by a near-death experience. "He was loopy for a couple of series and then he went back in," said Nicholas.

Ben Davidson could kiss his ass, which had been kicked a lot harder by Frank Namath. Leave the game? Not in this life. He wouldn't give Davidson the satisfaction. Not then. Not ever.

■   ■   ■

After their dismal start the Jets finished yet another season at 5–8–1. For all the hype, one could argue that the "Go Go Jets," as the 1965 team was advertised, were in a holding pattern. But that missed the point. Chuck Knox had now completed the foundation of what would soon become a superb offensive line. Don Maynard, who seemed to catch nothing but boos in the first half of the season, finished with 68 catches for 1,218 yards and 14 touchdowns, tying for the league lead. On defense the Jets were buoyed by Hudson and Atkinson—a painfully shy, God-fearing, baby-faced rookie whose vicious hitting made Wahoo expendable—and Verlon Biggs. At six-four, 275 pounds, all of it muscle, Biggs was a prototype for a new, athletic defensive end. Back at Peekskill, his sculpted physique prompted Dr. Nicholas to ask if he lifted weights. "No, Doc, nothing like that," said Biggs. "I just live." In body and spirit, the Jets defensive ends were opposites. Gerry Philbin, who relied on sheer ferocity, once said of Biggs: "If I was that big, people would have to pay me to let them live."

Biggs might have been a candidate for the top rookie honor if not for his teammate. Despite his limited action, Namath finished as the AFL's third-leading passer with 2,220 yards, with 18 touchdowns and 15 interceptions, and became the first quarterback in either league to be named a Rookie of the Year. A professional quarterback takes years to develop. Namath was still learning to play a game he had already changed.

As a measure of that change, consider the first week of December, 1965. The Jets were practicing in Los Angeles, where they stayed between the San Diego and Oakland games. Namath's 4-F classification had just become the subject of debate in Congress. "It was a beautiful, sunny afternoon, and all of a sudden you see a powder-blue Cadillac convertible drive out onto the field, top down," recalled John Schmitt, then a $9,500 backup center. "And out comes Mamie Van Doren."

She wore white boots, very short shorts, and a sweater. "Unbuttoned down to *here*," said Schmitt. "You could see everything that she had."

The abundant gifts that made Miss Van Doren a star of such classics as *Vice Raid, Sex Kittens Go to College,* and *Guns, Girls and Gangsters* were now on display for the New York Jets football club. "It was probably the most disorganized practice we had all week, because you couldn't concentrate," said Schmitt. "Even the coaches were watching her." They were only human. Mamie, on the other hand, was a kind of bombshell goddess. She wasn't just *blond.* Her hair was the color of light. Mamie Van Doren was a gift from Fame herself.

At the end of practice, players ran their laps, all except Joe. His knee hurt. Instead, still in uniform, he proceeded directly to Mamie and her powder-blue top-down Caddy.

The coaches started waving good-bye, like envious fathers watching their sons leave on dates. "Have a good time, Joe. See you tomorrow."

As the Cadillac churned dust, one imagines them murmuring a variation on a phrase middle-aged men were then wont to say. "How you like them salted apples?"

In the summer of '65, Giants coach Allie Sherman was re-signed to a ten-year deal worth an estimated $500,000. It was a lot of money, but Sherman had put a lot of years into the Mara family business. After joining the club as an assistant in 1949, Sherman became personnel director, offensive coordinator, and in 1961, head coach. Since then, his teams had made it to the championship game three times. The ten-year contract was Wellington Mara's idea. His brother Jack, the team president, had just died of cancer, and Wellington—who assumed Jack's responsibilities in addition to his own—wanted to ensure the franchise's long-term stability. The agreement was also an attempt to recall the most halcyon period of the House of Mara. "Football," he said, "is not a hobby to us."

Mara's was an obvious reference to Werblin and all the white-shoed harm he threatened to inflict on the game. He still refused to acknowledge the Jets owner, much less the $400,000 mascot. His fellow NFL owners, however, didn't share Wellington's reticence. Yet even as they decried Sonny and Joe for vandalizing the economic foundation of *their* sport, they were moving to cut another kind of deal. That spring, Werblin disclosed that several NFL owners had been calling around, floating the idea of a peace accord between the leagues.

These calls were unofficial and surreptitious. The NFL guys came on very nice. But their good manners were a sign of fear. Implicit in their overtures was an acknowledgment that the good old days were irretrievable.

The real meaning of Namath's contract was something the Maras could not bring themselves to fathom. Far from being profligate, it paid immediate dividends. The Jets sold 2,500 season tickets the week it was announced, an amount that would more than cover Namath's first-year salary. But that was just the beginning. Though most of the contract wasn't due for years, the season ticket money kept rolling in. With Namath's arrival, attendance at Shea averaged almost 60,000—better than most NFL teams.

Then there was the TV subsidy. The NBC bankroll wasn't about to dry up

24. NO GUARANTEES

anytime soon. True, some AFL owners were indeed losing money, but Sonny had been right on that count, too: Most of the NFL guys couldn't buy shoe polish from them. In 1960 H. L. Hunt learned that his son Lamar had lost a half-million dollars in his inaugural season. "At that rate," said H. L., "he can't last much past the year 2135 A.D."

The old man wasn't kidding, and neither was the AFL. Mickey Mouse football—as the NFL called it—was here to stay. The problem was, this continued competition for college kids—none of whom had Namath's box-office potential—wasn't good for anyone's business. In 1966 Texas linebacker Tommy Nobis signed a reported $600,000 deal with the NFL's Atlanta Falcons. Vince Lombardi, coach and general manager of the Green Bay Packers, committed about a million dollars on a couple of rookie running backs, fullback Jim Grabowski and halfback Donny Anderson. With the bidding getting too rich for most owners' blood, Lamar Hunt and Dallas Cowboys general manager Tex Schramm met secretly on April 6 under a statue of the Texas Ranger at Love Field.

The next day, in a move that was unrelated but long expected, AFL commissioner Joe Foss resigned. The Congressional Medal of Honor winner was replaced by Al Davis. The former Raiders coach won the job with a strong recommendation from team owner Wayne Valley and the blessing of Sonny Werblin (who had been working behind the scenes to hasten Foss's departure). Like most football coaches, Davis could speak in a southern dialect if need be. But at thirty-six, with sideburns and the remnants of a pompadour, he preferred to cultivate his reputation as a street fighter from his native Brooklyn, a characterization that few AFL coaches would dispute. Guys like Ben Davidson were players after Davis's own heart. He'd do anything for an edge. For years, teams visiting Oakland were convinced that Davis had bugged their locker room.

By May the discussion between Hunt and Schramm had evolved into an actual negotiation regarding a merger. Then the Giants announced that they had signed a soccer-style kicker named Pete Gogolak, who had played out his option with the Buffalo Bills. In the AFL's seven-year existence, this situation had never arisen. No matter how many dirty tricks were used in the procurement of college kids, a gentlemen's agreement between the leagues prohibited them from going after each other's veterans. Mara, so bound by his sense of honor and tradition, wouldn't normally have been one to violate such an agreement. But these were extraordinary circumstances. With Hunt and Schramm getting closer to a deal, the Gogolak signing was seen as Mara's desperate attempt to scotch the merger. He didn't want to play in a league with those Mickey Mouse teams, and he didn't want to share a city—especially not with a team with that silly white-shoed quarterback whose name he would not mention.

"It was a declaration of war," Davis told Bob Curran, author of *The $400,000 Quarterback,* a history of the AFL. "We had to do what the generals do in a war. Go after the supply lines. Hit the enemy where it hurts most."

"The NFL had struck a blow and we reacted," said Al LoCasale, a Chargers assistant who became Davis's consigliere. "They had taken a shot using a revolver, and Al shot back using a machine gun."

Davis wasted no time requesting contacts and phone numbers for NFL players. He wanted to know whose contracts were up when. Don Klosterman, a veteran front-office man with the Chargers and the Chiefs, was dispatched to make his way around the country and acquire NFL talent. The plan was to go after their stars, their quarterbacks. The Raiders signed Roman Gabriel of the Los Angeles Rams. John Brodie, of the San Francisco 49ers, signed with the Oilers for a reported $1 million. Meanwhile, Werblin pursued a couple of Lombardi's defensive stars.

It didn't take long before the NFL cried uncle. On June 8 it was announced that the leagues would merge by 1970. By January there would be a common draft and an interleague championship game. Pete Rozelle would serve as the commissioner of this expanded version of the NFL. There was one final point. The AFL would pay an $18 million indemnity to the teams that would now have to share their territories. Ten million would go to the Giants, and the rest to the 49ers. The settlement left three very unhappy people.

"Munich," said the Jets president, invoking Neville Chamberlain's appeasement of Adolf Hitler. Werblin also likened the deal, somewhat more accurately, to Gimbel's paying Macy's. For Sonny, it came down to money: "Why should we pay them any?"

"Why should we give in?" Wellington Mara asked in turn. "We never had it so good." The Giants were less concerned with the $10 million windfall than they were with the prospect of competition from the Jets. Mara was so worried about Werblin's outfit that he seemed oblivious to the state of his team, which was about to embark on a worst-ever 1–12–1 season despite the services of his new kicker.

For his part, Al Davis was livid. He won the war, only to be sold out in the peace. What, he should go to work for Rozelle? Not in this lifetime. He wouldn't even attend the press conference announcing the merger. Instead, he made plans to return to the Raiders as an owner. His team would prosper, and he'd be a pain in Rozelle's ass for the rest of his days. Now that was a happy ending.

In fact, all the old AFL teams would eventually do well in the new configuration. One wouldn't have known it at the time, but in due course they would all earn their full share of money and respect. There were a lot of reasons for this. But in retrospect, Davis found one better than others.

"Namath made us," he said.

■   ■   ■

The AFL's reigning rookie of the year, though surprised that the merger had happened so soon, said he'd look forward to that interleague "title game"— even if it was a contest that most people couldn't take seriously. Still, for a guy who figured so heavily (if symbolically) in the negotiations, Namath wasn't overjoyed with their outcome. You didn't have to be a hustler to see the owners' angle. "Large contracts will be harder to come by for everybody without competition between the leagues," he noted.

Namath had spent the winter in Florida, which was to become his primary off-season residence. He lived at the swanky Palm Bay Club, not far from Sonny's place on Golden Beach. Joe loved Florida. The sun and all it touched, especially the girls (Eastern Airlines stewardesses all got their wings in Miami), were a kind of antidote for a childhood spent amid black snow. From Florida, he went to Tuscaloosa, where he stayed in a two-bedroom apartment with a plastic Virgin Mary atop the TV. He liked to get ready for the season in Alabama.

That July, he reported to Peekskill with his significant other, an Irish setter named Fancy Pharaoh. Physically, Namath felt very good, although "good" was already a relative term when it came to appraising his health. He was already suffering from bursitis in the left knee, probably the result of overcompensating. It wasn't unusual for his left knee to feel worse than the surgically repaired right one, which had to be taped and braced before he even stepped onto the field.

"I'm not the player I was," he said. "But it's enough to win."

Namath was missing more than a medial meniscus. Like most twenty-three-year-olds, he lacked a sense of irony. That summer, watching Mickey Mantle hit an opposite-field home run, Joe would remark: "Just think how much better he would be with two good legs."

Just think: this was the same kid, his reputation for drinking and carousing now fully established, who sought an obedience school for Pharaoh. The dog didn't do much to endear Namath to his teammates, some of whom still considered him the owner's pet. There happened to be a prohibition against pets at training camp. The subject came up at a team meeting.

"What about Namath's dog?" asked a veteran of the defensive line.

"That's different," said Weeb, thinking fast. "That's our mascot."

Fancy Pharaoh never quite caught on as a symbol of team unity. Rather, as the clubhouse kids learned, he came to represent something else entirely. "We were told to keep a really close eye on that dog," says Kevin Barry, an academy student who worked as a ball boy during training camp. "Some of the veterans would throw rocks at it."

There were two codes of behavior on the New York Jets: one for Joe and one for everybody else. Though not all the Jets subscribed to Sonny's star system, it was a universally held belief in Birmingham, where they traveled that August for an exhibition against the Houston Oilers. Joe was front-page news in the local papers. Stores were selling $9.95 Joe Namath football shoes and $10.95 Joe Namath football helmets. The town was full of signs advertising places where the game would be shown on closed circuit television: "See Joe." *Joe.* The Jets might as well have been his backup singers. But it was Joe—and only Joe—who drew 57,205 fans to an exhibition between a couple of faraway teams from the American Football League. Birmingham was a big party, and the guest of honor would drink to that, thank you very much.

"Namath stumbled into a quarterback meeting the night before the game drunk off his ass," Art Donovan, a former Colts tackle who worked with the Jets, recalls in his autobiography. "Walt Michaels, then an assistant coach, wanted to kill him. As Michaels began to rise from his chair, he said to me, 'Look at that sonofabitch. I'll nail his ass.' But I pulled him back into his seat and told him, 'You better not unless you want to get fired.' Throughout the entire meeting Weeb wouldn't even look at his starting quarterback, he was so pissed." Stories of Namath drinking on duty, like the debate these stories engendered, would follow him throughout his career with the Jets. "But what the hell," concluded Donovan, himself known as a hell-raiser. "The kid was the franchise."

And the franchise's fortunes were greatly imperiled when, thirteen minutes into the game with Houston, Matt Snell took a handoff for no-gain to the Oilers' 23-yard line. Later, Snell would say he heard a referee whistle the play dead and gave up the ball. The Oilers' Ernie Ladd, however, thought it might be a fumble. He picked up the ball, and after a moment's deliberation, began running the other way. Ladd, a 315-pound tackle, was among the few defensive linemen who had shown Namath mercy and even admiration. "I would never want to hurt him," he had said the year before. "He has so much natural ability, it's unbelievable." Still, between the white lines, compassion was in short supply. As Ladd turned upfield, the Oilers' Don Floyd, a 245-pound defensive end, put a block on Namath, who nevertheless managed to make the tackle. Ladd suffered less than his tackler. Namath had to be helped off the field.

"He was frightened to death," said Dr. Nicholas, who quickly conducted a locker-room examination of the right knee. "I really had to convince him it was just a minor strain and that he'd be all right by the Boston exhibition."

Boston was September 1. As it happened, Namath wouldn't be ready for that game. He wasn't even expected to play in the season opener in Miami against the Dolphins, the AFL's newest team. Short of surgery, there was no way to determine the extent of the damage. It was left to Namath to determine when, or if, he could play. That would remain the case through the season. Often, Namath couldn't decide if he could play until the morning of the game. By now, Joe had an impressive grasp of the medical terms associated with his orthopedic maladies. Still, he preferred to frame his own diagnosis in layman's terms: "Man, my knee's completely fucked up. As far as I'm concerned, it's ruined for life. I couldn't play anything but quarterback."

■   ■   ■

Thanks in large measure to Broadway Joe, quarterback is the most glamorous position in American sports. Perhaps it is also the most ridiculed. For years, defensive linemen have derided quarterbacks as pretty boys. In fact, the good quarterback must be a good bit tougher than his pursuers. He knows he will be hit, and knows that the hit will be administered by men much larger and stronger than he. Often, it comes from the blind side. Those are the worst; the hits you don't see are the hits from which you don't get up. But unlike players at any other position, the quarterback has no recourse. He cannot defend himself. He never gets a chance to hit back. Rather, he is measured by his composure in the face of violence. He is simply expected to take it.

And this was more true of Namath than the others. As he became the game's most famous quarterback, he also became its most vulnerable. "Joe liked to call those patterns that took a while to develop," says George Sauer. "He'd already made the decision: He would take the hit to make the completion." But unlike the new breed of scramblers, Joe couldn't run from trouble. He couldn't dance or dodge. There wasn't anything he could do but take it. Taking it artfully became his art.

Athletes are artists whose skills perish with age. But again, Joe's was an extreme case. Broadway Joe might have been a symbol of youth, but Joe Namath grew old while still very young. "I can't do the things I used to," he said that summer, already a fatalist at twenty-three. Mickey Mantle might've had his problems running after a baseball, but Mantle's great years were behind him. Joe was only at the beginning of his career. Each hit he took could be his last. He knew it; the guys hitting him knew it.

He was trying to elude time as much as he was any tackler. Namath could take shots, but only so many. With no means of escape, he had only one recourse, a single, slightly masochistic form of revenge. He had to keep getting up. This was best done with a smile. Don't let them know. That was the heart of this hustle.

■   ■   ■

In anticipation of Namath's sophomore debut, NBC elected to air the Jets' season opener against the Miami Dolphins on a Friday night, nationally broadcast in living color between *The Huntley-Brinkley Report* and *The Man from U.N.C.L.E.* Unfortunately, the game was not fit for prime time. The Jets began with Mike Taliaferro at quarterback. By the time Namath came on to relieve him in the third quarter, Taliaferro had already missed 13 of 17 passes. After a month off, Namath—still hobbling on his "wrenched knee," as the papers were calling it—wasn't much better. One of his jump passes was intercepted and returned twenty-seven yards for a touchdown. Another team might have beaten the Jets that night. But the Dolphins, 16-point underdogs, were an expansion team playing in only their second game. The Jets' eventual victory owed a great debt to Johnny Sample, a big trash-talking defensive back who had played for Ewbank in Baltimore and made two interceptions that night. Still, the evening was considerably less than the network hoped for when it preempted the first twenty minutes of *The Man from U.N.C.L.E.*

If only the NBC gang could have waited a week. The next game was a rematch: Namath versus Houston, the team that damaged his knee in Birmingham. The Oilers had a great defense, having already held Denver without a first down and the Raiders without a point. The crowd at Shea—54,681—established an AFL record for opening-day attendance. Bookmakers saw the game as "a betting tossup," according to the *Times.* Of course, Namath saw it differently. This time, just five weeks removed from his injury in Birmingham, he threw for five touchdowns to four receivers: Sauer (sixty-seven yards), Snell (twenty-five), Maynard (fifty-five and thirty-seven), and a thirteen-yarder to Pete Lammons, the rookie tight end who had played so well for Texas in the '65 Orange Bowl. Lammons wasn't the Jets' only promising rookie. Emerson Boozer, an abundantly talented sixth-round pick from Maryland Eastern Shore, ran for a thirty-nine-yard touchdown after sliding off four would-be tacklers on a draw play. The only thing Boozer couldn't do yet was block. But his teammates, particularly Matt Snell, would fix that.

"We worked on it every day, every day, during practice and after practice," says Boozer. "In college I didn't have to worry about blocking. If we ran forty plays, I carried the ball thirty of them. But the Jets were a passing team. I had to block."

You couldn't play for the Jets if you couldn't block. "The whole point was to protect Joe at all costs," says Snell.

The Jets couldn't run sweeps like Vince Lombardi's Green Bay Packers, but they were well schooled in pass-blocking techniques, and the backs knew how to pick up blitzing defenders. Namath benefited greatly from those who came before him. Sherman Plunkett was more than big; he was a fine protector of quarterbacks. Dick Wood, the starting quarterback before Namath, had two ruined knees. "He wouldn't get on the plane unless Sherman had already boarded," says Chuck Knox. Together, Knox and Plunkett trained the man who became responsible for Namath's blind side, left tackle Winston Hill. "They were the ones who told me I could play," says Hill, who arrived in 1963 with everything but confidence. "I had already been released from Baltimore. I was an offensive tackle trying to take Sherman's job, and it didn't faze him. He would spend time with me after practice. I remember once, I had a lousy day and I was the first one off the field. And Sherman Plunkett called me back and embarrassed me in front of everybody and said, 'Get back there. You know you didn't do anything all day.' We started step by step, making corrections." With the Jets, Hill had to relearn the position. "In college," he recalls, "everything was three yards and a cloud of dust." That was blocking for the run. Pass-blocking was different, less crude. Defensive linemen could play in a rage. But pass-blocking required a more even temperament. Against all instinct, the offensive lineman can't charge. You begin by giving ground. "It's a matter of technique," says Hill.

And the Jets' technique was a little different. Most pass blockers were then taught to keep their fists against their chests. "The defensive man would put his hands on your arms and it was like he had you by the wing," says Knox. "You could not protect the passer that way, not against a modern pass rush."

So Knox instructed his linemen to extend their arms, and keep their hands open. It was a trick he had learned as an assistant at Kentucky, and was not, strictly interpreted by the rulebook, a legal move. But if the lineman kept his arms parallel, inside the confines of the defensive man's body, officials tended not to call it. Soon, they stopped calling it altogether. "It caught on because it's the best way to protect the quarterback," says Knox.

In addition to gifted athletes like Hill—a tennis player of some renown in high school—the Jets had players like John Schmitt and Dave Herman, in whom technique was fortified with an unnaturally intense desire. In 1964, Schmitt's rookie year, an encounter with Ernie Ladd had left his knee all but destroyed. He wasn't expected to return. Then again, as an undrafted lineman out of tiny Hofstra on Long Island—no one's idea of a football school—he should never have made the team. By 1966 Schmitt was the Jets' starting center, a position he would hold for many years. As for Herman, he came from a renowned football school, Michigan State. But as a twenty-seventh-round pick, Haystack, as he came to be called, was not forecast for great things. His talents were not easily discerned. He wasn't particularly big, and didn't have the grace or balance of a Winston Hill. But intensity is a talent, too—and no one played with more than Herman. "In his early days as a pro," wrote Larry Fox, who had been covering the team since 1961, "his claim to fame was the number of helmets he broke—yes, broke—lunging headlong into enemy players."

"The mix was perfect," Knox says of his former charges. "They had a special job to do. They knew Joe Namath was going to make the difference, and we had to be able to protect him. All our guys felt like that."

There were still other techniques available when Knox's repertoire failed. "It was just kind of understood that if a guy started beating you—grab him and tackle him," said Randy Rasmussen, who joined the line the following year. "You couldn't let him get to Joe. Take fifteen yards, but don't let him get Joe. It was just a thing you picked up. You felt it."

In Schmitt's ten seasons with the Jets, he was often asked if they blocked better for Namath than their other quarterbacks. "Absolutely not," he would say. But the game films reveal a different story. "When you look at the film, yeah, we do block better for Joe than we block for anybody else," said Schmitt. "If you had to bite a guy in the gonads to take him down, you'd take him down before you'd let him get to Joseph."

Not only did these linemen relinquish their resentment of Joe, he became their cause. They were unlike their quarterback in every way: superior in size, opposite in temperament. There are no stars on the offensive line. But Joe made them special. In this kingdom, they became elite troops, royal bodyguards posted at the palace gates. Their bond with the quarterback, and the fellowship among themselves, intensified in proportion with their opponents' determination to down Namath. The Raiders weren't alone in that respect. Most teams agreed: the best tactic was to knock his gimpy ass into a state of submission. The Broncos went so far as to codify the strategy with a locker room sign: "Get Namath."

The linemen took that kind of thing personally. As it happened, Namath passed the ball 471 times that season, more than any quarterback in either league. Taliaferro threw another 41 passes. But the Jets allowed only 9 sacks, then a record in either league. Namath took his share of hits; all quarterbacks do. But he wasn't sacked for a loss until the seventh game of the season.

"That offensive line played as well as any offensive line could play," says Knox. "It was a very special group."

■   ■   ■

The rematch with the Oilers was held on October 16 in Houston. The Jets were 4½-point favorites. With four wins and a tie, they were off to the best start in the team's brief history. But the second-year quarterback, always good for a thrill of some kind, remained enigmatic. There seemed to be two Namaths, and sometimes they would show up for the same game. Against Boston, for example, he was intercepted three times as the Patriots took a 24–7 lead going into the final quarter. The fans at Fenway Park were jeering him wildly as Namath theatrically cupped his hand to his ear, an invitation for more. Then he went to work, throwing 14 completions for 205 yards in less than a quarter. A tie never seemed so dramatic.

Unfortunately, there was nothing he could salvage against Houston. Namath threw four interceptions, and the Jets were shut out, 24–0. Late in the game Ernie Ladd put him down hard. "I thought about staying down," he said later, "but I heard them yelling and I wasn't going to lay there."

Getting up was all the satisfaction he would get out of that day. As the players dressed, one of the assistants started complaining about guys "drinking and running around." Earlier in the week, Billy Mathis had thrown a party at his apartment, and Namath didn't look very sharp at the next day's practice. That didn't discourage him from further nocturnal forays. On Thursday, he accommodated a magazine writer with a late-supper interview over martinis. Then he met up with jockey Bill Hartack, a friend of Joe Hirsch's better known as the pugnacious winner of four Kentucky Derbys. Namath and Hartack had a late date with a couple of hot sisters, and Joe wound up spending the latter part of the evening, and a good bit of the following morning, shuffling between the Pussy Cat and the Copa. By his own account he got in about five A.M. He partied the next night, too. Then he got some sleep and boarded the team flight to Houston, which he seemed to enjoy, puffing away on Salems while ogling the stews. Namath had last been seen at the hotel bar with a cute blondie on his arm. But now, after the loss, all this talk about drinking and running around pissed him off. "This isn't high school," he said.

The reporters wanted to know about the interceptions.

What was to know? It was a bad day.

Yeah, but what *happened*?

Now what the fuck kind of question was that? They got beat. *He* got beat. He'd just had his worst day as a pro. Ernie Ladd had been pressing him into the dirt. Everything hurt. It was all plain to anybody who had bothered to watch the game. Now these guys want to know *what happened*? Joe knew just what was happening. Earlier that week *Sports Illustrated* had come out with a cover story about him staying out all night. Actually, the story was about more than his late hours and dating habits, but that's all anyone would remember. You could never trust these sportswriters. They didn't really want to know what happened; they wanted more booze and broads.

"I wasn't up to the game," Namath snapped. "We didn't prepare. We were out all night carousing, getting drunk."

There, that good enough for you fuckers? Where was Joe Tronzo when you needed him? Namath had begun to dislike the disheveled squadron of heralds who seemed to follow him everywhere. What he said and how it read in the papers were not necessarily the same. Still, in this instance, the press treated his remarks with great discretion. His easily misconstrued diatribe didn't appear in the *Times* or the *News*. It did run in the *World Journal Tribune,* but only with reporter Dave Eisenberg's astute disclaimer: "He lashed out with the fury of a loser who hates himself more than anyone else in the world. . . . Namath sounded as if the reporters wanted a sensational headline, and in his anger about losing he would oblige by going a step further in what he said than did *Sports Illustrated* in this week's cover story."

Joe's anger was short-lived. There was plenty of beer and liquor on the flight home, as the players celebrated tight end Dee Mackey's thirty-second birthday. The kid quarterback led the celebration, wishing everyone well over the plane's intercom. Not long after that, he cramped up. It was his "good" leg this time, the one with bursitis. Joe got up to walk it off and found himself leaning on a magazine writer, John Skow.

"I'm so racked up," he said. "This is the first time in my life I've ever thought about quitting football."

"You serious?" asked Skow.

"Yeah."

"You want that in the magazine?"

"I don't give a damn."

■ ■ ■

Namath didn't throw an interception the following week. Instead, as if his purpose were to gall those trash-talking bullies on the Raiders line, he ran for two touchdowns, a bootleg, and a sneak. Still, that wasn't enough. The Raiders rallied and won on a touchdown with two seconds left. A fan doused Namath with coffee as he walked off the field.

Namath was 19 for 32 that day, 272 yards. The defense gave up 17 points in the final quarter. But it was the quarterback who assumed the blame. "I didn't get enough points," he said, asking the press not to take his words out of context. "I'm not worth a damn."

The next week, Namath's self-esteem took another blow when he threw five interceptions against Buffalo. The Bills defensive line had established a pool, $10 a man, with the proceeds going to the guy who dropped Namath for the biggest loss. The winner was Ron McDole, a 250-pound defensive end who sacked Namath for a fifteen-yard loss in the third quarter. "When McDole arose," noted Dave Anderson, now writing for the *Times,* "he went around shaking his teammates' hands with the enthusiasm of a man who had broken the bank at Monte Carlo."

It was the only sack of the day. Namath immediately got up and hit Sauer with a twenty-nine-yarder. Two plays later, he lofted a beautiful ball for Lammons, a thirty-four-yard touchdown. Stick that in your winner's pot. But the damage was already done. As McDole noted after the game, "Quite a few times we hit him just as he passed."

"We go after Namath more than any other quarterback," admitted Tom Day, the Bills' other defensive end. "He has a quicker release than anybody in pro ball." That included the great Johnny Unitas. "He's far better than Unitas was at the same stage of his career."

Namath wasn't flattered by the comparison, even after throwing for 343 yards. "Just great," he said. "How about those five interceptions? Maybe they're a record, too."

In fact, even with great protection, Joe was throwing more interceptions than anyone in the league. The booing at Shea grew louder. Namath claimed not to care. And perhaps that was the best explanation.

The interceptions were due to a number of factors. There were the occasional broken patterns and bobbled balls. There was the pain in both knees. It was hard enough taking steps and getting in and out of cars, much less playing ball. Inexperience accounted for some of his problem. He was still twenty-three, still learning the position, and for all his gifts, he hadn't been a professional quarterback long enough to be authentically proficient. But more than all that was Namath's peculiar temperament. He still played as he partied, lacking a sense of moderation. "How do I know," he had said, gesturing to his Lincoln, "that all of this won't end tomorrow? It could, you know. It really could." He was young, rich, outrageously talented, and acutely aware that everything could be taken away in a moment. There were no guarantees. In the meantime, he might as well let it fly. Fuck it. Give the people what they want: booze, broads, and bombs. The bomb. No one threw the long ball like Joe Willie. He would challenge anyone with that arm. Frank Cicatiello, who followed Joe closely, observed as much: "A lot of times he was intercepted just because he thought he could beat everybody."

The interceptions reflected a young man's arrogance, some of which he would never shed. Namath played with the instinct of a gambler and the fatalism of one who believes he has nothing to lose. He led the league that season with twenty-seven interceptions, including another five in the rematch against Oakland.

Again, Namath had dared the Raiders by running against them. This time, he set up a touchdown with a thirty-nine-yard dash on a muddy field, disregarding Weeb's frantic exhortations to get out of bounds. "When a quarterback runs," Weeb liked to say, "finally he doesn't get up." In Namath's case, though, *finally* could come at any moment. Watching him, there was always a sense that the next run, the next hit, the next play, could be his last. The Jets came away with a tie that day, as Namath hit George Sauer for a two-point conversion in the game's final minute. After the five interceptions, they were lucky to get that much. But the game also eliminated their once-strong playoff hopes.

The Jets had gone to Houston in mid-October as a first-place team, with four wins, but they'd only prevail in another two games. The first was against the woeful Miami Dolphins. Namath needed a pain-killing shot in his "good" knee just days before the game. The other win came in the season finale against Boston. He was feeling no pain for that one, either.

It was December 17, 1966. Boston had a lot riding on the contest. A win would put the Patriots in the championship game and give each player a chance at a $6,000 bonus. The Jets, whatever the outcome, would finish in second place.

"We were out all night," says Frank Cicatiello, who was visiting. "I mean, *all* night." Joe went from drinking B & B to Sambuca to Grand Marnier. For a while, he was with a girl named Patty.

"I remember calling home, Youngstown, and speaking with my buddy, Mikey," says Cicatiello. "He said Boston was favored by seven or ten. I said, 'You got to give the points.' He says, 'Why?' I say, 'We're not home yet.' It's like six-thirty in the morning.

"We went from one place to another. Ray was already waiting when we got home. I don't know how Joe played that game. I don't see how he even got dressed to play. I'll guarantee you he don't remember the first half."

Namath didn't throw an interception that day. At twenty-three, at the peak of his recuperative powers, in that twilight between sobriety and intoxication was an unbothered state, a higher, almost meditative consciousness. He connected on 14 of 21 passes, his highest percentage all season. He threw for 287 yards and three touchdowns. There was no stopping the Jet offense on such a day, not with Boozer and Snell each running for more than 120 yards. The Jets won 38–28.

Namath likes to say there was nothing at stake against Boston that day. But in fact, everything was at stake. Namath had a pretty good idea what was about to happen. For all he knew, the Boston game might have been his last. In a few days, he'd be going back to Lenox Hill. The "minor strain" that Dr. Nicholas diagnosed back in Birmingham was really more torn cartilage, and would have to be removed. Namath had already spoken with the *News*'s Dick Young, whose loyalty to the Werblin regime had been rewarded with a gig as a radio commentator on Jets games.

"I want to have it done," said Joe.

Young figured he wanted to be a complete football player again.

"I'll never be that," said Namath. "I just want it to be better than it is."

Young tried to get Joe to set the odds. There was a chance that an operation could provide some relief. But there was another chance that he'd never play again.

"They can't guarantee a thing," said Namath.

It could all end tomorrow. And if that was the case, you might as well get drunk, have a good time.

Namath could live with the surgery. He could live with the risk. What really pissed him off, though, were the reporters who called him in Beaver Falls just before Christmas. The club was confirming Young's story. This seemed to upset Joe more than the booze and broads stuff. This hurt his only true girl. "I'm damn mad," he said. "I asked them not to say anything until after Christmas so my mother wouldn't worry."

■   ■   ■

The second operation was considerably more complicated than the first. Once again, loose bodies of crumbled cartilage were removed. But this time a piece of tendon was transferred from the back of his leg to the patella region to provide Namath with greater rotational stability in the joint. In terms of publicity, this surgery wasn't exploited as the first one had been. By now, everybody knew Broadway Joe. What other ballplayer would show up for surgery with a beatnik goatee? There was no need for heavy-duty press agentry. Nor was there any need for his mother, or anyone else, to worry. "We expect Joe to be much better for four or five or six years," said a team spokesman. The operation was a huge success. At least, that's what it said in big bold type on the back page of the *Daily News*.

It was October, an autumn for all that Jimmy Cannon held dear. A quarter of a century had passed since Joe DiMaggio's hitting streak, and fifteen years since Joe Louis's last fight. The athletes Cannon commemorated as avatars of the strong, silent virtues were no longer athletes. Like him, they were on the far side of middle age.

Cannon was fifty-six. His column now appeared in something called the *World Journal Tribune.* Nicknamed "the Widget," it was a hastily assembled combination formed from the remains of the *Journal-American,* the *World-Telegram and Sun,* and the *Herald Tribune.* Those papers, like so much of Cannon's New York, had been rendered obsolete or extinct in this age of television. The Widget itself only had a few more months to live.

25. BOOZE AND BROADS

Today, October 17, 1966, Jimmy Cannon was scheduled to interview Joe Namath. If it were his call, they probably would've met at Shor's. But it wasn't his call, was it? The kid had only been here two years, but already he was as big as Mickey Mantle, which was to say, bigger than anyone else in town. Namath wanted to meet at a joint on Forty-ninth off Second. They ought to call this kid Second Avenue Joe. Broadway Joe? Kee-rist. What would Runyon have said? Runyon was Cannon's rabbi in the newspaper business. Then again, Runyon had been dead twenty years.

The sky was a flash of periwinkle—"Garish dusk," as Cannon would describe it. The joint was called the Pussycat. The short, sweet-faced girl at the hat check was called JoJo, and her boyfriend, a corpulent Lucchese gangster, was known as Mr. Gribs. His real name was Carmine Tramunti. He was treated with great respect in the Pussycat, as was another wiseguy, Tommy (Tea Balls) Mancuso. But none of that concerned the old sportswriter or the young quarterback. Joe was much more interested in the Chinese food, spare ribs with duck sauce and mustard and pork fried rice. The Pussycat aspired to be like Jilly's with a younger crowd. The girls were a good draw. The dancers from the Copa ate for free. The Bunnies from the Playboy Club were on scholarship, too. Namath liked the girls even better than the pork fried rice.

The bartender was setting up for cocktail hour. They didn't have bartenders like this in Cannon's day. Her name was Linda. The way she was dressed reminded Cannon of a bathing suit with stockings. He was a long way from Shor's.

Though Cannon wouldn't know it, Namath disliked Shor's. Al Hassan had begged Joe to take him there, so they went with his brother Frank. Big disappointment: Toots talking loud, stirring his drink with his finger. Who needed the place? The food was lousy, and the famous owner—who thought himself hilarious for spilling a drink on Mike Bite—was just a common slob. Namath could have overlooked that much, but not the fact that there weren't any broads.

Now, at the Pussycat, Namath ordered a beer.

Cannon, who hadn't had a drink in years, was obliged to give the kid his due. "This guy doesn't try to duck it," he would write. "He knew what I intended to interview him about. This is where he chose to meet me. It was as though he would be a phoney if he had steered me to a squarer place."

The meeting had been occasioned by Namath's performance in Houston the day before. The issue wasn't the four interceptions, but the bitterly facetious remarks about booze and broads that required clarification. The partying, Namath declared, had nothing to do with the defeat. "Why don't they accept we just got beat?" he asked.

Namath insisted he'd never do anything to jeopardize his career. He studied the game. He got his sleep. "I'm not going to let having a good time affect my physical status," he said. "The way some people put it, they got me an alcoholic."

Namath tapped his beer glass with his thumb, as if to remind the columnist that this had all been caused by the insidious politics of appearance, the gossip that fills the gaps between reputation and reality. Cannon gladly took Joe at his word. Then again, there was a reason ballplayers weren't supposed to hang out in places like the Pussycat.

"I'm no hypocrite," said Namath. "I don't hide anything."

That was a curious concept for a man of Cannon's generation, for whom subterfuge was an accepted practice, especially for a star ballplayer dealing with the rigors of public life. Shor's, and all the places like it, were men's clubs. Booze was the sacrament. But broads were something different. Broads were mostly a secret vice. How many times had DiMaggio borrowed the keys to Cannon's room at the Edison Hotel? In public, DiMaggio appeared regal and expressionless. He considered fame an irritant, an embarrassment. Fame was a bright beam in his eyes. But when the lights went down, the Dago came alive. In the shadows, DiMagg was a world-class humper.

Joe Louis was another one who epitomized the wordsmith's notion of wordless grace. Louis would die before running at the mouth like that Cassius Clay. It was Cannon who framed the idea of Louis's universal dignity: "Yes, he's a credit to his race, the human race." But the maintenance of such dignity was a burden. For Louis, the price of fame remained a secret—just like all the tea he smoked to ease his mind.

And now this Namath had the balls to sit there with a beer and proclaim: I have nothing to hide.

He resided in a penthouse with a llama-skin rug that looked like dry ice—or so all the magazines said. There was an oval-shaped bed with a mirror suspended above. Who'd have thought Cannon would live to see a football player living like a space-age pimp? Still, unlike these other creatures of television—Clay and the unspeakable Howard Cosell—Cannon couldn't help but like the kid.

"He doesn't have to sneak around," he wrote. "He goes where the action is."

Even as he sat there with his beer, Namath posed the question: Was something a vice if you didn't have to lie about it? Or was the real sin, as Cannon might have put it, phoniness?

In Namath, one saw fame without fear. In the men's clubs Cannon inhabited, booze was an end in itself. But in Joe's New York, booze and the broads ran together, everything from the same spigot.

How many years had it been since Cannon himself had had a drink? Aww, who was counting? Linda the barmaid was some kind of pussycat. Cannon would know. He used to go with Joan Blondell, the movie actress. But that, too, was long ago.

As garish dusk gave way to another moist night, the old sportswriter had to be wondering: What was it like to be a prince of this new city? What was it like to be Broadway Joe of Second Avenue?

■   ■   ■

Booze and broads were similar opiates, administered differently. They eased the pain. They eased the nerves. Where there had been an arthritic vise or a knot in the gut, they left a spray of endorphins. Booze and broads were to be taken liberally and casually, for medication and recreation. "I drink for the same reason I keep company with girls," Namath once said. "It makes me feel good. It takes away the tension." Tad Dowd, who didn't drink, came up with a name for Namath's girls: "tension easers." Namath, to his later chagrin, had started calling them foxes.

First among Joe's foxes was the wondrously named Suzie Storm. One of the magazine writers assigned to profile Joe that season described her as "a rock-'n'-roll chickie." But that doesn't begin to do her justice. She was a navy brat from Pensacola, still in college, majoring in French. She enjoyed museums as much as she did bars. Suzie Storm was the pure drug, uncut: slim but ample-chested, with straight blond hair. She was southern groovy, and she could sing her ass off. "I don't know where she got it from," says Dowd, who was still managing Mary Wells. "But that voice was like the white woman's answer to Tina Turner."

Eventually, Joe would talk of marrying Suzie Storm. But such talk was still a few years away, for he was too busy sampling the many and varied gifts bestowed upon him at night. "I don't like to date so much as I just like to kind of, you know, run into somethin', man," Namath told Dan Jenkins, a *Sports Illustrated* writer who would go on to further elucidate the nexus between football, booze, and broads in his blockbuster novel *Semi-Tough.*

Broadway Joe couldn't help but run into something. The girls were just *there*—at the Open End, where the pimps hung out; at the western-motifed Dudes 'N Dolls, where they worked as teepee dancers; at Mr. Laff's and the Pussycat and the Cheetah and Small's Paradise up in Harlem. Namath made the same connection as his father, finding something almost patriotic in the pursuit of pussy. "Seems almost un-American to me for a bachelor not to go around having a drink with a lady now and then," he once said through his signature grin, part put-on, part leer.

The rube from Alabama had learned fast. By '66 Joe knew his way through the Manhattan night. Tad Dowd recalls bouncing around town with Namath and Tom Jones, another of his pals. They were leaving a place called the Phone Booth. Tad was trailing the Namath entourage when he spied that famous duo, Emeretta and Winona, looking as good as ever. But they were already comfortably ensconced at a table with Mick Jagger and the Stones. "C'mon, girls, let's go," said Tad, gleefully waving his stogie. "We're having a party at Joe's place."

Winona and Emeretta promptly picked up their purses and followed him out the door. "What were they going to say?" asks Tad. "You want to be with Jagger and the Stones? Or you want to be with Joe Namath?"

The quarterback or the skinny English kids? It wasn't much of a choice. An invitation to Joe's place was not to be passed up.

"I was a healthy young American boy," he said.

There was Darryl Shane, the most beautiful girl dancing in the Copa line. There was Francine Lefrak, who made her debut in polite society that December, at a disco, wearing a paper gown, with none other than Andy Warhol in attendance. Her dates with Joe, she once said, "usually amounted to drinking until six in the morning." And don't forget Carol Doda, proud owner of America's most famously augmented 44D's, the trailblazer credited with popularizing topless waitress service. They met at the Plaza, with critics from both the left and right (Max Lerner and William F. Buckley) looking on. The introduction was made by a lisping press agent, presumably in the employ of

Miss Doda. Then again, a woman of her vocation already understood how to get good press. By now, Tom Wolfe had celebrated Miss Doda's parabolic dimensions as she stood under a "yum-yum tree."

The guys who bitched about the women's libbers missed the whole point. Let Jimmy Cannon put a nickel in the jukebox to hear Sinatra lament the loser, "Set 'em up, Joe." The new city's anthem had just been released. It was James Brown, one of Joe's favorites, belting out "It's a Man's Man's Man's World." This was Men's Lib. You could get everything you wanted, booze and broads, under one roof.

"It was great," said Art Heyman, a professional basketball player who had a piece of a bar called the Bishop's Perch. "All the girls wanted to get laid by Joe. Everybody got leftovers."

Being around Joe meant your cup runneth over with yum-yum.

"I was taught that sex is a mortal sin," says David Kennedy, for whom confession was a weekly event. He went late Saturday afternoon, mostly to St. Patrick's, hoping to find an indulgent priest, a father who might've been young once, the kind who'd let you slide with six Our Fathers and six Hail Marys. He didn't want the ones who made you feel as if you would dwell for eternity in a lake of fire, even though anyone who'd seen Winona and Emeretta in their prime wouldn't find lakes of fire to be much of a deterrent. But even as he confessed, Kennedy knew that in a matter of hours he'd be with Joe and the boys, eagerly committing the same sins for which he was now repenting. For years, he was conflicted, racked with guilt. But it was a lot easier to stop going to confession than to stop going out.

Namath, for his part, suffered no such guilt. He blamed the priest who told him that a confession was in order every time he had been with a woman. This would have been spectacularly time-consuming. The real sin, in Namath's estimation, was hypocrisy. He said a prayer of thanks most nights, but would not ask to be forgiven for fornication. "So I stopped going to church," he said. "I wasn't going to go to confession and lie."

■   ■   ■

Thus said the high priest of lush life, a man who thought nothing of ordering beer for breakfast, just to get his bearings after a rough night. "A Miller, right away, no coffee," recalls Spiros Dellartas, a waiter at the Green Kitchen who became a friend. The Green Kitchen was near the corner of Seventy-seventh and First. By then, Joe, Ray, and Joe Hirsch (when he was in town) were living down the block, at 370 East Seventy-sixth Street, in the penthouse of the Newport East, an exclusive new apartment building teeming with stews and nightclub owners. Renting for $500 a month, their apartment had an expansive terrace affording a great view of the Manhattan skyline. The penthouse became a kind of temple—a high-rise shrine to the Hefneresque ideal. It even featured a couple of oil paintings of Joe as rendered by a hot *Playboy* illustrator, LeRoy Neiman, whom Sonny had commissioned as the Jets' in-house artist. The coffee table and chandelier were glass. The leather bar and the mirrored bed were round. Joe's sheets were green satin; his wallpaper silk, his floors marble. The sofa and ottoman were brown suede. The fixtures in the john were eighteen-carat gold. A miniature Spanish galleon Namath bought in Cincinnati rested atop a French provincial cabinet. What would they think in Beaver Falls? Broadway Joe was the king of this jungle: Siberian snow leopard throw pillows, cheetah-skin bench, an easy chair and drapes in a brown-and-white jungle-cat print. And of course: the llama-skin rug. It looked like a patch of exotic marine life or furry tentacles from a cheap science fiction movie. The shaggy strands were about six inches long, deep enough for one of David Kennedy's cuff links—a gift from his father, appropriately enough—to vanish without a trace. "It's with the God of the llama rugs now," Kennedy says wistfully. Like the white shoes and the green Lincoln, the rug is recalled with great affection by men of a certain age.

The penthouse proved a bit of unwitting brilliance, as its exotic furnishings became centerpieces in a new flurry of Broadway Joe columns and feature stories. It even merited a big spread in the women's page of the *Times,* which thought to pose Joe in the easy chair as he looked up (somewhat less than pensively) while reading *Catch-22.* It was good old-fashioned movie mag stuff: the star at home. This bachelor pad was straight out of the MCA playbook.

The only wonder was that Sonny didn't think of it. Rather, getting a place in the Newport East was all Bobby Van's idea.

■   ■   ■

As it pertained to the marriage of booze and broads, Bobby Van might be considered a ringbearer. He was born Robert Vannucci in Island Park, Long Island. While Bobby was still in grade school, his overworked father decided on a career change. He sold the family's textile mill in Greenpoint, Brooklyn, and bought a dude ranch upstate, in a tiny town called East Jewett. "Why a dude ranch?" says Bobby. "I never knew." He never complained, either. He had his own horse, which he would ride into town to pick up the mail. Bobby was a fine baseball player, but an even better cowboy. With more daring than the average dude, he became the ranch's champion rodeo rider.

Sitting atop an untamed animal requires more than mere physical skill. One needs a certain indifference to consequence, a fearlessness that Bobby would put on grand display when he came to New York. He was about twenty when he arrived in 1959 or '60. He rented a little office on Forty-second Street, from which he sold vacation packages to the dude ranch. Bobby loved New York. He loved playing softball for the Broadway Actors' League, and loved going to places like the Flick, an ice cream parlor on the East Side. The Flick had no liquor license, but it did have great-looking girls. Unfortunately, wherever there are girls, there are also the requisite number of assholes, some of whom started brawling one autumn night in 1962. Though Bobby tried to intercede as a peacemaker, the Flick's management didn't appreciate his efforts, and he and his friends were barred from the place. "Fuck you," he told the owner. "We'll open our own joint."

That was not an idle threat. Bobby was selling plenty of dude ranch vacations, and his friends were doing even better. Soon, they opened Table Talk, an ice cream and babes joint on Second Avenue between Thirty-eighth and Thirty-ninth Streets. Their gimmick was a phone on each table. See a cutie? Call her table. Bobby's actor friends came by. So did Danny Stradella, owner of Danny's Hideaway, a showbiz hangout. Little Danny brought the girls from the Copa to the opening night. About fifteen minutes later, Sinatra's sidekick, Jilly Rizzo, walked in. All of a sudden, Table Talk was as hot as ice cream has ever been.

About six weeks later, a guy came in and started a fight, just like the fight at the Flick. Van began escorting him from the premises when the provocateur took a swing at him. Bobby swung back. "I hit him," says Bobby. "He goes through the window."

But the broken window wasn't a sufficient deterrent. As Bobby was learning, some guys just weren't content with ice cream and broads. They cost him a couple nights' business and at least one other window. Next, Bobby got a visit from another guy whose kids had gone to the dude ranch. "Listen," he said. "We can help you with these fights."

After telling the guy to get the hell out of his ice cream parlor, Bobby received a call from his stepfather, a state supreme court judge. "Don't you know what you're getting into?" asked the judge. "This is what you call organized crime."

Just as Bobby was beginning to understand, he was also tiring of the ice cream business. There was something better out there. Who wanted an ice cream parlor when you could have a discotheque? "It looked like a lot more money," he explains.

Bobby already had a place picked out: a broken-down Chinese restaurant on Fifty-eighth between Madison and Park that, as good fortune would have it, was very close to the Playboy Club. The Ginza, as it was called, had two levels. Reconfigured by Bobby and his partner (a Jewish kid from Boston named Gordy), the bar and dining area would overlook the dance floor. Suspended above the dance floor was a wooden cage—Bobby built it himself—which would house some of the most attractive go-go girls New York had ever seen. It turned out that guys liked go-go girls even more than ice cream, and soon it was hard even to get a seat for lunch.

"We didn't know what to do with the money," says Van.

But then he started seeing some of the same faces he'd seen at the Flick and Table Talk. By now he knew their names, guys like Fat Gigi and Johnny Echo from East Harlem. They left big tips but caused bigger problems. One night a bartender went over the balcony, landing on the dance floor. He was lucky to have survived. The Chinese guys, who still owned the place, thought Bobby and Gordy were trying to muscle them out. Bobby, who was working for a percentage of the day's receipts, told the DA he had nothing to do with the bartender's misfortune. That was the truth. He had always told the Chinamen that he would walk if they were unhappy with him, so walk he did . . . right into a short-term lease at Fiftieth and Third. The building was slated to be demolished in a few years, but in the meantime, Bobby Van would throw a hell of a party there.

The new joint, which opened in September of 1965, was called Dudes 'N Dolls. It was fashioned with a Western motif after Bobby's own heart. "Word got out pretty fast," he recalls. "I had the best-looking barmaids, the best-looking waitresses, and the best-looking dancers." An assortment of go-go squaws and cowgirls, outfitted to conjure prurient visions of Pocahontas or Calamity Jane, could be found frugging in teepees or atop tom-tom drums. Among them was a young dancer named Goldie Hawn.

Soon, Tad Dowd was bringing in stars like Tom Jones and Bill Hartack. Mickey Mantle loved Dudes 'N Dolls, even if it wasn't the kind of place where Yankees should be seen. After midnight, Jilly Rizzo would show up with Sinatra's date, this skinny young kid, Mia Farrow. The singer himself wouldn't arrive until much later, maybe two-thirty in the morning, when Bobby would meet him at the side entrance. Though Sinatra could have used the front door, he insisted on sneaking in, maintaining a cover that was inevitably blown as soon as he started throwing firecrackers at the dancers.

Dudes 'N Dolls was also a big hit with the "the same wiseguys from East Harlem who broke up the Ginza." For some reason, they didn't recognize Bobby from the Chinese disco; to them, he recalls, "I was the kid from Table Talk who threw the guy through the window." As the injured party wasn't one of their crew, Johnny Echo and the boys took no offense. In fact, it gave the crazy cowboy some cachet. When another crew from Mulberry Street moved in on Dudes 'N Dolls, Johnny Echo voluntarily interceded—free of charge, says Bobby—on his behalf. "We know this kid," warned Johnny Echo. Translation: "Back off. He's a nice kid. And this is a nice place."

And so it went. Joe Namath first paid a visit during his rookie season, when Tad Dowd pressed him into service as a celebrity judge of a dance contest. The other judges were Hartack and Joey Villa, whom Dowd was touting as "the next Jerry Lewis." He might have been off about Joey Villa, but he was right about Joe. Joe loved the place.

"From the time he stepped into Dudes 'N Dolls it was his place, his hangout," says Bobby Van, who appreciated the way Namath handled himself in a bar. Unlike a lot of ballplayers, Joe always picked up the check. ("Nobody was quicker on the draw," says Al Hassan.) He liked late hours and the people who kept them. Like Bobby, he went by the code of the stand-up guy. "I don't care what a man is as long as he treats me right," Namath declared in '66. "He can be a gambler, a hustler, someone everybody else thinks is obnoxious, I don't care so long as he's straight with me and our dealings are fair."

Nightlife soothed him. "He seemed to have a comfort factor," says Bobby. "He used to tell me, 'The only way I can relax is with a girl and a bottle of Johnny Walker Red.' . . . He could drink a bottle and still get up and play football."

Bobby and Joe started hanging out quite a bit, tough mama's boys with common interests in booze and broads. After that first season, they hung out in Florida. At Bobby's suggestion, Joe moved into the Newport East. Bobby's apartment was 1401B, right across the hall from Sammy Davis Jr., whose mother worked as a hatcheck at Dudes 'N Dolls. Bobby put a lot of people to work, especially Joe's friends. By the end of the '65 season, Ray Abruzzese was already thinking of a vocation after football; as Joe told Bobby, "My roommate wants to learn how to tend bar." By '66 Ray was the off-season bartender at Dudes 'N Dolls. Soon Jimmy Walsh, who graduated from the University of Alabama law school that year, did shifts as a part-time maître d' while studying for the bar exam. Tad picked up some work there, too. Friends do for friends.

On any given night these friends would bounce back and forth from Dudes to the Pussycat to the Open End, on First Avenue between Seventy-sixth and Seventy-seventh streets. The Open End, within stumbling distance from both the Newport East and the Green Kitchen diner, catered to a crowd that kept especially late nights, an eclectic assortment of pimps, gamblers, detectives, ballplayers, and at least one late-night talk show host. *The Tonight Show,* starring Johnny Carson, was shot live in New York. Sometimes, in the hours that followed, Carson went live at the Open End. One such session resulted in what Art Heyman recalls fondly as a crucial juncture in television history—"the night Bobby Van saved Johnny Carson's life."

Bobby Van doesn't disagree with Heyman's characterization: "Johnny was seeing two beautiful black sisters, Ida and Chiquita. They were, like, five-eight, five-nine, gorgeous. One of them grabs me and says, 'Come outside, Johnny's about to get hurt.'

"I go out, and Johnny's falling off the curb. He's trying to argue with this guy. But he's so drunk. I grab him so he doesn't fall, and the guy whacks *me* across the nose, smashes my nose right across my face."

Bobby got in a couple of good shots of his own before retreating to the

Newport East to get supplies: cotton for his nose and a baseball bat to pulverize the son of a bitch who had sly-rapped him. But a friend intercepted him before he could reenter the bar, where guns had already been drawn.

"Bobby, don't get involved," said the friend, who went by the name of Brownie. "Let me do what I have to do."

Brownie was a pimp and a bookmaker, probably a numbers man, too. But he never caused a beef. "A stand-up guy," says Van.

The incident had embarrassed Brownie. About two weeks later, he tapped Bobby on the shoulder. Brownie told him to forget about the guy who had cracked him in the nose. He would never again be seen in the Open End.

Bobby asked what that meant.

Don't ask, said Brownie. "Don't worry."

But then, who was worried? No matter how late it got, the nights seemed as young as its players. What great nights those were. All you needed was a bar; from there, all good things flowed. During the off-season in Florida, Bobby convinced Joe to come in as his partner in a new place. They'd lease the commercial space adjoining the Newport East. Why not? They decided to call it "the Jet Set," and be up and running by '67. Ray would have a piece, too. Joe loved the idea of owning a joint: friendship, money, kicks under one roof. Who cared what people said?

"I can do anything I like," said Joe.

Almost anything. "At the last minute," recalls Bobby, "Sonny Werblin nixed it. Sonny didn't want Joe to get in the booze business."

Sonny didn't mind if Joe had a few too many, and he didn't care about the women. After all, booze and broads were part of the image he had cultivated. But the bar business was another matter entirely. Sonny loved bars, but for drinking, not owning. A lot of people come in after dark. When it got that late, how did you tell the good guys from the bad? Not everyone observed that stand-up designation Namath held so dear. The wee hours aroused, among other things, man's most larcenous instincts. Sonny knew that much as a kid, running for his life from a dance hall with a fist full of cash.

Jack Danahy believed in God and country, in Jesus Christ and J. Edgar Hoover. The son of a business agent for the marble workers union, he grew up in the Bronx, gladly serving 7 A.M. mass to the Carmelite nuns cloistered in a convent on Gun Hill Road. Jack was an excellent student, graduating from St. Brendan's grammar school, All Hallows High School, Georgetown University, and, in 1939, Columbia University School of Law. However, something about his experience on Morningside Heights offended his sensibilities. Though he came from a union family, he found some of the professors "far out to the left," and frowned on their concern with process over punishment. Danahy was never comfortable with the idea of defending the guilty. That was not a sin he'd want to confess. So he turned down the big-money law firms and joined Hoover's FBI.

26. LIAR'S POKER

"Loved every minute of it," he says.

The bulk of Danahy's career as a G-man reflected the director's concern with spies, Communists, and those alleged to be. "I was a longtime supervisor in the Soviet espionage squad," he says proudly. Agents were trained to catch spies by spying: following them, establishing a network of suspicious associations, then leveraging the appearance of guilt into confessions. Danahy worked on some of the bureau's biggest cases, helping debrief erstwhile spies like Whittaker Chambers and Elizabeth Bentley, known as "The Red Spy Queen."

Danahy liked to be out in the field, not in an office. But when the need arose, he demonstrated a certain flair for memo writing. By 1961, he was working out of bureau headquarters in Washington, an assignment he did not particularly care for. He missed the action of working in New York. So, fully aware that the new attorney general, Bobby Kennedy, was pushing Hoover to get tough on organized crime, Danahy wrote a memo to the director. He suggested that agents investigate gangsters with the same techniques they used to investigate Communists. "Strictly a bullshit memo," Danahy chuckles. "But it worked." Hoover sent him to New York to set up and run an organized crime detail. The years that followed were good ones for Danahy. He was a field boss again, and as such got to meet a lot of interesting people, men who straddled the line between fame and infamy, everybody from Joe Valachi, star stool pigeon, to Joe Namath, star quarterback.

■　　■　　■

Danahy met Namath at the Pussycat. It was late 1966, or maybe early '67, soon after Namath had gotten out of the hospital. The date is less clear than the hour: very late. Danahy was making the rounds with one of his agents, Billy Kane, nicknamed Captain Midnight for the hours he kept. The Pussycat was on their list of establishments that warranted a regular drop-in. "Every now and then I liked to get out on the street and get a look at these guys," says Danahy. "So I know what they look like."

Namath, at first glance, was looking like a loser. "I think he had half a bag on," recalls Danahy, who found him sitting at the bar. "Although it was hard to tell, because Joe had adopted that half-ass southern accent and he had those crazy eyelids that were hanging down below his belt somewhere."

At either side of Namath, says the former agent, "were capos in the Lucchese family." One of them, he believes, was Carmine Tramunti, Mr. Gribs. Joe and the gangsters were playing Liar's Poker. The hand you were dealt came from the serial numbers on bills drawn from the cash register. The bartender (no girls in bathing suits now—this was a guy) was serving as the dealer, and getting quite nervous about it: Danahy and Captain Midnight were obviously cops of some sort.

But Namath seemed oblivious to everything but his losing streak. Danahy, who enjoyed his Dewar's with water, had no objection to a man's spending time at the bar. Nor did he have anything against gambling per se. The director himself loved going to the track. As for Liar's Poker, Danahy had played quite enough back in the Bronx. "But that was an *honest* game," he says.

It still pisses him off, remembering those hoodlums at the bar: "I think Joe was being taken. That's just like them. Even if it's just a dollar—they gotta win. Punks."

Now Danahy, as he recalls, "was out to break balls." He turned to Namath. "I know you," he said.

The quarterback grunted and went back to his losing streak.

"Yeah," said Danahy, "you're an athlete, right?"

Athlete, not ballplayer. Another grunt.

"Wait, don't tell me . . . you're a . . . tennis player?"

Tennis player. That got Namath's attention. That was a slur to which Namath responded by introducing himself amid a stream of profanities.

"Glad to know you," said Danahy, and then, gesturing at the Lucchese gangsters, "Now, do you know who these guys are?"

"What the fuck business of it is yours?" Namath barked.

"You should be hanging out with a better class of people," answered the G-man, who turned to leave before any fisticuffs could break out.

It would be a couple of years before Danahy met up with Namath again. By then, he would be the NFL's director of security. In the meantime, though, he doesn't recall paying the kid much mind. He had *real* bad guys to worry about. Besides, Jack Danahy was a Giants fan.

■ · ■ ■

Maybe Danahy didn't feel any need to keep an eye on him, but someone in Washington certainly did. On January 30, 1967, the Federal Bureau of Investigation created a dossier, a new entry in a body of work known as "Hoover's Files":

JOE NAMATH

Captioned individual, a member of the New York Jets of the American Football League, has never been the subject of an FBI investigation. However, earlier this month information was received from a reliable source indicating that he frequents The Pussycat Bar in New York City. It is understood that The Pussycat is actually owned by Carmine Tramunti, who is allegedly a member of the Lucchese "family" of La Cosa Nostra (LCN); Dave Iacovetti, allegedly a member of the Gambino "family" of LCN; and Anthony Napolitano, who is also an alleged member of the Gambino "family." Jack Lambert reportedly manages The Pussycat for the three LCN members mentioned above and Lambert's name is on the license for this establishment. Joe Namath reportedly shares an apartment in New York City with Jack Lambert.

Namath has been observed intoxicated on several occasions and also reportedly had an affair with an airline stewardess who became pregnant as a result of this association. It is alleged that an abortion was arranged for this girl by the wife of Jilly Rizzo, the operator of a restaurant-bar in New York. It is understood that the abortion had to be postponed due to the arrest of Jilly Rizzo's wife on charges stemming from an abortion ring operating in the New York area.

It has been reported that Jack Lambert has recently received a beating from Carmine Tramunti since Lambert wants to leave The Pussycat and operate a bar which will be financially backed by Joe Namath.

A check with the New York office of the FBI on January 27, 1967, disclosed that Namath has been a devotee of discotheques since arriving in New York City two to three years ago and has been interested in starting his own discotheque. A reliable source who is acquainted with Namath's activities has advised the New York office that on one occasion

Namath planned to open a discotheque called the "Jet Set." However, Namath's associates in the proposed venture are all New York underworld figures. When the owner of the New York Jets learned of this proposed adventure he ordered Namath to disassociate himself from plans he had regarding the new discotheque.

This same source also advised that there have been rumors among members of the New York sports world that Namath had "thrown" several games while quarterbacking the New York Jets during the 1966 season. It is also understood that Namath's association with "hoods" and cheap gamblers will soon be revealed publicly in New York City.

Attached is a copy of the FBI Identification Record Number 505 524 F which may be identical with Joe Namath.

The Namath dossier reveals more about the director than about the "devotee of discotheques." It should have been no surprise that Hoover was keeping files on Martin Luther King and his associates. After all, they wanted to free the colored man. However, the football player posed other risks. If this Joe Namath had his way, everybody would be whoring and drinking right out there in the open. And that hair! It seemed to be growing by the hour. Namath was the antithesis of the G-man, a Ken doll after Hoover's own fantasy. "You won't find long hair or sideburns à la Joe Namath here," he once said. "There are no hippies in the FBI. The public has an image of what an agent should look like."

Image was everything to Hoover, and Namath's image violated the director's sacrosanct notions of secrecy and morality. "He was a great moral judge of everybody but himself," says Jack Anderson, the syndicated columnist who eventually broke the story of Hoover's secret files. The director was delighted to learn of the rich and famous conducting themselves in ways weak and depraved. "Hoover loved to be titillated," says Anderson. As he dealt in rumor and reputation (he understood the press even better than Sonny), his files observed no distinction between minor truths and major lies. The celebrity dossiers were a kind of supermarket tabloid written for an audience of one. As Anderson recalls: "The troops knew what the boss liked to read."

After reviewing the Namath file, Danahy concludes that its author was a Washington-based supervisor responding to a higher-up (perhaps Hoover himself) who asked: "What do we know about this Joe Namath?"

What, exactly, prompted the request is unclear. But it would seem to have something to do with the confrontation at the Pussycat, an evening Namath himself came to consider as the origin of Danahy's "vendetta against me." They were each scotch-drinking former altar boys who had been declared 4-F by the army. (Rheumatic fever had left Danahy with a heart murmur.) But against the backdrop of the 1960s, Namath and Danahy were also perfectly matched antagonists. Danahy, who later found Joe to be "a pretty decent guy," chuckles at the idea of a vendetta. But he allows that Hoover—"who gets a bad rap all the way"—would have been apprised of his encounter with Namath at the Pussycat. "I would have stuck that in the next day's teletype," says Danahy, referring to daily summaries that kept the director abreast of events in the field. "That would incite Hoover's interest."

Still, the specifics of the Namath report escape Danahy. "A lot of stuff in there I never heard of." For instance, he recalls Carmine Tramunti, the Lucchese boss, as "a mean sonofabitch," but knows nothing about him beating up Jack Lambert, the Pussycat's titular owner.

"Carmine Tramunti was like a father to me," says Lambert. "He never put a finger on me. I was never, ever, ever touched by any wiseguy. It was an unwritten law: you never touched Jack Lambert. I was cared about by people."

Tramunti became acting boss of the crime family when its namesake leader, Thomas Lucchese, died of a brain tumor in 1967. According to the 1970 New York State Joint Legislative Committee Report on Crime, Tramunti's interests included numbers, narcotics, and "one of the big floating crap games in the city, the so-called 'Harlem Game.' . . . He is also one of the more important underworld investors in bars and restaurants in the city." His muscle in this endeavor was identified as Tommy (Tea Balls) Mancuso.

Lambert, who denies having had any financial relationship with Tramunti, insists that it was Mancuso who was his partner at the Pussycat. "Tommy Tea Balls was the closest friend I had," he says. "Look, I'm a Jew. I'm not involved in whatever you would call 'the organization.' I knew a lot of people. A lot of people hung out in my bar. Every showgirl, every Playboy Bunny, every entertainer in New York hung out at the Pussycat. It became *the* spot to hang out. . . . A lot of people wanted to hang out where the wiseguys hung out. And this *was* the wiseguy hangout. But Joe was never, never, never, never, never involved with the wiseguys. Never."

Lambert knew Mancuso wasn't a saint, but beatification wasn't a requirement for being a stand-up guy. As Lambert recalls: "Tommy Tea Balls came to me one day and said, 'Do Joe a favor and keep him away from us. For his sake. He doesn't need to be around any of us.' That's the kind of guy Tommy T. was."

Mancuso wasn't alone in his regard for Namath. While much of America dismissed Namath as a kind of hippie, a lot of wiseguys—who fancied themselves connoisseurs of things tough and cool—were quite taken with him. "They never touched him," says one well-connected, old-line bookmaker. "They never even tried. They *liked* the guy."

And for a time, the feeling was mutual. As Danahy once said, "Joe liked hoodlums." Lambert would have characterized himself and his associates differently: "I was a knockaround-type guy back then." Still, he allows,

"We weren't the type of people Joe should have been running around with."

Lambert relayed Tommy Tea Balls's message. But Joe refused to stay away. "Joe liked the excitement," says Lambert. "Joe liked to be involved with dangerous things."

Hanging out with mob guys didn't make him one of them. Hell, what if he liked to drink with Communists? What would that make him? "I'm not doing anything wrong," Namath insisted.

■   ■   ■

Even if he had wanted to, it would have been very difficult for Joe to avoid Jack Lambert. For the better part of a year, from 1966 through much of '67, Jack slept on the couch at the famous bachelor pad. "Joe and Ray took me in at a time when things were going very poorly for me," he says.

While correctly describing Lambert as Namath's roommate, the FBI report seems less accurate in other areas. Among Joe's old friends, Lambert is not alone in dismissing the part about Jilly Rizzo's wife, Honey, and the abortion. "That's a damn lie," he says. "Honey never had anything to do with that."

Rather, Lambert fondly recalls poker games up at the apartment and trips to Puerto Rico, where Joe had a dynamite girl who danced at the Americana Hotel in San Juan. Joe had so many women, but he had some funny ideas about marriage, like it had to be so pure. "He wanted to marry a virgin," says Lambert. "That's the truth of the matter. We talked about it a lot."

Jack used to kid Joe: He wasn't going to find many virgins at the Pussycat or Dudes 'N Dolls. But then, what was the rush? Jack figured their run would last forever. And it just might have—if not for a bet. They were playing pool. Jack wasn't a great player, but he still took the bet once Joe spotted him about 25 balls out of 100. The stakes were a trip to Puerto Rico. "He kicked the shit out of me," says Lambert. "At that time, I just didn't have the money to pay."

Joe didn't care what the FBI called you, a hoodlum or a Communist. He cared about your word. Your word was your bond. If you broke it, you were out.

To this day, Lambert speaks of Carmine Tramunti and Tommy Tea Balls with reverence and affection. But this episode with Joe continues to embarrass him. "I didn't act as a good friend," he says. Jack Lambert, of all people, understood the reason for his banishment. Welshers were not to be tolerated. Men revealed themselves in the way that they gambled.

■   ■   ■

Of all the allegations in Namath's file, the ones most often echoed by the public (the betting public, mostly) concerned his "association with 'hoods' and cheap gamblers" and the "rumors" (even the Feds felt some compunction to be circumspect in this instance) that he had "thrown" ball games. Danahy, who as the NFL's director of security would become an expert on football gambling, says categorically: "I have never heard a word about Joe Namath being dishonest."

But honesty wasn't the issue; associations were. And Namath's were already in violation of league policy as stipulated in his archaically worded contract, right under his signature: "Players must not enter drinking or gambling resorts nor associate with gamblers or other notorious characters."

The games athletes play are inevitably subject to the games gamblers play. The relationship between football and gambling is as old as the sport itself. Consider this front-page account of a hotly disputed loss by Geneva College in the November 16, 1903, edition of the *Beaver Falls Daily Tribune*: "The spectator who attended the game and wagered his money on the result is entitled to fair treatment and a hearing in the matter, and when he sees a deliberate attempt made to carry off his money, he has a right to ask for the appointment of an impartial committee." Failure to investigate, writes this correspondent, "will injure the great college game."

A betting sport, by its nature, faces perennial suspicion and periodic scandal. In professional football, allegations of fixes date back to a 1906 game between the Canton Bulldogs and the Masillon Tigers. In 1943 the *Washington Times-Herald* reported on persistent rumors that Redskins quarterback Sammy Baugh—whose team had lost to heavy underdogs from Pennsylvania that season—was uncomfortably close to a known gambler. (In fact, this gambler had both a bookmaking conviction and ties to the New York mob.) The association wasn't proof of wrongdoing, but that did little to bolster public confidence in the National Football League. In 1947, after Manhattan district attorney Frank Hogan won the conviction of four mob-connected gamblers, NFL commissioner Bert Bell indefinitely suspended two New York Giants, quarterback Frank Filchock and fullback Merle Hapes, for failure to report bribe offers.

By 1963 the league had a new commissioner, Pete Rozelle, who suspended two of the game's biggest stars, Green Bay running back Paul Hornung and Detroit defensive tackle Alex Karras, for an entire year because of their gambling. Hornung, football's golden boy, made a good show of his repentance. "I made a terrible mistake," he told reporters. "I am truly sorry." Nevertheless, Rozelle remained troubled by Hornung's habitual betting and his "associations" in Las Vegas, where his wagers were placed. It didn't help that Hornung had only bet on the Packers. Betting on one's own team wasn't like betting on a horse. "They don't have point spreads on horses," Rozelle once said. "If you openly stated you bet on your own team, there will be suspicion, depending on what happened in the game, that maybe you bet the other way." With the bettor's spread in the balance, every play could undermine the confidence in Rozelle's product. Victory became a relative term. Now, even casual gamblers were concerned with the margin of victory. Was it more or less than the spread? Every call—on the sidelines, in the huddle, and by the officials—became a potential conspiracy.

Karras—less of a star, but also less publicly repentant—didn't bet against his team either. He also bet less than Hornung—reportedly only $50 on six games. But the commissioner didn't appreciate the company Karras kept, nor did he approve of the Grecian Gardens restaurant where the Lions were known to hang out with some undesirable gambling types. Five of Karras's teammates were fined for betting on NFL games in which they did not play. The Lions' organization was fined $4,000, because the coach had failed to report what the commissioner called "certain associations by members of the Detroit team."

Like Bert Bell—who maintained a private hotline to keep him apprised of suspicious behavior and fluctuations in the odds—Rozelle consolidated his stature and authority in the course of a gambling scandal. Pro football had evolved; it was no longer a minor-league sport. Television had conspired with the point spread to transform the professional game. The Tube and the Spread were yin and yang; from their harmony flowed football's sudden hegemony in American sport.

"Wherever there was a television set, there was a new type of sports wire service," write professors Richard O. Davies and Richard G. Abram in *Betting the Line: Sports Wagering in American Life*. "Television dramatically changed the world of sports betting by democratizing the process and opening up sports for all to see. It gave everyone a chance to scout teams and ponder future wagers. Coupled with the steady expansion of sports reporting in daily news-papers, television provided the information that gave a new generation of gam-blers confidence—sometimes false—in their own abilities as handicappers."

Between TV and the point spread, all the work was done for you. You could sit in the comfort of your own easy chair, with your own beer. And even as you belched and scratched, you could fancy yourself a sage gambler, without having to spend all that time figuring the odds. No longer did one have to con-sider game-time temperatures, injuries, and tendencies with Talmudic serious-ness. With a point spread, either team represented a plausible wager. No matter what, you were in the game. There were no long shots anymore.

But if Everyman could be a wise man, he could also be a conspiracy theo-rist. It is perfectly apropos that the 1958 sudden-death championship—the game that seemed to announce pro football's arrival as a nationally televised sport—also aroused great popular mistrust. With the game tied and the Colts 3½-point favorites, Baltimore went for the touchdown instead of the field goal. The decision cast suspicion on Ewbank, the coach; Unitas, the quarterback; and Carroll Rosenbloom, the Colts owner, said to have bet $1 million on the game. Though Rosenbloom was a big gambler with an abundance of questionable associations, there was never even the slightest evidence to question the integrity of his coach or the quarterback.

Still, in this new world, proof mattered less than perception. Suggestion became its own reality. "The essential fact is that many people believed that gambling helped determine the outcome of the most famous professional game in history," write Davies and Abram. "At the heart of these speculations stood the new system of the point spread and how it created new expectations and pressures upon coaches and players. . . . The cold reality, NFL executives understood as never before, was that professional football and gambling were, like Siamese twins, inextricably linked."

It is no coincidence that Rozelle, the first NFL commissioner to fully understand the power of television, also became the league's most relentless opponent of gambling. Rozelle worked under the same theory as Hoover: the questionable association was tantamount to guilt. The commissioner ordered his league's ever-growing security force to report "even the suspicion of evil." "The key to interest in pro football is the honest competitive aspects of it," he once said. "If we lose that, there would be no compensation features to keep us at the level we are now."

People had to believe the games were honest. If not, pro football would soon be fighting for its life with that other great experiment in televised sports—roller derby.

■　　■　　■

"Joe used to put all the bets through me with the bookies," says Art Heyman, an avid bettor then knocking around the lower rungs of professional basketball. "He used to bet all the football games."

When asked to define "all the football games," Heyman issues a quick qualification: "College. He did all the college games."

How much Namath bet—Heyman recalls his usual wager as $200 a game—and whom he bet on remain unclear. There is no question, however, that he enjoyed gambling. If it wasn't football, it was pool, or horses. He even bet on the fortunes of red ants. "They had these big ones down South," says Fred Klages, recalling his trip through Tuscaloosa as a minor-leaguer. "You could kill them with a dart. Of course, Joe killed the most of anybody." Namath could never abide the Protestant notion of gambling as a vice. This was, remember, a boy who delivered his sainted mother's best hopes to the numbers man. Like Coach Bryant, Namath enjoyed the occasional trip to Vegas. And like his own father, he enjoyed wagering on a ball game. As a son of the Lower End, Joe didn't consider betting any more sinful than drinking. But as pro football's first full-blown TV star, Namath also became a lightning rod for suspicion.

Allegations that he had taken part in a "fixed" game dated back to his Alabama debut, the three-touchdown performance against Georgia. The Tide, 17-point favorites, won 35–0—not the kind of numbers that suggest a fix. Still, the *Saturday Evening Post* breathlessly accused Coach Bryant of obtaining secret pregame information from Georgia athletic director Wally Butts: "Not since the Chicago White Sox threw the 1919 World Series has there been a sports story as shocking as this."

Bryant and Butts, Georgia's busted-out former coach, were actually old friends who often spoke before games. That contest was no exception, but for the fact that an insurance salesman named George Burnett claimed that a telephone operator had accidentally transferred him into their conversation. Burnett also claimed to have taken concurrent notes detailing the Bryant-Butts plot. Desperate to reverse rapidly declining circulation trends, the *Saturday Evening Post* paid Burnett $5,000 for the article—a pretty good score, considering the man had absolutely no proof of a fixed game. Editors at the magazine, which had only recently accused Bryant of teaching "brutal" football, never even asked Burnett to produce his notes. Butts would eventually come away with $460,000 in damages, while Bryant ended up with a $320,000 settlement.

The magazine might have saved a bundle if someone had checked with Namath. "I called every play of that game," he said. "I knew the game wasn't fixed."

The incident would inform Namath's eventual contempt for what he called "the Northern press." Still, it also should have provided him a valuable lesson: gambling conspiracies were everywhere, bounded only by human imagination and libel law.

Recall the line from Namath's FBI file, regarding "rumors among members of the New York sports world" that he had "thrown" games. On this topic, Danahy—who created a gambling squad as part of the organized crime section—is adamant. " 'New York sports world' means gamblers—not necessarily bookies," he explains. "The biggest source of rumors—and I know this from personal experience—is losing gamblers. A guy loses a bet, or the Jets didn't cover the spread, and in his mind the game was thrown on him."

Namath had been confounding bettors and bookies since high school, but New Yorkers had never seen anything like him. Everyone in town, it seemed, had a story about betting the wrong way based on Joe. Barry Skolnick, a bar owner who lived in the Newport East, recalls Joe staggering into his place, the Golden Twenties, one night with Mickey Kearney, a part-time boxer and full-time hoodlum often found in the quarterback's company. Namath slurrily ordered Grand Marnier from the bar. "He couldn't walk, he couldn't talk," says Skolnick. "When Joe got into the Grand Marnier, that meant it was time for everyone to go home." But because it was Joe, everyone stayed, until about five A.M., when Mickey Kearney finally carried him out. Skolnick didn't even charge for the drinks, though he did put $25 on the tab for a bathroom partition Namath had tried to punch out. The following morning, a game day, Skolnick called his bookie. "Believe me," he says, "I didn't like to bet against the Jets." But opportunities like this didn't often present themselves.

Of course, Namath had a great day, throwing for what Skolnick remembers as "a bunch of touchdowns." Skolnick doesn't recall the stats or the score or any of the numbers beyond the one denoting the magnitude of his loss. That much he remembers exactly. "Do you know," he asks, "how much a thousand bucks was back then?"

At least Skolnick had a sense of humor. Most members of the aforementioned New York sports world were terribly poor losers. David Kennedy recalls an evening spent with Namath, Tad Dowd, and the jockey Bill Hartack following a Jets loss. As Namath wanted to douse his wounds in relative obscurity, they chose a lonely-looking joint in the East Forties, not one of their usual spots. It was empty, save for a few guys at the bar, one of whom came over to the table, drunk. "You know how much money I lost on you today?" he said.

Namath rolled his eyes. How many times had he heard that line? He waited for the guy to finish. But the drunk kept on berating him until finally Hartack leaped up and cracked him across the jaw. The drunk collapsed on impact, making for a suddenly adrenalized moment of unspoken mirth. Forget Sherman Plunkett, Winston Hill, or Dave Herman. Forget the goon, Mickey Kearney. In a cantankerous 117-pound jockey, Namath had found his fiercest bodyguard.

It took a while and some effort for the drunk to pick himself up. Before staggering back to the bar, he warned the Namath camp that retribution would be coming in short order. Kennedy watched as the nervous-looking bartender placed a call. Next thing he remembers hearing was the screech of tires as a large sedan came skidding to a halt outside. Three men got out, two big guys and a little guy. Kennedy, concerned for the condition of his mortal soul, remembers thinking: *Great, we're gonna get shot by some hoods.* The little guy, wearing a camel-hair coat and fedora, approached their table alone as the big guys went straight to the bar, grabbed the drunk, and escorted him into the car. "I'd like to apologize for my friend," said the little guy. "It'll never happen again."

Of course, it did. It happened again and again and again. Joe would be having a drink, and certain "members of the New York sports world" would start right in, as if he had personally robbed them. Most of the time, Joe ignored these complaints. Occasionally, he managed to grin or grit his teeth through their bitter monologues. The mob guys might've liked his style, but they were notorious for their hubris as handicappers. One night after a game,

Tad Dowd recalls, "a real Joe Pesci type" came barreling through the door at the Pussycat. From the bar, Lambert could see him, too. "He was a pretty bad guy," he says.

Immediately, he started into Namath. "You cost me a lot of money today," he said. "A fucking bundle."

The Jets had just lost. Namath, thirsty for a drink, was in acute pain. Still, everything seemed basically normal—except for Joe's response. "Who the fuck told you to bet?" he snapped. "I hope you lost your house." A bundle? Good. "I hope you lost *your mother's* house."

It wasn't the brightest thing Joe could've said. Lambert was quickly summoned to a meeting. "Some people—I can't say who—spoke to me," he says. "They felt Joe had acted very fresh." Lambert was instructed to deliver a message to the quarterback: "Shape up, get in line, behave yourself."

But Lambert never mentioned it to Namath. "Joe had every right to talk that way," he insists.

Joe told off the wiseguy same as he had the G-man. It was, after all, a matter of principle.

At 10:00 P.M. on January 5, 1967, ABC aired *Pro Football's Shotgun Marriage: $onny, Money and Merger,* narrated by Howard Cosell, a frequent, though uninvited, guest at Namath's bachelor pad. There was by now a general consensus that Sonny's signing of Namath was the biggest thing to have happened to professional football since the 1958 championship game. Even establishment types like Arthur Daley, the *Times*'s Pulitzer Prize winner, had come to understand: "With one gesture, he saved the Jets, saved the A.F.L. and set the wheels spinning inexorably along the road to merger."

The following morning Namath was released from Lenox Hill Hospital, where he had just undergone his second knee surgery in as many years. With his body's fate in doubt, his mind became quite clear. For all the publicity surrounding his signing, and for all its renowned significance,

27. THE STAR SYSTEM

he was no longer the game's highest-priced player. The famous $400,000 contract seemed almost obsolete to him. Soon Namath would be telling people, "It wasn't enough." The fresh lump of scar tissue on his knee was only a reminder that Sonny hadn't been giving anything away in the first place. Joe had to make a financial score while he still could, for his sake and his family's.

He would buy his mother a house and had already set up Frank in the insurance business, which made sense for his brother. Insurance was for responsible people, providers. Everybody should be insured. In a way, it was the opposite of the numbers business. The numbers guy played off your sense of hope; the insurance broker played on your sense of inescapable reality. And in Joe's own actuarial estimation, the inevitabilities included a young death with old knees. Joe couldn't see himself living to fifty. Hell, he'd count himself lucky if his knees survived to twenty-five. So based on these and other calculations, he came up with some figures of his own. In April, he met with Sonny at the Palm Bay Club to discuss his future. According to one account, Joe wanted a million bucks. He didn't deny it, either. Like Coach Bryant used to say: it didn't hurt none to ask.

■   ■   ■

That same month, Namath quit smoking. Connie Dinkler, the socialite whose husband owned the Palm Bay Club, wagered that he couldn't stop for five years. The price was $5,000, and Joe even worked his mother into a side bet, as he wanted her to quit, too. Joe didn't have much of a problem giving up the smokes; he just substituted snuff for the Salems. By July, when he arrived in Peekskill for training camp, he'd put on some weight. But from all the talk you'd think the extra pounds were in his hair, which was now vaguely Beatle-like. The back no longer bore razor traces. Even worse, he had grown side-burns. And while the fashion would have been unremarkable in another twenty-four-year old, it was regarded as yet another blasphemy Namath had committed in violation of the gridiron's regimental etiquette.

The first Monday of camp was picture day. The photographer was already on his way when Weeb, who still wore a flat-top, implored Joe to get his hair cut. Unfortunately, the barbershops were closed on Mondays. Sonny was ready to send up a barber from Manhattan by limousine, but then Weeb found one right there in Peekskill. Everything was set. There was just one problem: Weeb's guy was a nonunion barber.

No union, no haircut. "My father told me never to go non-union," said Namath, who was photographed sideburns and all.

"Some image," complained Ewbank.

One imagines Wellington Mara nodding in agreement. At the dawning of the Age of Aquarius the Giants were coming off a 1–12–1 season, a campaign so disastrous that Mara was finally forced to acquire a quarterback. Fran Tarkenton was among a new breed at the position, a slight and speedy scram-bler. In all other ways, though, he seemed to embody the virtuous, God-fearing image that Mara held so dear. He lived with his wife (who, as one writer noted, "wore his Sigma Alpha Epsilon pin for three years at Georgia") and young daughter in a rented English Tudor in New Rochelle. He didn't drink or smoke. He wore ties in public. He belonged to the Fellowship of Christian Athletes. "In my way," he once said, "I'm preaching a sermon when I play on Sunday." Tarkenton's esteem only grew by the inevitable comparison to Namath, whose own appearance had become freighted with counterfeit meaning.

Yet while Middle America saw something sinister in sideburns, Joe's team-mates perceived something more complex. Joe had emancipated them from some of the sport's sillier rules. (The standard contract still mandated the wear-ing of "coats and neckties in hotel lobbies, public eating places, and on all public conveyances.") But his look—everything from Edwardian jackets to Bermuda shorts—was yet another expression of Sonny's separate standard, the star system. "Before Joe got here, everything was cut and dried," Dave Herman once said. "Chewing tobacco was a $100 fine. Sonny Werblin had team blazers made up, matching coat and tie. But then Joe came along. Joe was Sonny's boy."

■   ■   ■

By August 3, the day before the Jets' first exhibition game, Sonny's boy finally had his new contract, already typed out and awaiting his signature. Under its terms, the Jets would pick up their one-year option on Namath for the 1968 season. Then a new no-cut, no-trade contract would kick in, running from '69 to '71. His salary would be raised to $35,000, but once again, the big bucks were in the bonuses. He would receive $10,000 for 1967, $25,000 for the 1968 option year, and a deferred payment of $150,000 that wasn't due until 1972. The total came to $340,000.

It wasn't what Namath had asked for, nor did it reflect his economic value. But "economic value" was still an esoteric concept in pro football. By the prevailing standards, Namath's deal remained outrageously lucrative. More than that, it provided the insurance he most wanted; the money was guaranteed even if he was physically unable to play. All in all, it wasn't a bad deal, considering that Namath had to negotiate without benefit of a bidding war.

In contrast to the first contract, this one went unpublicized, which was fine by Namath, who didn't like the way he was being quoted anyway. Not only did Sonny fail to alert the press, he didn't even inform his own partners, who after all were footing nearly four-fifths of the bill. Sonny, like Joe, was a star, accountable to no one.

But Namath didn't sign that day. Instead, after practice, he went to Ewbank and requested permission to leave Peekskill. "He came to me in the afternoon and he was upset about some personal problems," Ewbank said the following day. "He said he had to just go into the city."

Weeb was hardly a disciplinarian, but on the eve of the Jets' first exhibition he denied permission. There was already talk around camp that Namath had missed bedcheck the previous week. Now the coach told him if he left, he'd be fined.

Namath went anyway. What was $340,000 minus fifty bucks? His brother Bobby had just come down with that mysterious family curse, the Doylestown flu, his legs suddenly gone numb. And what Bobby couldn't feel, Rose could. It was tearing her up. To hear Namath's account, he seemed more worried about his mother than his brother, whose condition was later attributed to a herniated disc. "Her brother died that way ten years ago," he later explained. "He stood up in the kitchen, his legs went dead and he died. She's awfully worried about that."

In typical Namath fashion, he sought solace at the bar. On August 4, between 1:45 and 3:00 A.M. he was at the Open End, where he met Charles

Parmiter, sports editor of *Time* magazine. Parmiter wasn't working on a tip that night, but had been bouncing around himself, from a party on Eighty-fifth Street to a pop at Mr. Laff's. Now, seeing Namath at the Open End, he introduced himself, hoping he could get an interview. After all, Parmiter knew Bear Bryant—sort of. Bryant held clinics at the private school his father ran in Hawaii. The coach had even been to the Parmiter residence.

Namath, however, was not impressed. It was late, he'd been drinking, and he was AWOL from camp. The last guy he wanted to see was some writer from *Time* magazine saying they had a "mutual friend" in Bear Bryant.

What happened from there was a matter of debate, legal and otherwise. According to Namath's affidavit, Parmiter asked why he wasn't in training camp. The quarterback said he didn't want to talk about it. Parmiter asked again. "At that point," said Namath, "I told him to leave me alone and I walked to the other side of the room where there was a small service counter. Parmiter followed me and again asked me why I was not in training camp. I told him that I did not want to be interviewed and that I was not going to answer any questions and I wanted him to leave me alone. However, he insisted on repeating his questions and remained standing closely in front of me. At that point I brushed Parmiter aside so that I could pass by."

Not long after that, he left the Open End with Mike Bite, Art Heyman, and Mickey Kearney to get a late snack.

Parmiter's affidavit is more eventful. According to the former *Time* correspondent, Namath refused his offer of a handshake, grabbed him by the lapels, and pushed him up against the cigarette machine. "Namath proceeded to hold me in this position for a period of approximately the next ten to fifteen minutes." During this time, Parmiter contended, Namath continued to threaten, throttle, and strike him. The "highly intoxicated" quarterback seemed particularly incensed by Parmiter's vocation, issuing a very Sinatra-esque proclamation: "I don't need any of you one-hundred-dollar-a-week creeps to go around writing about me."

In Parmiter's version Namath had two accomplices in "this coordinated, vicious and cowardly gang attack." One of them, never identified, warned the newsman to keep quiet or "something could happen to your family." The other was Mickey Kearney, who identified himself with characteristic modesty as "a professional boxer and shouted that he was going to break every bone in my body. . . . Whenever I attempted to shield myself from injury by raising my hands up toward my face, 'Mickey' forced me to keep my hands down and stated that if I brought my hands above my waist, he would kill me."

The intervening years have done nothing to clarify what exactly happened during the wee hours of August 4, 1967. Who was telling the truth? Or perhaps, the better question: Who was telling less of it?

Namath could get mean after drinking, but actual violence seems out of character. He wasn't a bully, much less the type to hold a smaller man down. There's no medical evidence in the form of a doctor's or hospital report to corroborate Parmiter's story of being smacked around for that long. By the standards of saloon altercations, ten to fifteen minutes is an epoch. On the other hand, Art Heyman—whose affidavit stated that Parmiter "was not struck, choked, or assaulted by Namath or anyone else"—now allows that "Joe swung at him."

"I didn't get paid a dime," says Parmiter, who has since written for a variety of publications from *Reader's Digest* to the *National Enquirer*. Parmiter, who has lived in the south of Spain for many years, can no longer recall why the case was dropped. Maybe he came to feel that the publicity itself was enough of a punishment for Namath. Maybe he, or the lawyers, simply tired of the matter.

Parmiter's suit and Namath's countersuit for defamation meandered their way through Manhattan State Supreme Court for a couple of years before an official "Stipulation of Discontinuance" was entered into the record without further notation on April 9, 1969. By then the case was moribund. Namath's attempt to depose Parmiter had been denied. Parmiter's attorney had been unable to secure the depositions he sought, mostly notably Kearney's. One assumes Namath's people wanted it that way, as there is substantial agreement on the subject of Mickey Kearney.

"Fucking lowlife," says Art Heyman.

"Drug addict," says Barry Skolnick.

"Bad kid," says Bobby Van. "Mickey had a quick first punch. He was a bully. If you hit him back, though, he wouldn't get up."

The sneaky first punch was Mickey's preferred method for shaking down bar owners. Mickey was a jack of many criminal trades: enforcing, collecting, thieving, and dealing. But he liked to be known, as Parmiter discovered, as a professional fighter. He trained at a Parks Department gym in Manhattan, where he wore his fight-night robe, a white terry-cloth number with his name on the back, just to work out. Kearney went five-eleven, about 210 pounds, a heavyweight. But his name does not even merit an entry in *The Ring Record Book*. The only mention of Mickey Kearney is a bout on March 26, 1968, in Secaucus, New Jersey. He was disqualified in the first round against Ronnie Williams of Brooklyn, N.Y. It was Williams's only win in five fights that year.

Mickey's talents were better suited to the street. You didn't want to crowd Joe when Mickey was around. Mickey was a scary guy. A mobster called Johnny Fats "sort of controlled him," says a bookmaker who grew up with Kearney. "Mickey would've been like half a made guy. But after a while, the guys realized they couldn't control him. He was too fucking crazy, too fucking wild."

But Joe didn't seem to mind. Bodyguard, gofer, pal—whatever function it was that Mickey actually served—Joe seemed to like his company. For a while, Mickey went everywhere with him. Wherever you saw Joe—in Vegas, tossing a football in Central Park, even on the Jets' sideline—you saw Mickey. The guy might've been bad news, but he was always around.

■   ■   ■

Just hours after Parmiter introduced himself at the Open End, the Jets played an exhibition in Bridgeport, Connecticut, where the fans took up a chant: "Namath needs a haircut." Much to their dismay, the shaggy quarterback didn't play beyond the first quarter. The Patriots, who lost 55–13, didn't offer much of a challenge. For Joe, the reckoning was still to come at a team meeting. Word of an altercation at the Open End was just trickling out, and his teammates were angry, as was Weeb. "I want a day off myself," said the coach. But Sonny was already campaigning for his star's inalienable right to be a star. "You can't treat him the same as anyone else because he's not the same," argued Sonny. "He's a superstar. You have to compare him with the DiMaggios, the Mantles and the Ruths."

Werblin had a point, but this wasn't the kind of logic that made the Matt Snells and Gerry Philbins very happy. "A lot of players resented the way Sonny treated Joe," says Snell. "But what were you going to do?" Says Philbin: "There were two sets of rules: one for all the other Jets, and one for Joe Namath. Because of Sonny Werblin, Weeb was afraid to discipline him."

Namath made his own case at a players-only meeting. His teammates accepted the apology as genuine. Joe's eyes were rimmed red, as if he'd been weeping. His act of contrition did not go into specifics, and that seemed to be okay with most of the guys. They didn't need to know exactly what was happening with the man's family, or what went down at the bar. (It would be another three weeks before Parmiter filed court papers.) But they did need Namath to be a leader. As Johnny Sample reminded him, that was part of the job description. It went with money and fame.

Namath could live with that. But his notion of leadership was a qualified one. "I like the idea of being a leader," Namath said after the meeting. "But what I do off the field is my business."

Weeb's business was to levy the fine, somewhere between $200 and $500. The Jets guarded the number as carefully as their quarterback. Considering all the factors, Weeb went as easy as he could, but it was still not easy enough for the boss. "If it were up to me," said Werblin, "I would not have fined Namath."

Then again, Sonny would be making it up to him very soon. On August 22, Namath finally signed his new deal, which included $185,000 in bonus payments alone.

That same day, the Jets cut Ray Abruzzese, who had been struggling with a muscle pull. "Worst move I've ever seen," remarked Namath. Weeb was clearing roster space for a rookie named Henry King, a six-four, 205-pound defensive back who had arrived in Peekskill with a healthy signing bonus. As a senior, King led the nation in interceptions. But Namath didn't care about that. To Namath, King—whose pro career would last all of thirteen games—was just "some rich rookie."

It is difficult to imagine an activity more deleterious to the human knee than professional football. Jets veteran left guard Sam DeLuca, captain of the offense, ruined his in the preseason. Cornerback Cornell Gordon's season ended when he took a vicious shot to the knee while running back an interception during the opener at Buffalo's War Memorial Stadium. With two minutes left in that game, Matt Snell tore up *his* knee. Just for good measure, the Jets lost that afternoon. A game that began with a pair of Namath-to-Maynard touchdowns—one of them a fifty-six-yard bomb—ended with New York blowing a 17-point lead.

But through the first part of that 1967 season the Jets seemed to have an answer for everything. In place of Gordon, Ewbank decided on Randy Beverly, an undrafted twenty-three-year-old from Colorado State whose career would last far beyond the thirteen games played by "rich rookie" Henry King. To assume DeLuca's duties, he came up with Randy Rasmussen, a twelfth-rounder from Kearney State via Elba, Nebraska, population 184. With nineteen-inch calves, Rasmussen had the squat, big-legged build the Jets preferred in their pass blockers. Though Chuck Knox had already left for the Detroit Lions (New York was fine and all, but it remained his dream to coach in the more respected National Football League), the 255-pound rookie was easily indoctrinated into the principles that governed the lives of Jets linemen. "I know if my man hits Joe," he said, "*I'm* in trouble."

In Snell's absence, Boozer's talents became even more apparent. He wasn't as big as Snell, and he didn't have a sprinter's speed, but his steps were endowed with an unusual combination of toughness and guile. Around the goal line or the first-down marker, Boozer ran like a man much bigger than his listed weight of 195. He could also break off big gains in the open field. A shake of his shoulders misdirected many a pursuing linebacker. And Boozer was great off the draw play, waiting that split second as the pursuing defenders

28. THE BEAUTY OF JOE

formed his angle of escape. After only half a season, Boozer would have thirteen touchdowns. The AFL single-season record was nineteen. But more important was the way his running enhanced Namath's passing.

After squandering that 17-point lead in the opener, the Jets rallied from 17 down to beat the Denver Broncos 38–24 on the road. Namath threw for 399 yards—a personal best and new team record. But that mark would last only a week, as the following Sunday saw him throw for 415 yards and three touchdowns against Miami. The Dolphins weren't good, but neither were they bad enough to diminish Namath's accomplishment. Four-hundred-yard games were a rarity in 1967. And though the AFL was known as a passer's league, Namath became the first of its quarterbacks in three years to throw for over 400 yards. He played the position with a new sense of daring and distance. One had the impression that, unlike any other quarterback, he could score from anywhere at any time. In just that second quarter against the Dolphins, Namath threw for 216 yards.

Numbers like those made the Raiders ever more eager to pound him. And though they may have had the league's best defense, Namath would frustrate their worst intentions. Their game was scheduled for a Saturday night at Shea. A swirling wind, arriving in great gusts off Jamaica Bay, made passing difficult for both quarterbacks. The wind was an occupational hazard at Shea, one that Namath had been dealing with since his rookie year. By now, he knew this much: if you can't throw a good game, you can call one, which is precisely what he did. The Raiders kept blitzing, and Namath kept calling 25 Lag, a delay that gave him a series of options. Mostly, he opted to run Boozer on the draw. Without so much as a touchdown pass, the Jets won 27–14. Even Namath's best-known tormentor, Ben Davidson, had to admit, "He called a nice game." The Raiders' offense was in a less charitable mood, as the Jets had done to their quarterback what Davidson & Co. had planned for Namath. Daryle Lamonica was sacked four times. "Their defense didn't show me anything and their offense was holding on every play," said guard Gene Upshaw. "Wait until we get them back in Oakland."

That engagement was still a couple months off. In the meantime the Jets were now 3–1, in sole possession of first place. Namath was still setting new marks, still establishing the outrageous boundaries to his game. One came the very next week against Houston at Shea. The Jets jumped out to a 17–0 lead. Then, on taking his third snap of the second half, Namath threw for Maynard, who had already caught one touchdown. But the ball was picked off by Miller Farr, an Oiler defensive back who returned it fifty-one yards. It was Namath's first interception of the afternoon, and his sixth of the season (an improvement over the previous season's pace). With the Jets driving on their next possession, Namath again threw for Maynard. And again, he found Farr. Infinitely more horrifying to the Jets' high command, however, was the sight of Namath himself making the tackle sixty-seven yards from the point of interception. The risk was for naught; Houston scored five plays later. And before the third quarter was over, Namath would throw another. This one, intercepted by Ken Houston, was returned forty-three yards for a touchdown.

Oblivious to the boos, Ewbank kept Namath in the game. And Namath, never one to disappoint, kept on throwing interceptions. There would be three more, including another two picked off by Miller Farr. Meanwhile, the Jets had scored a field goal, a touchdown, and a two-point conversion as Namath, undaunted by Farr's three previous interceptions, finally caught him with his back turned. "I just floated the ball up," he said. Maynard's catch—despite an interference call on Houston's Larry Carwell—tied the score at 28.

With five seconds left, Namath dropped back to his own 28-yard line to throw his final, and most dramatic, interception of the day. Unlike the five others, though, this one was not really his fault. The best he could do, under the circumstances, was throw the ball high and far in the direction of George Sauer. W. K. Hicks intercepted at the Oiler 25, and the gun sounded as he ran toward the goal. At the Jet 35, Hicks lateraled to Ken Houston. At the 29, amid a cloud of dust rising off the Shea infield, Houston lateraled to Carwell. As he sprinted down the sideline, Carwell picked up a bodyguard, 240-pound middle linebacker Garland Boyette. "That big Boyette," said Namath. "That's all I could see."

Namath shrugged off big Boyette and brought down Carwell four yards from the end zone. For a few long moments, the quarterback remained face-down in the dirt. The 245 yards Houston tallied on interceptions set a new AFL record. But more astounding was Namath's line on the game: 49 attempts, 27 completions (the season high, in both leagues), 6 interceptions (also, a season high), and 2 tackles, the last of which saved the game and kept the Jets in first place.

In fact, there was still more to it. "Joe broke a small bone in his ankle on that play," Dr. Nicholas would recall. "No one knew about it. We kept it quiet."

Namath gave no hint of the injury, even as he cut the tape from his ankles in the locker room. He seemed merely despondent. The hustler had been hustled. The Oiler backs, particularly Farr, had picked up his tendency to throw quick outs. On one interception a receiver broke the wrong way; another came on a ball that was deflected. Then there were some plain old bad passes, and finally, the one he threw into the crowd. But that was more detail than most people, particularly newspaper guys, could digest. "There was a reason for every one of those interceptions," Namath said glumly. "Stupidity."

The explanation did nothing to disband the humid scrum gathered around his locker. LeRoy Neiman was drawing furiously, putting colored chalk to paper. Namath took a dip from his tin of Skoal and a sip of orange soda. The writers were still scribbling, still wanting more.

What the hell was he supposed to say, booze and broads?

Actually, he might have. Art Heyman remembers bumping into Joe the night before. He was loaded. You got to go home, said Heyman. But Joe wasn't in the going-home mood and instead ended up crashing on Heyman's couch. The next morning, as Heyman recalls, Joe had an unusual pregame request: "a shot of peppermint schnapps for his breath."

■   ■   ■

The second half of the season began in Kansas City. Though the Jets were still in first place in the Eastern Division with a 5–1–1 record, the Chiefs were favored by a touchdown. As Namath went, so did the spread. The truth of his injured ankle—the fracture had been grudgingly described as a "bruise"—was a secret to everyone but the bookmakers, who stopped taking bets when Namath didn't appear at practice earlier in the week. Only after he returned did the game go back on the boards.

But even with Namath, the Jets would need a lot more than a touchdown against Kansas City. If the Chiefs didn't have the meanest defensive line, they certainly had the biggest, a group that now included Namath's old friend Ernie Ladd and 287-pound Buck Buchanan, who batted back four of his passes that day. For Jets fans, the highlight of the game might have been their quarterback's thirteen-yard run for a first down. In fact, "run" is a charitable description. With the fractured ankle, Namath's sprint was another man's hobble. He was more vulnerable than ever, a fact of which the Chiefs took full advantage. Then again, at least he was able to hobble off the field under his own power. Emerson Boozer had to be carried off after Chiefs cornerback Willie Mitchell, who had already intercepted Namath twice, delivered a blind shot to the running back's right knee. The impact of the collision ripped the ligaments. Through the first half of the season, Boozer had been the Jets' best player. But now, following this 42–18 defeat in Kansas City, it looked as if his season was over.

Matt Snell returned the following week against the Bills. Though the Jets won 20–10, with Namath throwing for 338 yards, Snell himself couldn't manage more than six carries. The following week, in a win against hapless Boston, he left the game with a concussion after just two. This was not a good sign for the Jets.

A healthy Snell could run, catch, and block. He would contribute as much to Namath's accomplishments as anyone who ever played for the team. But theirs was a curious relationship. Snell had been Sonny's first star, the prize Werblin took from the Maras. But the signing of Namath had made him just another highly skilled member of the Jets' supporting cast. While Snell always considered Namath a superior talent—never given his proper credit as a student of the game—he disliked the flagrant double standard. Snell was a consummate football player, fluent in every aspect of the game. As far as he was concerned, Joe could be a movie star on his own time. But now, as he tried to come back on his bad knee, Snell couldn't help but empathize with Namath. The feeling was most acute when Dr. Nicholas pulled out his syringe. Aspiration had become a ritual they shared.

"It's like a horse needle, looks like a sipping straw," says Snell. "They got to get that sucker all the way in there. They give you a local anesthetic, but it still hurts. I've always been afraid of needles. But the biggest thing is when you hear that needle breaking through the tissue, into the joint capsule itself. You can hear it as they push in–pop. *Pop*. It's almost like popping a balloon."

Nicholas would draw back the plunger, and the tubes would fill quickly with a yellowish brown liquid. It was not unusual for the fluid to spurt three or four inches as he replaced full tubes with empties. "That's how much pressure builds up in the knee," explains Snell. Nicholas told him that the fluid was the body's way of defending the wounded joint, which was one way to look at it. But there was another. In those tubes was a spirit distilled from pain. It looked like sewer water.

■   ■   ■

On December 3 the Jets hosted the Denver Broncos, losers in 10 of 12 games. The bookmakers favored the Jets by two touchdowns. The fans favored staying home. It was a miserable, rainy day, and the Giants—still New York's most popular football team—were on television, live from Cleveland. Shea was half empty, with 28,712 no-shows. For once the fans showed better sense than the bookies. Of Namath's sixty attempts, four were intercepted in the second quarter. Each of the "mudballs," as one columnist called them, led to Denver scores. "The ball was so caked with mud I don't see how he could throw it," said George Sauer. The final was 33–24, Broncos.

By now, it wasn't just the fans who were booing Namath. Some of his own teammates had joined the chorus.

"He was out drinking with Sonny the night before and came in late to the locker room," recalls Paul Zimmerman, then the *Post*'s beat man and an ardent defender of Namath.

"I'm not going to say he was drunk, he might have overslept," says Gerry Philbin. "All I know is, he came in late, when everybody was already dressed. Prima donna."

"I saw a situation where Joe came straight from being out with Sonny, drinking all night, into a game on Sunday," says Snell. "He had to get in the sauna. You could just smell the booze. You knew it wasn't good for him. But sometimes he played better. And sometimes he didn't. Sometimes, you know, he'd throw five interceptions."

Namath once claimed he rarely took a third drink the night before a game, but preponderance of anecdotal evidence suggests otherwise. "He was boozing," says Jack Lambert. "But there was also a reason for the boozing. His legs would swell up like balloon legs. Then they'd stick him with those six-inch needles. It was a terrible, agonizing situation."

Besides, it wasn't as if Namath had invented this form of pain management. "We were *supposed* to drink," says Larry Grantham. "We were following the heritage of the pro athlete going back to Babe Ruth. You punished your body. It was so ingrained: you played ball until you couldn't play anymore." After that, you headed for the bar.

Bartenders seemed to know Joe. They were his medicine men, purveyors of elixirs that soothed all that could ail a man. The medical doctors gave him cortisone and Butazolidin. Alcohol—whether wine, beer, Sambuca, Grand Marnier, Johnnie Walker Red, vodka, blackberry brandy—was just his way of supplementing the treatments. This much he knew for sure: "Alcohol helps as a painkiller."

Still, his pain was constant. That wicked stepmother never let him out of her sight. But Namath made little, if any, distinction between the tremors that ran through body and mind. It was all routed through nerve tissue, and it all hurt.

Al "Tank" Passuello, who ran a bar Namath would frequent for years, recalls a particular late evening with the quarterback drinking Johnnie Red. He ordered another and another, and so on, until finally Passuello was moved to remark, "Jesus Christ, Joe, you got a game tomorrow."

Suddenly, the bar became a kind of confessional partition. "I got so much fucking pain," Namath confided. "This is the only thing that calms me down. If anything, I won't be jittery."

The barman seemed to understand what Namath was saying. What was the difference between ache and anxiety? Why not dose them the same way? Relief was a state of relaxation. Passuello poured another round. Cheers. "I'm a better man for it," said Joe.

■   ■   ■

As the Denver game ended, Namath took a hit that left him seeing double, but that was the least of his problems. His vision would clear; neurologically, he'd be fine. Orthopedically, however, he was more of a mess than ever. There was the ankle, and of course, the knees, with the "good" left one now hurting more than the "bad" right one. The most immediate concern, though, was the thumb on his throwing hand, which had become so swollen that it was first thought to be broken. Once again, the Jets managed to keep it a secret from everybody but the bookies. Namath didn't practice until Friday, when the *Post*'s Paul Zimmerman—who wrote a football gambling column called "Pigskin Prophet"—broke the story. And again, the bookies didn't start taking action on Sunday's game with Kansas City until Namath could be seen practicing with the team.

Unfortunately, this encounter with the Chiefs proved a less than a sporting proposition. With Namath's mangled right thumb, the Jets weren't much of a threat to pass—certainly not with ten-knot winds coming off Jamaica Bay. And without Boozer or a healthy Snell, they couldn't run. On this particularly frigid afternoon, they couldn't even block. Buck Buchanan and Ernie Ladd attacked with an intelligent ferocity that made Randy Rasmussen look like a chump rookie, and Sherman Plunkett a fat old man. Namath was sacked five times.

"He took one hell of a beating and he didn't say a word," Buchanan noted after the game. "Even when he got the ball away we were close enough to hit him."

"If anybody rated that $400,000, he sure did," said Ladd. "He was in pain. . . . He came up limping and you could see it."

Certainly, the Raiders took note of his agony while watching game films that week. Their strategy hadn't changed since '65: take out Namath, and you take out the Jets. In all that time, the Jets had only beaten the Raiders once— back in October, at Shea, still Oakland's only loss of the season. "This is the game we've been looking forward to all year," said Davidson. "Joe's a marked man," said Dan Birdwell, who'd be lining up across from Sherman Plunkett. "Joe knows it. We know it."

Everyone knew it. But after the Chiefs had gotten through with him, there wasn't much left. Then again, what Namath lacked in mobility, he'd make up for in motivation. With two games left in the season, the Jets and Oilers were now tied for first place, and vying for that single play-off spot from the Eastern Division. Then there was the Jets-Raiders rivalry. What had begun with Namath and Davidson in the mud on old Frank Youell Field now engulfed both teams with seething animosity. The coaching staffs had long accused each other of spying. But even spies respected certain rules of engagement, which was more than could be said for the Raiders and the Jets. The Raiders were cheap-shot artists; the Jets would grab and hold. The Raiders went so far as to charge the officials with conspiring in the plot to protect Namath at all costs.

Oakland had the AFL's best defense that year. Nicknamed Eleven Angry Men, they took particular pride in an emerging statistic: the quarterback sack. Their front four had already notched a record sixty-one of them, dropping AFL quarterbacks for a total of 581 yards in losses.

Through the first half of the game they didn't put much hurt on Namath, leaving the Jets up 14–10. Namath had thrown for one touchdown, a twenty-nine-yarder to Maynard, and rushed for another as he picked up a fumble on the 1-yard line and dove into the end zone. Then, early in the third quarter, Namath dropped back to pass and took a huge hit from Ike Lassiter. Unlike Ben Davidson, Lassiter didn't have a handlebar mustache, nor did he entertain reporters with stories of drinking tequila and riding his motorcycle through Mexico. Davidson may have been a great, glib character, but Lassiter was the superior football player. And all of him—six-five, 270—was directed at Namath, full stride, full speed, full force. There was a strange perfection to the way Lassiter hit him straight on, a forearm to the face delivered at the quarterback's most vulnerable moment, just as he began to uncoil. Namath never saw the resulting interception. What he really saw in that moment must be unknown even to him.

With seven more plays, the Raiders had a touchdown and the lead. The Jets came back, a long completion to Sauer giving them first-and-goal from the Raider 10. Namath tried to run in off a roll-out, but was stopped at the 1. Neither Bill Mathis nor Matt Snell could make that yard.

The Raiders kept adding to their lead. By early in the fourth quarter the score was 31–14, a differential ensuring that Namath would be passing after almost every snap. Though Namath had been sacked just once (by right tackle Tom Keating for a fourteen-yard loss), the trench warfare had been especially furious that day, full of grappling, stomping, punching.

With 11:43 remaining and the Jets with the ball on their own 12, Namath dropped back again. Winston Hill braced himself for yet another charge by Davidson. "I blocked him," recalls Hill. "In fact, I thought it was one of the better blocks I made." "He had a hold of me for a while," recalls Davidson, but a "while" is relative, a tricky measure of time. In the midst of a game, seconds can feel like years. Hill finally lost track of his quarterback as Joe fled the pocket, unable to find a receiver. It was now a broken play, though the full dimensions of its brokenness remained to be seen.

Another "while" passed. Davidson trailed Namath to the other side of the field. He was too late to make a sack or bat down the pass, which would fall incomplete. But by that point, Davidson was no longer concerned with the football. "You get a shot at him and you got to relieve your frustrations," he said after the game.

The offending blow was a left to the head. It was a cheap shot, and a late one, too. But most of all, it was spectacularly theatrical. Namath was left splayed facedown on the turf. The force of the blow had knocked the helmet off his head. There he was: with white shoes and mod hair, but already channeling the spirit of the bald and bloodied Y. A. Tittle. At the tender age of twenty-four, Namath would become supplicant to the Hit. Or would he? This was going out live on NBC, an early if unplanned experiment in Reality TV.

Namath tried to rise, finally succeeding, then staggering toward the Oakland sideline. He was weaving like a busted-out drunk, but with each step he collected a ransom in respect. Finally, he caught himself, redirecting his path back to the huddle. Dr. Nicholas made him count backward. A fighter would've been counted out; but Namath was counting himself in.

"I don't know how much more the guy can take," Oakland's Birdwell said after the game. "One time he looked right at me and grinned and said something, but he could have been talking in a foreign language. . . . It was like he was punchy or something."

Joe hit Pete Lammons for nine yards on the play immediately following Davidson's hit. But by then, recalls Davidson, "The game degenerated into a brawl." He brawled with Dave Herman. He brawled with Winston Hill. But through it all Namath kept throwing. He had two more touchdowns and a 2-point conversion left in him that day. He finished with three touchdowns, three interceptions, and tied his season-high of 27 completions for 370 yards, most of them to Sauer and Maynard.

But the Jets' eventual loss, 38–29, combined with Houston's win over San Diego, all but ended their once-strong play-off hopes. Still, the postgame talk was less concerned with the team's collapse than the quarterback's courage. "His right cheek looks like he's carrying a baseball in it," wrote the *Post*'s Paul Zimmerman, who compared the discoloration to a West Coast sunset.

"It has to be broken," said Dr. Nicholas.

Namath was asked when it happened. "This morning," he said, telling the writers that he bit into an especially tough steak for breakfast.

He'd let Davidson hit him again before giving that big bastard any satisfaction. He tried to grin. "That's what the game's all about—hitting," he said. "If you can't take it don't play." Namath could take it with style. They wanted to know where it was broken, the cheek or the jaw. They wanted to know how he could possibly play against the Chargers next week. What was the difference? "Got to play," he said. "Even if the damn jaw's broken off."

Later, Namath made an appearance in the bar of the Jets' hotel. He wore a snappy silk jacket and a funky French-cuffed shirt. While it was his habit to brood after a painful loss, that night was an exception. Even the newspaper guys just happened to see him with a glass in his hand. For a guy with two bad knees (the left now required aspiration as well), a chipped ankle bone, a mangled thumb and, as X-rays would soon reveal, a freshly fractured cheekbone, Namath looked to be in a great mood, which was just how he wanted it, too. Let the newspaper guys write. Let people talk. Joe himself couldn't have been more chatty as he sipped his scotch and signed autographs, his very public graciousness a spectacular "Fuck you" to the Raiders. He finally limped out holding his rocks glass and stepped into a waiting cab. Most of his teammates were going to Escondido, where the Jets would stay before playing the Chargers. But

Namath and Hudson, who had been knocked out of the game with a dislocated hip, were flying to Vegas. "He never said a word about the pain," says
Hudson. "The only thing he ever complained about was losing money."

Even when he lost, though, Joe loved Vegas. One time, a guy there gave
him a hooker as a present. She was from Freedom, Pennsylvania, not far from
Beaver Falls. They had some drinks, talked for a while. It was a good time:
kind of funny, kind of nice. Good for the healing process. Good for the soul.
He should've sent Ben Davidson a postcard: *Wish you were here . . .*

When he got to Escondido, Namath learned that his teammates had voted
Don Maynard the Jets' most valuable player for 1967. He had no quarrel with
that. Maynard would finish the season leading the league with 1,434 receiving
yards, better than 20 yards a catch. George Sauer, who led the league with
seventy-five catches, would've been a good choice, too. Namath himself finished sixth in the balloting among his teammates. Who knows why? Maybe
they were still pissed about his hanging out with Sonny before the Denver
game. Joe had more important things to worry about. He was having his helmet fitted with a "protective" face mask—"a birdcage," as he called it.

After the X-rays came back positive for a fractured right cheekbone, people
around the team assumed that Namath would play only if the Dolphins beat
Houston on Saturday night, thereby keeping the Jets' slim play-off hopes alive.
But as it happened, Houston won big. Sauer wept at the news. "It was all for
nothing," he said.

Namath did play, though. The following day, he threw for 343 yards and
four touchdowns without an interception in a 42–31 Jets win. That gave him
4,007 yards on the season. No one had ever passed for 4,000 yards in a single
season. In fact, nobody had come within 250 yards of that figure. Namath's
record would stand until 1979, after the NFL season had been expanded from
fourteen to sixteen games.

■   ■   ■

All these years later, at the start of a new millennium, Ben Davidson would
like to correct the record. In many ways, Namath made him a celebrity. The
publicity bestowed upon him that day in Oakland has lasted a lifetime. Davidson has appeared in movies and starred in beer commercials. For years a photograph of his helmet-jarring hit on Namath occupied a prominent place in
the Raiders' corporate headquarters. But in fact it wasn't he who broke Namath's cheekbone. It was Ike Lassiter. "Poor Ike," says Davidson. "To this day,
he thinks if the press had gotten it right, he would have been the one who got
the Lite Beer commercials."

Lassiter's hit came early in the third quarter, meaning that Namath played
almost the entire second half with a busted face. But he never identified
Lassiter as his assailant. That refusal of an acknowledgment was the subtlest of

insults, Joe's way of saying: That all you got? Whatever abuse had been inflicted on his skeletal system, Namath was careful never to give the perpetrators any satisfaction. "I never thought we got to Joe," says Davidson. Now, as ever, the idea of an unbowed, purple-faced quarterback enjoying himself at the gaming tables fills Davidson with a kind of awe. "That was the beauty of Joe," he says. "God bless him."

A portion of Namath's upper jaw remained numb until well after Christmas, a fact he encouraged correspondents to neglect. "I don't want the guys who did it to get any satisfaction," Namath explained.

It was too late for that. The Raiders' defensive line seemed to be everyone's story leading up to the second annual AFL-NFL championship in Miami. Though the game was being hyped as "the Super Bowl"—the name owing to Lamar Hunt's daughter, and her fascination with the high-bouncing rubber Super Ball—the case for superlatives escaped most observers. The first such interleague championship, held amid a local TV blackout, was so eagerly anticipated that 32,000 seats went unsold at Los Angeles Memorial Coliseum. Those foolish enough to pay $12 for a ticket—an outrageous sum in those days—were rewarded with the Green Bay Packers' less-than-exciting win over the Kansas City Chiefs, 35–10, a score that seemed to vindicate the notion of the AFL as a Mickey Mouse league.

29. BOSSES

The second Super Bowl figured to be just as competitive. To most fans, the championship had already been decided when the Packers beat the Dallas Cowboys in subzero temperatures, a game immortalized as "the Ice Bowl." With two weeks to defrost, Green Bay would easily overwhelm the Raiders. Jimmy "the Greek" Snyder, a good oddsmaker with a great talent for publicity, favored the Packers by "a strong 14." Vince Lombardi's charges had perfected the Power Sweep, as predictable as it was powerful, and yet another indication of the NFL's vast superiority.

In the meantime, the press had to manufacture demi-celebrities like Jimmy the Greek and Gentle Ben Davidson, who was pleasantly accommodating when recounting his adventures in quarterback bashing and motorcycle riding. Davidson was quick to discern the comedic elements of this preposterously named event, at which writers and cameramen seemed to outnumber the fans. Of course—the sports media had nothing better to do. Pro basketball, still a fledgling professional sport, didn't arouse much interest in January, and spring training didn't start for another couple of months. Besides, the weather really was super.

Typically, the media types would intercept Davidson as he made his way from his hotel room to the dining hall. "When he sits down by the pool it's an automatic signal for a press conference to begin," noted the *Post*'s Paul Zimmerman. Davidson understood his role: *someone* had to entertain all these guys. Someone had to feed this beast for whom foils, dupes, and jesters were delicacies. The year before it had been Fred "the Hammer" Williamson, who used the inaugural Super Bowl as an audition tape for a career well spent in blaxploitation films. "The Packers? Shee-it," Williamson had said. "Lombardi? Sheeit. We're going to whip their asses. . . . I'm going to lay a few hammers on 'em."

Before it ended, Williamson had been knocked out by the Green Bay sweep and had to be carried off the field.

Davidson and the Raiders wound up faring only a little better—at least Big Ben was able to leave under his own power. The final was 33–14, Green Bay. As the Packers had only beaten the Raiders by 19, one might argue that the NFL's margin of victory was actually shrinking. Then again, the Raiders had beaten the Oilers by 33. One didn't need to be schooled in higher branches of mathematics to appreciate the statistical implications. Even sportswriters understood. The results seemed to ratify a prediction made the year before when William N. Wallace, the *Times*'s chief football correspondent, wrote: "These Super Bowl games will now go on year after year, but it may be some time before an American League team will be good enough to win one."

■   ■   ■

Not long after the Hammer regained consciousness, Namath's "good" leg was placed in a cast extending from thigh to ankle. A "small tear" to a tendon had been causing chronic pain and inflammation below his kneecap. Bursitis was nothing to be overly concerned about. "The injury," according to the *Times,* "is akin to a tennis elbow." That assessment might have been of greater comfort if Namath were a tennis player. Still, it was hoped that immobilization for a period of three to four weeks would have a corrective effect.

Unfortunately the bursitis remained long after the cast was removed. A decision was then made to repair the "small tear" on his now-atrophied leg. Dr. Nicholas performed the thirty-minute surgery March 20 at Lenox Hill. With no reported complications, the operation was considered to be yet another success. This time around, there was little media coverage. Though they belonged to the world's only 4,000-yard passer, Namath's knees had become a dreadfully familiar subject. Even Werblin, with his great talent for press agentry, would have had problems turning another operation into an event. Besides, by then Sonny was having problems of his own.

■   ■   ■

Werblin's partners had never shared his kinetic ambition. They had never considered the commercial potential of fertilizing sports with showbiz. They were not particularly concerned with football's place in a televised world. Unlike Sonny, none of them saw the Jets as a second career. The Jets were supposed to be merely a good time.

"The social aspect of it was very important," says Michael Martin, who like his father, Townsend, was an heir to the fortune of Henry Phipps, Andrew Carnegie's partner in the steel business.

The families of Martin, Leon Hess, and Phil Iselin knew the Werblins from Monmouth Park, a beautiful track on the Jersey Shore. Donald Lillis, the other partner, also had an interest in horse racing. They all figured that a day at Shea would be very much like a day at the races. In their view, stock in the Gotham Football Club Inc. was like membership in a good club. "They got into it to have fun," says Lillis's daughter, Helen Dillon.

In the beginning, the arrangement fulfilled each partner's expectation. Pregame festivities were held on the press level at Shea, in what they called the Directors' Room. "It was exciting," remembers Dillon, "because Sonny always had show business people there." The other owners were only too happy to have him as their front man. He kept interesting company and he knew how to deal with the press. Besides, who really wanted to run a football team?

But the relationship began to change when the newspapers that Sonny had cultivated so skillfully started referring to him as *the* owner. After a while, he could no longer be considered first among equals. The way Sonny reconfigured the team, he had no equals. The Jets were *his* team.

"All of a sudden," Dillon remembers, "he had his own pregame party. They were in another room."

"I think it was symbolic of what was happening," says Martin. "Instead of all the partners being together, Sonny had his own group, physically someplace else. It was almost like a class thing."

The irony isn't lost on Martin, for whom class is a matter of ancestry. But apart from the irony, the fact is that Sonny, usually so sensitive to the value of manners in commerce, should have known better. His partners were men of varied temperaments who acquired their fortunes through varied endeavors: inheritance, stock, oil and garment businesses. But when it came to second-class treatment, they were of one mind. The resentment was said to be particularly acute among the wives, who felt they were being shown up by Mr. and Mrs. Sonny Werblin. "He degraded us," said Bette Iselin. "He made us feel really nothing. It became an intolerable situation for all of us. He hated the idea he had partners."

There was no question, even among those increasingly dissatisfied partners, that Sonny Werblin had substantially saved New York's AFL franchise. Perhaps, given the NBC contract, he had even saved the AFL. But the ultimate expression of his promotional brilliance had also become the great symbol of his hubris. With regard to Broadway Joe, Sonny didn't care what his partners thought, just as he didn't care what his players thought. Going into the '68 season, it was expected that the Jets would have to renegotiate Namath's contract. But Sonny never even told his partners—who owned more than 75 percent of the team—that he had already renegotiated the previous August when Namath was making headlines for breaking camp and beating up sportswriters. Sonny didn't realize that by giving Namath his security he would sacrifice his own. His partners were furious when they found out about Namath's secret deal. At Monmouth Park, such an expenditure would never have been approved without the board of directors. Why should the rules be different at Shea?

"We just wanted to know what was happening before it happened," said Townsend Martin.

"What disturbed us," said Phil Iselin, "was not the lack of identity or publicity, but a lack of knowing what was going on."

The most outraged of the group was Donald Lillis. He, too, was self-made: having dropped out of college, he wound up as a partner in Bear, Stearns & Co. with his own seat on the stock exchange. Lillis, who had also been president of Bowie Race Course in Maryland, was a 145-pound end in high school. Now, at sixty-six, he was a widower in poor health in quest of a few kicks. "My father was such a frustrated football player," says Helen Dillon. As such, he didn't need Sonny making him a frustrated owner.

An ultimatum was issued in short order: He's out, or I'm out, said Lillis.

The best on-the-record explanation of subsequent events appeared in Milton Gross's *Post* column, which quoted Iselin as saying: "My job was to try to save it for Sonny. I tried to get him to buy the team at a fair price for him, $7,000,000. He offered $1,500,000 down and seven years to pay the balance. It wasn't satisfactory. There was no guarantee on the payment of the balance. He got his all in cash."

With his MCA training, Sonny knew better than to play at these games with his own money. Instead he sold his share, receiving a reported $1,638,000 on an initial investment that slightly exceeded $200,000. Of his former partners, Sonny said: "You didn't see them in Kansas City when it was fourteen below." Sonny loved the Jets. But he loved being the boss even more. "You can't run any venture by committee," he said.

On May 18, 1968, just before the sale was finalized, Sonny leaked word of Namath's new contract, making it sound as if the deal had just been concluded. The rushed timing of the announcement, which did not even include the terms, seemed to make little sense. The Preakness would lead the papers that Sunday. The Yankees had made a trade. Even the Mets had won. On another day, Sonny could have had the back pages to himself. But he knew what he was doing. On the eve of his buyout, the newspapers were still identifying Werblin as *the* owner. "It suddenly dawned on me," he said, "why should I let them have the pleasure of announcing it?"

The report was particularly galling to Lillis, who succeeded Werblin as team president. His daughter, Helen, liked Namath well enough. She even went out with one of his friends, a handsome record executive named Bob Skaff. "We double-dated with Joe one time, and I *still* have a hangover," she says. "He was *something*." But her father was of another mind: "With the women and the booze, Joe was not your All-American football hero. And that kind of teed my father off."

Lillis was determined to acquire the services of a disciplinarian, and the most renowned of them was Vince Lombardi, living symbol of NFL supremacy. Among Lillis's first acts as team president was to offer Lombardi a job, either as coach, general manager, or both; whatever the title, Lombardi would be the boss. But the offer was promptly refused, and Lillis wouldn't have another chance. The Jets would never get that authority figure he had envisioned, one who could rule the team and rein in its quarterback. Lillis's tenure as team president lasted exactly two months. On July 23, he died of a heart attack.

His daughter inherited his share of the Jets; Phil Iselin was appointed president. While Iselin didn't want the job, Townsend Martin and oilman Leon Hess—each of whom had more than double his stake in the team—didn't want it even more. "My father would have been a much tougher owner," says Helen Dillon. Unlike his predecessors, Iselin didn't fancy himself as either a football guy or a showbiz guy. He just sold dresses.

■　　■　　■

Having unloaded his interest in the Jet Set, Bobby Van had nothing better to do than hang out with Joe, now rehabilitating from his third surgery in as many years. The regimen wasn't always orthodox. Joe and Bobby occasionally rented a two-seater bicycle for kicks, but mostly they just walked, mile after mile. Those were some hot spring days, and it was their habit to break for a beer along the way. Among their stops was a bar at Sixty-second and Lexington Avenue, the Margin Call. It was owned by some stockbrokers and managed by a guy named Danny who lived in the Newport East. One day Danny came over and bought a round. The brokers were looking for a buyer, he mentioned. Was Bobby interested?

Yes, he was interested. Ray Abruzzese would be interested, too. And don't forget Joe. When Werblin sold out, Namath lost the closest thing he'd ever have to a boss, someone who would set him straight. Werblin was the guy who told him not to slouch. Werblin was the guy who reprimanded him for allowing himself to be photographed with Barbra Streisand without a tie. And Werblin was the guy who told him to stay out of the bar business. But now Werblin was out.

Bobby managed the place for a couple of weeks while they thought it through. Then again, what was to think? This was the joint they'd been waiting for. All they needed was a name. The Goal Post, offered Ray. Nah, that was kind of corny for three swinging bachelors. What about something with "bachelors"? The Bachelor Pad? Three Bachelors?

How about Bachelors III?

Why not?

About the only thing Joe would apologize for was not earning his degree. "I've been standing still intellectually," he admitted to Dave Anderson. "I don't improve myself mentally . . . scholastically," he told Dick Young.

As it did not concern his sideburns or occasional goatee, this was not the kind of confession most locker-room moralists wanted to hear. What's more, it belied his own unusual intelligence.

Back in 1965, three days after Namath's arrival in Peekskill, the Jets were tested on their knowledge of the playbook, then about an inch and a half thick. The exam consisted of 106 questions, of which Namath answered 104 correctly. The two he missed concerned the blocking sled and proper stances for linemen, information a quarterback would never need. The rookie's score only confirmed what Paul Bryant and Larry Bruno had known for years: Joe's genius for football was as much mental as physical. For Namath, football

30. STUDENT OF THE GAME

was a branch of Pool Hall Geometry, part mathematics, part psychology. Interestingly enough, it was that great young arm—the raw, arrogant force behind so many interceptions—that often obscured his true aptitude for the game.

"He could sit down and listen to some football concept for the first time, and snap, snap, he'd have a mental picture of every phase of it," recalled Bryant.

When obliged to discuss football with civilians or—worse yet—sportswriters, Namath found it was best to use few words. "I can explain things to people with diagrams," he said. His take was visual, not verbal. Joe *saw* the game: movement charted against time. It was not unusual for him to borrow a waiter's pencil and diagram plays on cocktail napkins. When it came to football, Joe had that gift of the highest order—imagination.

The question, however, was whether he had leadership. With two Super Bowls now entered into evidence, the football establishment regarded Namath's

4,000-yard season as a counterfeit record set against inferior competition. In raising the mark, he had generated less praise than debate, prompting Dave Anderson's cover story for *True* magazine, "Could Swinging Joe Namath Make It in the Tough NFL?" In an issue timed to hit the stands just as the 1968 season began, Anderson polled six current or former NFL head coaches, among whom there was agreement on the subject of Namath's physical talent. "His arm, his release of the ball are just perfect," said Lombardi, the most effusive in his praise. "Namath is as good a passer as I've ever seen."

But Redskins coach Otto Graham, a Hall of Fame quarterback who did the commentary on Jets radio broadcasts during Namath's rookie year, harped on the fact that the guys in his own locker room had never selected him as their most valuable player. "To me," he said, "this proves that he does not have the respect he should from his teammates. It's tough for the Jets to win if their quarterback doesn't have that respect. Being out the night before a game does not generate it."

The respect accorded Joe was a curious commodity; how much he had depended on whom you asked. It almost seemed as if people were judging two ballplayers. There was Broadway Joe, the guy who stayed out too late; there was Namath, diligent student of the game. Yet even his critics recognized the knowledge he acquired through long hours of preparation. "People talk about Joe partying," says Snell, "but he had to spend a lot of time watching film and going over game plans." As conspicuous as the llama rug in his apartment were the reels of film and the movie projector he kept there. Typically, he'd put in a couple hours watching game films before going out. "The one-eyed monster," he called the projector. "It doesn't lie."

Joe the hustler was an assiduous observer of opponents' tendencies and flaws. Defensive backs were conditioned to think that a receiver would make his move within fifteen yards of the line of scrimmage. Maybe, if the guy was special, he'd go at eighteen. But beyond that distance, a receiver who hadn't made his move was sprinting for the end zone. Quarterbacks didn't throw twenty-yard square-outs. Even if they had the arm, they wouldn't have the time.

The Jets were an exception. Not only did they have a twenty-yard square-out in the playbook, within a year of Joe's arrival they were running twenty-five-yard square-outs. "Joe and I worked it out ourselves," explains George Sauer. "He was one of the few quarterbacks who could make that pass, and our offensive line was good enough to give him time. Guys like Winston Hill and Dave Herman could give him four whole seconds. And, gosh, those backs of ours could block. They could pick up anybody on the blitz."

To see it work in a game—the defensive back hauling ass upfield as Sauer suddenly made his move—was a thrill, a brainy triumph in a brawny sport. Namath and Sauer put in many hours after practice, as their sessions became known for an emphasis on precision. They also had a good effect on

Maynard, who had been unfairly pegged as a sprinter in receiver's clothes. Sometimes, Weeb would actually run them off the field. "Save your legs for Sunday," he'd say.

But why quit when the work was so much fun? "We would invent patterns," says Sauer. There were endless variations and combinations: corner routes and post routes, head fakes and shoulder fakes, stops and starts, ins, outs and curls. Typically, their creations were based on something Joe had seen on the films, specific moves for specific defensive backs. The twenty-five-yard out, for example, worked very well on Buffalo's Butch Byrd.

"The timing was perfect," says Snell. "That's the kind of stuff that impressed you. Joe worked at his craft."

■   ■   ■

The summer of '68 afforded the Jets a new start. Training camp was held at Hofstra University in suburban Hempstead, Long Island. The players lived in an air-conditioned dormitory, Tower D. There was a bar called Bill's Meadowbrook right across the main local drag, Hempstead Turnpike. Not only had the Jets left their squalid quarters at Peekskill, they had forgotten some of the old grudges against Joe. Though Sonny was gone, his star system would remain, a fact of life for the New York Jets. But more than ever before, players wanted to hitch a ride on Joe's star. As the roster became a little younger, there came an acknowledgment that the players' lot was tethered to Namath's. The more he got, the more they could get. A couple of the guys still didn't like him and never would. But their opinions were not offered for public consumption.

As for the coach, Weeb got a little tougher that summer. When Sherman Plunkett, who'd already lost a step, reported to camp at 337 pounds, Ewbank told him he'd have to pay the Jets $15 a day in "training camp expenses" until he made weight. When that didn't work, Ewbank cut him and replaced him with Sam Walton, a rookie out of East Texas State. Weeb did much the same with defensive tackle Jim Harris, who was replaced by a rugged, undersized second-year man out of Texas, John Elliott. With Sonny's departure, Weeb even took on the press. The training room, where tape and physical therapy were dispensed, was now off-limits. Reporters were further ordered to vacate the locker room within an hour of kickoff on game days. Finally, Ewbank went so far as to ban hard liquor on team charter flights. The rule was supposed to apply to everyone, though Joe was never known to observe it. There were limits to Ewbank's sudden display of power. With his new contract, Joe had something Weeb hadn't had since the team missed the 1967 play-offs: job security.

As the Jets opened their exhibition season in Houston, the coach and the star could be seen arguing in the locker room before the game. Namath, whose left knee was swollen, had unilaterally declared himself ineligible to play just before the game. Starting quarterback duties would be assumed by one of his childhood idols, the recently acquired Babe Parilli, a great old ball handler from Rochester, Pennsylvania, trained by Paul Bryant at Kentucky. The only question, as Ewbank would soon concede, was whether Namath should operate the sideline telephone in street clothes or in uniform. As Ewbank explained, "I wanted him to suit up because I thought it would look better to his teammates. He would be one of them."

It was, in fact, a little late for Joe to be one of the guys, and he eschewed the uniform for a double-breasted chalk-stripe jacket with matching tie and handkerchief. On the sidelines Namath looked like the result of an experiment that had cross-pollinated Al Capone with a British rock star. The single item of football attire was his white shoes, but taken with the rest of the ensemble, they seemed an especially flagrant challenge to the coach's authority.

Dick Young, doing "color commentary" for WOR-TV, claimed that Namath's absence from the game had less to do with his knee than Sonny Werblin, who as part of their earlier deal had promised to pay him a $3,000 bonus for each exhibition game. This supposed handshake deal was categorically denied by Namath, Iselin, and Ewbank. "Mike Bite did talk to me about it once and I turned him down," Werblin told Young the next day. "I guess he has renewed it with the new owners."

Young was still Sonny's guy, and his scoops meant nothing but trouble for Werblin's former partners. "If Joe wants money let him come to me," shot back Ewbank, still the team's general manager. "I'm the man he has to negotiate with now." If that was Ewbank's bid for respect from the star, it was a transparent failure. If Joe didn't respect Ewbank enough to suit up for a game, then he would never deign to negotiate with him. Besides, the template had already been cut: Joe didn't deal with management; he did his business with ownership. It seemed as if the former owner, working through Young, was putting the world on notice: They'll never be able to deal with Sonny's star without Sonny.

The potential for a locker-room crisis was clear. Everyone had reason to be offended, from the emasculated coach to the underpaid players. None of Namath's teammates—who were making between $125 and $250 for exhibitions, based on seniority—could simply *decide* not to play. "The New York Jets would do well to trade Joe Namath right now," wrote the *Times*'s football columnist, William N. Wallace, who considered the quarterback's attitude a greater detriment than his knees. "The athlete's scant respect for the coach has so diminished that Namath calls the shots as to when he will play or not play."

Still, the controversy remained louder in the press room than the locker room. A few Jets muttered their muted approval of Wallace's sentiments, but none were sufficiently angry or indiscreet enough to speak for the record. The story didn't bother the team as it would have a year or two before.

"The boy says he's hurt and I believe him," said Paul Rochester, the defensive tackle and captain. "He knows his own knees. If I were hurt I'd hate to have people telling me I had to play."

"I believe Joe's side of it," agreed Dave Herman, the guard who never stopped protecting him. "I've seen him play too many times when he was hurt to think he'd do a thing like this to us when we're all going for the championship and working like hell."

Namath, for his part, never claimed his knee was in especially bad condition. It may have been a little more swollen than usual. But something bothered him practicing on the Astroturf. Why take the risk for an exhibition game? In each of the past two seasons, Namath had injured his knees playing in games that didn't even count. For all anyone knew, it was the injuries he suffered in the preseason that had kept the Jets out of the postseason. "Doesn't it make sense for me to take care of my knee now so I can be ready for the regular season?" he asked. "If these were regular season games, I'd play even though the leg was broken."

Nobody, not even his remaining detractors in the locker room, would doubt that. They had seen him wrapped and taped and braced and aspirated. They had seen him play on ruined knees and with broken cheekbones. They'd seen him hit. They'd also seen how he got up.

"He just didn't feel pain like other people," says Jim Hudson, who played quarterback in Texas' 1965 Orange Bowl win over Alabama. Hudson, now a hard-hitting safety, roomed with Namath on the road, where Joe paid the difference between a suite and a regular room. In fact, Hudson knew that Joe felt plenty of pain. Joe just didn't like to talk about it.

Hudson himself had a well-earned reputation for toughness. Pete Lammons, the Jets tight end who had played with him at Texas, liked to tell the story about something that happened earlier that summer. They were in Austin when a black widow bit the safetyman. The spider's bite can be fatal, but all Hudson got was a swollen leg. As for the black widow, Lammons told everyone she just went off and died. That's what you got for messing with Hud.

Hudson's endorsement carried a lot of weight, particularly among the team's assortment of Texans. The Lone Star Jets included Curley Johnson and Don Maynard, both former Titans, and four members of the Orange Bowl team that beat Alabama. On the subject of Namath, the Texans were in substantial agreement. "You couldn't ask for a better football player," says Sauer.

But the Texans were only one faction in a locker room that, like most locker rooms, was fraught with intramural politics. Namath, unlike any other player, could traverse the lines between each group while belonging to none. His linemen saw him as a prize to protect. His receivers loved him, too. It was no different than high school: Namath was cool. He was cool with southerners and northerners, with whites and blacks. "He really got along with the black guys," recalls Paul Zimmerman. "He'd come off the cafeteria line with his tray and go straight for the black table, integrating it. I saw him do that so many times I know it wasn't an accident. He was way ahead of his time."

Watts had burned in '65; Detroit and Newark were set ablaze in '67. Now, in the summer of '68, the Jets' chances for success depended, in some measure, on their ability to get along better than the rest of the country. The raceless sensibilities Namath acquired in the Lower End would have a salutary effect on the team as a whole. Even guys like Larry Grantham, instructed in staunch segregationist ways as a child in Mississippi, came around. "By then, I had completely changed," says Grantham. The primary agent of his enlightenment was not Namath, but another Mississippian, Verlon Biggs. As an undersized linebacker, Grantham profited greatly from playing behind an oversized defensive end. "Big and strong as Verlon was, we got to be real good friends," recalls Grantham. "I could just lay back and hide behind his big ass."

The Jets would benefit from new, more tolerant standards in everything from race to commerce. Three days after refusing to play in the exhibition against the Oilers, Namath was photographed at camp wearing a $5,000 mink coat with an eager, impish furrier tugging on the garment's hem. Like the white shoes and the llama-skin rug, the mink would become famous through its association with Namath. The coat had been constructed as per his specifications: double-breasted, center-vented, tapered at the waist. Furs were another flagrant violation of the football player's code of standards. Not that Joe cared. Let the fans call him a fag. His teammates—most of them, anyway—knew better. Wearing mink took balls. Besides, the coat looked great, and when he tired of it, he'd have it refitted for his mother. But best of all, it didn't cost him anything. The furrier was paying him.

By now, there were plenty of guys rooting for Joe to hustle all he could while he could, as envy had given way to admiration. Refusing to play in Houston might even have helped more than it hurt his stature in that locker room. Joe's toughness was no longer a subject of debate. The real issue, as far as the players were concerned, involved Weeb: Why insist that a gimpy-kneed man risk his livelihood playing on Astroturf in a game that didn't even count—and for only $250? Even if Namath's refusal was an attempted shakedown, well, so what? Joe was only doing what others would have done if they had the chance. Most guys would rather see the money go to Joe than stay with Weeb. At least he'd buy a round.

Weeb knew a lot about talent and the odd places it could be found. That summer, he talked Bob Talamini, Houston's former all-league guard, out of a short-lived retirement. But Weeb was also the tightest sumbitch in football (with the possible exception of Don Maynard, who demanded ten-cent receipts from the Triborough Bridge to claim on his income taxes). Negotiating with Weeb wasn't easy. Most ballplayers knew they were disposable, to be used up, thrown out, and replaced. But Weeb's willingness to fight over that last nickel was an additional indignity that the Jets had to endure, and a lot of them were getting tired of it. On the eve of their season opener in Kansas City, five of the team's best players remained unsigned and unhappy: Biggs, Maynard, Sauer, Snell, and Johnny Sample. Weeb controlled everyone's playing time and money—except for Joe's. In a peculiar way, Namath had come to articulate every player's unspoken desire. At some point in their careers, they all want to tell coaches and management to fuck off.

At their final practice before Kansas City, the Jets held another players' meeting. Johnny Sample was elected captain of the defense; Namath was elected captain of the offense.

"No one gave a shit if Joe stayed out all night," says Curley Johnson, the punter and substitute tight end who had been with the Baltimore Colts and Titans. "Long as we won. Long as he kept throwing those touchdowns."

Joe was flattered to tears, his eyes welling up as he left the meeting. Not even Sonny could have bought this election. It wasn't Sonny's team anymore; it was his team.

The 1968 season began with the Jets' new captain missing on six of his first seven passes. The eighth was a fifty-six-yard touchdown that Maynard caught in full stride, the first of two he would catch that day. Maynard would leave Kansas City, where the Jets were 6½-point underdogs, with 203 yards in receptions. But the most encouraging sign came at the end of the game, with the Jets clinging to a 1-point lead, 20–19. On second down and eleven from their own 4-yard line, it was beginning to feel like the previous season's opener: the Jets were about to blow the lead and the game. With almost six minutes left, all the Chiefs needed was a field goal from Jan Stenerud, their soccer-style kicker. With the strongest leg in the game, Stenerud had already kicked four that afternoon.

31. FU MANCHU

On second down, Namath called a slant-in for Maynard. Incomplete. Now, on third and eleven, with failure to make a first down all but guaranteeing a Chiefs field goal, he called the same play. This time the Maynard slant-in went for seventeen yards.

Kansas City never got the ball back. "That last drive by Namath was fabulous," said Chiefs coach Hank Stram. "I felt there was no way they could go from their four and maintain possession to the end of the game. I'd have given hundred-to-one odds."

Stram's team had beaten the Jets twice, by an average of 17 points, during the previous season. But suddenly, last year seemed long ago. The Jets' good cheer was based on more than Captain Namath's six-minute drive. Despite an injury that kept middle linebacker Al Atkinson out of the game, the Jets defense hadn't allowed a touchdown. Walt Michaels's unit wasn't big, but with guys like Philbin and John Elliott up front, Hudson and Sample in the secondary, and Grantham calling the signals, they played with crafty aggression.

The Jets followed their win over Kansas City with a drubbing of Boston, 47–31. Joe underwent his usual postgame ritual; the bar was a place to both celebrate and medicate. But then, after returning for practice on Tuesday, Hudson had an idea. "I think we ought to stop drinking," he said. "We're just drinking too damn much."

Namath had a better idea. How about they just cut down a little?

Hud hadn't felt too good out there at practice. "I think we better stop," he repeated.

Namath counteroffered again: wine instead of scotch.

"Hell, that's not quitting."

Finally, Namath agreed to give it a try. He'd stay sober at least through the next game against winless Buffalo. The Bills had already lost their first- and second-string quarterbacks to injury. The line, which opened with the Jets as 17-point favorites, was 19 by Sunday. The way Joe figured, a rookie quarterback would be going up against the league's best defense. "I don't know how they're gonna score," he said.

But Namath took care of that himself. He threw seven touchdowns that day, three of which came on interceptions. In the second quarter, with the Jets in position for a touchdown, Buffalo's Steve Janik returned a Namath pass from one end zone to the other, 100 yards for the score. In the fourth, which began with the Jets down 23–21, Namath threw two more interceptions for touchdowns—within 62 seconds. The day ended with the score 37–35, Buffalo's only win of the season. Namath's line: 19 of 43 for 280 yards, four touchdowns, five interceptions.

Afterward, Ewbank kept the locker room closed for a good long time. Rather than reprimanding Namath, he focused his unhappiness on his offensive lineman, Sam Walton. Unable to contain Buffalo's Ron McDole, the rookie tackle had finally tackled him. "Tackling a man like that is a confession that you can't handle him," said Ewbank, always concerned about pass protection. In addition to the interceptions, Namath had three balls batted down near the line of scrimmage.

Finally the locker room opened, and reporters who had been listening through the door asked the quarterback for his take. Was it bad protection? Was it overconfidence? No, said Joe, "It's all the dumb guy sitting right here."

Right around then, with the reporters huddled around the quarterback, the Jets' new president appeared in the doorway. While Sonny had commandeered the locker room as if it were backstage, Sam Iselin thought to ask Ewbank: "It is all right if I come in now?"

Outside, as the Jets made their way to the team bus, Murray Janoff of the *Long Island Press* caught up with Namath's father. John Namath, still working in the mill, tried to attend all Joe's games, as he had always loved watching his son play. But it didn't seem much like play anymore. The father was grim-faced watching Joe navigate the steps leading down from the locker room at War Memorial Stadium, leaning on both banisters so as not to bend his knees. "Look at him," said the father. "He can hardly get down the stairs. I want him to give up football."

John Namath, for whom sports was so sacredly American, couldn't have been more serious. He had been asking Joe to quit since the previous December, after the Oakland game. In fact, he had told Joe that's what he wanted for Christmas. "The best gift he could give me would be to quit," he said. Forget the money, the fame. Forget all that. Quit. Walk away. Hobble away, while you still can, son. "I can't stand to watch him play anymore," he said. Almost half a century had passed since John Namath arrived on the SS *Rotterdam,* but only now was he beginning to understand his own parents' fear. He didn't want his son to be crippled.

Joe, for his part, would recall leaving Buffalo with different concerns. Four and a half days of sobriety had exacted an awful price. "I started drinking again that night," he said, "and I drank right through the following Sunday when I threw no interceptions and we whipped San Diego."

By now, the 3–1 Jets were talking among themselves about the possibility of a championship. Next up was dog-ass Denver, with a defense that hadn't intercepted a pass all season. Once again, the Jets were 19-point favorites. Once again, Namath—who spent most of the time between games in bed with the flu—didn't take a drink for almost the entire week. Finally, as if to complete the trinity of coincidence, he threw another five interceptions. The Broncos won 21–13. The only one more disgusted than the 63,052 fans at Shea was Namath, who refused to take questions after the game. "Not this time, please," pleaded the quarterback, whose knee had to be drained after the game. "Just say I stink. I fucking stink."

Namath had now thrown a dozen interceptions in little more than a third of the season, ten in only two games. Walt Michaels had a talk with Joe, and then, for good measure, Michaels also spoke to Jim Hudson: "You need to tell your roommate how to be a quarterback. . . . All he needs to know is that every time he goes out there, the other quarterback is gonna try to outdo him, so he doesn't need to do anything. All he has to do is have some more patience, not force the ball so much, and let the defense force the other team into mistakes. Tell him to just let the defense help him win the football game and he'll be the greatest quarterback of all time."

This wasn't the kind of suggestion that Namath would ordinarily entertain, much less accept. But these weren't ordinary circumstances. "I don't think I ever played any worse than in that game against Denver," he admitted. It had started well enough, with a sixty-yarder to Maynard, but then, without warning, he just came apart. Now, for the first time, Namath seemed shaken. With that fractured confidence, however, came a new willingness to temper his nature, the conviction his own father had instilled, that old belief that he could beat anyone, anywhere, anytime. It turned out that the Denver defeat was exactly what Namath needed.

Both the quarterback and the team emerged from that game with a new resolve, a final acknowledgment that mere talent was no longer enough. At the following Tuesday's practice, Verlon Biggs appeared unshaven and announced that he would remain so until the team clinched the divisional championship. As such pronouncements were not Biggs's style, the rest of the team took note. Then Hudson decided that he wouldn't shave, either. For years, beards had been against league rules. But all of a sudden, they had become a sign of team unity. Even Namath joined in, growing what would soon become the most famous mustache in the Western Hemisphere.

In the league office, his Fu Manchu might have been considered subversive, but on the field, Namath became downright conservative. He started throwing less and winning more. Over the next four games, Namath was intercepted only three times. And though he didn't throw a touchdown pass during this period, he didn't need to: the Jets won all four.

At 7–2, the Jets were off to their best start ever. Still, not everybody in New York seemed happy with the quarterback. For one thing, Joe was being followed. He didn't know who—it could have been the district attorney's office or the FBI—but they were some kind of cops. The interceptions he'd thrown against Buffalo and Denver had probably given rise to allegations of some vast gambling conspiracy. Whoever it was, Joe and Ray stopped bullshitting about the point spread on the phone.

Then there were the fans and the sportswriters. They weren't very happy with Joe, either. "We're winning and they boo me because I'm not throwing touchdown passes," said Namath. "When we were losing and I was throwing two or three a game they booed louder."

"We were all writing: 'What's wrong with Namath? He can't find the end zone,'" Zimmerman recalls. "In retrospect, he had become much more disciplined. But we were too fucking stupid to see it."

Joe would ultimately go six consecutive games without a touchdown pass. Perhaps he was just looking for the right occasion. If so, the Jets' annual trip to Oakland would do just fine. On the day of the annual grudge match, *Daily News* readers were treated to this description of Al Davis's new team headquarters: "It is decorated in a silver-black modern Mussolini style. The art work consists of huge football action pictures. At the head of the stairs, leading to the coaches' offices, is that classic from last year's Jets-Raiders game featuring Ben Davidson flying through the air after fracturing a dazed Joe Namath's cheekbone. Namath is on all fours after the blow."

The night before the game, Al Davis just happened to be in the Jets' hotel, where he just happened to bump into the Jets' quarterback. Davis had been a great fan of Namath's since Alabama and knew how much the kid had meant to the AFL. Unfortunately, he explained to Joe, that sentiment wasn't shared by certain members of his defensive line. They were out to get him, said Davis, one guy in particular. Of course, Oakland's managing partner was duty bound not to reveal his identity. He just didn't want to see anything unfortunate happen to good ol' Joe. "Better be careful," remarked Davis.

Of course, the Raiders weren't the only team out to do violence the following day. The Jets would set a new team record: 13 penalties for 145 yards. Five times they were whistled for face-masking, the most crucial of these calls going against Hudson in the third period. It came off a third-down flare pass to Raiders fullback Hewritt Dixon, when Hudson came up from his strong safety position to tackle Dixon at the Jets' 11, a couple yards short of the first down. Grantham got a piece of Dixon, too, and could feel the blow's aftershock, which pinched a nerve in his neck. Hudson felt something else—the *ping* of the referee's weighted penalty flag against his helmet. He had been mistakenly called for tackling Dixon by the face mask. "He never grabbed the mask," Dixon admitted later. "His arm was under my chin." Then again, the two opposing players needed little provocation to start jawboning. "He was saying he was gonna whip my ass and I was yellin' I was gonna whip his ass, and flags started flying all over the place," remembered Hudson, who figured that the back judge was just another guy Al Davis had put on the pad during his term as commissioner. Hudson then engaged the official in a shouting match, an exchange resulting in another penalty for unsportsmanlike conduct and the strong safety's expulsion from the game. For good measure, Hudson gave 53,318 Oakland fans the finger as he was escorted from the field. The penalties gave the Raiders a first down on the Jets' 3-yard line. They scored a touchdown on the next play.

The score was 22–19, Oakland. There had already been four lead changes, and Namath was about to make it five. Gerry Philbin recovered a fumble deep in Jets territory, a mere ninety-seven yards from the goal line. No problem: Namath gained that ground with two passes to Maynard, who was having his way with Oakland's rookie cornerback George Atkinson. The touchdown pass, covering fifty yards, was Namath's first in seven games. It was now well into the fourth quarter. Jim Turner added a twelve-yard field goal for the Jets with 8:49 to play. But the lead was never safe. The Raiders came back with Daryle Lamonica passing to Fred Biletnikoff for a touchdown that tied the game. The Jets answered with another field goal, a twenty-six-yarder, Turner's fourth of the day. The score was now 32–29 with 1:05 left. Namath had already recorded his best statistical game of the season: 381 yards (228 of them to Maynard), 19 completions on 37 passes without an interception. He had even run for a touchdown (he always seemed to have at least one good carry against the Raiders), a 1-yard bootleg in the second quarter. It was looking as if the Jets might finally beat the Raiders in Oakland.

But then, following the kickoff, Raiders halfback Charles Smith took a short pass twenty-one yards. The Raiders were going right at Hudson's replacement, rookie Mike D'Amato. Another face-mask penalty brought the ball to the Jets' 43. There were 50 seconds left. The game had run late, what with all those penalties. And now, at 7:00 P.M. EST, NBC cut to its previously scheduled program.

Heidi, the saga of a pigtailed orphan girl in the Swiss Alps, was sponsored by Timex, a company with an obvious interest in punctuality. "You treated a sponsor like that very carefully because you wanted them to come back," said Dick Cline, NBC's supervisor on-duty. "And since it was 'only' AFL football and nobody was really sure how many viewers watched it anyway, it seemed like the thing to do."

Frantic NBC executives watching at home couldn't get through to the office. The deluge of calls from outraged football fans literally blew out the network's switchboard. "I just sat there and screamed at the television set," recalls Chet Simmons, the network's sports director.

In the meantime, Daryle Lamonica threw again for Smith, who beat D'Amato for a touchdown. To make matters worse, the Jets' Earl Christy fumbled the ensuing kickoff, which the Raiders ran in for a touchdown. Oakland had now scored two touchdowns in nine seconds, a remarkable feat missed by the millions who had been watching at home. All across the country, football fans began to curse the little Swiss girl. This was the Jets and the Raiders, after all, with New York giving 7½ points. People had *money* riding on this. As Dick Young astutely pointed out, the first touchdown cost Jets fans the game. The second cost them their bets.

NBC attributed the mishap to "forgivable human error." Sonny Werblin must've had a good chuckle. This would never have happened if he were still running the network.

"The Heidi Game," as it came to be known, had several consequences. The first was a pledge by NBC to let every game remain on the air until its conclusion. The second was a substantial fine levied by NFL commissioner Pete Rozelle against the Jets. Hudson had to pay a total of $200 for being thrown out and making "obscene gestures" while leaving the field. Walt Michaels owed $150 for berating the officials. (Michaels, fired after a brief career as a Raiders assistant in '63, was perhaps the foremost expert in conspiracy theories involving Al Davis.) John Elliott faced an automatic $50 fine that came with his ejection, prompted by an illegal blow to Raiders center Jim Otto late in the game. Dismayed by the outspokenness with which Ewbank and Michaels had criticized the officials, Rozelle also levied a whopping $2,000 penalty against the Jets organization for what he termed "extreme bad manners." Never mind that an irate Dr. Nicholas had stormed the officials' dressing room; what particularly galled the commissioner was the fact that Ewbank had shown the game film to the New York beat writers, fomenting newsprint indictments of the officials, the Raiders, and the Rozellian idea of good, clean competition. "I remember it like it was yesterday," says Zimmerman. "Weeb showed it to us later that week at a hotel in Escondido before the San Diego game." The most arresting image was that of Raiders tackle Dan Birdwell and Namath, who had just released the ball. Having arrived too late to inflict any sanctioned pain,

Birdwell balled up his fist and gave it a full wind-up, delivering something like a bolo punch. "The film showed him hitting Namath as hard as he could," says Zimmerman. "Right in the balls."

Typical of Namath, he was never heard complaining about the low blow. He was much more concerned about his right thumb, which had been jammed for the third time that season. His foot was sore, too. Sam Walton, who spent the afternoon getting beat by Ike Lassiter, had fallen on it. But those were details lost amid all the discussion generated by the network's mistake. "It made the front page of the *New York Times*," says Simmons. "It's not remembered as a great moment for NBC. But it was crucial for accentuating the importance of pro football and the AFL. It showed that people wanted to see the AFL."

In fact, most people wanted to see AFL games only if there were no NFL games available. The AFL continued to be regarded as an inferior product, a prejudice that extended to the media as well. "The Jets were still seen as second sisters," says Sal Marchiano, a sportscaster with New York's CBS affiliate. The toughest thing about covering the Jets, Marchiano found, was waiting for Namath to emerge from the sauna. Eventually, Marchiano developed a friendship with the quarterback. Marchiano liked covering the Jets. They were a good bunch of guys, and they seemed genuinely flattered by the attentions of a television correspondent, particularly one from a station associated with the "other" league. But Marchiano also found himself wondering if these assignments were bad for his career: "You wonder: are they watching? The network guys. The fans. You were perceived as covering the wrong camp. Covering the NFL was still considered the thing to do."

The week after the Heidi Game, the Jets played a San Diego team quarterbacked by Namath's pal John Hadl, who was leading the league in passing yardage. The Chargers desperately needed a win to keep pace with the Raiders in the Western Division. The Jets needed a win to earn at least a tie for first place in the East. The stakes were high, but the most suspenseful moment of the afternoon occurred before the game, when Namath went into the bathroom with a razor. AFL president Milt Woodard had been petitioning the Jets for some time to attend to their grooming. On the subject of facial hair, Woodard was like Hoover, wanting the Jets to "conform with the generally accepted idea of an American athlete's appearance." Of course, this only guaranteed that the Fu Manchu, like the white shoes and the fur coat, became a sensation. Tad Dowd, now the PR man for a suddenly famous booze-and-broads emporium called Bachelors III, was inundated with requests from photographers who wanted to shoot regular updates gauging the mustache's progress.

Now, as Namath made his way toward the sink, reporters started to scurry.

Was he finally bowing to pressure from the league office? Was this the end for Fu Manchu?

No, boys. Fu Manchu still lived. It was merely a trim.

Then Namath went out—still in flagrant noncompliance with that "accepted idea of an American athlete"—and threw for 337 yards and a pair of touchdowns, one of them an 87-yard bomb to Maynard. The Jets, with a defense that intercepted the Chargers' John Hadl four times, won 37–15.

As it happened, the Giants were out on the coast, too. While the Jets were beating the Chargers, the Giants were losing to the Rams. The Jets were finally going to the play-offs, but the Giants were going nowhere—for the fifth straight year. Still, it was the Giants who won big in the ratings. CBS attracted an audience of 34 million for the Giants-Rams game, while NBC got only 15 million for the Jets-Chargers. In the New York metropolitan area, the ratio was 2.3 million to 1 million. In other words, fans still preferred a mediocre Giants team to a good Jets team by more than two to one.

On Thanksgiving, the Jets gathered in the Diamond Club at Shea to watch the Chiefs beat the Oilers, a game that gave them sole possession of the divisional championship. A good time was had by all. The menu included turkey, cake, and champagne, a bottle of which was emptied on Weeb. At the following day's practice, Jim Hudson, receiver Bake Turner, and defensive back Cornell Gordon finally shaved, a public ritual sponsored by Remington razors. Each player received $250 for the use of his likeness in print ads.

Joe, too, was ready to shave—but not for a piddling $250. He had already asked Jimmy Walsh to call around and see what was available. Jimmy, who had graduated from Alabama law school in 1966, had been kicking around New York for most of the time since. He slept on Eddie Jaffe's couch for a stretch. He stayed with Tad for a while at the Edison Hotel. He tended a little bar for Bobby Van, served sandwiches at the penthouse poker games, and worked briefly for a jack-of-all-trades lawyer named Weinberg. On June 24, 1968, he was finally admitted to the bar. "A quasi-lawyer," was how Jimmy would later describe himself. In fact, though, he was already known as the man to see for those wanting an audience with the quarterback. "I got great access to Joe because of Jimmy," Marchiano recalls.

In response to Joe's query, Jimmy called Tad, who called Eddie Jaffe, who knew a guy at Schick, a company that made electric razors. On December 11, the morning after appearing on *The Tonight Show,* Namath went to a video production studio on East Seventy-eighth Street. There, Fu Manchu finally met its match. Namath didn't like anybody telling him how to wear his hair. But there was a higher principle at stake here: money. Nobody knew it, but the world was about to witness a watershed moment in sports marketing. Broadway Joe was like pornography for admen; he gave them hard-ons. His naturally rakish smile could be used to sell just about anything. A shit-eating grin of this magnitude required a proper medium, a dimension beyond mere print ads. Joe was TV. Unbelievable, the kind of stuff you could sell on TV. You could sell a football league. Or you could sell men's grooming products. Once again, Broadway Joe was changing that generally accepted idea of the American athlete. In the not too distant future, athletes would be judged not by their play but by the merchandise they moved. The fee for the mustache was ten grand. The way the newspapers figured, it came to about ten bucks a hair. The shaver, however, was just the beginning. It was a good score for Joe, but it was a great score for Jimmy.

■   ■   ■

The Jets won their last three games of the regular season, beating the new Cincinnati Bengals franchise once and the still-hapless Dolphins twice. They finished 11–3, 8–1 since Namath had thrown the five interceptions against Denver. In those nine games, he averaged only 1 interception for every 42 attempts, the best such ratio in all of pro football. But more important than these numbers were the drives, usually late in the game, marches of Namath's conception, providing the margin of victory. It began with the six-minute drive against Kansas City. Against San Diego, the Jets were down 4 when he led them seventy-five yards for the winning touchdown. In Houston, with about four minutes left, he went eighty yards for the victory. As a quarterback, Namath was at his best under the most difficult circumstances.

That year there were two polls for MVP awards—one for sportswriters and broadcasters, another for coaches. Namath won both by comfortable margins. Even his teammates finally voted him most valuable. Walt Michaels's advice had been sage. But behind the cult of Joe lay another truth: the Jets had the best defense in the league. Even by the standards of the day, Jets defenders bordered on scrawny, but they gave up the fewest yards of any team in the league. Michaels's unit had developed its own fierce ethos. "We had an undersized defense," says Gerry Philbin. "But everybody was tough. And everybody played injured."

Now, as Namath went off to Puerto Rico for a few days, Kansas City and Oakland would play for the right to play the Jets. Weeb instructed his players not to express a preference in opponents. But the Jets got their wish anyway. Oakland won 41–6. The following Sunday would be the Jets and the Raiders at Shea. This was a box office hustler's wet dream, a grudge match so perfect as to border on absurdity, a sequel more eagerly anticipated than the original: Heidi Meets Dr. Fu Manchu.

On the morning of December 29, 1968, following the completion of his midnight tour, a rookie cop named John Timoney exited the Seventeenth Precinct on the corner of East Fifty-first Street near Lexington Avenue. As this was early Sunday, shortly after 8:00 A.M., the last person the cop figured to see was the high priest of lush life. But there he was, leaving the Summit Hotel by the side entrance that faced the precinct. "Looked like he'd been partying all night," recalls Timoney, who describes the girl on Namath's arm as "a model type, a chichi East Side type of girl."

The intervening years have dimmed the memory at its edges. Was Namath holding a whiskey bottle? Was he wearing his fur coat? As for the girl, Timoney seems to recall "Nancy Sinatra–type boots." But what's unchanged and immutable is his recollection of the look on Namath's face. It still makes him want to cheer. "He looked like a young guy should look after he's been out all night," says Timoney, who would rise to positions of great prominence in the NYPD. "He looked disheveled. Disheveled, but happy."

32. DISHEVELED BUT HAPPY

Timoney quickly alerted his brother officers to Broadway Joe's condition. They told him he was crazy. In a few short hours Namath was due at Shea, where the championship of the American Football League was to be settled. Everybody knew that. Kickoff was 1:00 P.M.

Some months later, the writer Jimmy Breslin would quote Namath: "The night before the Oakland game, I got the whole family in town and there's people all over my apartment and the phone keeps ringing. I wanted to get away from everything. Too crowded and too much noise. So I went to the Bachelors Three and grabbed a girl and a bottle of Johnnie Walker Red and went to the Summit Hotel and stayed in the bed all night with the girl and the bottle."

Timoney would make sure Breslin's piece made the rounds in the precinct.

It was a good read, casting Namath as a kind of Babe Ruth with psychedelic lighting, extolling the medicinal virtues of blended whiskey. "It's good for you," said Namath. "It loosens you up good for the game."

But the rookie patrolman's vindication was still months away. In the meantime, John Timoney bet the Raiders. How could he not? Besides, he was getting 3 points. This oddsmaker the papers liked to quote, Jimmy the Greek, was picking the Jets by a field goal. Of course, Jimmy the Greek didn't see Broadway Joe disheveled but happy just a few hours before kickoff. But it didn't take a bookie to know that disheveled but happy did not a good quarterback make.

Then again, considering what was in store for Namath, why not? He might as well get his pregame dose. Enjoy that kind of funny, kind of nice while he still could. Joe Namath was about to take the beating of his life.

■   ■   ■

Though there is no record of the wind-chill factor that day, it is clear that nature was in the meanest of moods. With temperatures hovering around the freezing mark, the wind buffeted Shea in squalls up to fifty miles per hour. Game films reveal an oddly ravaged field: soggy in some places, hard as concrete in others. A barren dust rose from the baseball diamond. The field was quickly pocked with large divots.

The Jets and the Raiders had played seven times since Namath first donned Sonny's colors in 1965; the Jets had won just once. The teams knew each other as well as an old married couple, each incapable of altering its fundamental nature. The Raiders, as their pirate logo suggested, played like marauders, confusing defense and violence. The Jets were still the quarterback's team. But this particular contest would offer a few new twists. The Raiders arrived in New York with the AFL's number-one-ranked offense.

What's more, the Jets were suddenly weak where they had been strong—at right tackle. Having watched Ike Lassiter have his way with Sam Walton during the Heidi Game, Weeb wasn't about to let that happen again—so he moved Dave Herman over from guard to tackle. The shift was more difficult than it may sound. Guard and tackle are played at different angles, requiring men of different proportions. Herman would be giving away about twenty pounds to Lassiter. He'd have to make up for that deficit with desire. Lassiter was big and mean and strong. But at least he wasn't one of those guys you had to find to block. He came right at you.

And that's just how the Jets came at Oakland: fifty-six yards in four plays, a drive that ended with a fourteen-yard touchdown pass. Don Maynard, nursing a bad hamstring since early December, always made it look easy against Oakland's rookie George Atkinson, who lost his footing on the Shea infield. Late in that same quarter, Jim Turner added a field goal. But the Raiders came back with 10 points in the second quarter, 6 on a twenty-nine-yard touchdown from the AFL's top-rated passer, Daryle Lamonica, to Fred Biletnikoff. Just as Maynard owned Atkinson, Biletnikoff owned Johnny Sample, who was now benched for the first time in his career. Sample's benching was the least of the Jets' problems, though. Now as ever, their foremost concern was protecting a quarterback who couldn't protect himself. Ewbank's instinct in replacing Walton with Herman was sound, but every scrum was an opportunity for the Raiders to inflict pain and suffering. As one such pile cleared, Lassiter was suddenly overjoyed, jumping up and down, pointing at Joe, whose left middle finger was now perilously unhinged.

The finger elicited several graphic descriptions from the press box. It was likened to a snake, an "S," and "a broken board on a picket fence." Namath, for his part, didn't know quite what to make of it. "Never saw a finger like that on me before," he said. "It was bent three ways."

Trainer Jeff Snedeker popped the dislocated digit back into place on the sidelines. Later, he would tape Namath's middle finger to the ring finger. It was also treated with a shot of xylocaine, a numbing agent. Unfortunately, there was nothing to be done for Namath's right thumb, which had been badly bruised again, the fourth time that season. This was his throwing hand. As any magician would tell you, Namath needed his touch. "I was afraid to get a shot in it because I figured it would numb up and I wouldn't get the feel of the ball," he said.

The Raiders were about to administer numbness of a different kind. Late in the second quarter, Namath was hit again, his prone body marking the spot where Davidson and Lassiter met in a pincerlike movement. It was Oakland's only sack of the day. A look at the film suggests an airborne Davidson hit Namath with a knee to the head. Once again, the Raiders had taken him to that place where man is liberated from his senses. The most pungent description of the following moments belonged to the *Post*'s Paul Zimmerman, who wrote of Lassiter standing over Namath "like a gladiator waiting for Nero to give the thumbs-down sign."

The Raiders had already begun to celebrate. Namath was slow to rise, unaware that he had a concussion. Concussions weren't then part of the football vernacular. "A little punchy," is how Babe Parilli put it after the game. "He just didn't seem right." Parilli reminded Namath that he was ready to relieve him, if only until he could clear his head. But Namath declined the offer.

He could hear another voice besides Parilli's. The concussion was speaking to him in a dreadful percussive language. "There was a bad throbbing in my head," said Namath. It would last the rest of the game.

As the first half came to an end, Namath remained in a weakened state, mentally and physically. His passes were no match for the swirling winds. He was glazed. Finally, on the next-to-last play, an incomplete pass to Sauer, Lassiter cracked him again. Dr. Nicholas escorted Namath off the field. The score was 13–10, Jets. "In the locker room," wrote Larry Fox, "the Jets suddenly realized that Namath was acting strangely. He didn't know where he was! Had he been knocked silly by Lassiter's blow or had it been an accumulation of previous clouts by the Raiders? Nobody could be sure. Dr. Jim Nicholas and Jeff Snedeker led Namath off to a side room, where they ministered to him like seconds treating a dazed fighter who's just been saved by the bell. Just before the team started getting ready to go back on the field, Dr. Nicholas warned Ewbank, 'You may have to go with Parilli.' "

But Parilli was thirty-eight. His time had already passed. Now was Joe's time. The medicine men tended to him with great care. Namath would recall three painkilling shots, one for the finger and another for each knee. Gradually, he came to discern yet another voice apart from the tom-tom beat in his head. Again it was his father, was what his father had instilled in him as a Little Leaguer, an expression of nature and nurture, Namath family values. "It's hard sometimes when you're hurting physically to be able to work your mind properly and overcome the pain," Joe said, recalling that halftime. "It comes from the bloodline, from the family, from the teachings you've had." The bruising of his brain and body had rendered Namath in an almost hypnotic state. "What you should feel," John Namath had said, "is that you are better than anyone out there," Joe remembered.

His father and brothers were in the stands, but they weren't his only sources of inspiration. As an older man, Namath would say: "If it wasn't for my teammates and my family, I believe I would've quit in the second quarter." Herman was more than holding his own against Lassiter. But on that day, none set a higher standard than Jim Hudson, Namath's sometime roommate and closest friend on the team, the man who had been ejected from the Heidi Game. In the third quarter, Oakland had a first and goal on the Jets' 6-yard line. After three straight Hudson tackles, it was fourth and two. Oakland had to settle for a field goal that tied the game, though not for long.

Suddenly, Namath's arm and mind both came alive. Following Hudson's goal-line stand, he drove the Jets eighty yards in seven minutes, varying the modes of attack, using Boozer, Snell, and Maynard for first downs. He got lucky, too, when an Oakland defensive back dropped what should have been an easy interception. The final pass of the drive saw Namath roll left and throw across his body, hitting Pete Lammons in the flat. Lammons put his head down and ran it in for a touchdown.

As the fourth quarter began, Lamonica went back to Fred Biletnikoff, who beat Sample for fifty-seven yards. The Raiders had the ball on the Jets' 11-yard line. But again, their chances for a touchdown ended with Hudson, who broke up the pass, almost intercepting it at the goal line. Again, Oakland would have to settle for a George Blanda field goal.

The score was 20–16, Jets. Just as Lamonica went to Biletnikoff, Namath went back to Maynard, bad hamstring and all. But here was Namath's big mistake: a ball lofted too high, easily intercepted by Atkinson, who came sprinting full steam down the sideline. It was Namath who took him down, though this wasn't a feeble quarterback's approximation of a tackle. Instead of trying to push or angle Atkinson out of bounds, Namath put his shoulder down and simply decked him. He hadn't been watching Hudson for nothing. Atkinson told Namath he would kill him. Namath told the rookie to shut his mouth. On the next play the Raiders finally scored a touchdown as Pete Banaszak went over left tackle. The extra point made it 23–20, Raiders. If the game ended now, Namath's various wounds would have meant nothing compared to the insults he'd have suffered as the game's goat.

But there was still time. And Namath didn't need much—just enough for three completions. As he came to the line of scrimmage, he noticed that the Raider cornerbacks, Atkinson and Willie Brown, were laying off the receivers, playing seven or eight yards off the line, not wanting to get beat by the bomb. So Namath threw short, a quick out to Sauer for the first down. For the next play, the Raider corners positioned themselves right up close on their receivers. The quick out to Sauer had achieved its intended result. Atkinson and Brown were playing right into Namath's hustle. Earlier, Maynard had told him that when the right time came, he could get a step. Well, now was the time, with Atkinson playing all the way up. Namath had told the team to be ready for this call at the line of scrimmage. The backs would stay in for maximum protection. Maynard, Sauer, and Lammons would split the field on go patterns. Here it was, the bomb. "I didn't wind up, but I got a lot on it," said Namath.

The ball was intended for Maynard to catch over his left shoulder. But it drifted, left to right. "The wind caught it," says Maynard. "I revolve around and catch it at about two o'clock and go out of bounds on the six-yard line. If the wind hadn't caught it, I'd have gone right into the end zone."

"One of the greatest catches I've ever seen," said Namath. As he went upfield considering what to call next, he found himself thinking of Petey the Cabdriver. He didn't know why. He didn't even know Petey's last name. "He was just a little fat guy who liked to hang around the Bachelors III and talk football when he got finished driving his cab," recalls Bobby Van. Petey was always complaining to Joe about how the Jets were too conservative near the goal line, always running the ball. Petey was probably just another dissatisfied gambler. But in the biggest game of his life, Joe took his advice—calling a play-action pass, faking the handoff to Snell. The first option was Bill Mathis on the left side, but the safety came up to cover him. The next option was Sauer, who was also covered as he cut across the middle. The third option was Pete Lammons, moving right to left. But he, too, was covered.

This would be the last time Namath took advice from a cabbie. He might as well have let the girl in the Nancy Sinatra boots call the play. As he looked for an open receiver, Namath slipped on the Shea infield.

"I felt like I was blocking on that play forever," said Dave Herman.

Namath regained his footing as he spotted Maynard freelancing in the end zone. "I threw that ball as hard as I'd ever thrown a pass," he said. The path of the ball split three defenders. Maynard caught it in the back of the end zone. The extra point made it 27–23. The Jets had the lead again.

That touchdown drive dominates most memories of the game. But it only took 31 seconds off the clock, leaving almost 8 minutes to play in the final quarter. Again, the Raiders came downfield looking for a touchdown. In two plays, Lamonica—who passed for 401 yards on the day—had them on the Jets' 26. But once again the Raider offense stalled within striking distance of a touchdown. Verlon Biggs sacked Lamonica on fourth down, hitting him hard from the blind side. "He never saw me coming," said Biggs. But the Raiders would have yet another chance. This time, they advanced the ball to the Jets' 12-yard line. Lamonica went back to pass, and Biggs came charging again. This time the quarterback saw him. Fearing the sack, Lamonica threw behind Charlie Smith, his safety-valve receiver. The pass was ruled a lateral, and Jets linebacker Ralph Baker recovered the ball. That marked the fourth time the Raiders got inside the Jets' 20 without scoring a touchdown.

The final play of the game was recorded as a Hudson tackle. As endings go, this one couldn't have been more apropos. But the game would forever be associated with Namath. As viewed from his own locker room, he had done more than stand up to the Raiders. He had beaten them. Broadway Joe had become the Jets' saint of victory, the slayer of Al Davis's dragon. "If you don't feel you can come back," Namath said after the game, "then you don't belong on that field." What his father had given him, he now gave the Jets. "I'll tell you the biggest thing we have going for us," Gerry Philbin said after the game. "We have so much confidence in Joe." As long as they had Namath, they had a chance. The team now believed that—even if the rest of the world still found the idea a bit preposterous.

In the late game, the CBS game, the *real* game, Cleveland was already losing 17–0 to Baltimore, the Jets' next opponent. The Colts would win the NFL Championship in a rout. Talk had already begun about the upcoming mismatch. The way they were playing, the Colts made last year's Green Bay team look like weak sisters.

"I haven't seen enough of Baltimore to say anything about them," declared Namath before returning to the locker-room celebration. The clubhouse was foamy with champagne, a scene that did further damage to the AFL president's puritanical ideal of the American Athlete. It wasn't enough to play with poise and pain; ballplayers had to be phony exemplars of abstemious behavior. Weeb reminded Namath of the prohibition against alcohol in the clubhouse. To hell with that, Namath said. He'd pay the fine himself.

Namath kept swigging, but as he did, the photographers and their flash-bulbs began to annoy him. "Don't do that," he said, hiding the bottle. "Parents hate me enough as it is."

Later, the party moved to Bachelors III. It was an ordinary-looking joint save for Bobby Van's gorgeous bartendresses and a few LeRoy Neiman oil paintings of the saloon's most famous owner. Bachelors III had become a capi-tal for cool people and those who just hoped to be. Everybody, though, wanted to bathe in Joe's light. He poured champagne over Johnny Carson. "First time I ever knew you to waste that stuff," said the talk show host. Again, Namath cautioned the photographers. He didn't want to be seen in the papers with a drink in his hand. "Wait till I put the glass down," he said. "You know this isn't allowed."

The celebration didn't end until Monday evening, when the Jets held a team dinner in the Diamond Club at Shea. Weeb used it as an opportunity to thank the wives. The coach had something called the Tuesday Rule. He wanted his players to refrain from conjugal relations from Tuesday until after the game. Now, he thanked the wives for their patience and understanding.

Then Namath got up to make his toast. "I want to thank all the broads in New York," he said.

Especially the one in the Nancy Sinatra boots.

He got a big laugh. Amid all the celebration, Namath appeared in a higher state of disheveled but happy. However, one moment went unnoticed. His daddy had always told him he was the best. Now here was the proof. As he had left the field, Joe Namath was weeping with joy.

Jimmy the Greek wasn't the best oddsmaker; he was, however, the most famous. Born Demetrius Synodinus in Steubenville, Ohio, he had natural gifts for probabilities and self-promotion. After changing his name to "Snyder," he founded a Las Vegas "public relations firm" called Information Unlimited. Although he would set odds on just about anything, his specialty was giving prices to some of America's most influential sportswriters, like Furman Bisher in Atlanta, Blackie Sherrod in Texas, Will McDonough in Boston, and Dave Anderson at the *New York Times*. Like Sonny Werblin, Jimmy understood that he who controls the ink gets the credit. He was great with the press, and with his rolled collars and pinky rings, he looked the part, like those guys in the stands at New Castle, writ very large. In the minds of many, Jimmy the Greek was America's bookmaker.

33. THE POINTS

"The number is 17," the Greek declared. "The Colts by 17."

This proclamation was issued early Sunday evening, shortly after the league championship games. The Colts, in Snyder's estimation, were merely "the greatest defensive team in the history of football, better than the Packers."

Under Don Shula, Ewbank's successor, the Colts had allowed the fewest points of any team in the annals of the game. Having already won two play-off games, their record now stood at 15–1. The Colts had shut out four teams, including the Cleveland Browns, 34–0, in the NFL championship game. And though the Greek rated Namath as high as he rated any quarterback, he gave the Jets no advantage at the position. Unitas had spent most of the season on the bench, resting a torn tendon in his chronically sore throwing elbow. In his place, the Colts traded for Earl Morrall, a backup from the Giants. It was thought that Morrall's only resemblance to Unitas would be his crew cut. But contrary to every expectation, Morrall was named UPI's Player of the Year. Statistically, his season had been overwhelmingly superior to Namath's. Morrall had thrown eleven more touchdowns and two fewer interceptions. He had a higher completion percentage, 57.4 to Namath's

49.2, and averaged almost a yard more per attempt. What's more, after a season of rest, Unitas—still recognized as the game's greatest quarterback—was now ready to play. "Imagine," said the Greek, "having Unitas available as a backup."

Of course, Snyder's opinion was not the only one. The *Daily News,* which announced the opening line as a banner headline on its back page, cited a more conservative source: COLTS SUPER 16 OVER JETS. Even at 16, the Jets would be the biggest underdogs in the short but lopsided history of AFL-NFL championship games. But the line was still moving, and within a few days, the spread had gone to 18. Word was, the Jets could be 20-point underdogs by January 12, the day of the game.

It was around this time that Namath made an appearance in Bill's Meadowbrook, the bar near the Jets training facility at Hofstra. Tank Passuello poured him a Johnnie Walker Red.

"How you betting?" Joe asked.

"You guys, of course," said Passuello. He was betting with his heart. The Jets were good guys, and they'd been good for business. But Tank wasn't a dummy, either. "Give me eighteen points," he said. "I'll take that anytime."

Suddenly, a disgusted look flashed across Namath's face. "Points?" he said. "What are you talking about, points?"

"Well, I mean . . ." Tank started stammering. *Points?* It felt like Joe had just called him a pussy. "Well, you know, eighteen is a lot and, well . . ."

"We're gonna win straight," said Joe.

"Win straight?"

"Eighteen points," said Joe. "What's that in odds?"

"I don't know," said Passuello. "Maybe seven to one."

"Bet it," said Joe. "Bet the ranch."

"What the fuck," said Tank. "You sure?"

"Positive."

Joe started talking about how he'd seen the films. He'd studied the Colts' style, and he knew the Jets would beat them. But Tank didn't take note of what Joe was saying so much as how he said it. Joe had that look, a look so resolute it served as his marker. So Tank got everyone together—his partner, the waitresses, the chefs, the bouncers, even the busboys—raised about three grand among them, and bet the Jets to beat the Baltimore Colts at 7 to 1. The bookmakers, who loved nothing more than people betting with their hearts, gladly took their money.

The last big 7-to-1 proposition coming out of Miami was Cassius Clay over Sonny Liston in '64.

But that kind of thing happens once in a lifetime.

■   ■   ■

On the other side of the world, in a spooky place called the Cha Rang Valley, word started getting around Camp Addison that Joe Fucking Namath Himself grew up with a mess hall supervisor from the 523rd Transportation Company. The brother's name was Linwood Alford. And soon everybody was busting his chops, telling him that his boy Joe might be cool and all, but the Colts were going to take him out. Big Bubba Smith would maim his white ass.

"Let me see your money," said Linwood.

He'd already figured his angle. He'd go to every shylock on the base if necessary. He wanted all the action he could get. The official line was 18. But now Linwood came up with his own line: 12.

The money started rolling in. Seven, eight, nine hundred bucks. Maybe a thousand by game time. The stake was kept in an old footlocker.

GIs betting the Colts remarked on their inexplicable good fortune. Twelve points? Perhaps Linwood was suffering from shell shock.

In fact, he had never been more sane. In Linwood's estimation, Bubba Smith had about the same chance as that big kid who had once vowed to get Joe after school. It was ninth or tenth grade. Linwood had warned him not to mess with Joe, but this kid had to learn for himself. So right after school they went behind the building, and Joe knocked him out cold. Linwood stood over the prone body. "Told you not to mess with that little white boy," he said.

Now, a decade later, Alford was taking all the bets, convinced that the 12-point spread was a genius hustle. "I grew up with the guy," he says. "Joe was going to win. And even if he didn't, I knew he sure as hell wasn't losing by two touchdowns."

■　■　■

In the celebration that followed the Raiders game, Namath had mentioned that Daryle Lamonica was a better passer than Earl Morrall. A remark like that was seen as the height of bad form, and considering the Colts' capacity for vengeance, it wasn't very smart, either. Then again, perhaps it was just the champagne talking. So now, as the Jets' charter headed for Miami, Dave Anderson and some of the other beat writers gathered around and asked Namath if he wanted to set the record straight.

"I said it and I meant it," insisted Joe. "Lamonica is better." In fact, in Namath's estimation, there were at least three other guys better than the NFL's top-rated passer of 1968: John Hadl, Bob Griese of Miami, and Yours Truly. Actually, Namath was being charitable. "You put Babe Parilli with Baltimore and Baltimore might have been better. Babe throws better than Morrall."

Namath was nursing a scotch, but his mood was neither tipsy nor brash. His lack of diplomacy was, in fact, very deliberate. He already seemed very well schooled regarding the Colts, and his study of the films was obvious.

"When the Colts lost to the Browns at midseason, they didn't get beat by any powerhouse," he said. "I'm not going to take what I read about their defense. I'm going to go with what the one-eyed monster shows me. The one-eyed monster doesn't lie."

Why should he say different? The AFL had better quarterbacks. "I completed 49 percent of my passes this season," he said, "but I could have completed 80 percent if I dropped the ball off to my backs like they do in their league." With the Colts in mind, Namath was constructing both a paradigm and a challenge: Long balls mean big balls, real men throw to their receivers. And when it came to receivers, he said, "the Jets have the best."

Before the plane touched down, Namath had already set the agenda. Dave Anderson's interview would establish a tone for the entire week. The Colts would be furious, especially when they read the part about Parilli being better than Morrall. Parilli had been cut by Lombardi himself in 1959, when Namath was the backup to Rich Niedbala in Beaver Falls.

Who did this kid think he was?

Maybe just another guy sipping scotch on an airplane. Still, he was entitled to his opinion. "I value it very highly," said Joe. "Especially when I'm talking about football."

■ ■ ■

The Jets arrived ten days before the game and made Fort Lauderdale their base of operations. Workouts were held at the Yankees' practice facility, where Namath was assigned Mickey Mantle's spring training locker. At the Galt Ocean Mile, a seaside resort where the team stayed, Namath and Hudson checked into the Governor's Suite, a room that had been occupied by Vince Lombardi during the previous year's championship. Later, Namath would quip: "I'm not sure he would have approved of everything I did in his old room." But in fact, the NFL's reigning father figure would have found the game's profligate son somewhat less dissolute than advertised. Namath spent much of the week studying film, contemplating angles and edges. Lombardi admired the boy for his arm. But Namath was looking to beat the Colts with his head. He couldn't let anything distract him, not even a couple of J. Edgar Hoover's men. They showed up on Friday, the morning after the Jets checked in, and apprised Namath of a possible threat on his life. Someone in Miami—one of those organized crime types—had a problem with Joe. But this was just a routine warning; probably nothing. Besides, the FBI men seemed very pleased that Namath was in the Governor's Suite. Don't worry, they said. As his room faced the beach, and not the pool, a would-be assassin would have little place to hide. "He'll never get away," promised one of the G-men.

■ ■ ■

Dr. Nicholas started making his rounds on Saturday. He drained about two ounces of fluid from Namath's right knee before tending to some of his lesser-known patients. Middle linebacker Al Atkinson, another of the Jets' under-sized tough guys, received a cortisone shot for his ailing left calf. Don Maynard received a similar injection for his left hamstring. It had been a great season for Maynard, who had surpassed former Colt Raymond Berry as professional football's all-time leading receiver. He led the league with an average of 22.8 yards a catch. But for a month now, he had been playing on a hamstring that had gone from bad to worse. For all Namath's talk of Maynard and the deep threat he posed, the quarterback already knew that his flanker was already spent. There was a good chance that the fifty-two-yarder he caught against Oakland was all he had left. The whirlpools, the heating pads, the shots—nothing seemed to ease what kept grabbing at Maynard's hamstring. "I'm afraid to run on it," he admitted to Dr. Nicholas. The guy who was supposed to be on the receiving end of all those Namath bombs could, in fact, barely jog.

Of course, Maynard's injury status wasn't something Namath had shared with Dave Anderson, whose story was played across two pages in the *Times* that Sunday, the day the Colts arrived in Florida. The Colts were predictably outraged, and no one more so than Lou Michaels. The thickly built younger brother of the Jets defensive coach, Lou had grown up in Swoyersville, Pennsylvania. In some ways, he had a great deal in common with Namath. His father was a Polish immigrant who arrived at Ellis Island in 1911—the same year as Namath's paternal grandfather—and dropped dead after a quarter century in the coal mines. Like Namath's, Michaels's gift for the gridiron saved him from the horrors of industry. He played his college ball at Kentucky, where he came to know Frank Namath ("a down to earth guy . . . he didn't have the killer instinct . . . didn't have the talent his brother was given"). Lou made his professional debut as a defensive end for the Los Angeles Rams back in 1958. He was known to have a temper, and a pretty good mouth, too. But now, a de-cade later, his primary responsibility was as a place kicker, a holdover from an era when men played more than one position. And on the night of January 5, 1969, as Namath came into his sight at Jimmy Fazio's bar in Fort Lauderdale, the boy quarterback desecrated Michaels's every notion of what a football player should be.

The way Michaels remembers it, Joe was drinking near the waitress station, wearing his fur coat: "Joe was really looking for a fight. He pointed to me and said, 'We're gonna kick the shit out of you and I'm gonna do it.' That's the exact words he used, God strike me dead."

As it happened, God had a place in the debate that followed. "They got to arguing over Catholicism," says Hudson, who was out bouncing with Joe when they walked into Fazio's that night. "Over who was the best Catholic and who treated his mother the best. Then, of course, somebody said, 'Well, we'll be tearing your ass up come Sunday.' "

What most offended Michaels was Namath's lack of humility. "I told him my mother brought me up better—in so many words," says Michaels, still dismayed at the thought of Joe's ten-thousand-dollar shave. "He should have been thankful for the gift of being such a good athlete. Johnny Unitas never acted like that."

Joe retorted, "Unitas is an old man. He's over the hill."

That was about all Michaels could take: "It boiled my blood pressure over." The old lineman now offered to settle all their differences—theological, maternal, and athletic—out in the parking lot. "I really got mad," says Michaels. "If I went after him, no one would've been able to separate us."

Namath, who was giving away about 50 pounds to Michaels, declined the offer. The peacekeeping effort was aided by Hudson and Dan Sullivan, the Colts lineman. "We finally got to talking sensible," says Michaels. There would be no fight. For Joe, who seemed to be spoiling for one, there was no longer any need. He'd already won by making Michaels feel old and angry. He pulled out a hundred-dollar bill and paid for everyone's drinks before giving Michaels and Sullivan a lift back to their hotel. By the end of the evening, Michaels had to admit that Joe wasn't such a bad guy after all.

Lou didn't know it yet, but he'd been hustled. All these years later, that evening still rankles him: "I definitely know in my heart that I am a better Catholic than Joe Namath will ever be. He can't look me in the eye and tell me he goes to church every day."

■　■　■

The following morning was Picture Day, scheduled for 10:00 A.M. Three Jets didn't show: Snell and Boozer, roommates who slept through their wake-up call, and Namath, who refused Hudson's exhortations to rise and shine. "If they want pictures of me," he told Hudson, "they're going to have to take 'em later than ten o'clock."

But even in absentia, Namath was the news. Word of the previous evening at Fazio's was already leaking out. Michaels was being cast as the stooge who had been bought off with a $100 bill. That was twice the fine Namath would pay for missing the team picture. "Namath didn't show up for Photo Day?" asked Don Shula, the Colts' thirty-nine-year-old coach. "What the hell is Weeb doing?"

For Shula, who typically betrayed little emotion, the question qualified as a barbed remark. A substitute defensive back under Ewbank, Shula had been appointed his successor. Over six seasons, his team had won five more games than the Green Bay Packers. But on this particular Monday, as he sipped a glass of milk in the Statler Hilton's Don Quixote Room, his indignation seemed as evident as his success. Shula—who reminded one columnist of an ultra-efficient "regional sales manager"—began by lavishing praise on the Jets quarterback, noting his quick release and strong arm: "A great arm . . . sees the blitz . . . recognizes defenses and can pick them apart . . . knows where to go with the football." But Namath's transgression, according to Shula, was more than just a violation of etiquette. "I don't see how Namath can rap Earl," said the coach. Not only had Morrall led the NFL in passing, but Colts split end Jimmy Orr had averaged 25.6 yards a catch, almost 3 yards better than Namath's man, Maynard. "He's thrown for a great percentage without using dinky flare passes," said Shula, who'd already parsed Namath's critique of his starting quarterback. "We're proud of him. Anyone who doesn't give him the credit he deserves is wrong."

The veins were rising in the coach's neck. "Shula was steaming," says Anderson. He wasn't alone. Morrall, another one not given to displays of emotion, was furious, too. "Earl told me," says Lou Michaels, "'I want to beat these guys by 40.' I want to beat them bad."

■　■　■

This game wouldn't require the services of Fred Williamson or Ben Davidson. Namath kept the media beast well fed all by himself. The *Post*'s Larry Merchant declared it "Joe Namath Week." Typically, he would take a seat by the pool, his beach chair inevitably forming the epicenter of the media crush. Never had a man in a checked boxer-style bathing suit attracted such crowds, whether of reporters and cameramen and columnists or of kids and old ladies. "He has risen to the occasion," wrote Merchant, "simply by staying in character." Namath's grin seemed omnipresent. He made sure to address women as "ma'am" and even as the glare intensified was never seen in an awkward moment.

"He's never faced anybody like he's going to have to face in our defense," said Johnny Unitas. "From the films of games I've seen, the Jets haven't had much of a pass rush put on them. . . . They haven't really been put under that much pressure. Our pass rush will be something, I think, that Namath will remember a long time."

"I've never heard a quarterback make remarks like he's been making," said Billy Ray Smith, the Colts defensive tackle. "A lineman sure, he can protect himself. But a quarterback, it only takes one crack to put him out of commission. . . . There's nothing I like to hit more than quarterbacks, and when you get a mouthy one, it makes it that much better."

"On Sunday," said Norm Van Brocklin, the Hall of Fame quarterback then coaching the Atlanta Falcons, "Joe Namath will play his first professional football game."

Van Brocklin wasn't exactly going out on a limb with that judgment. Most of the reporters who had eagerly gathered about Namath at the pool were likewise predicting his inevitably humiliating defeat. While there were a couple of exceptions—George Usher and Stan Isaacs of *Newsday,* the Long Island paper, picked the Jets to win—but even Namath's most ardent supporters had a difficult time envisioning a Jets victory. Paul Zimmerman, a former college player who knew the sport as well as anyone in the press box, saw the game 27–16 Colts. Of fifty-five writers polled, forty-nine picked the Colts. Edwin Pope of the *Miami Herald* picked the Colts 42–13. *Sports Illustrated*'s Tex Maule, considered by many the dean of the football writers, had the Colts winning 43–0.

Namath was keenly sensitive to the prejudice, especially among those affiliated with the NFL and CBS. On Wednesday, the Jets PR man delivered word that Namath was "only going to talk to the writers he knows." But his boycott of the football establishment was short-lived. Most of the time, he treated his antagonists to a wink—like the Los Angeles–based TV correspondent who asked, "What about the people who expect a no-contest game?"

"Maybe we shouldn't play," said Namath.

"How about the big point spread?"

"Well, I don't know about odds or betting or things like that," he replied, slyly. "But it is a pretty big price."

■   ■   ■

Namath's week-long engagement at the Galt Ocean Mile was a kind of performance art. He purveyed his poolside persona with a rare combination of ease and outspokenness never before seen from an athlete, at least not with so many cameras around. If Namath were a wrestler, he'd be both the babyface and the heel. In the sportswriters' collective estimation, Namath was a guy who said whatever was on his mind. Even those who condemned glibness had to bless him for it, as he filled notebook after notebook.

Still, there were limits to his candor. Jerry Tallmer, a feature writer from the *New York Post,* caught up with Namath as he strolled out to the beach. The interview had already been arranged, and given what had already become a monotonous storyline, Tallmer figured his planned line of inquiry would come as some relief to the young star. He wouldn't even bother with a single question about Morrall. Rather, he was interested in Namath's life and times, growing up in Beaver Falls, the family, you know . . .

Suddenly, Namath's green eyes darkened.

His father, who had taken a couple of days off from the mill, would be arriving soon. His brother Bobby, now running a bar in Monaca, near Beaver Falls, would get in Friday night. Rose would be staying home, though. She would light a candle at the church and pray to St. Mary and St. Jude for a Jets victory. With the recent spate of hijackings, she said she was just too nervous to fly. As it was, she would need a "nerve pill" just to sleep the night before the game. Joe, who wanted to surprise her with a gold brooch bearing twelve diamonds, told her it was just fine to watch on TV like everyone else. The very last thing he wanted was a nervous mother.

But that wasn't anyone's business, certainly not this reporter's. Namath's poolside persona had vanished. Tallmer saw a different look, a marker of a different sort.

"I don't talk about that," said Namath. "We don't want to talk about any history or family or private things. . . . I don't."

The writer tried another approach. What was the first thing Joe remembered?

"What's that mean?" he asked suspiciously.

"You know . . . in your life?"

"We're not going to get anywhere," said Namath. The interview was over.

■   ■   ■

Joe had baited the hook. Baltimore bit. "Our football team is conscious of everything that goes on, everything that is written," said Shula. "Joe makes it more interesting."

As 18-point favorites, cast as guardians of their sport's honor and tradition, the Colts—their place at the forefront of football history already being considered—found themselves under enormous pressure. What some players could not acknowledge, their coach would make explicit. "Everything we accomplished this season goes on the line in this one," said a grim-faced Shula. "If we blow it, we destroy the whole season." Even a close game would be seen as a kind of defeat.

The Jets, on the other hand, were saddled with none of these expectations. Playing the Raiders at home for the AFL championship, now *that* was pressure. But the Jets were beyond that now. Besides, pressure doesn't always translate into motivation, something the Jets had in abundance. Guys like Grantham, Mathis, Maynard, and Curley Johnson were now playing a single game for a winner's stake of $15,000, more than they had ever made during an entire season with the Titans. Ewbank was coaching against his former player, his successor, and most of all, Carroll Rosenbloom, the man who fired him after winning two championships. Winston Hill would be lining up against Ordell Braase for the first time since 1963, when he was a rookie in the Colts training camp. "He was the guy who got me cut from Baltimore," said Hill. "I couldn't block him in practice." Now the debt was coming due. Johnny Sample, the roughhouse defensive back who probably talked even more than Namath that week, claimed to have been blackballed by the National Football League. He was another one for whom revenge and respect were now indivisible. Snell and Boozer were offended by Jimmy the Greek's assertion that Baltimore, with

Tom Matte and Jerry Hill, had the better backfield. Snell was sick of hearing the fair-haired NFL guys getting all the credit. "I read all the time about how great Tucker Frederickson is," he said. "He's been there four years, and I don't guess he's gained 1,000 yards all told." Snell had begun to collect offenses; he was looking for reasons to be angry. He had played in the same backfield with Tom Matte at Ohio State. Matte was a good enough football player, but he had three years on Snell, three years worth of hits. Now Jimmy the Greek was calling him "fantastic," and Snell found himself wondering: When the hell did he get to be some kind of superman?

"Booz," he said, "for the first time in my life, I'm going to be looking for people to run into. I'm going to be looking to punish people."

The Jets watched the films of the Colts every day in the Galt Ocean Mile's Imperial Room. Certain strategic concerns were obvious. The man who most concerned the defense was tight end John Mackey, whose talent there was no denying. "Heckuva football player," says Hudson, whose primary responsibility would be Mackey. "But with the type of offense they played and the routes they ran, we felt like we could handle them if we could get a pass rush." And for the Jets, whose defense was always overshadowed by the Joe Namath Show, that wasn't such a big "if." Gerry Philbin had 19 sacks alone that year. Biggs and John Elliott had combined for another 22.

On offense, Dave Herman would go at right tackle again. He would be giving away forty pounds to the man now regarded as the most fearsome defensive end in football, Bubba Smith. Like Herman, Smith had attended Michigan State. Herman was a senior when Smith was a freshman, but whatever psychological advantage that might have yielded was undone by their physical disparity. At six-seven, 295 pounds, Smith was like Verlon Biggs—just bigger, stronger, faster and meaner. His fans loved to chant: "Kill, Bubba, Kill." There were limits to what Herman could do on spirit alone, a fact even his own wife had to concede. The night before the game she found herself weeping, all the "Kill, Bubba, Kill" talk having finally gotten to her. "I don't want to be a widow," she said.

The Jets' other concern, at least in the minds of most experts, was Baltimore's vaunted safety blitz. Namath would be up against more than Bubba and Billy Ray, as Shula liked to use safeties Jerry Logan or, more likely, the harder-hitting Rick Volk, as human missiles. Their mission: seek and destroy opposing quarterbacks. "Volk was the guy who was supposed to bring the heat," says Snell.

But the more the Jets saw, the less they were impressed. By now, after all those hours of practice, Namath's receivers knew enough to recognize the blitz and slant in to an area vacated by the charging safety. "We kept watching them films," says Lammons, "and they kept running at the strong side of the defense. They couldn't see that they had to go to the other side. And they couldn't pass for shit. On defense, they all played zone. We could kill a zone. And they loved to blitz. Blitzing? Hell, that was the best deal in the world for us. Our backs could pick up anybody."

Weeb had trained them with just this situation in mind. "You got to find that fucking safety," says Boozer. "The hard part is you got all these guys in front of you, and you got to find him. Best thing to do is try to keep an eye on that sumbitch's feet. But Joe wasn't worried about getting hit by a blitzer. Blitzing linebackers and safeties, we were death on them. We *invited* them to come. It was like: 'come on in.' Soon as he pops that head of his out the doorway, you just tear it off. It was *fun*."

The rest of the team was now seeing what Namath had discerned even before he walked into Bill's Meadowbrook. The one-eyed monster demystified the Colts, most of whom had played for Weeb in what now seemed like a bygone era. The oddsmakers might have regarded Baltimore as the superior team, but as viewed in the Imperial Room, they were the older team. The crew-cut quarterbacks, Morrall and Unitas, had been in the league since 1956. Right linebacker Don Shinnick had already played twelve years, the same as Winston Hill's old pal Ordell Braase. Lenny Lyles, the right corner, had played eleven. Billy Ray Smith had been in the league ten years, Bobby Boyd, the balding left corner, nine.

"They looked slow, less inventive, both offensively and defensively," says Sauer, who recalls one particular film session in great detail. The Jets were studying the Colts 34–0 victory over Cleveland in the NFL championship. That contest—in which Leroy Kelly, the Browns' league-leading rusher, was held to twenty-eight yards—was considered incontrovertible proof of Colt superiority. But the ever-diligent Sauer noticed evidence of Baltimore's vulnerability. He recalls the Browns' Paul Warfield beating Lenny Lyles on a post-corner route, the same type of pattern he planned to run on Lyles. "We were so intense," says Sauer. "There was no sound in that room except the projector."

Playing quarterback for the Browns was Frank Ryan, the very same Frank Ryan who once proclaimed that if the rookie Namath was worth $400,000, then he was worth a million. Now, four years later, the Jets sat watching and waiting for Ryan to hit his receiver. "Warfield was so open he had time to catch a cold," says Sauer. All that could be heard was the projector, until finally Sauer spoke up, his voice thick with disdain: "Throw the damn ball already."

Demystification was giving way to a kind of contempt. What was the big deal about the NFL? The Colts had become yet another exemplar of an archaic sporting establishment. The signs were everywhere. Out in Los Angeles, the National Collegiate Athletic Association was debating whether student-athletes could have their scholarships revoked on account of unkempt or too-long hair.

J. Neils Thompson, representing the University of Texas, said, "Long hair and beards not only defy orderliness, but under certain circumstances can be detrimental to performance." That was Wednesday, January 8. On that same day, all the way across the country, another proud representative of the University of Texas stood up to address his colleagues. The Jets had just finished one more session examining the tendencies of those rapidly aging sumbitches, the Baltimore Colts. Now Pete Lammons, a Texas hero in the '65 Orange Bowl, was heard to drawl: "Damn, y'all, we gotta stop watching these films. We gonna get overconfident."

■   ▦   ▮

Following Thursday's practice, Dr. Nicholas drained Snell's knee again. The three fluid ounces he drew were a record for Snell. The doctor took it as a sign that the fullback had been exerting himself in practice. Then, as ever, he directed his attentions toward Namath.

Five syringes had been prepared. The first contained novocaine, injected below the left kneecap. The second, shot through the same needle, contained 25 milligrams of prednisone, a cortisone compound to relieve pain and inflammation in the left tendon. Then Nicholas drained off a couple of ounces of fluid from the right knee. Next, returning to the left, he shot the back of the knee with novocaine, followed by another 25 milligrams of prednisone to relieve inflammation in the bursal sac. Finally, the doctor offered a pain-killing injection for his right thumb. This, Namath declined. Rules of the Blue Room still applied. He would need all his touch for the game. Nicholas sent him away with a bottle of red pills, just in case the left knee acted up again.

Later that afternoon, Namath stopped by a team barbecue for some food and a beer. Everyone looked to be having a good time on the beach. It seemed as if Joe's linemen—Schmitt, Talamini, Herman—all had kids already. From that vantage point, family life looked pretty good. Joe would have liked to stay. But the Miami Touchdown Club had selected him for its annual FAME award as pro football's Player of the Year. It would be the first time such an honor was bestowed upon an AFL player, and the Jets' PR man, Frank Ramos, had persuaded him that attendance was obligatory. So Namath traded his beer for a paper cup filled with Johnnie Walker over ice. A turquoise Cadillac soon came to pick him up, and Dave Anderson, always Joe's favorite writer, even went along for the ride to Miami Springs Villas.

The Villas was a swanky place, though Tad Dowd recalls that night's crowd as "a lot of Kiwanis Club kind of guys." Namath was a big draw, and the place was already packed for cocktail hour, maybe 600 people. These included various members of the quarterback's entourage: Dowd, Joe Hirsch, and Bob Skaff, then the president of Liberty Records. Nicknamed "the Egyptian

Prince," Skaff had a perennial tan and had achieved some renown as a ladies' man. But as it pertained to betting, he wasn't possessed of the same confidence. On Namath's recommendation, Skaff had wagered $1,000 on the Jets at 7-to-1 odds. But he was more concerned with his boss, who bankrolled Liberty Records. Even with the points, this guy wasn't comfortable taking the Jets. "Skaff was being a nervous nelly," says Dowd. "He kept asking Joe if the Jets would cover. Cover? Finally, Joe says, 'Get your boss on the phone.' This was about ten steps from the main dining room. Skaff calls his boss, guy named Al. Now Joe, who's getting pretty worked up, takes the phone and says, 'Al, listen to me: You got nothing to worry about. Bet ten grand if you want. We will beat this team.'"

It was just about time for the prime rib dinner. Guests included AFL president Milt Woodard, astronaut Gordon Cooper, and Jim Rathman, winner of the Indianapolis 500. O. J. Simpson, selected as College Player of the Year, was unable to attend, but called during the banquet to express his thanks. The only real attraction, though, was Namath, who sat on the dais next to his companion for the evening, Mr. Johnnie Walker. He was drinking out of a rocks glass now, sipping and smiling as speakers took turns teasing him. "It became like a Dean Martin roast," says Dowd.

Namath began his own remarks by praising his family, Coach Bruno, Coach Bryant, Mr. Werblin, Weeb Ewbank, Phil Iselin and Company, and of course, his teammates. "This should be a most valuable player award for the entire team," he said.

He was still just getting started. "I'd like to personally thank all the single girls in New York for their contribution," he said.

At some point the expansive discourse was interrupted by a heckler yelling, "Sit down!"

"Who's that?" asked Joe. "Lou Michaels?"

The way Namath remembers that evening, it was the heckler who precipitated his pronouncement. Perhaps there was something in his voice, an echo of authority he found distasteful. Perhaps he heard strains of Hoover, Danahy, or Woodard in that voice. Who was this Colts fan? Another Kiwanis clubber who wasn't getting laid? To hell with him. If the nuns at St. Mary's couldn't embarrass Joe, this guy surely had no chance. The heckler hadn't seen the films. The heckler hadn't had five ounces of sewer water drained off his knee. He hadn't been shot up with prednisone. It was time for him to sit his tired old Baltimore Colts ass down. Everybody else might as well go and call the bookies.

"The Jets will win Sunday," announced Joe Namath. "I guarantee it."

What remained of his acceptance speech lacked the same focus. He said there were five defensive players better than anyone on the Colts. He said Super Bowl Week had been "the greatest time of our lives." And he chastised Milt

Woodard, who presented him with the award. "How can the league say it's wrong to have long hair?" asked Namath. "What's hair got to do with being a football player? . . . People say it creates the wrong image for the kids."

Image? Ask Y. A. Tittle about image. Everybody knew why people liked football. Everybody knew what drew fans to the game. It was just like he said on the plane ride down to Florida: the *real* image of football was brutal. It was mangled fingers, fractured cheekbones, purplish half-moons of scar tissue. And all the prednisone and novocaine and booze didn't help a bit unless you won. That's what they should be telling the kids.

"In closing," said Namath, "I don't like to agree with this saying, but I'm afraid it's true: the name of the game is kill the quarterback."

■ ■ ■

Memory is a hustler himself, perversely accommodating. One tends to remember what one wants to remember. Recollection, the most sentimental of wagers, is part wish. Those who were there for Super Bowl III, and those who only believe they were, tend to recall Namath's guarantee as the Biggest Thing about that epochal contest. They will nostalgically hold forth on the media's frenetic attempt to analyze—no, *deconstruct*—the words of a buzzed young man then twenty-five years old. They will swear in good faith to having read banner headlines and bulletins heralding the Guarantee. They will tell you of a morning after that rendered Namath bigger than the triumphant *Apollo 8* astronauts who had just circumnavigated the moon.

In fact, the astronauts—Colonel Frank Borman, Captain James Lovell Jr., and Lieutenant Colonel William Anders—were the story of the day. After President Johnson presented them with Distinguished Service Medals, they went to New York for a ticker-tape parade. There was other major news, such as a decision by the *Saturday Evening Post*—founded by Ben Franklin, but more recently famous for its persecution of Bear Bryant—to cease publication.

But Namath's remarks of the previous evening didn't rate even a single mention in the New York papers. They were to be found only in the *Miami Herald,* the bottommost story on the first sports page. The headline—I GUAR- ANTEE WE'LL WIN—NAMATH—ran above a mere twelve paragraphs that appeared in the *Herald*'s late editions. The byline belonged to Luther Evans, a sportswriter enterprising enough to duck out of the Villas' King Arthur banquet room and phone Namath's guarantee to his desk.

Among Namath's teammates, reactions were mixed. There were those who agreed with Don Shula, who said, "He's given our players more incentive." Some Jets saw another Namath hustle, worthy of mild amusement and, perhaps, applause. But those of the majority opinion no longer gave a shit. Joe was being Joe; there was a still a game to be played.

The New York media remained, for the most part, equally indifferent. The guarantee would eventually become the Guarantee, the most famous prediction since Babe Ruth's "Called Shot" home run in Game 3 of the 1932 World Series. In Ruth's case, the writers had the industriousness to make up a good story. In Namath's, they had a good story and ignored it. Or perhaps Namath himself was just too much of a good story. Though this was the first time he'd underwritten his comments with such a headline-friendly statement, he had been saying things like that for more than a week now.

Newsday, which circulated on Long Island, reported the Guarantee in a headline in its Saturday editions. *Times* columnist Robert Lipsyte also mentioned it in passing in the thirteenth paragraph of a column about Ewbank. There was yet another fleeting allusion to the Guarantee in the tenth paragraph of the standard game-day advance in Sunday's *Daily News.* On the eve of the big game, correspondents and editors seemed to dismiss Namath with a disdain born of familiarity. They had grown tired of his act and now waited for it to end.

For the record, Ewbank engaged in some halfhearted damage control: "I wouldn't give a darn for him if he didn't think he could win." But his team had more serious problems. The Jets' big weapon wasn't exactly a secret: the Bomb, Namath to Maynard. But here it was, the afternoon before the game, and football's all-time leading receiver still couldn't run. Earlier in the day he had taken a shot of xylocaine, and now it was time to test his damaged hamstring at the Jets' final practice. Maynard started jogging and making his cuts. But then he pulled up lame. "I felt something," he said. "I better not run anymore on it."

The hamstring wouldn't improve overnight, nor would the Jets' chances. It had been reasoned, with great unanimity, that New York's only hope was the Bomb. The long pass was more than the Jets' specialty; it was their identity. Namath had proclaimed as much ten days earlier on the charter flight. Long balls meant big balls. The Colts understood the message all too well. Of course, they were expected to win the game. But mere winning wasn't enough. After listening to Namath's bluster all week, they were determined to avoid the special ignominy associated with his bombs.

"Not one bomb has been made on us all season," said Bobby Boyd, Baltimore's thirty-one-year-old cornerback. After all that had happened, the Colts weren't going to allow Namath to succeed in doing what no other quarterback had done to them. It was a matter of pride.

Considering the circumstances, Bobby Boyd had no cause to be so concerned with his pride. For lack of a good hamstring, there would be no bombs. Namath should have been the one worrying. In a few hours he'd be engaged in a game of Kill the Quarterback with an 18-point price on his head. What's more, he'd be lacking his most lethal weapon in Maynard. Nevertheless, on the eve of the game, he would achieve a high state of relaxation right there in the Governor's Suite. As per his request, he had a film of the Colts' play-off win over the Vikings, a team quarterbacked by Joe Kapp. "Can't throw at all," said Namath. Everything was right. He had the one-eyed monster. He had his Johnnie Walker. And he had his kind-of-funny, kind-of-nice. Bobby Van would remember Joe ducking away with her early that evening: "About five-five, dark hair, a great-looking little girl. I think he met her at Fazio's."

On January 10, 1969, two days before the game, Pete Rozelle announced that the annual AFL-NFL championship would be known, henceforth and officially, as "The Super Bowl." Dick Young compared the commissioner's position to "the man who marries the gal on the child's third birthday." Rozelle, always concerned with appearances, had little choice. The term, he admitted, "seems to have taken hold." Unfortunately, with the approaching contest being forecast as the most lopsided in the game's short history, "super" verged on satire.

By most conventional standards—fumbles, interceptions, missed field goals, dropped passes—Super Bowl III would have been judged another dismal failure. The game was sloppy, full of folly, frustration, and squandered opportunity. One

34. SUPER

can argue that the most significant play was an incomplete pass. Neither team played near its potential. The game was super only in its defiance of expectations, all of which revolved around Namath. In short, this was the stuff of legends.

In 1967, more than 30,000 seats remained empty in the cavernous Los Angeles Coliseum. But this year the tickets—as printed, they referred only to the "Third World Championship Game"—were almost impossible to get. The $12 seats—a sum that roused charges of price-gouging at Super Bowl I—were now being scalped for $150. The sellout attendance was 75,377. But as Curt Gowdy, NBC's play-by-play man, said in his opening: "They could have sold 150,000."

Gowdy's was a prescient preamble, with Namath's braggadocio at the core: "He doesn't even predict it. He guarantees it." What's more, anticipating what the Super Bowl would become, Gowdy noted the peculiar feel of a commercial holiday. "The greatest three days in rental car history," as he described them. The point spread now had the Colts favored by as much as 20 points in some places. And though that hardly seemed like a sporting proposition, bookies would report wagering of historic proportions. There were those, like the loudmouth at the Touchdown Club, who wanted to see the Colts assault Namath, forcibly sit him down and shut him up. And there were others to whom the

Guarantee gave some slight, if sentimental, hope. The Guarantee was pure Namath—a violation of football's orthodoxies that generated interest. Even those who liked him had to wonder: Was Namath merely a raffish mascot of lost causes? Or could he actually underwrite his boasts?

"The Super Bowl is world theater," pronounced Marshall McLuhan, who deigned to talk to the *New York Times* during the game. "The games of every culture hold up a mirror of the culture."

Such was the case with Super Bowl III, a telecast sponsored by Chrysler, Pall Mall Gold, Salem, Winston, TWA, RCA, Schlitz, Phillips 66, and Gillette Techmatic razors at a rate of $135,000 a minute. The Colts and the Jets, meanwhile, were stereotyped as the crew cuts versus the longhairs. Maybe the players deserved better than that, but as seen on television—a medium about which McLuhan knew less than Werblin—they had come to represent opposite ends of the decade. Many boys of the baby boom would recall the game as a battle between sensibilities, or as they were known by the brand names, Square versus Cool.

Sunday, January 12, was an overcast, windy day, with gusts up to 15 miles per hour. Game-time temperature was 73 degrees. The *Apollo 8* astronauts, who looked not unlike Coach Shula, led the Orange Bowl in reciting the Pledge of Allegiance. Joseph P. Kennedy sat with his surviving son. And Bob Hope sat with the vice president–elect. "Just flew down with Ted Agnew," he announced merrily.

Ted? Ted was a big Colts fan. To review the broadcast is to wonder, as did so many kids Namath's age and younger, if the game hadn't been rigged for the Squares.

■　　■　　■

Perhaps it was that very sense of assurance that prompted Colts owner Carroll Rosenbloom to pay a call on his former coach before the game. A couple of nights earlier, at the NFL's Mexican-themed party on Miami Beach, Rosenbloom was overheard bragging that he had bet a quarter of a million on his team. Now, the man who fired Ewbank in 1963 was requesting his presence at a gala to be held that evening at the Rosenbloom home in Golden Beach. Weeb declined, politely but firmly. Then he made sure his team learned about his invitation to the big Baltimore victory party.

Weeb had been preaching "poise and execution" the whole week. But following his own advice was easier said than done. Earlier, the coach couldn't decide whom to introduce before the game, the offense or the defense. "What the hell, Weeb," said Joe. "Just introduce the seniors."

The coach's distracted state may have had something to do with the state of his senior-most starter. With Maynard's hamstring still casting doubt on his ability to play, Bake Turner had been expecting to start at flanker. But after a final consultation with Dr. Nicholas, Weeb decided to take his chances with Maynard. He'd be a decoy, if nothing else. The Colts didn't know the extent of his injury, and what they didn't know could hurt them an awful lot.

■   ■   ■

The scrapping of expectations began with the second play from scrimmage, a handoff to Matt Snell, who'd go left following the blocking of Winston Hill. "It wasn't in our game plan," says Snell. "Joe called the play at the line of scrimmage. We never ran sweeps and stuff like that, but it broke wide open." Snell, true to his word, was looking to punish people. Nine yards upfield he collided with Rick Volk, the Colts' star free safety. Snell put his helmet down, charging: "I think Volk was so shocked he never got in good tackling position. He ducked under, and I think I got him in the head with my left knee." The play ended with Volk facedown, concussed. He would return to the game, but he'd have no memory of Super Bowl III. It would be Monday before the safetyman got around to asking who won.

Though that first drive was short-lived, it would remain with the Colts the rest of the day. Delivered in the violent vernacular familiar to all players, Snell's message translated as:

Fuck you and your safety blitz.

The Colts came back with a fuck-you of their own, at least what seemed to be one. It started with a nineteen-yard pass play to John Mackey. Not only was Mackey the player the Jets most feared, but Larry Grantham, their most savvy defender, had uncharacteristically blown a coverage. In eight plays, Morrall had the Colts with a first down at the Jets' 19. Then the offense stalled. Lou Michaels came on to kick a field goal. At twenty-seven yards, it should have been a gimme, but there was something strange about the way the ball came off his foot: a misdirected loft, like a shank shot out of a sand trap, wide right.

"How *did* Lou Michaels miss that first field goal?" asks George Sauer. "It was a chip shot."

"I still say it was good in my sleep," says Michaels, who thought it was 3 points when the ball came off his foot. In his mind's eye, it drifted right, directly over the crossbar. The official may have even blown the call. "The wind took it," he says.

Wind? Perhaps there had been a wind that night at Fazio's.

■   ■   ■

Now eighty yards from the goal, Namath threw three short passes, the last of which found Billy Mathis for the first down. This was not what had been expected from a young man known, in the not so distant past, as the Hungarian Howitzer and the Beaver Falls Bomber. He was throwing under the defense, practically begging Baltimore to step up on his receivers. His strategy was like that of a fighter who sets up his right with a series of jabs. As soon as he established the rhythms of the short threat, Namath went deep. Both backs stayed to block as Namath took a long drop. In the meantime, Maynard sprinted past Bobby Boyd, who in accordance with the precepts of Baltimore's zone defense, released him to the strong safety, Jerry Logan. Despite the bad hamstring, Maynard outraced the safetyman, too, beating Logan by a couple of steps. But those steps were less than the distance by which Namath overthrew his ailing receiver.

"Damn," thought Ewbank. "If he's healthy, that's a touchdown."

Namath and Maynard had the same thought. The Colts, meanwhile, considered themselves very lucky. Namath had them beaten with the bomb. And he made it look so easy, as if he could do it anytime, with just a flick of the wrist. "That ball, in the air, was delivered fifty-five yards," marveled Gowdy.

Now the Colts renewed their vow of vigilance, to protect at all costs against the Namath bomb. But as they did, they changed the geometry of the field. "That might have been the most important play of the game because it determined what they did on defense," says Sauer, a math major at Texas. "The whole zone rotated to Don's side, which was the strong side."

The shift left Lenny Lyles all alone with a great split end on the weak side of the field. "It also," adds Sauer, "set the stage for the 19 Straight." The 19 Straight, as it was known in the Jets playbook, called for Snell to run left behind Winston Hill. It was an old-school, NFL-style play, and wasn't called too often during the season. But Baltimore's shift had exposed its weak side, which had already been weakened with age. Lyles, just a couple weeks shy of his thirty-third birthday, was matched against a twenty-five-year-old just coming into his prime, while linebacker Don Shinnick, also thirty-three, tried to contain Snell's power running. "They were very good," says Sauer, "but not quite as quick as they used to be." Finally, there was Ordell Braase, the defensive end, who had been such a menace to Hill back in the summer of '63. Now Hill would block him as if he were paving over the past.

■   ■   ■

Still, as the first quarter ended, it was the Colts who were threatening to score. After Sauer had fumbled deep in New York territory, a run by Tom Matte brought the ball to the 6. Then Morrall threw into the middle of the defense. Al Atkinson tipped the ball, a sudden misdirection that caused it to pop high off the pads of tight end Tom Mitchell and into the arms of Jets cornerback Randy Beverly, who downed it for a touchback. The play deflated Baltimore yet again.

There were now eighty yards between the Jets and the goal line. But the Colts, still reeling from the incomplete bomb to Maynard, played as if Namath could cover that distance in a single play. Instead, he called Snell to run left on four consecutive plays, a total of twenty-six yards. Then Namath got lucky, with Shinnick nearly intercepting a pass intended for Sauer. On the next play, with Snell on the bench sucking oxygen through a mask, the Colts came with a blitz. "Other quarterbacks wouldn't be able to handle it," said Shula. But Namath could recognize the blitz before it took shape. "Most of the plays were called at the line of scrimmage," he would recall. "We got out of the huddle early to see what they might show." The blitzes that broke most quarterbacks' composure were welcomed by Namath. Even as he called the signals, he was thinking: *Please let them blitz, please.*

Baltimore did not disappoint. This time the blitzer was a linebacker, Mike Curtis, nicknamed "the Animal." Namath remained free of his grasp just long enough to dump the ball off to Billy Mathis, who ran into Colts territory for the first time that day. Then Namath went weakside twice to Sauer—four yards, eleven yards. The possession would end as it began, with Snell running behind Winston Hill. The touchdown drive took 5 minutes and 57 seconds, but in that time, the Jets had demonstrated their best qualities of the day. As an athletic contest, Super Bowl III is less than its reputation, its beauty difficult to discern. But two men were brilliant that day: Namath, for his intelligence and poise, and Snell, for his physical valor.

The Colts answered with another sustained drive. Again, it ended with Lou Michaels missing a field goal. At forty-six yards, this one wasn't a chip shot. But the Colts weren't finished squandering opportunities. On their next possession, Tom Matte—who had already spent his $15,000 winner's share to build an extension on his house—broke off a fifty-eight-yard run, only to be caught from behind by Jets cornerback Billy Baird and Larry Grantham. As Matte tried to get up, Johnny Sample hovered over him, telling him how slow he was. They were still jawing when the officials separated them. But the last word would be Sample's, the former Colt who loudly advertised his dislike for all things NFL. A couple of plays later, with Morrall trying to pass for a touchdown, Sample stepped in front of Colts flanker Willie Richardson and made the interception at the 2.

But the worst was yet to come for Morrall. The last play of the half was the flea-flicker, an option to Matte, who lateraled back to Morrall, whose primary receiver was split end Jimmy Orr. Weeb knew it well. The flea-flicker had been in the Baltimore playbook since he had been coach. The Jets had defensed it all week in practice, with no success. Now, under game conditions, they reacted just as poorly. "All alone is Jimmy Orr," said Curt Gowdy. Orr was frantically waving his hands. "Orr could have walked in," the play-by-play man said moments later. "He was wide open at the 10-yard line, nobody within fifteen yards of him."

"I did everything but shoot up a flare," Orr would say after the game.

"I never saw him," said Morrall. "I saw the fullback open."

The fullback was Jerry Hill, but he wasn't open. As Morrall threw into the middle of the field, Jim Hudson jumped the route and made the interception.

"Earl wanted to win so bad he got away from winning," says Lou Michaels. "I think Morrall was overexcited."

■　　■　　■

At the half Baltimore's locker room was infested with a hint of doom. Michaels and Morrall had played like Namath's marks back in the days of the Blue Room. The Colts had now blown five scoring opportunities. Three of Morrall's passes—each a potential touchdown—had been picked off. Namath was right: Babe Parilli would've done better. Bubba Smith, who had gone without a sack, started chain-smoking at his locker.

Meanwhile, in the Jets' locker room, Al Atkinson huddled with Dr. Nicholas. Just before the flea-flicker, he had suffered a separated shoulder, the kind of painful injury that could keep a player out for six weeks. But the Jets, with no backups at middle linebacker, didn't have a proper substitute for Atkinson. He pleaded with the doctor to keep his shoulder their secret. Nicholas warned him that hitting—the key part of a middle linebacker's job description—would cause excruciating pain.

"So let's get rid of the pain," said Atkinson.

Nicholas jabbed him with a syringe full of xylocaine. Then Jeff Snedeker taped his shoulder pads to his skin. "It was a remarkable display of courage," Nicholas recalled.

You had to be impressed. "I'm really shocked by this game," Bob Hope, king of the squares, told the NBC man at halftime. "These Jets are really doing something out there." With that, America's Comedian returned to his seat, joining his great good friend Ted Agnew and the secret service. The Florida A & M marching band had just concluded a rousing rendition of the "Battle Hymn of the Republic." The second half was about to begin.

On the Colts' first play from scrimmage, Tom Matte's fumble was recovered at the Colt 33. The short drive that followed—mostly running plays—saw Namath survive his first and only sack at the hands of Bubba Smith, and a near interception by Jerry Logan. Baltimore's strong safety had cut in front of Lammons with nothing but open space between him and the goal line. Logan got both hands on the ball, but couldn't hold on. Namath knew he shouldn't have thrown it, but he also knew that luck was part of the game. On the next play, Jim Turner kicked his first field goal, a thirty-two-yarder. It was 10–0, Jets.

Though Unitas was already warming up, Morrall remained at quarterback. He had three more plays. Then the Colts punted.

On the next series, Namath finally connected with Maynard. But again, the pass was too long. Maynard caught it on the far side of the end zone. As the official signaled the catch out of bounds, Namath was in great pain. He had reinjured his already aching thumb, jamming it on the helmet of oncoming Colts tackle Fred Miller. The hurt was bad enough for Namath to take himself out of the game, something he had refused to do against Oakland. Parilli came in without benefit of any warm-up and tossed an incomplete pass for Sauer. Then Turner came on to kick a thirty-yard field goal.

The score was now 13–zip, Jets. The Colts had begun to believe in the inevitability of the Jets' luck.

The third quarter ended without a Colt first down, and the Jets driving yet again. Namath returned to his game plan. "We worked that left side," he would say. "Wore it out as much as we could." Now the Colts looked their age. Sauer beat Lyles on consecutive plays, eleven yards, then thirty-nine. As the fourth quarter began, Shinnick and Ordell Braase, mainstays of Baltimore's weakside defense, were benched. The Jets were finally stopped at the 2-yard line, where Turner kicked yet another field goal, his third of five attempts on the day.

Now, as if to underscore the ironies inflicted by age, Joey U. was watching Johnny U. from the sidelines. It was obvious from the wobble on Unitas's passes that his elbow was still very sore. Baltimore managed to mount an equally wobbly drive. But the notion of Unitas as heroic javelin thrower was merely a memory, something to be mourned. With the ball at the New York 25, Unitas threw for Jimmy Orr in the end zone. His pass was intercepted, easily, by Randy Beverly.

"The world is a happening," McLuhan said that day from Toronto. "In the speed-up of the electronic age, we want things to happen. This offers us a mosaic that the fans love—everything is in action at once."

Translation: it was *live,* an authentic surprise experienced simultaneously all around the global village (especially where the sporting men took action). Up in the broadcast booth, Gowdy was saying: "You may be seeing one of sport's greatest upsets in history." At Bill's Meadowbrook in Hempstead, there was much joy among those who got in at 7 to 1. At Camp Addison, in the Cha Rang Valley, where GIs were listening over Armed Services Radio, Linwood Alford was already figuring how much of a score was stashed in that footlocker. Jimmy the Greek learned of the Jets victory in Cottage Hospital in Santa Barbara, where he had undergone emergency abdominal surgery. The famous oddsmaker blamed Morrall's interceptions in the end zone. Not even a wizard could have figured on that. But there went the point spread. "If they played tomorrow," he conceded, "I'd make the Colts 12-point favorites like I originally thought."

In fact, the Greek had nothing to worry about. The overpriced line would make him more famous than he ever imagined. You couldn't buy that kind of publicity.

For most bettors, the game had lost its suspense. But there remained some intrigue on the field. On his next possession, Unitas led the Colts on an eighty-yard touchdown drive. With 3:19 left, the score was 16–7. Now Lou Michaels came up with his best play of the day, an onside kick recovered by the Colts. As Unitas took the field again, an unconscious Rick Volk had to be dragged off by his teammates. Now, even Namath was nervous. But 1958 was a long time gone. On fourth and five from the Jets' 19, Grantham tipped Unitas's last chance for Jimmy Orr.

Namath concluded his play selection with six consecutive handoffs to Snell, who finished with 121 yards on thirty carries, and another 40 yards as a receiver. Those might have been MVP numbers. Even Sonny Werblin thought so. "I'll never forget," says Snell, "he told me, 'I thought it should have been you.' Then he sent me to a Cadillac dealership in Jersey where they gave me a green Eldorado." Sonny might have done this from the goodness of his heart, or maybe he was making a play to represent Snell. Whatever the case, the Super Bowl MVP was something of an MCA production. "Joe was the quarterback," says Snell, his shrug taken to mean: He was the leading man. Namath went 17 for 28, 206 yards, no interceptions. For some reason, the pain in his thumb made throwing to his left especially difficult. Despite that, he hit Sauer eight times for 133 yards. Maynard, who changed the game on an incomplete pass, didn't make a reception. Namath remains the only quarterback to be named Super Bowl MVP without throwing a touchdown. The best passer in the sport, a master of its angles, did not even attempt a pass in the fourth quarter.

As the game came to an end, Don Shinnick, a member of the Fellowship of Christian Athletes, offered his congratulations. "Always remember the Lord," he said.

"I'll remember that," Namath replied.

Then he walked off the field wagging his right index finger. What were the squares expecting, a peace sign? Nah. It was nothing like that. The Jets were number one. The Cool Kid had won. And so had those who just wanted to be cool. Namath's was a gesture that adolescent males—the most narcissistic of all creatures—found themselves mimicking in front of the mirror. They would do this for years, imagining themselves as Joe Willie, even as they became adults.

■　■　■

For years, there have been whispers that Namath and Michaels made a bet that night at Fazio's. And while owners like Rosenbloom could brag with impunity about a quarter-million-dollar wager, woe to the player who made any kind of bet. Pete Rozelle's league did not respect the customs of boys brought up in industrial Pennsylvania. Betting violated the NFL's strictest prohibition. "They made a bet someway," says Walt Michaels, uniquely positioned as Lou's brother and the architect of the Jets defense. "I know it wasn't on the game. They weren't betting on the game."

Maybe that's true. But Jim Hudson says otherwise. "There was a bet," he says. As per their agreement, he recalls Michaels giving him the money he now owed to Joe right after the game. Michaels was nothing if not an honorable loser. As for the amount wagered, Hudson says: "I don't even remember, to be honest. Back then we felt it was a lot. But it wasn't that much."

Whatever the amount, Hudson didn't want to be the one holding the money. He remembers giving it to Mike Bite, Joe's lawyer, after the game. "I don't have any recollection of that," says Bite. "And I can honestly say I never discussed that with Joe."

Lou Michaels, for his part, categorically denies the whole story. He says there was no bet and that he never gave Hudson any money for Joe. "If he got some money, he didn't get it from me," says Michaels. "Honesty is the best policy."

One can never really know the truth. Maybe Michaels's version is close. Or maybe he just got hustled—by Namath, and by time. After all, memory itself is a hustler, a sneaky pimp who knows more of his customers' innermost desires than they do. In his dreams, Michaels still swears that first field goal was good.

■   ■   ■

Now came the time for newsmen to collect their quotations. In the locker room, Johnny Sample produced an aging newspaper clipping with the headline: "Kansas City Not in Class with NFL Best—Lombardi." "I think the NFL will be ready for us in about two years," he said. Randy Rasmussen, the modest second-year pro who did an improbably fine job on Billy Ray Smith, observed: "I think I whipped him pretty good."

When asked if he was surprised, Gerry Philbin said, "Yeah, I'm surprised they scored on us."

"All you wrote was how great Matte and Hill were," said Snell. "Go talk to them now."

"I had no doubts," said John Namath, wearing a straw souvenir hat. "The boy can do anything he sets his mind on doing."

Namath himself chided the writers, especially those not from New York, for picking the Colts. Then he gave credit to his defense, while expressing regret that his comments had been taken as a "rap" on Morrall. He was just stating facts. That didn't mean he felt bad for the guy, either. "Better him than me," said Namath. The questioning continued: What about the two passes that were almost intercepted? What if the Colts had scored first?

"If a frog had wings," said Namath, "it wouldn't bump its ass."

Editors at the *Miami Herald* were already working on a banner headline to run across the top of the next day's sports section: JOE GUARANTEED IT. Less apparent in that same edition would be this brief item: "Wahoo McDaniel, former football star, makes his last appearance as a wrestler Wednesday night at the Miami Beach Auditorium." He would wrestle Boris Malenko, the Mad Russian.

"Eighteen-point underdogs," Namath finally shouted. "J-E-E-S-U-S K-E-E-RIST."

The only thing sillier than the price was the locker room. As per orders from the league president, champagne was not allowed. "Ridiculous," said Namath. The squares were still putting up a fight, still worried about that image.

Soon, as Namath was off partying with Suzie Storm and Joe Hirsch, Rick Volk was vomiting in his bathroom at the Statler Hilton. Then the man who began his day as Baltimore's big weapon—the safety blitzer—collapsed in the tub. The Colts team doctor, who had been in the next room, responded by jamming his left hand into Volk's mouth. Using a ballpoint pen, the doctor tried to prevent the safetyman from biting off his tongue. The doctor almost lost a finger. Eventually, the convulsions subsided and Volk was brought to Holy Cross Hospital, where a spokesman described his condition as "very satisfactory."

Namath, who knew better, sent flowers.

Sometime after the Super Bowl, Joe and Al Hassan were drinking at Jilly's South, Jilly Rizzo's place in Miami. The buzz began: Where's Frank? Frank? Frank's coming, Frank's coming. *Frank.*

Joe was buzzing, too. "As drunk as I've ever seen him," says Hassan.

Finally, Sinatra walked in with a guy who looked to be a bodyguard. Frank, rumored to have lost big money on the Colts, put out his hand. Joe got up to shake it and in the process knocked over every drink on the table. Sinatra, much to the waitstaff's horror, was dripping wet. An uneasy moment passed during which patrons couldn't help but think of the retributive possibilities stemming from a dripping and humiliated Frank, he of the legendary temper. Namath began to gargle an apology.

But then Sinatra stopped him: "Ah, Joe, don't worry about it."

The world had changed since January 12, 1969. In fame's pecking order, Namath suddenly outranked Sinatra. Actually, at that moment, he outranked just about everybody who wasn't a Beatle. But unlike the Beatles, whose confederation was approaching its sour end, Namath's party had really just begun.

35. AMERICA'S HERO

For years now, the handling of Namath, particularly on game days, involved logistics of Beatlesque proportions. Police escorts were mandatory. The team bus would have to drive directly onto the airport runway to keep Joe from being accosted in the terminal. John Free, the Jets' business manager, would spend Saturdays devising ways for the Jets star to exit the stadium without incident. His favorite trick was probably smuggling Joe out in the back of a laundry truck. But these crazy young girls were ever ready to test his ingenuity. Consider the cutie-pie who thought to lie down in front of the Jets' bus. "She told me she wasn't going anywhere until Joe came out to give her a kiss," says Free.

Dave Herman would recall a hotel lobby packed with young women "all

dolled up like they were waiting for a Hollywood producer." The Jets were in
Cleveland for a preseason doubleheader. But the mere suggestion of Broadway
Joe transformed it into an event. "When Joe Namath came off the elevator,"
said Herman, "it was like a stampede. People went crazy, screaming, climbing
over each other just to touch him."

On the morning of January 22, 1969, girls who once wept for John, Paul,
George, and Ringo flocked to City Hall, where Mayor Lindsay declared it
"New York Jets Championship Day." Namath, noted the next day's *Times,* "required a wedge of 12 policemen to cross a sidewalk thronged with female admirers." The old MCA formula that created Frankie and the bobby-soxers now
produced an outrageous, almost psychedelic, sense of possibility. The bobby-
soxers had ripened.

"We all had this feeling that Joe could get laid anytime he wanted," says
sportscaster Sal Marchiano. "He was *the* bachelor." Unlike other men, Joe
never had to hustle the girls. They were just *there,* around, available.

The 1969 Astrojet celebrity golf tournament, sponsored by American
Airlines, was held in February at La Costa in Carlsbad, California. Namath
was paired with his buddy Mickey Mantle. They were easy to spot out on
the course; their cart was the one being followed by another, this one carrying two amply bosomed blondes and a cache of cold beer. "We're waiting
for them to come in off the course to interview them," recalls Marchiano.
"But then they make a turn, go up a hill, leave the golf carts and disappear
with the girls for about an hour. Finally, they come back down, half-
crocked. The girls are still with them. Joe goes into the press area to be interviewed. And the first question—it was a classic: 'Joe, are you having
fun?' "

Namath almost spit up his beer. "Am I having *fun?*"

In April, he was picked up for drunk and reckless driving when his rented
Cadillac convertible was clocked doing about 70 miles per hour on Miami's
Seventy-ninth Street Causeway, a 40 mph zone. It was 4:05 A.M. "Sure I cussed
the cop and I was wrong to do it," Namath said later that morning. "But I was
sober." In fact, a sobriety test, taken about two hours later at the Dade County
Jail, revealed a blood alcohol level of .02, one-fifth the legal limit.

Throughout the day, reporters kept calling at the Palm Bay Club. To hell
with them. "Don't worry," he told his mother. "Don't believe everything you
read." Newspaper guys weren't going to ruin his good time. Instead, he drank
tequila while putting for dollars (the living room rug served as a green) with
Mike Bite, his Alabama lawyer, and Dick Schaap, who had been commissioned
to write his autobiography.

The fun season, such as it was, culminated on May 24, proclaimed "Joe
Namath Day" in Beaver Falls. Namath arrived bleary-eyed, having partied until about 7:00 A.M. that morning. His traveling squad included Johnny Sample,

George Sauer, Don Maynard, Tad Dowd, Dick Schaap, and a couple of tension-easers, one of whom wore a transparent blouse (though not for long). "It was wilder than I could write in the book," Schaap said later. "Joe brought back those two broads as gifts for his hometown buddies. One was a hooker. The other was just a dedicated amateur."

Joe Namath Day began with a motorcade. Passengers in Namath's convertible Chevy Impala included Wibby Glover and Big John Jackson, the Lower End's beat cop. Women threw flowers at Joe. Kids rushed up to the car to shake his hand. It took forty minutes for the Chevy to travel a mile and a half. Though the population of Beaver Falls had dropped below 17,000, a crowd of approximately 25,000 stood lining Seventh Avenue.

That evening 1,300 people paid ten bucks a plate to attend a testimonial dinner (the menu included braised steak and molded gelatin salad, music courtesy of Henry Garcia and the Tijuana Trumpets) in Namath's honor at the Geneva College gymnasium. The event was organized by the Beaver Falls Booster Club Committee; among its members was Keith Allen, whose son, Sam, used to put away Namath's equipment. Allen once slapped his son for letting Namath hustle him out of a buck or two in the Blue Room. Sam, the would-be poet who only played to please his father, was now living in Detroit, where he got a call from his sister. "You'll never believe it," she said. "Dad is bragging how you used to shoot pool with Joe Namath."

■   ■   ■

Namath's months-long party had paused just once, on account of the war in Vietnam. In February, he traveled with a USO tour that stopped at military hospitals in Japan, Okinawa, Hawaii, and Clark Air Force Base in the Philippines. Other members of Namath's delegation included Steve Wright of the Giants, Jim Otto of the Raiders, NBC announcer Charlie Jones, and Packer tight end Marv Fleming, who would become a friend for many years. Never had Namath been more grateful for the knee that disqualified him from military service. The players were supposed to cheer up the troops, but so many of them—bleeding or burned, without legs or ears or noses—seemed beyond consolation. And that hopeless feeling was almost contagious.

These mangled men incited great guilt in the Raiders' exceptionally rugged center. "I was an ROTC guy in college," says Otto, whose bad knees, like Namath's, had kept him out of the war. "Now I felt like I had let them down . . . like I was leaving them behind."

"I never felt guilt," says Fleming, who played on three Packer championship teams. "When you go into the hospitals and out in the field and you see these guys they're almost hypnotized. Like: *I'm here fighting for my country.* I was probably just as big and strong mentally and physically as any of them. But I remember thinking, 'God, I would not want to be here.' "

Like Namath, Fleming was ruled 4-F for the draft, though the decision stirred no debate on Capitol Hill. He had made sure to tell the army physician that the vertebrae he fractured in college still caused him great pain. "Plus," says Fleming, "I had the Green Bay people working with me. I took my physical in Wisconsin." To this day, he can't help but chuckle when he thinks about the examiners who designated him 4-F. "I think they all got season tickets," he says.

Lombardi's guys were the biggest thing in Wisconsin, where the only problem was the cold. In winter, that half-mile between the practice field and the locker room felt like Antarctica. Luckily, there was no shortage of local kids volunteering for taxi service. The kid who waited on Fleming had a red pickup. "He would have it all warmed up so I could ride shotgun from the field to the locker room," recalls Fleming. They got to know each other, the sandy-haired kid from Green Bay and a black ballplayer from Compton, California. The boy's father had left, and his sadness was apparent to Fleming. They'd go out to eat, mostly burger joints. Fleming recommended junior college, where the kid enrolled for a year before moving away. At least that's what Fleming heard when he showed up for training camp in the summer of '68.

Now, about six months later, as he deplaned after a seventeen-hour flight to Clark Air Force Base, a jeep was waiting. "Which one of you is Fleming?" barked an officer. "We have to hurry."

The Packers tight end would never forget the odor of the military hospital: "Boom, it hit you as soon as you walked in: marijuana. Everybody in there was smoking pot."

Otto and Namath followed him into a private room. There, a young man—minus a leg and an arm—was waiting, bandaged head to toe like a mummy. "Remember me?" he asked.

Fleming shook his head.

"Joe, you're great," said the patient. "But Marv here is *my man*."

Fleming still didn't understand.

The kid spoke again. "The red truck," he said.

Fleming turned back to Namath and Otto and asked for a moment alone. Namath and Otto stepped out of the room. Fleming and the boy said their thank-you's and I-love-you's. Then the boy died. He was nineteen.

"The whole thing took about two minutes," Fleming says.

Marv and Joe considered going home right then. But they stayed through the tour's end. When Namath returned to the States, he gave an interview to Dave Anderson. "Makes you wonder," he said, "what the hell we're doing there."

Those were the most politically charged words he ever uttered. And though the remark seems in keeping with the time, it was out of character for Namath. There is a tendency to group him with athletes far more radical in their leanings, as if his Number 1 sign was the white man's answer to the Black Power salutes delivered by sprinters John Carlos and Tommie Smith at the '68 Olympics. But even Namath's appearance at a riot in Harlem, where such disturbances seemed almost regular occurrences in those years, lacked any social agenda.

Joe went at the urging of Howie Evans, sports editor of the *Amsterdam News*. Earlier, as a favor to Evans—a good friend of Sherman Plunkett's—Namath had visited the Chargers, a youth football team in East Harlem. Now, as Evans saw some of these same Chargers tearing up the Jefferson projects, he headed down to Bachelors, waited for Namath, and convinced him that his presence would be appreciated.

"We got in a cab," says Evans. "Everything stopped when we got there. It was like: Who is this white guy, a cop? Nah, it was Joe Namath. He came out and he stopped the fucking riot."

According to Evans, Namath even got on the bullhorn, telling the kids to call it a night. "Why you want to burn down your own neighborhood?" he asked.

Broadway Joe had a soothing effect, and many kids in the crowd dispersed. Finally, Howie and Joe walked the twenty-plus blocks back down to Ninty-sixth Street, the northern border of white man's Manhattan, where cabs could again be had. "We done walked this far," said Evans. "Might as well walk the rest of the way."

"I ain't walking no more," said Joe. "My legs are killing me."

He had one request: that Evans wouldn't write about the evening. As Sherman Plunkett himself vouched for the sportswriter, Namath granted a favor. But he didn't want to see anything about it in the papers. He wasn't in the business of telling people how to act. He had neither a message nor a master. He wasn't Muhammad Ali.

And yet, Ali is the one with whom Namath is most often compared. Like Ali, Namath is credited with powers of prophecy, having predicted a win against a heavy favorite in Miami. And like Ali, he became a fetish for Howard Cosell. But there the comparison should end. The former Cassius Clay was a figure laden with race and militant politics, a dedicated disciple of Elijah Muhammad. Ali vowed to go to jail before he would ever go to Vietnam. Namath, whose brother John had now fought in two Asian wars, wanted only to avoid marriage. In many ways, he remained a blue-collared son of a mill town. Curiously, it was an old sportswriter who pegged Namath best in 1970. "He is something special," James Reston wrote in the *Times,* "a long-haired hard hat."

By then, a discussion of Namath on the op-ed page of the *Times* was nothing unusual. *Esquire* magazine had already devoted the better part of an issue to "The Higher Truth of Joe Namath." His cartoon likeness was celebrated on the cover: a fur-coated giant, clutching a blonde while swatting at biplanes atop the Empire State Building. Inside the magazine, William F. Buckley Jr. was among those who took his turn interpreting the affairs of Broadway Joe: "I saw him in person once, at the opening of *Oh! Calcutta!* . . ."

Namath had to laugh at this frantic search for his true significance. Let the rest of the world immerse itself in the symbolism of pro football. Let fashionable theorists offer metaphors for militarism and authority, with Lombardi as a stand-in for General Westmoreland. For Namath, the game was simply what it was. He took advantage of Weeb because he was allowed to, which is not to say that he didn't believe in the sanctity of authority. He was, after all, one of Bear Bryant's boys.

Most laughable was the notion of Namath as a hippie, more evidence that squares just didn't understand. His hair might've been longish, but it was carefully and expensively groomed. His taste in music was similarly subdued, running to Tom Jones and the Fifth Dimension. Hippies didn't play golf, nor did they sip blended scotch at the Palm Bay Club.

In retrospect, his Number 1 gesture anticipates the 1970s, the Me Generation, more than it figures in the '60s. He had no politics and, exempting booze and broads, belonged to no movement. Rather, in Namath's soul was a concern that the new Republican president would have heartily approved. His issue wasn't social justice; it was commerce.

■ ■ ■

The day after the Super Bowl, UPI moved an item about Namath's being offered a movie part as a French Resistance fighter. A piece in the *Daily News* noted that he had received "several" movie offers and speculated that the quarterback may have already taken his last snap. "You've got to make it while you're on top," said Namath, fueling the talk of his retirement. "Before you get destroyed." The idea of Namath as a movie star was initiated by Werblin back in '65. To an old MCA agent, star quality was a fungible commodity. Football star, movie star, same difference. Interestingly enough, Werblin was again trying to call the shots with Joe. "Agent isn't the proper word," he said, describing his new role when Namath was away on the USO Tour:

> All I'm trying to do is consolidate some of Joe's offers . . . the most fantastic I've ever seen—movies, books, TV specials, endorsements. We've heard from every major motion-picture studio—Universal, Paramount, Twentieth Century and Warner's. And from two or three independent producers. But the trick is not to make a freak movie, definitely not a football movie. Joe has sex appeal, that's the important thing, like Sinatra had. . . .
>
> Look at Cary Grant. He was an acrobat, and Rock Hudson, he was a truck driver. But they had sex appeal, and that's what counts. Somebody with guts who looks good has got it made.

As for the books, several major publishing houses have made offers, and the endorsement opportunities represent an awful lot of money. We want to try to have something that will be lasting, instead of 15 minutes of nothing. But no matter what happens, when Joe's three-year contract expires, I won't represent him in his negotiations with the team. I made that clear at the start. My role will be looking over his offers, and in all this I'll be working with Mike Bite and Jimmy Walsh.

The selling of Broadway Joe had begun in earnest. Still unknown, however, was the identity of the head salesman, a role for which Sonny was now making his play. He would secure Namath a supporting role in *Norwood*, a Hal Wallis production, playing Glen Campbell's ex-marine buddy. Namath's part—he shared an old-pal handshake with Campbell and tossed footballs through old tires—was short on dialogue and drama. This was only supposed to be a starter picture, nothing more. Al Hassan, now a theater instructor at the University of Maryland, accompanied Namath to Hollywood as his personal acting coach. Shooting would begin in the summer. It was six days' work for a reported $60,000, not to mention a dressing room with a tub full of vodka and beer on ice.

Then there was Broadway Joe's, an attempt to build a fast-food empire by selling Football Heroes, Quarterback Burgers, and B. J. Junior Burgers (shaped, of course, like minifootballs). The flagship franchise had opened the month before the Super Bowl on Miami's Seventy-ninth Street Causeway.

While Mike Bite, still based in Birmingham, was listed as secretary of Broadway Joe's Inc., the most active of Namath's people was Jimmy. He repped Joe with Braniff Airlines. He cut a deal with Rex International, the maker of Banlon shirts, for Namath's own line of knit shirts. The agreement was to guarantee him $100,000, with $25,000 up front and 5 percent of the net sales. On May 15, 1969, Jimmy signed papers to incorporate Namanco Productions Inc. Forming an entity like Namanco—short for Namath Management Company—was another old MCA move.

"Sonny Werblin had been my hero," Jimmy once said. "He was the greatest agent ever." Jimmy had been impressed with Sonny ever since Lyford Cay. But that didn't mean he had to do business with the guy. It seems that Sonny, for all his greatness, priced himself out of the market for Namath's services.

There was a meeting during which Sonny laid out his terms. "I wanted to see how it went so I go up to Joe's apartment," recalls Tad Dowd, who had no love for Werblin. "Mike and Jimmy were sick about it. They said Sonny wants fifty percent. I say, fifty percent of what? They say, 'everything.' I say, Fifty percent, tell him to go fuck himself.'"

At some point, somebody did, in so many words. And for his diversion, Sonny acquired a Thoroughbred named Silent Screen. The horse, he now

Above: The ascendant hustler, lower left, looking very cool in flat-top and shades. With Namath hitting better than .400, the 1961 Beaver Falls varsity baseball team won the Western Pennsylvania Inter-scholastic Athletic League championship.

(COURTESY OF THE BEAVER COUNTY RESEARCH CENTER)

Left: The basketball squad didn't fare as well, but the white boy had game.

(COURTESY OF THE BEAVER COUNTY RESEARCH CENTER)

Above: At the senior prom. To Namath's left is his star receiver, Tom Krzemienski.

(COURTESY OF THE BEAVER COUNTY RESEARCH CENTER)

Above: Levitating at Alabama. As Coach Bryant said, "Joe had more natural playing ability than anybody."

Right: A crestfallen Bryant walking off the field as Namath lay writhing in pain. It was October 10, 1964, the day he first hurt his knee. Joe felt as if he'd been shot; a team doctor said it was probably just a sprain.

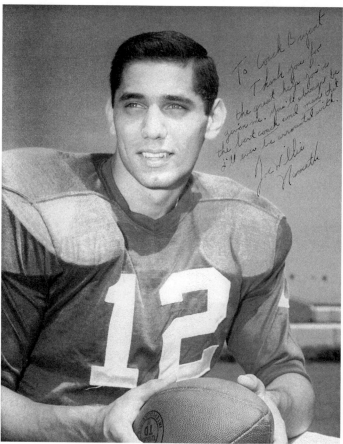

Above: Bryant consoling Joe after the loss to Texas in the Orange Bowl. Sonny Werblin was so taken with Namath's performance that night that he was heard to proclaim: "I'm not paying this kid enough."

(AP/WIDE WORLD PHOTOS)

Left: To Coach Bryant, father figure.

(COURTESY OF PAUL W. BRYANT MUSEUM/ UNIVERSITY OF ALABAMA)

Right: Joe with Sonny, who preached the gospel of Star Quality. Everything Sonny learned in his thirty-five years at MCA went into the selling of Broadway Joe. In turn, Namath would make Sonny a star in his own right.

(MEYER LIEBOWITZ/ *THE NEW YORK TIMES*)

Left: With Weeb Ewbank and the contract that changed everything.

(AP/WIDE WORLD PHOTOS)

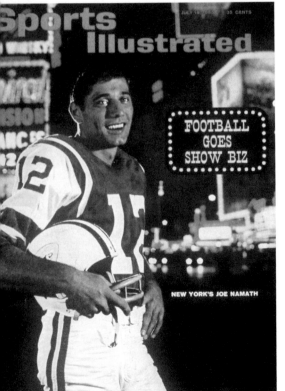

Above: Cool Joe taking a bite of the salted apple as he shows up at the Armed Services Induction Center, September 15, 1965.

(AP/WIDE WORLD PHOTOS)

Left: A star is born: Broadway Joe on the cover of *Sports Illustrated*, July 19, 1965.

(JAMES DRAKE/ *SPORTS ILLUSTRATED*)

Right: Looking good at a preseason workout at Shea, July 1965.

Above: The famous cheap shot from Ben Davidson in Oakland, 1967. Namath could take whatever the big guys were dishing out. "That was the beauty of Joe," remarked Davidson.

(RUSS REED/ OAKLAND TRIBUNE)

Right: Who needs a knee, anyway? The jump pass, 1966.

(BARTON SILVERMAN)

Left: The high priest of lush life enjoys a quiet moment at home with a good book and his llama rug.

(Bettmann/Corbis)

Right: Playing a game of touch football with the Playboy Bunnies, 1967.

(©*New York Daily News,* L.P. Reprinted with Permission/Jim Garrett)

Below: A man and his furrier, showing off the famous $5,000 mink, 1968.

(AP/Wide World Photos)

Left: Who says a guy can't have it all? Booze and broads in Miami, 1967.

(Joe Lippincott/ *The Miami Herald*)

Left: Bobby Van (left), legendary New York nightclub greeter Tony Butrico (right), and Joe getting ready for the grand opening of the Jet Set, before Sonny pressured his star quarterback to get out of the bar business.

(COURTESY OF BOBBY VAN)

Right: Outside Bachelors III, the hottest joint in town, June 1969.

(© ROY DECARAVA 2004. COURTESY, THE DECARAVA ARCHIVES, NEW YORK)

Below: For $1.10 a shot, you had to give the customers what they wanted: great-looking barmaids, spare ribs, and a chance to rub shoulders with The Man himself.

(NEAL BOENZI/ *THE NEW YORK TIMES*)

Right: Entertaining the media in the days before the Third World Championship Game, what the *New York Post*'s Larry Merchant called "Joe Namath Week."

(Walter Ioos, Jr./ *Sports Illustrated*)

Below: Who's afraid of Bubba Smith? Going deep against the Colts. January 12, 1969.

(AP/Wide World Photos)

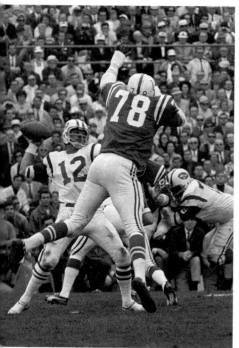

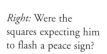

Right: Were the squares expecting him to flash a peace sign?

(Walter Ioos, Jr./ *Sports Illustrated*)

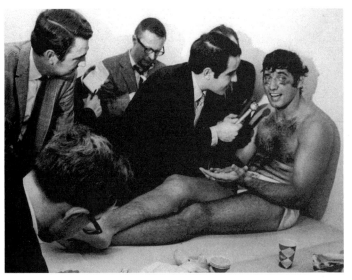

Left: Being interviewed by Sal Marchiano (with the microphone) and others after the big game.

(AP/WIDE WORLD PHOTOS)

Right: The Super Bowl MVP hugging the father who instilled his legendary confidence. "What you should feel," said John Namath, "is that you are better than anyone out there."

(AP/WIDE WORLD PHOTOS)

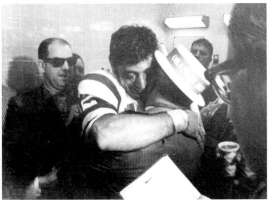

Left: Joe, you made us proud: The victorious motorcade down Seventh Avenue in Beaver Falls. May 1968.

(AP/WIDE WORLD PHOTOS)

Right: America's heroes: Joe with Mickey Mantle being mobbed by fans at the opening of a new office of their ill-fated employment agency, Mantle Men/Namath Girls.

(Bettmann/Corbis)

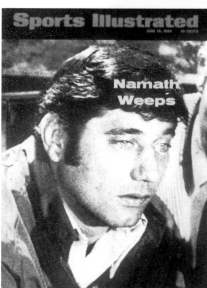

Left: "I'm not selling. I quit." Namath at the famous Bachelors III press conference, June 1969.

(United Press International/*Sports Illustrated*)

Right: Back at Bachelors, making the scene with Suzie Storm.

(©*New York Daily News*, L.P. Reprinted with permission/Carmine Donofrio)

Above: After being hit by Broncos tackle Dave Costa in Denver, September 1969. "The hardest hit I've ever seen a quarterback take," said the Jets trainer.

(AP/WIDE WORLD PHOTOS)

Above: A pregame ritual: getting the knee ready for action.

(TIME LIFE PICTURES/ GETTY IMAGES)

Below: Meet the press: Joe and some of his favorite people after a tough game.

(BARTON SILVERMAN)

Above: Leaving the field at Shea after losing 13–6 to the Chiefs, December 20, 1969. It was only Namath's third post-season game with the Jets, and his last.

(AP/WIDE WORLD PHOTOS)

Right: With Jimmy Walsh leading the way, Joe Namath sold everything from Ovaltine (below, top) to typewriters (below, bottom).

(AP/WIDE WORLD PHOTOS)

(COURTESY GEORGE LOIS)

(COURTESY GEORGE LOIS)

Below: The flagship franchise of the short-lived Broadway Joe's hamburger chain, Miami, 1969.

(TIME LIFE PICTURES/ GETTY IMAGES)

Left: In costume with Victoria George for Larry Spangler's spaghetti western, *The Last Rebel.*

(LARRY SPANGLER PRODUCTIONS/ *SPORTS ILLUSTRATED*)

Below: Backstage with Hoot Owl Hicks for *Damn Yankees,* Jones Beach, 1981.

(ROGER J. THURBER)

Below: With broadcast boothmates Frank Gifford and O. J. Simpson, a disastrous experiment for *Monday Night Football,* 1985.

(*SPORTS ILLUSTRATED*)

Above: Rehearsing for his appearance in *A Salute to Broadway,* a musical review staged at Great Adventure amusement park in New Jersey, 1982.

(AP/WIDE WORLD PHOTOS)

With three of the most important people in his life: *Left:* Joe, 41, and Deborah, 22, on their wedding day, 1984. *Below:* With dapper dad in the locker room after Namath had been so spectacular in a defeat against the 49ers, 1971. *Below, left:* Plugging his mother's book in 1975.

(*South Florida Sun Sentinel*)

(*New York Post*/William Jacobellis)

(AP/Wide World Photos)

Left: The newlyweds at Macy's for the launch of his underwear line.
(AP/WIDE WORLD PHOTOS)

Below: Family portrait: A bearded Joe and Tatiana (right), in costume for *The Seagull*, with daughters Jessica (left) and Olivia, New York City, 1997.
(HEINZ KLUETMEIER/
SPORTS ILLUSTRATED)

Above: With Broadway in the background, the proud father poses with his girls, June 25, 2003.

(ANTHONY J. CAUSI)

Below: Joe and Olivia. Fatherhood gave him "a love never felt before."

(DAMIAN/*SPORTS ILLUSTRATED*)

proclaimed, was preferable to the ballplayer: "In football your inventory can cause you trouble overnight. . . . They can stay out late, drinking. They can feud with each other. They can pop off and make controversial headlines. Silent Screen—he gets to bed early, gets up early, drinks water, keeps his mouth shut and does his work."

Mike Bite was still Joe's lawyer, but Jimmy had become his guy. Jimmy was there whenever Joe came calling, whenever someone came calling for Joe. Jimmy could hustle Joe because he believed in him. And if the hustle wasn't sufficient, he had no problem kicking someone in the balls on Namath's behalf. The gravedigger's son knew Joe was his ticket. Now, if you wanted to deal with Namath—even if you wanted the smallest piece of him—you had to deal with Namanco. If you dealt with Namanco, you were dealing with James C. Walsh, 274 Madison Avenue, New York, New York, 10016.

■   ■   ■

If not for Jimmy, Namath wouldn't have met George Lois.

Movies were nice, but the business of America, to paraphrase Calvin Coolidge, was advertising. And Lois, the basketball-playing son of a Greek florist from the Bronx, was the profane prince of admen. His first great coup for Doyle, Dane Bernbach came on the Volkswagen campaign. Fresh from the Goodman's Matzoh account, he had a unique appreciation for the agency's dilemma: "We have to sell a Nazi car in a Jewish town." They did better than that, transforming a Nazi car into an egalitarian, utilitarian hippie limousine.

Lois had a unique ability to vandalize the cliché. His best-known works were the designs he concocted for the covers of *Esquire*. He famously posed Sonny Liston—who embodied America's fear of the Negro hoodlum—with a Santa Claus cap. He shot Andy Warhol to look as if he were drowning in Campbell's soup. He presented Ali as a martyr to the Vietnam draft, shot full of arrows, posed like Saint Sebastian in Andrea del Castagno's fifteenth-century painting. He photographed Lieutenant William Calley, accused war criminal, with Vietnamese children, Roy Cohn with a halo, and Ed Sullivan in a Beatles wig.

Although his human props were varied, those he regarded with greatest affection were the athletes, particularly ballplayers. But there was a problem using ballplayers in ads. The formula hadn't really changed since the 1950s, when Dodgers centerfielder Duke Snider appeared with Captain Midnight on behalf of chocolate-flavored Ovaltine:

"Duke," asks Captain Midnight, "what do you do to keep yourself in top condition?"

"Well, Captain Midnight, I get plenty of sleep, exercise and the right kind of foods," replies the Duke. "And I drink chocolate-flavored Ovaltine."

Lois explains: "They'd have these guys doing testimonials. It was an insult to the ballplayer." Even worse, they violated the cardinal rule of advertising. "You can't make it look like a guy is doing it for the money. You have to make him look like he's doing it for fun."

Then came Namath. In shaving his Fu Manchu for Schick, he had unwittingly vandalized the conventions of advertising. "Watching that ad, you know he's doing it for the money," says Lois. "But he's doing it with a gleam in his eye and a grin on his face. He's having fun. The fact that he's getting the dough made it even more delicious. You actually feel good about the fact that he's getting paid. It's like: 'The league says I can't wear this mustache? Okay, then pay me.' It was a kind of fuck-you. But he delivered it so sweetly. Namath had real sugar."

Lois understood what was hip. But he also understood that the measure of a man was in the merchandise he moved, the stuff he sold. In Namath, Lois recognized qualities that would help determine the course of the quarterback's life—even as Namath was physically diminished, through retirement and beyond. He had something other men wanted. His endorsement was a promise, however false, that one could actually purchase just a bit of Broadway Joe's *je ne sais quoi.*

Lois was so taken with the performance for Schick that he called Jimmy, arranging for Namath to appear in the new Braniff campaign. With a running slogan of "If you've got it, flaunt it," these were hilarious commercials, set off by unlikely pairings of passengers in the first-class cabin: Warhol and Liston, Salvador Dalí and Whitey Ford, Mickey Spillane and Marianne Moore. But Namath, unlike the others, would appear alone in the first spot, the leadoff hitter in a new $10 million account for Lois's new firm, Lois, Holland, Callaway. Only weeks removed from the Super Bowl, Namath was America's No. 1 Flaunter.

Lois recalls the Namath shoot for several reasons. First was Gina Lollobrigida, another Braniff endorser, whose affections for the quarterback were obvious. Second, the grips and the gaffers kept asking for Joe's autograph; to them, he was the only famous guy. Third was Jimmy Walsh. They had been scheduled to start shooting around 8:00 A.M., but by 9:30 Joe still hadn't appeared. So Lois called Jimmy.

"We need more money," said Jimmy. *We.*

"I'm gonna fucking kill you," said Lois.

Soon enough, Jimmy showed up with his client. "And he was nice, you know?" says Lois. "He kind of shrugged and said, 'Well, I tried.'"

The Braniff campaign led to other ads and other deals. That summer Lois, who used Mickey Mantle in commercials for a brokerage firm, came up with a novel idea: an employment agency combining the luster of his two favorite stars. It would be called Mantle Men, Namath Girls.

"I know it sounds so obnoxious," says Lois, "but I wanted to be the one who made Mickey and Joe really rich. I loved those guys, everything about them. And I remember thinking: I don't want them to have to hustle for the rest of their lives." Mantle had recently retired after eighteen injury-filled years in the big leagues, and Namath's retirement was an ongoing possibility. But the worse they hurt, the harder they partied.

Lois would have them shoot commercials for the agency in the morning. Then typically Mickey would get up and say: "George, it's already eleven o'clock. Let's go to Seasons."

"Do you know how much fun it is," asks Lois, "to walk into the Four Seasons with Joe Namath and Mickey Mantle?"

Occasionally Lois would pull Joe aside, suggesting that he was drinking too much around Mickey. Joe would simply reply, "Gotta keep him company."

That's as far as Lois would go in interceding. You couldn't *tell* Joe what to do. Then again, maybe there was something more he could have said, a way to warn him. The truth was, Mickey Mantle was a walking warning for a guy like Joe. With his career over, there was nothing to keep him from drinking. Lois always returns to one particular story about Mantle:

He got a call to rescue Mickey at the Pierre Hotel on Fifth Avenue. George found him in the bar, drunk out of his mind. "There he is," recalls Lois, "telling his stories to thirty white guys in suits, all laughing and drinking."

Finally, Mickey noticed him. "George, what are you doing here?"

"Mickey," he replied, "you're late for your flight."

Mickey paid his tab, and the hostess, a knockout blonde, asked him for an autograph. It was for her son. Sure, said Mickey, as he touched her tits. Lois apologized profusely and began to push his stumblebum friend toward the door. He tipped the hostess, the bellhop, anybody who could help him remove Mickey Mantle from the premises. Finally, he got Mantle through the revolving door.

Mickey staggered into the street and fell. The day was gray, winter. It had just snowed.

"Jesus Christ, Mickey," said Lois. "Are you all right?"

His head was hanging over the curb, his face inches from the slush. Mantle looked up at Lois, a drunken drawl making its way through his grin: "Fine place for America's hero."

Bobby Van didn't have to come up with a gimmick for Bachelors III as he did for his other joints. In terms of decor, it was the Pussycat refashioned as a sports pub, with walnut paneling, red tablecloths, and a jukebox. The long bar led to a dining room festooned with a gallery of Namath's favorite athletes, guys like Mantle and Bill Hartack. The barmaids, who got $1.10 for a shot of bourbon, were known for low necklines and high skirts. The kitchen, featuring the ubiquitous spare rib entrée, stayed open quite late. But the real attraction was Broadway Joe, whose many idealized faces were featured in a painted montage above the cash register.

The place did a great tourist business, but even New Yorkers acted like tourists as they came in to ask, "Joe here?" "Joe around?" A good night at Bachelors III included a Namath sighting. To the public, Joe did for Bachelors III what

36. THE UNDESIRABLES

Frank had done for Jilly's. A rustle anticipated his presence. Everybody wanted to be there for that moment. Everybody. It was the same urge, somewhat transfigured, that made men want to shave with Schick or fly Braniff. "We had the hottest place in town," says Bobby Van.

He can remember getting a call from Jilly, who had gotten a call from Frank, who had gotten a call from someone with President Johnson. As Jilly explained it, the president's daughter Lynda Bird and her date would be in town. Bobby was to extend them every courtesy.

No problem, said Bobby, who gave them the big center booth. Everybody seemed to be having a good time. The place was packed. Bobby and Joe were drinking at the bar with Bing Crosby. ("I just wanted to see what all the fuss was about," Bing told them.)

At some point, a Secret Service man pulled Bobby aside and asked if the two tables on either side of Lynda Bird's party could be moved. No problem, said Bobby, but then he looked at the tables. On second thought, he said, you'd better talk to Joe. "He knows those guys better than I do." The agent asked to have a word with Joe. Joe had no problem with the request until he, too, saw who was sitting at the tables. One was occupied by Carmine Tramunti's main man, Tommy Tea Balls, and a wiseguy known as Angelo Cheesecake; the other belonged to Carmine "Junior" Persico, a fast-rising triggerman in the Colombo family.

"Junior was a steady customer who closed the place many a night," says Van. "Never caused any problems."

Then again, Joe wasn't taking any chances. Now it was his turn to get cute. Finally, he told the agent: "I got no problem if you want them moved, but you're going to have to ask them yourself. Now if you'll excuse me, I'm going to finish my drink with Bing Crosby."

Back at the bar, everybody had a good laugh. After all, the saloonkeepers had now accomplished what was previously thought impossible—offending the Establishment while having a cocktail with the venerable crooner. But looking back, Bobby Van considers that evening as a symbolic beginning of the pub's predicament: Bachelors' capacity for offense, and publicity, had put the establishment on law enforcement's radar.

Van had reason to expect trouble. The cops remembered Table Talk and the Ginza, and the State Liquor Authority had given him a hard time with the Jet Set and Dudes 'N Dolls. For that reason, he had kept his name off Bachelors' liquor license, identifying himself only as a "manager."

Nevertheless, by the spring of '69, Bachelors III already figured in investigations being conducted by at least three different agencies—the Manhattan district attorney, the NYPD, and Jack Danahy's old pals, the Feds. By now, Danahy himself had left Hoover's FBI for a job with Rozelle's NFL. But it was said that as the league's director of security, he still nursed a grudge born late one night at the Pussycat. "Ever since then," Namath would charge, "this guy has carried a vendetta against me and was dumb enough to admit it to several of the Jets. He told them how I'd told him to go fuck himself, that I was bad for the game and that as long as I stayed in pro football, I'd be a thorn in his side. This man started everything."

In Danahy's version, he was only trying to help Namath extricate himself from a long-developing and potentially damaging situation. It was right before the Super Bowl that Danahy had received a call from the NYPD's chief of detectives. "Enjoy the game," said the chief. "But let's have lunch when you get back."

"In my heart," says Danahy, "I knew it was Joe. He was the centerpiece of everything."

Later, over that lunch, Danahy was informed that Namath's regulars included con men, fences, bookmakers, and of course made men—exactly the kind of guys you'd expect to find in a hot East Side joint. The cops already had an undercover working inside, and the phones were tapped. "The police were giving me the heads-up with the agreement that I would get Joe off the license because they wanted to make a bust on the place," says Danahy. "They didn't want to embarrass the National Football League. It was a big favor to me."

Danahy maintains that he was only trying to pass the same favor on to Joe. But Joe would have none of it. In March, Namath was contacted through the Jets and presented with a list of unsavory patrons. He was then informed—by whom, he never specified—that these customers were suspected of using the establishment's phones to make or book bets.

Namath claimed not to recognize a single name on the list, but forwarded a copy to the district attorney's office, anyway.

"We asked the DA to put a detective here," Van told a reporter. "We sent registered letters."

Prosecutors failed to acknowledge their request, though that didn't mean they weren't interested. Some weeks later, Namath was shown a selection of photographs. Okay, he admitted, he'd met a few of these guys in his joint. He knew them by sight. Maybe he even knew their nicknames. But so what?

Finally, Rozelle decided that Danahy should confront Joe and deliver an ultimatum on the night of the Football Writers Dinner, June 3, at the Waldorf-Astoria. Before Namath received the George Halas Award as pro football's most courageous player, they all met up in a suite—Namath, Ewbank, Phil Iselin, Danahy, and a cop friend of his. Danahy related to Namath what he had been told. From now on, the men on the list and in the photographs were to be known as "undesirables," and contact with said individuals strictly forbidden. As far as the NFL was concerned, Joe's actual guilt or innocence was beside the point. Rozelle's standard was *appearance*, "the suspicion of evil," as the commissioner liked to put it. Danahy made sure Namath understood that he was speaking for Rozelle. As a "raid" was imminent, said the former FBI man, Joe had a day to sell his piece of the club.

Namath didn't like being pushed around and given ultimatums. That much was clear from his remarks after accepting the Halas award.

"Some of my friends among the sportswriters, some of the old-timers, were like, 'What the hell is he talking about?' " says Danahy. "He was really pissed off. I can't remember exactly what Joe said that night, but it was a ridiculous speech. It was all about civil rights."

The following afternoon, Namath, Mike Bite, and Jimmy Walsh met Rozelle and Danahy at the NFL's Park Avenue headquarters. Rozelle reminded the quarterback that under the standard player's contract he was forbidden from associating with "gamblers or other notorious characters." While that was the same standard contract prohibiting drinking and mandating the wearing of ties in hotel lobbies, such niceties hardly mattered under the circumstances. An undesirable was who or what Rozelle said it was;

the rule was his to interpret and enforce. The commissioner gave Namath another forty-eight hours, until week's end, to sell his shares. Failure to do so would result in his indefinite suspension.

Over the next couple of days, Danahy helped negotiate on behalf of Rozelle, assuming the "bad cop" role. But the Namath camp had a bad cop of its own. "With Mike Bite I had a friend," recalls Danahy. "Mike Bite was backing my argument: 'Joe, this is the only way to go.' But Walsh was saying, 'We're gonna fight this.' Jimmy and I had a mutual disregard for each other. As far as I was concerned, he was an interloper . . . a horseshit lawyer. Mike Bite was a well-established lawyer who had taken good care of Joe going back to college. Bite was the guy I wanted to do business with."

By not selling, Joe jeopardized everything from his salary to his endorsements, a figure Jimmy estimated at $5 million for the foreseeable future. Ray Abruzzese, being a stand-up guy, gave Joe his blessing to cash out, and finally Namath gave in. Mike and Jimmy started to draw up the papers. At 7:15 P.M. on Thursday, they informed Rozelle of their client's intention to divest his interest in Bachelors III by ten the following morning. Then Namath headed to the opening of Gerry Philbin's new bar in Amityville, Long Island, where it would attract little if any notice from the fraternity of undesirables or commissioners. Sipping white wine through the festivities, he didn't get drunk, but he did get mad. He didn't like bullies, and he didn't like hypocrites. Rozelle was being both. Tim Mara, the first owner of the Giants, was a bookmaker. Steelers owner Art Rooney bought his team with money he won at the track. Carroll Rosenbloom was a degenerate gambler. What made them so goddamn *desirable*?

"Fuck the money and everything else," Namath would say. "I was *right,* man."

Namath found no dissenters among his teammates at Philbin's party. By midnight, Tad was putting out the word: the world's most famous quarterback would announce his retirement at Bachelors III in a matter of hours. "The place could use some breakfast business," said Tad.

Namath got to bed just before dawn, and rose, groggily, about 9:00 A.M. The apartment was packed. The whole crew seemed nervous, especially Mike Bite. Coach Bryant called, urging Joe to reconsider. "No, sir," he said. "It's a matter of principle."

What followed was one of the great press conferences, at once surreal and sublime. Flanking Namath like crestfallen apostles were sportcasters Kyle Rote, Frank Gifford, and a ridiculously somber Howard Cosell, looking as mournful as an undertaker.

"I'm not selling," announced Namath, unable to hold back the tears. "I quit."

He had done nothing wrong. He hadn't gambled on football—even Rozelle conceded that much. But the presumption of innocence did not apply to Joe Namath. He had to *appear* innocent. Well, it was a little late for that.

If he hadn't shaved his goatee to look good for members of La Gorce Country Club, he wouldn't sell his stake to look good for Rozelle. Namath had had his fill of phony rectitude. Did Rozelle ask the gamblers to identify themselves before he had a pop at Shor's? What was so bad about gambling, anyway?

"Is there a man out there who has not bet on a football game?" he asked.

A cameraman raised his hand. "Damn right, Joe."

"My father's a gambler," said Namath.

Should he stop associating with him?

He argued well. But more striking than his gumption was his grief. It was a great performance because it wasn't performed. The tears streaming down his bloated face seemed antithetical to the public's notion of Broadway Joe. But a good many people seemed to enjoy the spectacle, a bell-bottomed bad boy acquiring humility the hard way. The line on the cover of *Sports Illustrated* read: "Namath Weeps." In fact, he was heartbroken. "Football is the thing I love to do most," he said. He would miss it all terribly, even those games of Kill the Quarterback.

■   ■   ■

Reaction to the news was varied. The only one to express relief was Joe's father. "He's all crippled up," said John Namath, who hoped only that his youngest boy would remain retired.

Weeb Ewbank, on the other hand, was taken by surprise. "This is what I have to put up with," said the coach, blurting out words he would regret.

The commissioner's office issued a nine-paragraph statement, reiterating Rozelle's position: "Continuation of such associations after learning of a person's undesirable background is cause for deep concern. Such conduct gives the appearance of evil."

"We have rules," said Giants quarterback Fran Tarkenton, "and we all know what these rules are."

"Man, you think NBC is going to sit still?" asked Johnny Sample.

On Wall Street, stock in Broadway Joe's Inc.—the publicly traded fast-food chain that peaked at 16 earlier that year—closed at 9.5, down a point and a quarter on the day.

In Washington, Namath's retirement warranted inclusion, along with the latest word on offshore drilling and Earl Warren, in the daily news summaries that were ready on the president's desk first thing in the morning. The president liked to annotate his news summaries. "Nixon was very aware of history," says John Dean, who would become famous as his White House counsel. "He liked to put his views down so they'd be there for posterity." A big football fan, Richard Nixon had strong views on the Namath affair. "Good riddance," wrote the president, underlining the words in the margin. "These guys must set an example."

■   ■   ■

It had taken the NFL to endow Namath with a bona fide cause. Suddenly, he became what he never aspired to be, leader of a movement. George Sauer, Pete Lammons, and Jim Hudson told reporters that they were quitting, too. "If Pete Rozelle gives Joe an ultimatum like that," said Hudson, "he's got to give one to me. I'm no different. I know gamblers. Everyone does. . . . Sixty-two thousand out there at the ball game and most of them have a bet. Some of the biggest names, some of the biggest places in town have gamblers."

That night, Bachelors was packed solid with a long line out the door. Shortly before 1:00 A.M., the place began to buzz. *He's here. It's him.* Namath arrived with Suzie Storm. He wore a double-breasted chalk-stripe suit with a tie and silk handkerchief, she a white dress and scarf. In photographs taken that evening, she looks like a southern-fried Catherine Deneuve. By 3:00 A.M., the early papers had hit the streets. Namath sat despondently at a table in the back, nursing a drink. Suzie massaged his shoulders as he stared at the image of his own weeping self on the front page. He was a week past his twenty-sixth birthday. He had been retired for sixteen hours. The feeling was undesirable.

■   ■   ■

Fame had thrown a great gala with Broadway Joe the guest of honor. Now came the hangover. It would linger, that toilet taste churned up from his gut. It would change him.

Namath flew off to Lake Tahoe, where he was one of several quarterbacks scheduled to play in Harrah's Invitational Golf Tournament. (Apparently, the NFL had no objection to players golfing with gambling *executives*.) But there was no escaping Bachelors III. Over the next few weeks, the stories came at a furious pace, and with them, Namath's everlasting fury at the press. Finally, the Fourth Estate had found an angle even better than booze and broads: gangsters. Each story triggered a flurry of denials and counteraccusations. The *Daily News* reported that Bachelors III's regulars included Tommy (Tea Balls) Mancuso and Carmine Persico, described as the Colombo family's "No. 1 hit man." *Newsweek* flagrantly misidentified Bobby Van as "a man who can always arrange a bet, no matter how large, handled by someone. Because of his knowledge of big gamblers, he has also helped to set up junkets of high rollers to Las Vegas." The magazine also said Tea Balls Mancuso had been quite careless in his use of a pay phone tapped by the FBI: "Mancuso frequently mentioned Van and hinted that he had inside knowledge of 'The Kid's' physical condition before a game."

Sports Illustrated ran a piece by a young freelancer claiming that Mancuso supplied protection for high-stakes crap games in Namath's penthouse apartment. The sources for the story were all unnamed. "My memory is I got it from bookmakers, wiseguys, and some cops, too," says the writer, Nicholas Pileggi, who went on to great success writing about the Mafia. "They were very solid sources at the time." The dice games were alleged to have taken place in January and February of 1969, a period during which Namath was rarely in New York. In those two months, he spent more nights in the Philippines and Okinawa than in Manhattan. "An out-and-out smear job," said Namath, who took great umbrage with *Sports Illustrated.* "Beats the hell out of me how they got the story, but the son of a bitch who wrote it ought to be working for Looney Tunes."

The same empire enlisted in his glorification now seemed to have a stake in his demise. The most damaging and detailed of the stories appeared in *Sports Illustrated*'s sister publication, *Life.* This piece even included a reference to the confrontation at the Pussycat. "An early warning," it read, "delivered by a federal agent who observed Namath sitting with Tramunti and Mancuso." Danahy wasn't mentioned by name until later in the story. "Within the law enforcement fraternity he commands great respect," wrote *Life*'s Sandy Smith.

"A good friend of mine," says Danahy. In fact, Smith was considered a friend by many FBI agents, including one who now worked as his investigator at the magazine. Billy Kane, aka Captain Midnight, had been one of Danahy's most trusted men and accompanied him the night he first encountered Namath playing Liar's Poker at the bar. Unlike most journalists, Captain Midnight had little trouble locating Tommy Tea Balls for a comment.

"Namath's a good kid," Mancuso told him. "Everybody is crucifying him now. It's a damn shame. He really ought to be left alone. . . . One day I sat down for two hours with Richard Nixon. He didn't know who I was. Just because I spent two hours with a guy, does that make him my friend?"

"That article," says Danahy, "is Billy Kane dictating to Sandy."

Though *Life* (among others) was apparently unaware of Namath's most frequently undesirable association—"Mickey Kearney? Never heard of him," says Danahy—it did place him squarely in the nexus of New York's criminal life. Aside from Tramunti, Mancuso, and Persico, Bachelors' roster of regulars included Fat Gigi and Johnny Echo (patrons of Bobby Van's establishments dating back to the Ginza), JoJo DiGiovanni, a bank robber said to be dismayed "over Broadway Joe's attentions to a woman," and Harry (the Hawk) Bernow, a jewel thief who, unbeknownst to *Life,* was a tenant of the Newport East and an habitual guest at the poker games in Namath's penthouse.

The Namath camp responded by hiring Jim Lynch, a former FBI agent recommended by Eddie Jaffe and Tad Dowd. "It is my plan to have men police the restaurant and check on customers with police records," said Lynch. "Namath would not necessarily know these disreputable people."

This "security plan" was an attempt to appease Rozelle. Still, some parties were already beyond mollification. The press, which Namath had regarded as a collective pain in the ass, now became something to despise. "The press doesn't care how much it hurts people like me," he said. "So long as there's a good headline." There were exceptions, notably the *Times*'s Dave Anderson. But for the most part, Namath would spend the rest of his career hating *them*: sportswriters, cityside reporters, gossip columnists. He considered them all jackals, eager to sniff at these sores that grew after Fame left his bed.

After reading the story in *Life,* his mother called, weeping with fear. She begged Joe to stay away from these people. She was worried for his safety. "When I heard her crying, I really got furious," Namath recalled. "My family was being affected."

■   ■   ■

Although Bachelors III was never raided, the spate of magazine stories had much the same effect. On June 20, National League president Warren Giles sent a memo to his baseball clubs advising players to stay out of the place. Baseball commissioner Bowie Kuhn requested that the American League follow suit, stating that penalties should be in order for players who disregarded the notice.

Meanwhile, Rozelle, who wanted the sport's most marketable star to return before training camp, asked for another meeting. On June 26, Namath was taken by car to the commissioner's apartment. The meeting, intended to be clandestine, followed an elaborately planned, high-speed, bait-and-switch getaway to elude the paparazzi. Also attending were Ewbank, Jimmy Walsh, and Dick Schaap, whose account of that afternoon would become a centerpiece of Namath's forthcoming autobiography. The commissioner began with a request: to sign a couple of photographs for his daughter and her friend.

"You're the biggest name we've got," Rozelle gushed.

But autographs were all he would get from Joe, who wasn't impressed with his representation of the facts. "Most of what he said," noted Namath, "actually seemed to be straight from the *Life* and *Newsweek* and *Sports Illustrated* stories."

The meeting resolved nothing, and the next morning Namath left to film his role in *Norwood.* A movie career would only increase his leverage with Rozelle, underscoring the point that Joe Namath didn't need to play football for money. His name sold everything from hamburgers to highballs. In fact, negotiations were already under way to open Bachelors III franchises in Boston and New Orleans.

With Joe in Hollywood, Jimmy kept talking with Rozelle. On July 12, the day before he was due in training camp, Namath flew to New York. A story in the *Post*—attributed to "one of the legal men behind the Super Bowl superstar"—said Namath would report to camp just to force Rozelle's hand, with the resulting suspension to be met by a lawsuit. The story, under a double-byline with Zimmerman and a cityside reporter, incensed Namath. He landed at Kennedy about 10:30 A.M., a crowd forming in the terminal around him. He signed autographs for the stewardesses. He shook hands with a baby. But he wouldn't answer any questions.

The Associated Press reporter, perhaps the last guy to be wearing a brimmed hat in July, asked: "What are your plans, Joe?"

Namath yanked the hat down over his eyes.

Instead of reporting to camp, he met again with Rozelle, who repeated his concern about the magazine stories. The commissioner also said he received "bad reports" on Bobby Van and Ray Abruzzese. The meeting lasted four hours. That night, Namath brought Bobby and Ray to Rozelle's apartment, where they were admitted through the service elevator. While Joe wanted them to make their cases in person, he also wanted them to make *his* case. Bobby and Ray weren't associates. They were his friends, and Joe wasn't giving them up. That much was nonnegotiable.

Over the next couple of days, in separate conversations with Namath and Walsh, Rozelle abandoned his opposition to Namath's partners. Meanwhile, Weeb, who didn't want to suspend his quarterback, granted Namath permission to remain out of camp. "He has a business deal he has to finalize," said the coach.

As usual, Weeb was less indulgent with the rest of his team. But the players' dissatisfaction, most of it still owing to the legendary Ewbank cheapness, was mounting. Bob Talamini and Mark Smolinski retired suddenly. Pete Lammons, whose cause now merged with Namath's, vowed to hold out until Weeb offered a decent contract. As one player put it: "We put him in the Hall of Fame when we won the Super Bowl. You'd think he'd put a little money in our pockets."

On Wednesday evening, Namath went out to Bill's Meadowbrook, where he met with teammates—most of whom were very sympathetic—and picked up his championship ring. The rings themselves had become symbols of the players' discontent. Although Weeb had wanted to give them watches, Namath insisted on diamond-encrusted rings, like the ones Lombardi's Packers had received. "Joe went in and talked to Weeb and Iselin and told them they were a cheap bunch of so and so's," said one veteran. "He forced them to give us rings."

The following morning, Mike Bite, just back from burying his mother in Alabama, came up with a solution. Namath would sell his interest in the

Lexington Avenue bar, but retain his right to franchise Bachelors III, with Bobby and Ray as his partners. Rozelle agreed, provided he had the right to reject any of Namath's potential investors. After a quick trip to the Coast, where he finished shooting *Norwood,* Namath showed up for camp on Monday night, arriving by limousine with Jim Hudson.

The conflicting principles, Rozelle's "appearance of evil" versus Namath's stand-up ethic, had finally given way to an even higher one: the harmony of self-interest. The NFL, NBC, and Namanco Productions, to name just a few, were all better off with Joe Willie playing this new game he had helped create.

The *Apollo 11* astronauts, then in lunar orbit, were informed that Namath and Rozelle had reached an accord.

Not long after they shook hands, Bobby Van showed up in New Orleans. The three bachelors were looking to open their next joint. Bobby had already located a prospective partner, known as Diamond Jim, who introduced him all around. It was a wonderful evening, concluding about 5:00 A.M. at a venerable establishment outside of town.

The next day, Bobby got a call from Jimmy, who'd already gotten a call. It seems that one of Bobby's new pals, the good old boy with the great old joint, was Carlos Marcello's son. Carlos Marcello was the Mafia boss of Louisiana.

"I didn't know," said Bobby.

"You can't open there," said Jimmy. "Forget New Orleans."

On the afternoon of August 8, 1969, the Jets flew to St. Louis for an exhibition with the Cardinals the following day. Exactly what happened over the next several hours remains unclear, or perhaps willfully forgotten. Both Hudson and Namath decided to turn in early, about 11:00 P.M. It was sometime after midnight that Hud, who slept closest to the door, woke to an insistent knock, a pounding, really. Opening the door, he was greeted by "a couple lunatics who'd been drinking too much." They demanded to see Joe. "I want to kill that son of a bitch," said the first, trying to push his way into the room.

Hudson punched him. Then the second drunk reached out and brushed him just below his right jawbone. Hudson clutched at his throat as the two men fled. He had never seen the blade. But now he saw the blood.

"Looked like he hit my jugular," he says. "Every time my heart beat, it squirted."

Joe, finally awake, got a towel to stanch the bleeding, and the Jets safetyman was taken to the hospital. "They gave me a lot of stitches," Hudson recalls. "Probably more than they had to." The Jets didn't want to involve the cops or the press, and Weeb never even told the other players what had happened. All they knew was, from that time on, a guard was posted outside Namath's suite on the road, and his name never again appeared in a team hotel's room manifest. Nobody asked too many questions. It was reported, in passing, that Hudson had suffered a laceration slipping in the shower.

The beat writers had more pressing concerns than Hudson's absence from a preseason game. "The World Championship of New York"—the Jets versus the Giants—was scheduled for the following Sunday at the Yale Bowl in New Haven. The drums had been beating in anticipation of this contest for some time now. Back in April, when Namath received the Hickok Belt as professional athlete of the year, he included the Giants among the NFL teams who'd

37. THE JOE NAMATH SHOW

"get killed" by most AFL competition. In July Namath told Howard Cosell, "I don't think too many people are ever going to take the Giants seriously." Just because Joe was grinning, using Howard as a straight man, didn't mean he was kidding. Normally, Namath offered the flimsiest of reasons to excuse himself from preseason action. This game was different, though. "I won't go out," he vowed on the flight back from St. Louis. "Weeb won't take me out."

Namath had been nursing a grudge against the Giants since late 1964, when Wellington Mara drafted Tucker Frederickson instead of him. Even so, his resentment was mild compared to the remaining Titans still on the Jets roster. The Jets, who made $15,000 a man for winning the Super Bowl, would receive $250, win or lose, for playing the Giants. But Bill Mathis spoke for the team when he said, "I want to win even more than the Super Bowl." For Don Maynard, ten seasons had passed since the Giants had cut him, but he still recalled Allie Sherman's slights as if they had been yesterday. "Wasn't the first mistake he made," said Maynard, now pro football's career leader in receiving yards. Grantham could still remember the Giants' Del Shofner, a fellow renter at the Concourse Plaza Hotel, being told to stop playing cards with members of the "other" team. "Giant fans still don't feel we're on a parity with their team and we feel we've got to prove it," Grantham said a few days before the game. "A lot of people, NFL fans, still regard the Super Bowl as a fluke."

The Giants, coming off consecutive 7–7 seasons, refused to say anything that might be construed as provocative. "It was like a heavyweight championship—but one guy was reluctant to admit there was even a fight," recalls Fred Dryer, then a Giants rookie. "You were up against the truth of what you represented. The Giants were old."

A couple of things about life with the Giants immediately struck Dryer, a talented defensive end from San Diego State. First were the old steamer trunks in the locker room, still bearing the names of great Giants long gone, guys like Gifford and Tittle. Second was *that guy*. Dryer was informed that white football shoes were prohibited, as they had been popularized by *that guy over there*. "In many ways, the Giants were defined by him," says Dryer. "But I never once heard Wellington Mara say the words: 'Joe Namath.'"

By contemporary standards, all the hype over an exhibition game may seem absurd. But after so many years of mutual rancor, it had taken on the air of a civil conflict, a struggle between two incompatible cultures, symbolized by Broadway Joe and Bishop Mara. The Giants' owner had gone so far as to accuse the *New York Times* (home to some of the most conservative sportswriters in town) of harboring a bias. His letter arrived at the sports desk during the '68 championship season, charging the paper had given more coverage to the Jets. A reporter was assigned to test Mara's allegation, and when the column inches were totaled, the Giants won by a few.

The grand old team's owner might have blamed himself before leveling accusations at the press. *Times* football columnist William N. Wallace, who had argued that the Jets should trade Namath the year before, now imagined a world in which Mara had drafted the quarterback out of Alabama. There had been no merger, no Super Bowl. NBC had been forced to sue CBS and Pete Rozelle for monopoly and restraint of trade. "Namath's late hours on the East Side and his girls caused comment in the Mara family's Catholic circles," wrote an amused Wallace. "Ever the pragmatist, Well Mara reached back for Lincoln on Grant: 'Tell me which airline's hostesses he dates and I'll send all my players on it.'"

Perhaps Mara had wished it so that savage summer day, August 17, 1969. With 70,074 fans gathered in 81-degree heat, the Yale Bowl had become unconscionably humid by the 2:00 P.M. kickoff. "I can remember this guy with zinc oxide on his nose, shitface drunk," says Dryer. "He was beating on the side of the locker room, a fan intimidating the Giants. The Jet fans were crazy. You know you're in trouble when your supporters are not as venomous as your foes."

"Everybody got drunk and threw up," says Helen Dillon, whose own recollection remains focused on "a bloody guy with half his teeth gone, shouting 'See you next year.'"

The ill-tempered louts from Queens were taking over, and the Jets themselves seemed possessed of their bloodlust. Now, ten seasons into his pro career, Billy Mathis took his first benny, short for Benzedrine, a form of speed. That's how much he wanted to kick Giant ass. Early in the game, the Giants came with a blitz. Mathis was supposed to pick up the linebacker, Ralph Heck. But even though Heck had gone down before Mathis could reach him, the Jets' back dove at him anyway, trying to spear Heck with his helmet. Fortunately, the linebacker rolled over just in time. Mathis headed back to the huddle with eyes big as silver dollars and a chunk of turf lodged in his face mask.

"Man, the Food and Drug Administration is gonna get you," said Heck.

Mathis, who scored two touchdowns on the day, always remembered that. It was the only funny line he ever heard on a football field.

The afternoon is not remembered for humor. More apparent was Namath's flirtation with perfection. His game, statistically abbreviated, was 14 for 16 with three touchdowns, the last of which concluded his afternoon midway through the fourth quarter. (Namath had refused Ewbank's suggestion to come out earlier.) By then, the Jets were winning 37–14, a margin less lopsided than the actual game. The Jets jumped out to a 24–0 lead when Mike Battle, a bellicose rookie who liked to eat glass, ran a punt back eighty-six yards, literally hurtling the punter en route to a touchdown. There were still more than twelve minutes remaining in the first half.

Namath wasn't intercepted or sacked. By contrast, Tarkenton, throwing under constant pressure, was 9 for 21. His second interception came on his last attempt, as Grantham hit him. "If I had a line like that in front of me, I'd be scrambling, too," said Namath.

As it ended, Don Maynard led the fans in a chorus of "Good-bye Allie." The Giants coach, in the fifth year of his ten-year contract, lasted another few weeks before his eventual firing. But it was the Jets who had finally done him in.

The Giants locker room was funereal. Wellington Mara stood with Father Dudley, as if the priest might deliver last rites. Most striking was the look on Mara's face. "Like Thomas Aquinas trying to separate reason and faith," says Dryer. "He was crushed. I saw a man who just found out what he thought was true, was not true. He was literally trying to figure out what happened. I felt so sorry for him, and at the same time I was also angry. It was like an elephant being in the room and no one wanted to talk about it. We were so outmanned, in spirit and personnel. We were just a lame football team from the fifties."

■　　■　　■

After winning the Super Bowl and beating the Giants, the Jets considered the regular season as something to be merely tolerated on their road to a second championship. Ewbank hired Ken Meyer, Namath's backfield coach at Alabama, to replace Clive Rush, now the Patriots' head coach. But the offensive schemes required no modification. What's more, with three lousy teams in their division—Boston, Buffalo, and Miami—and another two games against the hapless Cincinnati Bengals, the schedule gave the Jets a cushion. Still, each game came at a price, starting with the season opener, a 33–19 win in Buffalo. Namath, who sat out the final exhibition game with a strained tendon and blood clot in his right knee, hurt the knee again as Winston Hill and Bills tackle Bob Tatarek toppled onto him, pressing his heel against the back of his thigh. Tatarek clapped his hands as the quarterback writhed in pain. Namath needed about a minute to get up. "They knew I was hurt," said Joe.

In other words, he had the Bills right where he wanted. On the next play, he hit Maynard with a sixty-yard bomb.

The following week, in Denver, Namath took a good beating at the hands of defensive end Rich Jackson, nicknamed "Tombstone." Jackson's relentless pursuit of the passer resulted in two sacks and three holding penalties on the increasingly ineffective Sam Walton. But the hit of the game was delivered when Broncos tackle Dave Costa burst through the line and greeted Namath helmet first, where the rib cage meets the solar plexus. After the play was whistled dead, Costa looked down upon his work with remorse. It wasn't a cheap shot, he explained after the game. Joe knew that. Costa would never go for his knees. "He's done a hell of a lot for our league," said Costa.

But the extent of the lineman's admiration was not immediately clear in those moments after the hit. "The hardest shot I've ever seen a quarterback take," said Jeff Snedeker, the Jets' trainer, "I thought every rib in his body was broken."

Namath's legs began to jerk and jump, as if the pain circuits were over-loaded, the hurt escaping through the extremities. "Stay down," Costa told Namath. "You're hurt."

He stayed down, at the edge of consciousness, for approximately five fuzzy minutes. Namath wouldn't come back with the bomb this time. He couldn't. The Jets lost by 2 points. After the game, some of the guys flew to Vegas, but Namath couldn't even make the trip. "How long can you take it," asked a Denver writer, "getting banged up like this?"

"About fifteen more games," he said, "counting the two play-offs and the Super Bowl."

Beyond that, though, was anyone's guess. The ribs would heal. But the knees only continued to degenerate. To Namath, it felt as if each would re-quire another date with Dr. Nicholas's scalpel. After throwing for 344 yards in a loss to San Diego, Namath went to Boston, where he was opening another Bachelors III with Bobby, Ray, former Jets receiver Jim Colclough, and Boston Bruins hockey player Derek Sanderson. There, a local television station asked if he planned to retire after the season. "I can practically guarantee that," de-clared Namath. At practice the next day, he was asked what *practically* meant. "More than likely," he said. "My knees are hurting worse than ever."

■   ■   ■

Though diminished physically, his persona only grew larger. In October, Ran-dom House published *I Can't Wait Until Tomorrow . . . 'Cause I Get Better Looking Every Day* by Joe Willie Namath with Dick Schaap. The title appeared only on the back of the dust jacket, as the front was reserved exclusively for Namath's headshot. Schaap, a bright and exceedingly prolific former city editor and columnist at the *Herald-Tribune,* described the book as "part put-on." But it practically codified the Broadway Joe image, a testament to his principles and a kind of mission statement for his marketing plan. In the world according to Joe, booze and broads were good, while hypocrisy and sportswriters were bad. *Can't Wait* would become another artifact in the Namath archive. Even the chapter titles—"I Like My Girls Blond and My Johnnie Walker Red"—would be remembered as advertising slogans, eventually framing a nostalgic notion of Namath. Schaap, then thirty-five, had already collaborated with Packers guard Jerry Kramer on a best-selling diary of the 1967 season entitled *Instant Replay.* But the famous quarterback, celebrated for his alleged candor, proved a much more difficult subject. Schaap had great affection and admiration for Namath, and an appreciation for the quarterback's good manners, his generosity, and his loyalty. Namath, whom he often interviewed over several rounds of scotch, was good company. But the resulting one-liners seem less fun when read sober:

"If a doctor told me I had to give up women, I'm sure I'd give up doctors."

"I only drink on two occasions, when I'm with people and when I'm alone."

"The Only Perfect Man who ever lived had a beard and long hair."

The put-ons camouflage an intensely private man. Namath, who approved every word of the manuscript, had little tolerance for a biographer's invasive procedures. The dissolution of his parents' marriage—the central event in his emotional life—is dealt with in two sentences: "My mother and my father split up when I was twelve years old and eventually each of them remarried. I stayed close to both of them." In the same way, Coach Bryant's views on segregation and race go unmentioned. When it comes to those he loves, Namath can't bear to find or do any wrong.

Such is his characterization of Suzie Storm: "A girl I think I could spend the rest of my life with." But he wasn't ready. "I wouldn't be a good husband," he confesses. "I'd cheat." In Namath's canon of ethics, cheating—an especially virulent form of lie to John and Rose's youngest son—was infinitely worse than sportswriting. America's bachelor was an uncompromising advocate of marital fidelity. "If he told me once, he told me a million times: he wanted to go out as much as he could when he was single because he would never cheat on his wife," says Tim Secor, whose First Avenue bar, the Tittle Tattle, abounded with available women. "That was a really, really big thing in Joe's life: not to fuck around when he got married."

Meanwhile, the newly famous Suzie appeared in Baton Rouge with her band, the Laymen. It was homecoming weekend, the night before the LSU–Ole Miss game. But students were less interested in the pep rally than in seeing Joe's Girl sing "Baby, It's You." According to the *New York Times:* "Traditional cheerleader chants of 'We're No. 1' were drowned out by driving versions of 'We Want Suzie. We Want Suzie.'"

Much to the crowd's delight, Joe's Girl flashed the victory sign.

■　■　■

With *Can't Wait Until Tomorrow* awaiting publication, Jimmy Walsh got a call from an independent television producer. Larry Spangler, a former brush salesman, made his first big score selling the *Merv Griffin* and *Mike Douglas* shows into syndication. Now he pitched *The Joe Namath Show.* Namath gave the go-ahead as soon as he met Spangler, who shared the quarterback's interest in booze and broads. "You always had to get that silent nod from Joe," says Spangler. Beyond that, the most difficult part of the deal was convincing Jimmy and Mike Bite to agree. "They would bicker back and forth," says Spangler. "Bite changed his mind so much, you never knew what was what, and Jimmy wouldn't win Mr. Popularity. . . . He was always making demands, especially on the advertisers."

In due course, it was agreed that the show would be an equal partnership between Namanco and Spangler's company. And before another day had passed, Spangler secured a sponsor, Bristol Myers, makers of assorted men's grooming products. "Back in those days, Bristol Myers spent a fortune on television," he recalls. "They loved the idea, but they said they had to see Namath on camera first. I say, 'I can't get the guy to go on camera if you're not going to make the deal.'"

Bristol Myers made the deal. Schaap was chosen as a cohost, to be Namath's guide more than his sidekick. Louisa Moritz, a young actress who had perfected the dumb blonde role, would come on, usually in miniskirt and high boots, to giggle, read Joe's mail, and provide double entendres. Tad Dowd got the title of executive coordinator. Pierre Cardin supplied the wardrobe, and LeRoy Neiman painted the panels for the set. *The Joe Namath Show* debuted as a weekly half-hour talk show on Friday, October 10, at 8:30 P.M. in New York, where it aired on WOR-TV, Channel 9. Within a week, it was being seen on forty-five stations, all of which had purchased a fifteen-week package.

The critics were very encouraging. "Joe's show had an insouciance, a spontaneity and a genuine *joie de vivre* that even congenital Namath haters must have found infuriatingly engaging," said *Time.*

"His half hour had an almost amateurish naturalness because Mr. Namath refused to take himself or the occasion very seriously," wrote Jack Gould, TV critic of the *New York Times.* "The absence of slick video professionalism was not unappealing."

Namath's apparent ease on the air may have had something to do with the pregame festivities. The show taped on Monday, when Joe was still nursing his postgame aches and bruises. But Bristol Myers executives, who loved to drop by and rub elbows with the star and his burgeoning entourage, seemed to ease the path by insisting on good catering and a well-stocked bar. "Every taping was standing room only," says Spangler. "Reeves Broadcasting on Ninth Avenue was *the* place, a balls-out party from the time we got there, like Mardi Gras."

As a guest on the show, producer David Merrick said, "This is the first time I've been offered a drink *before* going on." The studio was the only joint in town where regulars included Mickey Kearney, Howard Cosell, and Roone Arledge, the president of ABC Sports. Arledge, already working on a project that would air pro football on prime-time Mondays, seemed particularly interested in the show's star.

But the broadcast's great asset was Schaap, who booked the guests. He was a dedicated but amused student of celebrity, with sensibilities not unlike George Lois's. Schaap's bookings resulted in some deliciously absurd pairings: Merrick and Mets first baseman Donn Clendenon, Bills rookie O. J. Simpson with Maximillian Schell, Truman Capote and Rocky Graziano.

"Truman," asks the former middleweight champ, "didn't I box you in Cleveland?"

In another show, Ann-Margret appears as a plant in the studio audience, done up as a shimmering hippie chick. "Tell me, Joe," she coos, "to what do you attribute your quick release?"

Two reasons, he says: "One, excitement. The other, fear."

Another memorable exchange occurred during the second taping, featuring Muhammad Ali and George Segal, about to film *The Owl and the Pussycat* with Barbra Streisand. The part would require nude scenes, the discussion of which seemed to deeply offend Ali. The man who vanquished Sonny Liston now sank back in his seat, hands by his thighs, looking down as if in prayer.

"When you start talking about all that naked stuff, I don't take part in that kind of conversation," he said. "Civilized people don't go around talking about that."

"Civilized people?" said Namath. "I beg to differ."

"I'm a religious man," said Ali

The former champ's religiosity had been less evident before the show, when he hit on Louisa Moritz. An enraged Spangler had allowed Ali to remain, but his bodyguards—"these goddamn Muslims with weapons"—were to leave the studio. The ordeal left Ali in a very pissy mood. Hence, his apparent displeasure with the discussion of George Segal's nude scenes.

"It's really disgraceful," said Ali.

"Well, I think you better go back to sleep then and not listen," said Namath, grinning awkwardly. Namath was highly averse to conflict, especially on the set, but Ali's hypocrisy must have been wearing on him. Joe had now picked up his coffee mug, and as it came within inches of the microphone, one heard the show's own distinctive background noise, almost a theme song—the unmistakable tinkle of ice cubes.

Namath's coffee cup, says Spangler, "was filled with alcohol. Always. We were the drinkingest show on television."

In retrospect, *The Joe Namath Show*, in all its naturally amateurish glory, looks like the greatest ever cable-access show. But beneath the merriment, the partying, and the put-ons were qualities lost on both the critics and the host's friends. Namath held a very big grudge. Barely a show went by without him decrying *Life* ("they don't print the truth"), *Sports Illustrated* ("the lousiest sports magazine, in all truthfulness, it really is"), or, his most frequent target, New York sportswriters, some of whom he refused to speak with. ("What do you expect? They do a good job for the kind of people they are.")

For a guy long accustomed to taking shots in the papers, Namath remained extremely sensitive to criticism or even the prospect of it. The eventual reception for *Norwood*, the release of which had been delayed, seemed to fill him with dread. "I have a feeling it's going to be pretty nasty," he said.

Norwood was, in fact, a bomb, but it was hardly his fault; Namath's was only a minor role. Even so, he knew that the enormous, contagious self-assurance he had on the field abandoned him in front of the camera. All these years later, reviewing old reels of *The Joe Namath Show*, one is continually aware of his self-consciousness. Those around him, those with a stake in him, those intoxicated by his presence, failed to see it. But Namath was nervous. That first show featured Yaphet Kotto, then starring on Broadway in *The Great White Hope*. In anticipation of the introduction, Namath had written the actor's name phonetically on his palm, but still managed to mispronounce it.

This was the last thing he wanted: to look foolish, to be the ignorant ballplayer, the object of a smirk. Ever since he met Sonny, people had been telling Joe he was a natural for show business. But he didn't feel very natural in front of the camera. "I'm a rookie in this business," he said apologetically.

Once, with Merrick in the guest chair, Schaap inquired about the possibility of Namath's performing in a musical about pro football. Joe, said Merrick, could be in a musical about anything. Then, turning to Namath, Merrick asked how he was enjoying show business.

"It is fun at times," he said glumly, "but I still don't feel comfortable."

Part of him never would. Namath was great at being Namath, and Broadway Joe was just Namath writ large. But acting was different. Whether you were playing an ex-marine or a talk show host, showbiz was a kind of lie. It was easier to act natural with ice cubes in your coffee mug.

■　　■　　■

Midway through the show's first and final season, Schaap turned to Namath and offered congratulations. "You've already proven yourself as probably the greatest quarterback in the history of football this year," he said. "You've won six straight games, five of them under the point spread."

"It is pretty difficult to do that," Namath agreed.

The margins of victory reflected the team's tendency to play just well enough. Beneficiaries of an easy schedule, the Jets finished the regular season 10–4, but did not beat a team with a better than .500 record. Over breakfast at the Green Kitchen diner, it was mirthfully concluded that the toughest opponent Joe had faced in all of 1969 was Janis Joplin.

The earthy singer, who showed up one night at Bachelors III, was not a prototype Namath bunny. But their assignation owed to Joplin's resolve—a fierce determination to bed Broadway Joe—and great quantities of tequila.

Namath survived the hangover, just as he endured all the game's hazards. In fact, Joe was in better shape than a lot of his teammates. Jim Hudson went down in the eighth game, an injury resulting in his third knee surgery. A few weeks later, Maynard suffered a fracture in his right foot. In the next-to-last game, Randy Rasmussen sprained an ankle, and Gerry Philbin dislocated his left shoulder. The Jets lost a lot of manpower, but coming off the Super Bowl and the Yale Bowl, they also lost some of their intensity. It affected even the most dedicated players. George Sauer went from 66 catches in 1968 to 45 a year later. Part of this owed to the fact that Namath, again voted the team's MVP, was throwing less than he ever had as a pro. But part was human nature. "I just didn't have that desire," says Sauer. "Where do you go after pulling one of the greatest upsets in history?"

As far as the team was concerned, the regular season had really been just a preamble to the Super Bowl play-offs. On December 19, 1969, as Joplin prepared to take the stage at Madison Square Garden, the sold-out crowd was informed that "Miss Joplin would like to dedicate the entire set to the New York Jets for their victory over the Kansas City Chiefs tomorrow."

The bookies, less confident in that outcome, had the Chiefs favored by four. The next day was another frigid one at Shea. Maynard would play only sparingly, entering the game late in the third quarter. Unlike the Colts, the Chiefs were aware of his injury, thereby compromising his effectiveness as a decoy. Better able to play was Gerry Philbin, his harnessed shoulder shot full of novocaine. Paul Zimmerman, a passionate observer of all things at the line of scrimmage, called it "perhaps his finest day as a pro." With swirling winds, December 20, 1969, was a day for defense. Neither Namath nor his receivers were sharp, and even the usually sure-handed Snell dropped a few passes. Through three quarters, neither team was able to score a touchdown.

But early in the fourth quarter, following a pass interference call, the Jets had a first down at Kansas City's 1-yard line. With the Chiefs barking out vows to keep the Jets out of the end zone, Namath called on Snell, who was stopped a foot or so from the goal. The next handoff went to Bill Mathis, who didn't make it either. The score was still 6–3, Chiefs. Now, on third down, Namath called a play-action pass. He faked the pitch to Snell, who was actually the intended receiver, and then faked the handoff to Mathis. The second fake was supposed to draw the linebacker, Bobby Bell. But Bell, refusing to be suckered, stayed with Snell as Namath rolled right. "He had no right being there," Joe said. "If he's not there, it's a touchdown." *If.* Now it was Namath's turn to play the sucker. He thought about running. But three red jerseys were closing fast. Namath got the ball away, barely and feebly, as Bell, defensive back Jim Kearney, and defensive end Jim Lynch, who had come from the other side of the field, converged on him. "I think the Fifth Army got me," said Namath. "I don't know who it was, but after it happened both my right hand and my head were hurting."

He walked off, dizzy, and Jim Turner came on to kick the tying field goal. But the tie was short-lived. The Chiefs had the wind at their backs. On their next play from scrimmage, quarterback Len Dawson—recognizing the Jets formation with only three defensive backs—hit split end Otis Taylor for sixty-one yards. Then he found Gloster Richardson, nineteen yards for the touchdown. The extra point made it 13–6.

The Jets weren't out of chances yet. They reached the Kansas City 20, only to see Namath throw three straight incompletions. One of them, to an open Sauer, simply died in the wind. Maybe Joe should have known better. With 1:55 left, he spit in the wind. It came right back on him, a sign of things to come. "You just couldn't throw the ball with that wind," Namath said later.

A penalty gave the Jets still another first down, thirteen yards from the goal line. But Namath was picked off in the end zone, his third interception of the day. He had completed 14 for 40 passes. The Jets' reign as champions came to an end. Ewbank, sixty-two years old, broke down weeping in the locker room.

"No one has to apologize for anything," Philbin said after the game. "We all went down together." However, the intervening years have harshened his assessement of the game. He blames Ewbank for being too cheap to bring back Bob Talamini, a guard who might have made a hole down at the goal line. And he blames Namath. "If the defense only gives up 13 points, you should win the game," says Philbin. "Joe couldn't move it one fucking foot with four downs to go."

Then again, the memory would plague Namath, too. A loser's humiliation knew no bounds. As if to prove that point, Mayor John Lindsay introduced himself in the locker room. "Don't be dejected," said Hizzoner. "I know what it's like to lose. You'll get 'em next year."

Yeah. Wait'll next year. What choice did he have?

When asked if he had played his last game, Namath said: "I hope not." In the next day's *Daily News,* Dick Young argued that Namath couldn't afford to quit. The stock price of his hamburger chain had plummeted. "He just hasn't put away enough to support himself in the manner that he and his hangers-on have become accustomed," wrote Young.

In fact, Joe had already made up his mind to play, but money wasn't the reason. His real concern was the storyline. Money couldn't cure this regret. This was no way for *The Joe Namath Show* to end. He couldn't fade away now, just hours after Joplin had been moaning into her microphone: "Joe, Joe, where are you, Joe?"

In the summer of 1970, Vince Lombardi checked into Georgetown University Hospital with an incurably advanced case of colorectal cancer. From his deathbed, in the twilight of his consciousness, he was heard to shout: "Joe Namath! You're not bigger than football. Remember that."

Having attained his own fame in the age of televised sports, Lombardi could have been more sympathetic to the young man's predicament. Namath, once again chosen by AFL coaches as the league's most valuable player, might not have been bigger than the game. But for a time, it certainly felt as if he was. Whatever the case, Namath would spend the rest of his career vigorously testing Lombardi's postulate.

As the old coach lay dying, Joe stopped at the Las Vegas Hilton, where the King was making a comeback. "Ladies and gentlemen," Elvis called from the stage in that bubba baritone of his, "I have a good friend here tonight. The greatest football player, the greatest quarterback, my hero, Joe Namath." Tad Dowd and Al Hassan, ranking members of the entourage that night, would never forget it. The King's hero was *Joe*. And how long was the ovation—five, ten minutes?

38. BIGGER THAN THE GAME

Soon Elvis's manager, Colonel Parker, came to request Namath's presence backstage. Namath didn't want to bring the whole crew; it wouldn't look right. He just wanted his father to meet Elvis. But Colonel Parker insisted: "Elvis don't care if you bring fifty."

When they got backstage, Elvis told his pretty young wife, Priscilla, to hit the casino. "This gonna be a man's night of talk," he said.

Then Elvis started apologizing. "Joe," he said, "I wasn't at my best tonight. I got a cold."

Presley, it turned out, never missed *The Joe Namath Show*. Hell, he told them, he had every one on tape. Elvis, who'd been looking forward to picking Joe's brain for a while, started to reel off all sorts of football questions. He'd even worn something green that night, in honor of the Jets. "Meeting Joe was clearly a big thing for Elvis," says Dowd.

By then, Broadway Joe and the King had more than enough in common. They had each been cited as a bad example for the nation's youth. They had the love of millions. They even had the same leading ladies.

Ann-Margret, Elvis's costar in *Viva Las Vegas,* hadn't made an American picture since 1966. With her career floundering, she put her hopes in a motorcycle picture written by her husband, Roger Smith. Allan Carr, her manager, was looking to match her with the right leading man, but most of the candidates were either too expensive or too old. Then one day, while taking a shower, Carr had an inspired idea. "It occurred to me," he said, "that the biggest celebrity in the country was probably Joe Namath."

Carr, who went on to produce the movie version of *Grease,* wasn't a football fan, but he had been greatly impressed with Namath's teary-eyed press conference during the Bachelors III affair. The strength of that performance meant one of two things: Namath was either a sincere and emotional man or "as good an actor as Richard Burton." Whatever the case, Broadway Joe was clearly the guy to play the title role of C. C. Ryder in his biker epic, *C. C. & Company.* Shooting began in the winter of 1970 in Arizona.

Not long afterward, Joe went to Italy to star in *The Last Rebel,* a spaghetti Western produced by Larry Spangler. His character, Hollis Burnside, was an old-boy version of C. C. Ryder. In *C. C.,* Joe played a biker who saves a fashion editor (Ann-Margret) from being gang-raped. In *Rebel,* he played a Confederate soldier who rescues an escaped slave from a lynching. Instead of a motorcycle, he rode a horse. Instead of a redhead, he got a blonde, the slinky Victoria George. She was the hooker who looks too good to be bad.

Eventually, Spangler would try to compensate for the picture's shortcomings (after seeing a rough cut, a studio exec told him it was "the worst piece of shit" he had ever seen) with a soundtrack by Tony Ashton and Jon Lord, of Deep Purple fame. Still, with Woody Strode as the escaped slave Namath's character saves from lynching and Jack Elam as the comrade who betrays him, *Rebel* is a better Western than *C. C.* is a motorcycle picture. Namath himself wasn't overly concerned with the quality of the script or the production values. For company, he brought a few members of the entourage, including Bobby Van, Mickey Kearney, and Al Hassan, who played a bartender. Rome wasn't his favorite place. The city was in the middle of a heat wave, and Bobby Van recalls being doused from a hose as they tried to catch a predawn nap at the bottom of the Spanish Steps. The girls didn't impress Joe, either. "American women are 10 times more beautiful than Italian women," he said. Then again, maybe they were just frequenting the wrong establishments. "Here they call them hookers," says Bobby Van. "There, they call them 'girls who need a ride home.'"

Whatever they were, Namath wasn't in Italy to meet chicks. He wasn't there for art's sake, either. He was there for the money.

It was Tad Dowd who had convinced him to take the *Rebel* part. Dowd's rabbi, Eddie Jaffe, had found the script and the two of them stood to split $16,000 from Spangler if Dowd could deliver Namath. Without Namath, Spangler had no shot at raising the money.

Tad, perpetually broke, declared his interest up front. In describing the concept for Joe, he spoke of "a poor man's version of *The Good, the Bad and the Ugly.*" Maybe it would be a decent picture, maybe not. The only sure thing was the money—about $150,000, the same as Joe made for *C. C.* "You're going to make 300 grand for ten weeks work," Dowd told him. "Think of your father. He didn't make that his whole life."

The logic was unassailable. Namath had to make it while he could. If nothing else, the hustler knew the value of a buck. He was getting $300,000 to play cowboys. He was getting $35,000 (not including bonuses, of course) to play quarterback.

His salary, as determined by his last deal with Werblin, was already a point of contention. By now, Namath had proclaimed his intention to play in the upcoming season. But that wasn't a guarantee. Unhappiness with his knees had been replaced by unhappiness with his contract. "I have a contract to fulfill, but I'm not getting enough to play," he told Dave Anderson that spring. "I wonder if it's right. I believe you should do what's fair and I'm trying to get it in my mind if it's fair. . . . I don't expect anybody to feel sorry for me, but my point is that at least 30 football players make more than I do in salary in a season."

Here was Namath's contradictory nature on full display. To play or not to play? Viewed from one perspective, he seemed like another bad actor doing *Hamlet*. These ponderously posed questions of right and fairness neglected the fact that in signing his contract he had given his word.

From another vantage point, his questions regarding worth were long overdue in a sport that routinely crippled players while affording them fewer protections than steelworkers. Though the economy was in recession, the NFL was still booming. The merger and the Super Bowl—both of them parts of the Broadway Joe legend—had translated into a windfall. Television money was coming in at ever-higher rates. Soon the NFL would be a prime-time property on ABC. Wasn't Namath entitled to his share? Wasn't true value, and his insistence on getting it, another principle?

Besides, making money wasn't as easy as it looked. His Broadway Joe's hamburger chain had turned out to be a disaster. According to information cited in *New York* magazine: "Broadway Joe's Inc., lost $243,978 on revenues of $667,952 in the eight months ended July 31, 1970, a rate that suggested a loss of 25 cents on each 75-cent Quarterback Burger sold."

At the time, fast-food franchises were a fashionable celebrity investment, and included such chains as Mickey Mantle's Country Cookin', Jerry Lucas Beef 'N Shakes, James Brown's Gold Platter restaurants, and Al Hirt's Sandwich Saloons. In January, shortly after the Chiefs beat the Vikings in the AFL's second consecutive Super Bowl upset, Namath testified before a Senate subcommittee investigating the ills of franchising. The hearing room was standing room only. Namath, wearing a powder blue Edwardian jacket and a polka-dotted shirt, swore that he was not out to make "a fast buck."

Namath told the senators he was Broadway Joe's largest stockholder, owning 19 percent, and a dedicated chairman of the board. He neglected to tell them, as the *Wall Street Journal* later reported, of the board meeting he conducted while showering in his penthouse apartment, hollering his approval from the bathroom whenever it was time to vote.

Then again, for all Namath's assurances that he would be an active owner, his only asset—indeed, the company's only real asset—was his name. For that reason Mike Bite, who delivered Namath, was given 95,000 shares. Their partners in the start-up were a couple of real estate promoters and a stockbroker, Thomas Marshall, who had been suspended by the SEC. Although Marshall left after the first fiscal year, during which the company lost $370,988 on revenues of $238,870, the problems remained after his departure. At its peak, Broadway Joe's Inc. had eleven franchises and a Quarterback Burger that food critic Gael Greene called a "dry, bland outrage." Namath was already thinking of how to make it right with friends, particularly teammates, who had invested with him. By the end of September, Namath and Bite would resign and "transfer" their all-but-worthless stock to the company's remaining director. Some years later, while driving past the original franchise on Miami's Seventy-ninth Street Causeway, Namath turned to a friend and said: "I paid off every penny. I'm damn proud of that."

■　　■　　■

Namath's frustration with his contract was hardly unprecedented. But unlike the rank and file of the NFL Players Association, he was among the very few able to address their own grievances. That summer, the players union began to talk of a possible strike. Rozelle and the owners reacted by locking veterans out of training camp. With Hofstra off-limits, the Jets—minus their captain quarterback, who remained at the Palm Bay Club—conducted their own informal practices at Adelphi College. But this routine was short-lived, as the Players Association backed down after a couple of weeks. At 8:00 A.M. on August 4, the morning after the settlement was announced, Super Bowl veterans Namath, Maynard, Grantham, Winston Hill, John Schmitt, Jim Turner, Bake Turner, and Dave Herman were scheduled to take their physicals. While Namath wasn't the only one who didn't show, he was only one of two players—middle linebacker Al Atkinson being the other—who couldn't be reached. "I started calling him about an hour after the settlement between the owners and the Players Association was announced," Mike Martin, now the Jets' assistant general manager, told the *Times*. "I tried first contacting his lawyer, Jim Walsh, and learned he was in Florida. I then heard Joe was in Boston and I tried there and was told he left for New York. I then tried to telephone his New York apartment. Someone answered and said Joe was expected later in the afternoon. I tried later and there was no answer."

Against most expectations, the owner's son was proving himself a solid front-office man. Martin's candor always endeared him to reporters, but in this case, Namath didn't appreciate it. "He didn't talk to me for that entire season," says Martin.

By contrast, Ewbank went out of his way to avoid any problem with his quarterback. "I am not going to levy a fine until I have talked to Joe," he said. "There may be extenuating circumstances."

In typically cryptic fashion, Namath tried to rationalize his absence by citing his "problems." "Football used to be No. 1 with me, but at this stage it's not my main concern," he told Dave Anderson, who reached him at his new townhouse on Eighty-second Street off Fifth Avenue, one of the city's most desirable addresses. "I honestly don't know what I'm going to do. I'm working to get my problems solved. Some of them are business problems, a lot are personal."

The following afternoon, Namath, Jimmy Walsh and Mike Bite went to see Phil Iselin. The Jets' team president, more conciliatory than he was likely to have been with hourly wage earners in his employ, cautioned against the condemnation of his star while expressing willingness to "help him with his financial problems." Over the next few days, as Namath missed the exhibition in Birmingham, Alabama, it was reported that he would return to the team only if granted a "big loan."

By now, Namath's teammates knew the drill. His preseason snit had become an annual event, but could usually be resolved for the right price. "Ever since Joe joined the club there has been a double standard," said Philbin. "We've come to expect it. . . . But as long as he can get ready for the first game of the season, we don't hold it against him."

Actually, players *were* holding it against him, and not jealous or aging veterans upset over the fresh kid's $400,000. For the first time, Namath's contemporaries were voicing displeasure with him. Most outspoken was Al Atkinson. Like Namath, Atkinson was a twenty-seven-year-old bachelor who had played through painful injuries, including a separated shoulder in the Super Bowl. But all similarity ended there; for Atkinson, a Philadelphian who once considered a career in the priesthood, belonged to the Fellowship of Christian Athletes.

"It bothers me that a lot of guys with kids and mortgages are working hard, hoping for a big payoff by winning the Super Bowl, but they're wondering where their leader is," Atkinson said after learning that Namath wouldn't be reporting on time. "I don't think it's fair and I'm saying so."

Atkinson, who had been deeply opposed to a players' strike, didn't want to go through another preseason melodrama starring Broadway Joe. Bachelors III had been enough. "It took away team unity," said Atkinson, who believed that a me-first attitude was partly to blame for the loss to Kansas City. As far as he was concerned, Namath's newfangled credo masked old-fashioned selfishness. "It used to kill me," said the linebacker, "to see this guy sit back on his TV show and think everything he does and stands for is justified as long as he comes right out and says it. He thinks it makes an indiscretion correct if you admit to it."

Atkinson had never been one to command the spotlight—it wasn't until 1967, his second season with the Jets, that he asked the PR staff to remove the words "exceptionally quiet" from his bio—but his words now carried great weight. He was the defensive captain. He organized team prayer services. He had suddenly become the unlikely protagonist in the Jets' experiment with protest politics. Instead of reporting to camp, Atkinson announced his own retirement. When it came to Namath, Atkinson considered himself a conscientious objector.

The linebacker's argument made Joe's absence even more difficult to defend. Even the *Times*'s Dave Anderson, whose even temper, good manners, and obvious sympathy had made him Namath's unofficial Boswell, seemed to be taken aback by the quarterback's behavior. Given a turn as a columnist, a departure from his usual beat writer's duties, he seized on that fundamental part of Namath's nature, the distaste for conflict. With training camp approaching, wrote Anderson, "he knew he had to make a decision. Instead, he refused, as if avoiding the confrontation with reality would make it disappear. During the pro football labor impasses, he could have joined the other experienced Jets in their informal workouts at Adelphi College, but he hid at the Palm Bay Club."

But this reproach from the normally admiring Anderson was gentle compared to what Namath would read elsewhere. The conflagration over Bachelors III had left him feeling suspicious, persecuted, almost Nixonian. The press, he believed, was out to get him. Namath had already cut off three writers: Paul Zimmerman, Larry Fox, and Dick Young, the most widely read columnist in town.

"Like him or not, you had to read him," says the *News*'s Bill Gallo, a great friend of Young's. "Dick was a must."

Young had grown up in Washington Heights, the son of a movie cameraman who left the family to work in Hollywood. "He used to talk about his old man, about not growing up with a father," Gallo recalls. "He didn't like any-one to know, but his mother had some kind of nervous breakdown. She wasn't able to take care of him. So Dick became a foster child and grew up half of his youth in two Catholic homes." One was Italian, the other Polish. The experi-ence left Young fluent in all the dialects spoken by New York's ethnic working classes. But unlike Jimmy Cannon, Young harbored no aspirations to be a poet. It was enough to be a newspaperman.

As a columnist, he was many things: irascible, sentimental, and hypocriti-cal. He was an objective newsman who had no problem accepting Sonny's largesse, a family man who liked his booze and broads. But he was also fiercely independent of the journalistic herd, an excellent reporter who knew how to leverage the size of his following to obtain fresh information. "We had two million readers, three and a half million on Sundays," says Gallo. "If you had a ball club, who would you go to?"

Young, who made his name covering the Brooklyn Dodgers, came of age when newspapers were the most powerful medium in sports. He despised tele-vision and all it begat, beginning with Cosell. "Howie the Shill," Young called him in print. Not long after Werblin lost his piece of the team, Young was re-leased from his Jets radio gig. The generally acknowledged culprit was his erst-while broadcast partner, Cosell, who had long since volunteered himself for service as a Namath acolyte. "The Young-Namath feud began the day Dick lost the radio job," says Larry Fox.

Then again, their grudge might well have been inevitable. In Namath, Young found a perfect target. Not only was he a creature of television, but Na-math's example anticipated a new generation of spoiled superstars. Just as Cosell became Howie the Shill, Namath became "Joey Baby." Now Young would give him a reason to feel persecuted.

In his parody of "the Joe Namath system," Young wrote: "It's the latest thing, stupid. You got problems, you don't go to work. You stay home and mope. . . . We got a place here in New York where lots of people with prob-lems never go to work. It's called the Bowery. They used the Joe Namath sys-tem in the Bowery long before Joe Namath was born."

Later, following a Sal Marchiano interview in which Namath suggested his absence was due to his painfully uncertain orthopedic condition, Young re-sponded: "A man who arrives with two lawyers is not there to talk medicine with his boss. He is there to talk money."

As for Namath's boycott, Young couldn't have asked for more from a ballplayer:

> He isn't talking to me. It's all right. I'll survive. Sometimes my wife isn't talking to me, and I number those among my fondest days. . . .
> Very early in life a newsman must make his decision: Will I sell out

my readers? Will I write only nice things, so that the athletes will talk to me? If the answer is no, he becomes a newspaperman. If yes, he becomes a hero worshipper, a house man, a sycophant, a dispenser of pap, and perhaps he goes on to radio and TV. . . . Howard Cosell must have guests. In order to get them, he must cater to them. He must fawn over them, sympathize with them, tell them how wonderful they are. If he doesn't, they don't go on and soon he has no show, for it would be punishing simply to look at Howard Cosell talking for five or 10 minutes.

On August 14, after ten days of retirement, Al Atkinson announced that he would rejoin the team. He explained the decision as a result of injuries to his replacement, Mike Stromberg, and Gerry Philbin, who was recovering from shoulder surgery. "Everything I've said I've meant, but I feel a responsibility to the team," he said. As for Namath: "If he wants to hide behind a bottle and soak his troubles in it, that's his business. I wish somebody would tell him that his real friends are out at Hofstra. All he had to do is come out there and join them."

Atkinson showed up at camp three days later, and within hours Namath ended his own hiatus, reporting to Dr. Nicholas's office for his physical. The next afternoon, following the morning practice session, Namath arrived at Hofstra. He pulled up in a mocha-colored Jaguar with Al Hassan and went to his room. Besieged with questions, he provided only a statement: "I'm here to prepare for the coming season."

After countless interview requests, Jets PR man Frank Ramos conferred again with the quarterback. "Joe said he would not talk if any of the writing fellows are around," Ramos told reporters.

The newspapermen would make do with quotes they scavenged from the radio and TV guys, including one gem from Ed Ingles, who worked for WINS radio. In their interview, Namath denied having tried to renegotiate his deal with the Jets. He hadn't yet recovered from the Kansas City game, he said, a loss that hurt him like an unfaithful lover. This wasn't about money, he insisted. This was about his relationship with football, and the price it exacted, both physical and emotional.

"I don't know whether I want to get up in the morning and be sick," said Namath. "Every time before a game, you can't even eat. You drink a cup of coffee and get sicker and I don't like that feeling . . . you get the chills in the morning and the stomach is upset. You wonder: is it worth it?"

Football was a commitment, requiring the kind of devotion that hurt his stomach.

In the end, Namath was never disciplined for missing camp. "It's a dead issue," declared Ewbank. As for the financial matter, no settlement was announced. Iselin, who had offered to "help," didn't want to be seen as capitulating. But on

January 3, 1971, the Jets sent a letter to Namath, in care of Jimmy Walsh, informing him that the club would award him with a $50,000 bonus. The first half was payable on January 5. The second half would arrive a year later. The bonus came with one notable condition: Namath had "to report and to remain at training camp at the times and places prescribed."

■   ▨   ■

Sports Illustrated celebrated Namath's return with a cover courtesy of Larry Spangler Productions: an adoring Victoria George eagerly invading the unshaven gunslinger's personal space. BACK TO WORK, JOE NAMATH! read the headline. END OF THE DOLCE VITA.

Of course, Joe's notion of training fell short of the Spartan ideal. His accomplice in escaping camp's rigors was a rookie cornerback named Steve Tannen. A first-round draft pick out of Florida, Tannen had driven north in a red Volkswagen van. He had a girl from college make curtains with red, white, and blue fabric that hung like bunting in the windows. He had an eight-track with an excellent selection of mellow sounds, including Spirit, James Taylor, and Traffic. And he had some of the best Colombian dope. "Every year I'd go to training camp, people would be waiting for me and my heavy trash can liners full of reefer," says Tannen.

Namath required only a little convincing to ride shotgun in the VW. He didn't like the feeling that there was nothing in front of the windshield, but soon got over it. The Jets practiced twice a day in camp, with their last meetings and film sessions ending around nine o'clock, two hours before curfew. "Then Joe and I would get in my van and take off on Hempstead Turnpike," says Tannen. "We'd drive an hour in either direction, smoking dope and listening to music. Then we'd drive an hour back, stop at Jack in the Box and get something to eat before we made curfew."

As vices went, dope smoking carried a greater stigma than drinking. It was still illegal and not widely accepted among players, especially the older white guys. "There weren't that many dopers, people were doing mostly uppers and speed," Tannen recalls. "The NFL turned a blind eye to pills. But *drugs* were anathema. Smoking marijuana was like being a murderer."

In hindsight, one can debate the relative benefits and ills: Was it better to smoke dope or pop bennies and greenies and reds? Namath liked to get high. Cannabis produced an amusingly curative vapor, especially therapeutic for Namath's love affair with the game. He wasn't the first to discover that marijuana is good for the treatment of pain. It also helps with nausea.

The Jets opened the 1970 season in Cleveland, a game that was featured as the inaugural telecast of *Monday Night Football*. A decade had passed since Roone Arledge submitted a memo to his boss at ABC, vowing "to add show business to sports." Given a sufficient number of cameras positioned at the proper angles, he reasoned, each game could be exploited as a real-time narrative. Now ABC, which had an enthusiastic sponsor in Ford, paid the National Football League $34 million for four seasons of Monday nights. The broadcasts would feature a three-man booth: Keith Jackson, former Cowboys quarterback Don Meredith, and Howard Cosell, whose ostentatiously nasal verbosity made him a new kind of heel for millions of fans watching at home.

39. THE AGONY OF DEFEAT

". . . *the premier quarterback, Number Twelve, Joe Willie Namath, of the Jets . . .*"

Monday Night Football would become an institution. But the star of that first evening, the protagonist around whom the network trained its cameras, was Namath. He was everything Arledge wanted. Cosell might have been fun to hate, but Namath still inspired the most extreme sentiments. In New Orleans, where a Jets preseason game drew 78,581, Namath left the game briefly after a hard hit to his right knee. This incited great glee among the fans, who threw tomatoes and beer cans at him. Later, when Namath appeared on the sidelines in street clothes, they took up a delighted chant from the stands: "We killed Joe, we killed Joe!" The following week, after receiving a threat on Namath's life, Dallas police greeted the Jets' plane and remained at the quarterback's side (even on the team bench) until he left town.

The Monday night crowd at Cleveland's Municipal Stadium—a new record, 85,703—was also energized by the prospect of Broadway Joe's failure. Late in the fourth quarter, a thirty-four-yard touchdown to Sauer cut the Browns' lead to 24–21. Soon Namath would have his chance to orchestrate a game-winning drive. But instead, hurried by a charging defender, he threw his third interception of the evening. Browns linebacker Billy Andrews returned it twenty-five yards for a touchdown that sealed the Jets' defeat. The cameras first focused on Andrews; next, the jubilant fans. Then Arledge, scanning the monitors, barked at his director, Chet Forte: "Look at Namath!"

Now the prime-time audience was shown Broadway Joe as it had never seen him before: motionless, hands on hips, head down, bowed, humbled. The posture was an unmistakable acknowledgment of his error. From *Monday Night Mayhem,* by Marc Gunther and Bill Carter: "The camera stayed right there, framing Namath, milking the image, as other players trotted on and off the field. . . . The Namath shot distilled into one arresting image Arledge's contributions to sports television: the human dimension, the climax of the drama, the agony of defeat."

Cosell remained stupefied just long enough for Keith Jackson to remark: "There's a depressed Joe Namath."

■　　■　　■

Unfortunately for Joe, there was more where that came from.

Going into the fifth week of the season, the Jets were one win against three losses, their sole reason for optimism being a seventy-two-yard touchdown pass to Rich Caster, a tall, talented rookie who had idolized Joe while growing up in Mobile, Alabama. In all other respects, the season was proving to be a disaster. The right side of the offensive line had been decimated with injury. Maynard was out, too. But worst of all, Matt Snell had ruptured his right Achilles tendon in the fourth quarter of a 34–31 defeat in Buffalo. Snell, averaging twenty-two carries a game, was the conference's leading rusher. Afterward, he sat sobbing in front of his locker, Dr. Nicholas unable to console him. "I'm finished, Doc," said Snell. "My career's finished."

Namath, who had spoken so cavalierly about quitting the game, felt different now. Suddenly he was ashamed to go into the trainer's room and ask for ice.

Two weeks later, the Jets faced the Colts in a rematch of Super Bowl III. As part of the realignment brought about by that game, the Colts had agreed to join the Eastern Division of the American Football Conference, descended from the AFL. This would be the first of Baltimore's semiannual dates with the Jets, and it went much like the game originally forecast by NFL fans for January 12, 1969. Johnny Unitas, now thirty-seven, maneuvered his team to an early 17–0 lead, and the Jets never recovered. Without Snell, Namath directed a predictably desperate offense. He threw 62 passes, completing 34 for 397 yards. He was also intercepted six times: two were returned for touchdowns, and two more stopped what seemed to be touchdown drives. Still, the Jets had a chance, down 29–22 late in the fourth quarter when Billy Ray Smith got to Namath. The impact of the fall broke the wrist on his throwing hand. The fracture, occurring at the base of the navicular bone below the thumb, would require a cast for at least six weeks.

In his five-plus seasons with the Jets, Namath had never missed a nonexhibition game due to injury, that streak being a remarkable testament to his toughness. But as it came to an end, Namath was done for the year. The new Jet quarterback was Al Woodall, a second-year backup from Duke whose professional career to date consisted of eleven passes.

■   ■   ■

Unlike other ballplayers, Namath at least had a second career.

The week leading up to the Baltimore game coincided with the New York opening of *C. C. & Company*. Arthur Knight of the *Saturday Review* declared it to be "the Ben-Hur of motorcycle movies," an assessment that appeared prominently, and quite alone, in the print ads. Other reviewers were not so sanguine. The *New York Times*'s Vincent Canby seems to have been in a charitable mood when he wrote:

> Here, at last, is the picture to name when someone asks you to recommend "a good bad movie." It's not very long; it pays attention to every hallowed idiocy of its genre and its characters talk a marvelously unreal type of movie repartee. . . .
> Even if that weren't enough (and it almost is) the movie stars Joe Namath and Ann-Margret, probably the only two people in the United States who have no identity problems, as, respectively, a nice, clean-cut long-haired Hell's Angel sort, and a high-fashion writer for—if I remember correctly—*Harper's Bazaar*.

A month later, in an effort to capitalize on the publicity created by *C. C.*, Paramount finally released *Norwood*, which included Namath's more modest role. "Big Joe," according to the *Times*, "has little to do and he does it well."

In fact, Big Joe was much tougher on himself than the *Times* had been. He didn't trust the reviewers any more than he had trusted the people on the set. After *Norwood*, he told *Playboy:* "I'm not sure that the movie people I've talked to aren't saying nice things just to make me feel good."

Unlike those around him, Joe the hustler understood where Sonny's theory was counterfeit; star quality wasn't a fungible commodity. Being a football star didn't make him a movie star, and it certainly didn't make him an actor. To develop his athletic gifts Namath had been tutored by family and coaches as long as he could remember. While he had been performing in front of crowds since Little League, he had never appeared in so much as a school play. Now the camera's presence made him desperately aware of his lack of training as an actor. He felt like an impostor. Joe had always enjoyed the movies. He liked the idea of being a cowboy or a war hero, but *acting* like one was not cool.

He dreaded having to sit through the rushes; after all, the one-eyed monster did not lie. "I felt like a fool watching myself talk," he said. "It didn't seem very natural to me." To prepare for a part, he would record and listen to his lines on a tape recorder. But playback was always a bitch. He particularly disliked the sound of his own voice.

Then again, he wasn't reading from great scripts. Typical was this from the mouth of C. C. Ryder, who waits for a long, leering moment before interrupting the gang rape of Ann-Margret: "You don't hurt something that looks that good. I mean, laying her is one thing, but bruising her, well, that's something else again."

It was hard not to wince. Joe had been scrutinizing his performances in game films for years. But that, Namath would explain, was "a whole different thing." He rather enjoyed watching himself play ball, for he could learn from his mistakes and appreciate deeds done well. But watching as he tried to be someone else filled him with a feeling very close to self-loathing. Game films were like silent movies. Athletic performance was authentic and natural. But these movie roles brought out another component of Namath's contradictory nature: along with the womanizer who longed to be faithful and the hustler who hated to lie was the performer who didn't like to act.

While he was still recovering from his injury, a crew from public television's newsmagazine *The Great American Dream Machine* arrived to film him shooting pool with Al Hassan. With the cameras rolling, Hassan persisted in asking Joe to perform a scene from *The Last Rebel*. Finally, Namath's indolent manner dissolved into anger. "No," he snapped. "I don't like to. And I don't want to. I'm not under contract. I have no confidence."

Some years later, he confessed: "I never saw *C. C. & Company* in full, or *The Last Rebel* or *Norwood*. I don't even watch myself on television shows when I do *Sonny and Cher* or Flip Wilson or Dean Martin or whatever. I sometimes turn it on and I look and then I cringe and then I turn it right off. I just get so paranoid. It's such a weird feeling."

■ ■ ■

Without their star quarterback, the Jets finished the 1970 season with a record of 4–10. When it ended, Namath headed south for the winter, where he was joined by Tim Secor, owner of the Tittle Tattle. The bar was Secor's job, but Namath was his calling. "As soon as you were in Joe's presence, you were young and famous," he says. "It was like coming from the planet Mercury."

Timmy familiarized himself with Joe's tastes: coed types and stewardesses (he papered the airports with notices entitling them to drinks on the house) were always the preferred choices, with blond hair and blue eyes for romance, and dark hair and brown eyes for sex. Timmy knew just what to do at the American Airlines golf tournament, now being played in Arizona, where Joe was again paired with Mickey Mantle. He gladly drove the cart, carried the liquor, and got the girls. "The broads took care of themselves," Secor recalls. "The booze was the hard thing because those guys drank fast—especially Mickey."

Another thing Timmy understood: don't ask. It didn't matter if Joe wanted a place to park his car (Secor had a garage on Park Avenue and Sixty-sixth Street), a ride to the Stadium, or a girl. "You didn't want to talk too much because he'd snap at you," he says.

So Timmy simply followed directions the day Joe said to pick him up at 7:00 P.M. with the Cadillac. Joe didn't say where they were going, just where to turn as the car made its way through Fort Lauderdale. Finally, they arrived at a dilapidated drive-in theater on the outskirts of town. Joe handed Timmy the money to pay for the tickets, and they parked, waiting for darkness to set in. "Usually Joe sits up straight in a car, but not this time," says Secor. "He slumps way down in the seat like he doesn't want anybody to see him. As the movie starts, he slumps down some more. . . . He don't say a fucking word the whole movie. He just sits there, almost like he's frightened that another car is going to spot him."

When Joe had seen enough, he asked Timmy to take him home. That was about all he said the entire evening. "He never talked about it," says Secor. "He never even mentioned it again."

What more was there to say? It was the *Ben-Hur* of motorcycle pictures.

■   ■   ■

The off-season was equally unkind to the Jets. Verlon Biggs, fed up with Ewbank's stinginess, became a free agent and signed with the Philadelphia Eagles. After three knee surgeries, Jim Hudson had to go in for an operation on his back. "The damn back hurt worse than the knees," he recalls. "I finally said, 'Enough is enough.'" He was finished with football. Unfortunately, football was not finished with him. Hudson would have to endure two more surgeries and, eventually, artificial knees.

More unusual was the retirement of George Sauer. He was halfway through a two-year contract paying him $40,000 a season, good money in those days, but his attachment to pro ball had been dissipating since the Super Bowl.

His father had also won a championship, and Sauer was always acutely aware of the comparison. George Sauer Sr. had been an All-American halfback at Nebraska. He played for the Green Bay Packers, then coached at Navy and Baylor before becoming personnel director for the Titans, and later the Jets. But the split end's retirement was nothing so crude or predictable as a good son's belated attempt at rebellion. "I see how hard other fathers push their sons in sports, but that never happened to me," he said. "Understanding might be the first act of love, and he understood that I was playing behind his name."

But Sauer, who had brought along a dog-eared copy of Camus's *Myth of Sisyphus* during Super Bowl week, kept asking himself why he was still playing. "I became embarrassed with military displays, jets flying over the stadium," he says. "Football is not, psychologically, my favorite sport. I started questioning a few things about the game, the ideas of aggression and the public spectacle. I had to wonder: is this a good thing for human beings to do? Some of the things I questioned were valid. But I think I wanted to get out for personal reasons."

The five-time All-Pro now declared his ambition to be a writer, a decision that puzzled teammates who respected him greatly. You could always be a writer, but football was something you had to do while you could. There were reasons, apart from money and adulation, that men willingly crippled themselves in the service of the game. There was a reason Matt Snell wept openly at the prospect of his forced retirement. Ballplayers had a chance to remain young, happy, and heroic in ways other men could not.

Sauer understood the dilemma. Even as he condemned some aspects of football culture, there were others he knew he would mourn. Late in July, with the Jets in camp at Hofstra, he showed up at Bill's Meadowbrook.

Back in '68, when the baby-faced receiver first walked into Bill's, Tank Passuello asked him for proof of age. Tank had seen many players come and go, but none whose exit would cause him more regret than Sauer's. "I can't begin to tell you about the conversations we had," says Passuello, who once staged a production of *Waiting for Godot* at the bar. "We used to talk about existentialism . . . religion . . . Beckett."

But now, as the ballplayer tried to say good-bye, he found there wasn't much to say. "We just sat around," Sauer recalls. "It was a little bit uncomfortable. You miss it. You miss the guys. I didn't want the guys to think I had deserted them. Of course, I had. I got pretty drunk and went home. Those were the days when you got pretty drunk."

Namath was there at Bill's that night. "I think he respected my decision enough not to start talking about it," says Sauer. "Although I doubt he agreed with it a hundred percent."

"I just said hello," Joe told Dave Anderson. "It happened to be one of the few times I've had a date here and I didn't want to leave my girl alone."

Despite his feelings for Sauer, Namath didn't want to get involved. After all the time he lost to injury, Joe had made his own peace with the game. Not playing made him realize how much he loved to play. Yes, it was love. Without him, the Jets lost to the Giants in an exhibition at Shea. "I had a sad feeling, my eyes were watery," he said. "Maybe I was being punished for getting too lackadaisical about football, too nonchalant, taking it for granted." Namath had been unfaithful, and now he wanted the game to take him back. Being a movie star didn't offer near as much fun or fulfillment as being a football star. Long before summer arrived, Namath cheerfully promised to be ready for the first exhibition game. By July, he broke with his own tradition and reported to camp on time and without complaint. Namath even declared a desire to recast his image, something the Jets' PR office tried to sell as the *new* Joe in a press conference. He no longer wanted to be known as a wise ass or a drinker. Hell, he'd even be glad to speak to the press. "My attitude is changed now," he declared.

He felt good. And relatively speaking, his legs felt good, too. Joe was actually looking forward to the preseason opener with the Detroit Lions. "Nowadays with these exhibition games you've got 60,000 people in the stands, and they're forming opinions about you," he said. "I'm going to convince them, starting this coming game, that we're the best and I'm the best. Yes, I want to show them that I'm the No. 1 quarterback in football."

There were, however, limits to the good humor of this new Namath—as the *Post*'s Paul Zimmerman discovered when he tried to ask a question.

"Now Paul," said Namath, a great fuck-you smile blooming across his face, "you know *we* don't talk."

Namath's feud with Zimmerman was many things: enduring, one-sided, vindictive, and unwarranted. Of the three newspapermen to whom he refused to speak, Zimmerman's case was the most curious. The mutual dislike between Namath and Dick Young seems as inevitable as it was intense; the *Daily News*'s Bill Gallo recalls the two having to be separated at the hotel bar during a golf tournament in Puerto Rico (Namath already had a couple of pops). On the other hand, Larry Fox, the *News* beat writer who had been covering the team since they were the Titans, never seemed fazed by the freeze-out. He figured the quarterback was probably upset by something he had written during the Bachelors III controversy. But Fox, who had never been overwhelmed by Namath in the first place, wasn't about to apologize for doing his job. "The only time I complained," says Fox, "was when he tried to get other guys not to talk to me. He doesn't have to speak to me, but don't let him interfere with me doing my job."

Zimmerman also recalls Namath's threatening to stop speaking to those newsmen he caught providing quotes to the three banned writers. Eventually, Namath even started telling younger players, "I don't want to see you talking to those guys."

"It was terrifying," says Zimmerman.

At six-one and 240 pounds, the *Post*'s beat writer was not easily terrified. But Zim was wired differently from Fox and Young, who advertised Namath's embargo like a badge of honor. Covering football was to Zimmerman what playing was to most athletes: his vocation, his passion, his obsession. Namath's boycott disturbed him greatly.

While covering Bachelors III, Zimmerman often had to "dump" his notes on a rewrite man who composed the finished product. As best he could tell, it was one of those stories—written by a cityside reporter ignorant of the nuances of locker-room politics—that began a grudge that never seemed to end.

"Zimmerman knows why I won't talk to him," Joe said some years later. "He is just a bullshit guy."

Whatever Namath's reasons, Zimmerman was an odd choice as one of his nemeses. He had grown up the son of a labor leader, the first vice president in the garment workers union, and attended the exclusive Horace Mann School in Riverdale. In high school, Zimmerman played football and boxed at George Brown's gym in Manhattan, where, at the age of fifteen, he sparred with Ernest Hemingway. (He was instructed not to hit Papa with any right hands, and to protect his balls, as that's where the Nobel Laureate would go in the clinches.)

After graduation, Zimmerman matriculated at Stanford, where he was expected to play on the offensive line, before transferring to Columbia, which he liked much better despite being unable to crack the starting lineup. That's not to say his undergraduate years were uneventful. Twice Zimmerman allowed researchers to dose him with LSD for a fee of $25. "I did such a good job of going crazy they gave me an extra five," he says. But soon the melting people began to concern him. "It scared the hell out of me. It takes some time for that stuff to wash out of your system."

Zimmerman kept playing football through an army hitch, a master's course at Columbia's Graduate School of Journalism, and his early years as a sportswriter. He appeared regularly on the semipro circuit until the age of thirty-two, though four years later he made a one-season comeback with the Morristown Colonials of the Atlantic Coast League. By then, Zimmerman (who had a side gig as the *Post*'s wine critic) was firmly ensconced in the press box. Like Namath, his career came of age with pro football. He was among the first generation of sportswriters who didn't view football as a stepping-stone to the baseball beat. With an elaborate system for charting games with color-coded pens, Zimmerman kept his own statistics rather than rely on team or league officials. On the subject of television, he felt not unlike Young, and was not above belting an overly aggressive cameraman. He was also possessed with an understanding that "the best reporters are the biggest pricks."

But Zimmerman's prickiness never extended to Namath. In fact, until the quarterback cut him off, Zimmerman had been his most passionate defender in the press box. He defended Namath after his altercation with *Time*'s Charles Parmiter. He defended Namath against cheap shots from *Esquire*. What's more, he understood the game. Namath was forever complaining that sportswriters who hadn't played football didn't know what they were seeing, the many facets of the game set into motion by the center's snap. In Namath's opinion, they couldn't distinguish between a bad pass and a great catch, a blown assignment and a justifiable interception. But these complaints didn't apply to Zimmerman, in whom Namath had everything he claimed to want in a correspondent: a meticulous reporter trained as an offensive lineman, a guy who knew football from the inside out. But there he was, forced to position himself inconspicuously at the outermost rung of the impromptu news conferences that formed around Namath's locker. No matter what tack Zimmerman tried—"Jimmy kept saying, 'I'll straighten it out' "—Joe wouldn't relinquish his grudge.

"I really did used to have nightmares about it," says Zimmerman. "You want to pretend it doesn't mean anything, but it fucking kills you."

■   ■   ■

For good luck, Namath drew a smiley face on the left knee of his practice uniform. He was eager for that exhibition with the Lions, feeling an old need to demonstrate his abilities as a player. But all that game ended up demonstrating was his vulnerability. Namath connected on seven of his first thirteen passes as the Jets jumped out to a 14–0 lead before a sellout crowd in Tampa. With the first half winding down, he had already proven enough for the preseason. Looking to leave the field without incident, Namath handed off to his fullback, Lee White. But White fumbled, and the ball was recovered by Lions linebacker Mike Lucci. Now Lucci came the other way, with fellow linebacker Paul Naumoff blocking for him. Namath, working on instinct that overwhelmed his common sense, tried to make a hit on Lucci (who went on to score anyway). But as he did, Naumoff put his helmet where the smiley face had been. "Dead on my left knee," Namath recalled. "Tore the cruciate and medial ligaments and some cartilage." Of course, he didn't know the extent of the damage as he walked haltingly to the locker room. At that point, he couldn't feel anything. Only later did the numbness give way to pain—not just Namath's, but the team's. Upon learning of the quarterback's condition, Don Maynard began to weep.

■   ■   ■

The first incision was scheduled for 7:00 A.M. the following morning, August 8, 1971, at Lenox Hill Hospital. In preparation, Namath asked the team's business manager, John Free, to call his mother. "I don't want her to hear it on TV," said Namath, who refused the wheelchair waiting for him at the airport. His father and brothers were all at his side by the time he came out of the operating room. John Namath reiterated his plea: "I want him to quit. We don't want him coming home with a limp or without his legs. What good is that?"

But Joe was already planning his return, and Dr. Nicholas said he might even be ready as early as mid-November. Soon, the Jets wheeled him out for a press conference. A reporter asked if it would have been better to stay on the ground, rather than walk off after the hit.

"It probably would have been as good as new," said Namath, oozing sarcasm. "Shit, I probably would have played this weekend."

His career as the "new" Namath had now officially ended. As the presser concluded, he was asked about the smiley button he was wearing. What did it mean?

"It means hate," said Joe. "And kill."

■   ■   ■

The Last Rebel, starring Joe Namath in the role of Burnside Hollis, was released during his convalescence. From Vincent Canby's review in the *Times*: "Joe Namath, in a style that might be identified as sheepish, plays a Confederate soldier who refuses to surrender when Lee does. Either Namath seems embarrassed (when he has to say something like "All right, men, guns on the table!") or else he simply grins, as if in acknowledgment of his great good luck to be making any movie at all."

■   ■   ■

Just as Burnside Hollis was less than Joe Namath, so was the movie less dramatic than his own life. As this was his fourth knee surgery, he thought he knew what to expect during the postoperative phase. But now, in addition to pain, there was paralysis. Shortly after the operation, he found himself unable to move his toes. Alone in his hospital room, he panicked, pushing the button by his bed for a nurse. Later, the doctors deduced that the force of the helmet blow had injured a nerve that ran to his foot. "That day I started getting electrical jolts up my body, every eight, ten, fifteen seconds," he said. "Morphine didn't help."

Neither did Percocet, which he was given upon his release from the hospital. "The worst pain I've ever had," Namath said a month after the operation. "I was 204 before the Lions game. The other day I was 192 with my cast on. The cast weighs eight or ten pounds. I hardly ever eat. I'm taking pills to kill the pain in my foot and all it's killed is my appetite."

By autumn, he had lost as much as thirty pounds. Finally, gaunt and weak, he stood over the toilet in his Manhattan townhouse, a container of Percocet in his hand. "Poured everything down the commode," he said.

Eventually the doctors prescribed a new medicine, Dilantin, an anticonvulsant given to epileptics. "That day those jolts went from every ten seconds or so to about every two and a half minutes, three minutes," Namath recalled.

"The next day, five minutes. The third day, maybe every ten, fifteen minutes. And then the jolts stopped completely. But the foot stayed hot, tingly and numb."

He was assured that the feeling would eventually return to his left foot. It could take a year, or it could take five. Fortunately, a ballplayer like Joe didn't need to feel much. The doctors were correct; the numbness did finally cease. But that hot, tingly feeling would stay with him, returning from time to time, on into the next millennium. The sensation was a strange relative of the Doylestown flu, something from those days when he could run and jump, like pinpricks to remind him who he used to be.

■ ■ ■

Rose came to New York in the hope that her cooking would help her son gain some weight. In the meantime, Joe worked diligently at his rehabilitation. Within a couple of months, he began throwing. But by November, the Joe-less Jets—who had also suffered injuries to John Elliott, Gerry Philbin, and Al Atkinson, among others—were 2–5, and without any realistic chance at the play-offs. Hence, the debate among the team's high command: Should Namath take off the rest of 1971? Why risk additional injury for a season that was already lost?

"I want to play," said Joe.

The question wasn't resolved until the afternoon of November 28, with the Jets hosting the San Francisco 49ers, a team leading the NFC in sacks and total defense. In the second quarter, the 49ers knocked Jets quarterback Bob Davis out of the game. Davis's plight was a fleeting concern among the sellout crowd, as Namath trotted onto the field amid wild applause. There was 10:30 left in the half. It was 1:41 P.M., a year plus a month and ten days since he last played in a regular season game. The effects of the layoff were obvious. He missed badly on his first two passes. On his second series, he threw an interception that resulted in a 49ers field goal. By his own admission, Namath was disoriented and nervous: "I was setting up too fast, not reading the defenses the way I should. The biggest problem was just controlling myself. I'd feel pressure coming from someplace, but I couldn't tell from where."

Through most of the first half, Namath seemed content to hand off to his big rookie fullback, the prodigiously talented John Riggins. But against the 49ers, Riggins wasn't enough. The third quarter began with the Jets losing 10–0. Then San Francisco added a touchdown. The great glee that greeted Namath had condensed into a murmur of acknowledgment: *Hey, the guy missed the last nineteen games. Whadjya expect?*

Then Namath threw for Richard Caster. He didn't like the way the ball felt leaving his hand, as if it had slipped, but Caster—the swift, six-foot-five-inch receiver with a reputation for dropping passes—caught this one in stride for a fifty-seven-yard touchdown. It was the first of two Caster would catch on the day. The other touchdown went to Eddie Bell, the speedy 5–7 split end who had replaced Sauer. Broadway Joe had returned intact: gunlike arm, quick release, uncanny composure. What doomed most quarterbacks was an expectation of the hit that caused them to panic or freeze. Namath, on the other hand, anticipated everything but pain. The film would show Namath oblivious to the charge of Cedrick Hardman—a defensive end known as "Nasty"—as he waited on Pete Lammons to get free. The play was right out of the old Jets-Raiders games. Namath would complete the pass at the expense of his jaw. "When Hardman hit me I started to feel for my teeth," he said. "I thought they were gone."

With 1:41 left, the Jets—who had scored two touchdowns in less than two minutes—got the ball back for their final chance. The score was 24–21, San Francisco, with the Jets on their own 28-yard line. The fans were standing, raucously enthralled, as Namath hit Caster for a first down. Then he hit Bell for twenty-one yards. Fifty-one seconds remained as he went back to Bell, throwing an incompletion to his now double-covered receiver. The next pass was picked off by linebacker Dave Wilcox—but the play was called back. In his rush to get the quarterback, Hardman had been offsides, nullifying the interception and giving the Jets the ball thirty-four yards from the end zone with 34 seconds on the clock. In the huddle, Namath called for a pass play. But something he saw at the line of scrimmage made him change his mind. There, he called for a "32 Trap," a running play for Boozer. Riggins couldn't believe what he was hearing, and thought Namath had made a mistake. He wouldn't call a running play now, he thought. The 49ers were of the same mind. Boozer ran fifteen yards, getting out of bounds at the 19 with 22 seconds remaining. Then Namath threw incomplete to Caster in the end zone. Now there was time only for a final play. The crowd stood, its collective heart thumping, as Namath again passed into the end zone, this time for Bell.

The following day, Namath would appear at Rockefeller Center to tape a television show. In preparation for his appearance, he would require special attentions from the makeup girl. Such was the condition of his swollen jaw. "He was pretty battered up," said Jeff Snedeker, the Jets' trainer. He had taken a painful blow to the elbow and his toes were black and blue, courtesy of a lineman who tried to leave his footprint.

But none of that hurt as much as the pass to Bell, which was intercepted by Johnny Fuller, a reserve safety.

The game ended on Namath's error, and what might have been a miracle finish became another Jets loss. "I didn't play well at all," said Joe. The records would reflect Namath's day as 11 for 27, 258 yards, three touchdowns, two interceptions. But now as ever, his numbers only revealed the true poverty of statistics.

"You're still my idol," said Cedrick Hardman, as they walked off the field. Even after all this time away from the game, Namath remained the quarterback defenses most feared. Was there a way to calculate that? The Jets liked their chances with Joe in the game, as did the fans. But there was no way to quantify what he had given them, an afternoon reaffirming their system of belief. Maybe one had to have been there, to have heard the odd sound emanating from the legions of ill-tempered jackals who so horrified the House of Mara. There was gratitude in their applause. So much for the agony of defeat. Joe hadn't been so loved for a loss since the '65 Orange Bowl.

"What that guy could do was unbelievable," said John Schmitt. "Fifteen minutes after that game was over, the people were still clapping."

Thirty years later, Schmitt's own sense of gratitude remains undiminished. Recalling the moment for a documentary, he seems jolly and bright. Then, without warning, a spasm crosses his face, a tremor in his remembrance. *What that guy could do . . .*

Suddenly, Schmitt finds himself trying to hold back the tears.

■   ■   ■

The San Francisco game established a tenor for the rest of Namath's career. In rooting for Namath, one was now rooting for the minor miracle. His injuries and layoffs made them less probable, but ever more desired. One could always hope for another brilliant comeback. After all, the man made his name mocking the odds. He was the fix to which both fans and front office types had become addicted. So had his teammates. "No one instills confidence or puts points on the board like Namath," said tight end Rich Caster, noting that guys practiced with more intensity when Joe was with the team. From ownership down, the Jets had come to think of Joe as the sole guarantor of their success. Without him, they were lost. "That was a problem: the team lived in the past," says Steve Tannen. "When Joe got hurt, everybody took a hike."

On January 27, 1971, a White House staffer named Malise C. Bloch sent a memo to George Bell, special assistant to the president. "Listed below," it began, "are the names of people whom we fell [*sic*] are not in sympathy with the policies and goals of the Nixon Administration." These included financial supporters of Democratic presidential hopefuls, union leaders who had declined to attend a Labor Day party at the White House, and a category called "Others." Among those in the latter grouping were such varied public figures as Bayard Rustin, Jane Fonda, Gregory Peck, and Joe Namath.

A couple of weeks earlier, Namath had appeared before a federal grand jury investigating league practices. "If you don't like your contract or the team that drafts you, what can you do?" he told reporters. And though the quarterback's opinions on free agency and players' rights—under questioning, he quickly conceded that these matters were "all over my head"—was an unlikely concern for the White House, Namath would remain an object of Nixon's attentions and ire.

40. THE SCORE

Some years later, the *Miami News* reported that Nixon was using a special Miami-based unit of the Internal Revenue Service to spy on prominent Floridians he considered his enemies. The paper's source said information concerning sexual, spending, and social habits "went directly to the White House." The unit's subjects included Miami mayor Maurice Ferre and Dolphins owner Joe Robbie, both Democrats, and Joe Namath, politically unaffiliated.

Nixon, like Hoover, wanted to stay apprised of Namath's affairs but never seemed to catch him in an actionable offense, which, considering the quarterback's lifestyle, shouldn't have been too difficult. Sal Marchiano recalls walking up Third Avenue with Joe: "It's the middle of the night, there's nobody out. But we can't light up a joint because it's too windy. So we duck into a store doorway and we're right in the middle of smoking this joint and all of a sudden there's a glaring light on us from a squad car."

They figured they're busted, the evidence smoldering between Joe's fingers. At any moment, two of New York's finest would tell them to put their hands in the air. Instead, they could hear the cops discussing the matter over the squad car's PA system.

"That him?" asked the first one.

"Nah," said his partner. "Can't be."

Then the policemen drove off.

Mort Fishman, Namath's good friend and frequent traveling companion, recalls a similar incident on a stopover in Dallas. Joe found a spot between two luxury cars in an all but deserted parking lot. There he pulled out his bag, maybe a quarter ounce of grass, rolled a joint, and lit it.

Then, without warning, the police cruisers appeared. "It was like they were coming from everywhere," recalls Fishman. Quickly, Namath stepped on the joint, kicking it down the drain, and shoved the baggie into Mort's pants. The pungent smoke still hung heavy in the air, but the cops seemed oblivious to the odor. At first, Mort didn't understand what had happened. The cops, it turned out, had been lying in wait for thieves breaking into cars.

"What are you talking about, 'break into cars'?" said Mort. "That's Joe Namath."

"Yeah, right," said the cop. "And I'm Bing Crosby."

In a matter of minutes, after providing the requisite autographs, Joe and Mort had their own police escort to make sure they wouldn't be late for their connecting flight.

When speaking of the good old days with Joe, Fishman seems as wistful as Marchiano. Mort was a father of two who had emerged from the wreckage of a divorce with solid credentials as both a golfer and a ladies' man, qualities that made him ideally suited for hanging out with Namath. It was, quite literally, a ball. But looking back, Fishman is struck by Namath's almost medicinal use of marijuana. Joe's dope-smoking, says Fishman, "depended on how much pain he was in. I think he smoked when he was in pain and I think he smoked to relax."

Then again, for Namath, relaxation and absence of pain had become one and the same thing.

■ ■ ■

Namath was now living sumptuously alone. The famous penthouse had been replaced by the town house at 14 East Eighty-second Street, full of Tiffany lamps, gilt clocks, and assorted floral and rococo trimmings. The decorator's concession to Joe's tastes was a game room that housed a pool table and his favorite shuffle bowling game, a gift from his father. As for women, Suzie Storm had been replaced, too. She had finally tired of waiting for Joe to settle down. Whatever he felt about Suzie's departure, Namath kept it to himself. For a while, he couldn't bear to hear Peter, Paul and Mary's 1970 hit, "Leaving on a Jet Plane."

"One day I was in Jimmy Walsh's office when that tune came on the radio and somebody says, 'Quick, turn it off, Joe's walking in,'" recalls Fishman. "It had something to do with Suzie."

Joe's new steady was the former Betty Lee Oakes, eight years his junior. A finely featured blond model who had graced the pages of *Cosmopolitan* and *Vogue,* she took the name Randi after her hometown of Randalia, Iowa. "Randi would have done anything for Joe," says Fishman.

When he was in the hospital, Randi would remain at his bedside, massaging his legs. Randi called Rose to get the recipes for Joe's favorite Hungarian dishes. And she came to accept, as Frances and Bebe and Suzie had before her, that being Joe's girl meant waiting your turn and sharing your man. Whether he was at the Tittle Tattle with Timmy Secor or bouncing around Bal Harbour with Mort, somehow the women always found him. Randi learned to keep an eye on the wine bottles he kept in his bedroom refrigerator. "When one of the bottles has been drunk or partly drunk," she said, "I know damn well what's been going on."

Still, Randi had little choice but to accommodate the notion of her man as every girl's dream. His body might have been in disrepair, but his image was more vital, and profitable, than ever. In the spring of 1972, Namath attended the Academy Awards with Raquel Welch. The date, as Tim Secor recalls, had been arranged by the studio that wanted to promote the soon-to-be released *Kansas City Bomber,* featuring Ms. Welch in the role of a roller-derby heroine. "The most amazing thing I've ever seen," he says. "We're walking to this circular bar in the middle of this huge room, and coming out of the woodwork there's Cary Grant, Burt Lancaster, Jimmy Stewart, Mike Nichols, Richard Widmark, Angie Dickinson, John Wayne. Every actor you ever saw and they all came up to Joe and said, 'I'd just like to shake your hand. I saw the Super Bowl and it was the greatest game I've ever seen.'"

Joe received the compliments graciously. Then he went back to the table to play footsie with Raquel.

That night, he presented the Oscar for Best Costume Design with Cybill Shepherd. "For those of you who don't have a program," he said, "my name is Joe Namath." His grin drew wild applause.

"He's great," gushed Andy Warhol. "He's the biggest star here."

Although Namath flubbed a line, calling his copresenter "Cheryl," nothing could diminish his fabulousness. The following day, a photo of him and Raquel on their way into the Dorothy Chandler Pavilion ran in newspapers around the world. The image might have provided the stencil for a Warhol silk screen or, just as easily, an advertisement for Broadway Joe.

Celebrity was a kind of brand name, and Namath was no exception. He had failed as a hamburger magnate, and his employment agency fell victim to Nixon's first recession. But under the aegis of Namanco and its sole director,

Jimmy Walsh, Namath was always open for business. "I was still at an age when I was trying to make a score," he said. "My father was still working in the steel mills." The idea of Babcock & Wilcox remained with him, always. Money was security, for him and the family.

By 1971, Bachelors III had locations in Boston, Tuscaloosa, and Fort Lauderdale, where Bobby Van, Ray Abruzzese, and Joe now spent their winters. Still, for Namath, selling liquor was less lucrative than selling his name. Namanco licensed a Joe Namath jigsaw puzzle and an electronic Joe Namath football game, for which he was to receive $100,000 in annual payments through 1976, plus a percentage of royalties. Yet for several years after his Super Bowl victory, most of his endorsements seemed to target a slightly older demographic, male consumers who wanted to purchase a little piece of Joe's cool. He sold La-Z-Boy recliners, Dingo boots ("The Dingo Man. He's no ordinary Joe"), Royal Pub Cologne ("The kind of guy who uses it doesn't need it"), Puma sneakers (Namath's model was called "Swinger"), and Noxzema medicated shaving cream.

For the Noxzema shoot, Joe and Hoot Owl showed up with six-packs of Budweiser at a Manhattan studio. There Namath met his newest costar, a little-known actress from Corpus Christi named Farrah Fawcett. "He absolutely loved Farrah," recalls Tony Jaffe, then the creative director for the William Esty advertising agency. "He just couldn't keep his eyes off her."

She was an amalgam of his favorite flavors at the time: blond and southern. Their apparent chemistry paid off in the commercial, which opens as Namath says, "I'm so excited, I'm gonna get creamed." Farrah, who had honed her skills as an Ultra Brite toothpaste model, then applies the balm with suggestive delight. "Let Noxzema cream your face so the razor won't," she coos.

"You've got a great pair of hands," says Joe.

The ad was a huge hit. What he lacked as an actor came naturally as a pitchman. Movie stars have million-dollar smiles. But Joe's money shot was a wink and a grin.

In 1972 George Lois concocted the slogan "Olivetti girls have more fun," part of a campaign to sell Olivetti typewriters to secretaries. The notion of secretaries as "girls" drew the ire of feminist groups, whom Lois appeased with a promise that the next such "girl" would be a guy. His colleagues were baffled, but Lois already had the storyboard in his head.

From one of the Mantle Men/Namath Girls commercials, he recalled that Namath (like most graduates of Beaver Falls High School) could type. So now Lois cast Joe as a secretary, taking dictation from a good-looking, well-dressed, middle-aged boss he addressed as "ma'am."

"I'm very pleased with your work, Joseph," she says, perusing his copy. "By the way, what are you doing for dinner tonight?"

Ever so slightly, Joe turns to the camera, his smile just less than a grin, his gesture just less than a shrug. Then one hears the sound of a typewriter going over the margin: *ding.*

"The typewriter does the wink," says Lois. "But no other ballplayer could have done that commercial. Hell, Robert Redford couldn't have done it. Paul Newman couldn't have done it. But, somehow, with Joe Namath, it worked."

Not everyone agreed. Lois remembers Gloria Steinem leading a delegation that stormed out of a screening in his office. "What's the problem?" he said. "The boss *always* tries to make the secretary."

Some people had no sense of humor. The feminists weren't the only ones pissed off by his use of Joe. That same year, in another Lois campaign, Namath started promoting Ovaltine, the chocolate-flavored milk supplement once endorsed by Captain Midnight and, before that, Little Orphan Annie. Lois's commercials placed Namath with an assortment of fresh-faced fourth- and fifth-grade boys: "Any friend of Ovaltine is a friend of mine," says Namath, infinitely more believable than Duke Snider. "Ovaltine is the only chocolate drink that gives you all the vitamins the U.S. government says you need all day. Nothing else comes close. My old pal Ovaltine."

The ads were straight and pure, the copy almost as corny as the old spots with Captain Midnight. Nevertheless, as Lois recalls, "A lot of people were furious. They were saying, 'Who is this sonofabitch? He's no example for our kids.'"

Though his own tastes now ran to vodka, Namath was still famous for taking his Johnnie Walker red and his girls blond. Thus, using him as a hustler of chocolate milk was informed with the same instincts that led Lois to present Sonny Liston as Santa and Ali as the martyred Saint Sebastian. The adman was subverting the old formula. The outrage might've been predictable, but it paled compared to the growth in Ovaltine's sales.

"They were looking to build another factory, for chrissakes," says Lois.

"We feel that Joe Namath has been to Ovaltine in 1972 what Little Orphan Annie was to Ovaltine back in the 1930s and '40s," said Paul Sullivan, the company's brand manager.

So much for the stigma of booze and broads. But just in case, Ovaltine ran another spot featuring Namath without the kids. This version, which ran during the Johnny Carson and Dick Cavett shows, was intended for the moms. Namath reminded them that he, too, drank Ovaltine as a kid. Moms liked hearing that. As always, moms loved Joe.

Namath's image was being framed in a way even Werblin would not have envisioned—through television commercials. Actually, it made perfect sense. Joe was made for TV, and TV was made for commercials. A whole generation was growing up with Namath. Boys who couldn't yet shave wanted to wear his Pumas. They were never hung up on his $400,000 contract. They didn't yet care for booze and broads, just chocolate milk. But they were reshaping the idea of

Broadway Joe, sanitizing his image in a way Pete Rozelle could never have done.

In anticipation of the 1971 Christmas season, Namath signed up to endorse Hamilton Beach's Butter-Up popcorn popper. It was a short-term deal, as the company was apprehensive about Namath's reputation as a carouser and the potential for bad publicity.

Hamilton Beach itself wasn't expecting too much; a bump in the Christmas retail season would have been just fine. All the home appliance companies, it seemed, had a version of the popper, and none managed to post better than modest sales. The Butter-Up variation tried to distinguish itself by offering a plastic butter dispenser.

"Any competitor could knock it off easy," says Hank Seiden, the creative director for Hicks and Greist, the company's ad agency. "But there was one thing they couldn't duplicate. We had Namath. The kids had to get the one identified with Namath. The product was such a big success they started making it all year round. Demand was so high distributors had to take it. We blew the top off the market."

At the advice of Charlie Skoog, who spearheaded the Hicks and Greist campaign, Hamilton Beach bought time on the first half of *Monday Night Football*. That time placement would allow kids to see the ads before they went to bed. Soon, Jimmy Walsh was negotiating a new deal. "I remember Charlie saying, 'This Jimmy is a tough little runt,' " recalls Seiden.

Namath's commercials, unlike his movies, had a good degree of authenticity. He liked Ovaltine. He liked popcorn. And though he didn't want to be a husband or a father, he loved kids.

Typical was Namath's reaction when Jack Danahy paid his first visit to the Jets' camp after the Bachelors III affair. Danahy brought two of his sons and a couple of their friends. "We saw each other and Joe ran into the training room," says Danahy. Rozelle's security chief—whom Joe blamed for the "vendetta" against him—expected nothing less.

"But the next thing I know, the door opens and Joe is calling the kids in," says Danahy. "They spent the afternoon in the training room with him. They took pictures. They got autographs. The kids never had such a day in all their lives."

In 1972, the Joe Namath Instructional Football Camp began operating at an old ski lodge in Vermont. The camp was a partnership with John Dockery, the Jets' Harvard-educated defensive back. It wasn't a big score, certainly not after paying the counselors and the rent. But it nourished a need in Namath. "That camp was one of his favorite things," says Hoot Owl Hicks, who frequently accompanied him there. "He loved working with kids."

The camp, which would change sites as it grew, offered several five-day sessions for boys. Mort Fishman's son attended the camp, as did Paul Zimmerman's, despite Namath's boycott of his father. "My kid went to his camp twice," says Zimmerman. "He loved it. And it was good for him."

In his first summer there, Zimmerman's son was chosen as the outstanding linebacker in his age group. A year later, he returned as a right tackle, and his father showed up for the final day's scrimmage. The sportswriter watched as his progeny made one block, and then another, before finally getting knocked down. As the play ended, Namath told the kid he could have made another block if he'd hustled more and stayed with the play downfield. "Maybe your team could've gained another ten yards," said Joe, who probably didn't know whose boy he was talking to.

It was a long ride home for the Zimmermans. At some point, the son felt a need to explain himself, why he hadn't made that third block. "Dad," he said, "I was tired."

Zimmerman knew his kid had played to exhaustion. What more could Joe want? "Now you know what I've been putting up with," he said.

■   ■   ■

Though his Jet contract ran through 1972, Namath fixed his negotiating position long before that year's training camp. "This is my option year but I'm not going to play unless I've signed a new contract," he told Dave Anderson. "And I'll say this: I think I should get more than any other player in the game."

Namath believed money had a therapeutic value: "Once I started making money, I figured, well, hell, I don't have to cheat or lie or bullshit anybody anymore." Money granted certain freedoms from worry and stress, and as such, he could no longer be happy without it.

But money was also a way to quantify one's respect and standing. Johnny Unitas, Fran Tarkenton, and Sonny Jurgenson were all reported to be making about $125,000 a year. Not including bonuses, that was considerably more than Namath's salary, and it pissed him off. He didn't need a new set of knees to be better than those guys. He was the best, and he wanted to get paid the best.

Jimmy Walsh, now working solo on Joe's contract, started by asking $1 million for three years. The Jets' lawyer, Dick Barovick, called that "absurd."

"We had to start somewhere," said Jimmy, slightly amused with himself.

Dave Anderson reported that Namath wanted "the highest annual salary in National Football League history, perhaps as much as $250,000."

"Believe me, this figure is not what we're talking about," Jimmy told Zimmerman. "It's purely conjecture."

Ewbank, who gladly deferred to Barovick in these negotiations, just as gladly granted Namath permission to report to camp a week late. On July 22, after appearing in a Bob Hope telethon, Namath arrived at Hofstra with

Jimmy. On his first day of workouts, he reiterated his position with the Jets: "As far as I'm concerned, they can stick it. I'm not going to play for an option clause. All that would be is the salary I got last year."

They would make him the game's highest-paid player, or he'd demand to be traded. "I don't know where the Jets would get another quarterback," he said.

Within a week Namath had his new deal. The terms were reported as being just what he wanted: two years for half a million. In fact, though, the contract was worth $600,000. It called for two annual payments of $200,000 plus another $200,000 after his playing days were over. The deferred money would come in four $50,000 installments over the first three years of his retirement. All Namath had to do was make up to four yearly appearances on behalf of his former team.

The Jets held a press conference in a staid dining room at Hofstra. On either side of Namath were Ewbank and team president Phil Iselin. Behind him was a crowd of boys pressing their noses to a glass door. There must've been about thirty of them, fresh-faced suburban kids. It looked like an Ovaltine commercial.

As the assistant general manager, Michael Martin had access to the files containing player contracts. "I could look up the terms of everyone's contract but Joe's," he says. "It was literally in a different place."

Metaphorically, this was also true of the man himself, as each new contract served to increase the distance between Namath and the rest of the team. The Jets had two kinds of players now: guys who had heard about the Super Bowl, and those who had actually been there. The veterans got older. Joe got richer. And Weeb, improbable as it seemed, got cheaper.

Gerry Philbin, like Namath, was going into his option year. Like Namath, he had been battling injuries for the past couple of seasons. His shoulder seemed to be in a perennial state of dislocation, and required a harness. His knee, with torn ligaments, needed a brace. He had sprained a foot and badly dislocated a finger. Over the past two seasons, Philbin had missed seven games. But he was also the most accomplished defensive lineman in team history, a stature he had attained through sheer will. Now the undersized defensive end was asking for what he called a "token raise," something in the neighborhood of $1,000. Nearing the end of his career, Philbin just wanted a little respect.

41. NOBODY'S PERFECT

Weeb told him he wasn't in the business of "making donations."

Later, Philbin told Paul Zimmerman: "Joe Namath missed nineteen games in those same two years and then he sat down and signed a half-million-dollar contract for the next two. I'm not saying he's not worth it, but he gets a $300,000 raise and I get zero."

"It was not fair," says Martin. "I respected Weeb as an individual, as an elder, an experienced person in the NFL. But there were times when I just had to bite my lip. Gerry's contract was certainly one of them."

Philbin, like others before him, no longer felt like a part of the team.

Namath, meanwhile, was starting to sound as if he *was* the team. There was an element of hubris, however unintended, in his preseason pronouncements, as he spoke of a long-held desire to play the perfect game: "It's always been a goal of mine." Another Super Bowl was not out of the question for the Jets. In Joe's view, it all came down to Joe. "I know if I play well we can win," he said. "I really believe I can win any game we play."

If such talk incited great expectations, who was to doubt him? The Jets won their opener 41–24 in Buffalo. Then they traveled to Baltimore. Since Super Bowl III, the Jets were 0–4 against the Colts. Unitas, still wearing his black high-tops, was now thirty-nine, but the Colts' zone was considered state-of-the-art. They had allowed just nine touchdown passes in all of the previous season. Faced with such a defense, a healthy Namath guaranteed nothing.

■   ■   ■

Later, Namath would speak of how ill prepared he was for this game. "I felt like a dog," he said. "I sat in the locker before the game trying to cram everything in, their formations and everything." He was furious with himself. Still, he managed to come up with a plan. Once again, he would attack the Colts' perceived strength. In the Super Bowl, he had hustled them short; now he would hustle them long. Namath would again use Maynard as a kind of decoy, stretching the zone to its limits, then throwing underneath the defenders. His target was usually Eddie Bell, the five-foot-seven-inch split end who had lined up in the slot position just inside Maynard. Bell's first touchdown was a sixty-five-yarder. It didn't hurt that Bubba Smith was in a wheelchair with a bad foot. "If you have time, all you have to do is send one or two people deep in one area and another deep underneath, and that man underneath should be open," said Namath.

Unitas, under intense pressure from Philbin all afternoon, came back with the flea-flicker. The play that Earl Morrall blew in the Super Bowl was now good for a forty-yard touchdown. Then the Colts added two field goals, making the score 13–7.

The Colts' lead was short-lived, though, as Namath hit Rich Caster—Pete Lammons's replacement at tight end—nine yards for a first down. John Schmitt was injured on the play. Now Namath considered what John Riggins had told him: the left-side linebacker was slacking off. When action resumed, Riggins ran a fly pattern straight out of the backfield. He beat the linebacker, then the cornerback. Namath hit him on the run, sixty-seven yards, touchdown.

The Colts' Don McCauley responded by taking the kickoff ninety-three yards into the Jets' end zone. Another quarterback might have been demoralized. Namath just returned to his hastily drawn plan, finding Bell "deep underneath" for forty-three yards. Then, as the defense moved closer to Bell, he hit Maynard, twenty-eight yards for the touchdown.

And following a Gerry Philbin sack that caused Unitas to fumble, Namath threw for yet another score, ten yards to Caster. He had thrown three touchdowns in a span of 89 seconds. The score was 27–20, Jets. At the half, Namath had already passed for 281 yards. But the game wouldn't get really interesting until the fourth quarter, when Johnny U. and Joey U. started going shot for shot.

With 8:05 left, McCauley dove into the end zone from a yard out, the fourteenth play of a sixty-six-yard drive meticulously crafted by Unitas. The Jets' lead had been cut to a field goal. The 56,626 fans at Memorial Stadium were united in raucous anticipation: Unitas would avenge the Super Bowl yet again.

On the next play, Namath called what Caster recalls as 63Q. "It was a read route," explains Caster. "If they were in double coverage I would stay to the middle, and if they went man-to-man I would take it to the corner. And Joe would read my moves."

With the defense tilted toward Bell and Maynard, the tight end faced single coverage. Caster sprinted past the safety, Rick Volk, for a seventy-nine-yard touchdown.

As a kid in Mobile, Alabama, Caster—who attended predominantly black Jackson State—grew up idolizing Namath. As a pro, he still looked up to him. "I was generally covered by linebackers and safeties," says Caster. "Joe felt I was supposed to beat those guys man-to-man." And if Joe felt that way, Caster did, too.

But then it was Unitas's turn again. He completed another masterful drive: eighty-three yards in ten plays, the finale a twenty-two-yard touchdown pass to Tom Matte. The Jets' lead was back down to a field goal.

As the Jets took the field, Namath was still contemplating what to call. He had a pretty good idea that the Colts, inspired by Unitas's drive, would be charging hard. In this situation the standard call was to take time off the clock. But Joe had another idea, a risky one, and in that moment he spoke to himself as his father would have: "If you ain't confident, you don't belong."

He had just noticed a substitute cornerback coming in at Caster's side. It was Rex Kern, a second-year player from Ohio State. Kern had been injured and hadn't played much. Namath could see that his jersey was still clean and white. The kid was cold. The kid was a mark. "I knew that's where I was going to go," said Namath.

Again, he called 63Q. He saw the blitz coming. "I knew Caster had to be one on one so I just hustled the hell back there, set up, let it go," he said.

Caster beat Kern. This time the touchdown went eighty yards. Namath would always recall the sight of Colts linebacker Mike Curtis giving chase, then falling, and finally, pounding the ground with his fist.

Johnny U. was finally out of comebacks, though in the end, that didn't seem to matter. September 24, 1972, was hailed as the best day of quarterbacking the game had ever seen. Unitas threw for 376 yards on a career-high 26 completions. Namath completed 15 of 28 passes for 496 yards, more than 33 yards per catch. He also threw six touchdowns. Someone asked if he had ever thrown that many before.

"Maybe back on Sixth Street," he answered. "In Beaver Falls."

Later that night, Joe sat in the back room at Bachelors III drinking Black Russians. Mickey Kearney was there, and some of the other guys. Dave Anderson, the only newspaperman still welcome at Joe's table, stayed past midnight.

"I got paid for it, I'm supposed to do the job," Namath told him. "I'm convinced I'm better than anybody else. I've been convinced of that for a while."

He smiled as another Black Russian was set before him. Swirling the fresh drink, he turned to Mickey the hoodlum, his little-known but frequent companion. "You want to take a sauna with me out at Shea tomorrow?" asked Joe. "By the time I'm finished tonight, I'll need a sauna."

He had to get rid of the toxins. He had a big day coming up. Namath was going to be a guest on *Sesame Street*. Broadway Joe would be appearing with Big Bird.

■   ■   ■

Namath led the NFL in passing yards (2,816), and touchdown passes (19) that year, 1972. But once again, the Jets couldn't beat a team that finished with a record better than .500.

They were 6–3, and still in contention for a play-off spot, when they arrived in Miami, where the Dolphins were undefeated. The Dolphins, now coached by Don Shula, were being quarterbacked by another former Colt, the still-crew-cutted Earl Morrall. Morrall had done a splendid job in relief of the injured Bob Griese, but these last few years had done nothing to dim his regret. "The Super Bowl is always there," he told the *Miami News* just days before the game. "I'll always remember it."

The same was true of his feelings for Namath. "I don't respect him," said Morrall. "His lifestyle, his actions. I wouldn't want to follow in his footsteps. I don't want to be like him and I hope my kids and the younger generation don't grow up to be like him.

"I don't think that's the style, for everybody to be big talkers, to be high-livers and to be out chasing."

Morrall's uncharacteristic candor (he claimed he hadn't known he was talking to a sportswriter) drew the expected reprimand from Shula. Namath, for his part, refused to shake his hand at the pregame coin-toss.

Morrall only chuckled. This wasn't revenge, but it was as close as he would get. Morrall, thirty-nine years old, ran for a thirty-one-yard touchdown that day.

As the game neared its end, the Dolphins held a 28–24 lead, but the Jets still had their chance, with the ball ten yards from the end zone. Namath, who couldn't be heard above the din of the crowd, twice called for the Jets to reconvene their huddle. Finally, an infuriated Nick Buoniconti, the Dolphins' middle linebacker, approached the line with Namath over center.

"Run the fucking play," said Buoniconti.

Namath ran the play. Buoniconti intercepted.

Miami went on to a perfect 17–0 season. The Jets lost four of their five remaining games, finishing 7–7.

There were plenty of reasons for their failure that season. Weeb, who had shown such skill acquiring fresh talent, fared less well replenishing the defense. Larry Grantham, who missed three games for the first time in his career, would retire after the season. Verlon Biggs was gone, and Philbin was old, playing his last season in New York. The Jets didn't rush the passer well. And their secondary, not a great one to begin with, had suffered a rash of injuries. By season's end, the Jets had given up more passing yards (2,888) than any team in the league.

New intramural conflicts were also developing. Riggins, who gained 944 yards in only twelve games, resented an offense so completely geared to the quarterback. The offense resented the defense; the old guys resented the new guys.

The game, too, had changed. The Jets didn't have the Dolphins to beat up on anymore. And these zone defenses were actually a lot trickier than Namath had made them look that day in Baltimore. There was a reason why running backs now dominated the game. In the three years since realignment, it had become rare for quarterbacks to throw 20 touchdowns in a season. Namath's 19 led the league, but he also had 21 interceptions.

"I don't think anybody can lay off a couple of years and come back with a good touch," said Ewbank.

As the season developed, Namath did seem curiously tentative. He was calling fewer plays at the line. But by his own estimation, his problem was more than a matter of touch. "There's nothing physically wrong with me," he said. "I guess I'm just not reacting to defensive changes the way I did before. Maybe the two years have taken something away."

■　　■　　■

On Saturday, December 9, the Jets' charter flight turned around on the runway at JFK. Namath had just arrived at the gate, half an hour late, and there was no way the team was going to Oakland without him. Riggins was already out; he would miss the last two games for "minor" surgery to repair cartilage damage in his right knee. But a victory on Monday in Oakland would keep the Jets alive for a wild-card play-off berth.

Certainly, Roone Arledge was thankful that Namath made his appointed flight. Broadway Joe was at his best that Monday night—despite a sore throat, five dropped passes (two in the end zone, according the *Post*'s Larry Merchant), and ankles that were badly twisted in the fourth quarter. The ankles forced him to leave the game briefly. He came back three plays later, on fourth and ten, and threw a fourteen-yard first down.

Namath threw for 403 yards that night. It was the second 400-yard game of 1972. Both went into the record books beside his name.

Once again, Arledge had his prime-time Achilles. Even Raider fans rose to cheer as Namath hobbled off the field on those bum ankles. "I was standing there on the sidelines in total awe of the guy," said Raiders offensive tackle Bob Brown. "He was like a magician."

"He can start off next season just where he left off this one," said Ewbank.

The newspaper guys recorded these observations with great gusto. But lost in this euphoric discussion was a startling contradiction of the Jets' central assumption, the conceit on which the team was based.

Namath was great. And they still lost.

The following June, former White House counsel John Dean appeared before the Senate's Select Committee on Presidential Campaign Activities, better known as the Watergate committee. His testimony introduced a series of memorandums Dean had filed as "Opponents List and Political Enemies Project." "I was not the compiler of the names," he says. "I was just the repository of this stuff."

The memos, comprising thirteen exhibits, became infamous as "The Enemies List." Nixon's foes were a varied bunch, numbering in the hundreds and drawn from the worlds of politics, labor, business, academia, and media. Under the heading "Celebrities" were ten performers, including Steve McQueen, Paul Newman, Bill Cosby, and Barbra Streisand. This category also included the single athlete to achieve enemy status:

"Joe Namath, New York Giants; businessman; actor."

Dean does not know exactly what prompted Namath's inclusion on the list, or his misidentification as a member of the Giants. The president himself, a fan so devoted he would call the Redskins coach to suggest plays, wouldn't have made that sort of mistake. Thus Dean believes that the quarterback's classification probably owed to zealous staffers who overheard Nixon make a crack about Namath.

42. DON'T TRUST ANYONE OVER THIRTY

Some athletes would have enjoyed the cachet conferred by inclusion on Nixon's list. "Ali," quipped Dave Anderson, "has been searching for new speechwriters, to make sure he's on the next updated list."

Former Cardinals linebacker Dave Meggysey probably wouldn't have minded Enemy status, either. "It is no accident that Richard Nixon, the most repressive President in American history, is a football freak," Meggysey wrote in his well-publicized book *Out of Their League*. In 1970, at the age of twenty-nine, he retired, explaining that "the glorification of individual and collective violence was a royal bummer."

There was a bunch of guys like Meggysey, who considered the NFL a clue to the American condition. But to Namath, they didn't make any more sense than the Fellowship of Christian Athletes, which urged ballplayers to "make yardage for the Lord." Namath wanted no part of these debates. Namath was only a symbol of Namath, assiduously apolitical, a model for future generations of high-priced athlete-endorsers. It wasn't his job to be *involved*. Politics was a dirtier business than shaving cream or chocolate milk, and certainly didn't pay as well, either. "I don't like to get involved in politics," said Namath at his football camp when the news broke. "I have my beliefs but they're private. I've been asked often to back people or to appear for them but I won't. I won't link my name to anything I don't know about."

For the sake of clarification, Jimmy Walsh added: "Joe Namath has never been critical of the President, his administration, the White House or anyone in government."

After all, Republicans bought popcorn makers, too.

■   ■   ■

Namath still partied plenty. But he did so with a greater sense of discretion, a newfound attention to the wholesome, and increasingly profitable, aspects of his image. The White House failed to realize that Namath was becoming, in many ways, a card-carrying member of the Establishment. He was a founding father of the Super Bowl, a game whose most recent vintage (in which the Dolphins beat Nixon's beloved Redskins) saw NBC ask sponsors for $200,000 per minute of airtime. Namath, long-haired hard hat, declared himself a big fan of "The Star-Spangled Banner." "Every time I hear it before a game," he said, "it reminds me of where we are in the world, in life. I kind of thank God that we're in this country. When I hear it, I get a chill."

Were those the words of a subversive? Would an enemy of the Republic appear on *The Brady Bunch*, as Namath did later that year? The episode, "Mail-Order Hero," is avidly remembered by the Butter-Up generation: Bobby Brady lies to his school pals, telling them he knows Joe Namath. Recognizing that her brother has gotten himself in too deep, Cindy Brady writes the football hero, informing him that Bobby is dying and that his final wish is to meet Joe (who'll just happen to be in town for an upcoming game). Somehow, "Mail-Order Hero" eventually gained status as classic TV. Namath himself seems comfortable in the role, at home amid the canned laughter. But then, he wasn't really acting; he was just playing Joe.

Ostensibly due to his television obligations, Namath was given his customary courtesy—an extra week to report to camp. After that term expired, his entrance aroused the usual fanfare. Receiver David Knight, a sure-handed rookie from William and Mary, likened seeing Namath in the huddle to seeing Jagger in concert.

The comparison was not unfounded. Namath, like Jagger, turned thirty that year. And while Bobby Brady loved him, there were other kids for whom puberty came laced with cynicism. They could now wonder about Namath, as they wondered about all the over-thirties: was this guy to be trusted?

Namath was more apart from the team than ever. In accordance with the NFL's collective-bargaining agreement, players received a 60-cent cost of living raise that summer, bringing their salary to $14.50 a day through training camp. At that rate, most guys had to eat in the cafeteria. But Joe ate most of his meals at Bill's Meadowbrook, where he also took his drinks. The bartenders knew to have a tall one ready for him when he came off the field. Joe usually took it to go, straight up to his dorm room.

Long gone were his days as the team's rebel, the standards for rebellion having changed. For the first time since '65, Namath wasn't the big story at training camp. That distinction now belonged to John Riggins. By comparison, Riggins made Namath look tame.

Namath's hobbies ran to golf and booze, same as most middle-aged businessmen. Riggins drove through Indian country on his motorcycle. Riggins's tastes ran to beer, silver jewelry with turquoise stones, and magic mushrooms. Riggins, who had no agent, did his own negotiating.

By a vote of his teammates, he was also the team's reigning MVP. Riggins had gained 944 yards in only twelve games before knee surgery ended his 1972 season. He took a real beating for his money; even Weeb acknowledged as much. Over the winter, he sent Riggins a $1,500 bonus, minus $600 for taxes. "It would have been higher if you got 1,000 yards," he wrote.

Riggins might well have, but Weeb's line was built to protect Namath, not to block for a back. Riggins might've been a stud, but he'd already seen what happens to studs. His locker had been near Matt Snell's. After snapping his Achilles, Snell spent the better part of three seasons trying to come back. But he never took another handoff, and instead was relegated to special-teams duty until finally he ruptured his spleen throwing a block on a kickoff return. Two ribs had pierced the organ. Dr. Nicholas ran out on the field to get him. "Let me up, Doc," Snell told him. "I want to walk off myself."

Riggins returned Ewbank's check, uncashed. He didn't want charity. He wanted a raise: from $25,000 to $150,000 per season, 100 times his "bonus." As Namath and the other veterans started working that summer, Riggins stayed home, hunting and fishing in Kansas. He sent Weeb a telegram: NEED MORE GREEN BEFORE I GET MEAN.

Ewbank replied that Riggins should be more realistic.

PLEASE DEFINE REALISTIC, Riggins wired back.

Almost two months would pass before Riggins signed a contract. The deal was finalized on September 13, just four days before the season opener in Green Bay, and was worth approximately $130,000 over two years. The 230-pound fullback arrived in Weeb's office bare-chested, in leather pants and a bowler hat. His bushy hair had been fashioned in a Mohawk.

No one had much to say about Namath's long locks anymore.

■   ■   ■

Later that day, the team arrived in full pads at Rikers Island, the city prison complex in Jamaica Bay, where Riggins entertained the inmates with an Apache-style war cry. The Jets, forced to vacate Hofstra before the college semester began, couldn't hold workouts at Shea until the Mets' season ended. Having to practice on the grounds of a penal colony was yet another indignity suffered by the players. For all the money they were paying Namath, Ewbank had hastened their transformation into a low-rent organization.

Ewbank was in his final year as coach now, and had already named his successor. Passed over were some of the wiser choices, including Chuck Knox (who would coach the Rams to a record of 12–2 that season) and Walt Michaels, greatly respected by most of the defensive players, in favor of Charley Winner. As a gunner in the Air Force, Winner had survived a stint in a German POW camp. As a coach in the NFL, he compiled a record of 35–30–5 in five seasons with the Cardinals. Black players were said to be unhappy in St. Louis, and none of Winner's teams ever qualified for the postseason. But he had one outstanding credential: Charley Winner was Ewbank's son-in-law.

Nepotism notwithstanding, Weeb's stamp of approval couldn't have done much to enhance Winner's standing among the players. That September, Ewbank traded Don Maynard to Philadelphia. Maynard had been in professional football since 1958, and had more catches and more receiving yards than anyone who'd ever played the game. There were still guys, like Larry Grantham, who swore they'd never seen Maynard caught from behind. But Weeb and his coaches wanted to make room on the roster for a kickoff-return specialist named Margene Adkins. The trade was Ewbank's way to avoid cutting a future Hall of Famer.

One account had Maynard tearfully pleading his case to an assistant coach as Namath looked away. "It was devastating," allows Maynard. "Ain't no one on that ballclub was faster than I was. I should've had a press conference and let the people go burn Weeb's house down."

Another fourteen years would pass before the Jets got around to retiring Maynard's number. The Giants would have done better; Wellington Mara was nothing if not loyal. But the Jets remained ever bound to Werblin's formula, a bit of old Broadway press agentry that measured a star by the demand for his publicity shot. The Jets received 40,000 requests a year for Namath's photo. Maynard was the next most requested player, with 300 requests.

■   ■   ■

The preseason itinerary included a stop in Tampa, where the Jets faced the Philadelphia Eagles. After only eight plays, Gerry Philbin, now of the Eagles, took his shot at Namath. It was a cheap one: Philbin hit him high, but late, after Namath had gotten rid of the ball. Not that it mattered to the ex-Jet. "He wasn't going to get away," says Philbin. Namath had come to represent everything that pissed him off about the Jets. Charity? Here's your charity, Weeb.

Namath got up and hollered at his former teammate, which only seemed to amuse Philbin. He had done what even Ben Davidson and Ike Lassiter had been unable to do. He had gotten to Joe. "For $250,000 a year," Philbin said after the game, "he can take a shot or two."

Still, despite the Philadelphia game, Namath emerged from the preseason in relatively good shape. He credited a new regimen of vitamins and Transcendental Meditation, which he learned from Bob Oates Jr., a semipro quarterback with whom he collaborated on a coffee-table book entitled *A Matter of Style*.

"I thought it would help him tremendously and I told him," says Oates, son of a venerable *Los Angeles Times* football writer. "Joe told me he used to throw up before every game and when he meditated, that just went away."

Meditation—when Namath remembered to practice it—provided him with what he'd been trying to get from money, liquor, and sex: freedom from worry, a higher state of relaxation. "Twenty minutes in the morning and twenty in the evening," Joe once said. "That's all you need. You'll feel better than you ever felt. . . . Your nervous system gets a state of rest that you never get at any other time. . . . The more you do, the more peace you have."

Unfortunately, TM was powerless against the orthopedic perils of football. Early in the second game of the season, with the Jets only five yards from Baltimore's end zone, the Colts sent both outside linebackers on a blitz. "Any man of decent mobility could have dodged the straight-line blitz of linebacker Stan White," wrote Dick Young, "but Joe can't move. He went into his turtle defense, pulling in his neck."

Rising from the turf after White had crashed down on him, there was something noticeably odd about the angle of Namath's torso. "Short season, wasn't it?" said one of the writers, watching from the press box.

The diagnosis was immediate: the impact had torn the ligaments of Namath's right shoulder, separating it from the socket. Under the best circumstances, a separated shoulder would cause him to miss between six and eight weeks. If it required an operation, he'd miss the entire season.

Frank Namath held his brother's hand in the locker room. Then he called their mother. Joe assured Rose that he would be fine.

As the Jets filed out of Memorial Stadium, Stan White was waiting for him. He wanted to say he was sorry. Joe told him not to worry.

On the way back to New York, Namath sat in the rear of the aircraft with Bob Skaff. Donald Lillis's daughter, Helen, who had dated the record company executive, brought them miniature bottles of vodka.

"How much can I drink before it affects the medication I'll get?" asked Namath, who was in obvious pain.

"If you drink enough," said Jeff Snedeker, the trainer, "you won't need any medication when you get to the hospital."

After five vodkas, Namath relented and took one of Dr. Nicholas's painkillers.

In just a few hours, it would be the first anniversary of Namath's 496-yard game against Unitas. As the flight neared New York, Paul Zimmerman made his way to the back of the plane. "If you rest your elbow on the tray table," he said, "it won't hurt as much."

Namath eyed him suspiciously. "How the fuck would you know?"

Zimmerman explained that he'd had the same injury, hoping that this might break the ice between them. But his was a misplaced hope. It would be another seventeen years before their next conversation.

■   ■   ■

The Mets made a surprise run to the World Series that year, which meant the Jets couldn't play a home game until the 28th of October. It didn't turn out to be much of a homecoming, a 40–28 loss to Denver. But by then, at 1–6, with Al Atkinson now out for eight games with a groin pull, the season was already a lost cause. Namath resumed practicing the following week, an experience that proved less than encouraging, as he watched his passes die in the wind. "Damn," he said. "It's like trying to throw a slingshot with a noodle."

Not long afterward, Namath sat down for an interview with Sal Marchiano, now with New York's ABC affiliate, for the eleven o'clock *Eyewitness News*. Namath said, quite clearly, that his shoulder was "very bad" and that he did not expect to return that season. Marchiano asked if he would return next year to play for Charley Winner's team. "It depends if the coach will have me back," said Joe. "I haven't played enough in the past few years to earn a spot on the team."

Marchiano's interview quickly gathered momentum as a big story: Namath forecasting the end of his season, and quite possibly, his career. But Joe denied it all the following day, dismissing the report as a hoax. "Everybody would be better off if they didn't take the news so seriously," he said.

Namath played that Sunday in Cincinnati, where the Jets finally ran out of time down six points and less than a yard from the Bengals' end zone. The Jets complained that they got no respect from the officials. More alarming, though, was their lack of respect from NBC, which two weeks later opted to bump a Jets-Colts game from its schedule in favor of a more meaningful contest between the Chiefs and the Browns.

The following Sunday featured a rematch with Gerry Philbin and the Eagles, but Namath's right knee was too sore to play. Aspiration three days before the game no longer did the trick, not at age thirty. Now came another flurry of stories, wondering if this was indeed the end for Joe.

"Sure this could be my last game," he said, days before the season finale against Buffalo. "But so what?"

Curiously, nobody seemed more mournful at the prospect of his retirement than Dick Young: "The last thing I want is for Joe Namath to be washed up. The fact that I cannot respect the man's philosophies, nor admire his unquenchable thirst for yes-men, for flattery, does not diminish the genuine appreciation for his abounding talents.

"I dread the day Joey Baby will be finished. Any newspaperman does. Namath is great copy. . . . He sells newspapers."

For now, though, only Weeb's retirement was certain. The Jets had given him an electric mower before his final game on a snowy Sunday at Shea. Weeb wept as he said good-bye to his players. "I failed you," he told them. But the coach who'd won championships for both the Colts and the Jets was himself overshadowed that afternoon, as the Bills' O. J. Simpson ran for 200 yards, making him the first back ever to run for 2,000 yards in a season.

The Jets lost 34–14, finishing the season at 4–10.

Late in the game, fans started to pelt the home team's bench with snowballs. One of them just missed Namath. The old quarterback picked it up and fired it back in the crowd.

Stupid kids.

Namath soon abandoned thoughts of retirement. He still couldn't rid himself of the desire to play, or, more precisely, his desire to play well. "It's a helluva lot easier to go out on a good year than a bad year," he said.

As usual, his off-season included a few rounds at the American Airlines golf tournament. Then he was off to the Bahamas, the waters off Great Harbor Cay in the Exuma Islands, where Joe and his pals traveled by boat. They liked to fish, and on this occasion, water-ski.

It was waterskiing, not football, that delivered the final insult to Namath's lower extremities. The tow rope, as Joe recalled, was brand-new. But just as he was getting up over the water, it snapped—and then so did his hamstring. As his concerned friends looked on from the boat, Namath managed to float and gave the thumbs-up sign. "I didn't want to get anybody upset," he would recall.

43. HIGH CONCEPT

He didn't know what was happening to him: "They helped me in the boat and my body just started vibrating and shaking. I went into shock and didn't realize it. Hey, you tear two of the biggest muscles in your body and you're shivering cold, freezing."

Two of the three muscles in his left hamstring had been severed. "Just rolled down like a window shade," he said. They settled in a mangled mass the size of a grapefruit behind his thigh.

Without a hamstring he would be literally unable to stride. But there was little that medical science could do for his shorn muscles: this wound was unhealable. It would limit his mobility even more than the knees. Still, Dr. Nicholas encouraged Joe to cheer up.

"You only need a hamstring to run," he said. "You're a quarterback, you don't need to run anyway."

■   ■   ■

Meanwhile, Namanco—dedicated to what Jimmy would call "the concept of Joe Namath"—continued to prosper. Walsh's chief deputy and occasional whipping boy was Jim Griffin, who went on to great success at the William

Morris Agency. The firm's vice president was Sam Iselin, brother of the Jets' president. Later, Jimmy would hire Mike Martin, who joined Namanco after a stint as director of football operations for the upstart World Football League. Given that several of Jimmy's clients were Jet players—including Emerson Boozer and Winston Hill, among others—Namanco's hierarchy seems a somewhat incestuous arrangement. But that never seemed to bother Jimmy.

A Walsh negotiation had a specific protocol. It began, recalls Martin, with "something outrageous, a figure that had no bearing on anything, just zeroes and zeroes." Typically, Jimmy's opening gambit resulted in shock, then dismay, and finally, stalemate. As the season drew near, Jimmy would give Martin new instructions: "Here's what we're gonna do: you're going to play the role of the ex-Jet employee." Martin's task was to assure his former colleagues that Jimmy might have been a little carried away—Jimmy was, after all, Jimmy—before throwing out a somewhat more reasonable figure. That's how the deals got done.

But the real business of Namanco, and its wholly owned subsidiary, Planned Licensing Inc., was always Namath. His endorsements now included a wide assortment of textiles. Franklin sporting goods made official Joe Namath uniforms. Arrow Shirts had an entire Joe Namath signature line with jackets, slacks, and sport shirts in a variety of gaudy synthetic prints. Fieldcrest Mills made Joe Namath bedsheets, part of "The Playmaker Collection."

Ad writers everywhere saw Namath as an imaginary friend—part man, part concept—who could make a product succeed. Among them was Peggy King, a copywriter with Long, Haymes & Carr, an agency in Winston-Salem, North Carolina. Peggy shared an office with a junior copywriter named Dave, whom she remembers as "a true son of the seventies, drifting from job to job and numbing the dread of real work with marijuana." One day Dave returned from lunch "in a sweet-smelling haze" complaining about the creative director, who wanted an outrageous new campaign for a rapidly declining brand, Hanes Beautymist pantyhose.

Peggy and Dave traded ideas across the partition that divided their workstations. "What about Burt Reynolds?" she said. It was a great idea. Reynolds had just appeared in *Playgirl*. But Dave did not respond. Finally, she looked around the partition and found Dave asleep on his typewriter.

That didn't mean he wasn't listening. At the next day's meeting, Dave offered the Burt Reynolds idea, which was enthusiastically received. But Reynolds wanted too much money, and again, Dave was stumped.

Not long after that, Peggy had occasion to be watching *Monday Night Football* and heard Howard Cosell opining about "the most abused legs in sports." Now *that* was an idea.

When she suggested Namath for Beautymist, the creative director was not impressed. "Yeah, everybody says, 'Namath,'" he told her. "That's obvious."

But then she told him her idea for the commercial, which wasn't so obvious. Soon the storyboard arrived at Namanco, where it sat while Namath and
Jimmy deliberated. It was a good goof, and a great gimmick, but they were
concerned about the public's reaction. Then Harry Benson, a photographer
who shot Namath for the cover of *Life* (and, later, *People*), came up with a visual solution: Have a great-looking woman sidle up to Joe in the final frame.
Her willing peck on his cheek would dispel any confusion.

And that's exactly how it was shot. As the commercial begins, the camera
moves in time with a cymbal roll: panning horizontally across pantyhose-clad
feet, calves, thighs, then green satin shorts and a familiar jersey to reveal the re-
clining, dimpled quarterback in full grin. "Now I don't wear pantyhose," he
drawls, "but if Beautymist can make *my* legs look good, imagine what they'll
do for yours."

Namath was less amused when he saw the final product. "I hated how I
looked," he said. "I hated how I sounded. I almost got sick."

But the commercial was huge, *huge*. Baby boomers would commit Namath's pantyhose hustle to their collective memory. It was right up there with
the Guarantee.

■   ■   ■

Of course, the squares would make their remarks. But then, who could really
question the manliness of Monday night's Achilles, the one who'd withstood
so many charges from Davidson and Lassiter? There was no shame in wearing
pantyhose; the only shame would have been not getting paid for it.

As the concept of Joe evolved, the likeness of Joe became a proprietary
matter. Namanco was absolutely determined not to give it away. In 1973, Namath sued *Sports Illustrated* and its parent company, Time Inc., for $2.25 mil-
lion for "wrongful and unauthorized use of his name." The charge arose from
ads for two subscription campaigns, each of which featured a photograph of
him that originally appeared in the magazine's Super Bowl III coverage. The
first was seen in *Sports Illustrated, Life,* and the *Daily News,* with the line: "How
to Get Close to Joe Namath." The second, which ran in *Cosmopolitan, Better
Homes & Gardens,* and *1001 Decorating Ideas,* targeted women: "The Man You
Love Loves Joe Namath."

The court papers left little doubt that Namath's fury over the Bachelors III
coverage, now four years past, had hardly subsided: "From June, 1969 to the
present, the defendants have conducted through the magazine SPORTS ILLUS-
TRATED, a malicious campaign to malign, disgrace and impugn the plaintiff's
integrity and honesty and in general to present to the reading public an untrue
and unfair representation of the plaintiff."

Namath continued the theme in his own affidavit, filed later in the proceedings: "It is well known among people in the sports, entertainment and

publishing industries that I have been grossly mistreated over the years by *Sports Illustrated* magazine. The magazine has always attempted to project me in the worst possible light."

Aside from the story on high-stakes craps games at his apartment, it is difficult to tell what so distressed Namath about the magazine's coverage of him. Though he was featured on seven *Sports Illustrated* covers—from the famous nocturnal shot on Broadway to the photo with Victoria George on the set of *The Last Rebel*—his court papers are willfully oblivious to their publicity value. What's more, he had also appeared in Harry Benson pictorials that ran on the covers of *People* and *Life,* both Time publications.

Although Time won its motion for summary judgment, Namath pursued the case all the way to the state court of appeals, a process that took almost three years. But this was a price he willingly paid, for again, he was defending one of his principles. Whether it appeared in spaghetti Westerns or pantyhose ads, his likeness was *his.* He wasn't giving it away, certainly not to a magazine he disdained. *That* was the concept of Joe.

In June 1974 he went to federal court to sue Topps Chewing Gum. Long the manufacturer of bubble gum trading cards, Topps bought the right to use players' photographs from the Licensing Corporation of America, which in turn had a deal with the NFL Players Association (NFLPA). The players union depended on this revenue. But Namanco wasn't representing the rank and file. Topps was warned by one of Jimmy's lawyers: "Namanco Productions, Inc. is party to an exclusive services contract with Mr. Namath and, therefore, is responsible for authorizing such usage. Your agreement with the N.F.L. Players Association has no force and effect since Mr. Namath is not a signatory to the Players Association licensing agreement."

Topps responded by asserting that its agreement with the Players Association gave it rights to "the pictures or likenesses of all of the football players in the National Football League." That included Namath, who had signed a standard players contract and still belonged (perhaps reluctantly) to the players union.

Namanco was particularly irked by the use of Namath's photo in a Topps puzzle game. Joe had already endorsed another puzzle, and no one had requested permission for this additional use. Jim Griffin wrote a letter to the union boss, Ed Garvey, saying that the NFLPA's conduct "indicates a blatant disregard for Mr. Namath" and an "attitude" that "we cannot tolerate."

In fact, Garvey had already asked Topps to cease using Namath in the puzzle, and Topps had agreed, believing that would resolve the matter. But Namath sued anyway, claiming that the company had been using his name and photo without "written consent" since his rookie year, 1965. Such unauthorized use constituted a violation of Namath's civil right to privacy, for which he wanted $750,000 in damages.

Namath's suit prompted Topps, in turn, to sue the licensing corporation, the president of the Players Association, and the NFL's treasurer. The adjoining cases were finally dismissed, by agreement of all the parties, in 1976. But Jimmy seemed to think all the time and money pursuing the case had been well spent. The concept of Joe demanded that he send a message: Anyone caught trying to use Namath's likeness without paying could expect a kick in the balls.

■   ■   ■

Roone Arledge, on the other hand, was more than willing to pay. For months, he courted Namath to replace Don Meredith, who left *Monday Night Football* after the '73 season. Cosell was all for the hiring of Namath. But Joe himself was more ambivalent. In anticipation of his eventual departure from the game, he had begun taking acting lessons. But his body was a lot closer to retirement than his mind. Joe still wanted to play, and Arledge was apparently willing to let him, offering a private plane to facilitate transit to and from the Monday night games. That wasn't all. "They offered many millions of dollars," Jimmy once recalled. "But not enough."

The word was Jimmy opened the negotiation by asking for $10 million, a figure he didn't deny: "If you don't ask for something, you can't get it." Jimmy also asked for low-interest loans and a percentage of ABC's Sports Division. By industry standards, Jimmy's price was crazy, but Arledge kept talking to him.

Finally, over Jimmy's angry objections, the Jets killed the deal. They didn't want a part-time quarterback, nor, in the end, did Joe want to be one.

Instead, Joe showed up for camp, where reporters first learned of his hamstring troubles. Namath admitted he wasn't yet dropping back as quickly as he'd like, but the press had no idea how severe the injury really was. The next day's papers described it as a "pulled" muscle. Otherwise, Namath looked to be in great shape, fit and tan, rested.

He had arrived in a chauffeured limousine with his lawyer, following what had been a short-lived strike by the Players Association. Other star quarterbacks—including Johnny Unitas, the Cowboys' Roger Staubach, and the Dolphins' Bob Griese—had broken ranks with the union and crossed the picket lines. Namath hadn't crossed the line, but he didn't picket, either. "Joe didn't come down on either side of the issue," says Steve Tannen, the Jets' player rep. While other Jets had been carrying signs at Hofstra, Joe had remained in Tuscaloosa on the advice of his attorney, Jimmy Walsh.

In anticipation of the 1974 season, Charley Winner wrote a letter to his players. The new Jets coach informed them that he expected, among other things, "100 percent of your time and attention to football." Winner wanted to put players on notice: the leniency and tardiness that characterized his father-in-law's regime would no longer be tolerated. Namath was not impressed. "I'll go out and do my job," he said, "but I don't need any jive."

The question soon arose, though, of just who was jiving whom. The Jets lost seven of their first eight games, a stretch during which Namath threw seventeen interceptions. Winner was politic enough to offer a couple of excuses— broken patterns and missed blocks—on behalf of his star. But even the most ardent Namath admirers had to admit that the end was at hand. This was his tenth season as a professional quarterback; the position now belonged to men who were bigger, stronger, faster, and most of all, younger. Concern for his knees missed the point; the more pertinent injury went unmentioned. That lump of herniated hamstring inflicted additional abuse to his already stooped gait; the erstwhile prince of cool, practitioner of the "we-bad strut," now moved with a stiff-legged hobble that was vaguely Chaplinesque.

44. MAGIC SIX

At one time, Namath couldn't move without great pain and effort. Now he simply couldn't move. Once, his interceptions were the sign of a young man's hubris. Now they signified an old man's desperation. Five of the Jets' first seven losses had been close games. In each of them, Namath's final pass was picked off.

He was generating more rumors than wins. There were stories of him playing out his last days for the World Football League, where his telegenic virtues might save a very sick enterprise, or for the Los Angeles Rams, now owned by Carroll Rosenbloom and coached by Chuck Knox. Rosenbloom, the big sport who used to own the Colts, couldn't forget Super Bowl III. Having been suckered by Namath, he coveted him still. But for most everyone else, the hustler's magic spell was finally wearing off.

On November 10, 1974, the Jets played the Giants for only the second time in the regular season. Again, the venue was the Yale Bowl. As the Giants were 2–6, only one game better than the Jets, this battle for bragging rights would leave even the winner with little to brag about. It drew almost 6,000 fewer fans than the first Jets-Giants exhibition, and was bumped off the air in New York.

The afternoon seemed to offer little more than vestigial emotion—an attachment to the rivalry, if not to the rivals themselves. But Namath felt a very old need bubble up. Losing bragging rights to the Giants would be like losing a rock fight for Jungle Hill.

A players-only meeting preceded the game. Emerson Boozer spoke first, followed by linebacker Ralph Baker, now in his eleventh season. They were tired of being called losers and wanted to win again. But these young guys didn't know about winning. They didn't know what the Giants meant. They didn't know shit.

Then Namath spoke. "This means a lot to us," he said quietly. "It's real, man."

There was something very different about the way his team charged onto the field that day. "I got a chill," recalled Charley Winner.

With Riggins injured, Namath completed his first seven passes. There was a touchdown to David Knight, and a ten-minute scoring drive in the third quarter. But with 8 minutes left in the game, the Jets were down 20–13. They had gone all the way to the Giants' 3, and it was now third down. In the huddle, Namath called 34 Wham. The call—Boozer off-tackle—was a nod to the good old days, when Boozer was virtually unstoppable near the goal line. Then, as Namath went to the line, he saw his angle. There were 64,327 fans in attendance. There was a press box packed with writers and broadcasters, coaches and scouts. There were dozens of players and personnel on the sidelines, twenty-two men on the field, and a crew of officials. There were guys selling pretzels and beer. But there wasn't anyone in that stadium with the ballsy imagination to envision what Namath had in mind. He had studied the Giants on film, and after three quarters, he'd seen enough of them up close. The weakside linebacker, Brad Van Pelt, had been cheating toward the middle. Now, near the goal line, Namath bet he would be coming hard again. Namath had been calling plays at the line all day, but this time, he stayed with what he had called in the huddle. He took the snap. The two lines came together in a grunting, armored collision. Boozer still recalls: "The way the defense was crashing in there, they're all going right to the ball." Boozer took a step across, then forward. He was to follow the fullback between the guard and the tackle. Then he cut through for the ball . . .

The ball . . . Where the fuck was it?

"I hit the hole and stopped," says Boozer. "I don't have the ball. I'm figuring it must've been a bad exchange between me and Joe. Now I'm looking for the ball on the ground."

He wasn't the only one.

"I almost fell out of the press box," said Ken Shipp, the offensive coordinator.

Here was the ultimate expression of his hustler's magic: the con man's instinct he honed in the Blue Room, the illusionist craft of misdirection he'd been taught by Coach Bruno. Joe began by faking his own guys, never telling them he was changing the play. "He had to make *us* believe we were running 34 Wham," says Boozer. If the Jets believed it, then so would the Giants.

"I hear the crowd roar," says Boozer. "Now I know something else is going on. Then I look up and see that sumbitch going into the end zone."

It was like high school. Everyone rushed to the scene of the fraud. Meanwhile, Namath had bootlegged to the weak side. But the fleet-footed boy could no longer run.

"Looked like he had a broom up his ass," said David Knight. "It must have taken him ten seconds to go five yards. . . . He could have gotten killed."

Namath's right flank was entirely exposed, defenseless. With a 1–7 record, in the midst of a season that seemed irretrievably lost, he put himself in a position where a hit could end his career. But there would be no hit. With casual aplomb, Namath waved off the Giant defensive backs as he crossed the goal line. A lot of defenders would have hit the man with the ball, just for good measure, but Spider Lockhart and Eldridge Small backed off. They had to respect the man's magic.

In accordance with new league rules, the game went into sudden-death overtime. Pete Gogolak, the Hungarian-born kicker Mara had signed back in '66, missed the first chance to win with a forty-two-yard field goal. It was close, and Gogolak thought the officials blew the call. But nothing he said could change the course of the afternoon. Namath, who hadn't been sacked or intercepted all day, began by sending Caster into the vacant precincts of the Giants' zone defense. That completion covered forty-two yards. Then he went to his big wide receiver, Jerome Barkum, for another thirteen. Finally, from the 5-yard line, he faked the handoff and hit Boozer in the end zone for the winning touchdown, and the league's first regular season sudden-death win.

Later, in the locker room at Lapham Field House, Namath was asked about a report that had him going to the WFL next season.

"Jimmy Walsh handles that," he said. "I don't think about it right now."

The broadcast noted that Namath would join the new league's Memphis franchise as an owner-player-coach.

Namath had to smile at that. Owner-player-coach? "That's some parlay," he said.

■ ■ ■

Particularly inspired by the win was the young defensive unit. The following week, the Jets intercepted the Patriots' Jim Plunkett four times as Namath threw another pair of touchdowns for a 21–16 win. Then the Dolphins, winners of consecutive Super Bowls, came to Shea. Something was wrong with Joe, though; his teammates could see as much as soon as he walked into the locker room. He kept his sunglasses on, and his thoughts to himself. "It wasn't like he had a bad night or something like that," said Boozer. "He just seemed down." Ken Shipp, the offensive coordinator, tried to go over the game plan with his quarterback. But it was useless. "He just ducked his head," said Shipp.

The crowd started booing Namath in the third quarter, after his third interception. "I was worried about Joe at that point," said Shipp.

Even Namath knew he wasn't right. "I was slow thinking," he'd say later. "My mind wasn't there at all." And yet, with the Jets down by 4 late in the game, he found Caster for a forty-five-yard touchdown. Namath hadn't beaten a winning team since the Super Bowl. But that pass to Caster provided the margin of victory against the defending champions.

Unfortunately, the victory did nothing to relieve Joe's obvious despondency. The night before he had learned that his father was in critical condition in Beaver County Medical Center. John Namath had been admitted with an acutely inflamed gallbladder, acute pancreatitis, emphysema, and an infection in his bloodstream. "His heart stopped last night but they got it going again," said Namath, his voice barely audible in the locker room. "They can't operate because he's having trouble breathing."

His mother had been at the game. "I'll have to tell her now," he said.

There were tears in his eyes as he left for the charter waiting to take him to Beaver Falls.

■   ■   ■

By the next morning, the retired steelworker's condition had been upgraded to "serious." John would continue to improve, as would the Jets. With a single play against the Giants, the transformation had begun. In the remaining six games of the 1974 season, Joe threw eleven touchdowns against only five interceptions (three of them that day against Miami). The Jets won all six. Their last six-game winning streak—six years earlier—culminated in a January victory over the Baltimore Colts. Now something in that bootlegger's magic allowed the franchise to revive a dormant belief.

■   ■   ■

On the season's next-to-last Sunday, Namath was interviewed by Dave Herman, now working for the WOR pregame show. Herman asked if he expected to return in 1975. "I really don't think so," said Joe. "I haven't talked with the owners. But I don't think I'll be back."

Two days later, at a press conference announcing his selection as team

MVP, Namath did an about-face: "I like this team. I don't want to leave the people here. I never have. I don't know a better situation for football."

After beating the Colts in the season finale—a game that saw him throw his eightieth consecutive pass without an interception—he repeated for emphasis: "I don't want to go anywhere else. I want to stay with the Jets. Ten years and I like it."

But even as the clubhouse kid came to take his game jersey for the laundry bin, Joe tucked it into his shaving bag. "I want to keep that," he said, rolling it up tight, a personal memento stuffed in between deodorant and toothpaste.

Once again, Namath's decisive brilliance on the field belied a sense of personal ambivalence. Should I stay, or should I go? Namath played the notes as wistfully as a ballad. But his habit of dropping hints and pronouncements, and their resulting interpretations, had long since become an exhausting ritual for both the Jets and the media.

It was time to negotiate another contract, and those last six games had given him great leverage. Once again, Joe was seen as the only player who could restore the team to health. But one man's cure is another man's fix, and the addiction to Joe—from fans to front office types—was revitalized with a vengeance. Under the right circumstances, it was argued, Broadway Joe could heal the Jets or the Rams or the entire World Football League.

Jimmy Walsh opened the negotiations by asking for $1 million—a year. "If Walsh thinks there is enough money in football to pay Namath a salary of a million dollars," said Phil Iselin, "I'll sell Walsh the club."

In fact, Jimmy was very keen on the idea of ownership. Years before, Tad Dowd had urged him to ask for a piece of the Jets, the right to buy a percentage of the team upon Namath's retirement. Now Walsh asked for "first right of refusal" if the team ever went on sale. In that case, Namanco would put together a bid. "It wouldn't be that difficult," said Jimmy.

The World Football League was already willing to make Namath an owner. The WFL was a curious creation, a crude, stripped-down expression of Sonny's old formula. While the league offered a couple of stars (most of them fading fast), it lacked any real foundation. Its first season, 1974, was a financial disaster, as unpaid players returned en masse to their former NFL teams. But the upstart league responded by procuring even more stars. The core of the Dolphins' championship offense—fullback Larry Csonka, halfback Jim Kiick, and receiver Paul Warfield—signed with the Memphis Southmen for a combined sum reported to be $3.3 million. Calvin Hill, Dallas's three-time Pro Bowl running back, signed with the WFL's Honolulu franchise. Anthony Davis, USC's first team All-American tailback, chose the Southern California Sun over the New York Jets. "They kept talking about New York, about how

Joe Namath had all these great deals," said his agent. "They never talked about why Anthony should play for the Jets."

Still, the centerpiece of the WFL's survival strategy was signing Namath. He had already saved one league. Now, coming off the enchanted six-game spell, he would save another. The plan called for Namath to play for a new franchise, the Chicago Wind. As yet, the team had no employees, no roster, and no stadium in which to play. In fact, the Chicago Wind's entire existence was contingent upon obtaining the services of Joe Namath. But once that happened, it was assumed that the details would magically fall into place.

Of course, that kind of magic didn't come cheap, and so the league owners pledged to personally honor their commitment to him even if their league went bust. "It was a 100 percent solid offer," Walsh would recall. "The most solid offer I've ever been involved with. It started at $4 million and developed into $5 million."

The deal included a $500,000 signing bonus, a $500,000 salary for three years, and a $2 million annuity, $100,000 a year for twenty years. "In all, there were 11 different contracts," said Walsh. Among them were terms for Namath's eventual ownership of a WFL franchise in New York.

Tad Dowd, who helped solicit the deal, urged Jimmy and Joe to take it. Their money was guaranteed, and if the league went under, Namath would become a truly free agent, with all NFL teams—not just the Jets—able to bid for his services. Having acknowledged the undeniable financial sense of it all, Namath began looking for a place in Chicago.

Then again, Chicago was cold. He'd be starting over. And in many ways, he'd be alone. "I think when you're famous, you're more susceptible to being alone," says Mort Fishman. "Joe didn't like being alone. And Jimmy was like an old bubby to him. He always tried to make sure someone was there for Joe." Usually that someone was Hoot Owl or Mort or Timmy Secor. In this case, it was Bob Skaff who considered moving to Chicago.

But at the last minute, Jimmy came up with another condition. "Walsh came up with a brand new demand that could have added another $18 million," a league official told Paul Zimmerman. "He wanted 15 percent of the WFL's total TV package."

That was the end of the deal. Perhaps Jimmy got greedy, but more likely, he knew exactly what he was doing. Joe felt about Chicago the way he felt about personal appearances. "Joe doesn't like to do them," Jimmy once told Dave Anderson. "So his fee is $25,000, and if anybody meets it, I'll raise it to $50,000." The WFL had met all his demands, so Jimmy raised them. Ultimately, the move to Chicago was too far, too cold, and too late for Joe to make.

He was an old thirty-two, and he didn't want to make that kind of change, not even for the money. "You can negotiate only so long and then you got to decide," Namath said later. For all the freedom money could grant, there were limits to the hustle.

Namath had, in fact, been looking forward to a season with the Jets. Those six victories had revived his football spirit. By Joe's account, the team felt better about itself going into '75 than it had going into '68. Hell, if he stayed healthy, the Jets could *win*. How great would that be? How perfect? What a story! Namath's sense of possibility didn't differ much from that of the owners or the fans. He was the fix. He was hooked. He was addicted to himself, as much as the game.

Dave Anderson went to Fort Lauderdale for an exclusive interview with the quarterback. Joe had a new drink, blackberry brandy, and a new club with his old partners, Bobby and Ray. It was called Bachelors III West, out on Oakland Park Boulevard in suburban Broward County. Anderson joined Namath at a dimly lit corner table. That night, Joe explained his reasons for turning down the WFL, while Jimmy revealed the deal that might have been. Jimmy had finally loosened his tie. Anderson could see that the long negotiation had finally left him drained.

"It cost me a couple million," said Jimmy.

■　　■　　■

Meanwhile, the Jets were still offering $1 million for three years. "I'll retire before I sign that contract," said Joe.

By July 15, the first day of training camp, Namath had yet to do either. Instead, he called a press conference for the Four Seasons. There, it was announced that Namath had signed with Fabergé, a cosmetics company with declining earnings. According to *Newsweek:* "The Namath deal is believed to be the biggest ever made with a celebrity spokesman." It reportedly guaranteed him $250,000 for a minimum of eight years, with two six-year options, a package worth between $2 million and $5 million. Jimmy had charmed and cajoled Fabergé owner George Barrie and his son, Richard, who proudly proclaimed that Namath was "what most men wish they could be and most women want."

Who needed the WFL? Who needed the Jets? Namath had Brut aftershave. "Joe told me if they came up with the money we were asking, he'd drink the stuff," said Jimmy.

There was also talk of developing a Namath line of men's cosmetics, perhaps a skin moisturizer. But the bulk of his promotional duties would be spent infusing Brut with the sweet smell of his success, the same whiff of magic that changed scrubs into studs. Look what it had done for his teammates.

"It's carried over from last season," said Namath, referring to the six-game streak. "You see, we had a lot of players who didn't know what it was to be a winner with the Jets. They weren't on the Super Bowl team. Now they know what it's like."

Still, a week later, he remained unsigned and absent from camp. The players held a meeting to discuss the matter among themselves. Rich Caster didn't understand why this year should be any different; Joe was always late. "Joe's being out of camp is his business," he said, "and we shouldn't put pressure on him."

But Riggins, who had called the meeting, said: "I feel Joe should be here. I want him to be here, going through what we're going through, right alongside the rest of us. . . . Joe's a very unusual person, and my idea is to make him more usual." That was a novel position for the team's erstwhile Mohawked holdout.

Namath, unmoved by any of his teammates' arguments, held fast to his own traditions, and did not report until July was all but over. His new salary was easily the league's highest, and more than six times what Riggins was making—even if it was less than Jimmy had been asking. After his opening salvo, Jimmy held firm at $1 million for two years. But Joe ended up settling for about $900,000.

Hey, sometimes you have to take one for the team.

In September 1975, on the eve of their final preseason game, the Jets were joined by a young writer named Rick Telander. He was twenty-six, a former All–Big Ten cornerback for Northwestern, and the author of an acclaimed memoir. A couple of years earlier, *Sports Illustrated* had assigned him a piece on basketball as played on the municipal playgrounds of black Brooklyn. Telander, still strumming his guitar for a band called the Del-Crustaceans, had been a literature major, his tastes ranging from Victor Hugo to Hunter Thompson. "I was going to live an artist's life," he recalls. Bed-Stuy was perfect. For a boy from Peoria, it seemed as exotic as Paris in the twenties.

The following summer, he returned with a mind to stay for a while. It was a great adventure, one he met with a great talent for listening and observing. "I just hung around," he recalls. "I was an expert at hanging around." As his passions and affections were genuine, he was

45. GARDEN CITY JOE

taken in by his subjects. For a while, Telander even coached them, a loose confederation of players called the Subway Stars.

The product of that summer, *Heaven Is a Playground,* set the standard for books on the urban American game, far exceeding the promise commensurate with a $4,500 advance. As it happened, his agent's husband, Tom Wallace, was an editor at Holt, Rinehart and Winston. He was also a huge Jets fan. Convinced that his team was finally going back to the Super Bowl, Wallace drafted Telander to document what the editor expected would be a historic season.

So Telander started hanging around the Jets. The players didn't see him as a writer. Sure, he was writing a *book,* but he could also take your confession. Talking to Rick wasn't like talking to Zimmerman or Larry Fox or Dave Anderson. The notes he took never appeared in the paper. Besides, Rick was like one of the guys, to the point that some of the coaches just assumed he was on the roster. Occasionally, he even filled in for an injured defensive back or wide receiver at practice.

The writer was on familiar ground. Ballplayers, as he himself knew, were still ballplayers, having been granted extended tours of adolescence. Teams were amalgams of their egos and talents, their insecurities and vanities. In many respects, the Jets were not unlike the Subway Stars. What made the Jets different from any other team, though, was the presence of Namath.

Telander met him at the Shoreham Hotel in Washington, D.C., on Saturday, September 6, 1975—the opening entry in the first of three composition books he would fill with notes that season. Telander hadn't been able to reach Namath on the house phone—the switchboard had been jammed since his arrival—so he got word to the Jets' PR man, Frank Ramos, who informed Joe that Dick Schaap had vouched for the young writer. Ramos called back, instructing Telander to be at the bar at 9:00 P.M. There he found Namath wearing a khaki leisure suit and drinking double vodkas with four black teammates. The quarterback then paid the tab and went to the dining room, where Telander, a columnist friend of his, and Namath were joined by Jimmy Walsh. Telander couldn't help but notice Joe's immense charm, even as he sent back his drink. "See if you can't fill it up or something," said Joe.

The waiter returned with a large glass filled to the rim with vodka. Now *that* was more like it. Joe was in a good mood. He spoke of his love for pecan pie in Tuscaloosa and bonefishing off Fort Lauderdale. Other subjects ranged from Richie Allen to Patty Hearst. "What is she trying to prove?" asked Joe. "If I found her in my bed I'd call the police. Hey, I believe in law and order. Damn right."

Namath was far more impressed with a girl he had spent the night with recently. He hadn't known what she looked like until he woke up with her. She wasn't Ann-Margret, put it that way. But he liked her, and he seemed to like her even more for turning down his request for her phone number.

Thoughout the meal, Namath remained the object of strangers' attentions. Girls sent willing glances; guys sent rounds of drinks.

Namath declined all of them graciously. He'd already ordered three carafes of wine for the four people at his dinner table. Besides, he'd been out late the night before. "If I hadn't had a couple Michelobs before practice, I never could have made it," he said.

Telander, who had been cut by the Chiefs after a brief stint in their '73 training camp, now recalled with awe the way some veterans could drink most of the night and still play the next day. Namath, he would write in his composition book, was "that type of athlete. How do they do it?"

Both Joe and Jimmy stiffened when Telander mentioned that he wrote for *Sports Illustrated,* but the chill seemed to pass soon enough. At the end of the meal, Joe paid the check for everyone and went up to his room. The following day the Jets were playing the Washington Redskins in the final exhibition of the preseason. Namath, on good behavior, made curfew with five minutes to spare.

■   ■   ■

Telander had planned on writing a book about the Jets, not Namath. Toward that end, he spoke to David Knight about Led Zeppelin. He spoke to Lou Piccone, an undrafted backup receiver from West Liberty State, about playing out his option. He spoke to Zimmerman about LSD. But somehow the topic of conversation always returned to Namath. Namath *was* the Jets. Telander came to find him immensely likable, and even admirable, but also at the root of the team's considerable dysfunction.

In order to understand the Jets, he excavated a good part of the quarterback's life. He went to Beaver Falls and spoke to Joe's father. He spoke to Butch Ryan and Rich Niedbala and the guys in the Blue Room. He spoke to Jimmy, who held forth on "the concept of Joe." Even Namath himself opened up, as unguarded as he had ever been, or ever would be for the record. He discussed money and Randi, TM and God, and that feeling he would get in his stomach. What emerged from Telander's work was a new portrait, demystifying the quarterback while humanizing him.

Tired of the commute to the Jets' practice facility, Namath had sold his posh Manhattan townhouse. Broadway Joe now rented a modest house on a quiet block in Garden City, Long Island, not far from Hofstra. The owners were an elderly couple, and one imagines they approved of their tenant, a nice boy who still made a habit of saying his prayers: two Our Fathers, two Hail Marys, an Act of Contrition, and a few words on behalf of his family. "That's if I'm not too drunk or if I'm not with a lady," said Joe. The house had a grandfather clock and floral-patterned furniture covers. The most plentiful item in Namath's refrigerator was Skoal, almost two dozen tins of the wintergreen-flavored snuff tobacco.

Telander had a good eye. The Jets locker room, for example, was stocked with Brut shampoo. But Joe, he noticed, was the only player who kept a bottle of antacid in his locker. Sometimes, though, Joe's head hurt worse than his stomach. For those occasions, he might have a beer and a few Bufferin before practice.

Namath's best friend on that '75 team was Richard Neal, the defensive end. Steve Tannen, now on injured reserve, had fallen out with him the year before. As Tannen recalls, they were drinking at Bills when he struck up a conversation with a girl Joe had been talking to: "He came over and grabbed my hair, pulled my head back and said, 'Don't be talking to her.' I said, 'You don't have to worry because I won't be talking to anyone who ever talked to you again.' And that was it."

Nothing like that ever happened with Neal. Unlike Tannen, who had begun to resent Namath's occasional smugness, Neal respected the boundaries between them. "Joe doesn't talk about his personal problems with anybody,"

Neal told Telander. "You don't want to get too deep with him, and he definitely doesn't want to get too deep with you."

Neal was 260 pounds, a black man from Louisiana. But his bond with Namath transcended race, geography, and football. They were both, as he put it, "lonely people." And they both liked to drink. "I'm one of the few dudes who can keep up with him," said Neal.

■   ■   ■

That September, the New England Patriots voted to boycott the final preseason game. More than a year had passed since the last job action—and the players association still hadn't negotiated a contract. Owners had ceased contributing to the pension fund, and players were no closer to gaining meaningful free agency. Within days, five teams voted to walk out in support of the Patriots. Among them were the Jets, who overrode their quarterback's strenuous objections.

"He had a profound attitude against the strike," said Caster. "He said it was not the right way."

With only four days before the season opener in Buffalo, there was a players-only practice at a public park. Only two Jets did not attend: Boozer, who was injured, and Namath. "I told Joe not to come out here," said Neal, the team's new union rep. "He's too valuable to this team to risk getting hurt."

That night, the players held another meeting. Once more, Namath was not present. "I don't think Joe knew about it," said Neal.

The strike, or what there was of one, would collapse within a day, and the Jets returned to work without incident. Then again, given the season ahead of them, a strike wouldn't have been such a bad idea.

■   ■   ■

Al Atkinson, the defensive unit's last link to the Super Bowl, had finally retired. In his wake came a porous unit, lacking both talent and toughness. The Jets allowed more rushing yards and points (an astounding 30.9 per game) than any team in the league. Their pass defense was no better, with opposing quarterbacks averaging better than nine yards each time they threw against the Jets.

These numbers seemed to predicate Namath's game. With the Jets always playing catch-up, he felt compelled to keep throwing long. "He thinks he can come back from three touchdowns behind," Ken Shipp said after the season. "You can't do that anymore. . . . Look around the league. All the quarterbacks are throwing short."

After eight games the Jets were 2–6. Namath led the league in interceptions with nineteen. The interceptions corresponded with another figure: sacks. The offensive line, the foundation of so many Jets teams, was crumbling. Winston Hill and Randy Rasmussen were old. Dave Herman, like John Schmitt, had retired. But the Jets had been unable to find adequate replacements. Namath had already been sacked nineteen times—as many sacks as he had taken in the entire previous season. He had been forced to run from the pocket another eight times—again, as many rushes as he had in all of 1974. Uncountable, though, were the total number of hits—cheap and otherwise—that he took in the course of each game. One particularly brutal afternoon in Baltimore prompted precautionary X-rays of the disjointed vertebrae in his neck. Against the Dolphins, down 20 points with six minutes left, Namath endured two sacks, one vicious hit after releasing the ball, and an interception. But Charley Winner still had him out on the field for a final play with 57 seconds left.

"You know where he's going to be all the time," said Dolphins linebacker Doug Swift. "He's handicapped."

"I'd like to say it can't get any worse," said Namath, whose left wrist was X-rayed after the Miami game. "But I am not really sure it won't."

In a season that lacked competitive suspense, Namath's fate became a gruesome guessing game. The *Daily News* posed the question in a headline: "How Much More Pain Can Namath Take?"

A lot. That was the answer. Namath would always recall seeing his brother Frank smash into a brick wall during a basketball game. "Damn," said Frank, realizing he had lost four teeth. But Frank kept right on playing, and so would Joe. That was the Namath way. It came from the way you were brought up. It came from the blood.

But then, mere physical pain, of which he had a practiced endurance, might have been the least of Namath's problems. There were other signs of his obsolescence. Less than a month into the season, the coaching staff started sending in plays for Namath to run. In a way, this was the cruelest insult for an aging hustler. The best calls in Jet history—the bootleg against the Giants, 19 straight against the Colts, Maynard down the sidelines against the Raiders— were all traps set with Namath's knowledge of the angles. But the coaches didn't want him playing the angles anymore; the spell had worn off. Worst of all, Joe offered no protest. "What scares me," one teammate told Paul Zimmerman, "is when Joe just accepts everything without saying a word. He might have his own thing in mind, something he wants to set up on his own, and when he just takes their play and runs it, it's like he's saying, 'The hell with it' and giving up."

What did they expect? He wasn't a young man anymore; he was Garden City Joe, a rare sight on his East Side stomping grounds. He couldn't stand the drive in from the suburbs. "Traffic's too damn bad," he said.

■　■　■

After losing 52–19 in Baltimore, a game in which Namath was sacked six times, the Jets finally fired Weeb Ewbank's son-in-law. Ken Shipp became "interim head coach," but the Jets kept losing. They were 3–9 going into their

Monday night game with the Chargers. San Diego meant a long plane ride. Of course, Joe and Richard Neal had devised a way to get around the team rule against drinking on the flight to away games: Neal would stash a bottle in his carry-on shoulder bag. Telander watched as they "managed to sip their way through a quart of vodka, after which Joe put on his sunglasses to conceal eyelids made of lead."

Two nights later, Namath missed curfew. Shipp actually fined him $500, and started the backup, J. J. Jones. Not since Bryant suspended him in 1963 had Namath missed any time for disciplinary reasons. The Chargers drew 52,446 that night, easily their biggest crowd of the season. The fans, especially those who came to boo Namath, voiced their displeasure at the announcement. Shipp had just wanted to make a point, though, and brought Namath on in the second quarter with the Jets down 7–3. They lost 24–16.

There was still one more game to play, a bitter cold date with the Cowboys at Shea. The temperature was around 20 degrees, with winds gusting up to 50 miles per hour, as Namath kept handing the ball to Riggins, who began the day fifty-seven yards shy of 1,000. Telander recalled that earlier in the season every player on the team had received a freebie shirt from Arrow's Joe Namath collection. But Riggins's shirt was still hanging, untouched, in his locker. In the second half, Riggins finally became the Jets' first 1,000-yard rusher (and would remain so for some time). That winter Riggins became a free agent. He told the Jets that he'd stay, but only for the same money as Namath. It was his way of getting out.

As for Joe, he didn't complete a pass against the Cowboys until the fourth quarter. He finished the game 1 for 8 for 7 yards, the worst day of his career. Finally, Dallas defensive end Harvey Martin laid him out on the frozen ground. Namath, with bruised ribs and a twisted knee, stayed down for an uncomfortably long while. Those moments provided little more than Telander's last frame. The writer was done hanging around. He had decided to call his book *Joe Namath and the Other Guys*. It was not the championship diary his editor had imagined. Telander might have done an even better job exploring the Jets locker room than the Brooklyn schoolyards, but who wanted to read about a guy who led the league in interceptions?

The book ends with Namath on the ground, having just endured the season's final, monstrous hit. A reserve running back recounts the scene: "Joe was sort of scrunched up on the ice, and I didn't know if he was hurt bad or what. When I could finally see his face, you know what I saw he was doing? He was *laughing*. The sonofabitch was lying there on the ice *laughing*."

For all of Namath's ambivalence about show business, both he and Jimmy had long spoken of their plans to go Hollywood once his playing days were over. In the meantime, the Los Angeles Rams seemed to offer everything he could want toward that end. The Rams practiced in hospitable weather. As they had just come off a 12–2 season, their Super Bowl aspirations did not challenge anyone's imagination. And owner Carroll Rosenbloom still coveted, as Dick Young once put it, "the thrill of parading Namath on his arm around the movie colony."

After the Jets' season ended, Namath began his own televised campaign, Hollywood or bust. "It would be a good idea for Rosenbloom to call me," he told Johnny Carson. Ten days later, on the Super Bowl pregame show, he was asked if he were going to be traded to the Rams. "I hope so," said Joe.

But even Hollywood fantasies are bound by budgets. Namath's salary for the 1976 season was $500,000— more than double that of the league's

46. HOLLYWOOD ENDING

second-highest-paid player, O. J. Simpson. The Jets were contractually obligated to pay him; Rosenbloom was not. As much as he loved the idea of bringing Joe to the Rams, he wasn't paying half a mil for a guy with no knees and no hamstring. Hollywood Joe was suspended in preproduction.

■   ■   ■

Namath's personal affairs had likewise come to a standstill.

Not every woman would be comfortable with a man who palled around with Joe, but Carol Erickson, Mort Fishman's longtime girlfriend, didn't have a problem with it. She got a kick out of Joe, even his habitual reading. "He wanted to obtain the knowledge that he didn't get through college," says Carol. "I admired that." Namath's self-imposed syllabus was heavy on travelers' guides, though Carol also recalls his enthusiasm for the novels of Richard

Bach, particularly a thin inspirational volume called *Illusions,* in which the messiah is a mechanic from Fort Wayne.

Over the years, the two couples spent a fair amount of time together, Mort and Carol and Joe and Randi. They played golf in Florida and watched sunsets in Connecticut, near the football camp. Randi stayed in Joe's cottage by the lake, which is where Carol first met her. "I remember she had a bandanna on her head," says Carol. "She was cooking dinner for everyone. She looked like the girl next door—but absolutely gorgeous."

Namath insisted on calling her "Betty," the name she was born with—Betty Lee Oakes. Carol was impressed, thinking: *He's calling her who she really is.*

Carol's own affections, like Randi's, were tempered by a sense of realism. Mort wasn't a one-woman guy, but she knew he'd settle down eventually. In the meantime, she had patience. Randi seemed equally pragmatic, but by the summer of 1976 her patience had been all but exhausted.

Carol still recalls the weekend: Randi was crying, sitting in that same kitchen where they had met. "She was devastated," says Carol. "She totally wanted to settle down with him. And I think he was totally in love with her, too. But he did not want to settle down. That weekend was going to be the last weekend she would be there. . . . It was really sad. It seemed like if it wasn't going to work out, then she wanted to get as far away as she could."

Randi was going to California. She wanted to be an actress. Joe, who was pretty broken up, too, promised to help any way he could.

"I love her and she loves me," he had said earlier that year. "But I know it is not permanent. I know it can't last because I'm going to keep moving."

He had settled on not settling down, running around but still running in place.

■   ■   ■

The Jets' new coach was Lou Holtz. At thirty-nine, he'd had some success at William and Mary, and more recently, at North Carolina State. Holtz was a proponent of the Veer Offense, which called for a quarterback with strong, young legs. The Veer was a college-style option, and Holtz was a rah-rah college-style coach. He was the kind of stickler who demanded that players give a properly spirited clap when breaking the huddle. He wanted socks worn at the same length, and jerseys tucked in just so. He even wrote a Jets fight song, to be sung after every win, to the tune of "The Caissons Go Rolling Along": *Win the game, fight like men, we're together win or lose, New York Jets go rolling along.*

Holtz envisioned numerous changes, beginning with Namath. Now thirty-three, Joe would no longer be a straight drop-back passer. "We'll make a half-roll," said Holtz. "If he can't do that, he needs Medicaid."

Of course, it behooved the coach to speak with his star quarterback before implementing these changes. "One of the first things I wanted to do when I took the Jets job was to talk to Namath," Holtz once said. "I called the Jets' office and asked a secretary for Joe's phone number. I was told no one had it, that it was classified information. She suggested I call Joe's lawyer, Jimmy Walsh.

"I called him, and asked for Joe's number. He said he couldn't give it to me. I said: 'Oh?'

"He told me if I wanted to talk to him, I should leave my number and if Joe could get back to me, he would."

■   ■   ■

The Jets' key acquisitions that off-season were Richard Todd, a quarterback drafted in the first round as an heir apparent, and Ed Marinaro, a running back the Vikings had been using primarily as a pass catcher. Both moves were fine with Joe. Todd, a big blond kid who had played for Coach Bryant at Alabama, already idolized Namath. And Marinaro, a football celebrity since his record-setting days at Cornell, was already a pal. Both players were also represented by Jimmy Walsh. Unfortunately, Holtz didn't know how to use either of them. Nor, for that matter, did he know how to make use of Namath.

Three times in the course of the Jets' 38–17 opening-day loss in Cleveland, Holtz substituted Todd for Namath near the goal line. Holtz wanted Todd to run the Veer, which worked on one of the three attempts.

"It is obvious we are not a big-play football team," declared Holtz. Uncomfortable with the long pass, he was planning to use the rookie even more. The following week in Denver, Namath left the game with an apparent concussion in the second quarter. In relief, Todd was 4 of 8 for 7 yards. By the time Namath returned in the third quarter, the Jets were down 29–3. Holtz then announced his intention to use Namath through entire games, in even goal-line situations, saying, "Joe gives us a mental lift down there."

What the coach failed to mention was a plan to usurp Joe's greatest privilege and call all the plays from the sideline. With Holtz sending his selections via the receiver-messenger, the Jets lost 16–0 to the Dolphins. Undaunted, Holtz resumed the play-calling in a 17–6 loss to the 49ers. Todd led the Jets to their only score. Namath, on the other hand, had now gone twelve quarters without the team scoring a touchdown. A new consensus had emerged: bench him. The truth was becoming impossible to ignore. Eventually, even loyalists like Dave Herman had to recognize it: "I'd tell him, 'Sit down, Joe Namath, your time's over with,' and he'll take it like a man." But Holtz just veered in another direction, using the opportunity to defend Namath. "It's difficult to throw out of a well or in a supine position," he said.

In the following week's home opener against Buffalo, Namath called most of the plays, and the Jets won by a field goal. Victories over the Bills, who finished 2–12, would account for two of the three Jets wins in 1976. The other was a 34–0 triumph over the Tampa Bay Bucaneers that November. Namath was coming back after having missed the previous two games with a sore right knee. But beating the Bucs, who didn't win a game that season, offered little consolation. More than 10,000 ticket holders didn't bother coming to Shea. Not that it troubled Joe, who had little to say on the subject, despite the calls for his benching. As Dick Schaap had written the week before: "Namath has cleaned up his act, and that is too bad, that is what hurts, that is what has diminished the appeal of the Jets."

With one game left on the schedule, Lou Holtz quit to take a position as head football coach at the University of Arkansas. Namath's status was far less certain. Given this debacle of a season, not even the Jets could be expected to pick up the option on his contract. By now it was commonly acknowledged, even among the Namath camp, that the Broadway Joe show had finally come to the end of its run. There might be an encore performance, but it would not be in New York. Namath was about to play his final game for the Jets—December 12 at Shea against the Cincinnati Bengals. Beyond that, there were no guarantees.

Though there were some homemade signs—"Thanks for the Memories, Joe"—his farewell was not officially observed. The Jets drew 31,067; a record number of season ticket holders stayed home. Who could blame them? It was wet, muddy, and cold. Namath was 4 of 15 for 20 yards. He was intercepted four times in the first half. Fans booed. He had defiled their memory of him.

Later, in the final moments of a 42–3 loss, a few hundred remaining fans struck up a chant of "We Want Joe!" But Joe was done.

Again, he had little to say. Only the sight of Paul Zimmerman seemed to animate him. Earlier in the week, Zimmerman had written about Namath as "a statue." In fact, he was a kind of monument. He could not move, and his time seemed long ago.

"I see that fat fucker who says I'm immobile, don't run the ball and look like a statue out there," said Namath. "But I saw this team winning with me the same way."

Suddenly, Joe was adamant. Give him some talent to work with. That's all he needed.

"I know I can play," he said.

Fuck the future. Long live the past.

"I throw as well as I ever did even if it might not look like it," he said. "My arm's good, period. And the leg's okay."

Broadway Joe had hustled himself, but good.

"What will you do now?" he was asked.

"Shower."

■   ■   ■

Not long after New Year's, 1977, Namath established a scholarship at Alabama in the names of Bessie Asbury, Ruth Burchfield, and Mary Krout, the widowed sisters who took such good care of him as an undergraduate. More widely known was his wish for an endowment from Carroll Rosenbloom. He had resumed his campaign for the Rams. "The only place I'd play is Los Angeles," he announced on Johnny Carson's *Tonight Show.*

"Now isn't that nice of him?" wrote Dick Young. "Joey Baby makes it sound as though he is calling the shots. . . .

"If you want the cold, unadulterated fact of it, Joe Namath has been fired."

In a matter of weeks, Namath dropped his Rams-only position. "It wouldn't be fair to the Jets," he said. The Jets, whose position had not changed, had no interest in picking up his option and only wanted to trade his rights. But Namath wasn't making it easy, as word spread that he didn't want to come off the bench or accept a salary cut. At those prices, there weren't any takers, not even the Rams.

It wasn't until the last week of March—after months of discussions between Jimmy Walsh, the Rams general manager Don Klosterman, and the Jets' Al Ward—that Namath finally consented (as per his contractual prerogative) to a trade. The negotiations had evolved into a game of chicken. The Jets retained Namath's rights until April 1, after which they would put him on waivers, effectively cutting him. In that event, Los Angeles would no longer have to compensate New York. But there was a risk—to both Namath and the Rams—that another team would claim him.

"I'm not the one saying so, mind you, but people tell me that Washington is interested and so is Denver," Jimmy told the *Times.* "I'm sure there are others."

The Rams wanted Joe to take a physical, a condition Jimmy refused. To the lawyer, it wasn't a medical issue: "His stature must be respected."

But the Rams remained firm: no exam, no deal. "Joe Namath isn't going to audition for a stethoscope," Jimmy shot back.

And so the most famous football player who ever lived went on waivers. Ten days later, at 4:00 P.M. on the afternoon of April 11, the claiming deadline passed without a single team putting in a claim on Joe. Jimmy had now run out of bluffs.

The Rams, who were also pursuing a deal for Houston quarterback Dan Pastorini, were divided on the subject of Namath. Don Klosterman, an old AFL hand, was still enamored of him. With the right protection, Klosterman figured, Joe could win again. But Rams head coach Chuck Knox—the former Ellwood City high school coach who first lobbied Werblin on Namath's behalf—had serious doubts. Knox, a conservative coach, believed in the running game, not old quarterbacks. He thought of himself as a realist, and in football, realism trumps all sentiments—except the owner's.

Carroll Rosenbloom's team had won its division for four consecutive years, with four different quarterbacks. But the Rams had yet to qualify for the Super Bowl, the previous season having ended with a loss to Fran Tarkenton and the Vikings in the NFC championship game. Quarterbacking duties had been shared by James Harris, a highly rated passer unable to shake the racist perceptions that seemed to doom all black quarterbacks, and Pat Haden, a blond Rhodes Scholar who led USC to three Rose Bowls. Haden—only twenty-three when he became the starter late in the season—was a fair-haired boy in every sense.

But listed at five-eleven, 182 pounds, he was also undersized. And Rosenbloom wanted big in every way. He had a better idea. "We made Joe Namath," he said, referring to his days as owner of the Colts. Now, as owner of the Rams, Rosenbloom had become a creature of Hollywood, and Hollywood people, like mobsters, believe their own bullshit. Rosenbloom wasn't about to let anything impinge on his fantasy of walking into the Polo Lounge with Broadway Joe on his arm. Another big *macher* in search of the perfect ending, Rosenbloom wanted the right script for his blockbuster: symmetry before subtlety, tie up all the loose ends. These young kids might think of Namath as a salesman of perfume and popcorn makers, but to Rosenbloom, he remained the sainted hustler who consecrated a gambler's holiday—at his expense. "Namath owes me one," he said.

■   ■   ■

The deal wasn't finalized until the middle of May. And though his new salary was reported to be a mere $150,000, Joe didn't seem to care. What was a $350,000 pay cut if you were having fun?

He reported on time to the Rams training camp weighing 187 pounds, almost twenty pounds less than he finished with the Jets. The bloat in his cheeks was gone. He hadn't been this light since sophomore year at Alabama. His daily workouts would begin at 8:15 A.M., an hour before most of his teammates. Joe quickly acclimated to life in southern California; he had a good tan and a driver for his Eldorado. Jimmy and Tad had spotted Wayne Lyttle some years before, a black kid from Queens asking for autographs outside the locker room at Shea. Jimmy took a liking to him and hired him at Namanco. Now Wayne had graduated to the position of Namath's personal attendant, with duties that included driver, gofer, and buffer. When practice ended, he would pull up on the field and drive Joe to the pool.

Namath could not run with the rest of the team, but he swam almost a mile a day as part of a new conditioning program the Rams had designed for him. "Joe was in that pool three times a day," says Fred Dryer, the former Giant defensive end who had become an All-Pro with the Rams. "He worked his ass off."

At thirty-four, Joe was the same age as Y. A. Tittle had been when he was traded to the Giants. Tittle went on to three straight championship games. With a little clean living, there was no telling what Namath could achieve. He would gladly pay the price, to use Coach Bryant's phrase. The work was a small down payment toward his happy ending. Not everyone shared his fantasy, though.

For the record, Chuck Knox says he had wanted Namath just as much as Rosenbloom. "I thought Joe could still play," he says. "I didn't know if he could be a starter." But others recall the quarterback as yet another source of contention between the coach and the owner, who had already prevented Knox from taking a lucrative offer to coach Detroit earlier that year.

"Chuck Knox never wanted him, and Rosenbloom insisted," says Larry Fox, who had known the coach from their first days with the Jets in '64. "Knox told me the story. He realized he had a dilemma. He said, 'If I start Pat Haden, every time he throws an interception, people are going to start yelling, 'We Want Joe!' The only thing to do is have Joe start the season and play himself out of a job.' "

■   ■   ■

As it happened, the cry of "We Want Joe!" was never heard in the Los Angeles Coliseum. The booing, however, began during the exhibition season, which the Rams concluded with a 1–5 record. Though used sparingly, Namath was sacked eleven times. Haden had played better, but when the season opened, Namath was the starter.

After three games, the Rams were 2–1. Despite his own respectable numbers—36 for 67, three touchdowns, one interception—Namath was already the source of much debate. He tried like hell to fit in with his new team, but there was only so much that trying could accomplish. Before each game, the Rams would charge out of the tunnel and sprint the length of the field, then line up for calisthenics. But Namath couldn't keep up. "Man, it was awful," he recalled.

He felt an unaccustomed need to defend himself: "I've got so much desire, so much pride. Some people don't think I can play anymore, but they're wrong and I'm going to prove them wrong."

Then, on a wet, windy Monday night, the Rams played the Bears in Chicago. Namath began well enough, and Los Angeles jumped out to a 13–0 lead. But as the drizzle became a driving rain, receivers started dropping balls. "Chicago's defensive backs had as much trouble handling Namath's passes as Ram receivers," noted the *Los Angeles Times*'s Bob Oates Sr., an ardent Namath admirer. Perhaps it was the wind, or the rain. Perhaps the problem was the slick field. "He couldn't plant his feet," says Dryer.

Or maybe it was just Joe. "The game plan was to run the football," says

Knox. "We were letting the quarterback call the plays. Joe saw some things he thought he could hit."

Namath threw four interceptions that night, finishing 16 for 40. With two minutes remaining, Bears linebacker Waymond Bryant hit him late and high, forcing Namath to leave the game clutching his throat. Though Haden came on to throw a touchdown, the Rams still lost, 24–23.

"I think Chuck wanted him to fail," says Dryer, who disliked Knox and his conservative schemes. "They left him out there to stick it up Carroll's ass."

Whatever the case, Namath was hurting a lot more than Rosenbloom. "He got beat up pretty bad," recalls Larry Fox, who covered the game.

By the time Joe came out of the shower, his locker was mobbed with reporters. The morning-paper deadlines had passed, but the day-after stories were already being prepared. While some would offer excuses for Namath, most would focus on his humiliation. Namath was surprised to see Fox so far from New York. Their eyes met for a moment. Namath had a peculiar look, as if to say, *Oh, shit.*

Fox barely got out the words. "Hello, Joe."

■　■　■

Several days later, the Rams informed the press that Haden would have to start the next game. Apparently, Namath had hurt his knee against the Bears. He could not recall having sustained the injury, which wasn't much worse than the usual postgame inflammation, but in Knox's mind, the distinction no longer mattered. The Chicago–L.A. game was history, mere memory, as irrelevant in its way as a junior high school contest between Ellwood City and Beaver Falls. The knee wasn't the issue. "It was a very, very tough decision for me," said Knox. "But it had to be made."

Joe Namath had been benched.

■　■　■

Under Pat Haden, the Rams won their next two games. "That puts an end to our quarterback controversy," declared Knox.

Namath kept his depression to himself. He stayed in shape and studied film, offering no complaint, just occasional counsel for his young replacement. In this way, he became a kind of team player he had never been. But from his new vantage point on the sidelines, he discovered that there was something even worse than not playing—not being listened to. "I suggested things," Namath said after the season. "Week in, and week out."

With the team winning, his suggestions were ignored. Once again, the Rams finished in first place; once again, they were knocked out in the playoffs. It was another rain-soaked contest, this time at the Coliseum. Haden, who had small hands for a quarterback, was having trouble holding on to the ball. With the Rams down two touchdowns to the Vikings, Namath and rookie Vince Ferragamo began warming up. Quarterback coach Kay Stephenson told Knox that Namath looked better and was ready to go. "He just nodded and walked away," said Stephenson. The players and the assistant coaches were expecting Namath to get the call, one last chance, and a good one at that, for a happy ending. But it never came. Knox stuck with his game plan.

"His downfall was his inability to understand the passing game," says Dryer. "That was the end of Chuck. And that was the end of Joe."

Minnesota won, 14–7. Knox was finished with the Rams. The game was finished with Joe.

■   ■   ■

At six feet, 225 muscular pounds, Mort Fishman was nicknamed "Jewish Tarzan." But on the afternoon of October 5, 1969, he must have looked like another ballplayer with a Jets shoulder bag. No one stopped him as he walked into the visiting team's locker room at Boston College Stadium and approached the quarterback.

"Mr. Namath?"

"Who are you?" asked Joe, wearing just a towel.

"Me? I'm nobody," said Fishman. "I'm from a hick town in Connecticut. But my son and six of his friends are outside, and I promised them I would try to get your autograph."

Joe seemed to appreciate Mort's manners, and at some level, to recognize the urgency of his mission. *The kids are big fans, Mr. Namath. It would mean the world to them.* In fact, it meant the world to Mort. Joe told him to go to the Bachelors III in Boston, where he saw to it that the kids were treated like princes.

It was the beginning of a friendship. "Turned out we had the same interests," says Mort. But those days of golf and girls were still yet to come.

At a table in the Boston Bachelors, Joe asked, "Where's your wife?"

"I'm going through a divorce," said Mort.

It was the divorce that led him into the locker room in the first place. "My son Scotty was in fourth grade," he says. "How could I say no to him? I just wanted him to enjoy a day without thinking about his parents getting divorced. The kid had a broken heart."

Divorce, as Mort was finding out, inflicted a peculiar pain. The former Mrs. Fishman had left him for a guy at their country club. The Silver Fox, Mort called him. Mort had always thought he knew something about women, but the divorce made him reconsider. He felt like the last to know. Ever since then, no matter what he did, the hurt never quite healed. The melancholy always returned. "I was at the bottom of the world," he says.

Almost eight years later in the winter of 1978, Mort could recognize some of the same symptoms in Joe. He recalls the night before they flew to Scottsdale for the American Airlines golf tournament. Namath had been sipping wine and brooding, distant and distracted, all week. They dined at a Polynesian restaurant. "Joe drank supper," recalls Mort. Then he drank some more. He didn't have much to say.

Joe didn't mention that he had already spoken with Dave Anderson, telling the *Times*man that he would not be playing "next year." He did not use the word "retirement."

Anderson asked if he ever wondered what he could have been with knees. "If I had good knees," he said, "I might've gotten killed in Vietnam."

Any regrets?

Just one, he said: "I wouldn't have gone water skiing that day."

■   ■   ■

The next morning, Mort placed a wake-up call. The phone kept ringing until finally Joe picked up. "Go on without me," he said. "I'll catch the next flight."

Mort was waiting for Joe when his plane arrived in Phoenix. He had a limo and some broads, friends of a friend. Good-looking, too. Mort had them wear Joe Namath T-shirts, figuring it would be a goof. Joe needed something to raise his spirits.

Joe wasn't in the mood, though. Mort could see what was happening as Joe got off the plane. The press converged on him. They kept asking about his retirement. Retirement? They wanted a retirement speech. What was he, Y. A. fucking Tittle?

Mort sent the broads home.

Meanwhile, the reporters were shouting questions. What will you be doing, Joe? Where will you go?

"Mars," said Joe. "I was going to the moon, but I decided Mars was better."

■   ■   ■

Among the publications covering Namath's retirement was *People*, whose correspondent at the golf outing wrote:

> The next morning he began drowning his sorrows in Coors. . . .
>
> His mood seemed to darken further as the tournament progressed, despite the arrival from Los Angeles of long-time girlfriend Randi Oakes, an actress and model. Playing poorly, Namath hit again and again into water hazards. . . . Several times he simply gave up, refusing to finish holes because neither he nor the ball was taking a straight course. He guzzled continuously, stashing the empties in his golf cart. On the final day of the tournament, which was sponsored by American Airlines, Namath threw an embarrassing snit because his beer was not properly chilled

when it was delivered to him on the first tee. He settled down only when his partner contacted a beer truck by CB radio and arranged for fresh supplies to be brought in.

"It's pretty tough for Joe right now," says his friend and business manager, Jimmy Walsh. "He has just made a major departure in his life."

It was a divorce, of sorts.

The Jets didn't need him. The Rams didn't need him. The game no longer needed him. If Namath wasn't the last one to know, then he was the last to admit it. He kept postponing the announcement, as if his words would make the retirement official.

"He still believed in his heart that he could get the job done," says Knox. "That's what made him such a great athlete in the first place."

Knox had been awed by him as a kid. Knox had been his first patron with the Jets. Finally, it was Knox who had benched him. But through it all, Namath's nature was unchanged. Of course, he still believed he could play. He had been taught as much, to have contempt for mere odds. *If you ain't confident, you don't belong. You are better than anyone out there. It comes from the blood.*

To retire was nothing less than to abandon the belief at his very core.

But the fucking press wouldn't be satisfied if he merely went away. They needed an announcement.

And what would that do? Annul the Guarantee?

Announcement was tantamount to renouncement. Yes, it was a divorce. Joe always said he couldn't get married while he was still playing. He didn't want to be unfaithful, and football was the closest thing he had to a marriage. Now they wanted him to relinquish his bond with the game, to repudiate his famous belief in himself, to admit he could come back no more. They wanted him to renounce a part of himself, as if it had never happened.

There was, it turned out, life after football. Sonny Werblin had sold Wellington Mara, of all people, on a new stadium built over a New Jersey salt marsh contaminated with industrial pollutants. Ben Davidson was doing Miller Lite commercials. And Ed Marinaro, cut by the Jets, landed a part as a gangster in a Harvey Keitel picture called *Fingers*.

Namath would do another movie, too. Later in 1978, he traveled to Germany for *Avalanche Express,* starring Lee Marvin, Robert Shaw, and one of his sometime girlfriends, Linda Evans. "I'm not carrying the picture by any stretch of the imagination," said Joe, who played "Leroy," an undercover CIA agent assigned to protect a KGB defector.

47. THAT'S ENTERTAIN- MENT

Movies, like real estate and restaurants (he was still partners with Bobby and Ray), were something to dabble in. But television was becoming a more serious pursuit. He was a creature of the medium, not by his own design but by an overwhelming consensus of the viewing public. The new commercial for Fabergé Organic Shampoo featured a screen that kept splitting until it contained thirty-six frames of Namath's face. On the eve of the championship game between the Cowboys and the Broncos, he cohosted a variety show, *Super Night at the Super Bowl.* He could even be seen by those watching *CBS News with Walter Cronkite.* In between word of a historic Egyptian-Israeli accord and Eric Sevareid's farewell, there he was: "I'm Joe Namath and this is the new Double Mac by Hamilton Beach. It makes two burgers in sixty seconds."

A decade after Super Bowl III, the edgier aspects of his image had all but worn away. He was softer, cornier, unobjectionable, ubiquitous. Perhaps, then, his course was inevitable: having begun as an experiment in live TV, he was doomed to become grist for a sitcom.

The Waverly Wonders—larcenously derivative of *Welcome Back, Kotter* and *The White Shadow*—aired, appropriately enough, on the old AFL network, NBC. Namath played the lead role: Joe Casey, a recently retired pro basketball player now teaching history and coaching at Waverly High School in Eastfield, Wisconsin.

Namath was ready, even eager, for the part. Except for the occasional glass of wine, he had quit drinking after returning from Germany. "Every night, Lee Marvin and Robert Shaw and I would go to the bar," he recalled. "Things started not to go so well. But that was the life I had always known, the party life. . . . One day in May, I just stopped drinking. I'm glad I drank, but I'm even happier I stopped. Every morning is nicer now that I don't have a hangover."

No more hangovers. No more blackouts. Instead, Namath spent a lot of time on *A Lotta Heart,* the nineteen-foot Boston Whaler he kept docked in Fort Lauderdale. Joe preferred the vessel because it was said to be unsinkable. He did a good bit of boating (often a straight shot all the way to Bimini), fishing, and snorkeling that spring. By the time he got to California to film the show, he was rejuvenated, the result of swimming, meditating, and drinking Perrier. Most days, he had a 7:15 A.M. wake-up call at the Beverly Hills Hotel and a tee time at Bel-Air.

This happy and healthy new Namath appeared on the cover of *People.* Just months after photographing him drinking and stumbling around the golf course, Harry Benson shot him again. The picture evidenced the reformation of Broadway Joe, for this was Namath as he'd never been seen. Among the many things Joe disliked about reporters was their insistence that he had blue eyes. They were, in fact, green. But there he was, on the cover of America's leading celebrity magazine: star of a new television series, smiling, invigorated, and very blue-eyed.

The piece noted Jimmy's business acumen and Joe's work ethic. "He's marvelous," said Dick Martin, the director best known as a host of *Laugh-In.* "He begs for direction. He's used to being coached." By all accounts, Namath was a model of diligence and professionalism on the set. "He's so damn sincere he doesn't belong in this business," said Joshua Grenrock, one of his costars.

Waverly Wonders debuted that September, an attempt by Lorimar Productions (the same company that produced *Avalanche Express*) and NBC to fill Friday nights with another half hour of situation comedy. Namath's character's situation included a basketball team that hadn't won in three years and a randy principal who wanted to sleep with him. The comedy, however, was less easily discerned. After three weeks, *Waverly* was canceled.

"The network loved the idea of Joe," says Mike Greenfield, a veteran Hollywood agent who worked with Namath and Walsh. "He was terrific in that show. The biggest problem, as with any half-hour show, is the writing. . . . Let's just say the concept and the writing didn't come together on the level that we hoped for. But let me tell you that most of them don't. The mortality rate in television is 90 percent."

Television produces more has-beens than football. As if to bear out this proposition, Namath concluded the year with a trip to the MGM Grand in Las Vegas. There, he was honored as the subject of a Dean Martin celebrity roast. It was typical of those affairs. "Besides being a great quarterback Joe was also a great swinger," said Dino, waving a cigarette. "He was the only one who had an electric scoreboard over his bed."

The night was full of lame jokes and canned laughter. The chief roaster's tipsy bit seemed to delight the usual suspects, old hands like Milton Berle, Red Buttons, and Joey Bishop. Also in attendance were Bruce Jenner, Jackie Gale, and Mel Tillis, the stuttering country singer. The dais was packed. But most of the guests were recognizable as the people they played on television: Bernie Kopell was the doctor on *Love Boat,* Lee Meriwether was the daughter-in-law on *Barnaby Jones,* Tom Bosley was Richie and Joanie's dad on *Happy Days,* David Doyle was the guy on *Charlie's Angels,* and Jimmy Walker was JJ, the skinny black kid from *Good Times.* Joe gave them all his trademark sheepish grin. They sat there and tittered, the backs of their chairs arrayed like tombstones in the vast wasteland.

For years, Namath had been asked why he didn't retire earlier. Why had he hung on so long?

Well, here was the reason. Look what happens to you. Look what they make you do on television. That night Joe might have foreseen his future: assisting Suzanne Somers as she hosted *The Second Annual National Collegiate Cheerleading Championships,* interviewing O. J. Simpson as the Juice spoke of his fervent desire to work *behind* the camera. It was all part of the same roast. The game was *live.* It was real. The rest was cold, canned crap. A month from now, Nielsen families everywhere would watch Dino's tribute to Broadway Joe, a showbiz night of the living dead.

At the far end of the dais sat the straight man. Once a good-looking kid himself, he had become immense. He lumbered to the podium in his tuxedo, a black, scarflike pilgrim's tie around his neck. A younger generation knew him only as a professional narrator and pitchman for wine that came in a screw-top jug.

Orson Welles still had that magnificent voice. That night he used it to great effect, narrating a highlight reel set in rhyming verse against the music from Sergei Prokofiev's *Peter and the Wolf.* Namath's presence was announced by the string section previously reserved for Peter. The Colts were signified by the Wolf's French horns.

Then the house lights went up. They were on TV again. Welles, whose *Citizen Kane* was released in 1941, reached down to shake Joe's hand. They had more than a little in common, more than an invitation to the same roast. Welles began to trudge back to his seat, another American genius who had peaked at the age of twenty-five.

■ ■ ■

Neither the cancellation of *Waverly* nor the reviews of *Avalanche* ("Apparently told to do something, Joe looks hurt and surprised, as if no one wanted his autograph," wrote the *Times*'s Vincent Canby) shook Namath too badly.

"Joe was philosophical about it," recalls Mike Greenfield. "He figured we gave it our best shot."

Perhaps life with the Jets had taught him to keep defeat in perspective. But more than that, he lacked an actor's need. What most actors lust for, the desire that charges careers, Namath had long since tired of. "Enormous fame," says Greenfield. "He was already famous."

He didn't bug Greenfield for another script, another interview, another job. Instead, he returned to Fort Lauderdale, sober and solvent. Namath was living on Thirty-third Court, in a two-bedroom "penthouse" that went for about $300 a month. His father and Esther had moved in across the hall. One of Joe's best friends, Eddie Gerber, had the apartment next door. A writer on assignment from *Esquire* described him as "the key member of Namath's entourage in Fort Lauderdale, the man to whom all Namath's unwanted phone calls are referred, a steadying, calming influence."

"Eddie Gerber was with him all the time," says Mort Fishman. "It was like they were married. They did everything together."

Everything included fishing, snorkeling, golfing, smoking dope, and hanging out. Gerber came from a wealthy family in Connecticut. "He didn't want anything from Joe," says Fishman.

Their building, 2881 NE Thirty-third Court, was on the Intracoastal Waterway, a short walk from the Galt Ocean Mile, where the Jets stayed during Super Bowl week. But that distance was better measured in years, not blocks. "Living in the past is a way of life I would like to avoid," Namath told *Esquire*. "Except in business, of course. In business . . . I live on my past, and it is lucrative."

Bachelors III had been reincarnated yet again, as a $1.2 million Fort Lauderdale disco and restaurant that seated 450. Namath understood his duties there. "Kind of as an attraction," he said.

Never had a guy gotten so many girls drinking Sanka.

■ ■ ■

John Kenley wasn't much of a football fan, but he liked the Beautymist commercial. "Pantyhose," he says, "is the most sensible thing a person can wear." He was already in his seventies, his hair a striking shade of orange, when he brought Broadway Joe to the stage. Kenley, the son of a Pennsylvania miner, had been a vaudeville dancer and mimic before finding work with Lee and J. J. Shubert, czars of the Great White Way. While working for the Shuberts, whom Kenley recalls as avid humpers of aspiring actresses, he acquired his own expertise at the box office. In 1940, after going out on his own, Kenley produced a show called *The Barker* in Deer Lake, Pennsylvania. It starred Ann Corio, one of Eddie Jaffe's Broadway babes. Her presence had just the intended effect on lagging ticket sales. "Ann Corio stripped completely naked," recalled Kenley.

He would often use burlesque performers—many of whom, like Rose La Rose and Georgia Southern, were from Jaffe's stable—in his summer stock shows. But over the years, as Kenley settled in Ohio, he found a gimmick the public liked even more than strippers—TV personalities. "They laughed at me," he says of the theatrical establishment, as one wasn't supposed to raid the vast wasteland for stage talent. But Kenley knew what he was doing, especially when it came to Broadway Joe: "Namath was an *attraction*. He put people in the seats."

The role he had in mind for Namath was that of Hal Carter in William Inge's *Picnic*. "A guy without any roots, a guy who kissed and ran from town to town," says Kenley. "It wasn't miscasting."

The show, also starring Donna Mills, was well received. The highlight of the performance was the first scene, as Joe stripped to his waist. Noted one reviewer: "That alone was worth the price of admission for the host of young women in the opening-night audience."

Ann Corio and Rose La Rose would have approved. Kenley couldn't have been happier. "Joe was damn good," he says. "He was dedicated, and he didn't come off phony." Still, the summer stock impresario had never seen an actor quite like Namath. "He was in great pain all the time," recalls Kenley. "He had to wrap his knees with Ace bandages." The script called for Namath to jump over a fence. It wasn't easy, but he did it without complaint, every night and twice on Sunday. The show opened August 14 in Akron. Then it was on to Dayton before closing in Columbus.

■   ■   ■

Namath might have been the only performer whose adventures in summer stock could have gotten him on *The Tonight Show*. "Would you agree," asked Johnny, "that sex before a game is beneficial?"

"Depends on what kind," said Joe.

He nailed it that night on Carson. Obviously, the theater agreed with him.

It was good training and good fun. Life was better without the booze and those weekly orthopedic traumas inflicted by opposing linemen. Namath looked great in his blazer and cream-colored slacks. He was happily unmarried, and happy to be off Broadway.

"The play certainly doesn't rest on my shoulders," he said.

In January 1980, Namath began studying with Arthur Joseph, a renowned voice coach in Los Angeles. "He wanted to sing," says Joseph.

As a player, Namath had been too self-conscious to join in during the pregame national anthem. Now Arthur Joseph would have to train his confidence as much as his voice. Joseph might have seemed an unlikely tutor for Namath, much less one to fortify the ex-quarterback's legendary belief in himself. But Joseph himself had an unshakable belief in his own gifts. It was more than perfect pitch; he heard, as he often said, the sound of one's soul. For him, the voice told him of traumas and triumphs at a person's core. "When I hear a voice, I truly hear who a person is," he says. "And that's not bullshit."

48. SOUND OF THE SOUL

In Namath, he heard many things: "A man who was used to being in charge, to not being questioned, a leader. . . . He lived a very flamboyant life, but I also sensed a man who had a . . . family value system . . . a very caring person."

As for Namath's accents and inflections, the teacher discerned "a combination of blue-collar Pennsylvania with the long, drawn-out southern sounds. It wasn't an affectation, though. Joe wasn't affected in that way." Alabama had become part of him. New York, curiously enough, had not. "There was no New York accent," says Joseph.

Still, Namath had good reason to feel uncomfortable as a singer. Years of barking and shouting signals had injured his voice. "It's not inappropriate to say he had the poorest pitch discrimination of any singer I ever taught," says Joseph. "It was really hard for him to learn to sing in tune."

As an athlete, Namath had great gifts. As a singer, he had only dedication and desire. The sessions with Arthur Joseph were rigorous, but Namath accepted his authority more willingly than he had anyone's since Coach Bryant. "He was completely open with me, completely trusting of me," says Joseph. "He gave me complete access."

Joe got a guitar and learned to read music. He trained his singing voice five days a week, three when he was on the road. And gradually, a vocal style developed. It had an adequate vibrato and a Rex Harrison quality. "Speak-singing," says Joseph. "But always professional, always in tune."

Before long, producers wanted Namath for their musicals. These engagements made for an itinerant life, but he didn't travel alone. Namath had his valets, usually Hoot Owl or Wayne Lyttle, and his teacher Arthur Joseph. It was Joseph who personally rehearsed Joe. It was Joseph who'd pull aside the trumpet player on opening night and tell him what to play for Joe's opening melody line. It was Joseph who yelled, "Stop!" as his pupil struggled through "Luck Be a Lady" during the taping of a televised variety show, refusing to let Namath continue singing off-key. "It was going to affect his self-esteem," says Joseph.

In the summer of 1980, Namath sang the lead in a production of *Li'l Abner* that toured to Atlanta, St. Louis, Kansas City, and Tulsa. With each stop, Namath seemed to put more distance between himself and his former life. Still, there were always reminders. While singing a number in *Li'l Abner,* he recalled, "one of the pieces in the knee came loose" and required a draining. Osteoarthritis was also setting in, creeping into bones that had taken so many hits, in his fingers and his spine. Sometimes Namath would scream from the pain. One morning in 1981, he woke unable to move. "I thought I was paralyzed," he said.

■   ■   ■

As usual, he endured the pain, though it may have helped that he was having a few pops again.

His next starring role was Joe Hardy, an aging baseball fan who strikes a Faustian bargain with the devil in *Damn Yankees.* Namath got good money (a reported $10,000 a week) and good press for his work at the Jones Beach Theater in Wantagh, Long Island, not far from Hofstra. Of course, the reporters were eager to establish a connection between the first and second acts of his professional life, but Joe wasn't buying it. "I had as much confidence playing football as anybody ever did," he told Dave Anderson. "I can't talk about the theater like that."

From the *New York Times* review of *Damn Yankees*: "Mr. Namath has genuine charm. He smiles a lot. He sings in a light baritone, or, when he is having trouble, in an amiable bellow. His perfectly capped teeth are like little beacons on the vast Jones Beach stage, and when he appears bare-chested in a locker room scene people in the audience go, 'Ooooh.'"

Mustering all that charm wasn't as easy as it looked. It was not unusual for Namath to have a drink in his hand as he greeted well-wishers after the show. He earned that drink. "The hardest-working guy I've ever seen," said the show's producer, Richard Horner. Namath was training with more regularity and dedication than he had in all his years as a pro quarterback. But he was enjoying himself, too.

"He had completely changed his friends," recalls Tim Secor, who visited backstage at Jones Beach. "He was hanging out with these theatrical types. He looked so happy."

The *Times*'s Gerald Eskenazi brought his wife and son to the show. Eskenazi's tenure as a Jets beat writer coincided with Namath's frustrating, drawn-out descent as a player. But now, as Hoot Owl ushered him through the dressing room door, he noticed some changes in Joe. First was the hair, which was blow-dried. Second was the demeanor: Namath had finally found contentment on Long Island.

■   ■   ■

Not long after *Damn Yankees* closed, former NFL security director Jack Danahy was accosted by a mugger on the Upper East Side. The old G-man's assailant came out of a doorway with a knife. Danahy, then sixty-three, spun around, pulled his licensed .38, and shot him three times, once in the head. The mugger was pronounced dead at the scene.

Ten months later, cops found the body of Mickey Kearney dumped on the grounds of a housing project on the West Side of Manhattan. The best theory, as one detective recalls, had him finally ripping off the wrong drug dealer. Kearney had been shot twice in the head and stabbed three times. The stab wounds were serially arranged, three quarters of an inch wide, almost five inches deep, puncturing his chest, lungs, and heart. Kearney's blood tested positive for opiates, most likely heroin.

The murder of Mickey Kearney—a shakedown artist, among other things, who used to terrorize Tim Secor when Namath was out of town—didn't come as much of a shocker. There was, however, one special point of interest among the cops. "We heard," said the detective, "that he was Namath's bodyguard."

That was back in the good old days. Joe didn't miss them at all.

■   ■   ■

"Who would've thought," droned Howard Cosell, "that Randi Oakes and Eddie Marinaro would turn out to be bigger stars than Joe Willie Namath?"

Cosell was heard volunteering this assessment on the set of *Battle of the Network Stars XII,* an extravaganza he cohosted with Oakes. Joe's ex was now known as Officer Bonnie Clark, a blond motorcycle cop on the hit show *CHiPs.* That same year, Marinaro began his run as Officer Joe Coffey on NBC's *Hill Street Blues.* Unlike ballplayers, cops never got old on television. Soon, Fred Dryer would assume the identity of LAPD Detective Sgt. Rick Hunter. *Hunter* stayed on the air until 1991, not including periodic returns as a TV movie. Syndication offered a kind of immortality.

Joe did some TV, too, mostly as a guest star on series like *Fantasy Island* and *The Love Boat*. Apparently, there wasn't a suitable cop role for Namath, though there might have been a part as a barman. After reading scripts for a new show called *Cheers,* Mike Greenfield became convinced of two things: It would be a monster hit, and Namath would be great in the lead role. The part was Sam "Mayday" Malone, a retired Red Sox pitcher who had given up drinking and ran a bar in Boston. "Joe couldn't have been more right for it— ex-athlete, charismatic, handsome, rugged, fun loving," says Greenfield. "I wanted him to do some real serious studying and preparation for the reading. He read it. He liked it. But he was a bit skeptical about all of a sudden drop- ping everything he was doing."

Whatever his reasons, Namath never read for the part in *Cheers*. "That was the end of our relationship," says Greenfield. "He was really upset that I had made such a big deal about it."

The agent recalls Joe's telling him to speak to Jimmy. It was a testy con- versation.

"How do you know it's going to be a hit?" asked Jimmy.

"It's my job to know," said Greenfield.

"*Waverly Wonders* wasn't a hit," said Jimmy. "You got a guarantee?"

■   ■   ■

After 1981, Namath did mostly stage work. It was physical, it was live, and perhaps in a way it was less phony than television. It connected him to an au- dience, not a sound set. After *Li'l Abner,* he appeared in *The Rainmaker* in Dal- las and then toured as Sky Masterson in *Guys and Dolls.* Next came a *Salute to Broadway* musical review—"a nightclub act we developed," explains Arthur Joseph—at Great Adventure amusement park in New Jersey. Finally, in 1983, the former Broadway Joe made his official Broadway debut, joining the cast of *The Caine Mutiny Court-Martial.* The part of Lt. Stephan Maryk, charged as a mutineer, didn't give him many lines, but it kept him onstage for most of the show. He took the gig at the suggestion of his new theatrical agent, Robert Lantz. "He thought this was the best way for me to be presented at this stage of my career—not having the focus right on me," said Namath.

Robert Lipsyte, a former *Times* columnist who had covered Namath in his prime, wrote of a performance that was "schooled and workmanlike" but with "none of that magical madness that possesses and empowers the great actors." Not to mention great ballplayers. "Backstage we joked about his finally becom- ing Broadway Joe until I felt comfortable enough to steer the conversation to- ward pride and ambition and vanity." Lipsyte wanted to know if Namath could again become a star.

"I don't think that's going to happen," said Namath. "I just don't have those drives and hungers anymore."

■   ■   ■

He'd already played the role of a lifetime—Broadway Joe. Now, after so many years as the star of a drama, he found himself best suited for lighter fare. By 1984, the *Times* noted that "Mr. Namath grows more personable and persuasive with each musical stage appearance." This praise appeared in a review of *Sugar,* based on the classic cross-dressing comedy *Some Like It Hot.* The scaled-down musical version, which opened at the Claridge in Atlantic City before going to Los Angeles, featured Namath in the role played by Tony Curtis in the film, a musician who dresses as a woman to escape the mob.

"I don't see how he ever got in drag," says an admiring John Kenley.

Namath insisted on skirts that covered his unsightly right knee, and, as not many girl sax players wore Ace bandages, he had to forgo the usual wrapping of the joint. High heels presented other problems; Namath found that pumps made both walking and talking arduous tasks. "Maintaining the consistency of a high falsetto voice is a little tough," said Joe.

He did eight shows a week, including matinees on Saturday and Sunday. He went through a lot of ice—in bags for his knees and cubes for his drinks. One night after rehearsal, a reporter saw him "belting them down pretty good" at the bar.

"We were working on that choreography," explained Joe.

The door to his dressing room was marked with his name and a big gold star. Inside, he had a bar. He might have a couple before the curtain went up.

Audiences loved him. The former Joyce Hupp, Joe's date for the senior prom, saw *Sugar* with her husband. They had front-row seats alongside a group of doctors who were attending a convention. As soon as Joe came on in women's clothes, Joyce started to laugh uncontrollably. Finally, the doctors began giving her dirty looks. "I can't help it," she said. "He looks just like his mother."

■   ■   ■

It took a tough man to put on such a happy face, especially in pumps. But the orthopedic aftershocks of his football career seemed the least of his problems. For Joe, the early 1980s were laced with personal loss. The bar business had gone bad, and with it, his friendship with Ray Abruzzese. Mort Fishman remembers driving with Namath one night in Lauderdale. They pulled into the parking lot outside Bachelors III. "Wait here," said Joe. "I gotta talk with Ray."

He was back in a minute, trembling with rage. "It wasn't good," he said. "I didn't want you there."

Spiros Dellartas, the waiter from the Green Kitchen who used to stay with Ray in Florida, heard another a version. "You believe this fuck?" Ray told him. "He accused me of stealing money."

It never would have happened in the good old days, when Joe was known as a brother to Ray, and a stand-up guy to all. Spiros still remembered the poker games up at the penthouse in the Newport East. Once he found himself down $500, way too much for a guy who served coffee and toast for a living. Joe pulled him aside and wrote him a check. Spiros didn't have the bread to pay him back, but Joe never mentioned it.

That's the kind of guy he had been. But was he still? A lot of his old friends were beginning to wonder: What's the matter with Joe?

■   ■   ■

On December 19, 1982, Paul Bryant coached his final game, as Alabama beat Illinois in the Liberty Bowl. Less than six weeks into his retirement, he died of a heart attack. On Governor Wallace's order, the state flag flew at half staff. Namath was in rehearsal for *The Rainmaker* when he learned of the death. "One of the biggest disappointments in my life," he said. Ray may have once been like a brother, but Bryant always remained a surrogate father. Although the director offered the grieving Namath a leave from the production, Joe insisted on going on with the show.

The hurt was deep; he carried it with him. Some years later, one could still hear its sound in his soul. While making a speech in Canton, Ohio, Joe's voice would break at the mention of Bryant.

■   ■   ■

For Namath, 1983 ended as it began, with a death. On December 2, Eddie Gerber died of cancer. "There wasn't much you could say to Joe about it," recalls Mort Fishman. "He never wanted to talk about death."

The following August, Namath was arrested in West Hollywood for drunk driving, an offense he paid for with a $390 fine, three years' summary probation, and a promise to complete alcohol education classes. It was his second such arrest in a year. The previous September, he was pulled over in Florida, driving a 1980 Cadillac with an expired Pennsylvania license. From the police report: "Vehicle was swaying from inside lane to outside lane; also vehicle was traveling at a high rate of speed. . . . Defendant had slurred speech red glossy eyes and the odor of an alcoholic beverage on his breath . . . was unsteady on his feet using the vehicle for support."

However uncertain his bearings, the defendant still had enough presence of mind to refuse to submit to Breathalyzer or urine tests. He even refused to be fingerprinted.

Prosecutors soon dropped the drunk-driving charge for lack of evidence. Later, after a hearing in which Namath testified, a judge declined to suspend his license for not consenting to the Breathalyzer. The officers' instructions, he ruled, had been confusing.

Namath's own confusion was apparent only to those around him. No longer Broadway Joe, he was a modern vaudevillian, a peripatetic player pushing forty and struggling with sobriety, a grown man whose mother was bugging him for grandchildren. "His mother was wanting him to get married," says Hoot Owl Hicks. "Everybody who knew him wanted him to settle down."

For the first time in his life, Joe was looking.

It was Arthur Joseph who made the introduction, in the waiting room outside his studio. The space was adorned with photographs of famous students, among them Joe Namath, who arrived for his lesson just as Deborah Lynne Mays was finishing hers. Joe called her the next day, and they started dating.

Arthur's wife, Rebecca, was upset. "She's just a child," she told her husband. "Why are you introducing her to Joe?"

Deborah was, in fact, twenty-one; Namath was now forty. But the voice coach did not share his wife's misgivings. "I trusted Joe's values," he says. He trusted Deborah, too. She was just starting out, having appeared in a few commercials and a television series, *The Greatest American Hero,* about a high school teacher whom aliens have endowed with super powers. But she was keen and full of ambition, a striking girl with brown hair and brown eyes. "One had a sense about Deborah," says Arthur Joseph. "She was a very determined person. She was intense. She wanted what she wanted in life. And she went after it."

49. DEBORAH

Arthur and Rebecca thought enough of Deborah to have her babysit their sons. "She was like part of the family," he says. Of course, she came from a nice family herself. "Lovely people," says Joseph, who stayed with Deborah's parents when he traveled to North Carolina.

The Mayses were well-to-do: Deborah's father, Bud, had a restaurant in Manteo, on the Outer Banks of North Carolina. Her mother, Shirley, was involved in the restoration of historical waterfront property in the coastal town of Elizabeth City.

Deborah had spent most of her childhood in Ligonier, Pennsylvania, where her father was a partner in a plant that manufactured toner for copy machines. Ligonier is horse country; the Mayses belonged to the Pony Club and had access to a stable at a nearby estate. Deborah, the middle child, showed great talent as an equestrian, riding English style, foxhunting and eventing. In 1977 Bud Mays sold his interest in the toner plant, and the family moved to North Carolina. Deborah attended Northeastern High School in Elizabeth City, where she was known as Debbie.

"A very beautiful girl," says classmate Dwayne Crank—and a bright one, too. "She took some courses people don't usually take. I remember her being in calculus."

They sat at the same table for lunch, along the back wall of the cafeteria, where the cool kids hung out. Dwayne was a receiver on the football team. His best friend, Eric McDaniels, was the star quarterback and Debbie's boyfriend. She, too, was determined to be a star. She would talk about going to California to be an actress.

"Send me an autographed picture," said Dwayne.

With her accelerated courses, Deborah left high school early, enrolling at Sweet Briar College in Virginia, an exclusive women's school with a renowned equestrian program. But after only a year, she left Sweet Briar for Los Angeles. There she would meet another star quarterback. Aspiring actresses are often slaves to chance, hoping for that lucky break. But for Deborah, meeting Joe Namath wasn't luck so much as fate. She shared a dream she had had with her voice coach, who considered Deborah's conviction even more reason to make the introduction. "It was a vision of hers," says Arthur Joseph. "She wanted to marry a football player."

■   ■   ■

If Shirley Mays might have had misgivings about her daughter dating a world-famous ladies' man, she got over them soon enough. "I could not speak for Broadway Joe," says Shirley. "That playboy person, I did not know." But Joe Namath was a darling. "As respectful of parents as anybody I ever met in my life," she says. And there was something else Shirley liked. "Joe's a lot like my son—his mannerisms and his laid-back attitude," she says. "My son was extremely handsome. He had dark hair. He kept a lot of stuff inside, just like Joe." Deborah was very close to her brother, Jeffrey. "She worshipped him," says Shirley Mays. Jeffrey liked to fish and have a drink, too. He and Joe probably would've gotten along famously.

But on November 13, 1980, not long after Deborah moved to L.A., he set out with a friend from Cape Hatteras. Their voyage was described as a fishing trip, though some locals suspect they might've been running drugs. Late that day, Mays, twenty-one, and his friend, twenty-two, were seen about sixteen miles off the Hatteras Inlet by a commercial fisherman, who helped them repair a leak in the engine's cooling system. At 6:30 P.M., the two men were reported missing. Although they had no radio or flares, the twenty-three-foot *Sea Ox* was a sturdy craft, built to float like a Boston Whaler. "We've got some encouraging news in that the boat is supposedly unsinkable," said Lt. Tom Blisard, a spokesman for the local Coast Guard station.

The Coast Guard sent out C-130 planes and H-3 helicopters, which were soon joined by air force, Marine Corps, and navy aircraft, including E-2 radar surveillance planes that scanned 220,000 square miles without any sign of the missing *Sea Ox*. "The boat and pieces will float," said Captain Ed Midget, commander of the Elizabeth City Coast Guard Air Station. "We should have found something." But nothing was ever recovered, not a trace of the boat or the young men. The search, covering coastal waters from New Jersey to South Carolina, was called off after seven days.

"You can't fill a void," says Shirley Mays, who remains haunted by the idea that her son is still alive. "It's very difficult to live with the unknown. . . . Each of us is handling it in our own way, the best way we can."

By "we," she means the family, each of whom is defined by the missing son, the missing brother. "That is who we are. That is on our minds when we wake up at night. That creates the emotional fallout. . . . We were the all-American family. That blew us apart."

■   ■   ■

Namath's courtship of Deborah was a quiet one, his intentions remaining unknown even to his oldest and closest friends. In October 1983, just months after meeting Deborah, *People* asked him about the young actress who had accompanied him while he played in *The Caine Mutiny Court-Martial*, his first run on Broadway. No, said Joe, he still hadn't found the right girl: "That hasn't happened yet, but not because I'm ducking it."

In fact, he had spent the better part of forty years trying to duck it. For all the women he had had, he had never lived with one. That would change, though, as would his feelings for Deborah.

"No doubt about it, he loved her," says Hoot Owl Hicks. "And she loved him."

Joe had been in love before: Frances Pinchotti, Bebe Schreiber, Suzie Storm, Randi Oakes. But Deborah had something the others did not—good timing. Even the astrologer she had begun to see after her brother's disappearance predicted that Deborah would be married that year, 1984. "He was looking for a wife, he was ready to settle down," says Hicks. "And she was there."

For all but sixteen guests, the wedding remained a secret. It took place on November 7, 1984, at a home in Fort Lauderdale. The hosts were old friends of the Mays family. At the request of her daughter—"with Joe's permission"— Shirley took care of the arrangements, everything from flowers floating in the pool to the champagne toast. "I did exactly what the two of them wanted," she says.

John Namath and his wife, Esther, were in attendance. But Rose—happy as she was over the prospect of "a little Joey"—was not present, blaming a bad reaction to a flu shot. Jimmy Walsh was the best man, and Deborah's sister Mindy was maid of honor. The ceremony was performed by the Reverend E. B. McGahee, minister of Davie United Methodist Church.

"I took my time to find the perfect girl," Namath said afterward. "I waited and waited for a long, long time before taking this step. I've always said I'm going to get married only once. This is my first and last wedding."

■   ■   ■

Arthur Joseph learned of the nuptials in the newspaper. The voice coach might have once considered Joe and Deborah like family, but the more the couple saw of each other, the less he saw of them. After a while, they stopped their voice training entirely. He never heard from Joe or Deborah as to why. "I found it so mean," says Arthur.

The voice coach, who believes that Deborah created "a breach" between him and Namath, wasn't alone in his misgivings about the new bride. Linwood Alford was introduced to the new bride back in Beaver Falls, at a banquet honoring the Tigers' varsity football team, 1984 WPIAL champions. "You know who *he* is," said Joe.

Obviously, Joe had shown her photographs and told her the old stories. Linwood was beaming.

Deborah nodded. "Well," she said pointedly, "things sure won't be like they used to."

For some, the first meeting with Deborah would be the last. Marv Fleming, a friend of Joe's since their USO trip to Vietnam in 1969, recalls meeting Deborah at the Namath football camp. Later, he was walking across the practice field toward the locker room when Joe asked if he had called Deborah "Randi" by mistake.

"No," said Marv. "I did not."

"That's good," said Joe.

"I'll apologize to her if she thinks I did," said Marv. "But I didn't."

No need, said Joe. "Just be cool."

Marvin felt regret wash over him as they walked to the locker room. He wasn't a drinking buddy—"Once he got to like, five going on six, I'd say, 'Okay, gotta go, Joe'"—but more of a friend to go out to dinner and shoot pool with. They played for a quarter a game at Joe's place in Truesdale Estates in L.A. Taking a quarter off Joe Namath was about as much fun as you could have. But now, Marv Fleming knew those days were over. "I could see she was creating a problem, getting rid of everybody," he says, referring to Deborah. "I didn't want to be a problem. So I just faded away."

Mort and Carol Fishman also met Deborah—Jimmy had instructed them not to call her "Debbie"—at the football camp. Namath came off the practice field to greet them, clearly happy to see his old friends after so long. Mort had been in the hospital for months with a staph infection, and Joe had been out in L.A. Joe gave Carol a kiss on the cheek and a big hug, almost twirling her around. At Joe's insistence, they made plans for lunch and dinner that same night. Just then, Deborah approached. "You could see," says Mort, "she was boiling over."

She asked to have a word with Joe, and the two of them stepped away. When Joe returned a few minutes later, he told Mort and Carol, "Gotta take a pass on dinner tonight. Matter of fact, I won't be able to have lunch, either."

Now Mort was pissed. He went home thinking Joe would phone to apologize. He waited, but no call ever came. "Just like that," he says, "never talked to the guy again. I was brokenhearted."

■   ■   ■

Shirley Mays has heard some of this before, how her daughter drove off Joe's friends, but protests, "She's getting a raw deal all the way around." Deborah, she explains, didn't like big drinkers, or hangers-on. Having married a man who was famous for not marrying, Deborah also became acutely aware of all the women who had been cast in bit parts and supporting roles in the Broadway Joe story. She couldn't turn on the television without wondering whom he had been with. Even absolute strangers spoke to him with a degree of intimacy, as if they *knew* him. *I love you, Joe. Do you know how much you mean to me? You're my all-time favorite. . . . I was there when . . .* Namath was mostly polite about it: I'm getting chills, he'd say.

Old friends and old fans had staked their claim on Joe long before Deborah came into his life. She was only six when he won the Super Bowl, but now she was left to consider the question of his identity, to reconfigure borders between man and myth, public and private, between her husband and Broadway Joe.

"She got hurt from so many remarks," says Shirley Mays. Her daughter wanted a new life, as did Joe. "But he didn't have the courage to do it," she says. "He doesn't like to do distasteful things. He'd been a star so long. He would let someone else be the bad guy, and she became it."

A process that began with his work in the theater ended with his marriage to Deborah: He had cut his ties to the old days. The friends he kept were the ones who observed the rules without incident. "If you want to be around Joe," says Hoot Owl, "you do what makes him happy."

And the best way to do that was to make Deborah happy.

In her first public appearance as Mrs. Joe Namath, Deborah spent a day at the races. It had been more than twenty years since Joe's first Orange Bowl, when his winning bet at a Florida track raised concerns for the morals of minors. Now Gulfstream Park in Hallandale was paying him $50,000 a year to serve as its spokesman. As a Gulfstream official explained: "He gives you the feeling of good, clean, wholesome fun."

The newlyweds were next sighted at Macy's flagship store in Manhattan, where Namath unveiled his line of signature underwear. Unlike baseball pitcher Jim Palmer, who posed for the Jockey brand, this promotion stressed that Namath was more than a mere model. As per Jimmy's specifications, he had "total control" over the design of his briefs. And

50. OLD JOE

though his talent for designing men's haberdashery would remain unnoticed, Namath looked good enough on the advertising placard: a slice of well-aging beefcake, a man other forty-somethings would want to be as they sucked in their stomachs in front of the mirror. Still, the new Mrs. Namath was the star of this show. She claimed to know nothing of this Broadway Joe character, saying, "We've never gone to a bar." The man she knew woke at 6:00 A.M. He fished, he golfed, and as per her request, he always wore his seatbelt.

The couple made their stage debut in a Wilmington, North Carolina, production of *Cactus Flower,* a romantic comedy about a philandering dentist played by Joe. Deborah played his young girlfriend. "They were very affectionate, very lovey-dovey," recalls Chuck Kinlaw, one of the actors. "All Deborah talked about was how Joe was a god in New York."

He was big in Atlantic City, too, where the Claridge signed him for another musical, *Bells Are Ringing.* Originally, Namath and his bride were to appear together, but then Deborah decided against it. "She hasn't convinced herself that her singing and dancing is polished enough yet," explained Joe.

There was an even more compelling reason for pulling out of the show: she was pregnant. The baby was due in October. If it was a girl, it would be named Jessica Grace. If a boy, it would be John Jeffrey, after his father and her brother.

■   ■   ■

With her own career on hold, Deborah took charge of Joe's. It was plain to see from the way he watched all those games on TV that he missed football. He would question the coaches. He would disagree with the announcers. The blood rushed to his face as he provided his own spontaneous, unexpurgated color commentary.

Do it, she told him.

Soon thereafter, Jimmy Walsh began discussions with Roone Arledge, now in charge of both the news and sports divisions at ABC. Although *Monday Night Football* was about to head into a sixteenth season, Arledge's infatuation with Namath had hardly diminished. Jimmy, for his part, was now representing an actor of dinner-theater caliber, eight years removed from the game. But he played it as if the leverage were all his. ABC would have to finalize the terms of any prospective agreement before even talking to Joe. "The stupidest ass-backwards way of doing a negotiation ever dreamed of," said Arledge, who nevertheless accepted Jimmy's conditions.

The network boss had his reasons. Cosell had left *Monday Night Football* after the 1983 season. Don Meredith, whose "Dandy Don" act now seemed less dandy than bored, departed the following year. With ratings down 22 percent over three seasons, commercial time had been discounted. ABC was now owned by Capital Cities, a bottom-line outfit, which meant that the very survival of *Monday Night Football* was in doubt.

In Namath, Arledge saw the telecast's salvation. The man who saved a league could surely save the show. Joe, who had never broadcast a game, might have been a risk. But so what? Risk was at the core of Broadway Joe. Forget the points, take the long-shot odds. "It was worth the gamble," said Arledge.

The final deal stipulated that Namath would provide "color" in a booth with Frank Gifford and O. J. Simpson. Jimmy got him huge money, two years guaranteed at a reported $850,000 per. A press conference was held at "21," where the writers couldn't have been more impressed with Joe's wife. Who'd have thought? The girl had a good head on her shoulders. "I'm the one," said Deborah, then about midway through her pregnancy. "I pushed him into going for this. Blame me."

■   ■   ■

On August 3, 1985, Namath went on the air wearing a yellow blazer with the logo of ABC Sports. He was broadcasting live from the annual exhibition contest in Canton, Ohio, where earlier that day he had been inducted into the Pro Football Hall of Fame. Namath's election had been the subject of substantial debate in football circles. In 1983, his first year of eligibility, he fell six votes short of the required twenty-three. The electorate consisted of a media representative for each team and one from the Pro Football Writers Association, a total of twenty-nine voters. Some of them, representing the league's oldest franchises, still had a beef with the AFL. Others hadn't been able to get past their image of Joe as a hippie smart-ass. Certainly, his reputation for surliness with the press didn't help. But the real case against Namath was made with numbers. His 27,663 passing yards were more than eight other Hall of Fame quarterbacks, and he was the first to throw for 4,000 yards. But he had also thrown many more interceptions (220) than touchdowns (173), and in twelve seasons with the Jets, he only played for three winning teams, a fact that could be argued two ways. Was he culpable for those losses? Or were his accomplishments in spite of them? He missed the better part of three seasons with injuries, and when he played, he played hurt. Interceptions were part of his game. In the first years they were mostly the result of a young man's hubris, his great gambler's confidence; later they became signs of an aging athlete's desperation. In his last two seasons in New York—a run that saw the Jets go 6–22—Namath threw forty-four interceptions and only nineteen touchdowns.

With numbers like those, he was voted down again in '84. The Hall of Fame selection committee, meanwhile, had seen fit to induct such household names as Arnie Weinmeister and Mike McCormack, both of whom began professional careers with the New York Yankees of the old All-American Football Conference more than half a century earlier. Broadway Joe would have to wait.

The decision had been noted with disapproval by Dave Anderson and the *Los Angeles Times*'s Bob Oates Sr., both fervent Namath loyalists. But there were others who questioned the committee's judgment, including the writer who took more grief from Namath than anyone. "Sure, I would have voted for him," says Paul Zimmerman. "You look at a guy's career and what it meant to the game."

By that standard, one is hard pressed to find a candidate more deserving than Namath. The edifice in Canton was, after all, a Hall of *Fame*. As Broadway Joe, Namath aroused a kind of interest the game had never before seen. He raised attendance, viewership, and wagers. In some sense, his election was irrelevant, for Namath had already been immortalized by the television ratings and the point spread. Those were the numbers that told the real story of his career. He had changed the game, elongated its dimensions, accentuated its drama, and consecrated its championship. He had endowed the National Football League with some of his cool magic, a fact that Roone Arledge understood as well as anyone.

By 1985, when the voters finally approved him, Namath's fellow inductees included his new broadcast partner, O. J. Simpson, and his favorite commissioner, Pete Rozelle. But the draw was clearly Joe. The annual festivities drew the biggest crowds ever, with more women than usual. "In terms of fan appeal," said one Hall of Fame official, "I'd say Joe is the most popular player we've had."

Bunny Kreshon, now a mother of three, drove to Canton with her kids. She got a glimpse of Joe as he walked to his car. "Joe . . . Joe," she called.

"Bunny, what are you doing here?"

"I love you."

She was dead serious. Then again, she wasn't the only one professing those sentiments. That day, everybody loved Joe.

Coach Larry Bruno made the speech introducing him. Joe accepted the praise with great gratitude for everyone, especially God: "He was kind enough to old Joe to let me find my wife, Deborah."

To hear "old Joe," as he now called himself, Deborah completed him. He knew all too well that not everyone could be so lucky. Even after all these years, his parents requested to be seated at separate tables during the various Hall of Fame banquets.

■ ■ ■

The *Monday Night* booth now featured a Hall of Fame backfield—Gifford, Simpson, and Namath—with unmatched endorsement power. Unfortunately, they didn't make much of a broadcast team. Gifford was ever the straight man. Simpson did his best work shilling for rental cars. As for Namath, two decades had passed since he was christened Broadway Joe, and the intervening years had taught him something about humility. But humility was of little use to him now. In fact, it was a detriment.

The network didn't offer him a lot of tutelage, as Arledge didn't want his man sounding too polished. He wanted Broadway Joe. The ABC boss, an otherwise shrewd judge of talent, had convinced himself that a forty-two-year-old expectant father could somehow morph back into the kid he used to be, as if it were still 1969. But instead of Broadway Joe, Arledge got Old Joe, this curiously deferential character who insisted on addressing him (as he always addressed his employers) as "Mister."

Old Joe Namath was not the character people liked to remember. As he kept talking about his responsibilities as a father and his lack of confidence as a broadcaster, perhaps his misgivings should have been apparent. "I have to convince myself I know what I'm doing," he said.

■ ■ ■

Deborah went out and got him books on how to speak. "She wanted him not to make mistakes," says Hoot Owl. Joe studied diligently, but Hoot Owl could never understand why Joe Namath of all people was worrying himself sick over his diction and his grammar.

"The greatest announcer that ever was, was Dizzy Dean," Hoot Owl told him. Diz was just a hillbilly from Arkansas, who barely spoke a word of proper English.

But Joe didn't want to be Dizzy Dean, or even Dandy Don. For that matter, he didn't want to be Broadway Joe, either. Speaking properly became a point of honor, as if it were the responsible thing to do. There was a problem with this approach, however: It wasn't him.

"If he'da just been Joe Namath, they would've loved it," says Hoot Owl. Hoot Owl could notice the change every time his friend went on one of those TV shows: "Joe don't act like himself."

■   ■   ■

Namath should have known as well as anyone: without the confidence, you don't belong. What was true for football was true for broadcasting. There was a counterfeit quality in his on-air demeanor, his insistent cheer and reluctance to criticize. "Inane," said the *New York Times,* noting Namath's unrelenting use of "heckuva" as his signature adjective. "Dwelled on the obvious," complained *USA Today.*

Those opening-night reviews stung, though not enough to make him work much harder. He remained ill prepared and preoccupied. Old Joe didn't want to be on the road, talking to players and coaches, when he should have been at home with his pregnant wife. After six games, *Sports Illustrated* declared: "*Monday Night Football* has a problem. It's the Joe Namath Problem, which is growing by the week."

Oh, what ABC would have given for the lout, the braggart, the shit-stirrer, the guarantor. But Old Joe didn't want to cause any trouble, as he now had responsibilities.

Typical was Namath's halftime interview with John Riggins, whom he recalled with suspect fondness and characteristic insight as "a piece of work." In the years since escaping Namath's shadow, Riggins had become a huge star for the Washington Redskins, with five 1,000-yard seasons. He had been the MVP of Super Bowl XVIII, and led the league in touchdowns for two years running. At thirty-six, Riggins was the NFL's oldest running back and its most publicized. He made headlines in the off-season, getting loaded at a Washington, D.C., banquet and addressing Supreme Court Justice Sandra Day O'Connor with the immortal words: "Loosen up, Sandy, baby." More recently, he had held out from training camp and been arrested for public drunkenness. But Namath wasn't going there. Instead, Old Joe asked Riggo how he managed to balance the demands of football and family.

From the *New York Post*, April 11, 1987:

BROADWAY JOE AND FIJI DEBBIE

Joe Namath isn't asking people he meets what their sign is, but he did go to the Fiji Islands last month because it was "in the stars." Broadway Joe and baby daughter Jessica were accompanying Joe's wife, Deborah Lynn Mays, who was making her annual "solar return." And what is a solar return? "Every year on your birthday, the planets line up in the exact same configuration as on your original birthday," Debbie said. But the line-up takes place in a different part of the world each year. And to derive maximum astrological benefit, you have to go to that place. Debbie said, "The place you are on your birthday makes a tremendous difference in what your next year will be like. I took the hour when I was born to meditate just by myself." The actress, who has been ruled by the stars for almost seven years, has help figuring out where to go each year on her March 6 birthday. Her astrologer, Signe Taff, fed Deborah's charts through a computer and targeted a two-mile square patch of the Fiji town of Nadi. "Astrology is kind of like religion," Deborah told PAGE SIX. She said her astrologer

51. FIJI

knew she'd tie the marital knot in 1984, but didn't predict who her groom would be. "They had predicted the marriage because of where I was that year. Had I gone someplace else, it could have completely changed what I had done that year," said Debbie. "You might have married another guy!" exclaimed Joe. "I'm not a flaky kind of person," said Pennsylvania-raised Deborah. "Astrology doesn't monopolize my time. It's kind of like going to a therapist."

Joe, for his part, didn't need a therapist or an astrologer to experience happiness or fulfillment; he had his girls, Deborah and Jessica Grace. The baby was born October 12, 1985, at Lenox Hill Hospital. Joe was present for the birth, the miracle of blood blessed with light. "A love never felt before," said Namath. Jessica began walking at seven months and three weeks, recalled Joe, who by then was well versed in the works of Dr. Spock. In the years to come, guests would be delighted to see that the erstwhile playboy had become such a dedicated parent. One of them recalled Jessica, then three, interrupting an interview to call her father on the speakerphone: "Daddy, could you come and wipe my bottom?"

"Of course I can," said Joe. "When do you want me to do that?"

"Now, Daddy."

There was nothing Joe wouldn't do for his girls. He was theirs to have and to hold, to serve and protect, to die for, if necessary. Deborah and Jessica were his stars, the constellations by which he was guided, the basis for his system of belief.

Unfortunately for Joe, a happy home life didn't translate into professional success. ABC fired him after that disastrous first season, opting to pay the remaining year on his contract rather than put him back on the air. A month later, Fabergé officially dropped him as well, fearful that the scent of Brut would become associated with failure. In fact, Namath hadn't done a Brut commercial ("Today's your Brut day! It's your lucky Brut day!") since 1984. That was the year Fabergé was sold, and Namath was married. Sales had increased 16 percent without him. As an endorser, Old Joe just didn't have the requisite sex appeal.

He seemed to be generating more litigation than sales. ABC stopped paying him after he spoke disparagingly to a *Newsday* reporter at a dinner for Dr. Nicholas. ("I think it's boring," he said, when asked about the revamped edition of *Monday Night Football*. "They're so wrong on so many things.") Namath responded by suing the network. He likewise brought suit against Fabergé, winning a motion to have the case file kept confidential. His case against Nantucket Industries, which canceled his line of underwear, was also sealed. It had been filed through Namanco's wholly owned subsidiary, Planned Licensing, which also sued Noel Industries—makers of "Joe Namath" jeans—and Alpha Richard Corp., makers of "Joe Namath" sports jackets. Jimmy Walsh's plan for equity in both companies collapsed when the signature jeans, which sold poorly at Sears, were recommended for discount chains like Kmart.

None of these cases ever went to trial, though perhaps Namath's self-esteem had been put to the test. After ABC fired him, he received an offer to serve as a ring announcer for a pay-per-view wrestling event. Wahoo McDaniel would have gotten a kick out of that.

■   ■   ■

Joe wasn't exactly out of business. George Lois came through with some television spots for *USA Today* and Olympic Airways, the national airline of Greece. Namath also did some guest-starring on episodes of *The A-Team*, and *ALF,* a show about a furry alien living with an average American family. But he had no steady work, no real job, and spoke of his disappointment and boredom. He spent his days golfing and fishing. And he drank. Later Deborah complained to an old acquaintance of his how Joe would come home, fill a large glass with vodka, and drink until he slept.

Deborah didn't drink. She hadn't liked it when her brother drank, and now she didn't like it in her husband. "You act foolish when you drink," says Shirley Mays. "I'm talking about my son and Joe. It's embarrassing if you're looking at people you love. It was disappointing to Deborah."

She finally gave him an ultimatum, which Joe preferred to regard as "a bet." Joe would never welsh on a bet, especially not with Deborah. Welshing on your wife would be a form of infidelity. "If I lost," he said, "I was going into rehab."

"She couldn't save my son," says Shirley. "But she certainly saved Joe. He stopped drinking because of her."

"There's a whole lot to be said for being on the same page as your partner," reflected Joe. Quitting wasn't an inconsiderable challenge, but having a wife and kid made it infinitely easier. Abstinence from drink became another token of his devotion to the family. For more than a year, Namath wrote in a journal, each entry marking another sober day. He was living without alcohol, and he was living better. The first entry was dated March 24, 1987, not long after the family returned from Fiji.

■   ■   ■

Carol Weisman had never seen her husband so nervous, pacing the lobby in the Century Plaza as he waited for Joe Namath. Michael Weisman was regarded among the brightest talents in sports television, having already produced the World Series and the Super Bowl. Now, at thirty-seven, he was the executive producer of NBC Sports and looking to hire one of his childhood idols. It was Namath who should have been nervous. "Joe was damaged goods at the time," says Weisman. "He had been so beaten up at ABC. He just wanted to bounce back. He would've taken anything."

Still, Mike Weisman was a wreck. It was Joe. *Joe.* Weisman grew up in Queens, where his friends counted themselves as Giants fans, though none had actually attended any of the team's sold-out games at Yankee Stadium. His father was a public relations man who took a job with the AFL when the Jets were still the Titans. But then came Namath, and suddenly none of his friends even cared that they couldn't get tickets to the Giants. "Joe was cool," he says. "And we all wanted to be cool." Weisman would always remember Namath as he was dressed for a particular interview with Curt Gowdy: bell-bottom jeans, Pumas, and a long blue wool coat, like an officer's coat. Weisman went out and got the exact same outfit, wearing the coat with the collar turned up.

Weisman went to North Carolina on a baseball scholarship. All the frat boys there had grown up watching the Colts, whose games CBS aired as its regional telecast in the South. Before the 1969 Super Bowl Weisman warned them what would happen, what Joe would do to the Colts. By then his dad was working for NBC Sports, and had invited his son down for the game. That Sunday turned out to be the last time Michael saw his father, who died of a heart attack that spring. But it was a great time, thanks in good measure to Joe.

And now Namath was coming to pick *him* up at the hotel. Namath had insisted on taking him and Carol to dinner. "I had these fantasies that he would arrive in a Maserati or something," says Weisman. "But he came in a four-seat family car, nothing flashy. It was above a Buick but less than a Mercedes."

Joe chose Mr. Chow's. They talked over dinner. Weisman explained that before Namath went back on air, he wanted him to work with someone, like a coach but for broadcasting. Unlike *Monday Night Football*, where three announcers fought for airtime, this would be only a two-man booth. Namath wouldn't be on big national games, either. Weisman would start by assigning him to the Jets, who weren't very good, but afforded Namath the luxury of playing to an audience that already loved him. He wouldn't have to be Edward R. Murrow or Howard Cosell or even Broadway Joe.

This was all to Namath's liking. For once, the matter of salary never came up, as Jimmy had already assured Weisman: "Money won't be an issue." Joe, who couldn't have been nicer or more receptive, made it clear he just wanted another shot.

But Joe's cordiality is not what stands out in Weisman's recollection of the evening. Rather, it's Deborah, or as Carol called her once by mistake, "Debbie."

"My name is not Debbie," she said. "It's Deborah."

The severity in her tone caused conversation to come to a momentary halt. "It got our attention," says Weisman. "She was very serious." Weisman thought Joe might say something to break the tension; after all, it had been an honest mistake. But Joe remained silent.

Later that evening, Deborah mentioned that she met her husband at a class. "Oh," said Weisman, trying to make conversation, "you're going to be an actress."

"No," she said sternly. "I *am* an actress."

Then followed another awkward lull, which Joe again ignored until the small talk resumed. Before the evening was over, though, Weisman told Joe how much he had meant to him, growing up in Queens. He told him about the bell-bottoms and the Pumas and the long blue coat. He told him about the Super Bowl and his father. Weisman still remembered some of the NBC guys weeping with joy after the Jets beat the Colts.

"Mike," said Joe Namath, "you're telling me these stories, I'm getting goose bumps."

■   ■   ■

As he spent more time with Joe, Weisman discovered that there were a lot of guys who felt as he had. How many times had he seen it happen? A dozen? A hundred? And in how many cities? They approached like pilgrims. They felt a need to tell Namath where they were, who they were with, how they felt, what it meant, that they, too, had predicted it. They had been with him. They had been young.

"You're giving me goose bumps," Joe would say.

At first, Weisman was taken aback by Namath's apparent insincerity, but with time he came to think differently. Joe could have told these people, "That's nice," or simply have said nothing at all. But goose bumps were an acknowledgment that the stranger's confession had been heard. Joe might as well have said, "Go in peace."

"It was an act of kindness," says Weisman. "It made people feel good."

■   ■   ■

Marty Glickman, a longtime New York football announcer, was selected as Namath's tutor. Glickman dissected his performance after each game and forwarded a report to Weisman. It was Glickman who told Joe how to hold the microphone. Think of the camera as a person, he said. Don't call players by their numbers or their first names. Don't just mention, explain. What is a crossing pattern? What is an out? If possible, draw on personal experience.

Joe listened attentively. He studied, though never to excess, and became more proficient. Bob Oates Jr., his collaborator on a coffee-table book fifteen years earlier and, more recently, an instructional manual for kids, provided some journalistic legwork. Deborah did some coaching as well. Namath's broadcast partner, Marv Albert, noticed that he kept a notecard with the word *energy* in his line of sight. "My wife stays on me," said Joe, who had a habit of fading in the second half of a broadcast. "She wants me to sustain my energy."

Reviews were mixed. Namath still had his quirks, elongating his *l*'s, for instance, so that *play* became a three-syllable word, "puh-l-l-lay." But while he never became a star, he did attain a level of competence as a broadcaster. More than that, he was a pleasure to work with, regularly bringing coffee for the producers and the grips. Everyone on the set wanted to have his picture taken with Joe. "I found him to be a terrific asset," says Weisman. "Never gave me any trouble. He never called and complained—as almost every announcer does—about his assignment or his hotel room. He had already been a star. Joe was a national celebrity going back to Alabama. He didn't need to be doing the Super Bowl. He wasn't thinking, 'Boy, they'll all see me. I'll be famous. I'll get some commercials.' Joe *was* famous. He didn't have the need. He'd had his fill."

Namath the broadcaster was a committed team player, and spoke of wanting to be a color man for another twenty or twenty-five years. NBC was a great gig for Joe: no more than one date a week from August through December. It kept him in the game. There was little pressure, and a lot of time to stay home with the family. That was the cure, of course, domestic tranquility. It wouldn't mend his joints, but it soothed wounds he suffered as a boy at the top of the stairs. All he had deferred—from his wages to his wedding—was for this: to be a father, to have a family, to keep it healthy and whole.

The network paid him only a low-six-figure salary, but there was other money coming in. Jimmy, now raising a family of his own in New Orleans, had placed him in a wide array of investments over the years, from shopping centers in California to rental properties in Savannah, Georgia.

In 1988, Joe and Deborah bought a 4,356-square-foot home with an adjacent plot in Southport, Connecticut. By coincidence, Sal Marchiano and his wife lived about a mile away. The couples met waiting on line at a local movie theater, where Sal and Joe exchanged greetings and numbers. Sal kept calling. It was always Deborah who picked up the phone, and Sal would leave a message for Joe. But he never called. Finally, Sal asked Jimmy what the problem was.

"She doesn't want him hanging out with his old pals," said Jimmy. Deborah didn't want him "to get back into bad habits."

Deborah had other plans. "She wanted to live in Connecticut and take acting lessons in New York," says Hoot Owl.

For her sake, then, Joe would try to live as a country squire. "We've got a little white farmhouse with green trim on five acres," he told Dave Anderson. "We've got a couple of horses and we're getting some goats and pigs. We've got a dog and we're getting another dog." For years, Joe had mourned his Irish setter, Fancy Pharaoh, who died late in 1969. Mort Fishman once saw him slam on the brakes, dash out of his car, and jump off a footbridge to save a couple of kittens drowning in a canal. Joe had always loved animals, particularly dogs, who gave love unconditionally. But he never liked the cold, nor did he like snow, and Connecticut just had too much of both. So following a winter that intensified his arthritic aches, the little white farmhouse went on the market, where it fetched $1.75 million, a $500,000 profit.

The Namaths decided to raise a family in Tequesta, Florida, a quiet, affluent town in northernmost Palm Beach County. The home was four bedrooms, 6,813 square feet, with a pool, on the banks of the Loxahatchee River. Orange and mango trees dotted the property, but Deborah decorated with rustic European touches. "With an English garden for me," she said. "A rose garden." For Joe, the water was filled with flounder and snook. He fished off his dock, and off his boat. He bought a new twenty-five-footer Boston Whaler, naming it *Team Game Too*.

On December 11, 1990, Joe and Deborah had a second daughter, Olivia Rose. She looked like her daddy.

Joe taught his girls to handle live bait, shrimp from the bucket. Before she was nine, Jessica had caught a ladyfish just north of Jupiter Inlet. The ladyfish broke the water four times before Jessica got it to the side of the boat. Olivia was four when she caught her first snook. "Reel," said Joe, "reel!" It was, recalled the proud father, "the prettiest snook we had ever seen." Joe threw it back.

What was love? What would you die for? What would save you?

"Just having those little arms wrapped around you," he once said.

Bathing. Wiping. Feeding. Reading the stories. Tucking them in. Waking them up. Later, hobbling into the kitchen before dawn to make their lunch. Driving them to school. Picking them up. There were tennis lessons and soccer practice and ballet recitals. He helped with their homework. Broadway Joe became Mr. Mom.

What could the kingdom of television bestow upon him now? What did he care if he had a hard time using the telestrator?

Why would he ever need a drink?

"He was with those kids every day, every morning, every night," says Hoot Owl. "The happiest thing in his life was his kids. . . . I witnessed it. I was there."

Those were happy years, through the mid-1990s. Everybody seemed to notice his glow when he was around the family. Joe Hirsch, "Uncle Joe" to the girls, recalls Namath coming to Gulfstream Park one morning with his daughters. Hirsch took them to the stall of Skip Away, a big gray who would earn Horse of the Year honors. A champion like Skip Away could easily become temperamental and aggressive, but he was unusually compliant as he let the girls pet and brush him. "Everybody was feeling pretty good," says Hirsch. The early sunshine shot into the barn, tracing each of them with a shimmer. Hirsch watched Namath watching his daughters. They had known each other since December 1964, more than thirty years. And in all that time, Hirsch had never seen him so at ease.

"So content," says Tom Werblin, who would visit the Namaths while vacationing with his own family in nearby Jupiter. In Deborah, he saw "a sweet girl, totally devoted to Joe." Olivia and Jessica clearly worshipped their father. "You could see it in their eyes," says Werblin. Meanwhile, Joe had become someone Sonny's son had never imagined: frolicking with the kids in the pool, bringing them by Jet Ski to a tiny island in the inlet, taking them to the movies, teaching them how to cast. "My son caught his first fish, a snook, off Joe's dock," says Werblin.

What Deborah sought in Fiji, Joe found on his dock, harbor to his private paradise, where his own stars were harmoniously aligned. Of all his guests in Tequesta, perhaps the least likely was Paul Zimmerman. Zim was now writing for *Sports Illustrated*, where he was known as the famous pigskin prognosticator, "Dr. Z." Knowing that Zimmerman had covered the Jets' only championship team, his editors asked him for a "Where are they now?" piece for their annual Super Bowl issue. "You'll have to get someone else," he said. "Namath hasn't spoken to me since '69."

Still, Zimmerman made the obligatory call to Namanco, just to appease his editors. He couldn't have been more surprised when his request was granted. So there he was, on Joe's dock, catching up on years gone by. Namath said his right knee hurt worse than ever; it would have to be replaced. But, then, no one had ever died of a bad knee. Joe hadn't done any stage work since Jessica was born, though again, not because of the knee. "What I want now is to be home with my family," he said.

Zimmerman couldn't get over Deborah, who was talking to the contractors. "I was very happy to see the kind of woman he had married," he says. "I always thought Joe would end up with a tootsie."

Manatees swam by, "almost close enough to pat." Namath kept a line in the water as he spoke of the Super Bowl. He recalled the afternoon from various vantage points: the field, the huddle, the sideline. "I never really knew," says Zimmerman. "He loved the game."

It took a while for the sportswriter to absorb the scene. He had imagined it many times, meeting Joe after all these years. But it had never been like this, a stunning, sunlit afternoon. Finally, Zimmerman asked: "Why . . . what did I do?"

Namath just shrugged. "Most of those grudges, well, I don't even remember what they were about."

As far as Zimmerman was concerned, those hours on the dock made up for years of hostility and aggravation. He was so happy for Joe. The famously gruff Dr. Z could feel himself welling up, then holding back tears as Namath went on about the Super Bowl.

"Look," said Joe, displaying a tanned arm. "Goose bumps."

In December 1991, Joe was assembling a swing set for the kids when his left knee gave out. The left was supposed to be his *good* knee, but it had been the one doing most of the buckling lately. Finally, the very notion of a good knee, however relative, had become as obsolete as the joints themselves. He fell by the swing set, in the backyard. He had never fallen before. For years, the doctors had been warning him that artificial knees were an inevitability. But only now, with his younger daughter a year old, did he opt for surgery.

"I didn't want to take any chances when I was carrying Olivia," he said. "I had to have this done."

His new knees were made of metal and plastic. The operation, performed at the Hospital for Special Surgery in Manhattan, took four hours. The rehabilitation lasted for months, during which time Joe Namath learned to use a walker.

52. TATIANA

Now as ever, his physical state had no bearing on his ability to move merchandise. In fact, the concept of Joe was undergoing something of a renaissance. He had reached a new level of ubiquitousness as the relentlessly cheery face behind Flex-All 454, an analgesic balm, and the Wiz, a New York–based consumer electronics chain. In 1992 Namath became the first corporate spokesman for NFL Properties Inc., the league's licensing arm. Jimmy Walsh, now with six kids of his own, was keeping busy. Later that year, Planned Licensing cut a deal for Namath to endorse Ambervision sunglasses, guaranteeing a minimum of $1.25 million over the next decade.

Like his contract with NFL Properties, it would provide a steady six-figure income into the next millennium—enough to help Namath take it in stride when NBC let him go the following year. After six seasons with the network, he had become a capable announcer, even providing an occasional whiff of the candor once associated with Broadway Joe. Early in his final season, for example, he was outspoken in assessing the state of his former team: "The Jets have been losing fans because they've been playing like mutts."

"Namath deserved better," says Mike Weisman. "But he got whacked for the same reason I got whacked. It was a new regime, and they just wanted to bring in their own guys."

Nevertheless Weisman's successor, Terry O'Neil, didn't want to be perceived as the guy who dumped Joe Namath, who had appeared only six times during the 1992 season. "It's an evolution toward what is an amicable parting," said O'Neil. Jimmy Walsh, who saw nothing amicable in NBC's actions, complained that O'Neil had always been intent on phasing out Joe. O'Neil responded that Namath had declined eight assignments. "All scheduling conflicts," replied Jimmy.

Namath, for his part, recalled having turned down a new contract that offered only eight games, half of a regular season schedule. He still liked the gig, but he had come to think of those weekends on the road as "a sacrifice." Fridays were a hardship. "The girls were crying when I was leaving," he said.

Their tears tempered whatever regret and resentment he felt for NBC Sports. "It's something you learn to live with," he said later. "Had I been a younger guy, I'd have been angry." Finally, he knew better. At fifty, he had learned who he was, and what he wanted.

■   ■   ■

Unfortunately, the same could not be said for his wife, who found that being Mrs. Joe Namath came with its own set of complications. "It's not easy being married to someone who's as big a legend as Joe," says Shirley Mays. "Not because he isn't nice and wonderful and everything else. But you kind of lose your identity."

Deborah would recall Joe playing in a celebrity golf tournament before they wed. A fan in the gallery kept hollering at him, telling him never to get married. The fan himself was wearing a wedding band, but considered that was beside the point. "Joe should never be married," he said.

Deborah advised him, none too gently, that Joe was getting married. Go live your life through someone else, she told him.

She was twenty-one when they met, twenty-two when they were married, and twenty-three when Jessica was born. Her own ambitions went into abeyance, melding with a legend that people regarded as public property. Still, she became far more than just Mrs. Joe Namath; she became his driving force. She wanted him to be well-spoken. She wanted him off the booze. And she got what she wanted, for hers was the approval he sought.

Early in the marriage, Namath had received a call from Howard Felsher, executive producer of the game show *Family Feud*. Felsher wanted to know if he was interested in replacing host Richard Dawson. "Just have breakfast with me," said Felsher.

"Can I bring my wife?" asked Joe.

The breakfast took place at the Beverly Hills Hotel. Something about Namath convinced Felsher that he was right for the show: "a nice human being, which is rare in our business." Joe seemed both intrigued and flattered by the attention. But Felsher quickly realized that Joe wasn't the one he needed to convince so much as Deborah. "She had great influence over him," says Felsher. "Every time he made a comment, he looked to her for approbation."

Deborah made herself clear: she did not have a high opinion of game shows. But no matter, her concern was Joe Namath. "It could do him a lot of harm if it fails," she said.

On the other hand, *Family Feud* was not without its enticements. As the show was a big hit, his salary would be big, too. Felsher convinced Deborah and Joe to take another breakfast meeting. Finally, with his wife looking on, Joe did some trial runs as a host. He was great; the contestants loved him. "Just charming," says Felsher. "He brought such a feeling of innocence to it." A deal was negotiated, with Felsher's boss, producer Bill Goodson, even agreeing to Jimmy's last-minute demand for a signing bonus. "Twenty-five thousand didn't mean that much," recalls Felsher. "But my boss got cold feet." Apparently, at the last minute, Goodson decided that *Family Feud* should have a more erudite host.

Deborah couldn't have spent too long mourning the sudden collapse of the deal. While the money might have been good, being the wife of a game show host was not what she had envisioned when she married Joe Namath. She had other aspirations.

"I was stunned when I first saw her," says Al Hassan. Without makeup and without that Nordic shimmer, she belied her husband's famously advertised preference for blondes. But she was gorgeous, and more than that, Hassan— who had staged Jean-Paul Sartre's *Respectful Prostitute* for his master's in theater arts at the University of Maryland—enjoyed their conversations. "She was a big foreign film buff," he says. They spoke of *Belle de Jour*, *The Bicycle Thief*, *Diabolique*, and *Divorce, Italian Style*. He found her equally knowledgeable when it came to the theater, as she spoke of playwrights Anton Chekhov and Eugene O'Neill. "She wanted to be an actress," he says.

Actually, she wanted to be a *serious* actress, and that was a problem. For while her husband could be a game show host or a football announcer or a pitchman for the Wiz, her own role—played in a quiet town ninety miles from Miami—remained the same. She would always be cast as Mrs. Joe Namath. Or, as some people still insisted on calling her, "Debbie."

How she hated that name. On April 1, 1992, she changed it, legally, dropping "Deborah" in favor of "May." Still, "May" did not achieve the desired effect, as a name or an identity. So on July 8, 1993, she again petitioned the court, and became "May Tatiana Namath," or, as she preferred to be known, Tatiana.

Perhaps she imagined herself a Russian princess. Maybe the name changes were inspired by her astrologer, Signe Taff, who believed in "moon wobbles" as a key determinant of human behavior. Whatever her reasons, says Shirley

Mays, "It's her God-given right." Tatiana's husband agreed, informing friends of her preference matter-of-factly, offering no explanation. Her name was her business; her happiness was his.

Butch Ryan, halfback on the 1960 WPIAL championship team, remembers bumping into Joe on the eighteenth green at the Blackhawk golf course back in Beaver Falls. He seemed so different from the brash kid who wore Italians and a letter jacket, telling the bookies in New Castle to fuck off. Joe mentioned that he was getting ready to move back to New York. He didn't want to go; he had gotten New York out of his system a long time ago. But Tatiana had her heart set on it.

"I'm only doing it for her," he said.

In January 1995, the Namaths bought a two-bedroom apartment in the Dakota, at Seventy-second Street and Central Park West, one of Manhattan's most exclusive addresses. Florida remained the family's primary residence, where Joe did his fishing and golfing and where the kids went to school. But Tatiana's acting lessons were in New York, and she commuted there regularly.

In a city fueled by ambition, however, her own aspirations remained unfulfilled. Among her teachers was E. Katherine Kerr, who found her to be a trying student. Tatiana—who asked that Kerr call her "Anna" for a while—did not lack talent. Rather, the problem was "this enormous tension she walked around with." "When it comes to acting you have to be open and vulnerable," says Kerr. "She was shut down."

The notable exception came in an autobiographical monologue she prepared, "a beautifully written piece," as Kerr recalls. It was all there, a series of emotional dislocations: her brother's disappearance, her mother's denial, and her parents' eventual divorce. It was clear that Tatiana had issues with her mother. Just as clear was her profound sense of loss, undiminished by the passage of time. She idolized her brother Jeffrey. And as Kerr got to know her better, she couldn't help but thinking that Joe had become something of a brother figure to Tatiana.

■   ■   ■

At 152 West Seventy-first Street, the Church of the Blessed Sacrament houses two tenants in its basement. One is a transitional residence for men who have tested HIV-positive and proven themselves clean and sober. The other, with a seating capacity of 100, is the ArcLight Theater, managed by Michael Griffiths, an actor who played safety for the University of Tulsa. In the spring of 1997, Tatiana paid him a visit. She knew him, though not well, through a drama coach they had once shared in the Village. Now Tatiana told him, at some length, of her plans to produce and star in a production of Anton Chekhov's *Seagull*.

"She was very attractive," recalls Griffiths. "I was smitten."

Tatiana paid on the spot, a week's rent to reserve the theater. He looked at her name on the check. "Namath?" he said. "I've never heard that name before except—"

"Except my husband, Joe," she said.

The family came to New York in preparation for the show, a run of four performances in late June. In addition to her duties as producer, Tatiana would play Nina, a young actress victimized by her own illusory ideals of romance and art. The role of Arkadina, also an actress, went to Katherine Kerr, who doubled as the director. Joe, at the request of both Tatiana and Katherine, accepted the role of Dr. Dorn. Chekhov's character was fifty-five, a year older than Namath. He was, like Joe, a handsome, worldly ladies' man now leading a contented, reflective life. Namath grew a beard for the role, which came in white. Other than that, recalls Griffiths, "he looked like any other Upper West Side dad." He always seemed to be taking his daughters somewhere. "He was Mr. Mom. And he liked it. You could see he definitely liked it."

Namath was also a pleasure on the set, much of which was built by Tatiana's father, Bud. One day Joe poked his head into the men's shelter, asked if anybody needed anything.

"Yeah. A TV," came the response.

The next day Blessed Sacrament's transitional residence received a delivery from the Wiz, a thirty-seven-inch Sharp with a VCR.

Namath seemed determined to create an atmosphere of harmony on the set. His concern wasn't for Chekhov, but for Tatiana. "I felt he could give a shit how the play was going as long as she was happy," says Griffiths.

But Tatiana's happiness, like Deborah's, was a complicated proposition. Where Katherine Kerr saw an actress who was tense and blocked, Griffiths saw a beautiful woman "searching for something."

"I think she wanted to have a real experience as an artist," he says. But accompanying that want was a desire to achieve her own fame. On that point, both Kerr and Griffiths would agree: Tatiana considered this production as her chance to be discovered. "She had a will to be a celebrity on her own, not just Mrs. Joe Namath," he says. "She felt now was her time."

For Tatiana, the production was a supremely serious matter. She rehearsed. She argued with her director. She seemed preoccupied with her husband's performance. "Do you think he'll be all right?" she asked.

As it happened, Joe was just fine. He made a very good Dorn, and it was arguably the finest performance of his dramatic career. After all, at this point in his life, playing Dr. Dorn was less of a stretch than playing Broadway Joe. Still, that's who people came to see, the ex-quarterback; the theater was packed for the four performances. "It was painful to Tatiana that she wasn't as good as

Joe," says Katherine Kerr. "Joe got the attention. Joe got the affirmation. I almost think she was jealous. She wasn't expecting him to be that good; I don't think anybody was."

Katherine never saw Tatiana again. She called a couple of times but got no response. Perhaps there had been too many disagreements between the two. Or perhaps Katherine's closed-down student had finally opened up. One morning while still in rehearsal for *The Seagull*, they were having breakfast on Columbus Avenue when Tatiana announced that she had met someone. The attraction, she added, was instantaneous. It might have been fated; he was, of all things, an expert in the field of identity modification. Katherine did not approve. "It was clear," she says, "there was some bad shit afoot."

Rose's old friend, Zoltan Kovac, came to visit her at the Beaver County Medical Center. He brought his wife, whom Rose had schooled as a cook all those years ago. "How good you two look," said Rose. At eighty-five she had been ill for some time, and now her time was all but done. She asked Zoltan and his wife to pray with her. "In Hungarian," she said.

Mr. and Mrs. Kovac each clasped one of her hands. They said a Hail Mary and an Our Father in the Magyar tongue. Rose seemed pleased. She died the next morning, October 21, 1997.

The funeral mass was held at the old St. Mary's, now called Divine Mercy. After the burial, mourners returned to the church for a repast. There, Coach Bruno tried to entertain Joe's daughters with some of his old coin tricks. The girls seemed to appreciate his skill for misdirection, even if it was only a short routine. "You can't do too much magic at a funeral," he says.

Joe didn't say much; perhaps he knew there wasn't much to be said at these occasions. By now, he had some experience with this kind of grief. His father had passed away a couple of years earlier, in Akron, Ohio, where he was living with Esther, who herself died just eight months later. Joe had his own family to fortify him through the loss of his father. But now, as his mother died, that family was itself fracturing. This was what he most feared, the curse revisited upon the boy who once cried at the top of the stairs.

53. A VINCULO MATRIMONII

■ ■ ■

Hoot Owl Hicks wasn't too surprised by the gossip he heard after "that Russian play," as he calls it. He felt bad for Joe, and part of him wanted to call an old friend, but by then it was too late. Hoot Owl was long gone. For thirty years, he had looked after Joe—a friend, valet, and sidekick, dating back to the

Pennsylvania kid's freshman year in Tuscaloosa. "I did things that he needed done," says Hicks. "I was there to make him happy and comfortable." But around 1991, Joe accused him of stealing. "He believed I did something I didn't do," says Hoot Owl, who speaks of the episode cryptically. "When I traveled with Joe I got expenses . . . I had a receipt for everything I turned in. I didn't do anything wrong, and if he thinks I did, well, that's on him."

Two people had Joe's ear. One was Jimmy. "As far as I know, he never said anything in my defense," says Hoot Owl. The other was Mrs. Namath. "I don't think she cared for me being around," he says.

With no patron in the Namath camp, Hoot Owl left. It caused him great grief. Still, he refuses to speak badly of Joe. "I think it bothers him, too," he says. "He was under a lot of pressure."

Hoot Owl had perceived a shift in the marriage's balance of power, with Joe increasingly desperate to please. "In the beginning, I would've never thought she'd have left him. But later on, I knew she was," he says. "She once told me that her and Joe would never make it. . . . Why'd she tell me that? I don't know. . . . I don't believe she was ever happy."

Whatever the case, Hoot Owl had seen the split coming years before. Joe and the girls went back home a couple of months after *The Seagull.* But Tatiana stayed behind in New York, returning to Tequesta only briefly the following summer. Then she left for California. "The Wife," as she was called in Joe's eventual petition for divorce, "left Florida in September of 1998, and except for infrequent visits to Florida to visit the parties' children, she has remained in California. To the best of her Husband's knowledge, it is the Wife's intent to remain in California."

Namath didn't file divorce papers until March 19, 1999, and the action didn't become public knowledge until the April 13 issue of the *National Enquirer.* The tabloid paid for a tip that yielded a photograph of Tatiana with her love interest, the man about whom she had spoken with Katherine Kerr. He was Dr. Brian Novack, a Beverly Hills plastic surgeon who specialized in the enhancement of breasts and penises. "The tip came from someone who knew the plastic surgeon," says the *Enquirer's* reporter, John South. "We caught them driving down the street. It was after that, that I spoke with them."

As South quoted Tatiana:

Joe loves being out on the golf course all day, or watching sports on TV, while I love museums, art galleries and the theater. Florida was too boring for me.

After I moved to Los Angeles, I met Brian Novack. Now I'm in love with him.

Brian is totally different from Joe. Joe's a jock and Brian's more of an artist than a surgeon. He wears his hair long for a doctor and he's very sensitive.

Tatiana described case #99-4051, now on the docket in Broward County, as "a friendly divorce."

After his account of Broadway Joe's being "sacked" by a plastic surgeon, South noticed that women around the office—the *Enquirer* was based in Palm Beach County, Florida—seemed particularly saddened by the news. "They would see him dropping the girls off for soccer practice," says South. "Total family man. Quite the doting father."

In the following week's *People,* Tatiana spoke of becoming a playwright. "It's better for my kids to see me happy and fulfilled," she said. As for Joe: "He's proud of me for making a difficult decision to reach my potential. He just wishes it wasn't this way, I'm sure."

Again, Namath would not comment.

■   ■   ■

He sought custody as "primary residential parent subject to a Plan of Shared Parental Responsibility, which gives the Wife full access to the children and full parental rights." Tatiana never contested the divorce, and on May 17, she entered into a settlement agreement. That document, along with other exhibits noted by the court, was to be kept out of the court file, at the office of Namath's divorce lawyer, James Fox Miller. A judge signed the final "dissolution of marriage" on June 8. "Less than four months," wrote one gossip columnist. "A record of sorts in Broward courts."

The legal papers cited a Latin term: *a vinculo matrimonii.* Namath had been released from the bonds of marriage. The dissolution left him in a position much like his mother had once been in. *A vinculo matrimonii.* The worst was still yet to come.

Joe was awarded custody of the two girls and the house in Florida. He had been the primary parent since Tatiana left in 1998. But by 2000, his daughters, now fourteen and nine, came to him with a request. They wanted to join their mother in Beverly Hills.

Here was irony in its cruelest form. He loved the girls more than anything; that much was beyond question. But after all that had happened, did he love them enough to let them go?

"He was never going to let them go until he realized that he could mess things up by not letting them go," surmises Hoot Owl. "Joe had lived through a broken marriage himself. He knew it wasn't good. He realized that they still loved their mother. You couldn't keep kids from their mother."

Namath would call his daughters' departure "the most devastating thing I've ever gone through." The pain could not be considered in relation to mere football injuries. It was beyond calibration, beyond metaphor, almost beyond words. "I can't compare family to athletics," he said. "There's a lot more . . . boy, I don't know . . . *love.*"

Love. He let the girls go because he loved them. That was about as much love as he could survive.

Now he couldn't sleep. He'd wake in the middle of the night unable to breathe. The attacks were without pause. "First thing in the morning, it's on your mind," he said. "You're consumed." Then came the pressure on his sternum. Once, the chest pains lasted for two straight days. Finally, he went to a doctor who put him through a battery of tests, none of which uncovered the slightest cardiovascular problem.

Not long after the kids left, Joe received a visitor. Sal Marchiano had been in Florida, palling around with some of the old crew; he pulled up in a rental car. Though Sal can't remember the time, it felt late. Sundial shadows cut across the Loxahatchee River and all through the house in Tequesta. The new millennium had just begun, and here they were: a couple of guys in their fifties comparing notes on daughters and divorce. Sal had been through his some years earlier, and survived it. "One day," he told Joe, "you'll be sitting with your daughters in Paris, laughing about all this."

That was not a day Joe could envision. His devastation was plain to see. They were sitting in the kitchen with a counter between them. Sal was struck by how neat everything was, meticulously clean, unnaturally quiet.

"Do you want a drink?" asked Joe.

"Ice water."

Joe served Sal, and then pulled out a bottle of vodka, pouring one over ice for himself.

Everybody reaches for something, thought Sal. He'd been there.

"I know it's not good for me," said Joe, shrugging with the peculiar insouciance of a condemned man.

"Well, since you brought it up," said Sal, "you better be careful."

Careful? What did they think of careful when they were young? Remember the cops in the squad car, the smoke from the smoldering joint in the headlights? Funny. They remember other things, too, not as funny. A lot of late nights, risky nights. "Every time I fly into New York and see the skyline, I think about how lucky we are to be alive," said Joe.

He didn't look so lucky, drinking in the shadows. Joe couldn't understand how it had happened, his daughters leaving.

"You know what the answer is," said Sal. "You got to go there, live near them."

"I hate Beverly Hills," said Joe. "That's why I got out of there. I don't want them growing up there."

They talked some more, then Joe walked him to his car. "If you ever need anything, call me," said Sal. "You can't be sitting alone in this house. Don't do this to yourself."

Joe nodded.

"C'mon," Sal said, finally. "You're *Broadway Joe.*"

Namath smirked, signaling contempt for his own mythic self.

"Joe!" said Sal, trying to get his attention. "Everybody loves you, Joe."

Sal got in his rental and started to drive. He was approaching the Intracoastal Waterway when he thought to look back. Who'd have thought it would be like this, Joe Namath alone, drinking in the shadows. So there were no guarantees, after all. Sal drove over the bridge thinking: *What just happened?*

■   ■   ■

"Depression," Namath would say, "has a way of sneaking up on you." Eventually, a doctor would prescribe an antidepressant. In the meantime, Joe did what he knew how to do. He had been medicating himself for most of his adult life. The oldest pain he knew came with a silent call: *A vinculo matrimonii. Heal thyself. Start sipping, Old Joe.*

On August 23, 2000, the Miami Dolphins hosted A Tribute to Dan Marino at Pro Player Stadium. Marino, now retired after seventeen seasons, had been to the Super Bowl, but had not won. It was the single cause for regret in a career that set records for attempts, completions, passing yardage, and touchdowns. Marino, who grew up in Pittsburgh, was the most prolific passer in NFL history, and his might have been the best arm ever to come out of western Pennsylvania, a quarterbacking fraternity that included Hall of Famers George Blanda, Johnny Unitas, Joe Montana, and Joe Namath. For years, Namath had bemoaned the state of quarterbacking: "You see guys throw the football and wonder who taught them. It's appalling to see the techniques used in high school and even college." Marino was the exception. Joe liked Marino, and everything about his game. "The throwing motion, the quick release, yes, they remind me of me," he once said.

Namath was scheduled to speak as part of the tribute. But just minutes before he was to go on, 52,000 fans were told that he had run into "transportation problems." In fact, according to the *Sun-Sentinel,* Namath "was so disoriented he could barely stand up or talk."

A man named Kevin Barry saw him in the VIP room before the festivities. Barry had wanted to tell him that he had been a Jets' ballboy at Peekskill Military Academy, and especially wanted Joe to know that he had taken good care of his dog, Fancy Pharaoh. But Joe didn't look to be in a conversational mood. He sat near a corner of the room, a good-looking middle-aged blond behind him. Joe was slumped in his chair, head down, a glass in his hand.

■   ■   ■

A few months after the Marino tribute, Namath was seen staggering around Giants Stadium, a concrete bowl in New Jersey where the Jets played their home games. "Barely able to stand straight," noted the *Sun-Sentinel.* The Jets won that night. Down 30–7 in the fourth quarter, the team mounted the great-est comeback in the history of Monday night football. Joe watched and drank from the owner's box. Every so often, his elder daughter would touch him on the elbow, as if to let him know she was still there.

Sadly, such Namath sightings became commonplace. Tank Passuello, for instance, saw him at a banquet for John Schmitt and Mike D'Amato, both Hofstra alums who played on the Jets' Super Bowl team. The honorees, as Pas-suello pointed out in his speech honoring them, were good family men who had been married for "a total of seventy years."

At that point, Passuello was interrupted by a sound that was part groan, part sigh. It was Joe, whose own remarks later would prove somewhat redun-dant. For some reason, Namath kept introducing Dr. Nicholas. "He was a lit-tle woozy, to say the least," says Passuello. "He came up and started babbling, but nobody gave a shit because they all loved him."

Everybody still loved him. Everybody wanted to help. But he was deaf to the best of wishes. He had become like a fugitive to some of his oldest friends, always changing his phone number. Finally, Al Hassan called the Namanco office in Manhattan and asked Jimmy's secretary if it was okay for him to have the new number, which she gave him. Al left three messages, none of them re-turned.

"I can take a hint," he says, trying to hide his own hurt. "But the next time I see Joe, it will be like it never happened."

After fifteen years, Mort Fishman had heard enough to stop waiting for an apology. "How could I hold a grudge?" asks Mort. "Joe has a good heart. He was probably just embarrassed." With two recently replaced hips, Mort drove to the camp. A caretaker recognized him from the old days and gave him di-rections to the house where Joe was staying. There, Mort met Jessica and Olivia and entertained them with magic tricks as they waited for Joe.

Joe seemed happy to see an old friend and gave Mort a big hug. They talked golf and even made a tee time. But when Mort came to pick him up the next day, he discovered that Joe and the girls had already left town earlier that morning.

"I remember thinking: what would he do now?" says Mort. "I mean, a guy his age." Maybe Joe was having similar thoughts, or maybe he had come to re-alize it was just easier to drink with strangers. If only Mickey Mantle were still around. The Mick could've told Joe: Sometimes strangers are the best kind of old friends.

He was sitting at the bar in the Polo Lounge when a man introduced him-self as Bob Gutkowski. "Excuse me, Mr. Namath. I don't mean to bother you, but I used to serve you at Bill's Meadowbrook." Gutkowski had been working his way through college then, and always took care to have a tall one ready for Joe when he came in off the practice field. After college, he had a job with

Chet Simmons at NBC, and later, as president of Madison Square Garden, Gutkowski ran the Knicks and the Rangers. In all those years, he couldn't remember ever having asked for an autograph. Now, though, he asked. "Joe wrote a marvelous note to my son," recalls Gutkowski. "Then we talked for about twenty minutes. It was early evening, maybe six-thirty. I said I had to go. He said he was going to stay and have a few more.

"There was a sadness in his eyes."

To a man of Gutkowski's generation, it was an odd, troubling image—not the drinking, but the sight of Namath by himself. He wasn't waiting for anyone. He didn't have anywhere to be. So he just stayed, alone at the bar, a fine place for America's hero.

For almost twenty years, the fifteen episodes of *The Joe Namath Show* were kept in a garage in New Canaan, Connecticut. Every so often, producer Larry Spangler would get a call from the garage's owner, a former employee who complained that "the Namath stuff" was taking up too much space. The guy's wife was getting on his case.

"Your wife?" said Spangler. "Aren't you the man of the house?"

Finally, the place in New Canaan was sold. If Spangler wanted the tapes, he'd have to fly in from California and pick them up himself. Recorded on two-inch-thick reels, the entire run of shows weighed more than 200 pounds. Spangler had them packed in steamer trunks and shipped to his home in Malibu.

54. CLASSIC SPORTS

"What's *that*?" asked his young girlfriend.

"Joe Namath," he said.

"Who?"

Now the reels went into Spangler's garage, where they were kept along with tapes of another project close to his heart, a blaxploitation picture starring Fred Williamson, *The Legend of Nigger Charley*. Spangler himself was often tempted to be rid of the cumbersome steamer trunks, but eventually he opted for storage over destruction. He had this funny idea: one day he would donate the fifteen Joe Namath shows to the Library of Congress.

Instead, he found an even better home for them. Classic Sports Network, a cable channel, had made a business of baby boom's need for nostalgia. There was Classic Rock, Classic R & B, and Classic TV, so why not Classic Sports— old games, old clips, even old commercials? A game's outcome no longer mattered. For aging baby boomers, suspense was less important than the comfort of familiarity. "It's like watching *Casablanca*," explained Brian Bedol, one of the channel's founders. "You know how it ends every time, but every time you've got to watch it."

Namath was among the first ex-athletes to sign a promotional deal with Classic Sports, which first aired on an Oklahoma cable station in 1995. Demographically, he was a perfect choice. By now, the Guarantee, the pantyhose, and *The Brady Bunch* had become part of a generation's background noise. Not only did baby boomers love him, but through the years their kids also became fascinated with Broadway Joe. His animated likeness would appear on *The Simpsons*. An assortment of Namath relics—popcorn makers, shirts, cards, puzzles—would be sold and resold on E-bay as objets d'art. *Maxim* included the Guarantee as one of "The 50 Greatest Guy Moments of All Time," somewhere between D-Day and the O. J. Simpson car chase. *Stuff* magazine cited two television commercials featuring Namath and Farrah Fawcett—the Noxzema ad and their 1981 reunion on behalf of Fabergé shampoo—among "The 10 Sexiest Commercials Ever." Gen-Xers could find the virtue in Namath's cheesiness: "Cheesiness is the fate of every youthful American icon who makes it to middle age," wrote *GQ*'s Andrew Corsello. "The important thing is that, through more than two and a half decades, Namath's appeal hasn't faded."

By the late 1990s, Spangler's reels could satisfy both the viewing public's kitschy yearnings and a fledgling network's need for programming. If people sat happily through old sitcoms and game shows, they'd feel blessed to watch Namath and Dick Schaap, in their Pierre Cardin wardrobes, bullshitting with everyone from Cosell to Capote.

The Joe Namath Show, along with old fight footage, comprised a prominent part of Classic Sports' programming. As Spangler recalls, the new network bought the full run of fifteen episodes for three airings. Then, in late 1997, ESPN bought Classic Sports. Spangler and Jimmy Walsh decided to sell *Joe Namath* outright to Disney, ESPN's corporate parent. "We milked it," says Spangler, who split his take with Namanco. "When it was all done, we probably took down half a million."

Not a bad score for the contents of two trunks that would otherwise be collecting dust. Namath, who had become a corporate spokesman for Classic Sports, retained his position after the sale to Disney. Broadway Joe became another knight in the kingdom of Mickey Mouse. His position would make it difficult, if not impossible, to turn down an interview request from ESPN-Classic, which was producing a series of one-hour documentaries on the outstanding sports figures of the twentieth century.

The shoot was scheduled for November 9, 2000, in Tequesta. One subject Namath would not talk about was the divorce. "He made it clear that he didn't want to get into that," says Craig Mortali, the producer.

Mortali had been apprised of Joe's drinking and depression, but saw signs of neither. Namath couldn't have been more charming. Before long, he knew the names of the cameraman and the audio technician. Anything you guys need? Glass of water? Joe wanted everyone to be comfortable.

The producer had grown up a Giants fan. Still, it was Namath, and none of the Giants, who had inspired him to wear Pumas and grow a beard in high school. Now, Mortali found himself slightly disappointed to discover that the house in Tequesta contained no evidence of the cool life. There wasn't even a pool table. Rather, the playroom had dolls and a kitchen set. "It was still very much a home for children," he says.

At the producer's request, Namath thumbed through a box of old photographs. He stopped cold on an image of the whole family—himself, Tatiana, and the kids. He made a face and mumbled something; then, gathering himself, he moved on.

The shoot went smoothly, pausing only to change film, and once, when the phone rang. It was Olivia on the answering machine. "Daddy," she was heard to say. "I was just thinking about you."

As requested, Mortali didn't ask about the divorce. "Having gone through one myself," he says, "I was very conscious and respectful of his issues." Instead, he tried another approach, asking Joe to tell him about his daughters.

"What else would you give your life up for?" asked Namath. On most subjects, he already had his lines down pat: Old Joe was in the third quarter of his life and planned on living to be a hundred. He got goose bumps just thinking about the Super Bowl. It was his version of a soft-shoe act, the latest rendition of Broadway Joe. But this answer about his daughters cut through all the background noise; he had chosen to frame it as a matter of life and death.

"You don't flinch, right?" he said, his eyes suddenly glassy and his voice thick, as if something had lodged in his throat. "You'd sacrifice your life for your children."

The interview concluded shortly thereafter. They shot six reels that day, almost three hours' worth of footage. Dusk approached, but Namath had brightened again. He explained that he had "an appointment" that evening, and that he wanted to do his exercises. Namath had an elliptical trainer, which didn't put much stress on the joints. He liked to keep in shape, an hour a day.

The crew packed up and left, but Mortali lagged behind. There was something he was still curious about, a rooting interest he wanted to satisfy. His rented Taurus was still in park when Joe's "appointment" arrived. He could make out the silhouette: beautiful, blond, very leggy.

"Good boy, Joe," he said, addressing the rearview mirror. "You still got it."

■   ■   ■

Almost a year later, at Chicago's Union Station, Rick Telander introduced Namath as the guest of honor at a black-tie gala for the Arthritis Foundation. Twenty-five years had passed since the publication of *Joe Namath and the Other Guys*. Telander, now a columnist for the *Chicago Sun-Times,* had spent many seasons covering the Bulls' Michael Jordan, as the basketball star became the most famous and lucrative venture in the history of team sports. Still, Telander wondered: if not for Broadway Joe, would there have been an Air Jordan? "Out of Namath, came all the others," he says.

Joe was drinking wine that night, and seemed to ramble a bit while delivering his speech. More striking, thought Telander, was Jimmy Walsh. Namath had aged. His face was tanned, deeply lined, almost leathery. But Jimmy looked just as he always had: freckled, frenetic, on the heavy side. "Same old Jimmy," says Telander. "He was still protecting Joe, kind of like Joe's handler, telling him when to go here and there. If there's a trouble-maker, Jimmy gets the guard. I was shocked to see them in the exact same roles that I had seen them in a quarter of a century before. Joe has ceded a very important part of his persona and his life to Jimmy."

It was difficult to distinguish between Jimmy and the concept to which he had dedicated his life—the idea of Joe. Where did one end and the other begin? Jimmy had long since taken custody of the Broadway Joe image. He was its disciple and defender. Back in 1992, when the Pro Set trading card company issued Joe Namath commemorative cards without Namanco's permission, Jimmy made sure it had to answer in federal court. The makers of Ambervision sunglasses also found themselves in federal court after they stopped paying on their contract with Namanco's subsidiary, Planned Licensing. The case against Pro Set was dismissed with a summary judgment, but Ambervision agreed in a settlement to make good on the balance of the contract, $504,722 plus legal fees. Win or lose, there was a principle at stake: If you messed with Joe, you were messing with Jimmy. Whether the occasion called for a slap on the back or a kick in the balls, Jimmy was always there, watching over his guy.

Namath received the Arthritis Foundation's Freedom of Movement Award that night in Union Station. Joe was no stranger to charity work, having given freely of his time and his likeness to the March of Dimes. But arthritis was more than a charitable mission. Planned Licensing had a deal with Boehringer Ingelheim Pharmaceuticals and Abbott Laboratories to promote an osteoarthritis medication, Mobic. Namath's appearances were well attended by senior citizens as he traveled the country, urging his fellow Americans to join him in the "Arthritis Huddle." The erstwhile apostle of booze and broads now advocated a "winning game plan" that included proper diet, exercise, and consulting with your doctor. This was one celebrity spokesman who knew whereof he spoke. Artificial knees were the least of his problems; osteoarthritis had wedged into joints traumatized by years in the game—his spine and his thumbs. He could no longer make a fist. He was often irritable. "It was never—never—out of your mind." Chronic pain, Namath warned, "can damage some relationships, not only with friends but even with family. When you're always grumpy or when you're always tied up with pain, it's a tough deal on everyone around you."

To hear him speak of the disease's emotional toll was to wonder how much his arthritic aches had contributed to the breakup of the marriage. On the other hand, if he had to suffer, he might as well get paid for it. Joe might be hurting, but Jimmy was always open for business.

Back in 1994, Jimmy had helped secure financing for a new Internet venture called Sportsline.com. In return for finding investors and for Namath's services as a spokesman, Jimmy and Joe were given a reported 20 percent stake in the company. Planned Licensing would receive 15 cents for every $4.95 monthly subscription sold after Sportsline went online in August, 1995. By October 16, 1999—a couple of years after CBS bought a stake in the company—the deal was amended. Planned Licensing would receive $1 million in cash over five years and options on 30,000 shares at $26, the stock price when the amendment went into effect. Jimmy and Joe could purchase up to 6,000 shares every October 16, starting in 2000. *Fortune* noted that "Namath received stock and warrants worth about $8 million today." SportsLine was then selling for about $35 a share. But by the first option date in mid-October, the price was down to $9.54. A year later, in 2001, it had fallen to $1.81, a victim of the NASDAQ implosion. It never recovered, hovering around $2 for the next couple of years.

No matter. Jimmy came up with another score. Michael Shustek, chairman and CEO of the Las Vegas–based Vestin Group, was a huge Namath fan. Vestin, a real estate company formerly known as Del Mar, had earned a reputation for double-digit returns and periodic attention from state regulators. In 1999, Nevada's Financial Institutions Division seized control of Del Mar for questionable accounting and management practices.

"Maybe we were growing a bit too fast, and that concerned the state," Shustek told the *Las Vegas Review Journal*. "The state made sure our books— our record keeping, not our finances—were up to date."

After suing the state, Shustek reached a settlement with regulators. He regained control of his company and took it public. Del Mar became Vestin, and in 2001 Namath became its spokesman. Shustek was enamored with the idea of Joe. "I don't know how many times I've seen that *Brady Bunch* episode," he says.

Once, in Tequesta after a day of golf, Shustek asked to see Namath's trophies. Namath responded by bringing Shustek into a room where his daughters' school art projects remained on prominent display. "There," said Joe. "Those are my trophies."

Of course, the Vestin arrangement had less to do with Namath's family values than his value as an endorser. Vestin sought aging baby boomers, those who would take Joe Namath's word on mortgage funds as they once did on popcorn makers and shavers. "He's perfect for our demographic," says Shustek.

Vestin agreed to pay Namanco $1 million a year through 2005, a total of

$5 million. Jimmy Walsh was named to Vestin's board of directors, and Planned Licensing Inc. was given warrants to purchase up to 1.2 million shares, or 16.2 percent of the company. In return, Namath would do a variety of ads and appearances. The man who made Nixon's Enemies List could now be seen on the Fox News Channel, a stars-and-stripes graphic fluttering in the background, as he applauded Washington's response to the terrorist attacks of September 11, 2001: "I think the president has done a wonderful job," said Joe. "Football taught me about life. . . . It's been a terrific team effort." Unlike the other stock touts who appeared on the show, Namath tendered his bullishness with certain caveats. "These gentlemen know far more about the economy than I do," he said. "But real estate, the way we're dealing with it . . . is very strong." There was cause for optimism, in the nation's leaders and its markets. "Americans have a certain strength," he said. "We're going to continue to get stronger."

■   ■   ■

Namath's fortieth high school reunion was held on Saturday, August 11, 2001, at the Beaver Falls Holiday Inn out on Route 18. Rumor had it that Joe would finally attend. He had been in Pittsburgh the day before, promoting his arthritis medicine. "There were probably twenty people who stayed late at the bar," recalls Cathie Smith, the hotel's lounge supervisor. "One guy kept saying that he had talked to Joe personally, and that Joe was going to show up. They were all waiting for Joe Namath. They all kept saying he was going to show. And then he didn't. They weren't too happy about it."

Namath might have had a good time. Despite the divorce, he could have counted himself lucky to still be a prince in a room full of bad toupees and missing fingers (the telltale sign of a life spent in the mill). But reunions were curious propositions for him, as he was the one through whom everybody summoned dormant memories. He had to be *on*. He had to be Broadway Joe. The act was more difficult to pull off with old friends than strangers.

Every year, Namath would receive an invitation to play in the annual Larry Grantham Celebrity Golf Classic, which reunited the Super Bowl team at Fiddler's Elbow Country Club in Bedminster, New Jersey. The goal was to raise money for Freedom House, a residential treatment center for recovering alcoholics and drug addicts seeking reconciliation with their families. Grantham organized the event in 1992, his sixth year of sobriety.

"The drinking just kind of crept up on me," says Grantham. "There were family problems, financial problems, DUIs."

Becoming an ex-drunk, he figures, was almost as tough as becoming an ex-ballplayer. After retiring from football, he went back to his native Mississippi, where he has worked as a banker in the years since. Even with a little weight around his belly, Grantham seems impossibly small to have been a linebacker. He carries no trace of a ballplayer's musculature. He still smokes.

In retirement, though, he acquired a kind of grace he never had as a player, even delivering the eulogy for his fellow Mississippian, Verlon Biggs, who died of leukemia.

"Larry became one of the best guys you'd ever want to know," says Matt Snell. "There's nothing he wouldn't do for you."

By 2002, he was trying to do for Sam Walton, the tackle who had lost his starting spot two weeks before the Super Bowl. Walton was living in Memphis, where he got by on social security checks and booze. "I went downtown looking for him, ten, maybe twelve times," says Grantham. "A bunch of us had some money to get him situated. But we never could find him." In May, Walton was found dead of a heart attack in an abandoned apartment.

That same spring, also in Memphis, Grantham paid a visit to Namath, who was in town to hawk his arthritis medicine. Grantham would have called first, but Joe's number kept changing. Instead, he arrived with a golf shirt bearing his tournament's logo. Grantham talked up Freedom House and the country club benefit and how much it would mean to everyone if Joe showed up.

Namath couldn't have been nicer, and Grantham went home thinking this would be the year that he finally made it. More than twenty guys from the Super Bowl team attended the affair at Fiddler's Elbow. Don Maynard played in his usual outfit: old red shorts and white cowboy boots fitted with golf spikes. Curley Johnson and Pete Lammons reminisced while sipping Coors Light over ice. Residents and graduates of Freedom House smoked cigarettes on a veranda overlooking the fairways and greens. It was a great day, lacking only for the greatest of Jets. Namath's absence hung over the clubhouse, unmentioned, unavoidable.

"I know Joe is special," Grantham says. "I know his popularity is a lot more than ours. But he's the one missing out by not being with the guys."

He was never one of the guys. He couldn't have been then, and he wasn't going to start trying now. "We always ask Joe, and he always says, 'I'll be happy to come, talk to my agent,'" says Fred Reihl, the director of Freedom House. "Then we talk to his agent, Jimmy, and Jimmy says, 'It'll cost you sixty grand for the day.' That's what he wanted this year. Joe stayed clear of it. Sixty grand? Sixty grand is what we clear for the day. We couldn't give away our proceeds just to have Joe Namath. The other guys come for free. It wouldn't be fair to them."

A few days later, Gerry Philbin was still pissed at Joe: "If he was there, I wouldn't go."

"Sixty grand to play charity golf with ex-teammates," Matt Snell says disdainfully. "Joe can blame it on Jimmy Walsh if he wants. But the truth is, what the truth is."

Philbin and Snell always had their issues with Namath. But the truth about Joe Namath, now as then, remains an ambiguous proposition. Former friends understood this better than ex-teammates. He might have lived off the past, but not in it. The good old days and the good old guys had little hold on him. A couple of years after Namath's divorce, Ray Abruzzese became ill with Parkinson's disease. He suffered tremors and anxiety attacks. Word got around, and friends called with best wishes. But not Joe.

"I'm shocked," says Bobby Van. "They were comrades."

Tim Secor knew how it felt. Some years before, he had been hit by a truck, an accident that left him a paraplegic. Some guys visited in the hospital. Others called. Again, not Joe. Tim never once heard from Joe.

Namath's friendships didn't have second acts. Ray, Timmy, Hoot Owl, Mort Fishman, Arthur Joseph . . . whatever they meant to him, they had one thing in common: they weren't blood.

Everything came down to blood—even the money. But hadn't Joe always known that? Going back to the first big deal, Sonny Werblin's concern was publicity, while Joe's was providing for his family. The Super Bowl, and the myths it spawned, made him a good living. But his life—what made Joe Namath weep and tingle—was the two girls. They were his blood.

The money helped, but it didn't cure anything. Joe still had to negotiate his own kind of truce with the bottle. He had to learn how to be a divorced dad. "Some pain never goes completely away," he said. "But you learn to deal with it."

After the girls left, he began flying out to the coast "every couple of weeks or so." Then, in January 2002, he bought a condo in Brentwood. The county assessor's office valued it at $610,980. But for Namath, it proved invaluable, as he was spending more and more time in Los Angeles with his daughters.

He was a better man when they were around. He even went back to school that fall, taking tutorials to finally earn his degree at Alabama. Namath hadn't forgotten the promise he made to his mother, but even more compelling than that assurance was a remark Jessica had made. She said she would be the first college graduate in the family.

"You want to bet?" said Joe.

■   ■   ■

It was right around that time when Tad Dowd ran into them in Century City. It was a Friday, early evening. Tad had stopped at Johnny Rockets, a hamburger joint in the mall. He was ready to sit down and study the *Racing Form* when he spotted Joe in the baseball cap. Joe introduced him to his daughter as "Mr. Dowd." The two men had seen each other perhaps a half dozen times over the last two decades. Still, they talked for the better part of an hour before Joe finally said good-bye. "Make sure to call the office and leave your number," he said.

He was taking Jessica to a movie, a big picture with a handsome young star his daughter liked.

Going back all those years, Tad had never seen any woman have this effect on Joe. "There was a lightness to him," he says. "A glow."

Tad made a point to watch them as they walked toward the multiplex, father and daughter, blood and light, dissolving into the crowd at the mall. Then he spread out his *Racing Form,* ready to ponder the odds.

■   ■   ■

In another year's time, Namath's daughters would return to live with him in Tequesta. But by then he couldn't seem to stay sober for long. Old friends would hear things through the grapevine. He drank too much wine at Michael's in Santa Monica. He was pounding vodka tonics at Clarke's in Manhattan. Early one morning at Reagan National Airport in Washington, he was seen wearing a baseball cap and sunglasses, nursing a beer at the bar.

An appearance for College Sports Network—a new venture from the creators of Classic Sports—was cut short after too many vodka tonics. Producers of a promotional interview featuring Namath complained that their footage was useless, as he wasn't making much sense. "He was definitely pretty soused," says Christian Red, a *Daily News* sportswriter who attended the event. During the taping, a bloodshot Namath even asked Red's girlfriend to fetch him a drink. "More vodka than tonic," he said.

Twelve days later, December 20, 2003, Namath attended a game as a member of the Jets' Four Decades Team. It was a night game, and he had been drinking steadily since that afternoon. Before the first half ended, ESPN sideline reporter Suzy Kolber asked him for a few words about the struggling Jets. "I want to kiss you," slurred Namath. "I couldn't care less about the team struggling."

Within a month, Namath was an outpatient at Hanley-Hazelden, a West Palm Beach rehabilitation facility specializing in the treatment of older adults. "I've embarrassed my family," he told Jeremy Schaap, his biographer's son, now a reporter for ESPN. "Every time in my life that something has gone askew, alcohol has been involved. . . . I'm convinced that I need help."

Namath's request for a smooch quickly became fodder for late-night monologues and drive-time rants. Just as inevitable were references to the sideline incident as a "wake-up call." Perhaps, it was a curious bit of good fortune for Sonny Werblin's creation to be seen drunk on national television. Maybe that was the only place for him to hit rock bottom, there in the vast wasteland.

■   ■   ■

So what about Joe Namath?

What becomes of him?

The clues, the signs of his ever-potent magic, are there on the morning of June 25, 2003, some six months before the incident on ESPN. The Jets are hosting a press conference at the Renaissance Hotel in Times Square. Its ostensible purpose is to announce that Joe Namath has been named the team's "ambassador-at-large." In fact, this event is a press agent's creation, an old-fashioned hustle that Sonny Werblin or Eddie Jaffe would have greatly admired. The Jets are now owned by Robert Wood Johnson IV, the billionaire heir to the Johnson & Johnson fortune. Though he is affectionately known as "Woody," taxpayers have little affection for subsidizing the construction of his new stadium. For nineteen years, the New York Jets have played in Giants Stadium. But the indignity of playing in New Jersey, more than forty miles from their Hofstra practice site, in an edifice named for their archrival, was not sufficient to justify underwriting a new Jets stadium—certainly not after the 9/11 terrorist attacks had left New York City unable to pay for schools and firehouses. Jets president Jay Cross grew frustrated with state officials, who were the key to developing a plot on Manhattan's West Side. "The state," he noted disdainfully, "is bereft of any kind of talent." So now, forty years after Harry Wismer's Titans became the Jets, the decision has been made to bring in real talent, Broadway Joe.

"Four decades of Jets football, absolutely wonderful," says Namath. "I get goose bumps thinking about it."

He speaks from a lectern. Behind him, beyond the wraparound window: Broadway. "I was standing right outside, *there*," he says, referring to the famous nighttime shot on the cover of *Sports Illustrated*. From there to here, night to day, then to now, Broadway is transformed. It is not unlike the Super Bowl: well lit, huge, homogeneous, a corporate theme park. The Olive Garden chain of restaurants, one of them situated directly below Namath, now provides the universally accepted standard for Italian cuisine. Broadway's small-time hustlers have been replaced with big-time ones, their signs like the banners of nation-states: Morgan Stanley, McDonald's, Budweiser, and of course, Disney. This is the destination, what came from *Amerika-laz,* American fever.

The sportswriters are assembled in front of him. Former teammates sit in a section to his left. Finally, this is the year he will attend Grantham's golf outing. "There's not an 'I' in the word 'team,'" says Joe. "I am very fortunate to be here because of the people I have worked with."

He thanks them all, starting with Dr. Nicholas. He thanks Werblin. "It was his idea to create the star system," says Joe. It was also his idea to bring Mara to the Meadowlands. In June 1971, two months after Werblin became chairman of the New Jersey Sports Authority, the Giants signed a thirty-year lease to play in what was still swampland. In 1984, shortly after Leon Hess gained sole control of the Jets, he moved the team into Giants Stadium. These facts escape Namath, who has anointed Hess posthumously as the team's sainted owner.

"Bring our team back home to New York City," says Joe. "We're the New York Jets. We should have our own stadium."

Of course, he wasn't saying it for free. From Dave Anderson's column in the next day's *Times*: "The overall value of his contract, as negotiated by his longtime agent, Jimmy Walsh, is whispered to be in the same neighborhood as his original $427,000 deal, then the most expensive in pro football history."

Jimmy keeps a watchful eye on Joe, even as he works the room, meeting and greeting. This deal with the Jets includes yet another line of clothes, "high-end activewear" to be marketed under the "Broadway Joe" label.

Namath is effusive in his praise for Woody Johnson and the team president: "You reached out to bring back our history." In fact, the team's history is mostly dismal. The Jets, one of the sport's least successful franchises, never made it back to the Super Bowl. No team in any sport has remained so tethered, for so long, to the memory of a single star.

But, hey, he guaranteed it.

What's more, it's hard work being Broadway Joe. He's *on* today. The sportswriters remain obediently enthralled for the better part of two hours. Some of them were there way back when; others were just kids. But Joe appears to have aged better than them all: tanned, energized, healthy. He's wearing a green tie with a gray double-breasted suit. His teeth are as white as his shirt.

"Fuckin' great," says the writer who had interviewed him almost four years before, in the bowels of the Orange Bowl.

What about Joe Namath?

"We're gonna bring them a stadium somehow," he says. Now, at the age of sixty, he is finally leading a pep rally. So what if he's hustling? It's *his* hustle, in furtherance of a higher purpose. It has become part of his patrimony.

"The Jets are a family," he says.

He knows better. Family is blood, the ones you would die for. His daughters are in the audience. Olivia is twelve. She has big, bright eyes, and braces on her teeth. Jessica is slim, seventeen. Joe doesn't always approve of her taste in music—the lyrics these days. "I can hear that kind of stuff in the locker room," says Joe. The sportswriters laugh.

"Daddy," says Jessica. "Daddy." She is attentive, practiced at reading her father's body language. She hands him a soft drink. He's been talking for so long. He's still twinkling, though. Joe Namath is happy. He now spends more days with his daughters than away from them. Soon, they will come back to Florida for good.

The photographers start snapping their pictures, the girls modeling their father's new line of high-end activewear.

What would you die for?

Better to live.

It has rained steadily for almost a month. But today sunlight washes over everything. One imagines the father and his daughters strolling down Broadway, the distant fabled land now cleansed of all shadow, every trace of nocturnal life.

Was there a Hungarian word for this?

Did it matter anymore?

It was best for Joe Namath to speak as his forebearers had instructed. Speak American: Love.

Acknowledgments

What you hold is an accumulation of my debts. I owe much to many, beginning with Joe Namath. At the beginning of this project, I contacted Jimmy Walsh, who thought that access to Namath should be structured around a financial relationship and editorial control. Our discussions, such as they were, never progressed from there. Looking back, I like to think that Jimmy was only doing what he does best, looking out for his guy. He had reason to know that I couldn't accept his terms, as they would not make for an unbiased and disinterested account. Perhaps, though, I should have known that Joe Namath had little interest in volunteering the intimacies of his life.

It is, however, a life whose meaning merits both examination and celebration. And toward that end, I received great aid and comfort. Tad Dowd granted me access to his own remembrances, a voluminous oral history. He asked only that I buy lunch for Eddie Jaffe and check in on him from time to time. Years of sobriety have afflicted Tad with a keen memory and a big heart. As he became my guide through the good old days, he also became a friend.

Rick Telander went through his attic with an archaeologist's sense of purpose, recovering artifacts of his research for *Joe Namath and the Other Guys*. These included his composition books and dozens of interview transcripts, including thirty-four pages, most of them single-spaced, from his sessions with Joe (November 4 and 20, 1975) and John Namath (December 6 and 22, 1975). These interviews were invaluable. Telander wasn't much more than a kid when he wrote *Joe Namath and the Other Guys*. But more than a quarter of a century later, his work provided a kind of map for mine. What's more, the papers he sent were a constant admonition to listen well.

In Beaver Falls, it was my great fortune to meet Sam Allen, reference librarian at the Carnegie Free Library. He has an archivist's sense of exactitude, a reporter's curiosity, and a poet's soul. He can often be found at Mountaineer Park. Sam lives as he wagers, inevitably, on long shots of the sentimental kind. I am honored to have had him bet on me.

Some of Namath's old friends I now count among my own: Bobby Van, a gracious host with magnificent memories; Jack "Hoot Owl" Hicks, who had me all but weeping at a Tuscaloosa truck stop; Mort "the Jewish Tarzan" Fishman; Al "Hatchet" Hassan; Tim Secor; Linwood Alford, who welcomed me into his home on a cold, dark afternoon after nothing more than a knock on his door.

Among my own old friends, Dan Klores was there from the very beginning of this undertaking. He was unfailingly generous with his advice and counsel, unwavering optimism, and conceptual brilliance. He helped me to reconsider a set of ideas and images as a book.

Don Van Natta Jr. eagerly volunteered his services, poring through a manuscript in progress even as he traveled back and forth from London to Riyadh investigating global terrorism. He knows how much this meant to me, both the level of scrutiny he applied to those early pages and the extraordinary encouragement he offered.

Joe Sexton and Wallace Matthews were there with whatever I needed whenever I needed it. Better or more loyal friends there are not.

Stan Bregman, my father-in-law, had better numbers than a bookmaker, everybody from John Dean to Secret Service agents once assigned to the White House detail.

Bless the sporting press. In addition to their vivid and thoughtful recollections, Dave Anderson, Larry Fox, and Paul Zimmerman left a remarkably detailed record. Much of the guts of this book comes from their years on the Jets beat.

And as Jimmy Walsh once told Rick Telander, "Thank God for Dick Young."

I would agree, though for different reasons, and add Dick Schaap, Jimmy Cannon, and Milton Gross to the roster of those I thank God for.

And thank God for Joe Tronzo, too.

It was my honor to speak with W. C. Heinz.

The *Sun-Sentinel*'s Dave Hyde provided me with, among other things, a recording of his interview with Namath, who speaks with heartbreaking candor about his experiences with pain, both physical and emotional.

I owe *Sports Illustrated* for pieces ranging from Robert Boyle's "Show Biz Sonny" in 1965 to Leigh Montville's "Off Broadway Joe" twenty-two years later. But mostly, I owe executive editor Rob Fleder, who was a huge help, though only he knows just how much.

Bob Raissman delivered, always.

Don Elbaum made a lot of good things happen.

Thanks to Jack Anderson, a Hall of Fame investigative reporter, for putting up with months of phone calls. Thanks to his daughter, Tanya Neider, for never abandoning the search.

I shall always appreciate and admire Larry Grantham, Dave Haytaian, and the people at Freedom House.

The *New York Post* and its director of information services, Laura Harris, granted me run of the newspaper's library and files. What Laura did went well beyond professional courtesy.

Thanks to the *New York Times* and the staff of its vast clipping morgue; Dr. William Irion and Betty Conner of the Beaver County Research Center; the staff of the Carnegie Free Library; Kenneth Britten and the Beaver Falls Historical Society; Sam Rushay, archivist at the Nixon Presidential Materials Staff of the National Archive; August Molnar and the American Hungarian Foundation; Albert Tezla, professor emeritus of English at the University of Minnesota, Duluth, an authority on Hungarian literature, a man as kind as he is learned.

Bob Gutkowski, a gentleman, led me to other gentlemen, including Al Passuello and Chet Simmons, who led me to David Kennedy, whom I thank for the intelligence and passion that run through his memories, his relentless encouragement, and his good company.

For their graciousness and insight: Mike Weisman, Jack Danahy, Craig Mortali, and Matt Snell.

Thanks to George Lois: profane genius, pious hustler, solid guy.

Arthur Joseph kept his word; his is the sound of a good soul.

Among Sonny Werblin's many triumphs, perhaps the greatest was having a son like TD.

Things might have worked out better for the Jets if they had hired Michael Martin as general manager.

The time I spent with Coach Larry Bruno was indeed magic.

I thank Bebe Schreiber, Shirley Mays, Jack Lambert, Roland Arrigoni, Lou Michaels, Jim Hudson, Frank Cicatiello, and George Sauer for all those hours on the phone.

In Alabama, this New Yorker learned that southern hospitality is no mere myth. Thanks to Doug Segrest of the *Birmingham News*, and to Clem Gryska and the staff of the Paul W. Bryant Museum.

My debt to Sal Marchiano is eternal.

Kevin Barry has been looking out for me since 1989, when he hooked me up with a basketball player named Lloyd Daniels. This time around, he hooked me up in Florida, making sure I had everything I needed, from the interviews to the great meals at Café Martarano.

Books are credited in the notes, but special thanks are due for *Total Football II*, Larry Fox's *Broadway Joe and His Super Jets*, Dave Anderson's *Countdown to Super Bowl*, Rose Szolnoki and Bill Kushner's *My Son Joe*, Namath and Schaap's *Can't Wait Until Tomorrow*, Keith Dunnavant's *Coach*, Gerald Eskenazi's *Gang Green*, Zimmerman's *The Last Season of Weeb Ewbank*, Kay Iselin Gilman's *Inside the Pressure Cooker*, Stephen Hanks's *The Game That Changed Pro Football*, Mark Gunther and Bill Carter's *Monday Night Mayhem*, Dennis

McDougal's *The Last Mogul,* and Professor Tezla's *The Hazardous Quest.* Also, Nick Tosches's *Dino,* David Maraniss's *When Pride Still Mattered: A Life of Vince Lombardi,* and Richard Ben Cramer's *Joe DiMaggio: The Hero's Life.*

Those who granted withdrawals (usually several) from the favor bank: Tyler and Bess Abell; Tracy Ahringer at the *Sun-Sentinel*; Gary Baronofsky; Ron Berger; Bill Boyle of the *Daily News*; Ace Cacchiotti of NFL Films; Frank Cerabino of the *Palm Beach Post*; Drew Champlin of the *Crimson-White*; Blossom Colley; Colin Cumiskey of St. Peter the Apostle High School; Luke Cyphers; Bob Drury; Fred Dryer; Julian Eure of the *Daily Advance* in Elizabeth City; Ed Fay; Carol Fishman; Marv Fleming; Beth Flynn; Bill Gallo; Wibby Glover; Joe Goldstein; Mike Greenfield; Art Heyman; Joe Hirsch; Zoltan Kovac; Charles Land; Jake Lotz; Bill Madden; Sam Marchiano; Ray McCormack; Steve McFadden; Phil Mushnick of the *New York Post*; Dr. John N. Perry Jr. of Greensboro, North Carolina, and John N. Perry Sr. of Ellwood City, Pennsylvania; Tom O'Hara and Joe Ellen Corrigan of the *Cleveland Plain Dealer*; Tommy O'Neill; Joe Ponzi of the Brooklyn DA's Office; Tom Robbins of the *Village Voice*; Lindsey Rogers and the Orange Bowl Committee; Alex Rosenzweig; Adam Rubin; Bob Skaff; Larry Spangler; Jerry Steinberg; Steve Tannen; Barry Weiss.

Thanks to some wonderful, stand-up guys in sports television: Tim Buckman of Fox Sports, Ray Stallone of HBO Sports; Jim Cohen and Gerry Matalon of ESPN Classic; Kevin Sullivan of NBC Sports, whose many good deeds included immediate delivery of a tape of the Super Bowl III telecast.

It is a privilege to live in a city with resources such as the New York Public Library (I made frequent use of the Science, Industry and Business Library and the Humanities and Social Sciences Library), the Brooklyn Public Library, and the Museum of Television & Radio.

I appreciate all the assistance I received from the staff of the National Archives and Records Administration on Varick Street in New York City; and from Esther, Dana, and Debbie at the Beaver County Prothonotary.

Of enormous help were notes on the first draft from Greg Drozdek, Carmen Rosenzweig, and Philip Ward, a fine teacher and an even finer friend.

Thanks to Harriet and Leonard Kriegel. My father gave the manuscript a good read, too, as he was uniquely qualified: a Namath fan, a man of letters, and an expert on the subject of courage.

At Viking, I thank Kate Griggs, Jesse Reyes, Jennifer Jackson, and the tireless, incomparable Alessandra Lusardi.

David Vigliano, my agent and friend, was at his best when it mattered most.

Writers who speak badly of editors haven't had the privilege of working with Rick Kot. The flaws in this book are mine. But all the good stuff had something to do with Rick—his faith, his dedication, his intelligence, his integrity.

Finally, my wife, Emily: beautiful mother of Holiday, goddess of long shots, dispenser of good judgment, possessor of patience, one hell of an editor, and always good for a few laughs, my love.

Source Notes

Unless indicated otherwise, all interviews were conducted by the author on the date specified.

Prologue

xiii "What about Joe Namath": Wallace Matthews interview, November 13, 2001. Matthews, then a sports columnist for the *New York Post*, is referred to as "the sportswriter."

xiii "The voice": Arthur Samuel Joseph, *The Sound of the Soul: Discovering the Power of Your Voice* (Deerfield Beach, Fla.: Health Communications, 1996), 1.

xv still drunk: Joe Willie Namath, *I Can't Wait Until Tomorrow . . . 'Cause I Get Better-Looking Every Day*, with Dick Schaap (New York: Random House, 1969), 97; Frank Cicatiello interview, July 2, 2002.

xv "I get a special feeling": Wallace Matthews, "Joe Still Feels Super Memories Last Forever," *New York Post*, January 28, 1999.

1. A Distant Fabled Land

1 February 11, 1911: *List or Manifest of Alien Passengers for the United States Immigration Officer at Port of Arrival*, February 11, 1911 (hereafter, *Pannonia* manifest). Available on microfilm, National Archives and Records Administration, Northeast Region, New York City (hereafter, NARA NYC).

1 The steamer had accommodations: American Family Immigration History Center, http://www.ellisisland.org.

1 Raho, a village of several hundred: August J. Molnar, president, American Hungarian Foundation, interview, November 6, 2002. During this interview, Molnar's reading and translation from the reference books in the foundation's archive provided background on the village once known as Raho and the town of Rima Szombat.

1 *Amerika-laz*: Albert Tezla, ed. and trans., *The*

Hazardous Quest: Hungarian Immigrants in the United States, 1895–1920: A Documentary (Budapest: Corvina, 1993), 28.

1 "Here you must live": Ibid., 30.

1 "not even Negroes": Ibid., 299

1 "in a distant fabled land": Professor Albert Tezla, an authority on Hungarian emigration and literature, now retired from the University of Minnesota, Duluth, interview, November 23, 2002. Tezla's translation of the verse came in an e-mail message December 14, 2002.

2 "My dad came to this country": John Namath, interview by Rick Telander (hereafter, RT), December 6 and December 22, 1975. Transcripts of the interviews provided by RT.

2 Janos was accompanied: *List or Manifest of Alien Passengers for the United States Immigration Officer at Port of Arrival*, December 4, 1920 (hereafter, *Rotterdam* manifest), microfilm, NARA NYC; Fourteenth Census of the United States, Pennsylvania, Beaver Falls, 6th Ward, Enumeration District 22 (hereafter, 1920 census), available online at the Irma and Paul Milstein Division of United States History, Local History and Genealogy, Room 121, New York Public Library, Humanities and Social Services Library, New York City (hereafter, NYPL).

2 Janos answered the same questions: *Rotterdam* manifest, NARA NYC.

2 Most immigrants left Hungary: Tezla, Molnar interviews. For additional background on Hungarian immigration I also used Tezla, *The Hazardous Quest*; Julianna Puskas, *Ties That Bind, Ties That Divide: One Hundred Years of Hungarian Experience in the United States* (New York: Holmes & Meier, 2000); Steven Bela Vardy, *The Hungarian-Americans* (Boston: G. K. Hall, 1985); and Emil Lengyel, *Americans from Hungary* (Philadelphia: J. B. Lippincott, 1948).

2 "Declaration of Intention": Citizenship documents including Nemet's "Declaration of Intention" and "Petition for Naturalization" on file at the Prothonotary, Beaver County Courthouse, Beaver, Pa. (hereafter, BCC).

2 The three other boys: 1920 census.

2 "When I first came here my father": John Namath to RT.

3 "He was tough": Jeff Alford interview, January 8, 2002.

3 granted by God: John Namath to RT.

3 it made steel: Kenneth Britten and the Beaver Falls Historical Society, "Industrial Heritage," in *Images of America: Beaver Falls* (Charleston, S.C.: Arcadia, 2000), 105–18. See also Kenneth Britten, *Beaver Falls: Gem of Beaver County* (Charleston, S.C.: Arcadia, 2002).

3 The Beaver Falls Athletics: Joe Tronzo, "Diamond's Golden Age," and Ted Houston, "Beaver Falls Athletics," in *Beaver Falls Area Centennial* (Beaver Falls, Pa.: News-Tribune, 1968), pp. 131–32. Beaver County Research Center, Carnegie Free Library, Beaver Falls, Pa. (hereafter, BCRC).

4 "My parents never allowed": John Namath to RT.

4 "To an old-fashioned Magyar family": Zoltan Kovac interview, December 17, 2002.

4 "I had a doctor change my birth certificate": John Namath to RT. On December 4, 1920, when he arrived at Ellis Island, John Namath was listed as eleven years old. However, his father's "Petition for Naturalization," signed May 25, 1921, gives his birthday as November 18, 1907. The 1930 census and his 1931 application for a marriage license also indicate that John A. Namath was born in 1907.

4 23 cents an hour: Denver and Eugenia Walton, *Rivers of Destiny* (Koppel, Pa.: Beaver County Historical Research and Landmarks Foundation, 1999), 42.

4 worked as a "heater boy": John Namath to RT.

4 Union Clothing Company: Beaver Valley Directory, 1925–26. Microform Reading Room, Room 100, NYPL.

4 Armstrong Cork: Beaver Valley Directory, 1927–28, NYPL.

4 survived by his wife: Obituary, *Beaver Falls Tribune,* November 12, 1926.

4 The cost of the funeral: Records of the A. D. Campbell Funeral Home, Beaver Falls, Pa.

4 about 50 cents an hour: Pay records of the J & L Steel Mill, c. 1926, from the Beaver County Historical Society. Also see Britten, *Images of America: Beaver Falls.*

4 lead story: "Falls Man Found Hanging in Cellar: Firemen Find Body Swaying From Rafters," *Beaver Falls Tribune,* May 17, 1927.

4 the entire burial cost less: Records of the A. D. Campbell Funeral Home, Beaver Falls, Pa.

5 Julia Namath would remarry: Marriage License, Register of Wills, BCC.

5 block populated by: 1930 census. Beaver Falls, 2nd Ward, Enumeration District 4-30, Microfilm, NARA NYC.

5 The Juhaszes owned their own home: Ibid.

5 her schooling was cut short: Rose Namath Szolnoki, *My Son Joe,* with Bill Kushner (Birmingham, Ala.: Oxmoor House, 1975), 8.

5 employed as a domestic: 1930 census.

5 "Women in mill towns": Szolnoki, *My Son Joe,* 8.

5 Beaver Falls Cardinals: John Namath to RT.

5 "He had a good job": Szolnoki, *My Son Joe,* 8.

5 married April 14, 1931: Marriage license, Register of Wills, BCC.

5 John Alexander Namath was born: Voter Registration, Bureau of Elections, BCC

5 Their newlywed years: Szolnoki, *My Son Joe,* 9.

6 Robert Namath was born: Marriage license, Register of Wills, BCC.

6 decided not to have any more kids: Szolnoki, *My Son Joe,* 11

6 birth of a third son, Franklin: Voter Registration, Bureau of Elections, BCC.

6 "I thought little girls": Szolnoki, *My Son Joe,* 13.

6 "I guarantee you": Ibid., 12.

6 "This couldn't be mine": Ibid., 13.

2. The Lower End

7 "He just cried": Szolnoki, *My Son Joe,* 14.

7 Who made us? Though the wording of the catechism varies, this version was found in the Carnegie Free Library, Beaver Falls. *The Official Revised Baltimore Catechism* (New York: W. H. Sadlier, 1945).

7 "They'd slap you": Frances Morelli-Pickard interview, February 4, 2002.

7 "All the stories": Frances Pinchotti-Slone interview, February 5, 2002.

8 "even the nuns were charmed": Joyce Hupp-Davis interview, February 7, 2002.

8 steelworkers' average annual earnings: Mark McColloch, "Consolidating Industrial Citizenship," in *Forging a Union of Steel,* ed. Paul F. Clark, Peter

Gottlieb, and Donald Kennedy (Ithaca, N.Y.: ILR Press, 1987), 48–87; Nelson Lichtenstein, *Labor's War at Home: The CIO in World War Two* (New York: Cambridge University Press, 1982), 111, cited in John P. Hoerr, *And the Wolf Finally Came: The Decline of the American Steel Industry* (Pittsburgh: University of Pittsburgh Press, 1988), 278.

8 with a quarter: Namath, *I Can't Wait,* 13.

8 "nice man at the corner drugstore": Szolnoki, *My Son Joe,* 83.

8 *kascinos:* Molnar interview.

9 deed to the property at 802 Sixth Avenue: Property records, Recorder of Deeds, Beaver County, BCC.

9 "There was the cutest": Szolnoki, *My Son Joe,* 14.

9 They were inseparable: Linwood Alford interviews, January 2, 5, 7, and 8, 2002, with regular follow-up phone calls.

9 "Hunky soup": Bill Braucher, "Young Joe Namath: Growing Up the Hard Way," *Newsday,* September 6, 1969.

10 "Joe's father gave us some whupping": Alford interview.

10 the hustlers knew how to tip.: Ibid.

11 bottle scam: Szolnoki, *My Son Joe,* 24.

11 "they were lyin' ": Ibid.

11 "If I brung a kid home": John Jackson interview, January 8, 2002.

3. Play Ball

12 "There was this basketball game": Morelli-Pickard interview.

12 box scores: *News-Tribune* (Beaver Falls), January 16, 1932, BCRC.

12 three years as a varsity linemen: *The Tiger,* Beaver Falls High School yearbook, 1949, BCRC.

12 "It was God's gift": All of John Namath's quotes in this chapter from interviews with Rick Telander.

14 "threw his bat over the railroad tracks": Interviewed by the author on December 12, 2003, nearly half a century later, Frank Walton had a vague recollection of being struck out by eight-year-old Joe. "The old man might be right," said Walton, who likely did break his bat and toss it onto the railroad tracks. "I certainly had the temper for that," he said. Walton doubts, however, that he actually could have sent the bat's remains *over* the tracks and into the Beaver River.

15 Bunny Hill and Jungle Hill: Alford interview. Also see Szolnoki, *My Son Joe.*

15 "developed my arm": Namath, *I Can't Wait,* 123.

15 "Third Street": Alford interview.

16 "Somebody had to pay the price": Benny Singleton interview, January 3, 2002.

16 "Joe's were a full knuckle bigger": Butch Ryan interview, January 6, 2002.

16 Joey was easy to recognize: Ryan and Alford interviews.

16 wizard of the sandlots: Wibby Glover interview, September 11 and 16, 2002, February 20, 2003; Alford and Ryan interviews.

16 "showed me how to grip": Namath, *I Can't Wait,* 83.

17 "Don't throw so hard": Braucher, "Young Joe Namath."

17 "Frank was *really* tough": Jake Lotz interview, December 15, 2002.

17 "he'd have killed me": Ibid.

17 homemaking club: *The Tiger,* 1955, BCRC.

17 "He was a strong kid": Dom Casey, interview by Rick Telander, undated.

4. Boy at the Top of the Stairs

18 "the last one from his family": *Broadway Joe: The Joe Namath Story,* written and produced by Keith Cossrow, guest host Al Michaels, A & E Biography, February 1, 2002.

18 still sobbing: Szolnoki, *My Son Joe,* 17–18; Alford interview.

18 "it got me scared": *SportsCentury: Joe Namath,* produced by Craig Mortali, ESPN Classic, January 22, 2001.

19 gin and Squirt: John Namath to RT.

19 "black snow": Samuel Allen interview, January 22, 2002. It's also worth noting that Henry Mancini, who grew up in nearby Aliquippa, composed an orchestral suite—*Beaver Valley '37*—based on his youth. The second part is called "Black Snow."

20 "is the top man": John Namath to RT.

20 2,100 degrees: *Visitor's Guide—The Babcock & Wilcox Tube Co., Beaver Falls, Pa.,* bulletin no. tb342, [c. 1950], BCRC.

20 "It's all that damn dirt": John Namath to RT.

20 "Daddy Will You Be My Valentine?": Ibid.

20 a puny trout: Joe Namath, "Fishing: Tales of the Sea," *Gourmet,* May 1995.

20 "It was terrifying": Ibid.

21 December 14, 1938: *Esther May Armour vs. Lawrence F. Armour,* Court of Common Pleas of Beaver County, Case No. 23, 1947, Prothonotary, BCC.

21 "such indignities": Ibid.

21 mind her own business: *Rose Namath vs. John Andrew Namath,* Court of Common Pleas of Beaver County, Case No. 344, 1959, Prothonotary, BCC.

21 world's best-dressed bowler: Ibid.

21 all over town: Ibid.

21 private detective: Ibid.

22 "Look what I found": Ibid.

22 It was over, he promised: Ibid.

22 "the saddest day of his life": Jack Hicks interview, March 17, 2002.

22 September 17, 1956: Property records, Recorder of Deeds, BCC.

22 "suddenly out on our own": Szolnoki, *My Son Joe,* 28.

22 "He got more affection": Kovac interview.

23 "those sleepy, mischievous eyes": Szolnoki, *My Son Joe,* 28.

23 "Joe never talked about it": Alford interview.

24 "He held it inside": Ryan interview.

5. Pint-Sized Quarterback

25 above a gin mill: Glover, Pinchotti, and Alford interviews.

25 115 pounds: Namath, *I Can't Wait,* 132.

25 "You couldn't hardly see him": Lotz interview.

25 "pint-sized Quarterback": "Falls Jr. High Nabs Second," *News-Tribune,* October 12, 1957.

25 a pair of touchdowns: Szolnoki, *My Son Joe,* 32.

26 Homeroom basketball: Lotz and Singleton interviews.

26 "Tommy, keep your hands up": Lotz interview.

26 "By ninth grade": Chuck Knox interview, June 30, July 10–11, 2002.

26 Joe was so hurt: Namath, *I Can't Wait,* 136.

26 a big mistake: Szolnoki, *My Son Joe,* 33

26 "too nice": Larry Bruno interview, January 5, 2002.

26 outscored 179 to 72: Scores totaled from results printed in *The Tiger,* 1960, BCRC.

26 didn't dress for all the games: Program for Beaver Falls–Ambridge game, October 3, 1958, BCRC.

26 "Mr. Ross gave me": Namath, *I Can't Wait,* 136.

27 "Mr. Schackern showed me": Ibid., 83.

27 "He just had a way with the ball": Lotz interview.

27 November 15, 1958: The date is specified in Namath's FBI report, obtained by the author from Jack Anderson's personal papers (hereafter Anderson papers).

27 "a bad influence": Lotz interview.

28 a $20,000 bonus: Namath, *I Can't Wait,* 134; Szolnoki, *My Son Joe,* 31.

28 "I think we made the right decision": Szolnoki, *My Son Joe,* 31.

28 Frank led the freshman baseball team: Details of Frank Namath's athletic career at the University of Kentucky from the 1956 and '57 football media guides and "Athlete Information Forms," dated August 30, 1955 and May 29, 1956. Provided by Tony Neely, Media Relations Director/Football, University of Kentucky.

28 "the third time, he went": Dude Hennessey interview, March 19, 2002.

28 April 27, 1958: Voter Registration, Bureau of Elections, BCC.

28 "almost like a father": Lotz interview.

29 Frank would kick Joey's ass: Glover interview.

29 "I could tell": Lotz interview.

29 "Some stuff": Alford interview.

29 "kind of funny": Namath, *I Can't Wait,* 90

30 men of a certain age remember: Allen interview.

30 "The first girl I ever loved": Cheryl Bentsen, "Namath Says Football Isn't His Whole Life," *Los Angeles Times,* February 23, 1976.

30 "She was waiting on the money": Rick Telander, *Joe Namath and the Other Guys* (New York: Holt, Rinehart and Winston, 1976), 207.

30 "she slaved over that stove": Glover interview.

31 stingy with the support money: *Namath vs. Namath,* BCC.

31 "He was pissed": Kovac interview.

31 "a lot of hate": Glover interview.

31 acted as his translator: Kovac interview.

31 finally filed for divorce: *Namath vs. Namath,* BCC.

31 joined in holy matrimony: Marriage license, Register of Wills, BCC.

6. Magic

32 Bruno played halfback: Larry Bruno interview.

32 129th pick: Bob Carroll, Michael Gershman, David Neft, and John Thorn, *Total Football II: The Official Encyclopedia of the National Football League* (New York: HarperCollins, 1999), 1451.

32 a full-time position: Joe Tronzo, "Namath, 600-plus to Honor Bruno Tomorrow," *Beaver County Times,* May 18, 1979.

32 The son of a tailor: Bruno interview. Unless otherwise noted, Bruno's background and quotes in this chapter are from that session, January 5, 2002.

32 rabbits from hats and doves from saucepans: Allen and Ryan interviews.

33 a special tutorial: Rich Niedbala interview, January 14, 2002: "Larry talked about faking being magic."

33 Bruno would phone third-stringers: Ernie Konvolinka and Joe Tronzo, "Sports Comment," *News-Tribune,* September 8, 1959.

33 very late hours: Ruby Finley (a high school friend of Joe's), interview, February 4, 2002: "Breaking curfew, he did that all the time. The ballplayers were supposed to be in and he was out drinking."

33 five-nine, 156 pounds: Program for the Beaver Falls–New Brighton game, November 13, 1959, BCRC.

34 "You could feel it": Niedbala interview.

34 "taking the ball to the goal line": Joe Tronzo, "Feelings Are Mixed as Men Return," *News-Tribune,* November 11, 1959.

35 first pass was a touchdown: Joe Tronzo, "Beaver Falls Defeats New Brighton," *News-Tribune,* November 14, 1959.

35 $900 a piece: Rick Halligan (Blue Room denizen with thirty years' experience in the pool table recovering business), interview, January 8, 2002.

36 Joe puffed Salems: Glover interview.

36 "high school diploma": Namath, *I Can't Wait,* 126.

36 "Italians were a big deal": Alford interview.

36 a game called Charlie: Rich Halligan and Gene Marx (another old denizen of the pool hall) interviews, January 8, 2002; Sam Allen, Rich Niedbala, Butch Ryan, and Linwood Alford interviews.

37 "twenty dollars in his pocket": Fred Klages interview, November 27, 2002.

37 "He had more guts": Ryan interview.

37 "a gimme": Niedbala interview.

37 "a boycott": Ibid.

38 girlfriends to do his homework: Hupp interview.

38 air force: Dan Jenkins, "The Sweet Life of Swinging Joe," *Sports Illustrated,* October 17, 1966.

38 "I'd even let him use my car": Telander, *Joe Namath,* 129.

38 Rose's court costs: The order was issued February 15, 1960, by Judge Morgan Sohn; *Namath vs. Namath,* BCC.

38 *"Famous* junk": Kovac interview.

38 siphon gas: Alford and Kovac interviews.

39 "Negley was a fifteen-minute drive": Niedbala interview.

39 driving to an American Legion baseball game: Niedbala and Ryan interviews.

39 "I mean *flying*": Ryan interview.

39 the Tommies won county, district, and area: *News-Tribune,* November 2, 1960.

39 five innings of one-hit ball: Casey to RT.

40 "false step": Namath, *I Can't Wait,* 180.

40 "on the sly": Alford interview.

40 "Bruno's the one": Tony Golmont interview, March 4, 2002.

40 "Larry's blocking schemes": Ryan interview.

40 these sessions were illegal: Bruno interview.

7. Joey U

42 studying Colts game films: Lotz interview, January 31, 2003.

42 A famous photograph: It was taken by Robert Riger and featured in *Best Shots: The Greatest NFL Photography of the Century* (New York: DK Publishing, 1999), 20–21.

42 against the urgings of his coach: Weeb Ewbank, *Goal to Go: The Greatest Football Games I Have Coached,* with Neil Roiter (New York: Hawthorn Books, 1972), 57–58. Ewbank says: "Unitas asked me what I thought we should do. I told him that we'd better keep the ball on the ground to avoid a mistake. . . . I nearly died when John threw that ball."

42 Unitas had noticed: Johnny Unitas, *Pro Quarterback: My Own Story,* with Ed Fitzgerald (New York: Simon & Schuster, 1965), 92.

43 reporters kept asking Unitas: Ibid., 93.

43 *The Pat Boone Chevy Show:* Ibid., 94–95.

43 As a high school sophomore: Allen interview.

44 It was unclear if he would even suit up: *News Tribune,* September 7, 1960.

44 "We were on the practice field": Allen interview.

44 "Tough people": Ryan interview.

45 38 Ride: Bruno interview.

45 "If this boy wants to be": Joe Tronzo, "BF Whips Midland: 'Take 'Em Tigers' on Scoring Spree," *News-Tribune,* September 10, 1960.

45 the bus ride back: Bruno interview; Namath, *I Can't Wait,* 180.

46 "Joe did his lines perfectly": Tim Wesley, "The Perfect Season," *Beaver County Times,* November 23, 1984.

46 Tronzo covered his first sporting event: Bill Swauger, "Tronzo: Colorful Columnist an All Around Joe," *Beaver County Times,* January 28, 1990.

46 "I was small": Ibid.

46 a mortar shell: Ibid.

46 Marsh Wheeling stogie: Joe Miksch, "Veteran Newspaperman Joe Tronzo Dies," *Beaver County Times,* May 5, 1999.

46 "Some I liked better than others": Swauger, "Tronzo."

47 Fame is a kind of poison: The idea comes from singer-songwriter Paul Simon, interviewed in 1998 about the impending death of Joe DiMaggio. See Mark Kriegel, "DiMaggio Was Perfect Fit for My Song, Simon Says," *New York Daily News,* November 27, 1998.

47 hadn't scored against the Castlemen since 1927: The scores of every Beaver Falls–New Castle game going back to 1915 were printed in the *News-Tribune* on September 22, 1960. Beaver Falls scored just 6 points on New Castle between 1922 and 1943.

47 "more nerve than a pickpocket": Joe Tronzo, "Tigers Powerful Offense All Set," *News-Tribune,* September 22, 1960.

47 "Don't worry coach": Bruno interview; Namath, *I Can't Wait,* 218.

47 About 8,500: Joe Tronzo, "Beaver Falls Wallops New Castle," *News-Tribune,* September 24, 1960.

47 "If he threw a pass that was intercepted": Bruno interview.

47 "We felt they were the one team": Ryan interview.

48 "The Ambridge stands": Joe Tronzo, "Sports Comment," *News-Tribune,* October 4, 1960.

48 "They thought they had us": Ryan interview.

48 "That's the play I remember most": Wesley, "The Perfect Season."

48 admits giving up on the ball: Klages interview.

48 "Speaking frankly": Joe Tronzo, "Beaver Falls Defeats Ambridge, 25 to 13," *News-Tribune,* October 1, 1960.

48 "His dad would keep a watchful eye": Ernie Neale interview, January 15, 2002.

49 "Joe crying": Bruno interview.

49 Dad's Night: Braucher, "Young Joe Namath."

49 "wasn't going to walk with his dad": Bruno interview, April 12, 2002.

49 "the Hungarian Howitzer and the Polish Picker": Joe Tronzo, "Beaver Falls Rips Butler," *News-Tribune,* October 8, 1960.

49 "Joe had a girl up there": Ernie Pelaia interview, January 15, 2002.

50 the bookies wore fedoras and slacks: Ryan interview.

50 hadn't beaten mighty Farrell since 1954: "Beaver Falls Will Meet Farrell Here Friday," *News-Tribune,* October 20, 1960.

50 How many points should we give you?: Ryan and Pelaia interviews.

50 had allowed a total of 19 points: *News-Tribune,* October 20, 1960.

50 "particularly young women": Bill Swauger, "Young People Dominate Sen. Kennedy Audience," *Beaver County Times,* October 17, 1960.

50 "The sleight of hand magician": Joe Tronzo, "Beaver Falls Whips Farrell High, 33 to18," *News-Tribune,* October 22, 1960. Tronzo spells "Namath" correctly in his lead, but reverts to the incorrect "Nameth" in the body of his story.

50 "a brash youngster": Joe Tronzo, "Beaver Falls Wallops Aliquippa," *News-Tribune,* October 29, 1960.

50–51 "Several times he could have selfishly": Joe Tronzo, "Beaver Falls Wins 'AA' Title! Whips Ellwood City, 26 to 0," *News-Tribune,* November 5, 1960.

51 "the best high school quarterback": Walton interview.

51 "He acts like he is the best": Joe Tronzo, "Beaver Falls Wins."

51 Seven of the town's eight voting precincts: "Tabulation of Voting in Beaver County," *News-Tribune,* November 9, 1960.

51 "common occurrences": Joe Tronzo, "Sports Comment," *News-Tribune,* November 8, 1960.

8. Small-Town Hero

52 "That Namath is no good": Allen interview.

52 "The word spread": Namath, *I Can't Wait*, 128–30.

53 butcher knife: Ibid.

53 Probably more rumors have cropped up: Tronzo, "Sports Comment," *News-Tribune*, November 11, 1960.

54 Unmentioned in the column: In his autobiography, Namath says the incident took place after the Tigers "had just won" the championship. Wibby Glover recalls that there was one more game to play. That would have been the New Brighton game, played a week after Beaver Falls won the WPIAL title, and three days before Tronzo's column appeared.

54 guns drawn . . . until coach Bruno arrived: Namath, *I Can't Wait*, 122–23. Wibby Glover has a different recollection. He says that the cops didn't draw their guns, just a flashlight. Bruno, he adds, didn't come to the police station, either. Rather, he recalls the police chief saying, "Wib, Joe's got a game to play, get him the hell out of here."

54 "A lot of people were jealous": Bruno interview.

54 "I'd like to ask you something": Hupp interview.

55 "Some of my teachers": Ibid.

55 "You know how black guys talk": Ron Davis interview, February 7, 2002.

55 Joe never showed: Ibid.

55 "I'm not aware of that": Pinchotti interview.

55 "he began to wait for me": Bunny Kreshon Stanko interview, February 11, 2002.

55 "Lot of stories about Joe and the girls": Ryan interview.

56 "Joe kind of floated": Niedbala interview.

56 "Joe wasn't hung up on girls": Alford interview.

56 "Everybody in Beaver Falls": Ruby Jean Finley Ramsey interview, February 4, 2002.

56 "My father went to his grave": Ibid.

56 "I was all over him": Ray Brokos interview, November 14, 2002.

56 19 points a game: Season statistics for WPIAL Section III, *News-Tribune*, February 28, 1960.

57 "Let me take him": Brokos interview.

57 "Joe Namath of the Tigers": John Carpenter, "Beaver Falls Edges Ambridge," *News-Tribune*, December 28, 1960

57 " 'Give me the ball!' ": Singleton interview.

58 "He could stop his dribble by palming": Roland Arrigoni interview, January 23, 2002.

58 In 1958 . . . By 1961: Jan Hubbard, ed., *The Official NBA Encyclopedia*, 3d ed. (New York: Doubleday, 2000).

58 only white starter: Namath, *I Can't Wait*, 134.

58 288–103: Joe Tronzo, "Tiger Five to Play at Hickory Gym," *News-Tribune*, December 2, 1960.

58 thirteen sectional championships: "Lippe Coached for 26 Years," *Beaver County Times*, January 26, 1979.

58 He disdained the newfangled game: Alford, Ryan, and Singleton interviews.

58 "I fooled around a lot": Namath, *I Can't Wait*, 135.

58 "Lippe really screwed him": Arrigoni interview.

59 "Joe threw the ball": Alford interview.

59 "He just didn't give it": Ryan interview.

59 "It was a shock": Allen interview.

59 "I did not see it due to my position": Joe Tronzo, "In the Shower Room," *News-Tribune*, February 4, 1961.

59 Wilson Young of 3407 Sixth Avenue: Young's letter printed in Joe Tronzo, "In the Shower Room," *News-Tribune*, February 8, 1961.

60 "Joe Namath being on school probation": Ibid.

9. Higher Education

61 "He wasn't a good student": Mervin D. Hyman and Gordon S. White, Jr., *Joe Paterno: "Football My Way"* (New York: Macmillan, 1971), 103.

61 "He didn't bother": Namath, *I Can't Wait*, 126.

61 "I got six hundred bucks": Bruno interview.

61 "Dago didn't do so bad": Ibid.

61 "as much money as my father made": Namath interviewed by Lawrence Linderman for *Playboy*, December 1969 (hereafter, *Playboy* interview).

62 "we could have used the money": Joe Namath (hereafter, JN) interviews with RT, November 4 and 20, 1975. Transcripts provided by RT.

62 St. Louis Cardinals: *Playboy* interview.

62 "They told me they had a women's college": *Playboy* interview.

62 "Deep down in Joe's heart": Bruno interview.

62 "Everybody was pissed off": Golmont interview.

62 scholarship offers at fifty-two: *Playboy* interview.

62 "I'm playing Christ": Telander, *Joe Namath*, 126.

62 "I got to get Joe out of here": Niedbala interview.

63 "It would have made our program": Lee Corso interview, January 15, 2002.

63 "His home life was not the greatest": Arrigoni interview.

63 "Best thing you can do": Bruno interview.

63 Almost every Sunday: Arrigoni interview.

63 Joe was embarrassed: Ibid.

63 "Why don't you finish your beer": Ibid.

64 peaked-bill beret: Corso interview.

64 "That's bullshit": Tim Secor interview, November 29, 2001.

64 "It was a big weekend for us": Al Hassan interview, August 5, 2002.

64 "put out the cigarette": Ibid.

64 "He shows up half gassed": Dick Young, "Young Ideas," *Daily News*, August 30, 1967.

64 "Look, Mister": Ibid.; Klages interview.

65 "He just sat on the bench": Larry Merchant, "A Kid from Wampum," *New York Post*, June 15, 1972.

65 On April 15: Marriage license, Register of Wills, BCC

65 "He would sit in my kitchen": Pinchotti interview.

65 hitting a ball over 400 feet: *News-Tribune,* June 6, 1961.

65 Joe was 2 for 3 that day: *News-Tribune,* June 13, 1961.

65 .450 mark: Namath, *I Can't Wait,* 133.

65 $50,000: In his autobiography, Namath writes: "I heard rumors that I could have gotten as much as $50,000 if I'd turned pro." In his *Playboy* interview, published in December 1969, he says, "the big offer I got was in my senior year, when the Chicago Cubs offered me $50,000."

65 Oldsmobile Starfire: Jerry Heasley, "1961 Oldsmobile Starfire Convertible," http://popular mechanics.comautomotive/sub_coll_/1999/6/61_ olds_starfire.

65 "He would drool": Hassan interview.

65 "I knew he was never": Pinchotti interview.

65 "We *all* knew": Hupp interview.

66 "He has a rich opportunity": Tronzo, "Sports Comment," *News-Tribune,* November 15, 1960.

66 "It was *very* important": Hassan interview, April 26, 2003.

66 "when I graduated from the twelfth grade": Szolnoki, *My Son Joe.*

66 St. Mary's never went beyond eighth grade: *St. Mary's* (Hackensack, N.J.: Custombook, 1972), BCRC. The book makes no mention of the school ever providing secondary education. Conceivably, Rose could have attended St. Mary's "commercial school," in which students received instruction in secretarial skills such as typing, bookkeeping, and shorthand. The commercial school was founded in 1925 and lasted until 1931. See Joe Tronzo, "Bells of St. Mary's," *Beaver County Times,* May 30, 1984.

66 occupation as "domestic": 1930 census.

66 "the most competitive guy I've ever seen": Hassan interview.

66 August 2: A copy of the agreement Namath signed with Maryland was provided by Arrigoni, from his personal papers.

66 Joe had already signed another letter committing to Notre Dame: In the December 17, 1964, editions of the *Tuscaloosa News,* columnist Charles Land interviewed Namath and wrote: "Joe visited Notre Dame and was impressed enough to sign a letter of intent there. But the romance cooled and Namath fell in love with Maryland."

66 He asked Joe to write Notre Dame: Arrigoni interview, February 23, 2003.

66 "She was upset about it": Ibid.

67 Joe had scored in the low 730s: Namath, *I Can't Wait,* 147.

67 "unofficial tutor": Szolnoki, *My Son Joe,* 42

67 "'Cause I get better looking every day": Hassan interview.

67 still fell a few points short of the 750: Namath, *I Can't Wait,* 147.

67 "If I don't go to college this year": Arrigoni interview.

67 "I'd like to congratulate you": Ibid.

67 "That's Bear Bryant, isn't it?": Ibid.

68 paid Coach Bruno a visit: Bruno interview; Clem Gryska interview, March 15, 2002.

68 "I'm gonna sign with the Cubs": Arrigoni interview.

68 "My job was to get Joe to Alabama": Howard Schnellenberger interview, January 30, 2002.

68 "If it weren't for Frank": Schnellenberger interview.

68 "Finally, his mother invited me": Ibid.

68 "My mother took a liking to Coach": Namath interview by Chris Russo and Mike Francesa, *Mike and the Mad Dog,* WFAN-New York, 660-AM, January 3, 2003 (hereafter, *Mike and the Mad Dog* interview).

10. The Tower

69 "I had longish hair": W. C. Heinz, "Countdown for Joe Namath," *Life,* August 29, 1965.

69 the real hustle had already been pulled off by Schnellenberger: Schnellenberger interview; see also Keith Dunnavant, *Coach: The Life of Paul "Bear" Bryant* (New York: Simon & Schuster, 1996), 205–6.

69 "It was a white shirt": Hennessey interview.

69 would much rather have faced a judge: Schnellenberger interview.

69 "Moro what?": Mickey Herskowitz, *The Legend of Bear Bryant* (New York: McGraw-Hill, 1987), 39.

70 "mostly sat around the house": Dunnavant, *Coach,* 17.

70 "I still remember the ones": Paul W. Bryant, *Bear: The Hard Life and Good Times of Alabama's Coach Bryant,* with John Underwood (Boston: Little, Brown, 1974), 21.

70 mean as hell: Dunnavant, *Coach,* 24.

70 "Sensing the need for a little more drama:" Ibid., 25.

70 "What's wrong with you": *SportsCentury: Bear Bryant,* produced by Vincent Cannamela, ESPN Classic, December 13, 2002.

71 Of the 115, 35 returned: Jim Dent, *The Junction Boys: How Ten Days in Hell with Bear Bryant Forged a Championship Team* (New York: Thomas Dunne Books, 1999), 290.

71 Junction wasn't much different . . . slide down the drainpipe: Schnellenberger interview.

71 "champions from the turds": Dunnavant, *Coach,* 69.

71 "what God looks like": Ibid., 71.

72 "The voice of God": Film clip at Paul W. Bryant Museum, Tuscaloosa (hereafter, PBM).

72 "You could hear that chain": Gryska interview.

72 "Everybody saw him as a savior": Clyde Bolton interview, March 22, 2002.

72 "Those were pretty lean years": Charles Land interview, March 26, 2002.

72 "The persona": Ibid.

72 "another country": Schnellenberger interview.

72 "Tilted": Gryska interview.

73 "A nigger sportswriter": Maury Allen, *Joe Namath's Sportin' Life* (New York: Paperback Library, 1969), 36.

73 "Y'all better not say anything": Hennessey interview.

73 "Everybody was just shocked": Hicks interview.

73 "It made you feel good": *SportsCentury: Bear Bryant.*

11. Colored Water

74 relayed Joe's request: Hicks interview.

74 didn't have a number 19: Ibid.

74 "Bryant had something to do with that": Gryska interview.

74 "As a quarterback, Pat": *Tuscaloosa News,* January 11, 1962, quoted in Dunnavant, *Coach,* 152.

74 "Word spread": Bolton interview.

75 "Colored water": Hicks interview.

75 "We just tried to be his friend": Ibid.

75 "more problems staying off the street than Joe": Schnellenberger interview.

75 "Ray had already proven": Hicks interview.

75 "But Joe ate 'em up": Gryska interview.

76 "Don't let that kid": Ibid.

76 A team that passed too much risked: Schnellenberger interview.

76 played a short three-game season: Though freshman standings are not readily available, Brad Green of the Bryant Museum researched the team's record.

76 "so option-oriented": Gryska interview.

76 "It's not your job": Namath, *I Can't Wait,* 181.

76 "Suddenly he grabbed hold": Ibid.

77 "Joe could dunk": Gryska interview.

77 "dunk it backward": Hicks interview.

77 "He used to brag": Butch Henry interview, June 10, 2002.

77 "In my freshman year": *Playboy* interview.

77 "he had three pictures on his dresser": Hicks interview.

78 "I wanted to quit": *Playboy* interview.

78 "You see how they treat the blacks": Hicks interview.

78 "Family was very important to him": Bebe Schreiber interview, June 8, 2002.

78 "Kids of divorce": Ibid.

78 "Bubba just pulled some money": *Playboy* interview.

79 they all jumped in Ray's car: Hicks interview.

79 He was 12 of 17: Charles Land, "Namath Pitches Whites In, 15–14," *Tuscaloosa News,* May 20, 1962.

79 "I will never, ever": Niedbala interview.

79 "He put the fear of God": Ibid.

12. Stud

80 Bryant still had six: *University of Alabama 1962 Football Information and Record Book,* PBM.

80 even Bryant had to acknowledge as much: Dunnavant, *Coach,* 162.

80 "out-mean people": Bryant, *Bear,* 184.

81 "commando training": Christ Vagotis interview, October 7, 2002.

81 Kill or Be Killed drill: JN to RT.

81 averaged 198 pounds: Charles Land, "Bryant: 'They Sure Do Look Good,' " *Tuscaloosa News,* September 1, 1962.

81 dismal forecast: Charles Land, "Bryant Paints Dismal Tide Picture," *Tuscaloosa News,* September 9, 1962.

81 biggest ever cross burning: Paul Davis, "Klansmen Meet Here for Rites," *Tuscaloosa News,* September 30, 1962.

81 "I can still see that first one": Gryska interview.

81 "Pat Trammell couldn't throw it like that": Richard Williamson interview, May 8, 2002.

81 "cocky 185-pound Yankee sophomore": George Smith, "Bama Romps Past Lame Bulldogs 35–0," *Anniston Star,* September 23, 1962.

82 "the best athlete I have ever seen": Bryant, *Bear,* 199.

82 "I would have *carried* him": Ibid., 200.

82 "He did beautifully": Land, "Bama Better Than Bryant Thought," *Tuscaloosa News,* September 23, 1962.

82 35-point favorite: Charles Land, "Tide Fights For 17–7 Win over Vanderbilt," *Tuscaloosa News,* October 7, 1962.

82 "I was having a miserable day": Namath, *I Can't Wait,* 182.

82 "You'll see it in the headlines tomorrow": Bryant, *Bear,* 201.

82 "I'd have loved to play another year": Williamson interview.

83 "I saw a guy who tips the field": *This Is the NFL: Joe Namath,* NFL Films, 75th Anniversary Series, 1994.

83 "Some people expect him to play like a senior": Charles Land, "Namath, Hurlbut Provide Solid 1-2 Punch for Tide," *Tuscaloosa News,* October 16, 1962.

83 "fell down trying to elude": Land, "Bama Whips Houston," *Tuscaloosa News,* October 14, 1962.

83 "going to make more money than any quarterback": Bryant, *Bear,* 202.

83 four straight incompletions: Charles Land, "Angry Tide Rips Hurricane, 36–3," *Tuscaloosa News,* November 11, 1962.

83 Ole Indian Joe: George Smith, "Tide Tames Hurricane in 36–3 Romp . . . Ole Indian Joe Outshines Mira," *Anniston Star,* November 11, 1962.

84 "Joe didn't have a bad day": Charles Land, "Inspired Tech Finally Stems Tide, 7-6," *Tuscaloosa News,* November 18, 1962.

84 hit Bryant twice with whiskey bottles: Bryant, *Bear,* 257.

84 "500 beautiful women": Lee Winfrey, "King Orange Peals in New Year," *Miami Herald,* January 1, 1963.

84 "I'm not impressed by Bryant's corn pone": Devine quoted in Charles Land, "Looking with Land: Miami Writer Blasts Bryant," *Tuscaloosa News,* December 30, 1962.

85 Miss Campbell to weep with joy: Gene Miller, "Now Who Could Resist a Strawberry Blonde?" *Miami Herald,* January 2, 1963.

85 "I've hugged Joe": Luther Evans, " 'That's N-A-M-A-T-H Son, But You'll Get to Know It,' " *Miami Herald,* January 2, 1963.

85 "I hold the Orange Bowl responsible": Associated Press, "Orange Bowl Is Warned after Joe's Track Win," *Birmingham Post-Herald,* January 5, 1963.

85 "undesirable types": Edwin Pope, "NFL Admits Probe of Betting; Senate Eyes Possible Scandal," *Miami Herald,* January 5, 1963.

13. Of Southern Comforts and the Schoolhouse Door

86 midnight mass at St. Philomena's: Kreshon interview.

86 "I'll regret that": Ibid.

86 "Son, be like Jesus": John Namath to RT.

87 "Any red-blooded American boy": Ibid.

87 front-page news: *Tuscaloosa News,* November 8, 1962.

87 *Corolla:* Yearbook on file at PBM.

87 "I like Southern girls": *Playboy* interview.

87 "Just to see how well I was doing": Ibid.

87 "This is the girl": Schreiber interview.

88 "He was never ready": Hicks interview.

88 "Those three little ladies": Schreiber interview.

88 pork chops and corn bread: Szolnoki, *My Son Joe,* 51.

88 "My family just adored him": Maury Allen, *Joe Namath's Sportin' Life,* 41.

88 *Gone With the Wind:* Szolnoki, *My Son Joe,* 60.

88 "a dorm with wall-to-wall": Paul Zimmerman, "Joe Namath: Caught Off Side?" *New York Post,* September 2, 1967.

88–89 as much as $50: Henry interview.

89 "You could get a hundred": Frank Cicatiello interview, July 2, 2002.

89 "Someone at my high school": Ibid.

89 "dead-end mill towns": Ibid.

89 "You know it's a tradition": Namath, *I Can't Wait,* 112–13.

90 Let's go to New Orleans: Ciciatello interview.

90 "We're just gonna ride": Ibid.

90 "Then Joe started having a few": Ibid.

90 knocking them cold: Ibid.

90 700 pounds of diesel-soaked burlap: Davis, "Klansmen Meet Here."

91 family that celebrated Emancipation Day: E. Culpepper Clark, *The Schoolhouse Door: Segregation's Last Stand at the University of Alabama* (New York: Oxford University Press, 1995), 175.

91 "I think I will get in": Associated Press, "Will Gain Admission to UA, Negro Feels," November 27, 1962.

91 "Those are chances": Vivian Malone Jones interview, May 13, 2002.

91 two private detectives: "Detectives Guarding UA Editor," *Tuscaloosa News,* November 13, 1962.

91 the imperial wizard had long been bragging: Clark, *The Schoolhouse Door,* 147.

92 wearing a microphone: Clarke Stallworth, "Wallace Bows after Troops Federalized," *Birmingham Post-Herald,* June 12, 1963.

92 "It was a thrill": *SportsCentury: Namath.*

92 "There were a group of us": Schreiber interview.

92 "There were threats": Malone interview.

92 "nervous breakdown": United Press International, "Hood Says He Plans Return to University," *Birmingham Post-Herald,* September 4, 1963.

92 a clinic in Montana: Bryant, *Bear,* 302.

92 "Branch Rickey": Ibid., 300.

92–93 boycotted the game: Dunnavant, *Coach,* 251.

93 Bryant and Governor Wallace . . . inextricably linked from 1958: Diane McWhorter, "Bama's Boys," *New York Times,* December 30, 1982.

93 "trusted his vision": *SportsCentury: Namath.*

93 "I get the hell out": JN to RT.

93 "Wow, eight years": Malone interview.

94 "I really did admire": Ibid.

14. Jimmy

95 wanted to attend Rutgers: Jimmy Walsh interviewed by RT, 1975. All of Walsh's quotes in this chapter are from that interview.

95 maiden name was Nagy: Elsie Nagy Walsh, Application for Account Number, May 20, 1937, Social Security Administration, Baltimore, Md.

96 "always studying": Hicks interview.

96 a hard time getting back to Tuscaloosa: Walsh to RT.

96 he needed money: Ibid.

96 July 2, 1899, in Charlestown, County Mayo: James Patrick Walsh, Application for Account Number, December 3, 1936, Social Security Administration, Baltimore, Md.

97 28 Main Street: Ibid.

97 Jimmy took after his father: Ed Susan interview, October 31 and November 1, 2002.

97 "It was the kind of work": Bill Carroll interview, November 1, 2002.

97 "He broke his back": Susan interview.

97 "Jimmy was the sixth back": Ibid.

97 "Pound for pound": Steve Baffic interview, November 9, 2002.

98 "There were three bullies": Ibid.

15. Sippin'

99 "It took us until Joe's junior year": Schnellenberger interview.

99 "the best college quarterback ever": Charles Land, "Athens to See Pitching Duel?" *Tuscaloosa News,* September 20, 1963.

99 "Namath has class": Charles Land, "Namath's Still a Dangerous Man," *Tuscaloosa News,* October 10, 1963.

100 "You just didn't": Land interview.

100 "Bryant didn't want you interviewing": Bolton interview.

100 "We gave plumb out": Delbert Reed, "Bryant Says Tide 'Gave Plumb Out,' " *Tuscaloosa News,* October 13, 1963.

100 the Volunteers' worst defeat: Charles Land, "Namath Fires Tide to 35–0 Win over Vols," *Tuscaloosa News,* October 20, 1963.

100 "Namath hurt his leg a little": Dick Looser, "Defense Terrible in Spots—Bryant," *Tuscaloosa News,* October 27, 1963.

101 "his finest hour": Land, "'Better Than I Thought,'" *Tuscaloosa News,* November 17, 1963.

101 Many recall the open date: Though Kennedy was shot on a Friday, Alabama students were expected back in class on Monday, the day of the president's funeral. As no football game was ever scheduled for that weekend, none had to be canceled.

101 "She loaned us some money": Hicks interview.

102 "Every football player on the team": Ibid.

102 "woman's store": Bryant, *Bear,* 202.

102 directing traffic while drunk: Namath, *I Can't Wait,* 185.

102 nauseated: Bryant, *Bear,* 202.

102 "A few sips": Namath, *I Can't Wait,* 185.

102 "Aw, Dude": Hennessey interview.

102 month's salary: Gryska interview.

102 "If it'd been me": Dunnavant, *Coach,* 208.

103 Perhaps he didn't want to be seen: Bryant, *Bear,* 203.

103 "Sir": Namath, *I Can't Wait,* 186.

103 call his mother: Dunnavant, *Coach,* 209; Szolnoki, *My Son Joe,* 57.

103 "Joe come out of there": Hicks interview.

103 "real bitter": Henry interview.

103 "She hid me out": B. J. Phillips, "Football's Supercoach," with Peter Ainslie, *Time,* September 29, 1980.

103 "You're just too good a boy": Ibid.

103 "I have thought about it": Charles Land, "Namath Suspended, to Miss Miami and Bowl," *Tuscaloosa News,* December 10, 1963.

103 "We know none of the background": Bob Phillips, "On the Roof," *Birmingham Post-Herald,* December 11, 1963.

104 "There were all these rumors": Henry interview.

104 "Never happened": Mike Fracchia interview, June 10, 2002.

104 "Joe had some other situations": Williamson interview.

104 "There have been ugly and unconfirmed rumors": Phillips, "On the Roof."

104 "The team was barely": Fracchia interview.

104 "I just felt like Coach Bryant": *SportsCentury: Joe Namath.*

104 "He was pushing his limits": Schreiber interview.

104 "One thing about Joe": Hicks interview.

105 "What the hell": Namath, *I Can't Wait,* 152

105 "We only had two": Ibid.

105 "Just be quiet": Hicks interview.

105 feet up on the cot: Ibid.

105 "taken off the line": Phillips, "On the Roof."

106 "What do you think their chances": Niedbala interview.

106 scrambling for the phones: Ibid.

16. Doylestown Redux

107 "Namath was terrific": Charles Land, "Namath Passes Reds To 17–6 Victory over Whites," *Tuscaloosa News,* May 9, 1964.

107 most well attended: Bill Lumpkin, "Namath Leads Reds by Whites," *Birmingham Post-Herald,* May 9, 1964.

107 1964 Crimson Tide football media guide: On file at PBM.

107 "Namath was the big difference": Paul Davis, "Disappointed Dooley Saw What He Expected," *Tuscaloosa News,* September 30, 1964.

107 "I speak for all of our backs": "Alabama Line Paved Way for 'Back of Week' Honors, Says Namath," *Tuscaloosa News,* September 23, 1964.

108 "I was at my peak": JN to RT.

108 "the men's wool suits": Paul Davis, "Don't Talk of Losing," *Tuscaloosa News,* October 11, 1964.

108 All week long: Golmont interview.

108 "It's my knee": Ibid.

108 like he'd been shot: Namath, *I Can't Wait,* 194.

108 "We were in the game": Golmont interview.

109 aspirated: JN to RT; Gerald Eskenazi, *Gang Green: An Irreverent Look behind the Scenes at Thirty-eight (Well, Thirty-seven) Seasons of New York Jets Football Futility* (New York: Simon & Schuster, 1998), 48.

109 "I was put in the hospital": Namath, *I Can't Wait,* 194–95.

109 "I always wondered whether his legs": Szolnoki, *My Son Joe,* 60.

109 he liked the look: *Playboy* interview.

109 "He moves like a human": Charles Land, "Bryant: All Games Big," *Tuscaloosa News,* October 23, 1964.

109 football parlay sheets: "Six Arrested Here in Gambling Raids," *Tuscaloosa News,* November 7, 1964. State Public Safety Commissioner Al Lingo, who had done his best to maintain the civil rights of white people, was quoted as saying: "These gamblers prey upon young people and cause delinquency and corruption and a moral breakdown in the community."

109 6½ points: Charles Land, Looking with Land, *Tuscaloosa News,* October 23, 1964.

110 reinjured as he scrambled: Charles Land, "Alabama Fights Off Gators, 17–14," *Tuscaloosa News,* October 25, 1964.

110 "He was really suffering": Schreiber interview.

110 "the money train": Ibid.

110 "They just didn't know": Eskenazi, *Gang Green,* 48.

110 "Pain": Hennessey interview.

110 with 1:45 left in the half: Charles Land, "Namath Tosses Spark Victory," *Tuscaloosa News,* November 15, 1964.

111 "If he doesn't sign one of the biggest": Associated Press, "Even Just for Seconds, Joe's Tough," *Tuscaloosa News,* November 16, 1964.

111 He didn't want any kids seeing him: Murray Olderman, "Tide's Namath Free Spirit of Football, Scribe Figures," *Tuscaloosa News,* November 22, 1964.

111 "colorful rogue": Bolton interview.

112 "A mild concussion": William N. Wallace, "Fumbles on Offense and Weak Defense Lead to Rout," *New York Times,* November 23, 1964.

112 the smart money: Murray Olderman, "Giants after Joe Namath?" *Tuscaloosa News,* November 26, 1964.

112 "If a pro team": Charles Land, "Tough Decision for NY Giants," *Tuscaloosa News,* November 27, 1964.

112 "That's class": Olderman, "Tide's Namath."

113 "The Best": The Oilers' scouting report appears in "Joe Namath: Mr. Big of the Bonus Baby War," *Life,* January 15, 1965.

113 Joe told Baugh not to bother: Eskenazi, *Gang Green,* 49.

113 "We chose the No. 1 player": " 'Best in Country,' Mara Brags of Frederickson," *Daily News,* December 1, 1964.

113 "National League all the way": Vic Ziegel and Leonard Lewin, *New York Post,* November 29, 1964.

17. Harry Wismer's Titans of New York

115 publicity stills of Wismer: For excellent background on Wismer and the Titans see Willliam J. Ryczek's *Crash of the Titans* (New York: Total Sports Illustrated, 2000); and Bob Curran, *The $400,000 Quarterback; or, The League That Came In from the Cold* (New York: Signet, 1969).

115 "a weasely intelligence": Larry Fox interview, June 4, 2002.

115 bogus "scoops": Jerry Izenberg interview, February 8, 2002.

115 "I ran faster backward": Don Maynard interview, May 11, 2002.

115 "It was embarrassing": Larry Grantham interview, May 8, 2002.

116 "It was a Giant town": Bill Mathis interview, April 9, 2002.

116 crowd of 10,200: *Total Football II,* 1759.

116 fingers instead of noses: Ed Gruver, *The American Football League: A Year-by-Year History, 1960–1969* (Jefferson, N.C.: McFarland, 1997), 87.

116 "You'd look up in the stands": Grantham interview.

116 "the stinking news media": Maynard interview.

116 "It would be better for New York": "Foss Favors Ouster of Wismer," *New York Times,* November, 24, 1961.

117 put the crowd at 7,175: *Total Football II,* 1761.

117 With the onset of twilight: Grantham interview.

117 He accused the Giants of conspiring: Curran, *The $400,000 Quarterback,* 129.

117 Longy Zwillman: Robert McDonald and Sidney Kline, "Wismer Secretly Marries Longie Zwillman's Widow," *Daily News,* July 25, 1962.

117 a very drunk groom: Joe Foss, *A Proud American: The Autobiography of Joe Foss,* with Donna Wild Foss (New York: Pocket Books, 1992), 272.

117 "chief executive officer": "Wismer's Wife Titans' Prexy," *Mirror,* November 1, 1962.

117 generated some optimism among the players: Mathis and Grantham interviews.

117 The list of creditors: Bankruptcy docket for Titans of New York Inc., on file at NARA NYC.

118 the Wismer Plan: Harry Wismer, *The Public Calls It Sport* (Englewood Cliffs, N.J.: Prentice-Hall, 1965), 91.

118 "Harry Wismer came up with an idea": Foss, *A Proud American,* 248.

118 Werblin's guest at "21": William O. Johnson Jr., *Super Spectator and the Electric Lilliputians* (Boston: Little, Brown, 1971), 131.

118 Sonny had been going to the track since Al Jolson: Joe Hirsch interview, November 27, 2001; Tommy Holmes, "The Sonny Side," *New York Herald Tribune,* July 29, 1965.

119 "a series of invectives": Foss, *A Proud American,* 272.

119 "They turned their backs": Wismer, *The Public Calls It Sport,* 2

18. Sonny, as in Money

120 "the appearance of roundness": Milton Gross, "Weeb Ewbank—Jet Pilot," *New York Post,* April 16, 1963.

120 "I've seen sicker cows": Dana Mozley, "Weeb, Jets Launch Titan Task," *Daily News,* April 16, 1963.

121 recommendation of Jimmy Cannon: "Weeb Ewbank," in Jimmy Cannon, *Nobody Asked Me, But . . . : The World of Jimmy Cannon,* ed. Jack Cannon and Tom Cannon (New York: Berkley, 1979), 277–79.

121 "Success will take time": Gene Ward, "Ward to the Wise," *Daily News,* April 15, 1963.

121 "Their popularity is spectacular despite": Jimmy Cannon, "New Shuffle," Sports Today, *Journal-American,* April 16, 1963.

121 a stringer extraordinaire: Ray Kennedy, "Miracle in the Meadows," *Sports Illustrated,* September 12, 1977.

121 accessibility: Izenberg interview. "The most available owner in the world," says Izenberg, who covered the Titans for the *Herald Tribune,* before becoming a columnist for the *Newark Star-Ledger.*

121 "It was writers in first class": Howie Evans interview, January 22, 2002.

122 "That horse would have to die": Izenberg interview.

122 "you get to play for the Giants": Matt Snell interview, May 21, 2002.

122 "Don't do anything": Ibid.

122 now highly regarded as a mentor: Gerald Eskenazi, *There Were Giants in Those Days* (New York: Simon & Schuster, 1987), 82.

123 "Jets" never crossed his lips: Snell interview.

123 "You're part of the family": Ibid.

123 "a procession of game shows": "Excerpts from Speech by Minow," *New York Times,* May 10, 1961.

124 "best salesman in the television industry": Al Rush interview, August 19, 2002.

124 died of a heart attack: Robert H. Boyle, "Show Biz Sonny and His Quest for Stars," *Sports Illustrated,* July 19, 1965.

124 would sit on a raised office chair : Dennis McDougal, *The Last Mogul: Lew Wasserman, MCA, and the Hidden History of Hollywood* (New York: Crown, 1998), 32.

124 "a kind of dysfunctional father figure": Ibid.

125 "I just grabbed whatever I could": Boyle, "Show Biz Sonny."

125 "nose job": Tom Werblin interview, November 16, 2001.

125 "Sonny could walk a cockroach": Chet Simmons interview, November 14, 2001.

125 "Werblin could play both sides": George Rosen, "Sonny . . . Just Like in Money," *Variety,* January 13, 1965.

126 a five-year deal worth between $6 and $7 million: David Gelman and Alfred G. Aronowitz, "MCA: Show Business Empire," article 2 of 5, *New York Post,* June 5, 1962.

126 Jack Benny's CBS deal: Ibid.

126 a multitude of programs: Boyle, "Show Biz Sonny."

126 Werblin asked NBC to renew: Gelman and Aronowitz, "MCA: Show Business Empire," article 3 of 5, *New York Post,* June 6, 1962.

126 "My dad would deliver": Werblin interview.

127 "People like to say": Rush interview.

127 the business left him cold: McDougal, *The Last Mogul,* 325.

127 tired of packaging: Werblin interview.

128 cryptic note: Johnson, *Super Spectator,* 133.

128 "You say the NFL got": Ibid., 134.

128 NBC cut five checks: William N. Wallace, "Pro Football Is Primed to Start Money War in Search of Talent," *New York Times,* November 25, 1964.

128 "Go get 'em": Ibid.

128 just another package: "Sonny looked on the AFL and the jets as another production another show," says Chet Simmons.

128 30,000 more than the year before: Based on attendance figures in *Total Football II,* 1761–62

129 Sonny wasted no time: Izenberg interview.

129 "Wahoo spells money": Milton Gross, "Jets' Wahoo—Time to Howl," Speaking Out, *New York Post,* September 14, 1964.

19. Happy New Year

130 "They let me soak": Jerry Rhome interview, December 8, 2002.

130 didn't do much talking: Ibid.

130 "the cardinal sin": Werblin interview.

131 "This is not the guy": Ibid.

131 Rush was less concerned with his knees: Walt Michaels interview, July 18, 2002.

131 the Jets' own scouting report: "Joe Namath: Mr. Big."

131 "I pushed Weeb very hard": Knox interview.

132 "Screaming like they were in agony": *This Is the NFL: Joe Namath.*

132 "Lincoln Continental": Ibid.

132 with Bryant's blessing: Bryant, *Bear*, 205.

132 He was already thinking long-term: Knox interview.

132 "we couldn't afford him": Charles Land, Looking with Land, *Tuscaloosa News,* December 20, 1964.

133 "St. Louis was the patsy": Michaels interview.

133 as if they needed permission: Larry Fox, *Broadway Joe and His Super Jets* (New York: Coward-McCann, 1969), 113.

133 "The latest rumor": Larry Fox, "Jets Have Huarte All Wrapped Up for '65," *World-Telegram and Sun,* December 19, 1964.

133 "There came a time": *Metro Sports Legends: Broadway Joe,* produced by Roman Gackowski Television, Metro TV, April 20, 2001.

133 "He's going to be at Tropical Park": Hirsch interview.

133 "Nah, that class was all filled up": Ibid.

134 "Why are we here?": Werblin interview.

134 an easy grace: snorkeling, lounging: Ibid.

134 "the *wives* would melt": Ibid.

134 he'd known for three weeks: Red Smith, "After Shuffle, Namath Ripe for Jet Set," *New York Herald Tribune,* January 8, 1965.

134 can't con a con man: Fox, *Broadway Joe,* 117.

134 "I just want to tell you not to worry": Smith, "After Shuffle."

134 on the advice of a smart lawyer: Werblin interview.

134 "He gave you his word": quoted in Larry Bortstein, *SuperJoe: The Joe Namath Story* (New York: Grosset & Dunlap, 1969), 57.

135 "Don't come home": Chuck Knox, *Hard Knox: the Life of an NFL Coach,* with Bill Plaschke (New York: Harcourt, Brace, Jovanovich, 1988), 104.

135 "You had to take care of Rose": Knox interview.

135 anything she wanted: Szolnoki, *My Son Joe,* 62.

135 "more like cops than babysitters": Knox, *Hard Knox,* 104.

135 writhing in pain: Charles Land, "Namath Injured Again: It's An Even Game Now," Looking with Land, *Tuscaloosa News,* December 29, 1964.

135 "I'm okay, coach": Associated Press, "Namath Lost For Bowl Tilt?" *New York Post,* December 29, 1964.

135 "an idiot": Land, "Namath Injured Again."

135 "Namath let it be known": Associated Press, "Cardinals Quit Trying for Joe," *Tuscaloosa News,* December 30, 1964.

135 a three-year deal: Leo Levine, "Namath Ready to Sign with Jets for $389,000," *Herald Tribune,* December 30, 1964.

136 "He hates to go to bed": Dick Young, Young Ideas, *Daily News,* December 31, 1964.

136 Kintner called the sports department: Kennedy interview.

136 "We *make* the goddamn TVs": Ibid.

136 $600,000: John Underwood, "Fabulous in Defeat," *Sports Illustrated,* January 11, 1965.

136 Orange Bowl Parade: Though NBC no longer has any tape of the game or the festivities, the Orange Bowl Committee copied what footage it had, from film reels to a VCR cassette, for the author. The tape (hereafter, OBT) includes the parade and game highlights.

136-37 Jesus and Mary was followed by Cinderella: OBT.

137 "I'm an incurable parade goer": Charles Whited, "Politics, Parade: They're Naturals," *Miami Herald,* January 1, 1965.

137 "Yes, sir": Charles Land, "Bryant Had Not Planned to Use Joe," *Tuscaloosa News,* January 2, 1965.

137 Jackie Gleason: OBT.

138 "It didn't hurt the storyline": Simmons interview.

138 "I've got a clean shot": George Sauer interview, June 4, 2002.

138 "Reminds me of Unitas": Underwood, "Fabulous in Defeat."

138 "By this time": Charles Land, "Longhorns Hold Off Fighting Tide, 21–17," *Tuscaloosa News,* January 2, 1965.

138 "How do you stop him?": Pat Putnam, " 'Namath One of Greatest I've Ever Seen'—Royal," *Miami Herald,* January 2, 1965.

138 "I thought I saw an opening": Joe Namath, as told to Neil Amdur, "Knew I Was Over for TD, But Ref Said No—Namath," *Miami Herald,* January 2, 1965.

138 three fingers: Pete Lammons interview, July 17, 2002.

139 applaud him: Charles Land, Looking with Land, *Tuscaloosa News,* January 1, 1965.

139 television pilot: Fox, *Broadway Joe,* 116.

139 "I'm not paying this kid enough!": Hirsch interview.

20. Four Hundred Grand

141 "as high as $800,000": "Mr. Werblin: 'Flo Ziegfeld' of Pro Football," *National Observer,* January 25, 1965.

141 "a great harm": Associated Press, "Namath's 400G Pay "Ludicrous': Modell," *Daily News,* February 18, 1965.

141 "Utterly ridiculous": Arthur Daley, "It's Only Money," Sports of the Times, *New York Times,* January 4, 1965.

141 "I guess I'll have to ask for a raise": United Press International, "Ryan Says Ryan Is Worth Million," *St. Louis Post-Dispatch,* January 5, 1965.

141 "It sounds impossible": Associated Press, "Not Scared of Pro Football, Says Joe," *Tuscaloosa News,* January 8, 1965.

141 "I don't see how anybody": Ibid.

141 "If I prove myself": Associated Press, "What's Ahead for Joe Namath Now?" *Tuscaloosa News,* January 10, 1965.

141 "Best passer": Ibid.

141 "The guy Sonny targeted": Paul Zimmerman interview, April 12–13, 2002.

141 "girls and golf": Boyle, "Showbiz Sonny."

141 Schweickert: Though he played quarterback in college, Schweickert was never projected as one in the pros.

142 NYU or Columbia: Dana Mozley, "Jets Have Huarte—for 200G," *Daily News,* January 10, 1965.

142 the life of the contract: A copy of Namath's executed Standard Players Contract and the bonus clause Addendum, both dated January 1, 1965, were included in *Joseph W. Namath v. Topps Chewing Gum, Incorporated,* 74C-953, US District Court, Eastern District of New York, now located at National Archives and Records Administration, Lee's Summit, Mo. (hereafter, NARA, Lee's Summit).

142 be lucky to get four years: JN, interview by Sam Marchiano, *Goin' Deep,* Fox Sports Net, September 21, 1999.

142 "he started wanting to see his father": Hicks interview, May 18, 2002.

142 Frank, Bobby, and Rita's husband: Namath, *I Can't Wait,* 207.

143 "Dad, you look awful": John Namath to RT.

143 "For $400,000": Leonard Shecter, "Look of Eagles," *New York Post,* January 24, 1965.

143 monthly pension of $821: William N. Wallace, "Y. A. Tittle of Giants Retires after 17 Seasons," *New York Times,* January 23, 1965.

143 "This is a moment": Ibid.

143 "Terrible": Leo Levine, *Herald Tribune,* January 3, 1965

144 "Get a load of the fag tie": Bob Considine, *Toots* (New York: Meredith Press, 1969), 62.

144 "Before the drug culture": Frank Gifford, *The Whole Ten Yards,* with Harry Waters (New York: Random House, 1993), 210–11.

145 "ballplayers who don't play ball": Pete Hamill interview, December 3, 2001.

145 "a cleft in his chin": Shecter, "Look of Eagles."

145 How much?: Sam Goldaper, "New Boy in Town," *Herald Tribune,* January 23, 1965. "It wasn't very friendly," Goldaper wrote. "For the next two hours the major interest in Namath was trying to find out how close to the reported $400,000 he actually signed for."

145 ham sandwich: Maury Allen, *Joe Namath's Sportin' Life,* 70.

145 Joe simply refused: Leonard Lewin, "Publicity's Heat Falls on the Namath Knee," *New York Post,* January 24, 1965. Lewin writes, "they wouldn't let Namath eat. He had to tell them how much money he really got, which he refused to."

145 "I'll make it": Dave Anderson interview, February 8, 2002.

146 "If I had known this": Eskenazi, *Gang Green,* 50.

21. Now Appearing on Broadway: Mistress Meniscus

147 1.1 million: *Sports Illustrated,* circulation department.

147 6:30 A.M.: "A Joint for Next Season," *Sports Illustrated,* February 8, 1965.

148 Sonny and Mike Bite: Ibid.

148 "the knees of a seventy-year-old": Fox, *Broadway Joe,* 119.

148 "He's not as good-looking": "A Joint for Next Season."

148 fifty times a day: Ibid.

148 "I thought I'd die": Namath, *I Can't Wait,* 196.

148 "He was all drugged up": Hassan interview, April 26, 2003.

148 good-looking nurses: Namath, *I Can't Wait,* 196.

148 "Most girls are Beatle crazy": William N. Wallace, "Namath: Football Idol on Mend," *New York Times,* February 6, 1965.

149 "I already have a date": Maury Allen, *Joe Namath's Sportin' Life,* 73.

149 "A beautiful girl": Jimmy Walsh to RT.

149 "Some blondes, some brunettes": Vagotis interview.

149 fifteen hours short: Boyle, "Show-Biz Sonny."

149 made Joe promise: Szolnoki, *My Son Joe,* 130.

149 "I don't think he was real serious": Ibid.

149 "We boogied hard": Klages interview.

150 "I need a favor": Kennedy interview.

150 "Sure thing, Sonny": Ibid.

150 double-date . . . Tito Puente : Hirsch interview.

150 spit tobacco juice: John R. McDermott, "The Famous Mustache that Was," *Life,* December 20, 1968.

150 leer at the Bunnies: Former Playboy Bunny interview, May 9, 2002.

151 Tad Dowd had grown up: Tad Dowd interview, August 5, 2002.

151 Rosita's doves: Dennis McLellan, "Eddie Jaffe, 89; Old-School Publicist Got Ink for Such Clients as Dietrich, Duke," *Los Angeles Times,* March 29, 2003.

151 "the last of the old line": Robert Sylvester, "Dream Street," *Daily News,* July 12, 1955.

151 Marlon Brando, Julie Newmar, Dorothy Dandridge: Ralph Blumenthal, "Eddie Jaffe, the Press Agent of Broadway, Is Dead at 89," *New York Times,* March 27, 2003.

151 "I thought the kid had talent": Eddie Jaffe interview, April 8, 2002.

151 "The lines were around": Dowd interview.

152 legends for their beauty: Dowd, Kennedy, Bobby Van interviews.

152 "Honey": Dowd interview.

152 "how do you meet girls": Ibid.

152 "the magic hour": James Drake interview, June 27, 2002.

153 "The NFL couldn't buy shoe polish": Boyle, "Show-Biz Sonny."

153 a delicate operation: Drake interview.

153 a big Italian dinner: Glover interview.

153 "It wasn't supposed to look": Drake interview.

22. Wampum

154 "Don't see why he's so early": Fox, *Broadway Joe,* 121.

154 "Drive up in something more modest": W. C. Heinz interview, May 7, 2003.

155 "I got news for you": Ibid.

155 " 'Shit, man' ": Ibid.

155 "I could see where it would be upsetting": *Playboy* interview.

155 each player's locker: Leigh Montville, "Off Broadway Joe," *Sports Illustrated,* July 14, 1997.

155 "Look at him": Evans interview.

155 "We have the rights to this kid": Grantham interview.

156 Weeb didn't even bother: Ibid.

156 $10,000 and $15,000: Heinz, "Countdown for Joe Namath."

156 feeling unappreciated: William N. Wallace, "Wahoo on Warpath for Wampum," *New York Times,* March 17, 1965.

156 "He hit him anyway": Grantham interview.

156 Wahoo jumped him: Namath, *I Can't Wait,* 162.

156 "The veterans": Mathis interview.

157 "You could see it": Snell interview.

157 getting rid of the ball too fast: Dave Anderson, "Ewbank 'Seconds' Namath's Motion," *(New York) Journal-American,* July 20, 1965.

157 wasn't following through: Heinz, "Countdown for Joe Namath."

157 "You don't have to show me your arm": Dave Anderson, *Sports of Our Times* (New York: Random House, 1979), 65.

157 "*Nobody* overthrew Maynard": Anderson interview.

157 Hud as the sleeper: Dave Anderson, "Jets Two-Way Hudson Looms As Sleeper," *Journal-American,* August 5, 1965.

157 brace of aluminum and elastic: Dave Anderson, "Namath 'Moved Offense' in Test," *Journal-American,* July 29, 1965.

157 "What's the matter, rookie?": Namath, *I Can't Wait,* 161.

157 "My main interest": Boyle, "Show-Biz Sonny."

158 "Wait'll Huarte gets here!": Fox interview.

158 "Yeah, you can go ahead and print that": Larry Fox, "Is Joe Namath Being Spoiled by Success?" *New York World-Telegram and Sun,* August 6, 1965. In his copy, Fox thought to substitute "frazzle" for Namath's profanity.

158 "There were little kids and mothers": Fox interview.

158 "Larry didn't go for it": Bill Hampton interview, July 18, 2002.

158 four more calls: Fox interview.

159 a Churchillian masterpiece: William Randolph Hearst Jr., "Editor's Report: The President's Finest Hour," *Journal-American,* August 1, 1965.

159 "I'd rather fight those reds": Dave Anderson, "Jets' 'Golden Arm' Joe Namath May Be Playing for Uncle Sam," *Journal-American,* August 11, 1965.

159 "very imminent": Ibid.

159 "That's classified": Dave Anderson, "Huarte Stays Mum on Draft Status," *Journal-American,* August 12, 1965.

160 "I was a phys. ed major": Anderson, *Sports of Our Times,* 64.

160 after calling eight consecutive running plays: Dave Anderson, "Namath: A-Plus," *Journal-American,* August 14, 1965.

160 "I can still see": Anderson interview.

160 "reflected the racial tone of the country": Winston Hill interview, July 18, 2002.

160 "a lot of hatred": Snell interview.

160 "Go find your own bar": Paul Zimmerman, *The Last Season of Weeb Ewbank* (New York: Farrar, Straus and Giroux, 1974), 62.

161 "You have to look at my history": Grantham interview.

161 "We had a little wide receiver": Snell interview.

161 "I want to see Sonny": Ibid.

161 "I don't see why Matt": Alphonzo Lawson interview, June 18, 2002.

161 "I was in the whirlpool": Ibid.

162 He told the guys: Namath, *I Can't Wait,* 163.

162 "A lot of the guys were shocked": Snell interview.

162 "I thought he could handle himself": Grantham interview.

23. Salted Apples

163 "I can't see why": Milton Gross, "Joe Namath—Girl Talk," *New York Post,* July 21, 1965.

163 "I love them all": Ibid.

163 "I was still dating Joe": Schreiber interview.

164 his shoes were to be laced: Hampton interview, July 29, 2002.

164 "No, it's for Namath": Ibid.

164 "I used to feel bad": Barry Skolnick interview, April 24, May 2, 2002.

164 "I don't punk out": *This Is the NFL: Joe Namath.*

164 "You wear black": Ibid.

164 "babysitter": Van interview, April 23–24, 2002.

164 "I think everybody understood": Snell interview.

165 "Just think": Leo Levine, "Namath: Apple of Army's Eye?" *Herald Tribune,* September 16, 1965.

165 "I always eat apples": Ibid.

165 "The apple?": Ibid.

166 Unlike most second exams: "Namath's Knee: A 2d Army Look," *Herald Tribune,* October 9, 1965.

166 "It may seem illogical": Army statement printed in "Namath's 4-F Knee: The Army Punts," *Herald Tribune,* December 9, 1965.

166 "I blame it on gutless draft boards": Williams quoted in Arthur Daley, "Namath and the Draft," Sports of the Times, *New York Times,* December 10, 1965.

166 "If I say I'm glad": Dan Jenkins, "The Sweet Life of Swinging Joe," *Sports Illustrated,"* October 17, 1966.

167 if it wasn't for that knee: Namath, interviewed on *Metro Sports Legends: Broadway Joe,* said: "If I hadn't had a knee injury I know where I would have been: over there."

167 January 20, 1966: Pat Palmer, "Army Gets Namath Case," *Fort Lauderdale Sun-Sentinel,* January 21, 1966.

167 "I would like to know": Associated Press, "House Asked to Look into Namath's 4-F," *New York Post,* January 21, 1966.

167 "Why me?": Robert Lipsyte, "Clay Reclassified 1-A by Draft Board; Fighter Charges Board with Bias," *New York Times,* February 18, 1966.

167 52,680 fans: *Total Football II,* 1763

167 "If I had to pick": Leonard Shecter, "Poor Joe," *New York Post,* September 2, 1965.

167 smoking cigarettes: Sauer interview.

168 teammates were somewhat amused: Dick Young, Young Ideas, *Daily News,* September 15, 1965.

168 "We want Joe!": Fox, *Broadway Joe,* 131.

168 "I made a lot of mistakes": Gene Roswell, "Namath: Lost, But . . ." *New York Post,* September 27, 1965.

168 "I can't complain": John Huarte interview, May 1, 2002.

168 "Mike could throw": Snell interview.

168 "one bomb after another": Fox, *Broadway Joe,* 133.

169 "falling off a barstool": Ibid.

169 "He recognized the defenses": Roswell, "Namath Handled Blitz Like a Pro," *New York Post,* November 15, 1965.

169 "Whatever tastes the worst": Montville, "Off Broadway Joe."

169 "He called a tremendous game": Frank Litsky, "Namath Has Proved That Price Was Right," *New York Times,* November 11, 1965.

169 "I'm checking off more": Ibid.

170 watching game films: Ibid.

170 "We isolated the cameras on him": Simmons interview.

170 "Lot of green stamps": Fox, *Broadway Joe,* 134.

170 "if we could intimidate him": Ben Davidson interview, September 13, 2002.

170 "no class at all": Roswell, "Namath Raps Raider Head-Hunting (His)," *New York Post,* December 13, 1965.

171 "Just trying to do my job": Ibid.

171 "Did you know that he nearly died": Paul Zimmerman, "Namath's Injuries," *New York Post,* August 19, 1975.

171 "Go Go Jets": *1965 New York Jets Season Highlights,* NFL Films.

171 "No, Doc": Dave Anderson, "A Biggs Man on Campus," *Journal-American,* August 11, 1965.

171 "If I was that big": Zimmerman, *Last Season of Weeb Ewbank,* 56

171 the first quarterback: *Total Football II,* 389. The award begins in 1955.

172 "It was a beautiful, sunny afternoon": *Metro Sports Legends: Broadway Joe.*

24. No Guarantees

173 "not a hobby": "Sherman Signs for 10 Years," *World-Telegram and Sun,* July 26, 1965.

173 Werblin disclosed: Milton Gross, "Sonny Werblin Calls the Play," *New York Post,* April 28, 1965.

173 sold 2,500 season tickets: Curran, *The $400,000 Quarterback,* 152.

174 "At that rate": H. L. Hunt quoted in Gruver, *The American Football League,* 56.

174 Love Field: Ibid., 158.

174 Davis had bugged: Dave Anderson, "Jets-Raiders Recalls the Distractions from Al Davis," *New York Times,* January 13, 2002.

175 "a declaration of war": Curran, *The $400,000 Quarterback,* 229.

175 "The NFL had struck": Gruver, *The American Football League,* 160.

175 "Munich": Al Buck, "Mara, Werblin Ask Why?" *New York Post,* June 9, 1966.

175 "We never had it so good": Ibid.

175 "Namath made us": Davis quoted in Gruver, *The American Football League,* 199.

176 "Large contracts": Associated Press, "Jets Namath Surprised at News of Merger," *New York Times,* June 9, 1966.

176 a plastic Virgin Mary: John Bowers, "Joe Namath: How Long Will the Glory Last?" *(New York) World Journal Tribune,* October 16, 1966.

176 It wasn't unusual for his left knee: George Usher, "Happiness Is Namath—Leading a Dog's Life," *Newsday,* July 1966.

176 "I'm not the player I was": Frank Litsky, "The Knee," *New York Times,* July 29, 1966.

176 Just think: Ibid.

176 "What about Namath's dog?": Mathis interview.

176 "veterans would throw rocks": Kevin Barry interview, February 22, 2002.

177 Stores were selling: Frank Litsky, "Welcome Is Warm for Quarterback," *New York Times,* August 14, 1966.

177 "Namath stumbled": Arthur J. Donovan Jr. and Bob Drury, *Fatso* (New York: Morrow, 1987), 210.

177 "never want to hurt him": Roswell, "Namath Praised by Ernie Ladd," *New York Post,* December 6, 1965.

177 "He was frightened": Leonard Cohen, "Namath Settling for 2 to 3 Weeks," *New York Post,* August 15, 1966.

177 Often, Namath couldn't decide: Dr. Nicholas quoted in Zimmerman, "Namath's Injuries": "Remember that exhibition game in Birmingham in 1966, when Don Floyd blocked Joe and hurt his knee? We didn't know from week to week whether Joe would play of not after that. Every week, he had to decide himself, right before game time."

178 "Man, my knee's completely": Bowers, "Joe Namath."

178 "Joe liked to call those patterns": Sauer interview.

178 "I can't do the things": Litsky, "The Knee."

178 *The Man from U.N.C.L.E.:* Frank Litsky, "Jets Win Opener From, Dolphins, 19 to 14," *New York Times,* September 10, 1966.

179 "We worked on it every day": Emerson Boozer interview, July 17, 2002.

179 "The whole point": Snell interview.

179 "He wouldn't get on the plane": Knox interview.

179 "They were the ones": Hill interview.

180 "The defensive man": Knox interview.

180 "his claim to fame": Fox, *Broadway Joe,* 100.

180 "It was just kind of understood": Randy Rasmussen interviewed by Rick Telander, December 17, 1975.

181 "When you look at the film": *Broadway Joe: The Joe Namath Story,* A & E Biography.

181 "Get Namath": Al Buck, "Namath Is Tough Going Uphill, Too," *New York Post,* September 26, 1966.

181 wasn't sacked for a loss until the seventh game: Milton Gross, "Joe Namath—Still Cool," *New York Post,* October 25, 1966.

181 4½-point favorites: Dave Eisenberg, "Jets Pick, but Oilers Can Be Rough," *World Journal Tribune,* October 16, 1966.

181 The fans at Fenway Park: Fox, *Broadway Joe,* 146

181 "I thought about staying down": John Skow, "Joe, Joe, You're the Most Beautiful Thing in the World," *Saturday Evening Post,* December 3, 1966.

182 Namath didn't look very sharp: Maury Allen, *Joe Namath's Sportin' Life,* 92.

182 "This isn't high school": Skow, "Joe, Joe."

182 "I wasn't up to the game": Dave Eisenberg, "Namath a Hard Loser," *World Journal Tribune,* October 17, 1966.

183 "I'm so racked up": Skow, "Joe, Joe."

183 doused Namath with coffee: Fox, *Broadway Joe,* 147.

183 "I didn't get enough points": Gross, "Joe Namath—Still Cool."

183 "When McDole arose": Dave Anderson, "Bills Defense Enjoys Namath Pool," *New York Times,* October 31, 1966.

183 "How about those five interceptions": Dana Mozley, "Joe Says Interceptions Came on 'Good Pitches,' " *Daily News,* October 31, 1966.

184 It was hard enough taking steps: Namath in Dana Mozley, "Heart Belongs to AFL—But Namath Picks GB," *Daily News,* January 5, 1967: "I was having trouble with such daily things as stepping off the curb, walking up and down steps, and getting in and out of cars."

184 "How do I know": Bowers, "Joe Namath."

184 "A lot of times": Cicatiello interview.

184 "When a quarterback runs": Gross, "Joe Namath—Still Cool."

184 needed a pain-killing shot: Dick Young, "Doc Aids Namath Prep for Dolphins," *Daily News,* November 11, 1966.

185 B & B to Sambuca to Grand Marnier: Cicatiello interview.

185 "favored by seven or ten": In fact, according to Joe Trimble, "Jets, Giants in Eastern Title Games," *Daily News,* December 16, 1966, the Patriots were favored by seven points.

185 "I want to have it done": Dick Young, Young Ideas, *Daily News,* December 21, 1966.

185 "They can't guarantee a thing": Ibid.

185 "I'm damn mad": Dave Anderson, "Jet Doctor Finds a Torn Cartilage," *New York Times,* December 22, 1966.

186 greater rotational stability: Norm Miller, "Namath Has 2 Operations on Knee to Restore Agility," *Daily News,* December 29, 1966.

186 "We expect Joe to be much better": Frank Litsky, "Namath of Jets Undergoes Surgery," *New York Times,* December 29, 1966.

25. Booze and Broads

187 Second Avenue Joe: Anderson interview.

187 "Garish dusk": Jimmy Cannon, "Namath Says Booze Did Not Beat Jets," *World Journal Tribune,* October 18, 1966.

187 Jojo: Jack Lambert interview, June 7, 2003.

187 The Bunnies: Playboy Bunny, Lambert interview.

188 stirring his drink with his finger: Hassan interview.

188 "Why don't they just accept": Cannon, "Namath Says."

188 "I'm no hypocrite": Ibid.

188 Cannon's room at the Edison: Richard Ben Cramer, *Joe DiMaggio: The Hero's Life* (New York: Simon & Schuster, 2000), 194.

189 fame an irritant: Cannon, "Joe DiMaggio," in *Nobody Asked Me*, 42–44.

189 "He doesn't have to sneak": Cannon, "Namath Says."

189 "I drink for the same reason": Namath, *I Can't Wait*, 96.

189 "rock-'n'-roll chickie": Skow, "Joe, Joe."

189 majoring in French: Namath, *I Can't Wait*, 101.

190 "the white woman's answer": Dowd interview.

190 "I don't like to date": Jenkins, "The Sweet Life."

190 "Seems almost un-American": The quote is from footage of JN shooting pool used in *Broadway Joe: The Joe Namath Story*, but originally aired as a segment on the *Great American Dream Machine*, executive producers Jack Willis and Al Perlmutter, WNET, January 13, 1971.

190 "We're having a party at Joe's": Dowd interview.

190 "I was a healthy young American boy": *Metro Sports Legends: Broadway Joe*.

190 wearing a paper gown: *New York Post*, December 27, 1966.

190 "drinking until six": "Joe's Girls," *Esquire*, October 1969.

190 They met at the Plaza: Barbara Long, "Joe Namath," *Vogue*, February 1, 1967.

191 "It was great": Art Heyman interviews, January 22, May 17, 2002.

191 "I was taught that sex": Kennedy interview.

191 "So I stopped": Namath, *I Can't Wait*, 14.

191 "A Miller, right away": Spiros Dellartas interview, September 18, 2002.

191 The penthouse: Details on the apartment in Judy Klemesrud, "The Penthouse of Joe Namath: First There's the Llama Rug . . . ," *New York Times*, December 12, 1967; Skow, "Joe, Joe."

192 whom Sonny had commissioned: Eskenazi, *Gang Green*, 69.

192 "Why a dude ranch?": Van interview.

193 Jilly Rizzo: Ibid.

193 "This is what you call organized crime": Ibid.

194 Fat Gigi and Johnny Echo: Ibid.

194 September of 1965: "Dudes 'N Dolls Opens with a Bang," *Night Beat*, October 1, 1965.

194 throwing firecrackers at the dancers: Ibid.

194 celebrity judge: Dowd interview.

195 "Nobody was quicker": Hassan interview.

195 "I don't care what a man is": Jenkins, "The Sweet Life."

195 " 'The only way I can relax' ": Van interview.

195 part-time maître d': Dowd and Van interviews.

196 guns had already been drawn: Heyman and Van interviews.

196 Brownie: Van interview.

196 "I can do anything": Bowers, "Joe Namath."

196 "Werblin nixed it": Van interview.

26. Liar's Poker

197 "Loved every minute of it": Jack Danahy interviews, January 30, 2002, and January 13, 2003.

197 "Strictly a bullshit memo": Ibid.

198 "I think he had half a bag on": Ibid.

198 "you're an athlete, right?": Ibid.

199 "Captioned individual": "Joe Namath," an FBI memo dated January 30, 1967, obtained from Anderson papers.

200 "You won't find long hair": Hoover quoted in Larry Merchant, *. . . And Every Day You Take Another Bite* (New York: Doubleday, 1971), 117.

200 "He was a great moral judge": Jack Anderson interview, September 5, 2002.

200 After reviewing the Namath file: Danahy interview.

200 "vendetta against me": Namath's version from *Playboy* interview:

NAMATH: . . . About four years ago, this guy supposedly came over to my table at a restaurant, pulled out his identification and told me the people I was with were mob guys, that I shouldn't be seen talking to them and that he didn't *want* me to talk to them. I supposedly told him, "Listen, when I'm not on a football field, I hang with whoever I want to hang with; and as long as it doesn't affect what I do on the field, you can just go fuck yourself." Since he supposedly was with a couple of people at the

time, he took that badly and got very, very upset. PLAYBOY: You say this confrontation "supposedly" took place. Did it or didn't it?
NAMATH: Maybe it did, maybe it didn't; I can't remember all the people I've talked to over the past four years and what I've said to 'em. Anyway, ever since then, this guy has carried a vendetta against me and was dumb enough to admit it to several of the Jets. He told them how I'd told him to go fuck himself, that I was bad for the game and that as long as I stayed in pro football, I'd be a thorn in his side. This man started everything.

201 "That would incite Hoover's interest": Danahy interview.

201 "Tramunti was like a father": Jack Lambert interview, June 7, 2003.

201 "one of the big floating crap games": The report, and background on Tramunti, were provided from the files of Doug LeVien, executive assistant to the district attorney, Kings County, New York. LeVien, an expert on organized crime, was an undercover agent in the successful prosecution of the Lucchese leader.

201 "Tommy Tea Balls was the closest friend": Lambert interview.

201 "They never touched him": Bookmaker interview, May 9, 2002.

201 "Joe liked hoodlums": Dan E. Moldea, *Interference: How Organized Crime Influences Professional Football* (New York: Morrow, 1989), 203.

202 "I'm not doing anything wrong": Lambert interview.

202 Lambert is not alone: "Never heard that, never," says Bobby Van. "And I was very close with Jilly." "All the years I was around Joe I never heard anything about an abortion," says Tad Dowd. "Not once."

202 "a virgin": Lambert interview.

202 "I just didn't have the money": Ibid.

203 stipulated in his contract: Standard NFL contracts were almost the same, word for word. Rule 3 in the NFL contract: "Players must not frequent gambling resorts nor associate with gamblers or other notorious characters."

203 "The spectator who attended the game": "Football Was Jolted: Unfair Tactics by W. & J. Players Greatly Deplored by Those Who Saw the Game," *Beaver Falls Daily Tribune*, November 16, 1903, BCRC.

203 ties to the New York mob: Moldea, *Interference,* 55.

203 conviction of four mob-connected gamblers: Moldea, *Interference,* 57-59.

203 "They don't have point spreads": Leonard Shecter, "Does Pete Rozelle Run Pro Football? Ask Joe Namath," *New York Times Magazine,* August 17, 1969.

204 "certain associations": Moldea, *Interference,* 125.

204 maintained a private hotline: Ibid., 63

204 "Television dramatically changed the world": Richard O. Davies and Richard G. Abram, *Betting the Line: Sports Wagering in American Life* (Columbus: Ohio State University Press, 2001), 87.

204 said to have bet $1 million: See "Rosenbloom in the Bahamas," in Moldea, *Interference.* Rosenbloom, a heavy gambler with an abundance of questionable "associations," was investigated but never punished by Rozelle, suggesting that the standards for players were less forgiving than for owners.

205 "the suspicion of evil": Shecter, "Does Pete Rozelle Run Pro Football?"

205 "Joe used to put all the bets through me": Heyman interview.

205 $200 a game: Ibid.

205 the fortunes of red ants: Klages interview.

206 paid Burnett $5,000: James Kirby, *Fumble: Bear Bryant, Wally Butts, and the Great College Football Scandal* (San Diego, New York: Harcourt, Brace Jovanovich, 1986), 61; also Dunnavant, *Coach,* 246.

206 "I called every play of that game": *SportsCentury: Bear Bryant.*

206 "The biggest source of rumors": Danahy interview.

206 "He couldn't walk, he couldn't talk": Skolnick interview.

207 "You know how much money I lost": Kennedy interview.

207 "I'd like to apologize": Ibid.

208 "I hope you lost your house": Dowd and Lambert interviews.

208 "Shape up, get in line": Lambert interview.

27. The Star System

209 "With one gesture": Arthur Daley, "$onny, Money and Merger," Sports of the Times, *New York Times,* January 6, 1967.

209 "It wasn't enough": Klemesrud, "The Penthouse of Joe Namath."

209 set up Frank in the insurance business: Bowers, "Joe Namath"; John Lake, "Two for the Football Show: The Swinger and the Square," *New York Times Magazine,* November 5, 1967.

209 Joe couldn't see himself living to fifty: Bowers, "Joe Namath."

209 wanted a million bucks: Roswell, "Namath Wants 1 Million," *New York Post,* April 24, 1967; Roswell, "Namath—He's One in a Million," *New York Post,* April 25, 1967.

210 Namath quit smoking: According to Namath, *I Can't Wait,* 87, the date was April 12, 1967.

210 get his hair cut: Wallace, "Joe Namath, The Pro," Sports of the Times, *New York Times,* July 27, 1967. See also Fox, *Broadway Joe,* 155.

210 "My father told me": Wallace, "Joe Namath."

210 Sigma Alpha Epsilon pin: Lake, "Two for the Football Show."

210 "I'm preaching a sermon": Ibid.

210 "Before Joe got here": Zimmerman, *Last Season of Weeb Ewbank,* 219.

211 new contract, already typed out: Copies of the contract, addendum, and accompanying documents are included in *Namath v. Topps,* The agreement was originally dated August 3, 1967. The date has been crossed out and replaced with a "22," the date Namath eventually signed.

211 He would receive: Addendum to Standard Players Contract, Bonus Clause, signed by Werblin and Namath, *Namath v. Topps.*

211 the money was guaranteed: *Namath v. Topps.* As with Namath's first contract, pararaph 6, pertaining to his physical condition, has been excised; see also Namath, *I Can't Wait,* 209.

211 "He came to me in the afternoon": Leonard Lewin, "Will Jets Fine Namath?" *New York Post,* August 5, 1967.

211 missed bedcheck: Ibid.

211 "Her brother died": Ibid.

212 a party on Eighty-fifth Street: Affidavit of Thomas O'Toole, December 1, 1967, *Charles Parmiter against Joe Namath,* Case No. 14213, 1967, Supreme Court of the State of New York, County of New York, Clerk's Office.

212 hoping he could get an interview: Charles Parmiter interview, December 19, 2002.

212 Namath's affidavit: Affidavit of Joe Namath, November 2, 1967, *Charles Parmiter against Joe Namath.*

212 Parmiter's affidavit: Parmiter's affidavit, sworn to December 28, 1967, is essentially the same as the affidavit of his attorney, Stuart Speiser, which was sworn to four months before, on August 25, and reported in the newspapers three days later.

213 "was not struck, choked, or assaulted": Affidavit of Arthur Heyman, October 31, 1967, *Charles Parmiter against Joe Namath.*

213 "Joe swung at him": Heyman interview.

213 "I didn't get paid a dime": Parmiter interview.

213 "Stipulation of Discontinuance": Clerk's Minutes of Supreme Court Actions and Proceedings 1967, New York County.

213 "Fucking lowlife": Heyman interview.

213 "Drug addict": Skolnick interview.

213 "Bad kid": Van interview.

213 a jack of many criminal trades: Kearney's criminal record of twenty-one arrests and seven convictions goes back to October 13, 1962, when he was picked up for burglary. He was then twenty.

213 a white terry-cloth number: Ray McCormack interview, January 30, 2002. McCormack, a former Golden Gloves fighter, recalls Kearney from the Parks Department gym.

213 It was Williams's only win: Nat Fleischer, ed., *The 1970 Ring Boxing Encyclopedia and Record Book* (New York: Ring Bookshop, 1970), 608.

213 "Mickey would've been like half a made guy": Bookmaker interview. The bookmaker grew up with Kearney in Manhattan. Other background on Kearney is based on interviews with Tim Secor, a former bar owner and close friend of Namath's; Ray McLees, former investigator with the Manhattan District Attorney's squad, January 16, 2002; and former NYPD detective Don McCrindle, October 17, 2002.

214 in Vegas, tossing a football in Central Park: Secor interview.

214 his teammates were angry: Fox, *Broadway Joe,* 157.

214 "You can't treat him the same": Frank Litsky, "Jets Ace to Explain Reported 'Night on the Town,'" *New York Times,* August 6, 1967.

214 "A lot of players resented": Snell interview.

214 "There were two sets of rules": Gerry Philbin interview, July 22, 2002.

214 as if he'd been weeping: Larry Merchant, "Namath's Day of Reckoning," *New York Post,* August 8, 1967; Fox, *Broadway Joe,* 158–59.

214 "I like the idea of being a leader": Merchant, "Joe Namath's Day."

214 "If it were up to me": "Jets' Namath Thrown for $mall Loss," *Daily News,* August 8, 1967.

214 August 22: *Namath v. Topps.*

215 "Worst move": Dave Anderson, "Namath Criticizes the Jets for Dropping Abruzzese," *New York Times*, August 27, 1967.

215 "some rich rookie": Ibid.

28. The Beauty of Joe

216 his dream to coach: Knox interview.

216 "if my man hits Joe": Edwin Shrake, "The Plays Go for the New Joe," *Sports Illustrated*, October 16, 1967.

217 thirteen touchdowns: Fox, *Broadway Joe*, 170.

217 400 yards: According to the Elias Sports Bureau, there were three 400-yard passing games in 1967. Johnny Unitas threw for 401 against the Atlanta Falcons on September 17 and Sonny Jurgensen threw for 418 on November 26 against Cleveland. Prior to Namath's 415-yard performance, the AFL's last 400-yard game was recorded by Len Dawson, who threw for 435 yards November 1, 1964, against Denver.

217 216 yards: Litsky, "415 Yards Gained in Air By Namath," *New York Times*, October 2, 1967.

217 25 Lag: Edwin Shrake, "The Plays Go for the New Joe."

217 "He called a nice game": Ibid.

217 "holding on every play": Ibid.

217 17–0 lead: Fox, *Broadway Joe*, 166–69.

218 "I just floated": Milton Gross, "The Eye of the Storm," *New York Post*, October 17, 1967.

218 a cloud of dust: *1967 New York Jets Season Highlights*, NFL Films.

218 "That big Boyette": Dave Anderson, "Houston Runner Stopped on the 4," *New York Times*, October 16, 1967.

218 "Joe broke a small bone": Zimmerman, "Namath's Injuries."

218 "There was a reason": Milton Gross, "Namath: 'I Was Ridiculous', " Speaking Out, *New York Post*, October 16, 1967.

219 "a shot of peppermint schnapps": Heyman interview, May 17, 2003.

219 back on the boards: "Namath, Ankle Improved, Is Set to Play—Kansas City One-Touchdown Choice," *New York Times*, November 5, 1967.

219 batted back four of his passes: Fox, *Broadway Joe*, 172.

220 "a horse needle": Snell interview.

220 28,712 no-shows: Fox, *Broadway Joe*, 174.

220 "The ball was so caked with mud": Paul Zimmerman, "Shocked Jets Face Uphill Road Now," *New York Post*, December 4, 1967.

220 "He was out drinking with Sonny": Zimmerman interview. Zimmerman's recollection is nothing if not consistent. On November 15, 1975, in an interview with RT, he said: "In '67 he partied all night with Sonny Werblin and blew a game which might have knocked them out of it . . . the Denver game." That same year, Werblin offered a different version of his night out with Joe: "I got blamed for that. What happened was, Dan Seymour had a cocktail party for his ad agency, J. Walter Thompson. Namath and his date and Namath's father and I went. Joe and his date left, and I stayed with the father. Weeb told everybody I kept Joe out. I'm still accused of it." Dick Young, "Jets Need Wrecking Ball," *Daily News*, December 17, 1975.

220 "Prima donna": Philbin interview.

220 "You could just smell the booze": Snell interview.

221 Namath once claimed: *Playboy* interview.

221 "His legs would swell up": Lambert interview.

221 "We were *supposed* to drink": Larry Grantham interview, July 18, 2002.

221 "Alcohol helps": *Playboy* interview.

221 "I'm a better man for it": Al "Tank" Passuello interview, June 13, 2002.

222 seeing double: Zimmerman "Shocked Jets Face Uphill Road Now," *New York Post*, December 4, 1967.

222 broke the story: Zimmerman, "Jets Got a Secret: It's Namath's Thumb," *New York Post*, December 8, 1967.

222 the bookies didn't start taking action: Fox, *Broadway Joe*, 175.

222 sacked five times: Milton Gross, "No Downing This Jet," *New York Post*, December 19, 1967.

222 "He took one hell of a beating": Milton Gross, "Joe Namath—On the Bottom," *New York Post*, December 11, 1967.

222 "If anybody rated that $400,000": Ibid.

222 "This is the game": Paul Zimmerman, "Big Ben Out to Toll Final Hours for Jets," *New York Post*, December 15, 1967.

222 "Joe's a marked man": Paul Zimmerman, "Jets Are Limp after the Raid," *New York Post*, December 18, 1967.

222 notched a record sixty-one: Milton Gross, "Joe: 'If You Can't Take It, Don't Play,' " *New York Post*, December 18, 1967.

223 first-and-goal from the Raider 10: Fox, *Broadway Joe,* 179.

223 "I blocked him": Hill interview.

223 "He had a hold of me": Davidson interview.

224 Dr. Nicholas made him count: Milton Gross, "No Downing This Jet," *New York Post,* December 19, 1967.

224 "I don't know how much more": Zimmerman, "Jets Are Limp."

224 Joe hit Pete Lammons for nine yards: Fox, *Broadway Joe,* 179.

224 "The game degenerated": Davidson interview. "If you can't take it": Gross, "Joe: 'If You Can't Take It.'"

224 "Got to play": Zimmerman, "Jets Are Limp."

225 "never said a word": *New York Post,* December 18, 1967.

225 gave him a hooker: Namath, *I Can't Wait,* 89.

225 sixth in the balloting: Paul Zimmerman, "Jets Can't Afford to Lose Altitude," *New York Post,* December 19, 1967.

225 Sauer wept: Fox, *Broadway Joe,* 180–81.

225 "Poor Ike": Davidson interview.

226 "the beauty of Joe": Ibid.

29. Bosses

227 "I don't want the guys who did it": Anthony Burton, "One Evening at Home with Jet-Set Namath," *Daily News,* December 28, 1967.

227 $12 for a ticket: *Total Football II,* 113.

227 "a strong 14": "Odds Maker Picks Packers by 14 and Says They'll Hold the Line," *New York Times,* January 4, 1968.

228 "When he sits down by the pool": Paul Zimmerman, "El Grandote," *New York Post,* January 11, 1968.

228 "The Packers?": Williamson quoted in Gruver, *The American Football League,* 174.

228 "These Super Bowl games": William N. Wallace, "Green Bay Wins Football Title," *New York Times,* January 16, 1967.

228 "akin to a tennis elbow": "Namath Is Facing Surgery on Knee," *New York Times,* March 8, 1968.

229 "The social aspect": Michael Martin interview, October 23, 2002.

229 "They got into it to have fun": Helen Dillon interview, October 28, 2002.

229 "his own pregame party": Ibid.

229 "I think it was symbolic": Martin interview.

229 "He degraded us": Milton Gross, "The Battle in the Sky," Speaking Out, *New York Post,* June 18, 1968

230 "What disturbed us": Ibid.

230 The most outraged of the group: Martin and Dillon interviews. As Milton Gross wrote: "All the partners agree that Lillis brought the situation to a head."

230 145-pound end: Fox, *Broadway Joe,* 187.

230 a reported $1,638,000: The best estimates of Sonny's take are in Gross, "Battle in the Sky," and Fox, *Broadway Joe,* 185.

230 "You didn't see them in Kansas City": Fox, *Broadway Joe,* 183.

231 "It suddenly dawned on me": Dick Young, "Would Sonny Swap His $2 Million Now?" *Daily News,* December 1, 1968.

231 "We double-dated with Joe one time": Dillon interview.

231 Among Lillis's first acts: William N. Wallace, "Lombardi Rejects Jet Offers," *New York Times,* May 23, 1968.

231 break for a beer along the way: Van interview.

232 Bobby managed the place: Ibid.

30. Student of the Game

233 "I've been standing still": Dave Anderson, "Could Swinging Joe Namath Make It in the Tough NFL?" *True,* September 1968.

233 "I don't improve myself": Dick Young, "Joe Namath/How It Really Is," *Daily News,* September 13, 1968.

233 106 questions: Heinz, "Countdown for Joe Namath."

233 "he'd have a mental picture": Bryant, *Bear,* 199.

233 "I can explain things to people with diagrams": Robert Lipsyte, "Recess," Sports of the Times, *New York Times,* November 16, 1967.

234 "His arm, his release": Anderson, "Could Swinging Joe Namath Make It?"

234 "he does not have the respect": Ibid.

234 "he had to spend a lot of time": Snell interview.

234 Defensive backs were conditioned: Sauer and Snell interviews.

234 "Joe and I worked it out": Sauer interview.

235 "Save your legs": Ibid.

235 "The timing was perfect": Snell interview.

235 $15 a day: Fox, *Broadway Joe,* 191.

235 Weeb even took on the press: Ibid., 187.

235 arguing in the locker room: Dick Young, "Weeb, Joe on Collision Course, Jets in Middle," Young Ideas, *Daily News*, August 14, 1968; Fox, *Broadway Joe*, 195.

236 "I wanted him to suit up": Young, "Weeb, Joe on Collision Course."

236 $125 and $250 for exhibitions: Gordon S. White Jr., "Werblin Denies Any Namath Deal," *New York Times*, August 14, 1968.

236 "The New York Jets would do well to trade Joe": William N. Wallace, "Trading of Namath Is Suggested to Solve Friction with Jets," *New York Times*, August 15, 1968.

236 "The boy says he's hurt": Paul Zimmerman, "Jets OK Joe—With Reservations," *New York Post*, August 15, 1968.

237 "I believe Joe's side": Ibid.

237 In each of the past two seasons: In 1966, Namath hurt his right knee against Houston making a tackle on Ernie Ladd. The result was postseason surgery. In 1967, in an exhibition game against the Philadelphia Eagles, he hurt the left knee, possibly resulting in the torn tendon.

237 "Doesn't it make sense": Zimmerman, "Jets OK Joe."

237 "He just didn't feel pain": Jim Hudson interview, July 21, 2003.

237 a black widow: Stephen Hanks, *The Game That Changed Pro Football* (New York: Birch Lane Press, 1989), 30.

237 "You couldn't ask for a better": Sauer interview.

237 "He really got along": Zimmerman interview.

238 "I had completely changed": Grantham interview.

238 double-breasted, center-vented: "That Touch of Mink," *Newsweek*, August 26, 1968.

238 Let the fans call him a fag: Dick Young, "Joe Namath," *Daily News*, September 13, 1968. JN quotes fan reaction: "You don't need a mink coat, you fag!"

239 "No one gave a shit": Curley Johnson interview, July 16, 2002.

239 his eyes welling up: Fox, *Broadway Joe*, 197.

31. Fu Manchu

240 missing on six of his first seven: Dave Anderson, "Namath Throws 2 Scoring Passes," *New York Times*, September 16, 1968.

240 "I think we ought to stop drinking": Namath, *I Can't Wait*, 94; *Playboy* interview; Hudson interview.

241 "I don't know how they're gonna score": Hanks, *Game That Changed*, 63.

241 within 62 seconds: Larry Fox, "Nightmare in Buffalo: Bills Intercept (5) Jets, 37–35," *Daily News*, September 30, 1968.

241 "Tackling a man like that": Larry Fox, "Walton Eager to Make Amends," *Daily News*, October 10, 1968.

241 "the dumb guy": Fox, *Broadway Joe*, 202.

241 "Look at him": Murray Janoff, "Quit—Joe's Dad," *Long Island Press*, September 30, 1968.

242 "I started drinking again that night": Namath, *I Can't Wait*, 94–95.

242 in bed with the flu: Ibid., 95.

242 "Just say I stink": Fox, *Broadway Joe*, 205.

242 "You need to tell your roommate": Hanks, *Game That Changed*, 65.

242 "I don't think I ever played any worse": Ibid., 64.

243 could have been the district attorney's office: Namath, *I Can't Wait*, 52–53.

243 "We're winning and they boo me": Paul Zimmerman, "Oilers Next in Namath Puzzle Play," *New York Post*, November 9, 1968.

243 "We were all writing": Zimmerman interview.

243 Al Davis's new team headquarters: "Jets-Raiders: Who's Gonna Hurt?" *Daily News*, November 17, 1968.

243 "Better be careful": Fox, *Broadway Joe*, 216. Fox's version comes from Ewbank, and eyewitness. But Namath related another of Davis's thinly veiled threats in Dave Anderson's *New York Times* column of January 13, 2002: "Al told me that some of the Raiders pass rushers wanted to knock me out of the game, but he didn't want 'em to do that because I was too valuable to the American Football League."

244 Grantham got a piece . . . Hudson felt something else: Hudson and Grantham's account of the play from Hanks, *Game That Changed*, 66–67.

244 "He never grabbed the mask": Zimmerman, "Lamonica All Right Shooting Jets Down," *New York Post*, November 18, 1968.

245 "You treated a sponsor like that very carefully": Hanks, *Game That Changed*, 68.

245 "I just sat there and screamed": Simmons interview.

245 cost them their bets: Dick Young, "Jets 32,

Oakland 29, Heidi 14," *Daily News,* November 18, 1968.

245 a substantial fine: Larry Fox, "Oakland Aftermath: Rozelle Fines Jets $2G," *Daily News,* December 3, 1968.

245 "extreme bad manners": Dave Brady, "Rozelle Cites Raps at Refs," *New York Post,* December 3, 1968.

245 "Weeb showed it to us": Zimmerman interview.

246 "It made the front page": Simmons interview.

246 "The Jets were still seen as second": Sal Marchiano interview, November 25, 2002.

246 "conform with the generally accepted idea": Dave Anderson, "Namath Takes It Off—At $10 a Clip," *New York Times,* December 12, 1968.

246 updates gauging the mustache's progress: Dowd interview.

246 Namath made his way toward the sink: Fox, *Broadway Joe,* 219.

247 fans still preferred a mediocre Giants: "Giants Beat Jets (on TV)," *New York Post,* November 25, 1968.

247 He slept on Eddie Jaffe's couch: Dowd interview.

247 June 24, 1968: Attorney Registration Unit, New York State Unified Court System, First Department of the Appellate Division.

247 "A quasi-lawyer": Jimmy Walsh to RT.

247 "I got great access": Marchiano interview.

247 Jimmy called Tad, who called Jaffe: Dowd and Jaffe interviews; Walsh to RT.

248 1 interception for every 42 attempts: Paul Zimmerman, "Joe Willie's Finest Season," *New York Post,* December 28, 1968.

248 "We had an undersized defense": Philbin interview.

32. Disheveled but Happy

249 "a chichi East Side type": John Timoney interview, November 22, 2002.

249 "the girl and the bottle": Jimmy Breslin, "Namath All Night Long," *New York,* April 27, 1969.

250 Jimmy the Greek: Dave Anderson, "Raiders Wary of Namath Arm," *New York Times,* December 29, 1968.

250 an oddly ravaged field: *A Stunning Prelude: The 1968 A.F.L. Championship, Oakland vs. New York,* directed by Jimmy Balder, NFL Films, 1968.

250 He came right at you: Fox, *Broadway Joe,* 226.

250 lost his footing: *A Stunning Prelude.*

251 "Never saw a finger like that": Larry Merchant, "They Beat Joe, He Beats Them," *New York Post,* December 30, 1968.

251 a shot of xylocaine: Dave Anderson, "Namath Connects for 3 Touchdowns," *New York Times,* December 30, 1968.

251 "I was afraid to get a shot": Paul Zimmerman, "Joe's Super Effort Reaps a Crown," *New York Post,* December 30, 1968.

251 "like a gladiator": Ibid.

251 "A little punchy": Ibid.

251 "There was a bad throbbing": Merchant, "They Beat Joe."

251 Dr. Nicholas escorted Namath: *A Stunning Prelude.*

252 "In the locker room": Fox, *Broadway Joe,* 229.

252 three painkilling shots: JN to RT.

252 "It comes from the bloodline": Ibid.

252 "If it wasn't for my teammates": Namath interview by Dave Dilorenzo and Todd Skowron, *Old Pro Sports Radio,* WALE-Providence, 990-AM, November 29, 2002; http://oldprosports.com/interviews.htm (hereafter, Old Pro Sports Radio interview).

253 Namath told the rookie: Namath, *I Can't Wait,* 81.

253 Maynard, Sauer, and Lammons would split the field: *Old Pro Sports Radio* interview.

253 "I didn't wind up": Hanks, *Game That Changed,* 76.

253 "The wind caught it": Maynard interview.

253 "a little fat guy": Van interview.

253 Petey was always complaining: Hanks, *Game That Changed,* 77; Old Pro Sports Radio interview.

253 The first option. . . . The third option: Hanks, *Game That Changed,* 77.

254 "I felt like I was blocking": Ibid.

254 "I threw that ball as hard": Ibid., 78.

254 "He never saw me coming": Paul Zimmerman, "Joe's Super Effort Reaps a Crown," *New York Post,* December 30, 1968.

254 "If you don't feel you can come back": Phil Pepe and Joe Trimble, "Image of Colts Limits Jets' Joy," *Daily News,* December 30, 1968.

254 "I'll tell you the biggest thing": Ibid.

254 "I haven't seen enough of Baltimore": Ibid.

255 He'd pay the fine: Dave Anderson, "Joe Namath: Man of Defiance Faces Biggest Challenge," *New York Times,* January 5, 1969.

255 "First time I ever knew you to waste": Zimmerman, "A Happy Joe Bubbles Over," *New York Post,* December 30, 1968.

255 "Wait 'till I put the glass down": Ibid.

255 "I want to thank all the broads": Fox, *Broadway Joe,* 233.

255 Joe Namath wept: Namath, *I Can't Wait,* 84.

33. The Points

256 the best oddsmaker: At the time, the man regarded as America's best bookmaker was Bob Martin, a transplanted Brooklynite who worked out of Churchill Downs Race and Sports Book in Las Vegas.

256 his specialty was in giving prices: Hank Goldberg interview, June 5, 2002.

256 "The number is 17": Dave Anderson, *Countdown to Super Bowl* (New York: Random House, 1969), 5.

257 a banner headline: *Daily News,* December 31, 1968.

257 could be 20-point underdogs: "Colts by 18," *Daily News,* January 4, 1969.

257 "How you betting?": Passuello interview.

257 "We're gonna win straight": Ibid.

258 soon everybody was busting his chops: Alford interview.

258 The money started rolling in: Ibid.

258 "I grew up with the guy": Ibid.

258 "I said it and I meant it": Anderson, "Joe Namath: Man of Defiance."

259 "I'm not sure he would have approved": Namath, *I Can't Wait,* 51.

259 "He'll never get away": Anderson, *Countdown,* 19; see also Namath, *I Can't Wait,* 52.

260 He drained about two ounces: Anderson, *Countdown,* 59.

260 "I'm afraid to run": Anderson, *Countdown,* 58.

260 "a down to earth guy": Lou Michaels interview, July 23, 2002.

260 "Joe was really looking for a fight": Ibid.

260 "They got to arguing over Catholicism": Hudson interview.

261 "Unitas is an old man": Lou Michaels interview.

261 "We finally got to talking": Ibid.

261 "If they want pictures of me": Anderson, *Countdown,* 86.

261 "Namath didn't show up": Ibid., 89.

261 his team had won five more: As Anderson notes, the Colts were then 63–18–3 under Shula, while the Packers were 58–21–1.

262 "regional sales manager": Robert Lipsyte, "Simply Super," Sports of the Times, *New York Times,* January 11, 1969.

262 "A great arm": William N. Wallace, "Shula Is Critical of Jet Star's Downgrading of Colts' Passer," *New York Times,* January 7, 1969.

262 "Shula was steaming": Anderson interview.

262 "Earl told me": Lou Michaels interview.

262 "Joe Namath Week": Larry Merchant, "His Week," *New York Post,* January 10, 1969.

262 "He's never faced anybody": Red Barber, "Four Months . . . and Unitas Still Waits in Wings," *Miami Herald,* January 12, 1968.

262 "I've never heard a quarterback make remarks": Norm Miller, "Colts on Joe: Good Passer, No Humility," *Daily News,* January 10, 1969.

262 "On Sunday": Norm Van Brocklin, quoted in Curran, *The $400,000 Quarterback,* 14.

263 George Usher and Stan Isaacs: "Jets Get 2 of Our Votes," *Newsday,* January 11, 1969.

263 Of fifty-five writers polled: Norm Miller, "Jets Find Out How Super They Are Today," *Daily News,* January 12, 1969.

263 picked the Colts 42–13: Edwin Pope, "Talk Not Cheap, Joe Will Find," *Miami Herald,* January 12, 1969.

263 "only going to talk to the writers he knows": Larry Fox, "Now Namath Isn't Talking," *Daily News,* January 9, 1969.

263 "Maybe we shouldn't play": Paul Zimmerman, "Joe Puts Some Swing in Super Bowl Scene," *New York Post,* January 8, 1969.

263 "Well, I don't know about odds": Ibid.

263 St. Mary and St. Jude: Szolnoki, *My Son Joe,* 87.

264 just too nervous to fly: Anderson, *Countdown,* 140.

264 "I don't talk about that": Jerry Tallmer, "Joe Namath's Closed World," *New York Post,* January 11, 1969.

264 "Our football team is conscious of everything": Luther Evans, "Is Namath's Lip Action Kiss of Death for Jets?" *Miami Herald,* January 11, 1969.

264 "Everything we accomplished": Roswell, "Shula

on the Points: 'Too Much Emphasis,' " *New York Post,* January 11, 1969.

264 "I couldn't block him": Winston Hill to RT.

265 "I read all the time": Dick Young, Young Ideas, *Daily News,* January 9, 1969.

265 Snell found himself wondering: Snell interview.

265 "looking to punish people": Anderson, *Countdown,* 184.

265 "But with the type of offense they played": Hudson interview.

265 "I don't want to be a widow": Anderson, *Countdown,* 203.

265 "Volk was the guy": Snell interview.

265 "We kept watching them films": Lammons interview.

266 "You got to find": Boozer interview.

266 "They looked slow": Sauer interview.

266 "Throw the damn ball": Ibid.

267 "Long hair and beards": Associated Press, "NCAA Considers Ban on Longhairs," *Miami Herald,* January 9, 1969.

267 "we gotta stop watching these films": Lammons interview.

267 Five syringes: Anderson, *Countdown,* 157.

267 attendance was obligatory: Ethan J. Skolnick, "SBIII: The Guarantee; Namath's Best Call," *Palm Beach Post,* January 25, 1999.

267 A turquoise Cadillac: Anderson, *Countdown,* 160.

267 "a lot of Kiwanis Club": Dowd interview.

268 $1,000 on the Jets at seven to one: Skaff interviews, October 9-10, 2002.

268 "a nervous nelly": Dowd interview.

268 Mr. Johnnie Walker: Skolnick, "SBIII: The Guarantee; Namath's Best Call"; Anderson, *Countdown,* 162.

268 "This should be a most valuable player award": Anderson, *Countdown,* 163.

268 "Who's that?": Namath in Luther Evans, " 'I Guarantee We'll Win'—Namath," *Miami Herald,* January 10, 1969.

268 "The Jets will win Sunday": Ibid.

269 the *real* image of football: As Namath had said, "You know what the real image of football is, it's brutality. Why don't they tell the kids like it is?" Dave Anderson, "Joe Namath: Man of Defiance."

269 "In closing": Evans, " 'I Guarantee.' "

270 In Ruth's case: Robert W. Creamer, *Babe: The Legend Comes to Life* (New York: Simon & Schuster, 1974), 361–68.

270 Saturday editions: George Usher, "Can the Jets Win? Joe Guarantees It," *Newsday,* January 11, 1969.

270 thirteenth paragraph: Robert Lipsyte, "Simply Super."

270 "I wouldn't give a darn for him": Evans, "Namath's Lip Action."

270 "I felt something": Anderson, *Countdown,* 189

270 "Not one bomb": Gene Roswell, "Boyd Alerts Bomb Squad," *New York Post,* January 10, 1969.

271 "Can't throw at all": Dick Young, "Namath Is Fresh, Honest, Always in Trouble," *Daily News,* January 12, 1969.

271 "I think he met her at Fazio's": Van interview.

34. Super

272 "the man who marries the gal": Dick Young, "It's Official: Super Bowl It Is," *Daily News,* January 11, 1969.

272 scalped for $150: *Miami Herald,* January 13, 1969.

272 "They could have sold 150,000": All Gowdy's quotes are from a videotape of NBC's broadcast of Super Bowl III, January 12, 1969, provided by NBC Sports (hereafter, NBC tape).

272 wagering of historic proportions: " 'Vig' Betting," *Daily News,* January 13, 1969.

273 "The Super Bowl is world theater": Gerald Eskenazi, "Viewers Drink In Underdog's Victory," *New York Times,* January 13, 1969.

273 Chrysler, Pall Mall: NBC tape.

273 $135,000 a minute: "Jets' Super Bowl Victory May Lead to Price Boost of AFL TV Minutes," *Advertising Age,* January 20, 1969. The rate SBIII was $15,000 less than the previous year's championship game on CBS.

273 "Just flew down with Ted": NBC tape.

273 Rosenbloom was overheard bragging: Marchiano interview.

273 big Baltimore victory party: Anderson, *Countdown,* 214; Hanks, *Game That Changed,* 116.

273 "What the hell, Weeb": Anderson, *Countdown,* 205.

273 Bake Turner had been expecting to start: Anderson, *Countdown,* 215; Hanks, *Game That Changed,* 129.

274 "It wasn't in our game plan": Snell interview.

274 "How *did* Lou Michaels miss": Sauer interview.

274 "I still say it was good": Lou Michaels interview.

275 "If he's healthy": Hanks, *Game That Changed,* 129.

275 the same thought: Anderson, *Countdown,* 64.

275 "That might have been the most important play": Sauer interview.

275 "not quite as quick": Ibid.

276 "Other quarterbacks": *The NFL's Greatest Games: Super Bowl III,* NFL Films, Polygram Video, 1997.

276 "Most of the plays were called": Ibid.

276 *Please let them blitz:* Namath, *I Can't Wait,* 64.

276 who had already spent his $15,000: Hanks, *Game That Changed,* 166.

276 The flea-flicker had been in the Baltimore playbook: Ibid., 135.

276 "I did everything but shoot up a flare": Dick Clemente, "Morrall Gloomiest of All Gloomy Colts," *Newsday,* January 13, 1969.

276 "I never saw him": Ibid.

277 "Earl wanted to win so bad": Lou Michaels interview.

277 chain-smoking at his locker: Hanks, *Game That Changed,* 140.

277 "So let's get rid of the pain": Ibid., 139; Anderson, *Countdown,* 225–26.

277 "I'm really shocked": NBC tape.

277 Namath knew he shouldn't have thrown: Namath, *I Can't Wait,* 67.

277 Unitas was already warming up: Ibid.

278 "We worked that left side": *The NFL's Greatest Games: Super Bowl III.*

278 "The world is a happening": Eskenazi, "Underdog's Victory."

278 listening over Armed Services Radio: Alford interview.

278 "If they played tomorrow": Anderson, *Countdown,* 241.

279 Grantham tipped: NBC tape.

279 " 'it should have been you' ": Snell interview.

279 "I'll remember that": Anderson, *Countdown,* 236.

279 "They made a bet": Walt Michaels interview.

280 "There was a bet": Hudson interview, July 21, 2003.

280 "I don't have any recollection": Mike Bite interview, July 21, 2003.

280 "If he got some money": Lou Michaels interview, May 9, 2003.

280 "I think the NFL will be ready for us": Dick Young, "Johnny Gives Sample of Jokes by Winners," Young Ideas, *Daily News,* January 13, 1969.

280 "I think I whipped him": "Super Jets," *Newsweek,* January 27, 1969.

280 "Yeah, I'm surprised": Anderson, *Countdown,* 237.

280 "I had no doubts": Bill Braucher, "Namath's Dad a Man of Steel, Was Sure Joe 'Can Do Anything,' " *Miami Herald,* January 13, 1969.

280 "Better him than me": Larry Merchant, "A Time for Gloating," *New York Post,* January 13, 1969.

281 "Wahoo McDaniel, former football star": "Wahoo Maps Last Stand," *Miami Herald,* January 13, 1969.

281 "Eighteen-point underdogs": Milton Gross, "Namath Just Did His Thing," *New York Post,* January 13, 1969.

281 vomiting in his bathroom: Anderson, *Countdown,* 243–44.

281 "very satisfactory": "Volk Hurt," *Daily News,* January 13, 1969.

281 sent flowers: Anderson, *Countdown,* 244.

35. America's Hero

282 "As drunk as I've ever seen": Hassan interview.

282 "Ah, Joe": Ibid.

282 "She told me she wasn't going anywhere": John Free interview, July 28, 2002.

283 "all dolled up": Ray Didinger, "The Mild Side of Broadway," from the Super Bowl XXVIII program; collected in John Wiebusch, ed., *The NFL Super Bowl Companion* (Chicago: Triumph Books, 2002).

283 "a wedge of 12 policemen": Joseph Durso, "Namath Is Hero of the Hour as Jets' Day Is Celebrated," *New York Times,* January 23, 1969.

283 "We all had this feeling": Marchiano interview.

283 "Am I having *fun*?": Ibid.

283 "Sure I cussed the cop": Associated Press, "Namath: I Was Sober," *New York Post,* April 15, 1969.

283 "Don't worry": Namath, *I Can't Wait,* 271.

283 Namath arrived bleary-eyed: Dave Anderson, "25,000 Turn Out to Hail Namath," *New York Times,* May 25, 1969.

284 "It was wilder than I could write": Dick Schaap to RT.

284 a crowd of about 25,000: Anderson, "25,000 Turn Out."

284 Henry Garcia and the Tijuana Trumpets: "Beaver Falls Area Booster Club Testimonial Dinner in Honor of Joe Willie Namath," program dated May 24, 1969, BCRC.

284 "Dad is bragging": Allen interview.

284 "I was an ROTC guy in college": Jim Otto interview, September 14, 2002.

284 "I never felt guilt": Marv Fleming interview, August 6, 2002.

285 "I had the Green Bay people": Ibid.

285 "Which one of you is Fleming": Ibid.

285 "The whole thing took about two minutes": Ibid. When informed of Fleming's account, Otto says: "I can remember that conversation. Something to that effect."

285 "Makes you wonder": Dave Anderson, "Vietnam Victims Gain Namath's Salute," *New York Times,* February 16, 1969.

286 "We got in a cab": Evans interview.

286 "I ain't walking no more": Ibid.

286 "He is something special": James Reston, "Joe Namath, the New Anti-Hero," *New York Times,* August 21, 1970.

287 "I saw him in person": William F. Buckley Jr., "Toward an Imperfect Understanding of the Namath Affair," *Esquire,* October, 1969.

287 "You've got to make it while you're on top": Larry Fox, "Namath Jilting Jets for Movie Deal?" *Daily News,* January 23, 1969.

287 "Agent isn't the proper word": Dave Anderson, "Making It," *New York Times,* February 1, 1969.

288 a tub full of vodka and beer on ice: Associated Press, "Joe Namath on the Set: 'Terribly Shy,' " *New York Post,* April 14, 1969.

288 secretary of Broadway Joe's Inc.: Florida Department of State, Division of Corporations, Corporations Online Public Inquiry, *http://www.sunbiz.org.*

288 $100,000, with $25,000 up front: "Agreement" of June 4, 1969, from *Joseph W. Namath vs. Spartans Industries, Inc. (Rex International Division),* Case No. 023189, 1972, Supreme Court of the State of New York, County of New York, Clerk's Office.

288 "Sonny Werblin had been my hero": Dave Anderson, "The Man behind Joe Namath's Deals," *New York Times,* July 17, 1975.

288 "I wanted to see how it went": Dowd interview.

289 "In football your inventory": M. R. Werner,

"Sonny . . . Just Like in Money," Horse Racing, *Sports Illustrated,* October 20, 1969.

289 274 Madison Avenue: Incorporation papers for Namanco Productions, Inc., No. 757928, on file at State Supreme Court Building, 60 Centre Street, New York, New York.

289 "We have to sell a Nazi car": George Lois, *George, Be Careful,* with Bill Pitts (New York: Saturday Review Press, 1972), 59.

289 for the covers of *Esquire: Covering the '60s: George Lois, the Esquire Era* (New York: Monacelli Press, 1996).

289 Duke Snider appeared with Captain Midnight: *Classic Sports Commercials from the Fifties & Sixties,* VHS, produced by Ira H. Gallen and Rona Y. Gallen, Moon River Inc., Tamarac, Fla., 1993.

289 "They'd have these guys": Lois interview, October 29, 2002.

290 "We need more money": Ibid.

291 "George, it's already eleven o'clock": Ibid.

291 "Gotta keep him company": Ibid.

291 "Fine place for America's hero": Ibid.

36. The Undesirables

292 $1.10 for a shot: Robert Lipsyte, "Night Thoughts," *New York Times,* June 14, 1969.

292 a call from Jilly: Van interview.

292 Lynda Bird Johnson: Lynda Bird, contacted through her former social secretary, Bess Abel, can't recall the evening at Bachelors III. However, a former member of her security team (interviewed August 8, 2003), who wishes to remain nameless, recalls her being there with a date.

292 "I just wanted to see": Van interview.

293 "I got no problem": Ibid.

293 kept his name off Bachelors' liquor license: Ibid.

293 "Ever since then": *Playboy* interview. See also Namath, *I Can't Wait,* 19; Namath says Danahy told his teammates, "I'm going to get that punk."

293 "Enjoy the game": Danahy interview.

294 "It was a big favor": Ibid.

294 Namath claimed not to recognize a single name: Namath, *I Can't Wait,* 17; also Milton Gross, "Joe Namath Makes a Case," *New York Post,* June 7, 1969.

294 "We asked the DA": Bobby Van to Arthur Greenspan, "memo to desk," June 16, 1969, from the files of the *New York Post.*

294 Prosecutors failed to acknowledge: Earl Wilson, "Namath, in Tears, Quits," with William H.

Rudy, Milton Gross, Leonard Katz, Leonard Lewin, Maury Allen, and Kenneth Gross, *New York Post,* June 6, 1969.

294 "He was really pissed off": Danahy interview.

295 "With Mike Bite I had a friend": Ibid.

295 estimated at $5 million: Dave Anderson, "Courage of Convictions Could Throw Namath for $5-Million Loss," *New York Times,* June 7, 1969.

295 "I was *right*, man": *Playboy* interview.

295 "The place could use some breakfast business": Dowd interview.

295 "No, sir": Ibid.

296 "Is there a man out there": Namath, *I Can't Wait,* 25.

296 "My father's a gambler": Wilson, "Namath, in Tears."

296 "Namath Weeps": *Sports Illustrated,* June 15, 1969.

296 "Football is the thing I love": Tom Renner, "Police Seek Namath Bar Hoods," *Newsday,* June 7, 1969.

296 "He's all crippled up": Ibid.

296 "This is what I have to put up with": Dave Anderson, "The Quarterback," *New York Times,* June 8, 1969.

296 "appearance of evil": "Text of Statement by Commissioner on Namath's Case," *New York Times,* June 7, 1969.

296 "We have rules": Larry Fox, "Fran Respects Namath but Backs Rozelle," *Daily News,* June 15, 1969.

296 "Man, you think NBC": Milton Gross, "Joe Namath: The Belief," *New York Post,* June 10, 1969.

296 down a point and a quarter: Dick Young, "Joe's Sense of Loyalty Will Bring Him Back: Young," *Daily News,* June 7, 1969.

296 "Nixon was very aware": John Dean interview, October 17, 2002. Though not yet White House counsel, Dean became quite familiar with Nixon's news summaries. When told what Nixon wrote in the margin, he said: "He knew exactly what he was doing when he wrote that. He was doing that for posterity."

297 "Good riddance," wrote the president: White House Special Files, Staff Member and Office Files, President's Office Files, Annotated News Summaries, June 1969, Nixon Presidential Materials Staff, National Archive at College Park, Maryland.

297 "If Pete Rozelle gives Joe an ultimatum": Sid Friedlander, "3 Jets Walk Out with Joe," *New York Post,* June 6, 1969.

297 Suzie massaged his shoulders: William Woodward and John Mullane, "Joe Hitting the Old Line," *New York Post,* June 7, 1969.

297 "No. 1 hit man": Edward Kirkman, "Joe's Bar Plus a Dash of Mafia," *Daily News,* June 12, 1969.

297 "a man who can always arrange a bet": "Blues for Broadway Joe," *Newsweek,* June 23, 1969.

298 *Sports Illustrated* ran a piece: Nicholas Pileggi, "The Game Was Up at Namath's," *Sports Illustrated,* June 23, 1969.

298 "very solid sources": Nicholas Pileggi, interview, March 15, 2004.

298 "An out-and-out smear job": Namath, *I Can't Wait,* 31.

298 "Beats the hell out of me": *Playboy* interview.

298 "An early warning": Sandy Smith, "Broadway Joe: Rebel with a Nightclub for a Cause," *Life,* June 20, 1969.

298 "A good friend": Danahy interview.

298 now worked as his investigator: Ibid.

298 "Namath's a good kid": Sandy Smith, "Broadway Joe."

298 habitual guest at the poker games: Dowd and Heyman interviews.

299 "It is my plan": Sam Goldaper, "Lynch to Devise Security Plans," *New York Times,* June 16, 1969.

299 "The press doesn't care": *Playboy* interview.

299 "When I heard her crying": Namath, interviewed by Johnny Carson, *The Tonight Show with Johnny Carson,* July 20, 1979 (hereafter, *Tonight Show* interview). Viewed at the library of the Museum of Television and Radio, New York City (hereafter, MTR).

299 National League president Warren Giles: Norm Miller, "Giles Tells Players to Avoid Joe's Pub," *Daily News,* June 25, 1969.

299 Bowie Kuhn requested: United Press International, "Namath Thrown a Curve," *New York Times,* June 28, 1969.

299 elude the paparazzi: Namath, *I Can't Wait,* 35–36.

299 "You're the biggest name": Ibid., 40.

299 "Most of what he said": Ibid., 38.

300 "one of the legal men": Lee Dembart and Paul Zimmerman, "Will Rozelle Suspend Joe?" *New York Post,* July 12, 1969.

300 Namath yanked the hat: Larry Fox, "Namath's in Town: Pete's Big Hurdle," *Daily News,* July 13, 1969.

300 concern about the magazine stories: Van says also says Rozelle "blamed the magazine articles, especially *Life*."

300 "bad reports": Namath, *I Can't Wait*, 42.

300 Rozelle abandoned his opposition: Ibid., 43.

300 "He has a business deal": Dave Anderson, "Coach Says Star Plans to Report," *New York Times*, July 14, 1969.

300 "We put him in the Hall": Dave Anderson, "Namath Back in City—In Silence," *New York Times*, July 13, 1969.

300 "He forced them": Arthur Greenspan and Paul Zimmerman, "Namath Sticking to Original Play," *New York Post*, July 14, 1969.

301 The *Apollo 11* astronauts: "Lunar Joe," *Daily News*, July 22, 1969.

301 "I didn't know": Van interview.

31. The Joe Namath Show

302 "a couple lunatics": Hudson interview.

302 "I want to kill that son of a bitch": Jeff Miller, *Going Long* (Chicago: Contemporary Books, 2003), 182–83.

302 "Looked like he hit my jugular": Hudson interview.

303 "get killed": Dave Anderson, "Namath: A.F.L. Clubs Can 'Kill' Giants," *New York Times*, April 30, 1969.

303 "to take the Giants seriously": Norm Miller, "Giants Won't Take Joe's Bait," *Daily News*, August 1, 1969.

303 "I won't go out": Dave Anderson, "Namath Set to Go All Out," *New York Times*, August 11, 1969.

303 "I want to win even more": Larry Fox, "All-Out Namath May Put Giants' Defense to the Test," *Daily News*, August 11, 1969.

303 "Wasn't the first mistake": Larry Fox, "Jets Want This One, Like Bad," *Daily News*, August 14, 1969.

303 "Giant fans still don't feel": Ibid.

303 "It was like a heavyweight championship": Fred Dryer interview, December 22, 2002.

303 "I never once heard Wellington Mara": Ibid.

303 accuse the *New York Times*: Larry Merchant, "The Sacrifice—I," *New York Post*, September 17, 1969.

303 when the column inches were totaled: Eskenazi, *Gang Green*, 55.

304 "Namath's late hours": William N. Wallace,

"If Namath Were a Giant," Sports of the Times, *New York Times*, August 17, 1969.

304 "guy with zinc oxide on his nose": Dryer interview.

304 "Everybody got drunk": Dillon interview.

304 Billy Mathis took his first benny: Mathis interview.

304 trying to spear Heck: Ibid.

305 "If I had a line like that": Bill Surface, "Pro Football's Broken Men," *New York Times Magazine*, October 26, 1969.

305 "Good-bye Allie": Maynard interview.

305 "Like Thomas Aquinas": Dryer interview.

305 "They knew I was hurt": Dave Anderson, "Namath Strikes Back after His Injury," *New York Times*, September 15, 1969.

305 "He's done a hell of a lot": Paul Zimmerman, "Costa Joe's 1st Super Highway Crash," *New York Post*, September 22, 1969.

305 "The hardest shot": George Usher, "Namath 'Guarantees' He'll Quit," *Newsday*, October 2, 1969.

306 "Stay down": Dave Anderson, "Namath's Career Is Resting on Blocks," *New York Times*, September 25, 1969.

306 "About fifteen more games": Paul Zimmerman, "Costa Joe's 1st Super Highway Crash."

306 "I can practically guarantee": Associated Press, "Namath May Quit After '69," *New York Post*, October 1, 1969.

306 "More than likely": Dave Anderson, "Namath Says It's 'More Than Likely' He Will Retire as Player after Season," *New York Times*, October 2, 1969.

307 "My mother and my father split": Namath, *I Can't Wait*, 125.

307 "I could spend the rest of my life": Ibid., 101.

307 "I wouldn't be a good husband": Ibid., 102.

307 marital fidelity: As Namath told *Playboy*: "I think you're supposed to be married and that's it—no clowning around."

307 "If he told me once": Secor interview.

307 "'We Want Suzie'": "L.S.U. Pep Rally Plays Second Fiddle to Suzie Storm," *New York Times*, October 26, 1969.

308 "You always had to get that silent nod": Larry Spangler interview, April 10, 2002.

308 forty-five stations: "Broadcast Joe," *Time*, October 17, 1969.

308 "amateurish naturalness" Jack Gould, "TV: A Three-Way Battle," *New York Times*, October 12, 1969.

308 "Every taping was standing room only": Spangler interview.

308 "This is the first time": *The Joe Namath Show* (hereafter, *JNS*), October 31, 1969. All fifteen shows were viewed in their entirety at ESPN Classic, Bristol, Connecticut, on March 1, 2002.

308 Mickey Kearney, Howard Cosell, and Roone Arledge: Spangler interview.

309 "Truman": *JNS*, December 19, 1969.

309 "Tell me, Joe": *JNS*, October 24, 1969.

309 Muhammad Ali and George Segal: *JNS*, October 17, 1969.

309 An enraged Spangler: Spangler interview.

309 the unmistakable tinkle: *JNS*, October 17, 1969.

309 "filled with alcohol": Spangler interview.

309 "they don't print the truth": *JNS*, October 17, 1969.

309 "the lousiest sports magazine": Ibid.

309 "What do you expect?": *JNS*, October 31, 1969.

309 "pretty nasty": *JNS*, December 19, 1969.

310 written the actor's name phonetically: "Broadcast Joe," *Time*, October 17, 1969.

310 "I'm a rookie": *JNS*, November 7, 1969.

310 "I still don't feel comfortable": *JNS*, October 31, 1969.

310 "It is pretty difficult": *JNS*, November 14, 1969.

310 a fierce determination to bed Broadway Joe: Joplin saw Namath as a notch in her belt. See Elice Echols, *Scars of Sweet Paradise: The Life and Times of Janis Joplin* (New York: Henry Holt, 1999), 201; Myra Friedman, *Buried Alive: The Biography of Janis Joplin* (New York: William Morrow, 1973), 183; Ellis Amburn, *Pearl: The Obsessions and Passions of Janis Joplin* (Boston: Little, Brown, 1992), 260–61.

311 throwing less than he ever had as a pro: In his rookie year of 1965, Namath averaged 26.15 attempts per game. In '69, he averaged 25.78.

311 "Where do you go": Sauer interview.

311 "Miss Joplin would like to": Johanna Schier, "Riffs," *Village Voice*, December 25, 1969.

311 "perhaps his finest day as a pro": Paul Zimmerman, "'Still My Champs,' Weeb Tells Jets," *New York Post*, December 22, 1969.

311 "He had no right": Murray Chass, "Wary Bell Foiled Jets, Says Namath," *New York Times,* December 21, 1969.

311 "I think the Fifth Army": Ibid.

311 only three defensive backs: Larry Fox, "Chiefs Un-Super Jets in 13–6 Playoff," *Daily News*, December 21, 1969.

312 simply died in the wind: Ibid.

312 "You just couldn't throw": Phil Pepe, "Can't Wait until Tomorrow 'Cause Yesterday Was a Horror," *Daily News*, December 21, 1969.

312 broke down weeping: Zimmerman, "'Still My Champs.'"

312 "No one has to apologize": Ibid.

312 "Joe couldn't move it": Philbin interview.

312 "Don't be dejected": Pepe, "Can't Wait."

312 "He just hasn't put away": Dick Young, "Namath's Last Game? . . . Don't You Believe It," Young Ideas, *Daily News*, December 21, 1969.

312 already made up his mind: After the game, Namath told his teammates, "We gotta win next year. I'll be back." Murray Chass, "Namath Is Hoping to Play Next Year," *New York Times*, December 22, 1969.

312 "Joe, Joe": Friedman, *Buried Alive*, 186.

38. Bigger Than the Game

313 "You're not bigger than football": David Maraniss, *When Pride Still Mattered: A Life of Vince Lombardi* (New York: Simon & Schuster, 1999), 496.

313 "Ladies and gentlemen": Tad Dowd and Al Hassan interviews.

313 "This gonna be a man's night": Dowd interview.

314 "the worst piece": Spangler interview.

314 "American women": Reynolds Packard, "Namath as Film Lover Boy," *Daily News*, June 21, 1970.

314 "Here they call them hookers": Van interview.

315 the two of them stood to split $16,000: Dowd interview.

315 about $150,000: Dowd recalls that Namath was paid $150,000. Spangler says it was "between $100,000 and $150,000." Both remember that Namath would not settle for less than he made for *C.C.*

315 "I have a contract to fulfill": Dave Anderson, "Namath, the Actor, Unsure of His Role in Pro Football," *New York Times*, May 27, 1969.

316 "lost $243,978 on revenues of $667,952": Richard Cohen, "How Wall Street Mousetrapped Broadway Joe," *New York*, November 30, 1970.

316 board meeting he conducted while showering:

Lancaster, "Thrown for a Loss," *Wall Street Journal*, January 4, 1971.

316 $370,988 on revenues of $238,870: Cohen, "How Wall Street Mousetrapped."

316 Namath and Bite would resign and "transfer": "Namath Quits as Chairman of Broadway Joe's Chain," *New York Times*, September 30, 1970; "Jets' Namath Rolls Out of Broadway Joe's Chain That He Headed," *Wall Street Journal*, September 30, 1970.

316 "I paid off every penny": Mort Fishman interview, September 9, 2002.

317 "I started calling him": Sam Goldaper, "Passer Here on Business," *New York Times*, August 5, 1970.

317 "He didn't talk to me": Martin interview.

317 "I am not going to levy a fine": Leonard Cohen, "Atkinson Quits Jets; And Where Is Joe?" *New York Post*, August 5, 1970.

317 "Football used to be No. 1": Dave Anderson, "Problems Cited By Quarterback," *New York Times*, August 6, 1970.

317 "help him": Paul Zimmerman, "Jets Will Help Namath," *New York Post*, August 6, 1970.

317 "big loan": Dave Anderson, "Namath to Return to Jets If They Grant 'Big Loan,' " *New York Times*, August 9, 1970.

317 "Ever since Joe joined the club": Leonard Cohen, "Atkinson Quits Jets."

318 "It bothers me": Dave Anderson, "Passer's Actions Termed 'Unfair,' " *New York Times*, August 6, 1970.

318 "It used to kill me": Paul Zimmerman, "Jets Will Help Namath," *New York Post*, August 6, 1970.

318 "exceptionally quiet": Fox, *Broadway Joe*, 141.

318 "he knew he had to make a decision": Dave Anderson, "Namath: Never a Quiet Crisis," Sports of the Times, *New York Times*, August 7, 1970.

318 "Like him or not": Bill Gallo interview, June 25, 2002.

319 "If you had a ballclub": Ibid.

319 The generally acknowledged culprit: Dick Barhold interview, July 2, 2003. Barhold is an authority on the history of New York broadcasting. Also see David J. Halberstam, *Sports on New York Radio: A Play-by-Play History* (Chicago: Masters Press, 1999), 123.

319 "The Young-Namath feud": Fox interview.

319 "It's the latest thing, stupid": Dick Young, "You Got Problems? . . . Let the Boss Worry," Young Ideas, *Daily News*, August 12, 1970.

319 "A man who arrives with two lawyers": Dick Young, Young Ideas, *Daily News*, August 19, 1970.

319 "He isn't talking to me": Dick Young, "Joey Baby Fools Everybody but Himself," Young Ideas, *Daily News*, August 22, 1970.

320 "Everything I've said I've meant": Dave Anderson, "Atkinson Says He'll Rejoin Jets, Citing 'Responsibility to Team,' " *New York Times*, August 15, 1970.

320 "Joe said he would not talk": Leonard Cohen, "Namath in Camp," *New York Post*, August 18, 1970; also see Norm Miller, "Namath Joins Jets at Camp: May Sit Out Giant Tilt," *Daily News*, August 19, 1970.

320 "is it worth it?": Miller, "Namath Joins Jets."

320 "It's a dead issue": Cohen, "Namath in Camp."

321 "to report and to remain": Copy of the letter, dated January 3, 1971, in *Namath v. Topps*.

321 "full of reefer": Steve Tannen interview, August 10, 2002.

321 "*drugs* were anathema": Ibid.

39. The Agony of Defeat

322 A decade had passed: Marc Gunther and Bill Carter, *Monday Night Mayhem: The Inside Story of ABC's Monday Night Football* (New York: William Morrow, 1988), 18–19.

322 "We killed Joe": Milton Gross, "Why Namath?" *New York Post*, September 11, 1970.

322 a threat on Namath's life: Associated Press, "Cops Guard Joe in Dallas Threat," *New York Post*, September 14, 1970.

323 "Look at Namath!": Gunther and Carter, *Monday Night Mayhem*, 68.

323 "There's a depressed": *The 25th Anniversary of ABC's Monday Night Football*, ABC Sports/PolyGram Video, 1994.

323 averaging twenty-two carries: Paul Zimmerman, "Jets without Snell, What?" *New York Post*, October 5, 1970.

323 "I'm finished, Doc": "Snell Weeps in Locker Room; Fears Injury Ends His Career," *New York Times*, October 5, 1970.

323 ashamed to go into the trainer's room: Zimmerman, "Jets without Snell."

324 "Here, at last": Vincent Canby, review of *C. C.*

and Company, directed by Seymour Robbie, *New York Times,* October 15, 1970.

324 "Big Joe": Howard Thompson, review of *Norwood,* directed by Jack Haley Jr., *New York Times,* November 26, 1970.

324 "I'm not sure": *Playboy* interview.

325 He liked the idea of being a cowboy: JN to RT.

325 "I felt like a fool": *Playboy* interview.

325 disliked the sound of his own voice: Earl Wilson, "It Happened Last Night," *New York Post,* July 8, 1969: "When I memorize my speeches and play them back on the tape recorder, I think they're awful."

325 "You don't hurt something": *C. C. and Company,* Avco Ambassy Pictures Corp., MGM Home Entertainment, 1970.

325 "a whole different thing": JN to RT.

325 "I have no confidence.": Fred Ferretti, "Part of N.E.T. 'American Dream': Angry Namath," *New York Times,* December 29, 1970.

325 "I never saw *C. C.*": JN to RT.

325 "As soon as you were in Joe's presence": Secor interview.

326 "You didn't want to talk too much": Ibid.

326 "He never talked about it": Ibid.

326 "The damn back hurt worse": Hudson interview.

327 "I see how hard other fathers": Dave Anderson, "Sauer Leaves Father's Shadow Behind," *New York Times,* November 24, 1968.

327 "I became embarrassed": Sauer interview.

327 "I can't begin to tell you": Passuello interview.

327 "We just sat around": Sauer interview.

327 "I had a sad feeling ": Dave Anderson, "Namath Asks Jets to Acquire Hayes," *New York Times,* May 6, 1971.

328 cheerfully promised to be ready: Ibid.

328 the *new* Joe: Zimmerman interview; Vic Ziegel interview, November 13, 2001.

328 no longer wanted to be known: Jim O'Brien, "Meet the New Namath," *New York Post,* August 4, 1971.

328 "I'm going to convince them": Ibid.

328 "Now Paul": Ziegel and Zimmerman interviews.

328 having to be separated at the hotel bar: Gallo interview.

328 "The only time I complained": Fox interview.

328 "I don't want to see you": Zimmerman interview.

329 "Zimmerman knows": JN to RT.

329 instructed not to hit Papa: Zimmerman interview.

329 "the best reporters": Zimmerman to RT, November 15, 1975.

330 "You want to pretend": Zimmerman interview.

330 a smiley face: Dave Anderson, "The Night They Wiped the Smile off Namath's Knee," *Life,* August 20, 1971.

330 "Dead on my left knee": Joe Namath interviewed by Dave Hyde, columnist for *Lauderdale Sun-Sentinel,* April 30, 2002, at the Omni Colonnade Hotel, Coral Gables, Fla. A microcassette recording of the interview was provided by Hyde (hereafter, Hyde tape).

330 he couldn't feel anything: Dave Anderson, "Namath Injured; Operation Today," *New York Times,* August 8, 1971.

330 Maynard began to weep: "Namath Undergoes Surgery; Future in Football Uncertain," *New York Times,* August 9, 1971.

330 "I don't want her to hear it": Anderson, "The Night They Wiped."

330 "I want him to quit": John Mullane, "Joe's Dad: He Should Quit," *New York Post,* August 9, 1971.

331 Dr. Nicholas said: "Namath Undergoes Surgery; Future in Football Uncertain," *New York Times,* August 9, 1971.

331 "good as new": Philip Werber, "Broadway Joe: Off-side and Out of Sorts," *Village Voice,* August 26, 1971.

331 "It means hate": Ibid.

331 "might be identified as sheepish": Vincent Canby, review of *The Last Rebel, New York Times,* September 25, 1971.

331 "Morphine didn't help": Hyde tape.

331 "The worst pain": "Namath Suffers His 'Worst Pain,' " *New York Times,* September 10, 1971.

331 "Poured everything down": Hyde tape.

332 that hot, tingly feeling would stay: Ibid.

332 her cooking would help her son: Dick Young, Young Ideas, *Daily News,* November 5, 1971.

332 "I want to play": Dave Anderson, "Namath, Jets Debate His Return," *New York Times,* November 2, 1971.

332 leading the NFC in sacks: *NFL Game of the Week No. 11: 49ers at Jets,* NFL Films, 1971.

332 "I was setting up too fast": Paul Zimmerman, "Namath Had the Crowd—And His Nerves—Jumping," *New York Post*, November 29, 1971.

333 "When Hardman hit me": Milton Gross, "Beautiful," *New York Post*, November 29, 1971.

333 Riggins couldn't believe: Murray Chass, "Namath Gets More 'Treatment,' " *New York Times*, November 30, 1971.

333 "pretty battered up": Ibid.

333 "I didn't play well": Dave Anderson, "Namath: 'We Didn't Win, I Didn't Play Well at All,' " *New York Times,* November 29, 1971.

334 "You're still my idol": Gross, "Beautiful."

334 "What that guy could do": *Broadway Joe: The Joe Namath Story.*

334 "No one instills confidence": Dave Hirshey, "Namath Arrives 'Early' at Jets Camp," *Daily News,* July 23, 1972.

334 "That was a problem": Tannen interview.

40. The Score

335 a White House staffer: White House Special Files, Staff Member and Office Files, Charles Colson, Black List, National Archive, College Park, Maryland.

335 "If you don't like your contract": Associated Press, "Star Cites Draft and Players Pacts," *New York Times,* January 14, 1971.

335 spy on prominent Floridians: Dick Holland and Chris Sanson, "IRS spied on Namath, Robbie, Gerstein as Nixon Enemies," *Miami News*, February 1, 1975.

335 "It's the middle of the night": Marchiano interview.

336 "like they were coming from everywhere": Fishman interview.

336 assorted floral and rococo trimmings: See pictorial by Harry Benson, "Namath: The Juicy Rewards of a Painful Life," *Life*, November 3, 1972.

337 "One day I was in Jimmy Walsh's": Fishman interview.

337 Randi would remain at his bedside: Kay Iselin Gilman, *Inside the Pressure Cooker: A Season in the Life of the New York Jets* (New York: Berkley/Putnam, 1974), 114–20.

337 "When one of the bottles": Ibid., 116.

337 "The most amazing thing": Secor interview.

337 footsie with Raquel: Ibid.

337 "He's great": With a camera and tripod, Warhol videotaped himself and friends as they watched the 44th Academy Awards, April 10, 1972; MTR.

337 "Cheryl": Ibid.

337 sole director: *Namanco Productions, Inc. v. Munro Games, Inc.,* Case No. 20179, 1976, Supreme Court of the State of New York, New York County, Clerk's Office. In his deposition, taken March 8, 1977, Walsh identifies himself as Namanco's "sole director."

338 "My father was still working": *Metro Sports Legends: Broadway Joe.*

338 $100,000 in annual payments: *Namanco Productions v. Munro Games.* Contract between Namanco and Munro is dated September 1, 1972.

338 Royal Pub Cologne: Royal Pub Cologne, Grey Advertising Reel, MTR.

338 six-packs of Budweiser: Tony Jaffe interview, March 11, 2004.

338 "I'm so excited": Noxzema, William Esty Commercial Reel, MTR.

338 already had the storyboard: Lois interview.

338 "I'm very pleased": Olivetti Typewriters, George Lois Reel, MTR.

339 "What's the problem": Lois interview.

339 "My old pal Ovaltine": Ovaltine, George Lois Reel, MTR.

339 "looking to build another factory": Lois interview.

339 "We feel that Joe Namath": *Ovaltine: A Friend for Life*, Ira H. Gallen, archivist, Rona Y. Gallen, producer, Ovaltine Products, Video Resources, New York, 1972.

339 intended for the moms: Ibid.

340 potential for bad publicity: Hank Seiden interview, October 28, 2002.

340 a bump in Christmas sales: "We were just looking for a bump around Christmas," Seiden says. "Popcorn wasn't that popular."

340 "Any competitor could": Seiden interview.

340 "The kids never had such a day": Danahy interview.

340 "one of his favorite things": Hicks interview.

341 "My kid went to his camp": Zimmerman interview.

341 "This is my option year": Dave Anderson, "Namath to Ask Record Salary," *New York Times*, January 23, 1972.

341 "Once I started making money": JN to RT.

"We had to start somewhere": Dave Anderson, "Namath Reaching for $250,000," *New York Times,* June 4, 1972.

341 "Believe me": Paul Zimmerman, "Figuring Namath," *New York Post,* July 11, 1972.

342 "they can stick it": Paul Zimmerman, "Namath Balks at Exhibitions," *New York Post,* July 24, 1972.

342 "get another quarterback": Al Harvin, "Namath Won't Play without Contract," *New York Times,* July 25, 1972.

342 worth $600,000: Contract, dated August 1, 1972, and amending letter, dated August 22, 1972 in *Namath v. Topps.*

342 boys pressing their noses: Gerald Eskenazi, "Namath Gets Record Pact of $500,000 for Two Years," *New York Times,* August 2, 1972.

41. Nobody's Perfect

343 "everyone's contract but Joe's": Martin interview.

343 "making donations": Philbin interview.

343 "Joe Namath missed nineteen games": Zimmerman, *Last Season of Weeb Ewbank,* 56.

343 "It was not fair": Martin interview.

344 "I know if I play well": Leonard Lewin, "Joe Sees Super Season," *New York Post,* September 11, 1972.

344 "I felt like a dog": Paul Zimmerman, "Namath's Finale?" *New York Post,* January 13, 1973. Also, speaking of his lack of preparation, Namath told Francesa and Russo in *Mike and the Mad Dog* interview, "I was so angry at myself and so teed off."

344 "If you have time": Dave Anderson, " 'If You Ain't Confident, You Don't Belong,' " *New York Times,* September 26, 1972.

344 what John Riggins had told him: "Joe Namath and the Jet-Propelled Offense," *Time,* October 16, 1972.

345 following a Gerry Philbin sack: *NFL Game of the Week No. 2: Jets at Colts,* NFL Films, 1972.

345 "It was a read route": Rich Caster interview, June 25, 2003.

345 sprinted past the safety: *Jets at Colts.*

345 "I was generally covered": Caster interview.

345 "If you ain't confident": Anderson, " 'If You Ain't Confident."

345 "I knew that's where": "Joe Namath and the Jet-Propelled Offense."

345 "Caster had to be one on one" Anderson, " 'If You Ain't Confident.' "

346 pounding the ground: *Mike and the Mad Dog* interview.

346 "Maybe back on Sixth Street": Paul Zimmerman, "Anywhere Is Joe's Zone," *New York Post,* September 25, 1972.

346 "I'm convinced I'm better": Anderson, " 'If You Ain't Confident.' "

346 "I don't respect him": Al Levine, "Namath Gets No Respect from Morrall," *Miami News,* November 16, 1972.

347 refused to shake his hand: Dave Hyde, *Still Perfect! The Untold Story of the 1972 Miami Dolphins* (N.P.: Dolphin/Curtis, 2002), 171.

347 "Run the fucking play": Ibid., 176.

347 "I don't think anybody can lay off": Larry Fox, "Is Joe Losing His Touch? He & Weeb Blame Layoff," *Daily News,* November 30, 1972.

347 "There's nothing physically wrong": Ibid.

347 turned around on the runway: Larry Merchant, "The Magician," *New York Post,* December 12, 1972; "Joe's Late," *Daily News,* December 11, 1972.

348 "in total awe": Paul Zimmerman, "Namath Leaves 'Em in Awe," *New York Post,* December 12, 1972.

348 "He can start off next season": Milton Gross, "Joe," *New York Post,* December 14, 1972.

42. Don't Trust Anyone Over Thirty

349 "I was not the compiler": Dean interview.

349 "Joe Namath, New York Giants": Senate Select Committee on Presidential Campaign Activities, Watergate and Related Activities, book 4, The Richard Nixon Library & Birthplace, Yorba Linda, California.

349 probably owed to zealous staffers: Dean interview.

349 "Ali": Dave Anderson, "Political Football," *New York Times,* July 1, 1973.

350 "The glorification": Dave Meggysey, *Out of Their League* (Berkeley, Calif.: Ramparts Press, 1970), 253. Also see Robert Lipsyte, "Changing Seasons," *New York Times,* August 10, 1970.

350 "I don't like to get involved": News Dispatches, "Apolitical Namath Sees Enemy Listing as 'Crazy,' " *Washington Post,* June 30, 1973.

350 "Joe Namath has never been critical": Ibid.

350 $200,000 per minute: "Super Bowl Is a Sell-out; 28 Sign Up," *Advertising Age*, January 1, 1973.

350 "I get a chill": Dave Anderson, "Political Foot-ball," *New York Times*, July 1, 1973.

350 later that year: *The Brady Bunch*, ABC, episode 97, "Mail Order Hero," September 21, 1973; http://www.tvtome.com.

351 Jagger in concert: Gerald Eskenazi, "All's Well with Jets: Namath Arrives," *New York Times*, July 24, 1973.

351 $14.50 a day: Robin Herman, "And in Jet Camp, Where Both Star and Rookie Earn $101.50 Week, the Instinct Is for Survival," *New York Times*, July 21, 1973.

351 have a tall one ready for him: Bob Gutkowski, who worked his way through college as a bartender at Bill's Meadowbrook, interview, November 6, 2001.

351 magic mushrooms: Tannen interview.

351 minus $600 for taxes: Zimmerman, *Last Season of Weeb Ewbank*, 70.

351 "It would have been higher": Eskenazi, *Gang Green*, 118.

351 "Let me up, Doc": Paul Zimmerman, "Snell's Career Over," *New York Post*, October 10, 1972.

351 NEED MORE GREEN: Zimmerman, *Last Season of Weeb Ewbank*, 97.

352 tearfully pleading his case: Iselin Gilman, *Inside the Pressure Cooker*, 67–68.

352 "It was devastating": Maynard interview.

353 40,000 requests: Gerald Eskenazi, "Jet Picture Day: 'Let's Have a Big . . . ' " *New York Times*, July 17, 1973.

353 "He wasn't going to get away": Philbin inter-view.

353 "For $250,000": Zimmerman, *Last Season of Weeb Ewbank*, 176.

353 vitamins and Transcendental Meditation: Es-kenazi, "All's Well with Jets."

353 "Joe told me he used to": Bob Oates Jr. inter-view, July 12, 2002.

353 "Twenty minutes in the morning": JN to RT.

353 "Any man of decent mobility": Dick Young, Young Ideas, *Daily News*, September 28, 1973.

353 "Short season": Zimmerman, *Last Season of Weeb Ewbank*, 202.

354 Joe assured Rose: Iselin Gilman, *Inside the Pres-sure Cooker*, 95.

354 "If you drink enough": Dave Anderson, "The

Trophy's in Lenox Hill Again," *New York Times*, September 26, 1973.

354 After five vodkas: Iselin Gilman, *Inside the Pressure Cooker*, 97.

354 "How the fuck": Zimmerman interview.

354 "a slingshot with a noodle": Dave Anderson, " 'Namath's World,' " *New York Times*, November 10, 1973.

354 "It depends": Dave Hirshey, "TV Comedy: Joe Laughs Off 'I Quit' Hoax," *Daily News*, November 13, 1973.

354 "Everybody would be better off": Ibid.

355 Aspiration three days before: Zimmerman, *Last Season of Weeb Ewbank*, 298.

355 "could be my last": Larry Fox, "Namath: Don't Know If I Want to Play," *Daily News*, December 13, 1973.

355 "I dread the day Joey Baby": Dick Young, ". . . Where Has Joey's Fastball Gone?" Young Ideas, *Daily News*, November 27, 1973.

355 "I failed you": Zimmerman, *Last Season of Weeb Ewbank*, 250.

355 fired it back: Iselin Gilman, *Inside the Pressure Cooker*, 248.

43. High Concept

356 "It's a helluva lot easier": Larry Fox, "Joe: NY Is Where I Want to Be," *Daily News*, August 15, 1974.

356 "I didn't want to get anybody upset": Hyde tape.

356 "You only need a hamstring to run": Ibid. "I swear to God that's what he said," said Namath.

356 chief deputy and occasional whipping boy: Secor, Fishman interviews.

356 vice president: Walsh deposition, *Namanco Productions v. Munro Games*.

357 "something outrageous": Mike Martin interview.

357 "a true son of the seventies": Peggy King, e-mail message to author, October 7, 2002.

357 asleep on his typewriter: Peggy King interview, October 8, 2002.

358 a visual solution: Harry Benson interview, De-cember 10, 2002.

358 "Now I don't wear pantyhose": http://www.commercialcloset.org.

358 "I hated how I looked": *Metro Sports Legends: Broadway Joe*.

358 "wrongful and unauthorized use of his name": *Joseph W. Namath against Sports Illustrated*, Verified Complaint, Case No. 015283, 1973, Supreme Court of the State of New York, County of New York, Clerk's Office.

359 "I have been grossly mistreated": Namath affidavit, December 9, 1974, *Joseph W. Namath v. Sports Illustrated*.

359 The players union depended: A letter from Richard A. Berthelsen, assistant to executive director, NFL PA, to Joe Namath, June 27, 1973, asks Namath to use his signature and likeness for a licensing deal with King Athletic Goods: "We need your cooperation more than ever with Association licensing projects like this one. Starting in early 1974 we will be negotiating a new Collective Bargaining Agreement with the owners, and we must preserve our licensing revenue to help finance those negotiations." *Namath v. Topps*.

359 "Mr. Namath is not a signatory": Michael S. Toorock, letter to Arthur Shorin, executive VP, Topps Chewing Gum, Inc., October 22, 1973. *Namath v. Topps*.

359 "the pictures or likenesses": George De Genaro, letter to Michael S. Toorock; Bushkin, Kopelson & Walsh, October 26, 1973. *Namath v. Topps*.

359 "indicates a blatant disregard": James M. Griffin, letter to Ed Garvey, National Football League Players Association, December 10, 1973. *Namath v. Topps*.

359 Garvey had already asked Topps: Garvey letter to De Genaro, November 2, 1973. *Namath v. Topps*.

359 believing that would resolve: De Genaro letter to Garvey, November 7, 1973. *Namath v. Topps*.

359 $750,000: Complaint, June 26, 1974, *Namath v. Topps*.

360 send a message: Garvey letter to James Walsh, February 19, 1975, reads: "During our last conversation about the lawsuit you indicated . . . that you were not going to pursue the matter, but were rather using it to police other people." *Namath v. Topps*.

360 "They offered many millions": Jimmy Walsh to RT.

360 "If you don't ask": Dave Anderson, "Joe Namath to Retire?" Sports of the Times, *New York Times*, June 2, 1974.

360 Arledge kept talking: Gunther and Carter, *Monday Night Mayhem*, 160.

360 Jimmy's angry objections: Howard Cosell,

Like It Is (Chicago: Playboy Press, 1974), 16; also, Gunther and Carter, *Monday Night Mayhem*, 161.

360 "Joe didn't come down on either side": Tannen interview.

360 on the advice of his attorney: Murray Chass, "Namath Returns," Sports of the Times, *New York Times*, August 15, 1974; "Joe Expects to Stay," *New York Post*, August 15, 1974; Fox, "Joe: NY Is Where."

44. Magic Six

361 "I'll go out and do my job": Anderson, "Joe Namath to Retire?"

361 Winner was politic enough: Murray Chass, "Interceptions Place Namath Under Fire," *New York Times*, November 9, 1974.

361 Namath's final pass: Paul Zimmerman, "Namath's Old Touch," *New York Post*, November 11, 1974.

361 the Los Angeles Rams: Paul Zimmerman, "Namath Headed for Los Angeles?" *New York Post*, October 22, 1974.

362 "This means a lot": Dick Young, "The Day the Jets Did a 180-Degree Bank," *Daily News*, December 10, 1974.

362 "I got a chill": Ibid.

362 cheating toward the middle: Paul Zimmerman, "Namath Fooled Them All," *New York Post*, November 11, 1974; Dave Anderson, "Pretzels, Fancy Pastry, Joe Namath," Sports of the Times, *New York Times*, November 11, 1974.

362 "The way the defense was crashing": Boozer interview.

363 "I almost fell out": Neil Amdur, "Jets Down Giants on Namath's Pass in Overtime, 26–20," *New York Times*, November 11, 1974.

363 "He had to make *us* believe": Boozer interview.

363 "Looked like he had a broom": Telander, *Joe Namath*, 56–57.

363 With a casual aplomb: *A Tale of Two Seasons*, directed by Bob Ryan, NFL Films, 1974.

363 "That's some parlay": Paul Zimmerman, "Namath's Old Touch," *New York Post*, November 11, 1974.

364 his thoughts to himself: Dave Anderson, " 'My Father's a Good Union Man,' " Sports of the Times, *New York Times*, November 26, 1974.

364 "He just seemed down": Paul Zimmerman, "For Joe, Winning Isn't Everything," *New York Post*, November 25, 1974.

364 "He just ducked": Ibid.

364 "His heart stopped last night": Ibid.

364 "I really don't think so": Murray Chass, "Namath Rallies Jets to 5 in Row," *New York Times*, December 9, 1974.

365 "I like this team": Murray Chass, "Jets Vote Namath No. 1 Man," *New York Times*, December 11, 1974.

365 eightieth consecutive pass: Murray Chass, "Jets' Happy Ending Only Half of Story," *New York Times*, December 17, 1974.

365 "I don't want to go": Paul Zimmerman, "Joe Leaves 'Em (Maybe) Laughing," *New York Post*, December 16, 1974.

365 "I want to keep that": Dave Anderson, "A Jet's Jersey to Remember," Sports of the Times, *New York Times*, December 16, 1974.

365 "If Walsh thinks": Dick Young, "Iselin: Namath Demanding $1M a Year for Openers," *Daily News*, January 12, 1975.

365 keen on the idea of ownership: He remained so. In 1978, Walsh helped form a syndicate in a brief, unsuccessful attempt to buy the New York Mets baseball club. See Maury Allen, "Namath Trying to Buy The Mets," *New York Post*, February 9, 1978.

365 buy a percentage of the team: Dowd interview.

365 "It wouldn't be that difficult": Dave Anderson, "Joe Namath, Club Owner," Sports of the Times, *New York Times*, January 19, 1975.

365 "They kept talking about New York": Dave Anderson, "Another Jets' Loss," *New York Times*, Sports of the Times, November 9, 1975.

366 pledged to personally honor: Dowd interview. "The most solid offer": Dave Anderson, " 'Too Big a Chance' for Joe Namath," Sports of the Times, *New York Times*, May 24, 1975.

366 began looking for a place in Chicago: Dowd interview.

366 "Joe didn't like being alone": Mort Fishman interview, November 20, 2002.

366 "He wanted 15 percent": Paul Zimmerman, "Did Joe's TV Demands Kill WFL Deal?" *New York Post*, May 23, 1975.

366 That was the end: Dowd interview.

366 "Joe doesn't like to": Dave Anderson, "The Man behind Joe Namath's Deals," Sports of the Times, *New York Times*, July 17, 1975.

366 "You can negotiate only so long": JN to RT.

367 revived his football spirit: Ibid.

367 "It cost me": Anderson, " 'Too Big a Chance.' "

367 "I'll retire": Dave Anderson, "The Jets 'Absurd' Offer," Sports of the Times, *New York Times*, May 25, 1975.

367 declining earnings: "Joe Namath Signs with Faberge Inc. as Sports Adviser," *Wall Street Journal*, July 16, 1975. According to the article, Faberge's 1974 earnings were down 36 percent from the year before.

367 "believed to be the biggest ever made": Lynn Langway, "The Rub-off," *Newsweek*, July 28, 1975.

367 "he'd drink the stuff": Anderson, "The Man behind Joe Namath's Deals."

367 "It's carried over": Gerald Eskenazi, "Cosmetic Deal Readies Namath for Jets," *New York Times*, July 16, 1975.

368 "his business"; Zimmerman, "Jet Players Hold Meeting Over Namath," *New York Post*, July 26, 1975.

368 "Joe should be here": Ibid.

45. Garden City Joe

369 "going to live an artist's life": Rick Telander interview, July 11, 2002.

370 three composition books: Hereafter, Telander notebooks I, II, and III.

370 "See if you can't fill it up": Telander, *Joe Namath*, 9.

370 "What is she trying to prove?": Telander notebook I.

370 "If I hadn't had a couple Michelobs": Ibid.

371 "That's if I'm not too drunk": JN to RT.

371 a beer and a few Bufferin: Telander notebook II.

371 "He came over and grabbed my hair": Tannen interview.

371 "Joe doesn't talk about his personal problems" Telander, *Joe Namath*, 204–5.

372 "He had a profound attitude": Paul Zimmerman, "Joe Shows Up at Practice," *New York Post*, September 18, 1975.

372 "I told Joe not to come": Ibid.

372 averaging better than nine yards: *Total Football* II, 1681.

372 "He thinks he can come back": Gerald Eskenazi, "Shipp Sees Vast Overhaul," *New York Times*, December 23, 1975.

373 forced to run from the pocket: Larry Fox,

"Sacked 19 Times, Pummeled Freely," *Daily News*, November 11, 1975.

373 precautionary X-rays: Ibid.

373 "You know where he's going to be": "Limping for Life," *Time*, November 24, 1975.

373 "I'd like to say it can't": Ibid.

373 recall seeing his brother Frank: Dave Anderson, "Joe Namath Is All Quarterback Again," Sports of the Times, *New York Times*, July 31, 1975.

373 "What scares me": Paul Zimmerman, "Namath's Not Calling His Own Game Anymore," *New York Post*, October 14, 1975.

373 "Traffic's too damn bad": "Limping for Life."

374 "managed to sip their way": Telander, *Joe Namath*, 204.

374 "The sonofabitch was lying there": Ibid., 243.

46. Hollywood Ending

375 "the thrill of parading Namath": Dick Young, Young Ideas, *Daily News*, December 11, 1974.

375 "It would be a good idea": "People in Sports," *New York Times*, January 9, 1976.

375 "I hope so": "Namath Wants Rams," *New York Times*, January 19, 1976.

375 $500,000: Associated Press, "Namath Pay: $500G," *New York Post*. March 16, 1976. The report was based on exhibits in the trial *Joe Kapp v. The National Football League*.

375 "He wanted to obtain the knowledge": Carol Fishman interview, September 9, 2002.

376 "She was devastated": Ibid.

376 promised to help: Mort and Carol Fishman interviews.

376 "I love her and she loves me": Cheryl Bentsen, "Namath Says Football."

376 *Win the game, fight like men*: Eskenazi, *Gang Green*, 132.

376 "If he can't do that": Ibid., 128.

377 "One of the first things I wanted to do": Holtz, quoted in Earl Gustkey, "The Battle for No. 1: USC vs. Notre Dame," *Los Angeles Times*, November 25, 1988.

377 "I should leave my number": Eskenazi, in *Gang Green*, 134, relates a similar story. Also, Tad Dowd recalls Jimmy Walsh laughing about not giving Holtz the number.

377 one of the three attempts: Paul Zimmerman, "Jets Veering from Joe?" *New York Post*, September 13, 1976.

377 "It is obvious": Larry Fox, "Jets Decide to Defuse," *Daily News*, September 16, 1976.

377 "Joe gives us a mental lift": Gerald Eskenazi, "Jets to Keep Namath In All the Way," *New York Times*, September 23, 1976.

377 a plan to usurp Joe's greatest privilege: Larry Fox, "Holtz Calls Plays, Jets Falter, 16–0," *Daily News*, September 27, 1976.

377 "I'd tell him": Steve Serby, "Herman: Bye, Joe," *New York Post*, October 27, 1976.

377 "It's difficult to throw": "Holtz Defends Namath," *New York Times*, October 6, 1976.

377 Namath called most of the plays: Larry Fox, "Reveal Joe Called Most Shots vs. Bills," *Daily News*, October 13, 1976.

378 "Namath has cleaned up his act": Dick Schaap, "Joe Namath: The Twilight of a God?" *New York Times*, November 7, 1976.

378 season ticket holders stayed home: Steve Cady, " 'Thanks for the Memories, Joe,' " Sports of the Times, *New York Times*, December 13, 1976.

378 "We Want Joe!": Eskenazi, *Gang Green*, 136.

378 "I see that fat": Bill Verigan, "Shadow Darkens over Namath," *Daily News*, December 14, 1976.

378 "Shower": Gerald Eskenazi, "Jets Routed by Bengals, 42–3, As Namath's Cloud Darkens," *New York Times*, December 13, 1976.

379 "The only place I'd play": "Namath Says He Wants Rams," *New York Times*, January 7, 1977.

379 "Now isn't that nice of him?": Dick Young, "Joey Baby's Bluffing His Way to LA," *Daily News*, January 10, 1977.

379 "It wouldn't be fair": "Namath Expresses Hope For a Place in the Sun," *New York Times*, January 28, 1977.

379 "people tell me that Washington": Gerald Eskenazi, "Quick Trade Is Sought as Clubs Meet Monday," *New York Times*, March 25, 1977.

379 "His stature": Ibid.

379 "Joe Namath isn't going to audition": Gerald Eskenazi, "Namath Is Placed on Waivers; Trade Talk with Rams Fails," *New York Times*, April 2, 1977.

380 "Namath owes me one": Joe Marshall, "Hollywood or Bust for Off-Broadway Joe," *Sports Illustrated*, April 25, 1977.

380 begin at 8:15 A.M.: Jerrold K. Footlick and Martin Kasindorf, "Hello, Hollywood Joe," *Newsweek*, August 22, 1977.

380 drive Joe to the pool: Ron Fimrite, "Giving

Joe a Big Hello," *Sports Illustrated*, August 15, 1977.

380 "Joe was in that pool": Dryer interview.

381 "I thought Joe could still play": Knox interview.

381 "Chuck Knox never wanted him": Fox interview.

381 sacked eleven times: "Namath Doesn't Deserve to Start," *New York Post*, September 13, 1977.

381 "Man, it was awful": Hyde tape.

381 "I've got so much desire": "Rough Start for Freeway Joe," *Time*, October 3, 1977.

381 "Chicago's defensive backs": Bob Oates, "Avellini's 2 Bombs Turn Rams into Losers 24–23," *Los Angeles Times*, October 11, 1977. It was Oates's son, Bob Oates Jr., who had collaborated with Namath on *A Matter of Style* (Boston: Little, Brown, 1973), and taught him Transcendental Meditation.

381 "He couldn't plant": Dryer interview.

381 "The game plan was to run": Knox interview.

382 "I think Chuck wanted him to fail": Dryer interview.

382 "Hello, Joe": Fox interview.

382 wasn't much worse than the usual: Skip Bayless, "Namath: I Could Play; Rams: We Didn't Lie," *Los Angeles Times*, October 15, 1977.

382 "a very, very tough decision": Knox interview.

382 "That puts an end": Leonard Koppett, "Haden Performance Puts Namath on the Sidelines," *New York Times*, October 26, 1977.

382 "I suggested things": Skip Bayless, "After 13 Years, Namath Plans to Call It a Career," *Los Angeles Times*, December 29, 1977.

383 "He just nodded": Mike Evans, "Aides: Knox Spoiled Namath's last Hurrah," *New York Post*, March 1, 1978.

383 "His downfall": Dryer interview.

383 "Who are you?": Fishman interview.

384 "If I had good knees": Dave Anderson, "Namath Is Retiring From Pro Football," *New York Times*, January 25, 1978.

384 "Go on without me": Fishman interview.

384 "Mars": Kent Demaret, "If Golf Is a Metaphor for Life, Joe Namath Is at a Dogleg, Wondering About His Next Shot," *People*, February 13, 1978.

384 "he began drowning his sorrows": Ibid.

385 "He still believed in his heart": Knox interview.

47. That's Entertainment

386 "I'm not carrying the picture": "Off the Screen: Joe Namath May Have Found a New Calling in Acting—Just so Long as They Don't Make Him Genuflect," *People*, July 17, 1978.

386 "the new Double Mac by Hamilton Beach": *CBS Evening News with Walter Cronkite*, November 30, 1977, MTR.

387 "don't have a hangover": Mary Murphy, "Joe Namath, Superhero Out of Season," *Esquire*, June 19, 1979.

387 No more blackouts: Kristin McMurran, "Joe Namath Used to Fear the Sack—Now It's the Bomb in His New TV Series," *People*, September 25, 1978.

387 Joe preferred the vessel: Fishman interview.

387 "He's marvelous": McMurran, "Joe Namath Used to Fear."

387 "The network loved the idea": Mike Greenfield interview, August 9, 2002.

388 "Besides being a great quarterback": *The Best of the Dean Martin Celebrity Roasts, Man of the Hour: Joe Namath*, produced and directed by Greg Garrison, Guthy-Renker Video, December 22, 1978, January 19, 1979.

388 interviewing O. J. Simpson: *Sportscene*, HBO, 1979. Tape provided by HBO Sports.

388 At the far end of the dais: *Man of the Hour: Joe Namath*.

389 "Joe looks hurt and surprised": Vincent Canby, review of *Avalanche Express*, directed by Mark Robson, *New York Times*, October 19, 1979.

389 "Joe was philosophical": Greenfield interview.

389 "the key member of Namath's entourage": Mary Murphy, "Joe Namath, Superhero out of Season."

389 "Eddie Gerber was with him": Fishman interview.

389 "Kind of as an attraction": Mary Murphy, "Joe Namath, Superhero out of Season."

390 "Pantyhose": John Kenley interview, August 22, 2002.

390 a vaudeville dancer and mimic: Peter Bellamy, "Mattress Bank to Fortune," *Cleveland Plain Dealer*, March 17, 1974.

390 "Ann Corio stripped": Scott Eyman, "John Kenley," *Cleveland Plain Dealer Sunday Magazine*, August 12, 1979.

390 "Namath was an *attraction*": Kenley interview.

390 "worth the price of admission": Michael Ward, review of *Picnic,* directed by Leslie B. Cutler, *Cleveland Plain Dealer,* August 16, 1979.

390 "Joe was damn good": Kenley interview.

390 "Depends on what kind": *Tonight Show* interview.

48. Sound of the Soul

392 "He wanted to sing": Arthur Samuel Joseph interview, September 26, 2002.

392 too self-conscious: Fred Ferretti, "Joe Namath Hopes to Score in the Theatrical Arena," *New York Times,* June 28, 1981.

392 "a combination of blue-collar Pennsylvania": Ibid.

392 "He was completely open with me": Ibid.

393 five days a week: Ferretti, "Joe Namath Hopes to Score."

393 "It was going to affect": Ibid.

393 "one of the pieces in the knee": Gerald Eskenazi, "Namath Still Part of the Game," *New York Times,* July 10, 1981.

393 "I thought I was paralyzed": Milan Simonich, "Namath Details Toughest Foe; Huddles Here with Fellow Osteoarthritis Patients," *Pittsburgh Post-Gazette,* August 10, 2001.

393 "I had as much confidence": Dave Anderson, "Joe Namath's Second Life," Sports of the Times, *New York Times,* June 29, 1981.

393 "Mr. Namath has genuine charm": John Corry, review of *Damn Yankees,* directed and chorographed by Frank Wagner, *New York Times,* July 2, 1981.

393 as he greeted well-wishers: Gerald Eskenazi, "About Long Island," *New York Times,* August 9, 1981.

393 "The hardest-working guy": Albin Krebs and Robert McG. Thomas Jr., "Joe Namath, Actor," *New York Times,* July 29, 1981.

394 "He had completely changed": Secor interview.

394 finally found contentment on Long Island: Eskenazi, "About Long Island."

394 pulled his licensed .38: Doug Feiden, "Ex-FBI Man Kills Mugger," *New York Post,* October 19, 1981.

394 The stab wounds were serially arranged: Ellen Borakove interview, May 16, 2002. Borakove, spokesperson for the Medical Examiner's Office, New York County, read from Kearney's autopsy, dated September 1, 1982.

394 who used to terrorize: Secor interview.

395 "Who would've thought": Dowd interview.

394 "Joe couldn't have been more right": Greenfield interview.

395 "a nightclub act we developed": Joseph interview.

395 "He thought this was the best way": Michael Small, "Joe Namath Powders his Nose," *People,* October 31, 1983.

395 "I don't think that's going to happen": Robert Lipsyte, "Joe Namath," *Sport,* December, 1986.

396 "Mr. Namath grows more personable": Alvin Klein, " 'Sugar'-by-the-Sea: How Sweet It Is," *New York Times,* June 10, 1984.

396 "I don't see how": Kenley interview.

396 "Maintaining the consistency": Patti Conley, "Namath Plays Atlantic City," *Beaver County Times,* April 15, 1984.

396 "We were working": Tom Wheatley, "Broadway Josephine," *The Pittsburgh Press,* April 22, 1984.

396 might have a couple before: Ibid.

396 "I can't help it": Hupp interview. Namath's prom date wasn't the only one. Al Hassan, who also saw the production, recalls thinking: "That's Rose Szolnoki."

396 "It wasn't good": Fishman interview.

396 "You believe this": Dellartas interview.

397 old friends were beginning to wonder: Fishman and Dellartas interviews.

397 "One of the biggest disappointments": Dave Anderson, "The Hall of Fame Snubs Joe Namath," Sports of the Times, *New York Times,* February 6, 1983.

397 the director offered: Dunnavant, *Coach,* 318.

397 Joe's voice broke: Audio of Namath's induction speech at the Pro Football Hall of Fame can be heard at http://www.profootballhof.com/.

397 Eddie Gerber died: Clerk of the Courts, Broward County 17st Judicial Circuit of Florida, probate records, case No. PRC880001462, http://www.clerk-17th-flcourts.org; death notices, *Miami Herdld,* December 6, 1983.

397 "There wasn't much you could say": Fishman interview.

397 $390 fine: Associated Press, A.M. cycle, April 4, 1984.

397 Defendant had slurred speech: Probable Cause Affidavit, September 23, 1982, Case No. 82-31181TT10, Broward County Courthouse.

397 refused to be fingerprinted: Ibid.; Jack Brennan, "Namath Charged in Drunk Driving," *Sun-Sentinel,* September 25, 1982.

397 officers' instructions: Helen Rojas, "Namath Keeps License in Courtroom Win," *Sun-Sentinel,* November 20, 1982.

398 "His mother was wanting him": Hicks interview.

49. Deborah

399 "She's just a child": Joseph interview.

399 most of her childhood: Shirley Mays interview, December 13, 2002.

400 "A very beautiful girl": Dwayne Crank interview, October 21, 2002.

400 "It was a vision of hers": Joseph interview.

400 "I could not speak for Broadway Joe": Mays interview.

400 sixteen miles off the Hatteras Inlet: Prentiss Findlay, "Hunt May End Today," *Elizabeth City (N.C.) Daily Advance,* November 21, 1980.

400 "We've got some encouraging news": Prentiss Findlay, "Search Area Widens for Lost Fishermen," *Elizabeth City Daily Advance,* November 17, 1980.

401 scanned 220,000 square miles: Prentiss Findlay, "Fruitless Search for Lost Fishermen Called Off," *Elizabeth City Daily Advance,* November 23, 1980.

401 "The boat and pieces will float": Ibid.

401 "You can't fill a void": Mays interview.

401 "That hasn't happened yet": Small, "Joe Namath Powders His Nose."

401 Even the astrologer: "Broadway Joe and Fiji Debbie," *New York Post,* April 11, 1987.

401 "He was looking for a wife": Hicks interview.

401 sixteen guests: Marianne Goldstein, "B'way Joe's Last Pass Intercepted by Former Actress," *New York Post,* November 8, 1984.

401 "I did exactly what": Mays interview.

401 blaming a bad reaction: "Joe Namath Is Intercepted for the Last Time, He Says, by Aspiring Actress Deborah Mays," *People,* November 26.

402 Reverend E. B. McGahee: Marriage Record, Office of Vital Statistics, Florida Department of Health.

402 "I took my time to find the perfect girl": Goldstein, "B'way Joe's Last Pass."

402 "It was so mean": Joseph interview.

402 "things sure won't be": Alford interview.

402 if he had called Deborah "Randi": Fleming interview.

403 "Gotta take a pass on dinner": Mort and Carol Fishman interviews.

403 "She's getting a raw deal": Mays interview.

403 "But he didn't have the courage": Ibid.

403 "If you want to be around Joe": Hicks interview.

50. Old Joe

404 "He gives you the feeling of good": Steven Crist, "Mellow Namath Enjoys Life After Football," *New York Times,* January 28, 1985.

404 "total control": "Namath's Line," *New York Times,* November 28, 1984.

404 "We've never gone to a bar": Ibid.

404 always wore his seatbelt: Martin Burden, "New Joe Belts Up & Belts 'Em Out at the Claridge," *New York Post,* April 5, 1985.

404 "All Deborah talked about": Chuck Kinlaw interview, September 19, 2002.

404 "She hasn't convinced herself": Jack Lloyd, "Broadway Joe Content with Family Lifestyle," *Beaver County Times,* April 14, 1985.

405 his own spontaneous, unexpurgated color: Rudy Martzke, "Joe Has Million Reasons to Work Monday Nights," *USA Today,* July 10, 1985.

405 "The stupidest ass-backwards way": Gunther and Carter, *Monday Night Mayhem,* 314.

405 ratings down 22 percent: Rudy Martzke, "Namath joins O. J., Gifford for New Era," *USA Today,* September 9, 1985.

405 "It was worth the gamble": Gunther and Carter, *Monday Night Mayhem,* 314.

405 "I'm the one": Phil Mushnick, "Joe's Eager to Tackle Role of Armchair QB," *New York Post,* July 10, 1985.

405 six votes short: Dave Anderson, "The Hall of Fame Snubs Joe Namath," Sports of the Times, *New York Times,* February 6, 1983. Anderson was a voter, designated by the Jets.

406 "You look at a guy's career": Zimmerman interview.

407 "In terms of fan appeal": Bob Oates Sr., "A Bit of Broadway Comes to Canton," *Los Angeles Times,* August 4, 1985.

407 "I love you": Kreshon interview.

407 "He was kind enough to old Joe": Text of Namath's Hall of Fame acceptance speech can be found at http://cbs.sportsline.com/u/fans/celebrity/ namath/super/hallfame.htm.

407 separate tables: Bob Oates Sr., "A Bit of Broadway Comes to Canton."

407 "Mister": Gunther and Carter, *Monday Night Mayhem*, 314.

407 "I have to convince myself": Skip Myslenski, "Namath Works on Game Plan for ABC Debut," *Beaver County Times*, July 30, 1985.

407 books on how to speak: Hicks interview.

408 "The greatest announcer that ever was": Ibid.

408 "heckuva": Michael Janofsky, "Namath: A 'Heckuva' Debut," *New York Times*, September 11, 1985.

408 "Dwelled on the obvious": Rudy Martzke, "Namath's Regular-Season Debut, Shaky, Promising," *USA Today*, September 10, 1985.

408 didn't want to be on the road: Gunther and Carter, *Monday Night Mayhem*, 316.

408 "Joe Namath Problem" William Taaffe, "Hey, Joe, Turn Out the Lights," *Sports Illustrated*, October 7, 1985.

408 "a piece of work": Rudy Martzke, "Namath's Regular-Season Debut."

408 managed to balance the demands: Janofsky, "Namath: A 'Heckuva' Debut."

51. Fiji

409 "A love never felt": Craig Davis, "Broadway Joe Is Still Super," *Sun-Sentinel*, January 19, 1989.

409 Dr. Spock: Jon Saraceno, "A Feat by No Ordinary Joe," *USA Today*, January 29, 1999.

410 "Now, Daddy": Craig Davis, "Broadway Joe Is Still Super."

410 fearful that the scent of Brut: Fabergé president Steve Manenti: "Namath is being phased out because of the ABC thing and also because of some ads he did in Florida for a racetrack that were not right for our image." Pat Sloan, "Fabergé Follows ABC in Sidelining Namath," *Advertising Age*, April 14, 1986.

410 Sales had increased 16 percent: Gary Slutzker, "Broadway Joe Doesn't Sell Here Anymore," *Forbes*, June 2, 1986.

410 "I think it's boring": Greg Logan, "Life's Dull, Monday's Worse, Namath Bored by Not Working, Monday Night Football," *Newsday*, September 25, 1986.

410 Namath responded by suing: *Namanco Productions Inc. and Joseph W. Namath v. Capital Cities, ABC, Inc. and ABC Sports*, Case No. 16948, 1987, Supreme Court of the State of New York, County of New York, Clerk's Office.

410 brought suit against Fabergé: *Planned Licensing, Inc. and Joseph W. Namath v. Faberge, Inc.*, Case No. 29586, 1987, Supreme Court of the State of New York, County of New York, Clerk's Office.

410 Nantucket Industries: *Planned Licensing Inc. v. Nantucket Industries*, Case No. 028996, 1987, Supreme Court of the State of New York, County of New York, Clerk's Office.

410 sued Noel Industries: *Planned Licensing Inc. v. Noel Industries, Inc.*, Case No. 25987, 1987; *Planned Licensing Inc. v. Alpha Richard Corp., Jerry Klanfer and Richard Stotter*, Case No. 014623, 1987. Supreme Court of the State of New York, County of New York, Clerk's Office.

410 ring announcer for a pay-per-view: Associated Press, "In This Corner . . . Joe Willie?" *Newsday*, March 26, 1986.

411 fill a large glass with vodka: Werblin interview.

411 "You act foolish": Mays interview.

411 "If I lost": Saraceno, "A Feat."

411 "There's a whole lot to be said": Montville, "Off Broadway Joe."

411 March 24, 1987: Namath gives the date in Saraceno, "A Feat," and Montville, "Off Broadway Joe."

411 "Joe was damaged goods": Michael Weisman interview, August 7, 2002.

412 "Money won't be an issue": Ibid.

412 "My name is not Debbie": Ibid.

412 "It was an act of kindness": Ibid.

413 journalistic legwork: Jim Baker, "Namath Bounced Back on NBC," *Boston Globe*, December 13, 1987.

413 "My wife stays on me": Rudy Martzke, "Namath Leaves Nothing to Chance in Comeback," *USA Today*, October 29, 1987.

413 regularly bringing coffee: Steve Danz, former NBC Sports field producer, interview, December 19, 2001.

413 another twenty or twenty-five years: David Fink, "Confident Namath Takes Second Shot at Sportscasting," *Pittsburgh Post-Gazette*, September 18, 1987; Rachel Shuster, "Namath Ready for NFL Comeback behind Mike," *USA Today*, August 27, 1987.

414 low six-figure: Weisman interview.

414 4,356-square-foot home: "A Gig Gainer for Namath and the Wife," *Daily News*, August 17, 1989.

414 "She doesn't want him hanging out": Marchiano interview.

414 "She wanted to live in Connecticut": Hicks interview.

414 "We've got a little white farmhouse": Dave Anderson, "The 'Super' Jets Question the Jets of Today," Sports of the Times, *New York Times*, August 7, 1988.

414 mourned his Irish setter: Saraceno, "A Feat."

414 jump off a footbridge to save: Fishman interview.

414 $1.75 million: "A Big Gainer."

414 6,813 square feet, with a pool: Palm Beach County Property Appraiser, Governmental Center, West Palm Beach, Fla.; also, http://www.co.palmbeach.fl.us/propapp.

414 "With an English garden": Paul Zimmerman, "Guaranteed Cool," *Sports Illustrated*, January 28, 1991.

414 Boston Whaler: Joe Namath, "Fishing: Tales of the Sea." "I like the boat for one main reason: it won't sink," Namath said. "It's made out of fiberglass with a Styrofoam core—you can cut it in half and it will still float."

415 "the prettiest snook": Ibid.

415 "Just having those little arms": Hyde tape.

415 "He was with those kids every day": Hicks interview.

415 "feeling pretty good": Hirsch interview.

415 "So content": Werblin interview.

416 "Namath hasn't spoken to me": Zimmerman interview.

416 "What I want now": Zimmerman, "Guaranteed Cool."

416 imagined it many times: Zimmerman interview.

416 "I don't even remember": Zimmerman, "Guaranteed Cool."

416 holding back tears: Zimmerman interview.

416 "Goose bumps": Zimmerman, "Guaranteed Cool."

52. Tatiana

417 "I didn't want to take any chances": Dave Anderson, "Joe Namath Receives a Brand-New Pair of Knees," Sports of the Times, *New York Times*, May 3, 1992.

417 $1.25 million: *Planned Licensing, Inc., v. Telebrands Advertising Corp,* Case No. 99 Civ 8597, Clerk's Office, U.S. District Court, Southern District of New York. License Agreement dated December 2, 1992.

417 contract with NFL Properties: Namath's contract with NFL Properties was a ten-year deal.

417 "playing like mutts": Rudy Martzke, "Sports on TV," *USA Today*, September 28, 1992.

417 "Namath deserved better": Weisman interview.

418 "It's an evolution": Bob Raissman, "NBC Should Leave Namath In," *Daily News*, July 23, 1993.

418 "All scheduling conflicts": Richard Sandomir, "Joe Willie Namath Is Now Free Joe Willie," *New York Times*, August 6, 1993.

418 "The girls were crying": Hyde tape.

418 "Had I been a younger guy": Ibid.

418 "It's not easy being married": Mays interview.

418 Go live your life: Montville, "Off Broadway Joe."

418 "Can I bring my wife?": Howard Felsher interview, September 5, 2002.

419 "It could do him a lot of harm": Ibid.

419 a more erudite host: Ibid.

419 "I was stunned": Hassan interview.

419 hated that name: *New York Post* files, entry dated April 17, 1987. After the *Post's* item about her astrological excursion to Fiji, she requested that the paper never again print her name as "Debbie."

419 April 1, 1992: Order Changing Name, Case No. CD 92-2198 FD, 1992, Palm Beach County Circuit Court, Clerk's Office.

419 July 8, 1993: Final Judgment Changing Name, Case No. CD 93-4638 FD, 1993, Palm Beach County Circuit Court, Clerk's Office.

420 "It's her God-given right": Mays interview.

420 offering no explanation: Hassan, Werblin, and Hicks interviews.

420 "I'm only doing it for her": Ryan interview.

420 the Dakota: Real estate records, City of New York, Department of Finance. Mortgage agreement with Arcs Mortgage was entered into on January 24, 1995.

420 commuted there regularly: Hicks and Hassan interviews.

420 "Anna": E. Katherine Kerr interview, February 20, 2002.

420 issues with her mother: Ibid.

421 "She was very attractive": Michael Griffiths interview, February 18, 2002.

421 four performances: Montville, "Off Broadway Joe."

421 a delivery from the Wiz: Griffiths interview. The television remains there, affectionately known as "The Joe Namath Special."

421 "searching for something": Ibid.

421 "Do you think he'll be all right?": Kerr interview.

422 she had met someone: Ibid.

53. A Vinculo Matrimonii

423 "How good you two look": Kovac interview, November 13, 2003.

423 October 21, 1997: Individual Record, Social Security Death Index, http://www.familysearch.org.

423 "You can't do too much magic": Bruno interview.

423 Joe didn't say much: Kovac, Alford, and Bruno interviews.

423 eight months later: Death notices in the *Akron Beacon-Journal* give dates as April 24, 1995, for John Namath and December 25, 1995, for Esther Namath.

424 "He believed I did something": Hicks interview, November 30, 2003.

424 "I think it bothers him": Ibid.

424 Tatiana stayed behind: Husband's Petition for Dissolution of Marriage, *Joseph William Namath and Tatiana Namath,* Case No. 99-004051, 1999, Broward County Circuit Court, Clerk's Office.

424 "The tip came from someone": John South interview, July 26, 2002.

424 "a friendly divorce": John South, "Wife Dumps Joe Namath—& Runs Off with a Plastic Surgeon," *National Enquirer,* April 13, 1999.

425 "They would see him": South interview.

425 "It's better for my kids": "Jilted Joe," *People,* April 19, 1999.

425 "primary residential parent": Husband's Petition for Dissolution of Marriage.

425 be kept out of the court file: On June 8, 1999, Judge Linda Vitale granted Namath's request to seal the court file. But on July 30—in response to a motion by the *Sun-Sentinel* and columnist Jose Lambiet—Judge Vitale vacated her own order. However, the settlement and some exhibits remained in Namath's attorney's office.

425 "A record of sorts": Jose Lambiet, "South Florida Insider," *Sun-Sentinel,* August 10, 1999.

425 "letting them go": Hicks interview.

425 "the most devastating thing": Hyde tape.

425 "*love*": Ibid.

426 The chest pains: Ibid.

426 "One day": Marchiano interview.

426 "I know it's not good": Ibid.

426 "Every time I fly": Ibid.

426 "I hate Beverly Hills": Ibid.

427 antidepressant: Hyde tape.

427 "You see guys throw": Mark McLaughlin, "Namath: QB's Today Lack Technique," *New York Post,* August 11, 1995.

427 "The throwing motion": Chuck Slater, "Broadway Joe Sees Himself in Miami's Marino," *Beaver County Times,* January 20, 1985.

427 "transportation problems": Jose Lambiet, "South Florida Insider," *Sun-Sentinel,* August 25, 2000; Greg Cote, "NFL Insider," *Miami Herald,* September 1, 2000.

427 Barry had wanted to tell him: Barry interview.

427 "Barely able to stand" Jose Lambiet, "Friends Say Broadway Joe Staggering Down Lonely Street," *Sun-Sentinel,* January 19, 2001.

428 "He was a little woozy": Passuello interview.

428 "I can take a hint": Hassan interview.

428 "a good heart": Fishman interview.

428 "Excuse me, Mr. Namath": Gutkowski interview.

54. Classic Sports

430 "Your wife?": Spangler interview, November 28, 2003.

430 "It's like watching *Casablanca*": *Adam Smith's Money Game,* transcript #111, June 27, 1998; http://www.adamsmith.net/transcripts/06_27_98.html.

430 among the first ex-athletes: The others were Ted Williams and Muhammad Ali.

431 "Cheesiness is the fate": Andrew Corsello, "He Makes You Feel *Good* Inside!" *GQ,* January, 1996.

431 "We milked it": Spangler interview.

431 "He made it clear": Craig Mortali interview, November 20, 2001.

432 "What else would you": *SportsCentury: Joe Namath.*

432 "You'd sacrifice your life": Ibid.

432 "still got it": Mortali interview.

433 "Same old Jimmy" Telander interview.

433 answer in federal court: *Joseph W. Namath v. Pro Set, Inc.*, Case No. 92-civ 0594, 1992, U.S. District Court, Southern District of New York, NARA Lee's Summit. Namath sued for $15 million, but the case was thrown out when a judge granted Pro Set's motion for summary judgment.

433 $504,722 plus legal fees: Settlement Agreement, dated January 6, 2000, *Planned Licensing, Inc. v. Telebrands Advertising Corp.*

433 make a fist: Dave Hyde, "Namath in Pain That Won't Stop," *Sun-Sentinel*, May 1, 2002.

433 "It was never": Hyde tape.

434 Jimmy helped secure financing: L.A. Lorek, "How Michael Levy Hit It Big with Sportsline," *Sun Sentinel*, October 18, 1998.

434 Planned Licensing would receive: "License and Consulting Agreement" between Planned Licensing, Inc. and SportsLine USA, Inc., dated August 10, 1994 available at http://contracts.corporate.findlaw.com/agreements/sportsline/namath.emp.1994.html. Also see John Lantigua, "SportsLine.com Shoots to Win," *Variety*, November 12, 2000.

434 6,000 shares every October: "First Amendment to License and Consulting Agreement" between Planned Licensing, Inc. and SportsLine.com, Inc. dated October 16, 1999, available at http://contracts.corporate.findlaw.com/agreements/sportsline/namath.emp.1999.10.16.html.

434 "Namath received stock": Andy Serwer, "Joe Namath Goes Long with SportsLine," *Fortune*, February 21, 2000.

434 $35 a share: $35.50 on February 18, 2000, according to Bloomberg Financial News.

434 hovering around $2: Bloomberg Financial News.

434 Del Mar: In February, 1999, Nevada's Financial Institutions Division seized control for what an official described as "a mismanagement problem." John G. Edwards, "Del Mar Mortgage Seized," *Las Vegas Review-Journal*, February 13, 1999; "State Announces Mortgage Company Takeover," News Release, Nevada Attorney General, http://ag.state.nv.us.agpress/1999/99_212.htm.

In April 2000, the same agency found Del Mar advertising misleading, ordering it to stop claiming that "no one has ever lost a penny" by investing with the company. John G. Edwards, "Del Mar Told to

Stop Running Ads on Investing History," *Las Vegas Review-Journal*, April 29, 2000. On October 3, 2003, Nevada's secretary of state announced that he had closed a year-long investigation into allegedly illegal campaign contributions made by Shustek and other Vestin employees. Neither Shustek nor Vestin was ever cited for any violations. Sean Whaley, "Campaign Contribution Probe: Heller Closes Investigation," *Las Vegas Review-Journal*, October 4, 2003.

434 "Maybe we were growing": Sean Whaley, "Vestin Chariman: Successes Lead Lender to Politics," *Las Vegas Review-Journal*, September 3, 2002.

434 "that *Brady Bunch* episode": Michael Shustek interview, November 30, 2001.

434 "my trophies": Ibid.

434 $1 million a year through 2005: Vestin's annual reports available on Yahoo!Finance.com; http://biz.yahoo.com. The 2001 Annual Report can be seen at http://www.edgaronline.com/bin/edgardoc/finSys_main.asp?dcn=0000950150-02-000309&nad.

435 "I think the president": *Cavuto on Business*, Fox News Channel, December 1, 2001. Videocassette courtesy of Fox News.

435 "These gentlemen know far more": *Cavuto on Business*, April 27, 2002. Videocassette courtesy of Fox News.

435 "Americans have": Ibid.

435 "There were probably twenty": Cathie Smith interview, January 3, 2002.

435 "The drinking": Grantham interview, July 18, 2002.

436 "Larry became": Snell interview.

436 social security checks and booze: Brad Hunter, "'69 Jet's Boozy Spiral to Death," *New York Post*, May 16, 2002.

436 "I went downtown": Grantham interview.

436 "I know Joe is special": Ibid.

436 "We always ask Joe": Fred Reihl interview, July 18, 2002.

436 "If he was there": Philbin interview.

437 tremors and anxiety attacks: Barry and Van interviews.

437 "I'm shocked": Van interview.

437 never once heard: Secor interview.

437 "Some pain": Steven Wine, "At 58, Namath Has Learned to Live with Pain," posted on Yahoo!Sports on May 10, 2002; http://ca.sports.yahoo.com/020510/6/mc1d.html.

437 "every couple of weeks": Hyde tape.

437 $610,980: Los Angeles County Assessor's Office. As of June 2002, the land was assessed at $424,830 and the improvements at $186,150.

437 "You want to bet?": Dave Anderson, "Namath, 60, to Earn Degree," *New York Times*, December 10, 2003.

437 "Make sure to call": Dowd interview.

438 "A glow": Ibid.

438 "definitely pretty soused": Christian Red interview, February 2, 2004.

438 "I've embarrassed my family": Namath interviewed by Jeremy Schaap, *Outside the Lines,* ESPN, January 25, 2004.

439 "The state": Jay Cross, e-mail to public relations consultant, June 27, 2003.

440 "The overall value": Dave Anderson, "Broadway Joe Wants a West Side Stadium," Sports of the Times, *New York Times,* June 26, 2003.

440 "I can hear that kind of stuff": Steve Serby, "Namath: Bring Jets to B'Way," *New York Post,* June 26, 2003.

Index